American Government and Politics Today

2018–2019 Brief Edition

Steffen W. Schmidt
Iowa State University

Mack C. Shelley II
Iowa State University

Barbara A. Bardes
University of Cincinnati

CENGAGE

Australia • Brazil • Mexico • Singapore • United Kingdom • United States

CENGAGE

American Government and Politics Today, 2018–2019 Brief Edition

Steffen W. Schmidt, Mack C. Shelley II, Barbara A. Bardes

Sr. Vice President, Higher Ed Product, Content, and Market Development: Erin Joyner

Product Director: Paul Banks

Sr. Product Manager: Bradley Potthoff

Project Manager: Julia Giannotti

Content Development Project Manager: Katy Gabel, Lumina Datamatics

Product Assistant: Danielle Gidley

Sr. Marketing Manager: Valerie Hartman

Sr. Content Project Manager: Martha Conway

Production Service/Compositor: Alison Kuzmickas, SPi Global

Copy Editor: Susan Bradley

Proofreader: Kristi Wiswell

Indexer: Terry Casey

Art Director: Sarah Cole

Text Designer: Dutton & Sherman Design

Cover Designer: Sarah Cole

Sr. Intellectual Property Analyst: Alexandra Ricciardi

Intellectual Property Project Manager: Betsy Hathaway

For product information and technology assistance, contact us at **Cengage Customer & Sales Support, 1-800-354-9706**

For permission to use material from this text or product, submit all requests online at **www.cengage.com/permissions**. Further permissions questions can be emailed to **permissionrequest@cengage.com**.

Library of Congress Control Number: 2017950885

ISBN:978-1-337-55970-6

Cengage
20 Channel Center Street
Boston, MA 02210
USA

Cengage is a leading provider of customized learning solutions with employees residing in nearly 40 different countries and sales in more than 125 countries around the world. Find your local representative at **www.cengage.com.**

Cengage products are represented in Canada by Nelson Education, Ltd.

To learn more about Cengage platforms and services, visit **www.cengage.com**

To register or access your online learning solution or purchase materials for your course, visit **www.cengagebrain.com**

Printed in the United States of America
Print Number: 01   Print Year: 2017

Contents in Brief

Contents

Justin Sullivan/Getty Images

Nikreates/Alamy Stock Photo

ZUMA Press Inc / Alamy Stock Photo

Chapter 4 Civil Liberties 66

Anadolu Agency/Getty Images

Chapter 5   Civil Rights   92

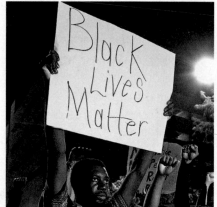

Charlotte Observer/Tribune News Service/Getty Images

PART II: THE POLITICS OF AMERICAN DEMOCRACY

Chapter 6   Public Opinion, Political Socialization, and the Media   118

Chip Somodevilla/Getty Images News/Getty Images

Chapter 7   Interest Groups and Political Parties   146

Pacific Press/LightRocket/Getty Images

Chapter 8   Campaigns and Elections   174

Chip Somodevilla/Getty Images News/Getty Images

PART III: INSTITUTIONS OF AMERICAN GOVERNMENT

Chapter 9 Congress 199

Zach Gibson/Getty Images

JStone/Shutterstock.com

Chapter 11 The Executive Branch 250

US Food and Drug Administration

Rena Schild/Shutterstock.com

Pool/ABACA/Newscom/Abaca Press/TAORMINA/Italy

Preface

In November 2016, Republican presidential candidate Donald Trump triumphed over Democratic candidate Hillary Clinton. The Republicans also maintained control of the U.S. Senate and House of Representatives, although they did suffer minor losses. Trump certainly has one of the most unusual backgrounds ever for a president, with no experience in elected or appointed public office. One consequence of his victory has been an explosion of interest in political news. Online news sites, including that of the *New York Times*, have experienced large increases in viewership. The same goes for cable news networks such as Fox News and MSNBC. For many people, American politics and government have never been more interesting.

Trump won the presidency by carrying the vote in the electoral college, even though Clinton's popular vote was more than 2 percentage points greater than his. Many have wondered how a candidate could become president while losing the popular vote, and that is one of many things that students will learn in this text. Now more than ever, it is important to understand America's complex and fascinating political system.

One thing was and continues to be certain: American politics today will never be without tension, drama, and conflict. Throughout this Brief Edition of *American Government and Politics Today*, you will read about how our government has responded to past issues and how it is responding to current conflicts.

This edition is basically a condensed and updated version of the larger editions of *American Government and Politics Today*. It has been created specifically for those of you who want a text that presents the fundamental components of the American political system while retaining the quality and readability of the larger editions. You will find that this edition is up to date in every respect. The text, figures, tables, and all pedagogical features reflect the latest available data. We have also included coverage of all recently issued laws, regulations, and court decisions that have—or will have—a significant impact on American society and our political system.

Like the larger editions, this volume places a major emphasis on political participation and involvement. This brief, fourteen-chapter text has been heralded by reviewers as the best essentials text for its affordability, conciseness, clarity, and readability.

New to This Edition

Of course, every chapter has been thoroughly revised and updated. But there is more.

Now in Full Color Throughout

A major objective of the Brief Edition has always been to provide students with an affordable textbook. To that end, previous editions have been limited to using a single color for contrast in most of the text. With this edition, however, we have been able—for the first time—to produce a text in full color and still keep it affordable. The use of color not only makes the chapters more attractive, but it also adds to the impact of the various charts and graphs that appear throughout.

Major Topical Updates

By far the most important change in American politics and government since the last Brief Edition has been the rise of Donald Trump. We give ample space to Trump's populist campaign and his use of the media, including Twitter. In *Chapter 1 The Democratic Republic* and *Chapter 6 Public Opinion, Political Socialization, and the Media*, we describe Trump's supporters and the problems facing the white working class. We describe the alleged scandals faced both by Trump and by Democratic presidential candidate Hillary Clinton, in particular concerning questions about Russian involvement in the 2016 elections. *Chapter 11 The Executive Branch* explains Trump's firing of FBI director James Comey. Other major new topics include:

- In *Chapter 3 Federalism*, the limits on what the national government can do to coerce the states.

- In *Chapter 4 Civil Liberties*, political correctness and government surveillance.

- In *Chapter 5 Civil Rights*, how black men are treated by the police. We also have a major new section on transgender individuals.

- In *Chapter 7 Interest Groups and Political Parties*, the growth in party polarization and the changing bases of the major parties.

- In *Chapter 8 Campaigns and Elections*, the limits of the "invisible primary," the role of superdelegates, and restrictions on the right to vote.

- In *Chapter 9 Congress*, the House Freedom Caucus and the conflict around replacing the late Supreme Court justice Antonin Scalia.

- *Chapter 11 The Executive Branch*, has been more appropriately renamed *The Executive Branch*. We focus on whistleblowers and those who leak national security information.

- *Chapter 13 Domestic and Economic Policy* describes the Republican struggle to replace the Affordable Care Act.

- Finally, *Chapter 14 Foreign Policy* highlights Trump's transactional foreign policy and trade issues with China and Europe.

Key to High Student Interest— Topical Debate-Style Features

Every *At Issue* feature focuses on a controversial topic and concludes with a *For Critical Analysis* question to invite critical thinking. Most of these features are new:

- Chapter 1: **Does Entitlement Spending Corrupt Us?**

- Chapter 2: **Is America a Christian Nation?**

- Chapter 3: **Should Recreational Marijuana Be Legal?**

- Chapter 3: **Should We Let Uber and Lyft Pick Up Passengers?**

- Chapter 4: **Do Police Use Excessive Force against Black Men?**

- Chapter 5: **Should We Deport Unauthorized Immigrants?**

- Chapter 8: **Can Money Buy Elections?**

- Chapter 9: **Is It Time to Get Rid of the Filibuster?**

- Chapter 10: **Should We Elect the President by Popular Vote?**

- Chapter 10: **Should President Trump Send U.S. Ground Forces to Syria?**

- Chapter 11: **Should We Simplify the Income Tax System?**

- Chapter 12: **Should State Judges Be Elected?**

- Chapter 13: **Should States Raise the Minimum Wage?**

- Chapter 14: **How Dangerous Is Putin's Russia?**

Making a Difference Features

At the end of every chapter, a feature entitled *Making a Difference* enhances our emphasis on student participation. These features provide newly updated, useful information for active citizenship. We offer tips on how to find information on issues, how to learn about your elected representatives, how to join and participate in advocacy organizations, how to protect your civil rights and liberties, and more.

Other Special Pedagogical Aids

The 2018–2019 Brief Edition of *American Government and Politics Today* retains many of the pedagogical aids and features of the larger editions, including the following:

- **Learning Outcomes**—A section-by-section focus on crucial questions that students should learn to address.

- **Key Terms**—Important terms that are boldfaced and defined in the text when they are first used. These terms are defined in the text margins, listed at the end of the chapter with the page numbers on which they appear, and included in the Glossary at the back of the book.

- **InterAct**—A mini-feature that directs students to selected websites and encourages them to take one or more actions when they get there.

- **Chapter Summary**—A point-by-point summary of the chapter text.

- **Test Yourself**—A quiz and an essay question at the very end of each chapter.

Appendices

The Brief Edition of *American Government and Politics Today* includes, as appendices, both the Declaration of Independence (Appendix A) and the U.S. Constitution (Appendix B). The text of the Constitution has been annotated to help you understand the meaning and significance of the various provisions in this important document. Appendix C presents *Federalist Papers* No. 10 and No. 51. These selections are also annotated to help you grasp their importance in understanding the American philosophy of government. Appendix D contains pie charts that explain the expenditures and revenues of the federal government.

MindTap

MindTap is here to simplify your workload as an instructor, organize and immediately grade your students' assignments, and allow you to customize your course as you see fit. Through deep-seated integration with your Learning Management System (LMS), grades are easily exported and analytics are pulled with just the click of a button. MindTap provides you with a platform to easily add current events videos and RSS feeds from national or local news sources. Looking to incorporate more recent and late-breaking news into the course? Utilize our KnowNow American Government Blog for weekly updated news coverage and pedagogy.

Instructor Supplements

The **Instructor Companion Website** (ISBN: 9781337559782) is an all-in-one multimedia online resource for class preparation, presentation, and testing. Accessible through Cengage .com/login with your faculty account, you will find the following available for download:

- Book-specific Microsoft® **Powerpoint® slides** of lecture outlines, as well as photos, figures, and tables from the text. These presentations make it easy for you to assemble lectures for your course.

- Cognero **Test Bank** (ISBN: 9781337559775): Multiple-choice and essay questions, along with their answers and text references, that are compatible with multiple Learning Management Systems.

- An **Instructor's Manual** that includes learning outcomes, chapter outlines, discussion questions, class activities and project suggestions, tips on integrating media into your class, suggested readings and Web resources, and a section specially designed to help teaching assistants and adjunct professors.

Acknowledgments

In preparing *American Government and Politics Today:* 2018–2019 Brief Edition, we were the beneficiaries of the expert guidance of a skilled and dedicated team of publishers and editors. We have benefited greatly from the supervision and encouragement provided by our project manager, Bradley Potthoff.

We are grateful to our content project manager, Martha Conway, for her ability to make this project as smooth-running and as perfect as is humanly possible. We are indebted to the staff at SPi Global. Their ability to generate the pages for this text quickly and accurately made it possible for us to meet our ambitious printing schedule. We also thank Katy Gabel, our content developer, for her work on the book's revision plan and project coordination. In addition, our gratitude goes to all those who worked on the various supplements offered with this text. We would also like to thank Valerie Hartman, marketing manager, for her tremendous efforts in marketing the book.

Many other people helped during the research and editorial stages of this edition. Gregory Scott coordinated the authors' efforts and provided editorial and research assistance. Sue Bradley's copyediting abilities contributed greatly to the book. We also thank Roxie Lee for her assistance, and Sue Jasin of K&M Consulting for her contributions to the smooth running of the project. Finally, we are grateful for the proofreading services provided by Kristi Wiswell.

We are also very thankful for the constructive comments and advice provided by our colleagues and peers, especially those whose thoughtful insights helped us shape this new edition:

Paul Blakelock, Lone Star College–Kingwood
Justin Deplato, Florida State College at Jacksonville
David Goldberg, College of DuPage
Tonya Gray, Central Carolina Community College
Robert L. Hall, Jr., Florida State College at Jacksonville
La Della Levy, College of Southern Nevada, Charleston
Charlotte Meador, Lone Star College–Kingwood
Don Mirjanian, College of Southern Nevada, Charleston
Azubike Kalu-Nwiwu, Erie Community College
Gwyn Sutherland, Elizabethtown Community and Technical College

Any errors, of course, remain our own. We welcome comments from instructors and students alike. Suggestions that we received on previous editions have helped us to improve this text and to adapt it to the changing needs of instructors and students.

S.W.S.
M.C.S.
B.A.B.

About the Authors

Steffen W. Schmidt

Steffen W. Schmidt is a professor of political science at Iowa State University. He grew up in Colombia, South America, and has studied in Colombia, Switzerland, the United States, and France. He has a B.A. from Rollins College and obtained his Ph.D. from Columbia University, in public law and government.

Dr. Schmidt has published 14 books and more than 130 articles in scholarly journals and major newspapers.

He is the recipient of numerous prestigious teaching prizes, including the Amoco Award for Lifetime Career Achievement in Teaching and the Teacher of the Year award.

Schmidt is a pioneer in the use of web-based and real-time video courses and is a founding member of the American Political Science Association's section on Computers and Multimedia.

He is known as "Dr. Politics" for his extensive commentary on U.S. politics and cyber threats in U.S. and international media. He comments on CNN en Español, Fox, Telemundo, Univision, and public radio, as well as CTV (Canada Cable TV) and the BBC. He has been quoted in every major news source in the world including *The Economist*, the *New York Times*, the *Washington Times, Kyodo News* of Japan, *Agence France-Presse*, Latin American news media, and others. He is the guest of two weekly radio shows on KASI Clear Channel and on Concord, New Hampshire, radio with Deborah "Arnie" Arnesen.

Dr. Schmidt is a founding member of the Department of Defense U.S. Strategic Command Academic Alliance, which focuses on cybersecurity policy.

He is on Facebook (SteffenWSchmidt) and Twitter (DrPolitics).

Mack C. Shelley II

Mack C. Shelley II is professor of political science and statistics at Iowa State University. After receiving his bachelor's degree from American University in Washington, D.C., he completed graduate studies at the University of Wisconsin at Madison, where he received a master's degree in economics and a Ph.D. in political science. He taught for two years at Mississippi State University before arriving at Iowa State in 1979.

Shelley has published numerous articles, books, and monographs on public policy. From 1993 to 2002, he served as elected coeditor of the *Policy Studies Journal*. His published books include *The Permanent Majority: The Conservative Coalition in the United States Congress; Biotechnology and the Research Enterprise* (with William F. Woodman and Brian J. Reichel); *American Public Policy: The Contemporary Agenda* (with Steven G. Koven and Bert E. Swanson); *Redefining Family Policy: Implications for the 21st Century* (with Joyce M. Mercier and Steven Garasky); and *Quality Research in Literacy and Science Education: International Perspectives and Gold Standards* (with Larry Yore and Brian Hand).

His leisure time includes traveling, working with students, and playing with the family dog and cats.

BARBARA A. BARDES

Barbara A. Bardes is professor emerita of political science and former dean of Raymond Walters College at the University of Cincinnati. She received her B.A. and M.A. from Kent State University. After completing her Ph.D. at the University of Cincinnati, she held faculty positions at Mississippi State University and Loyola University in Chicago. She returned to Cincinnati, her hometown, as a college administrator. She has also worked as a political consultant and directed polling for a research center.

Bardes has written articles on public opinion and foreign policy, and on women and politics. She has authored *Thinking about Public Policy; Declarations of Independence: Women and Political Power in Nineteenth-Century American Fiction;* and *Public Opinion: Measuring the American Mind* (with Robert W. Oldendick).

Bardes's home is located in a very small hamlet in Kentucky called Rabbit Hash, famous for its 150-year-old general store. Her hobbies include traveling, gardening, needlework, and antique collecting.

1

The Democratic Republic

People celebrating at a campaign rally in Brooklyn, N.Y., in 2016. *What do people mean when they wave the U.S. flag?*

Justin Sullivan/Getty Images

The five **Learning Outcomes (LOs)** below are designed to help improve your understanding of this chapter. After reading this chapter, you should be able to:

>>>**LO1** Define the terms *politics, government, order, liberty, authority,* and *legitimacy.*

>>>**LO2** Distinguish the major features of direct democracy and representative democracy.

>>>**LO3** Describe majoritarianism, elite theory, and pluralism as theories of how democratic systems work.

>>>**LO4** Summarize the conflicts that can occur between the values of liberty and order, and between those of liberty and equality.

>>>**LO5** Discuss conservatism, liberalism, and other popular American ideological positions.

Check your understanding of the material with the Test Yourself section at the end of the chapter.

Politics, for many people, is the "great game," and it is played for high stakes. After all, the game involves vast sums and the very security of the nation. In the last few years, the stakes have grown higher still. In 2016, American voters picked Republican Donald Trump to be the next president of the United States. Trump's political values and personal background were unprecedented among major-party presidential candidates. True, Democrat Hillary Clinton won more votes than Trump, but as we explain throughout this text, Americans choose their president through the *electoral college*, not the popular vote. Trump's electoral vote margin was decisive. While the Democrats picked up a few seats in Congress, Republicans still controlled both the U.S. House and Senate. A new era of conservative governance appeared certain, to the delight of some and the dismay of others.

Politics and Government

>>> **LO1:** Define the terms *politics, government, order, liberty, authority,* and *legitimacy.*

What is politics? **Politics** can be understood as the process of resolving conflicts and deciding, as political scientist Harold Lasswell put it in his classic definition, "who gets what, when, and how."[1] More specifically, politics is the struggle over power or influence within organizations or informal groups that can grant or withold benefits or privileges.

We can identify many such groups and organizations. In every community that makes decisions through formal or informal rules, politics exists. For example, when a church decides to construct a new building or hire a new minister, the decision is made politically. Politics can be found in schools, social groups, and any other organized collection of individuals. Of all the organizations that are controlled by political activity, however, the most important is the government.

What is the government? Certainly, it is an **institution**—that is, an ongoing organization that performs certain functions for society. An institution has a life separate from the lives of the individuals who are part of it at any given moment in time. The **government** can be defined as an institution within which decisions are made that resolve conflicts and allocate benefits and privileges. The government is also the preeminent institution within society because it has the ultimate authority for making these decisions.

Why Is Government Necessary?

Perhaps the best way to assess the need for government is to examine circumstances in which government, as we normally understand it, does not exist. What happens when multiple groups compete violently with one another for power within a society? There are places around the world where such circumstances exist. A current example is the Middle Eastern nation of Syria, run by the dictator Bashar al-Assad. In 2011, peaceful protesters were killed, which led to an armed rebellion. The government lost control of much of the country, and its forces repeatedly massacred civilians in contested areas. Some rebels, such as the so-called Islamic State (ISIS), were extreme Islamists. Others were more moderate. By 2013, rebels were fighting each other as well as the government. In much of Syria, law and order had broken down completely. By 2017, almost 500,000 people had been killed, and about half of the country's people had been driven from their homes.

As the example of Syria shows, one of the foundational purposes of government is the maintenance of security, or **order.** By keeping the peace, a government protects its people from violence at the hands of private or foreign armies and criminals. If order is not present, it is not possible for the government to provide any of the other benefits that people expect from it. Order is a political value to which we will return later in this chapter.

Limiting Government Power

A complete collapse of order and security, as seen in Syria, actually is an uncommon event. Much more common is the reverse—too much government control. In January 2017, the human rights organization Freedom House judged that forty-nine of the world's countries were "not free." These nations contained 36 percent of the world's population. Such countries may be controlled by individual kings or dictators. Saudi Arabia's king, Salman bin Abdulaziz Al Saud, and North Korea's Kim Jong-un are obvious examples. Alternatively,

Politics
The struggle over power or influence within organizations or informal groups that can grant or withhold benefits or privileges.

Institution
An ongoing organization that performs certain functions for society.

Government
The preeminent institution within a society. Government has the ultimate authority to decide how conflicts will be resolved and how benefits and privileges will be allocated.

Order
A state of peace and security. Maintaining order by protecting members of society from violence and criminal activity is the oldest purpose of government.

---

1. Harold Lasswell, *Politics: Who Gets What, When, and How* (Gloucester, Mass.: Peter Smith Publisher, 1990). Originally published in 1936.

a political party, such as the Communist Party of China, may monopolize all the levels of power. The military may rule, as in Thailand since 2014.

In all of these examples, the individual or group running the country cannot be removed by legal means. Freedom of speech and the right to a fair trial are typically absent. Dictatorial governments often torture or execute their opponents. Such regimes may also suppress freedom of religion. Revolution, whether violent or nonviolent, is often the only way to change the government.

In short, protection from the violence of domestic criminals or foreign armies is not enough. Citizens also need protection from abuses of power by their own government. To protect the liberties of the people, it is necessary to limit the powers of the government. **Liberty**—the greatest freedom of the individual consistent with the freedom of other individuals—is a second major political value, along with order. We discuss this value in more detail later in this chapter.

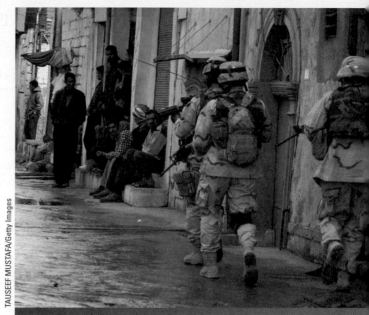

TAUSEEF MUSTAFA/Getty Images

U.S. soldiers in Mosul, Iraq. They are assisting Iraqi forces in a campaign to clear ISIS forces from the city. ISIS terrorists have become famous for their brutality. *What might inspire them to act in this way?*

Authority and Legitimacy

Every government must have **authority**—that is, the right and power to enforce its decisions. Ultimately, the government's authority rests on its control of the armed forces and the police. Few people in the United States, however, base their day-to-day activities on fear of the government's enforcement powers. Most people, most of the time, obey the law because this is what they have always done. Also, if they did not obey the law, they would face the disapproval of friends and family. Consider an example: Do you avoid injuring your friends or stealing their possessions because you are afraid of the police—or because if you undertook these actions, you no longer would have friends?

Under normal circumstances, the government's authority has broad popular support. People accept the government's right to establish rules and laws. When authority is broadly accepted, we say that it has **legitimacy**. Authority without legitimacy is a recipe for trouble.

Events in several Arab nations since 2011 can serve as an example. The dictators who ruled Egypt, Libya, and Tunisia had been in power for decades. All three dictators had some popular support when they first gained power. None of these nations had a tradition of democracy, and so it was possible for undemocratic rulers to enjoy a degree of legitimacy. After years of oppressive behavior, these regimes slowly lost that legitimacy. The rulers survived only because they were willing to employ violence against any opposition. In Egypt and Tunisia, the end came when soldiers refused to use force against massive demonstrations. Having lost all legitimacy, the rulers of these two countries then lost their authority as well. In Libya, the downfall and death of the dictator Muammar Gaddafi came only after a seven-month civil war. (As it happens, Egypt's shaky new democracy collapsed in 2013 when the army seized power.)

Liberty
The greatest freedom of the individual that is consistent with the freedom of other individuals in the society.

Authority
The right and power of a government or other entity to enforce its decisions and compel obedience.

Legitimacy
Popular acceptance of the right and power of a government or other entity to exercise authority.

Democracy and Other Forms of Government

>>> **LO2:** Distinguish the major features of direct democracy and representative democracy.

The different types of government can be classified according to which person or group of people controls society through the government.

Types of Government

At one extreme is a society governed by a **totalitarian regime.** In such a political system, a small group of leaders or a single individual—a dictator—makes all decisions for the society. Every aspect of political, social, and economic life is controlled by the government. The power of the ruler is total (thus, the term *totalitarianism*). Examples of such regimes include Germany under Adolf Hitler and the former Soviet Union under Joseph Stalin.

A second type of system is authoritarian government. **Authoritarianism** differs from totalitarianism in that only the government itself is fully controlled by the ruler. Social and economic institutions, such as churches, businesses, and labor unions, exist that are not under the government's control.

Many of our terms for describing the distribution of political power are derived from the ancient Greeks, who were the first Western people to study politics systematically. One form of rule was known as *aristocracy*, literally meaning "rule by the best." In practice, this meant rule by wealthy members of ancient families. Another term from the Greeks is *theocracy*, which literally means "rule by God" (or the gods). In practice, theocracy means rule by self-appointed religious leaders. Iran is a rare example of a country in which supreme power is in the hands of a religious leader, the Grand Ayatollah Ali Khamenei. One of the most straightforward Greek terms is *oligarchy*, which simply means "rule by a few."

The Greek term for rule by the people was **democracy.** Within the limits of their culture, some of the Greek city-states operated as democracies. Today, in much of the world, the people will not grant legitimacy to a government unless it is based on democracy.

Direct Democracy as a Model

The Athenian system of government in ancient Greece is usually considered the purest model for **direct democracy** because the citizens of that community debated and voted directly on all laws, even those put forward by the ruling council of the city. The most important feature of Athenian democracy was that the **legislature** was composed of all of the citizens. (Women, resident foreigners, and slaves, however, were excluded because they were not citizens.) This form of government required a high level of participation from every citizen. That participation was seen as benefiting the individual and the city-state. The Athenians believed that although a high level of participation might lead to instability in government, citizens, if informed about the issues, could be trusted to make wise decisions.

Direct democracy also has been practiced at the local level in Switzerland and, in the United States, in New England town meetings. At these town meetings, important decisions—such as levying taxes, hiring city officials, and deciding local ordinances—are made by majority vote. (In recent years, however, turnout for such meetings has declined.) Some states provide a modern adaptation of direct democracy for their citizens. In these states, representative democracy is supplemented by the **initiative** or the **referendum.** Both processes enable the people to vote directly on laws or constitutional amendments. The **recall** process, which is available in many states, allows the people to vote to remove an official from state office before his or her term has expired.

Totalitarian Regime
A form of government that controls all aspects of the political, social, and economic life of a nation.

Authoritarianism
A type of regime in which only the government itself is fully controlled by the ruler. Social and economic institutions exist that are not under the government's control.

Democracy
A system of government in which political authority is vested in the people.

Direct Democracy
A system of government in which political decisions are made by the people directly, rather than by their elected representatives.

Legislature
A governmental body primarily responsible for the making of laws.

Initiative
A procedure by which voters can petition to vote on a law or a constitutional amendment.

Referendum
An electoral device whereby legislative or constitutional measures are referred by the legislature to the voters for approval or disapproval.

Recall
A procedure allowing the people to vote to dismiss an elected official from office before his or her term has expired.

The Dangers of Direct Democracy

Although they were aware of the Athenian model, the framers of the U.S. Constitution were opposed to such a system. Democracy was considered to be dangerous and a source of instability. But in the 1700s and 1800s, the idea of government based on the *consent of the people* gained increasing popularity. Such a government was the main aspiration of the American Revolution in 1775, the French Revolution in 1789, and many subsequent revolutions. At the time of the American Revolution, however, the masses were still considered to be too uneducated to govern themselves, too prone to the influence of demagogues (political leaders who manipulate popular prejudices), and too likely to subordinate minority rights to the tyranny of the majority.

James Madison, while defending the new scheme of government set forth in the U.S. Constitution, warned of the problems inherent in a "pure democracy":

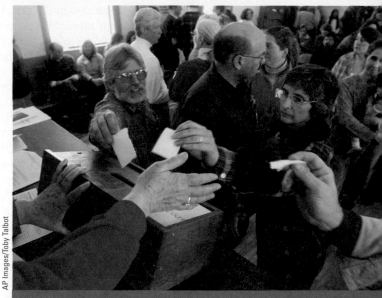

AP Images/Toby Talbot

These Woodbury, Vermont, residents cast their ballots after a town meeting to vote on the school budget and sales taxes. *What type of political system does the town meeting best represent?*

> *A common passion or interest will, in almost every case, be felt by a majority of the whole . . . and there is nothing to check the inducements to sacrifice the weaker party or an obnoxious individual. Hence it is that such democracies have ever been spectacles of turbulence and contention, and have ever been found incompatible with personal security or the rights of property; and have in general been as short in their lives as they have been violent in their deaths.*[2]

Like other politicians of his time, Madison feared that pure, or direct, democracy would deteriorate into mob rule. What would keep the majority of the people, if given direct decision-making power, from abusing the rights of those in the minority?

A Democratic Republic

The framers of the U.S. Constitution chose to craft a **republic,** meaning a government in which sovereign power rests with the people, rather than with a king or a monarch. A republic is based on **popular sovereignty.** To Americans of the 1700s, the idea of a republic also meant a government based on common beliefs and virtues that would be fostered within small communities.

The U.S. Constitution created a form of republican government that we now call a **democratic republic.** The people hold the ultimate power over the government through the election process, but all national policy decisions are made by elected officials. For the founders, even this distance between the people and the government was not sufficient. The Constitution made sure that the Senate and the president would not be elected by

Republic
A form of government in which sovereign power rests with the people, rather than with a king or a monarch.

Popular Sovereignty
The concept that ultimate political authority is based on the will of the people.

Democratic Republic
A republic in which representatives elected by the people make and enforce laws and policies.

2. James Madison, in Alexander Hamilton, James Madison, and John Jay, *The Federalist Papers,* No. 10 (New York: Signet, 2003), p. 71. See Appendix C of this book.

a direct vote of the people. Senators were chosen by state legislatures, although a later constitutional amendment allowed for the direct election of senators. The founders also established an *electoral college* to choose the president, in the hope that such a body would prevent voters from ultimately making the choice.

Despite these limits, the new American system was unique in the amount of power it granted to the ordinary citizen. Over the course of the following two centuries, democratic values became more and more popular, at first in Western nations and then throughout the rest of the world. The spread of democratic principles gave rise to another name for our system of government—**representative democracy.** The term *representative democracy* has almost the same meaning as *democratic republic*, with one exception. Recall that in a republic, not only are the people sovereign, but there is no king. What if a nation develops into a democracy but preserves the monarchy as a largely ceremonial institution? That is exactly what happened in Britain. The British, who have long cherished their kings and queens, found the term *democratic republic* unacceptable. A republic, after all, meant there could be no monarch. The British therefore described their system as a representative democracy instead.

Principles of Democratic Government. All representative democracies rest on the rule of the people as expressed through the election of government officials. In the 1790s in the United States, only free white males were able to vote, and in some states they had to be property owners as well. Women in many states did not receive the right to vote in national elections until 1920, and the right to vote was not secured in all states by African Americans until the 1960s. Today, **universal suffrage** is the rule.

Because everyone's vote counts equally, the only way to make fair decisions is by some form of majority will. But to ensure that **majority rule** does not become oppressive, modern democracies also provide guarantees of minority rights. If political minorities were not protected, the majority might violate the fundamental rights of members of certain groups—especially groups that are unpopular or dissimilar to the majority population, such as racial minorities.

To guarantee the continued existence of a representative democracy, there must be free, competitive elections. Thus, the opposition always has the opportunity to win elective office. For such elections to be totally open, freedom of the press and freedom of speech must be preserved so that opposition candidates can present their criticisms of the government to the people.

Constitutional Democracy. Another key feature of Western representative democracy is that it is based on the principle of **limited government.** Not only is the government dependent on popular sovereignty, but the powers of the government are also clearly limited, either through a written document or through widely shared beliefs. The U.S. Constitution sets down the fundamental structure of the government and the limits to its activities. Such limits are intended to prevent political decisions based on the whims or ambitions of individuals in government rather than on constitutional principles.

What Kind of Democracy Do We Have?

>>> **LO3:** Describe majoritarianism, elite theory, and pluralism as theories of how democratic systems work.

Political scientists have developed a number of theories about American democracy, including *majoritarianism*, *elite theory*, and *pluralism*. Advocates of these theories use them to describe American democracy either as it actually is or as they believe it should be.

Representative Democracy
A form of government in which representatives elected by the people make and enforce laws and policies, but in which the monarchy may be retained in a ceremonial role.

Universal Suffrage
The right of all adults to vote for their representatives.

Majority Rule
A basic principle of democracy asserting that the greatest number of citizens in any political unit should select officials and determine policies.

Limited Government
A government with powers that are limited either through a written document or through widely shared beliefs.

Some scholars argue that none of these three theories, which we discuss next, fully describes the workings of American democracy. These experts say that each theory captures a part of the true reality but that we need all three theories to gain a full understanding of American politics.

Democracy for Everyone

Many people believe that in a democracy, the government ought to do what the majority of the people want. This simple proposition is the heart of majoritarian theory. As a theory of what democracy should be like, **majoritarianism** is popular among both political scientists and ordinary citizens. Many scholars, however, consider majoritarianism to provide a surprisingly poor description of how U.S. democracy actually works. Policies adopted by the U.S. government are often strikingly different from the ones endorsed by the public in opinion polls. One example is religion in the public schools. Solid majorities have long advocated a greater role for religion in the public schools, even to the point of teachers leading students in prayer. Most elected officials, however, have tried to uphold the constitutional principle of "separation of church and state." Another example: the average voter supports programs such as Social Security, Medicare—and high taxes on the rich—far more strongly than do the nation's leaders. (We discuss programs such as Social Security and Medicare later in this chapter.)

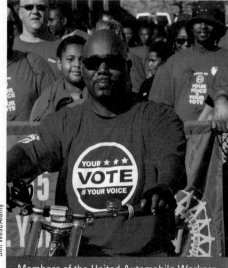

Jim West/Alamy

Members of the United Automobile Workers marching on Labor Day, 2016. They are encouraging union members to vote. *What kind of democracy are these citizens likely to support?*

Democracy for the Few

If ordinary citizens are not really making policy decisions with their votes, who is? One theory suggests that elites really govern the United States. **Elite theory** holds that society is ruled by a small number of people who exercise power to further their self-interest. American democracy, in other words, is a sham democracy. Few people today believe it is a good idea for the country to be run by a privileged minority. In the past, however, many people believed that it was appropriate for the country to be governed by an elite. Consider the words of Alexander Hamilton, one of the framers of the Constitution:

> All communities divide themselves into the few and the many. The first are the rich and the wellborn, the other the mass of the people. . . . The people are turbulent and changing; they seldom judge or determine right. Give therefore to the first class a distinct, permanent share in the government. They will check the unsteadiness of the second, and as they cannot receive any advantage by a change, they therefore will ever maintain good government.[3]

Some versions of elite theory assume that there is a small, cohesive elite class that makes almost all the important decisions for the nation,[4] whereas others suggest that voters choose among competing elites. Popular movements of varying political persuasions often advocate simple versions of elite theory.

Majoritarianism
A political theory holding that in a democracy, the government ought to do what the majority of the people want.

Elite Theory
The argument that society is ruled by a small number of people who exercise power to further their self-interest.

---

3. Alexander Hamilton, "Speech in the Constitutional Convention on a Plan of Government," in Joanne B. Freeman, ed., *Alexander Hamilton: Writings* (New York: Library of America, 2001).
4. Michael Parenti, *Democracy for the Few*, 9th ed. (Belmont, Calif.: Wadsworth Publishing, 2011).

Democracy for Groups

A different school of thought holds that our form of democracy is based on group interests. Even if the average citizen cannot keep up with political issues or cast a deciding vote in any election, the individual's interests will be protected by groups that represent her or him.

Theorists who subscribe to **pluralism** see politics as a struggle among groups to gain benefits for their members. Given the structure of the American political system, group conflicts tend to be settled by compromise and accommodation. Because there are a multitude of interests, no one group can dominate the political process. Furthermore, because most individuals have more than one interest, conflict among groups need not divide the nation into hostile camps.

Many political scientists believe that pluralism works very well as a descriptive theory. As a theory of how democracy *should* function, however, pluralism has problems. Poor citizens are rarely represented by interest groups. At the same time, rich citizens may be overrepresented. (Still, the unorganized poor do receive useful representation from religious and liberal groups.) There are also serious doubts as to whether group decision making always reflects the best interests of the nation. Indeed, critics see a danger that groups may grow so powerful that all policies become compromises crafted to satisfy the interests of the largest groups. The interests of the public as a whole, then, are not considered. Critics of pluralism have suggested that a democratic system can be almost paralyzed by the struggle among interest groups.

Fundamental Values

>>> **LO4:** Summarize the conflicts that can occur between the values of liberty and order, and between those of liberty and equality.

The writers of the U.S. Constitution believed that the structures they had created would provide for both popular sovereignty and a stable political system. They also believed that the nation would be sustained by its **political culture**—the patterned set of ideas, values, and ways of thinking about government and politics that characterized its people. Even today, there is considerable consensus among American citizens about certain concepts—including the rights to liberty, equality, and property—that are deemed to be basic to the U.S. political system.

Most Americans are descendents of immigrants who came from diverse cultural and political backgrounds. You can see how immigration will continue to change the composition of the nation in future years in Figure 1–1. Given the changing nature of our population, now and in the past, how can we account for the broad consensus that exists around basic values? Primarily, it is the result of **political socialization**—the process by which political beliefs and values are transmitted to new immigrants and to our children. The two most important sources of political socialization are the family and the educational system.

The most fundamental concepts of the American political culture are those of the dominant culture. The term *dominant culture* refers to the values, customs, and language established by the groups that traditionally have controlled politics and government in a society. The dominant culture in the United States has its roots in Western European civilization. From that civilization, American politics inherited a bias in favor of individualism, private property, and Judeo-Christian ethics.

Liberty versus Order

In the United States, our **civil liberties** include religious freedom—both the right to practice whatever religion we choose and the right to be free from any state-imposed religion. Our civil liberties also include freedom of speech—the right to express our opinions freely

Pluralism
A theory that views politics as a conflict among interest groups. Political decision making is characterized by bargaining and compromise.

Political Culture
The patterned set of ideas, values, and ways of thinking about government and politics that characterizes a people.

Political Socialization
The process by which people acquire political beliefs and values.

Civil Liberties
Those personal freedoms, including freedom of religion and of speech, that are protected for all individuals in a society.

on all matters, including government actions. Freedom of speech is perhaps one of our most prized liberties, because a democracy could not endure without it. These and many other basic guarantees of liberty are found in the **Bill of Rights,** the first ten amendments to the Constitution.

Liberty, however, is not the only value widely held by Americans. A substantial portion of the American electorate believes that certain kinds of liberty threaten the traditional social order. The right to privacy is a particularly controversial liberty. The United States Supreme Court has held that the right to privacy can be derived from other rights that are explicitly stated in the Bill of Rights. The Supreme Court has also held that under the right to privacy, the government cannot ban either abortion or private homosexual behavior by consenting adults.[5] Some Americans believe that such rights threaten the sanctity of the family and the general cultural commitment to moral behavior. Of course, others disagree with this point of view.

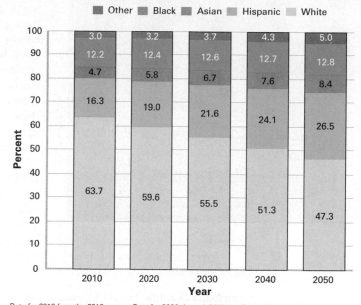

FIGURE 1–1 **Projected Changes in U.S. Ethnic Distribution**

What political changes could result when non-Hispanic whites are no longer a majority of the U.S. population?

Data for 2010 from the 2010 census. Data for 2020 through 2050 are Census Bureau projections.

Hispanics (Latinos) may be of any race. The chart categories *White, Black, Asian,* and *Other* are limited to non-Hispanics. *Other* consists of the following non-Hispanic groups: *American Indian, Native Alaskan, Native Hawaiian, Other Pacific Islander,* and *two or more races.*

Sources: U.S. Bureau of the Census and author's calculations.

Security is another issue that follows from the principle of order. When Americans have felt particularly fearful or vulnerable, the government has emphasized national security over civil liberties. Such was the case after the Japanese attack on Pearl Harbor in 1941, which led to the U.S. entry into World War II. Thousands of Japanese Americans were held in internment camps, based on the assumption that their loyalty to this country was in question. More recently, the terrorist attacks on the Pentagon and the World Trade Center on September 11, 2001, renewed calls for greater security at the expense of some civil liberties.

Liberty versus Equality

The Declaration of Independence states, "All men are created equal." The proper meaning of *equality*, however, has been disputed by Americans since the Revolution. Much of American history—and indeed, world history—is the story of how the value of **equality,** the idea that all people are of equal worth, has been extended and elaborated.

First, the right to vote was granted to all adult white males, regardless of whether they owned property. The Civil War resulted in the end of slavery and established that, in principle at least, all citizens were equal before the law. The civil rights movement of the 1950s and 1960s sought to make that promise of equality a reality for African Americans. Other

Bill of Rights
The first ten amendments to the U.S. Constitution.

Equality
As a political value, the idea that all people are of equal worth.

---

5. *Roe v. Wade*, 410 U.S. 113 (1973) and *Lawrence v. Texas*, 539 U.S. 558 (2003).

African Americans line up to register to vote in Selma, Alabama, following passage of the 1965 Voting Rights Act. *Why is voting so important for democracy?*

Bettmann/Getty Images

movements have sought equality for additional racial and ethnic groups, for women, for persons with disabilities, and for gay men and lesbians.

Although many people believe that we have a way to go yet in obtaining full equality for all of these groups, we clearly have come a long way already. No American in the nineteenth century could have imagined that the 2008 Democratic presidential primary elections would be closely fought contests between an African American man (Illinois senator Barack Obama) and a white woman (New York senator Hillary Rodham Clinton). The idea that same-sex marriage could even be open to debate would have been mind-boggling as well.

Promoting equality often requires limiting the right to treat people unequally. In this sense, equality and liberty can be conflicting values. Today, the right to deny equal treatment to the members of a particular race has very few defenders. Yet as recently as sixty years ago, this right was a cultural norm.

It can also be argued that liberty and equality are complementary. For example, people or groups cannot really enjoy liberty if they do not have equal rights under the law.

Economic Equality. Equal treatment regardless of race, religion, gender, or other characteristics is a popular value today. Equal opportunity for individuals to develop their talents and skills is also a value with substantial support. Equality of economic status, however, is a controversial value.

For much of history, the idea that the government could do anything about the division of society between rich and poor was not something about which people even thought. Most people assumed that such an effort was either impossible or undesirable. This assumption began to lose its force in the 1800s. As a result of the growing wealth of the Western world and a visible increase in the ability of government to take on large projects, some people began to advocate the value of universal equality, or *egalitarianism*. Some radicals dreamed of a revolutionary transformation of society that would establish an egalitarian system—that is, a system in which wealth and power were redistributed more equally.

Many others rejected this vision but still came to endorse the values of eliminating poverty and at least reducing the degree of economic inequality in society. Antipoverty advocates believed then and believe now that such a program could prevent much suffering. In addition, they believed that reducing economic inequality would promote fairness and enhance the moral tone of society generally.

Property
Anything that is or may be subject to ownership.

Capitalism
An economic system characterized by the private ownership of wealth-creating assets, free markets, and freedom of contract.

Property Rights and Capitalism. The value of reducing economic inequality is in conflict with the right to **property**. This is because reducing economic inequality typically involves the transfer of property (usually in the form of tax dollars) from some people to others. For many people, liberty and property are closely entwined. Our capitalist system is based on private property rights. Under **capitalism,** property consists not only of personal possessions but also of wealth-creating assets such as farms and factories. Capitalism is also typically characterized by considerable freedom to make binding contracts and by relatively unconstrained markets for goods, services, and investments.

Property—especially wealth-creating property—can be seen as giving its owner political power and the liberty to do whatever he or she wants. At the same time, the ownership of property immediately creates inequality in society. The desire to own property, however, is so widespread among all classes of Americans that radical egalitarian movements have had a difficult time securing a wide following in this country.

The Proper Size of Government

Opposition to "big government" has been a constant theme in American politics. Indeed, the belief that government is overreaching dates back to the years before the American Revolution. Tensions over the size and scope of government have plagued Americans ever since. Citizens often express contradictory opinions on the size of government and the role that it should play in their lives. Those who complain about the amount of taxes that they pay each year may also worry about the lack of funds for more teachers in the local schools. Americans tend to oppose "big government" in principle, even as they endorse its benefits. Indeed, American politics in the twenty-first century can be described largely in terms of ambivalence about big government.

Big Government and the Great Recession. In September 2008, a financial meltdown threatened the world economy. The impact of the Great Recession was so strong that even by 2016, the share of Americans with jobs was not yet back to the 2007 level, as you can see in Figure 1–2. In November 2008, the voters handed Democrat Barack Obama a solid victory in the presidential elections, and Democrats increased their hold on the U.S. House and Senate. Voters demanded government action to save the economy, yet major spending

---

FIGURE 1–2   **Employment Rates for U.S. Persons Aged 25–54, 1977–2015**

The growing number of working women from 1977 to 2000 reflects the movement to women's equality. Note also that despite recent economic growth, the job losses of the Great Recession have not been fully reversed. *What problems can result if large numbers of adults leave the workforce?*

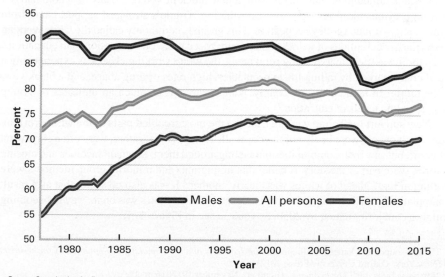

Source: Organization for Economic Cooperation and Development, Main Economic Indicators database dx.doi.org/10.1787/data-00052-en. © 2016 OECD, reprinted with permission.

programs aimed at accomplishing that goal were highly unpopular. In 2010, Congress and President Obama also approved a major health-care initiative that had no direct connection to fighting the recession. For many, this act completed the picture of big government out of control.

In November 2010, voters swung heavily to the Republicans, granting them control of the House. By 2012, however, a fear that Republicans would cut valued social programs may have balanced concern over Democratic affection for government. President Obama was reelected in November 2012, but the Republicans kept the House. The 2014 elections again favored the Republicans, who gained control of the Senate. One cause was low voter turnout by Democrats—turnout was lower than in any general election since World War II (1939–1945).

Who Benefits from Big Government?   The 2016 elections provided new information on popular attitudes toward the size of government. Donald Trump quickly established himself as the front-runner in the Republican presidential primaries. It soon became clear that neither Trump nor his followers were particularly enamored of the traditional small-government conservatism supported by most Republican officeholders. This attitude had also been common among supporters of the Tea Party, a conservative movement organized after Obama became president.[6] Most Tea Party supporters had no problems with programs such as Medicare and Social Security that benefited older voters, many of whom were white. They did oppose programs such as Obama's health-care plan that were seen as primarily benefiting poorer Americans in general and minority group members in particular. (Of course, other groups have had different issues with Obamacare.)

The question, in other words, was not so much the size of government but who *benefits* from big government. Trump's most ardent supporters largely shared this "who benefits" viewpoint. For more on programs such as Social Security and Medicare, see this chapter's *At Issue* feature.

Trump's Supporters.   Trump won in the November general elections in part because loyal Republicans rallied to his campaign. Still, a new block of voters—many of whom had not voted in previous elections—put him over the top. Trump's strongest support came from white voters without a college education. This group is commonly called the white **working class.** (Earlier definitions of *working class* were based more on occupation than education.) By 2016, it was clear that in many rural areas, the white working class was experiencing a social crisis marked by falling life expectancies, high rates of drug abuse, and a bleak view of the future. In fact, county by county, poor health was as much an indicator of Trump support as low levels of education.[7]

New support for Trump was not based in the most troubled parts of the white working class. Such people were likely not to vote at all. Trump voters, rather, were often somewhat better off, but saw their communities unraveling around them. Stagnant incomes and closing factories were part of the story. A belief that immigrants and minority group members were "cutting in line" ahead of whites was clearly another.[8] It was also no secret that as a result of population growth among minority groups, the United States was on its way to becoming a minority-majority nation by 2050, as you can see in Figure 1–1.

Working Class
Currently, those with no college education. Traditionally, individuals or families in which the head of household was employed in manual or unskilled labor.

6. Theda Skocpol and Vanessa Williamson, *The Tea Party and the Remaking of Republican Conservatism* (New York: Oxford University Press, 2012).

7. "Illness as Indicator," *The Economist* (London), November 19, 2016, p. 25.

8. Arlie Russell Hochschild, *Strangers in Their Own Land: Anger and Mourning on the American Right* (New York: The New Press, 2016).

Does Entitlement Spending Corrupt Us?

Certain federal benefits are called *entitlements* because you are entitled to receive them if you meet specific requirements. If you meet certain age and previous earnings requirements, you can receive a monthly Social Security check. If you lose your job, you may be entitled to unemployment benefits for a certain number of weeks. If your family income is below a certain level, you are typically entitled to benefits from the Supplemental Nutrition Assistance Program (SNAP, formerly called food stamps).

In recent years, federal entitlement spending has ballooned. Indeed, big government has gotten bigger in large part because Americans are receiving more entitlement payments every year. At all levels combined, government spending now has a value equivalent to about 36 percent of GDP. Some have argued that large-scale entitlement spending is corrupting us.

The More You Give People, the Less They'll Work

Conservatives point out that entitlement transfers—adjusted for rising prices and population growth—are now more than seven times what they were in 1960. (In part, this is because major programs such as Medicare and Medicaid were created in the 1960s.) Currently, almost half of Americans live in a household that receives at least one government benefit. If you count tax deductions, almost every household receives benefits.

Consider SNAP benefits. In 2007, 26 million Americans received them. By 2017, about 46 million Americans received them. The same story applies to Social Security disability payments. Four million people received disability checks in 1988. Today, disability checks are distributed to almost 11 million people. Fewer people are now in the labor force, and those who are work fewer hours per year. Since 2000, the labor force participation rate has fallen continuously, even during boom times. Many believe that increased entitlement benefits have reduced people's desire to join the labor force. In other words, entitlements corrupt.

Entitlements Are a Needed Part of the Social Contract

While the statistics just presented are accurate, political progressives do not accept the conclusions drawn. With an aging society, we should expect to pay more for Social Security. The same is true for government-financed health care. Health-care expenses are driven up not only by larger numbers of the elderly, but also by increasingly expensive (and effective) medical procedures.

Contrary to what some have argued, Americans are not divided between "makers" and "takers." At various times in our lives, we are all takers, and almost all of us are makers. As President Obama said in his second inaugural address, "The commitments we make to each other—through Medicare, and Medicaid, and Social Security—these things do not sap our initiative; they strengthen us. . . . they free us to take the risks that make this country great."

Americans believe in hard work as much as they always have. The Pew Economic Mobility Project sampled Americans on what is essential for getting ahead. More than 90 percent responded "hard work," and almost 90 percent answered "ambition." That doesn't sound like corruption.

FOR CRITICAL ANALYSIS
Who ultimately pays for entitlement programs?

Political Ideologies

>>> **LO5:** Discuss conservatism, liberalism, and other popular American ideological positions.

A **political ideology** is a closely linked set of beliefs about politics. The concept of *ideology* is often misunderstood. Many people think that only individuals whose beliefs lie well out on one or the other end of the political spectrum have an ideology. Actually, almost everyone who has political opinions can be said to have an ideology. Some people may have difficulty in explaining the principles that underlie their opinions, but the principles are there nonetheless.

Political ideologies offer people well-organized theories that propose goals for society and the means by which those goals can be achieved. At the core of every political ideology is a set of guiding values. The two ideologies most commonly referred to in discussions of American politics are *conservatism* and *liberalism*.

Political Ideology
A comprehensive set of beliefs about the nature of politics and the role of government.

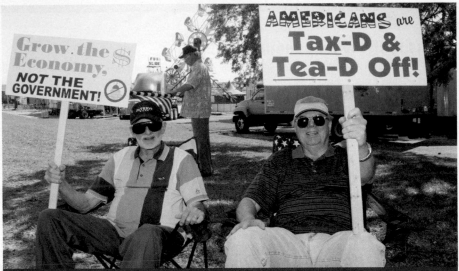

These members of the Tea Party movement in Florida assembled to voice their opposition to "big government." *What are some of the things paid for by our taxes?*

Cheryl Casey/Shutterstock.com

Conservatism

Traditionally, those who favor the ideology of **conservatism** have sought to conserve traditional practices and institutions. In that sense, conservatism is as old as politics itself. In America, limited government is a key tradition. For much of our history, limited government has included major restrictions on government's ability to interfere with business. In the past, enterprises were largely free to act as they pleased in the marketplace and in managing their employees. Government regulation of business increased greatly in the 1930s, as Democratic president Franklin D. Roosevelt (1933–1945) initiated a series of massive interventions in the economy in an attempt to counter the effects of the Great Depression. Many conservatives consider the Roosevelt administration to be a time when America took a wrong turn.

Modern Conservatism. It was in the 1950s, however, that American conservatism took its modern shape. The **conservative movement** that arose in that decade provided the age-old conservative impulse with a fully worked-out ideology. The new movement first demonstrated its strength in 1964, when Senator Barry Goldwater of Arizona was nominated as the Republican presidential candidate. Goldwater lost badly to Democrat Lyndon B. Johnson, but from that time forward *movement conservatives* have occupied a crucial position in the Republican Party.

Conservative Values. American conservatives generally place a high value on the principle of order. This includes support for patriotism and traditional ideals. As a result, conservatives typically oppose such social innovations as same-sex marriage. Conservatives strongly endorse liberty, but they generally define it as freedom from government support of nontraditional ideals such as gay rights or as freedom from government interference in business. Conservatives believe that the private sector probably can outperform the government in almost any activity. Therefore, they usually oppose initiatives that would increase the role of the government in the economy, such as President Obama's health-care reforms.

Conservatism
A set of beliefs that includes advocacy of a limited role for the national government in helping individuals, support for traditional values and lifestyles, and a cautious response to change.

Conservative Movement
An American movement launched in the 1950s that provides a comprehensive ideological framework for conservative politics.

Conservatives place a relatively low value on equality. Believing that individuals and families are primarily responsible for their own well-being, they typically oppose high levels of antipoverty spending and government expenditures to stimulate the economy, favoring tax-rate cuts instead. Trump supporters, with their anti-immigrant, nationalist views, emphasized different aspects of the conservative tradition than those championed by the conservative movement. Still, Trump's followers were clearly conservative in a broad sense.

Liberalism

The term **liberalism** stems from the word *liberty* and originally meant "free from prejudice in favor of traditional opinions and established institutions." Liberals have always been skeptical of the influence of religion in politics, but in the nineteenth century they were skeptical of government as well. From the time of Democratic presidents Woodrow Wilson (1913–1921) and Franklin D. Roosevelt, however, American liberals increasingly sought to use the power of government for nontraditional ends. Their goals included support for organized labor and for the poor. New programs instituted by the Roosevelt administration included Social Security and unemployment insurance.

Modern Liberalism. American liberalism took its modern form in the 1960s. Liberals rallied to the civil rights movement, which sought to obtain equal rights for African Americans. As the feminist movement grew in importance, liberals supported it as well. Liberals won new federal health-care programs such as Medicare and Medicaid, and the promotion of such programs became a key component of liberal politics. Finally, liberals reacted more negatively to U.S. participation in the Vietnam War (1965–1975) than did other Americans, and for years thereafter liberalism was associated with skepticism about the use of U.S. military forces abroad.

◐ Interact

The Pew Research Center asks, "Are you a Solid Liberal? A Steadfast Conservative? Or somewhere in between?" You may have a good sense of your personal political ideology. Then again, you may not. Pew has a "Political Typology Quiz" that you can locate by searching for that term in your browser. Take the quiz to find out how Pew classifies your politics. Alternatively, your instructor can set it up so that your entire class can take the quiz together (click on "start a new community group"). If your class takes the test, responses of individual students are anonymous.

Liberal Values. Those who favor liberalism place a high value on social and economic equality. As we have seen, liberals champion the rights of minority group members and favor substantial antipoverty spending. In the recent health-care policy debates, liberals strongly endorsed the principle that all citizens should have greater access to insurance. In contrast to conservatives, liberals often support government intervention in the economy. They believe that capitalism works best when the government curbs capitalism's excesses through regulation. Like conservatives, liberals place a high value on liberty, but they tend to view it as the freedom to live one's life according to one's own values. Liberals, therefore, usually support gay rights, including the right to same-sex marriage.

The Traditional Political Spectrum

A traditional method of comparing political ideologies is to arrange them on a continuum from left to right, based primarily on how much power the government should exercise to promote economic equality. Table 1–1 shows how ideologies can be arrayed on a traditional political spectrum. In addition to liberalism and conservatism, this example includes the ideologies of socialism and libertarianism.

  Socialism falls on the left side of the spectrum. Socialist parties and movements have been important in other countries around the world, but socialists have usually played a

Liberalism
A set of beliefs that includes advocacy of positive government action to improve the welfare of individuals, support for civil rights, and tolerance for political and social change.

Socialism
A political ideology based on strong support for economic and social equality. Socialists traditionally envisioned a society in which major businesses were taken over by the government or by employee cooperatives.

TABLE 1–1	The Traditional Political Spectrum			
What issues are not addressed by this spectrum?				
	Socialism	**Liberalism**	**Conservatism**	**Libertarianism**
How much power should the government have over the economy?	Active government control of major economic sectors.	Positive government action in the economy.	Positive government action to support capitalism.	Almost no regulation of the economy.
What should the government promote?	Economic equality, community.	Economic security, equal opportunity, social liberty.	Economic liberty, morality, social order.	Total economic and social liberty.

minor role in the American political arena. An obvious exception was senator and 2016 presidential candidate Bernie Sanders (D., Vt.), a self-proclaimed "democratic socialist." In the past, socialists typically advocated replacing investor ownership of major businesses with either government ownership or ownership by employee cooperatives. Socialists believed that such steps would break the power of the very rich and lead to an egalitarian society. In more recent times, socialists in western countries have advocated more limited programs that redistribute income.

On the right side of the spectrum is **libertarianism,** a philosophy of skepticism toward most government activities. Libertarians strongly support property rights and typically oppose regulation of the economy and redistribution of income. Libertarians support *laissez-faire* capitalism. (*Laissez faire* is French for "let it be.") Libertarians also tend to oppose government attempts to regulate personal behavior and promote moral values. We might expect, therefore, that a consistent libertarian would support same-sex marriage. Many libertarians are also skeptical about U.S. military interventions abroad.

Problems with the Traditional Political Spectrum

Many political scientists believe that the traditional left-to-right spectrum is not sufficiently complete. Take the example of libertarians. In Table 1–1, libertarians are placed to the right of conservatives. If the only question is how much power the government should have over the economy, this is where they belong. Libertarians, however, strongly advocate freedom in social matters. They oppose government action to promote traditional moral values, although such action is often favored by other groups on the political right. Their strong support for cultural freedoms seems to align them more closely with modern liberals than with conservatives.

Liberalism is often described as an ideology that supports "big government." If the objective is to promote equality, the description has some validity. In the moral sphere, however, conservatives tend to support more government regulation of social values and moral decisions than do liberals. Thus, conservatives tend to oppose gay rights legislation and propose stronger curbs on pornography. Liberals usually show greater tolerance for alternative life choices and oppose government attempts to regulate personal behavior and morals.

Libertarianism
A political ideology based on skepticism or opposition toward most government activities.

A Four-Cornered Ideological Grid

For a more sophisticated breakdown of recent American popular ideologies, many scholars use a four-cornered grid, as shown in Figure 1–3. The grid includes four possible ideologies. Each quadrant contains a substantial portion of the American electorate. Individual voters may fall anywhere on the grid, depending on the strength of their beliefs about economic and cultural issues.

Economic Liberals, Cultural Conservatives. Note that there is no generally accepted term for persons in the lower-left position, which we have labeled "economic liberals, cultural conservatives." Some scholars have used terms such as *populist* to describe this point of view, but these terms can be misleading. *Populism* more accurately refers to a hostility toward political, economic, or cultural elites, and it can be combined with a variety of political positions. In the 2016 presidential primary elections, both Donald Trump and Bernie Sanders made appeals that could be called populist, though their positions on the issues were radically different.

Individuals who are economic liberals and cultural conservatives tend to support government action both to promote the values of economic equality and fairness and to defend traditional values, such as the family and marriage. These individuals may describe themselves as conservative or moderate. They may vote for a Republican candidate based on

FIGURE 1–3   A Four-Cornered Ideological Grid

Can you name some celebrities or politicians who fall into each of these four categories? If so, who are they?

their conservative values. More often, they may be Democrats due to their support for economic liberalism. Many of these Democrats are African Americans or members of other minority groups.

Libertarians. As a position on the four-cornered grid, *libertarian* does not refer to the small Libertarian Party, which has only a minor role in the American political arena. Rather, libertarians more typically support the Republican Party. Economically successful individuals are more likely than members of other groups to hold libertarian opinions.

The Liberal and Conservative Labels. Even though all four ideologies are popular, the various labels we have used in the four-cornered grid are not equally favored. Voters are much more likely to describe themselves as conservative than as liberal. In the political battles of the last several decades, the conservative movement has consistently made *liberal* a term of derision, and they have succeeded in devaluing the term among much of the public. Indeed, few politicians today willingly describe themselves as liberal, and many liberals prefer to describe themselves as **progressive** instead. This term dates back to the years before World War I (1914–1918), when it referred to advocates of reform in both of the major political parties. Public opinion polls suggest that *progressive* is a relatively popular label.

Progressive
A popular alternative to the term *liberal*.

MAKING A DIFFERENCE

Seeing Democracy in Action

One way to understand the American political system is to observe a legislative body in action. By "legislative body," we don't mean only the U.S. Congress and the various state legislatures—there are thousands of elected legislatures in the United States at all levels of government. You might choose to visit the meeting of a city council or a county commission.

Why Should You Care? Local legislative bodies can have a direct impact on your life. City councils or county commissions typically oversee the police or the sheriff's department, and the behavior of the police is a matter of interest even if you live on campus. If you live off campus, local authorities are responsible for an even greater number of issues that affect you directly. Are there items that the sanitation department refuses to pick up, for example? You might be able to change its policies by lobbying your councilperson.

What Can You Do? To find out when and where local legislative bodies meet, call the clerk of the council or commission. If you live in a state capital, you can view a meeting of the state legislature instead. In many communities, city council meetings and county board meetings can be seen on public-access TV channels.

While attending a business session of the legislature, keep in mind the theory of representative democracy. The commissioners or council members are elected to represent their constituents (those who voted them into office). Observe how often the members refer to their constituents or to the special needs of their district. Listen for sources of conflict within a community. If there is a debate, for example, over a zoning proposal that involves an issue of land use, try to figure out why some members oppose the proposal.

To follow up on your visit, try to get a brief interview with one of the members of the council or board. In general, legislators are very willing to talk to students, particularly students who also are voters. Ask the member how he or she sees the job of representative. How can the wishes of the constituents be identified? How does the representative balance the needs of the particular ward or district that she or he represents with the good of the entire community?

Young students meet with Nancy Pelosi at the U.S. Capitol Building. Pelosi is the Democratic leader in the U.S. House of Representatives. *Why might elected officials be willing to meet with students?*

Bill Clark/CQ-Roll Call Group/Getty Images

Key Terms

authoritarianism 4
authority 3
Bill of Rights 9
capitalism 10
civil liberties 8
conservatism 14
conservative
   movement 14
democracy 4
democratic republic 5
direct democracy 4

elite theory 7
equality 9
government 2
initiative 4
institution 2
legislature 4
legitimacy 3
liberalism 15
libertarianism 16
liberty 3
limited government 6

majoritarianism 7
majority rule 6
order 2
pluralism 8
political culture 8
political ideology 13
political socialization 8
politics 2
popular sovereignty 5
progressive 17
property 10

recall 4
referendum 4
representative
   democracy 6
republic 5
socialism 15
totalitarian regime 4
universal suffrage 6
working class 12

Chapter Summary

≫ **LO1** *Politics* is the process by which people decide which members of society receive certain benefits or privileges and which members do not. It is the struggle over power or influence within institutions or organizations that can grant benefits or privileges. *Government* is an institution within which decisions are made that resolve conflicts and allocate benefits and privileges. It is the predominant institution within society because it has the ultimate decision-making authority.

Two fundamental political values are *order*, which includes security against violence, and *liberty*, the greatest freedom of the individual consistent with the freedom of other individuals. To be effective, government *authority*—the right and power to enforce its decisions—must be backed by *legitimacy*.

≫ **LO2** Many of our terms for describing forms of government came from the ancient Greeks. In a direct democracy, such as that of ancient Athens, the people themselves make the important political decisions. The United States is a democratic republic—also called a representative democracy—in which the people elect representatives to make the decisions.

≫ **LO3** Theories of American democracy include majoritarianism, elite theory, and pluralism. In majoritarianism, the government does what the majority wants. Under elite theory, the real power lies with one or more elites. Pluralism means that organized interest groups contend for power.

≫ **LO4** Fundamental American values include liberty, order, equality, and property. Not all of these values are fully compatible. The value of order often competes with civil liberties, and economic equality competes with property rights, which represent liberty to many people.

≫ **LO5** Conservatives advocate for a limited role for government, support traditional values, and are cautious about change. Liberals support government action to improve individual welfare, civil rights, and political and social change. Economic liberalism and conservatism can be analyzed separately from cultural liberalism and conservatism.

Test Yourself

1. When citizens of a nation do not enjoy liberty, the government frequently will:
   a. abolish the right to a fair trial.
   b. provide government funds to churches.
   c. engage in military aggression.

2. When authority is broadly accepted, we say it has:
   a. popularity.
   b. validity.
   c. legitimacy.

3. A principal characteristic of direct democracy is that:
   a. all lawful residents have citizenship rights.
   b. laws are made by the entire citizenry acting together.
   c. the power of the government is limited to protect minorities.

4. A democratic republic is based on all of the following principles except:
   a. popular sovereignty.
   b. majority rule.
   c. a limited monarchy.

5. A word or phrase used to describe our democratic system in terms of competition among groups is:
   a. majoritarianism.
   b. pluralism.
   c. elite theory.

6. Many of our basic guarantees of liberty are found in:
   a. the Bible.
   b. the Declaration of Independence.
   c. the Bill of Rights.

7. Our economic system, under which property consists not only of personal possessions but also of wealth-creating assets, is called:
   a. capitalism.
   b. industrialism.
   c. democracy.

8. A major theme of American politics during the twenty-first century has been:
   a. arguments over whether all citizens should have the right to vote.
   b. controversies over the proper size of government.
   c. disputes as to the role of the military.

9. Popular American ideologies include:
   a. conservatism, liberalism, and libertarianism.
   b. conservatism, liberalism, and socialism.
   c. conservatism, liberalism, and populism.

10. Important members of the conservative movement have included:
    a. President Franklin D. Roosevelt.
    b. Senator Barry Goldwater.
    c. President Lyndon B. Johnson.

11. Since the 1960s, most liberals have strongly supported all of these except:
    a. civil rights for African Americans.
    b. federal health-care programs.
    c. the use of U.S. military forces abroad.

12. A common term that has come to replace *liberalism* in current American politics is:
    a. populism.
    b. progressivism.
    c. libertarianism.

Essay Questions

1. In Australia and Belgium, citizens are legally required to vote in elections. Would such a requirement be a good idea in the United States? What changes might take place if such a rule were in effect?

2. In your own life, what factors have contributed to your political socialization? To what extent were your political values shaped by your family, by school experiences, by friends, and by the media?

Answers to multiple-choice questions: 1. a, 2. c, 3. b, 4. c, 5. b, 6. c, 7. a, 8. b, 9. a, 10. b, 11. c, 12. b.

2 | Forging a New Government: The Constitution

Independence Hall in Philadelphia. In this building, the founders signed the Declaration of Independence and wrote the Constitution. At the time, Philadelphia was the largest city in the country. *Why might the founders have placed the nation's capitol somewhere else?*

Nikreates/Alamy Stock Photo

The five **Learning Outcomes (LOs)** below are designed to help improve your understanding of this chapter. After reading this chapter, you should be able to:

>>> **LO1** Explain how the colonial experience prepared Americans for independence, the restrictions that Britain placed on the colonies, and the American response to those restrictions.

>>> **LO2** Describe the significance of the Declaration of Independence and the Articles of Confederation, as well as the weaknesses of the Articles.

>>> **LO3** Discuss the most important compromises reached at the Constitutional Convention and the basic structure of the resulting government.

>>> **LO4** Summarize the arguments in favor of and the arguments against adopting the Constitution, and explain why the Bill of Rights was adopted.

>>> **LO5** Describe the process of amending the Constitution and the informal ways in which constitutional interpretation has changed over time.

Check your understanding of the material with the Test Yourself section at the end of the chapter.

W*e the People of the United States, in Order to form a more perfect Union, establish Justice, insure domestic Tranquility, provide for the common defence, promote the general Welfare, and secure the Blessings of Liberty to ourselves and our Posterity, do ordain and establish this Constitution for the United States of America.*

Every schoolchild in America has at one time or another been exposed to these famous words from the Preamble to the U.S. Constitution. The document itself is remarkable. The U.S. Constitution, compared with others in the fifty states and in the world, is relatively short. Because amending it is difficult, it also has relatively few amendments. The Constitution has remained largely intact for more than two hundred years. To a great extent, this is because the principles set forth in the Constitution are sufficiently broad that they can be adapted to meet the needs of a changing society.

How and why the U.S. Constitution was created is a story that has been told and retold. It is worth repeating, because knowing the historical and political context in which this country's governmental machinery was formed is essential to understanding American government and politics today. The Constitution did not result just from creative thinking. Many of its provisions were grounded in the political philosophy of the time.

The delegates to the Constitutional Convention in 1787 brought with them two important sets of influences: their political culture and their political experience. In the years between the first settlements in the New World and the writing of the Constitution, Americans had developed a political philosophy about how people should be governed, and they had tried out several forms of government. These experiences gave the founders the tools with which they constructed the Constitution.

The Colonial Background

>>> **LO1:** Explain how the colonial experience prepared Americans for independence, the restrictions that Britain placed on the colonies, and the American response to those restrictions.

In 1607, a company chartered by the English government sent a group of settlers to establish a trading post, Jamestown, in what is now Virginia. Jamestown was the first permanent English colony in the Americas. The king of England gave the backers of this colony a charter granting them "full power and authority" to make laws "for the good and welfare" of the settlement. The colonists at Jamestown instituted a **representative assembly,** a legislature composed of individuals who represented the population, thus setting a precedent in government that was to be observed in later colonial adventures.

Separatists, the *Mayflower*, and the Compact

The first New England colony was established in 1620. A group made up in large part of Separatists, who wished to break with the Church of England, came over on the ship *Mayflower* to the New World, landing at Plymouth (Massachusetts). Before going onshore, the adult males—women were not considered to have any political status—drew up the Mayflower Compact, which was signed by forty-one of the forty-four men aboard the ship on November 11, 1620.

The reason for the compact was obvious. This group was outside the jurisdiction of the Virginia Company of London, which had chartered its settlement. The Separatist leaders feared that some of the *Mayflower* passengers might conclude that they were no longer under any obligations of civil obedience. Therefore, some form of public authority was imperative. As William Bradford (one of the Separatist leaders) later recalled, there were "discontented and mutinous speeches that some of the strangers [non-Separatists] amongst them had let fall from them in the ship; that when they came ashore they would use their own liberty; for none had power to command them."

Representative Assembly
A legislature composed of individuals who represent the population.

The Significance of the Compact. The compact was not a constitution. It was a political statement in which the signers agreed to create and submit to the authority of a government, pending the receipt of a royal charter. The Mayflower Compact's historical and political significance is twofold: it depended on the consent of the affected individuals (and thus served as an example of *popular sovereignty*), and it served as a prototype for similar compacts in American history.

By the time of the American Revolution, the compact was well on its way toward achieving mythic status. In 1802, John Quincy Adams, son of the second American president, spoke these words at a founders' day celebration in Plymouth: "This is perhaps the only instance in human history of that positive, original social compact, which speculative philosophers have imagined as the only legitimate source of government."[1]

Bettmann/Getty Images

The signing of the Mayflower Compact, by the American painter Jean Leon Gerome Ferris. *Was the Compact a constitution? Why or why not?*

Pilgrim Beliefs. Although the Plymouth settlers committed themselves to self-government, in other ways their political ideas were not those that are prevalent today. The new community was a religious colony. Separation of church and state and most of our modern civil liberties were alien to the settlers' thinking. By the time the U.S. Constitution was written, the nation's leaders had a very different vision of the relationship between religion and government. We look at some of the founders' beliefs in this chapter's *At Issue* feature.

More Colonies, More Government

Another outpost in New England was set up by the Massachusetts Bay Colony in 1630. Then followed Rhode Island, Connecticut, New Hampshire, and others. By 1732, the last of the thirteen colonies, Georgia, was established. During the colonial period, Americans developed a concept of limited government, which followed from the establishment of the first colonies under Crown charters. Theoretically, London governed the colonies. In practice, owing partly to the colonies' distance from London, the colonists exercised a large measure of self-government.

The colonists were able to make their own laws, as in the Fundamental Orders of Connecticut in 1639. The Massachusetts Body of Liberties in 1641 supported the protection of individual rights. In 1682, the Frame of Government of Pennsylvania was passed. Along with the Pennsylvania Charter of Privileges of 1701, it foreshadowed our modern Constitution and Bill of Rights. All of this legislation enabled the colonists to acquire crucial political experience. After independence was declared in 1776, the states quickly set up their own new constitutions.

---

1. Nathaniel Philbrick, *Mayflower: A Story of Courage, Community, and War* (New York: Penguin, 2007), p. 352. Today, the Mayflower Separatists are frequently referred to as the Pilgrims, but that name did not come into common use until two centuries after the colony was founded.

AT ISSUE

Is America a Christian Nation?

Christianity utterly permeated the world of the first English settlers. North and South, church attendance was often mandatory. Nine colonies had churches that were established by law.

The Declaration of Independence, however, makes no reference to Christ. The word *God* does not appear in the Constitution. By 1790, officially established churches were found only in Connecticut and Massachusetts, and the Congregational Church in Massachusetts had drifted so far from its Puritan origins that many of its members no longer accepted the divinity of Jesus. That is, they belonged to *Unitarian* congregations. One result of this development was that in the national elections of 1796 and 1800, neither major party fielded a presidential candidate who was, by modern definition, a Christian. John Adams, Unitarian, squared off against Thomas Jefferson, freethinker.

These facts raise the question: Just how Christian were the founders? More to the point, did the founders intend the United States to be a "Christian nation"? Scholars and school boards often differ on these issues.

One Nation, Under God

Christian conservatives point out that numerous American leaders throughout history have characterized the country as a *Christian nation.* The revolutionaries of 1776 often viewed the struggle in religious terms. Quite a few believed that God had a special plan for America to serve as an example to the world. The overwhelming majority of the colonists considered themselves Christians. Today, 71 percent of Americans identify themselves as such. If the term Christian nation merely identifies the beliefs of the majority, it is undeniably an accurate label.

To Christian conservatives who would like to change what is taught in the schools, however, the term means much more. They contend that American law is based on the laws of Moses as set down in the Bible. They also believe that America's divine mission is not just an opinion held by many people—it should be taught as literal truth. Finally, this group argues that "freedom *of* religion does not mean freedom *from* religion." The language of the First Amendment means only that the national government should not prefer one church over another.

Church and Government Must Not Mix

Mainstream scholars disagree with the previous arguments, often vehemently. For example, researchers have been unable to find American court cases that reference the laws of Moses. Ultimately, these people say, to argue that the founders were not serious about the separation of church and state is to ignore the plain language of the Constitution. True, most of the authors of the Constitution were Christians, but the founders were also steeped in *Enlightenment rationalism.* Enlightenment figures such as England's John Locke (1632–1704), France's Voltaire (1694–1778), and Scotland's Adam Smith (1723–1790) emphasized reason and individualism rather than tradition. Enlightenment thinking also rejected "enthusiasm" in religion. *Enthusiasm* referred to the spirit that allowed Protestant and Catholic Europeans to kill one another in the name of God over a period of two centuries. For the founders, mixing church and government was a recipe for trouble.

FOR CRITICAL ANALYSIS

Today, candidates for president benefit when they use religious language and when they are comfortable discussing their faith. Is this at all troubling? Why or why not?

British Restrictions and Colonial Grievances

The conflict between Britain and the American colonies, which ultimately led to the Revolutionary War, began in the 1760s when the British government decided to raise revenues by imposing taxes on the American colonies. Policy advisers to Britain's King George III, who ascended to the throne in 1760, decided that it was only logical to require the American colonists to help pay the costs of Britain's defending them during the French and Indian War (1754–1763). The colonists, who had grown accustomed to a large degree of self-government and independence from the British Crown, viewed the matter differently.

In 1764, the British Parliament passed the Sugar Act, which imposed a tax that many colonists were unwilling to pay. Further legislation was to come. In 1765, Parliament passed the Stamp Act, providing for internal taxation of legal documents and even newspapers. The colonists' Stamp Act Congress, assembled in 1765, called this act "taxation without representation." The colonists boycotted the purchase of English commodities in response.

The success of the boycott (the Stamp Act was repealed a year later) generated a feeling of unity within the colonies. The British, however, continued to try to raise revenues from the colonies. When Parliament passed duties on glass, lead, paint, and other items in 1767, the colonists again boycotted British goods. The colonists' fury over taxation climaxed in the Boston Tea Party: colonists dressed as Mohawk Indians dumped almost 350 chests of British tea into Boston Harbor as a gesture of tax protest. In retaliation, Parliament passed the Coercive Acts (the "Intolerable Acts") in 1774, which closed Boston Harbor and placed the government of Massachusetts under direct British control. The colonists were outraged—and they responded.

The First Continental Congress

New York, Pennsylvania, and Rhode Island proposed a colonial gathering, or congress. The Massachusetts House of Representatives requested that all colonies hold conventions to select delegates to be sent to Philadelphia for such a congress.

The First Continental Congress was held in Philadelphia at Carpenters' Hall on September 5, 1774. It was a gathering of delegates from twelve of the thirteen colonies (delegates from Georgia did not attend until 1775). At that meeting, there was little talk of independence. The congress passed a resolution requesting that the colonies send a petition to King George III expressing their grievances. Resolutions were also passed requiring that the colonies raise their own colonial militias and boycott British trade. The British government condemned the congress's actions, treating them as open acts of rebellion.

The Second Continental Congress

By the time the Second Continental Congress met in May 1775 (all of the colonies were represented this time), fighting had already broken out between the British and the colonists. One of the main actions of the Second Continental Congress was to establish an army. It did this by declaring the militia that had gathered around Boston an army and naming George Washington as commander in chief. Congressional participants still attempted to reach a peaceful settlement with the British Parliament. One declaration of the congress stated explicitly that "we have not raised armies with ambitious designs of separating from Great Britain, and establishing independent states." But by the beginning of 1776, military encounters had become increasingly frequent.

Public debate was acrimonious. Then Thomas Paine's *Common Sense* appeared in Philadelphia bookstores. The pamphlet was a colonial best seller. (To do relatively as well

MPI/Getty Images

The minutemen were members of a colonial militia that was ready to fight the British at a moment's notice. *In what ways might a local militia be less effective than an actual army in confronting the British?*

today, a book would have to sell between 9 million and 11 million copies in its first year of publication.) Many agreed that Paine did make common sense when he argued that Paine further argued that "nothing can settle our affairs so expeditiously as an open and determined declaration for Independence."[2]

> *A government of our own is our natural right: And when a man seriously reflects on the precariousness* [instability, unpredictability] *of human affairs, he will become convinced, that it is infinitely wiser and safer, to form a constitution of our own in a cool and deliberate manner, while we have it in our power, than to trust such an interesting event to time and chance.*[3]

Students of Paine's pamphlet point out that his arguments were not new. They were common in tavern debates throughout the land. Rather, it was the near poetry of his words—which were at the same time as plain as the alphabet—that struck his readers.

An Independent Confederation

>>> **LO2:** Describe the significance of the Declaration of Independence and the Articles of Confederation, as well as the weaknesses of the Articles.

On April 6, 1776, the Second Continental Congress voted for free trade at all American ports with all countries except Britain. This act could be interpreted as an implicit declaration of independence. The next month, the congress suggested that each of the colonies establish a state government unconnected to Britain. Finally, in July, the colonists declared their independence from Britain.

The Resolution for Independence

On July 2, the Resolution for Independence was adopted by the Second Continental Congress:

> *RESOLVED, That these United Colonies are, and of right ought to be free and independent States, that they are absolved from allegiance to the British Crown, and that all political connection between them and the state of Great Britain is, and ought to be, totally dissolved.*

In June 1776, Thomas Jefferson was already writing drafts of the Declaration of Independence. When the Resolution for Independence was adopted on July 2, Jefferson argued that a declaration clearly putting forth the causes that compelled the colonies to separate from Britain was necessary. The Second Continental Congress assigned the task to him.

July 4, 1776—The Declaration of Independence

Jefferson's version of the Declaration was amended to gain unanimous acceptance (for example, his condemnation of the slave trade was eliminated to satisfy Georgia and North Carolina), but the bulk of it was passed intact on July 4, 1776. On July 19, the modified draft became "the unanimous declaration of the thirteen United States of America." On August 2, it was signed by the members of the Second Continental Congress.

---

2. Thomas Paine, *Common Sense* (Ballingslöv, Sweden: Wisehouse Classics, 2015), p. 26.
3. *Ibid.,* p. 33.

Universal Truths. The Declaration of Independence has become one of the world's most renowned and significant documents. The words opening the second paragraph of the Declaration indicate why this is so:

> We hold these Truths to be self-evident, that all Men are created equal, that they are endowed by their Creator with certain unalienable Rights, that among these are Life, Liberty, and the Pursuit of Happiness—That to secure these Rights, Governments are instituted among Men, deriving their just Powers from the Consent of the Governed, that whenever any Form of Government becomes destructive of these Ends, it is the Right of the People to alter or abolish it, and to institute new Government.

Natural Rights and Social Contracts. The statement that "all Men are created equal" and have **natural rights** ("unalienable Rights"), including the rights to "Life, Liberty, and the Pursuit of Happiness," was revolutionary at that time. Its use by Jefferson reveals the influence of the English philosopher John Locke (1632–1704), whose writings were familiar to educated American colonists, including Jefferson. In his *Two Treatises of Government*, published in 1690, Locke had argued that all people possess certain natural rights, including the rights to life, liberty, and property.

Archive Images/Alamy

Benjamin Franklin, John Adams, and Thomas Jefferson work on the Declaration of Independence. *Why was that document so important?*

Locke went on to argue that the primary purpose of government was to protect these rights. Furthermore, government was established by the people through a **social contract**—an agreement among the people to form a government and abide by its rules. As you read earlier, such contracts, or compacts, were not new to Americans. The Mayflower Compact was the first of several documents that established governments or governing rules based on the consent of the governed.

After setting forth these basic principles of government, the Declaration of Independence goes on to justify the colonists' revolt against Britain. Much of the remainder of the document is a list of what "He" (King George III) had done to deprive the colonists of their rights. (See Appendix A at the end of this book for the complete text of the Declaration of Independence.)

The Significance of the Declaration. The concepts of equality, natural rights, and government established through a social contract were to have a lasting impact on American life. The Declaration of Independence set forth ideals that have since become a fundamental part of our national identity. The Declaration also became a model for use by other nations around the world.

Certainly, most Americans are familiar with the beginning words of the Declaration. Yet few Americans ponder the obvious question: What did these assertions in the Declaration have to do with independence? Clearly, independence could have been declared without these words. Even as late as 1857, Abraham Lincoln admitted, "The assertion that 'all men are created equal' was of no practical use in effecting our separation from Great Britain; and it was placed in the Declaration, not for that, but for future use."[4]

Natural Rights
Rights held to be inherent in natural law, not dependent on governments. John Locke stated that natural law, being superior to human law, specifies certain rights of "life, liberty, and property."

Social Contract
A voluntary agreement among individuals to secure their rights and welfare by creating a government and abiding by its rules.

4. David Armitage, *The Declaration of Independence: A Global History* (Cambridge, Mass.: Harvard University Press, 2007), p. 26.

Essentially, the immediate significance of the Declaration of Independence, in 1776, was that it established the legitimacy of the new nation in the eyes of the colonists themselves. In addition, the Declaration made it possible for foreign governments to recognize the United States as an independent nation. What the new nation needed most were supplies for its armies and a commitment of foreign military aid. Unless the United States appeared to the world as a political entity separate and independent from Britain, no foreign government would enter into an agreement with its leaders.

The Rise of Republicanism

Although the colonists had formally declared independence from Britain, the fight to gain actual independence continued for five more years, until British general Charles Cornwallis surrendered at Yorktown in 1781. In 1783, after Britain formally recognized the independence of the United States in the Treaty of Paris, George Washington disbanded the army. During these years of military struggles, the states faced the additional challenge of creating a system of self-government for an independent United States.

Some colonists wanted to form a strong central government even before independence from Britain. Others, who called themselves republicans (not to be confused with today's Republican Party), were against a strong central government. They opposed monarchy, executive authority, and virtually any form of restraint on the power of local groups.

These republicans were a major political force from 1776 to 1780. Indeed, they almost prevented victory over the British by their unwillingness to cooperate with any central authority.

During this time, all of the states adopted written constitutions. Eleven of the constitutions were completely new. Two of them—those of Connecticut and Rhode Island—were old royal charters with minor modifications. In most states, republican sentiment led to increased power for the state legislatures. In Georgia and Pennsylvania, **unicameral** (one-body) **legislatures** were unchecked by executive or judicial authority. In almost all states, the legislature was predominant.

The Articles of Confederation: Our First Form of Government

The fear of a powerful central government led to the passage of the Articles of Confederation, which created a weak central government. The term **confederation** is important. It means a voluntary association of independent **states,** in which the member states agree to only limited restraints on their freedom of action. As a result, confederations seldom have an effective executive authority.

Unicameral Legislature
A legislature with only one legislative chamber, as opposed to a bicameral (two-chamber) legislature, such as the U.S. Congress.

Confederation
A political system in which states or regional governments retain ultimate authority except for those powers they expressly delegate to a central government.

State
A group of people occupying a specific area and organized under one government. It may be either a nation or a subunit of a nation.

In June 1776, the Second Continental Congress began the process of composing what would become the Articles of Confederation and Perpetual Union, more commonly known as the Articles of Confederation. The final draft was completed by November 15, 1777, but not until March 1, 1781, did the last state, Maryland, agree to ratify the Articles. Well before the final ratification, however, many of the articles were implemented—the Continental Congress and the thirteen states conducted American military, economic, and political affairs according to the standards and the form specified by the Articles.[5]

The Articles Establish a Government. Under the Articles, the thirteen original colonies, now states, established on March 1, 1781, a government of the states—the Congress of the Confederation. The congress was a unicameral assembly of so-called ambassadors from each state, with every state possessing a single vote. Each year, the congress would choose

5. Keith L. Dougherty, *Collective Action under the Articles of Confederation* (New York: Cambridge University Press, 2006).

one of its members as its president of the congress, but the Articles did not provide for a president of the United States.

The congress was authorized in Article X to appoint an executive committee of the states "to execute in the recess of Congress, such of the powers of Congress as the United States, in Congress assembled, by the consent of nine [of the thirteen] states, shall from time to time think expedient to vest with them." The congress was also allowed to appoint other committees and civil officers necessary for managing the general affairs of the United States. In addition, the congress could regulate foreign affairs and establish coinage and weights and measures. But it lacked an independent source of revenue and the necessary executive machinery to enforce its decisions throughout the land. Article II of the Articles of Confederation guaranteed that each state would retain its sovereignty. Table 2–1 summarizes the powers—and the lack of powers—of congress under the Articles of Confederation.

Accomplishments under the Articles. The new government had some accomplishments during its eight years of existence under the Articles of Confederation. Certain states' claims to western lands were settled. Maryland had objected to the western land claims of Connecticut, Massachusetts, New York, and Virginia. It was only after these states consented to give up their land claims to the United States as a whole that Maryland signed the Articles of Confederation. Another accomplishment under the Articles was the passage of the Northwest Ordinance of 1787, which established a basic pattern of government for new territories north of the Ohio River. All in all, the Articles represented the first real pooling of resources by the American states.

Weaknesses of the Articles. In spite of these accomplishments, the Articles of Confederation had many defects. Although congress had the legal right to declare war and to conduct foreign policy, it did not have the right to demand revenues from the states. It could only ask for them. Additionally, the actions of congress required the consent of nine states. Any amendments to

TABLE 2–1   **The Confederation Congress—Powers and Limits**

Why would states be reluctant to forward taxes to the Confederation?

Congress Had Power to	Congress Lacked Power to
• Declare war and make peace.	• Provide for effective treaties and control foreign relations. It could not compel states to respect treaties.
• Enter into treaties and alliances.	
• Establish and control armed forces.	• Compel states to meet military quotas. It could not draft soldiers.
• Request soldiers and funds from states.	
• Regulate coinage.	• Regulate interstate and foreign commerce. It left each state free to tax imports from other states.
• Borrow funds and issue bills of credit.	
• Fix uniform standards of weight and measurement.	
• Create admiralty courts.	• Collect taxes directly from the people. It had to rely on states to collect and forward taxes.
• Create a postal system.	
• Regulate Indian affairs.	• Compel states to pay their share of government costs.
• Guarantee citizens of each state the rights and privileges of citizens in the several states when in another state.	• Provide and maintain a sound monetary system or issue paper money. This was left up to the states, and paper currencies in circulation differed tremendously in purchasing power.
• Adjudicate disputes between states on state petition.	

the Articles required the unanimous consent of the congress and confirmation by every state legislature. Furthermore, the Articles did not create a national system of courts.

Basically, the functioning of the government under the Articles depended on the goodwill of the states. Article III simply established a "league of friendship" among the states—no national government was intended.

Probably the most fundamental weakness of the Articles, and the most basic cause of their eventual replacement by the Constitution, was the lack of power to raise funds for the militia. The Articles contained no language giving congress coercive power to raise revenue (by levying taxes) to provide adequate support for the military forces controlled by congress. Due to a lack of resources, the Continental Congress was forced to disband the army after the Revolutionary War, even in the face of serious Spanish and British military threats.

Shays' Rebellion and the Need to Revise the Articles. Because of the weaknesses of the Articles of Confederation, the central government could do little to maintain peace and order in the new nation. The states bickered among themselves and increasingly taxed each other's goods. By 1784, the country faced a serious economic depression. Banks were calling in old loans and refusing to make new ones. People who could not pay their debts were often thrown into debtors' prison.

In August 1786, musket-bearing farmers led by former revolutionary captain Daniel Shays seized county courthouses and disrupted the trials of debtors in Springfield, Massachusetts. Shays and his men then launched an attack on the federal arsenal at Springfield, but they were repulsed. Shays' Rebellion demonstrated that the central government could not protect the citizenry from armed rebellion or provide adequately for the public welfare. The rebellion spurred the nation's political leaders to action.

The Constitutional Convention

>>> **LO3:** Discuss the most important compromises reached at the Constitutional Convention and the basic structure of the resulting government.

The Virginia legislature called for a meeting of all the states to be held at Annapolis, Maryland, on September 11, 1786—ostensibly to discuss commercial problems only. It was evident to those in attendance (including Alexander Hamilton of New York and James Madison of Virginia) that the national government had serious weaknesses that had to be addressed if it was to survive. Among the important problems to be solved were the relationship between the states and the central government, the powers of the national legislature, the need for executive leadership, and the establishment of policies for economic stability. The result of this meeting was a petition to the Continental Congress for a general convention to meet in Philadelphia in May 1787 "to consider the exigencies [needs] of the union."

The designated date for the opening of the convention at Philadelphia, now known as the Constitutional Convention, was May 14, 1787. Few of the delegates had actually arrived in Philadelphia by that time, however, so the opening was delayed. The convention formally began in the East Room of the Pennsylvania State House on May 25.[6] Fifty-five of the seventy-four delegates chosen for the convention actually attended. (Of those fifty-five, only about forty played active roles at the convention.) Rhode Island was the only state that refused to send delegates.

---

6. This was the same room in which the Declaration of Independence had been signed eleven years earlier. The State House was later named Independence Hall.

Factions among the Delegates

We know much about the proceedings at the convention because James Madison kept a daily, detailed personal journal. A majority of the delegates were strong nationalists—they wanted a central government with real power, unlike the weak central government under the Articles of Confederation. George Washington and Benjamin Franklin were among those who sought a stronger government.

Among the nationalists, some—including Alexander Hamilton—went as far as to support monarchy. Another important group of nationalists was of a more democratic stripe. Led by James Madison of Virginia and James Wilson of Pennsylvania, these republican nationalists wanted a central government founded on popular support.

Other factions included a group of delegates who were totally against a national authority. Two of the three delegates from New York quit the convention when they saw the nationalist direction of its proceedings.

SuperStock/Getty Images

George Washington, who would become the nation's first president, presided over the Constitutional Convention of 1787. It formally opened in the East Room of the Pennsylvania State House (later named Independence Hall) on May 25. *Why might Washington have been chosen to chair this convention?*

Politicking and Compromises

The debates at the convention started on the first day. James Madison had spent months reviewing European political theory. When his Virginia delegation arrived ahead of most of the others, it got to work immediately. By the time George Washington opened the convention, Governor Edmund Randolph of Virginia was prepared to present fifteen resolutions proposing fundamental changes in the nation's government. In retrospect, this was a masterful stroke on the part of the Virginia delegation. It set the agenda for the remainder of the convention—even though, in principle, the delegates had been sent to Philadelphia for the sole purpose of amending the Articles of Confederation.

The Virginia Plan. Randolph's fifteen resolutions proposed an entirely new national government under a constitution. Basically, the plan called for the following:

- A **bicameral** (two-chamber) **legislature,** with the lower chamber chosen by the people and the smaller upper chamber chosen by the lower chamber from nominees selected by state legislatures. The number of representatives would be proportional to a state's population, thus favoring the large states, including Virginia. The legislature could void any state laws.
- The creation of an unspecified national executive, elected by the legislature.
- The creation of a national judiciary, appointed by the legislature.

It did not take long for the smaller states to realize they would fare poorly under the Virginia Plan, which would enable Massachusetts, Pennsylvania, and Virginia to form a majority in the national legislature. The debate on the plan dragged on for a number of weeks. It was time for the small states to come up with their own plan.

Bicameral Legislature
A legislature made up of two parts, called chambers. The U.S. Congress, composed of the House of Representatives and the Senate, is a bicameral legislature.

The New Jersey Plan. On June 15, William Paterson of New Jersey offered an alternative plan. He proposed the following:

- The fundamental principle of the Articles of Confederation—one state, one vote—would be retained.
- Congress would be able to regulate trade and impose taxes.
- All acts of Congress would be the supreme law of the land.
- Several people would be elected by Congress to form an executive office.
- The executive office would appoint a Supreme Court.

Basically, the New Jersey Plan was simply an amendment of the Articles of Confederation. Its only notable feature was its reference to the **supremacy doctrine,** which was later included in the Constitution.

The "Great Compromise." The delegates were at an impasse. Most wanted a strong national government and were unwilling even to consider the New Jersey Plan. But when the Virginia Plan was brought up again, the small states threatened to leave. It was not until July 16 that a compromise was achieved. Roger Sherman of Connecticut proposed the following:

- A bicameral legislature in which the lower chamber, the House of Representatives, would be apportioned according to the number of free inhabitants in each state, plus three-fifths of the slaves.
- An upper chamber, the Senate, which would have two members from each state elected by the state legislatures.

This plan, known as the **Great Compromise,** broke the deadlock. (The plan is also called the Connecticut Compromise because of the role of the Connecticut delegates in the proposal.) It did exact a political price, however, because it permitted each state to have equal representation in the Senate. Having two senators represent each state diluted the voting power of citizens living in more heavily populated states and gave the smaller states disproportionate political power. Nonetheless, the Connecticut Compromise resolved the controversy between small and large states. In addition, the Senate would act as a check on the House, which many feared would be dominated by the masses and excessively responsive to them.

The Three-Fifths Compromise. The Great Compromise also settled another major issue—how to deal with slaves in the representational scheme. Slavery was still legal in several northern states, but it was concentrated in the South. Many delegates were opposed to slavery and wanted it banned entirely in the United States. Charles Pinckney of South Carolina led strong southern opposition to a ban on slavery. Furthermore, the South wanted slaves to be counted along with free persons in determining representation in Congress. Delegates from the northern states objected. Sherman's three-fifths proposal was a compromise between northerners who did not want the slaves counted at all and southerners who wanted them counted in the same way as free whites. Actually, Sherman's Connecticut plan spoke of three-fifths of "all other persons" (and that is the language of the Constitution itself). It is not hard to figure out, though, who those other persons were. The three-fifths compromise illustrates the power of the southern states at the convention.[7]

Supremacy Doctrine
A doctrine that asserts the priority of national law over state laws. This principle is stated in Article VI of the Constitution.

Great Compromise
The compromise between the New Jersey and Virginia plans that created one chamber of the Congress based on population and one chamber representing each state equally; also called the Connecticut Compromise.

---

7. See Garry Wills, *"Negro President": Jefferson and the Slave Power* (New York: Houghton Mifflin, 2003).

The Slave Trade and the Future of Slavery. The three-fifths compromise did not completely settle the slavery issue. There was also the question of the slave trade. Eventually, the delegates agreed that Congress could not ban the importation of slaves until after 1808. The compromise meant that the matter of slavery itself was never addressed directly. The South won twenty years of unrestricted slave trade and a requirement that escaped slaves in free states be returned to their owners in slave states.

Clearly, many delegates, including slave owners such as George Washington and James Madison, had serious objections to slavery. Why, then, did they allow slavery to continue? Historians have long maintained that the framers had no choice—that without a slavery compromise, the delegates from the South would have abandoned the convention. Indeed, this was the fear of a number of antislavery delegates to the convention. Madison, for example, said, "Great as the evil is, a dismemberment of the Union would be even worse."[8]

A number of historians have made an additional point. Many American leaders believed that slavery would die out naturally. These leaders assumed that in the long run, slave labor could not compete with the labor of free citizens. This assumption turned out to be incorrect.

James Madison (1751–1836) has been called "the master builder of the Constitution." *What did he do to earn that title?*

Other Issues. The South also worried that the northern majority in Congress would pass legislation unfavorable to its economic interests. Because the South depended on agricultural exports, it feared the imposition of export taxes. In return for acceding to the northern demand that Congress be able to regulate commerce among the states and with other nations, the South obtained a promise that export taxes would not be imposed. As a result, the United States is among the few countries that do not tax their exports.

There were other disagreements. The delegates could not decide whether to establish only a Supreme Court or to create lower courts as well. They deferred the issue by instituting a Supreme Court and allowing Congress to establish lower courts. They also disagreed over whether the president or the Senate would choose the Supreme Court justices. A compromise was reached under which the president would nominate the justices and the Senate would confirm or reject the nominations.

These compromises, as well as others, resulted from the recognition that if one group of states refused to ratify the Constitution, it was doomed.

Working toward Final Agreement

The Connecticut Compromise was reached by mid-July. The makeup of the executive branch and the judiciary, however, was left unsettled. The remaining work of the convention was turned over to a five-person Committee of Detail, which presented a rough draft of the Constitution on August 6. It made the executive and judicial branches subordinate to the legislative branch.

The Madisonian Model—Separation of Powers. The major issue of **separation of powers** had not yet been resolved. The delegates were concerned with structuring the government to prevent the imposition of tyranny, either by the majority or by a minority. It was Madison who proposed a governmental scheme—sometimes called the **Madisonian model**—to

Separation of Powers
The principle of dividing governmental powers among different branches of government.

Madisonian Model
A structure of government proposed by James Madison, in which the powers of the government are separated into three branches: executive, legislative, and judicial.

---

8. Speech before the Virginia ratifying convention on June 17, 1788, as cited in Bruno Leone, ed., *The Creation of the Constitution* (San Diego: Greenhaven Press, 1995), p. 159.

achieve this: the executive, legislative, and judicial powers of government were to be separated so that no one branch had enough power to dominate the others. The separation of powers was by function, as well as by personnel, with Congress passing laws, the president enforcing and administering laws, and the courts interpreting laws in individual circumstances.

Each of the three branches of government would be independent of the others, but they would have to cooperate to govern. According to Madison, in *Federalist Paper No. 51* (see Appendix C), "the great security against a gradual concentration of the several powers in the same department consists in giving to those who administer each department the necessary constitutional means and personal motives to resist encroachments of the others."

The Madisonian Model—Checks and Balances. The "constitutional means" Madison referred to is a system of **checks and balances** through which each branch of the government can check the actions of the others. For example, Congress can enact laws, but the president has *veto power* over congressional acts. That is, the president can reject the legislation. The Supreme Court has the power to declare acts of Congress and of the executive unconstitutional, but the president appoints the justices of the Supreme Court, with the advice and consent of the Senate. (The Supreme Court's power to declare acts unconstitutional was not mentioned in the Constitution, although arguably the framers assumed that the Court would have this power—see the discussion of *judicial review* later in this chapter.) Figure 2–1 outlines these checks and balances.

In the years since the Constitution was ratified, the checks and balances built into it have evolved into a sometimes complex give-and-take among the branches of government. Generally, for nearly every check that one branch has over another, the branch that has been checked has found a way of getting around it. For example, suppose that the president checks Congress by vetoing a bill. Congress can override the presidential veto by a two-thirds vote. Additionally, Congress holds the "power of the purse." If it disagrees with a program endorsed by the executive branch, it can simply refuse to appropriate the funds necessary to operate that program.

Similarly, the president can impose a countercheck on Congress if the Senate refuses to confirm a presidential appointment, such as a judicial appointment. The president can simply wait until Congress is in recess and then make what is called a "recess appointment," which does not require the Senate's immediate approval.

Checks and Balances
A major principle of the American system of government whereby each branch of the government can check the actions of the others.

Electoral College
A group of persons, called electors, that officially elects the president and the vice president of the United States. The electors are selected by each state and the District of Columbia.

The Executive. Some delegates favored a plural executive, made up of a committee. This idea was abandoned in favor of a single chief executive. Some argued that Congress should choose the executive. To make the presidency completely independent of Congress, however, an **electoral college** was adopted. This group would be made up of electors chosen by the states, and each state would have as many electors as it had members of Congress.

The founders hoped that through this system, the president would be elected by prominent citizens, not ordinary voters. In fact, for some years after the Constitution was adopted, electors in about half the states were chosen by the state legislature, not directly by the voters. Even in those states, however, the organization of political parties from 1796 on gave ordinary voters some input into choosing the president. A vote for a party's state legislative candidate, after all, was also a way to support that party's presidential candidate. By 1832, the South Carolina legislature was the only one still choosing electors.

FIGURE 2–1 Checks and Balances

The major checks and balances among the three branches of the U.S. government are illustrated here. The Constitution does not mention some of these checks. Checks and balances can be thought of as a confrontation of powers or responsibilities. Each branch checks the actions of the others. Two branches in conflict have powers that can result in balances or stalemates, requiring one branch to give in or both to reach a compromise. *Which result is more likely?*

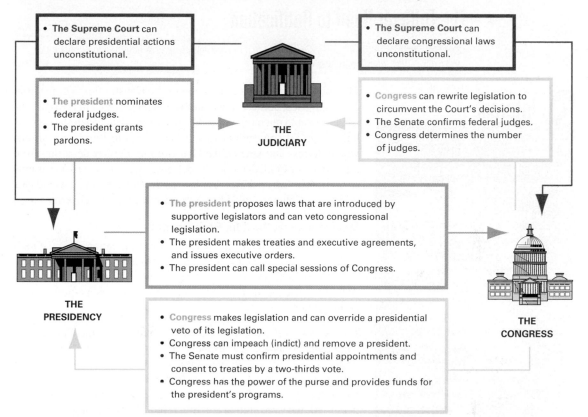

The Final Document

On September 17, 1787, the Constitution was approved by thirty-nine delegates. Of the fifty-five who had attended originally, only forty-two remained. Three delegates refused to sign the Constitution. Others disapproved of at least parts of it but signed anyway to begin the **ratification** debate.

The Constitution that was to be ratified established the following fundamental principles:

- Popular sovereignty, or control by the people.
- A republican government in which the people choose representatives to make decisions for them.
- Limited government with written laws, in contrast to the powerful British government against which the colonists had rebelled.

Ratification
Formal approval.

- Separation of powers, with checks and balances among branches to prevent any one branch from gaining too much power.
- A federal system that allows for states' rights, because the states feared too much centralized control.

The Difficult Road to Ratification

>>>**LO4:** Summarize the arguments in favor of and the arguments against adopting the Constitution, and explain why the Bill of Rights was adopted.

Interact

Our Constitution is based on the separation of powers, but in many other democracies, the legislative and executive branches are united. The chief executive, often called the prime minister, is also the leader of parliament (the legislature). In fact, parliament elects the prime minister. Research the government of Britain, Denmark, Poland, or another European country online. Use hyperlinks to learn the meaning of terms that are new to you. Consider—or discuss with your classmates—which constitutional principles of the country you chose to research would be surprising or unacceptable to Americans. How would the United States be different if the founders had adopted a parliamentary system?

Federalist
An individual who was in favor of the adoption of the U.S. Constitution and the creation of a federal union with a strong central government.

Anti-Federalist
An individual who opposed the ratification of the new Constitution in 1787. The Anti-Federalists were opposed to a strong central government.

The founders knew that ratification of the Constitution was far from certain. Indeed, because it was almost guaranteed that many state legislatures would not ratify it, the delegates agreed that each state should hold a special convention. Elected delegates to these conventions would discuss and vote on the Constitution. Further departing from the Articles of Confederation, the delegates agreed that as soon as nine states (rather than all thirteen) approved the Constitution, it would take effect, and Congress could begin to organize the new government.

The Federalists Push for Ratification

The two opposing forces in the battle over ratification were the Federalists and the Anti-Federalists. The **Federalists** favored a strong central government and the new Constitution. Their opponents, the **Anti-Federalists,** wanted to prevent the Constitution as drafted from being ratified.[9]

The *Federalist Papers*. In New York, opponents of the Constitution were quick to attack it. Alexander Hamilton answered their attacks under a pseudonym in newspaper columns and secured two collaborators—John Jay and James Madison. In a very short time, those three political figures wrote a series of eighty-five essays in defense of the Constitution and of a republican form of government.

These widely read essays, called the *Federalist Papers*, appeared in New York newspapers from October 1787 to August 1788 and were reprinted in the newspapers of other states. Although we do not know for certain who wrote every one, it is apparent that Hamilton was responsible for about two-thirds of the essays. These included the most important ones interpreting the Constitution, explaining the various powers of the three branches, and presenting the theory of judicial review. Madison's *Federalist Paper* No. 10 (see Appendix C), however, is considered a classic in political theory. It deals with the nature of groups—or factions, as he called them. In spite of the rapidity with which the *Federalist Papers* were written, they are considered by many to be perhaps the best example of political theorizing ever produced in the United States.[10]

---

9. There is some irony here. At the Constitutional Convention, those opposed to a strong central government pushed for a federal system because such a system would allow the states to retain some of their sovereign rights. The label *Anti-Federalists* thus contradicted their essential views.
10. Some scholars believe that the *Federalist Papers* played only a minor role in securing ratification of the Constitution. Even if this is true, these writings still have lasting value as an authoritative explanation of the Constitution.

The Anti-Federalist Response. Many of the Anti-Federalists' attacks on the Constitution were also brilliant. The Anti-Federalists claimed that the Constitution was written by aristocrats and would lead to aristocratic tyranny. More important, the Anti-Federalists believed that the Constitution would create an overbearing central government hostile to personal liberty. (The Constitution said nothing about freedom of the press, freedom of religion, or any other individual liberty.) They wanted to include a list of guaranteed liberties, or a bill of rights. Finally, the Anti-Federalists decried the weakened power of the states.[11]

The Anti-Federalists cannot be dismissed as unpatriotic extremists. They included such patriots as Patrick Henry and Samuel Adams. They were arguing what had been the most prevalent view in that era. This view derived from the French philosopher Baron de Montesquieu (1689–1755), an influential theorist. Montesquieu believed that a republic was possible only in a relatively small society governed by direct democracy or by a large legislature with small districts. The Madisonian view favoring a large republic, particularly as expressed in *Federalist Papers* No. 10 and No. 51 (see Appendix C), was actually an exceptional view in those years. Indeed, some researchers believe it was mainly the bitter experiences with the Articles of Confederation, rather than Madison's arguments, that persuaded the state conventions to ratify the Constitution.

Library of Congress Prints and Photographs Division: LC-DIG-det-4a26166

Alexander Hamilton was among those who wanted a monarchy. About two-thirds of the *Federalist Papers* were written by Alexander Hamilton. *What was the impact of that writing on American political thought?*

The March to the Finish

The struggle for ratification continued. Strong majorities were procured in Connecticut, Delaware, Georgia, New Jersey, and Pennsylvania. After a fierce struggle in Massachusetts, that state ratified the Constitution by a narrow margin on February 6, 1788. By the spring, Maryland and South Carolina had ratified by sizable majorities. Then on June 21 of that year, New Hampshire became the ninth state to ratify the Constitution. Although the Constitution was formally in effect, this meant little without Virginia and New York. Virginia ratified it a few days later, but New York did not join in for another month.

The Bill of Rights

The U.S. Constitution would not have been ratified in several important states if the Federalists had not assured the states that amendments to the Constitution would be passed to protect individual liberties against incursions by the national government. Many members of the Constitutional Convention had not thought that a Bill of Rights was needed, or even desirable. Some argued that listing particular rights might imply the absence of rights that were not mentioned. Still, a Bill of Rights turned out to be a political necessity.

Many of the recommendations of the state ratifying conventions included specific rights that were considered later by James Madison as he labored to draft what became the Bill of Rights. Madison had to cull through more than two hundred state recommendations. It was no small task, and in retrospect he chose remarkably well. One of the rights appropriate for constitutional protection that he left out was equal protection under the laws—but that was

---

11. Herbert J. Storing edited seven volumes of Anti-Federalist writings and released them in 1981 as *The Complete Anti-Federalist*. Political science professor Murray Dry has prepared a more manageable, one-volume version of this collection: Herbert J. Storing, ed., *The Anti-Federalist* (Chicago: University of Chicago Press, 2006).

not commonly regarded as a basic right at that time. Not until 1868 was the Constitution amended to guarantee that no state shall deny equal protection to any person.

On December 15, 1791, the national Bill of Rights was adopted when Virginia agreed to ratify the ten amendments. On ratification, the Bill of Rights became part of the U.S. Constitution. The basic structure of American government had already been established. Now the fundamental rights and liberties of individuals were protected, at least in theory, at the national level. The proposed amendment that Madison characterized as "the most valuable amendment in the whole lot"—which would have prohibited the states from infringing on the freedoms of conscience, press, and jury trial—had been eliminated by the Senate. Thus, the Bill of Rights as adopted did not limit state power, and individual citizens had to rely on the guarantees contained in a particular state constitution or state bill of rights. The country had to wait until the violence of the Civil War before significant limitations on state power in the form of the Fourteenth Amendment became part of the national Constitution.

Altering the Constitution

>>> **LO5:** Describe the process of amending the Constitution and the informal ways in which constitutional interpretation has changed over time.

As amended, the U.S. Constitution consists of about seven thousand words. It is shorter than any state constitution except that of Vermont. The federal Constitution is short because the founders intended it to be only a framework for the new government, to be interpreted by succeeding generations. One of the reasons it has remained short is that the formal amending procedure does not allow for changes to be made easily. Article V of the Constitution outlines the ways in which amendments may be proposed and ratified.

The Formal Amendment Process

Two formal methods of proposing an amendment to the Constitution are available: (1) a two-thirds vote in each chamber of Congress or (2) a national convention that is called by Congress at the request of two-thirds of the state legislatures. This second method has never been used.

Ratification can occur by one of two methods: (1) by a positive vote in three-fourths of the legislatures of the various states or (2) by special conventions called in the states and a positive vote in three-fourths of them. The second method has been used only once, to repeal Prohibition (the ban on the production and sale of alcoholic beverages). That situation was exceptional—prohibitionist forces were in control of the legislatures in many states where a majority of the population actually supported repeal.

Congress has considered more than eleven thousand amendments to the Constitution. Only thirty-three amendments have been submitted to the states after having been approved by the required two-thirds vote in each chamber of Congress, and only twenty-seven have been ratified—see Table 2–2. It should be clear that the amendment process is very difficult. Because of competing social and economic interests, the requirement that two-thirds of both the House and the Senate approve the amendments is hard to achieve.

After an amendment has been approved by Congress, the process becomes even more arduous. Three-fourths of the state legislatures must approve the amendment. Only those amendments that have wide popular support across parties and in all regions of the country are likely to be approved.

TABLE 2–2	Amendments to the Constitution		

Why have so few amendments been adopted?

Amendment	Subject	Year Adopted	Time Required for Ratification
1st–10th	The Bill of Rights	1791	2 years, 2 months, 20 days
11th	Immunity of states from certain suits	1795	11 months, 3 days
12th	Changes in electoral college procedure	1804	6 months, 3 days
13th	Prohibition of slavery	1865	10 months, 3 days
14th	Citizenship, due process, and equal protection	1868	2 years, 26 days
15th	No denial of vote because of race, color, or previous condition of servitude	1870	11 months, 8 days
16th	Power of Congress to tax income	1913	3 years, 6 months, 22 days
17th	Direct election of U.S. senators	1913	10 months, 26 days
18th	National (liquor) prohibition	1919	1 year, 29 days
19th	Women's right to vote	1920	1 year, 2 months, 14 days
20th	Change of dates for congressional and presidential terms	1933	10 months, 21 days
21st	Repeal of the Eighteenth Amendment	1933	9 months, 15 days
22d	Limit on presidential tenure	1951	3 years, 11 months, 3 days
23d	District of Columbia electoral vote	1961	9 months, 13 days
24th	Prohibition of tax payment as a qualification to vote in federal elections	1964	1 year, 4 months, 9 days
25th	Procedures for determining presidential disability and presidential succession and for filling a vice-presidential vacancy	1967	1 year, 7 months, 4 days
26th	Prohibition of setting the minimum voting age above eighteen in any election	1971	3 months, 7 days
27th	Prohibition of Congress's voting itself a raise or cut in pay that takes effect before the next election	1992	203 years

Why was the amendment process made so difficult? The framers feared that a simple amendment process could lead to a tyranny of the majority, which could pass amendments to oppress disfavored individuals and groups. The cumbersome amendment process does not seem to stem the number of amendments that are proposed in Congress, however, particularly in recent years.

Informal Methods of Constitutional Change

Looking at the sparse number of formal constitutional amendments gives us an incomplete view of constitutional change. The brevity and ambiguity of the original document have permitted great alterations in the Constitution by way of varying interpretations over time. As the United States grew, both in population and in territory, new social and political realities emerged. Congress, presidents, and the courts found it necessary to interpret the Constitution's provisions in light of these new realities. The Constitution has proved to be a remarkably flexible document, adapting itself time and again to new events and concerns.

Congressional Legislation. The Constitution gives Congress broad powers to carry out its duties as the nation's legislative body. For example, Article I, Section 8, of the Constitution gives Congress the power to regulate foreign and interstate commerce. Although there

"Remember, gentlemen, we aren't here just to draft a constitution. We're here to draft the best damned constitution in the world."

Peter Steiner The New Yorker Collection/The Cartoon Bank

is no clear definition of foreign commerce or interstate commerce in the Constitution, Congress has cited the *commerce clause* as the basis for passing thousands of laws.

Presidential Actions. Even though the Constitution does not expressly authorize the president to propose bills or even budgets to Congress,[12] presidents since the time of Woodrow Wilson (1913–1921) have proposed hundreds of bills to Congress each year that are introduced by the president's supporters in Congress. Presidents have also relied on their Article II authority as commander in chief of the nation's armed forces to send American troops abroad into combat, although the Constitution provides that Congress has the power to declare war. Presidents have also conducted foreign affairs by the use of *executive agreements*, which are legally binding understandings reached between the president and a foreign head of state. The Constitution does not mention such agreements.

Judicial Review. Another way that the Constitution adapts to new developments is through judicial review. **Judicial review** refers to the power of U.S. courts to examine the constitutionality of actions undertaken by the legislative and executive branches of government. A state court, for example, may rule that a statute enacted by the state legislature violates the state constitution. Federal courts (and ultimately, the United States Supreme Court) may rule unconstitutional not only acts of Congress and decisions of the national executive branch, but also state statutes, state executive actions, and even provisions of state constitutions.

The Constitution does not specifically mention the power of judicial review. In 1803, the Supreme Court claimed this power for itself in *Marbury v. Madison*,[13] in which the Court ruled that a particular provision of an act of Congress was unconstitutional.

Through the process of judicial review, the Supreme Court adapts the Constitution to modern situations and changing values. For example, it ruled in 1896 that "separate-but-equal" public facilities for African Americans were constitutional. By 1954, however, the times had changed, and the Supreme Court reversed that decision.[14] Woodrow Wilson summarized the Supreme Court's work when he described it as "a constitutional convention in continuous session." Basically, the law is what the Supreme Court says it is at any point in time.

Interpretation, Custom, and Usage. Changes in ways of doing political business have also led to reinterpretation of the Constitution. For example, the Constitution does not mention political parties, yet these informal, "extraconstitutional" organizations make the

---

Judicial Review
The power of the Supreme Court or any court to examine and possibly declare unconstitutional federal or state laws and other acts of government.

12. Note, though, that the Constitution, in Article II, Section 3, does state that the president "shall from time to time . . . recommend to [Congress's] consideration such measures as he shall judge necessary and expedient." Some scholars interpret this phrase to mean that the president has the constitutional authority to propose bills and budgets to Congress for consideration.
13. 5 U.S. 137 (1803).
14. *Brown v. Board of Education of Topeka*, 347 U.S. 483 (1954).

MAKING A DIFFERENCE

How Can You Affect the U.S. Constitution?

The Constitution has survived more than two hundred years of turbulent history. It is also an evolving document, however. Twenty-seven amendments have been added to the original Constitution. How can you, as an individual, help to rewrite the Constitution?

Why Should You Care? The laws of the nation have a direct impact on your life, and none more so than the supreme law of the land. The most important issues in society are often settled by the Constitution. For example, for the first seventy-five years of the republic, the Constitution implicitly protected the institution of slavery. If the Constitution had never been changed through the amendment process, the process of abolishing slavery would have been much different and might have involved extraconstitutional measures.

What Can You Do? Various groups support or oppose a number of constitutional amendments. One proposal would create a constitutional requirement to balance the federal budget. If such an amendment sounds like a good idea to you, there are a variety of organizations you might investigate, including Americans for a Balanced Budget Amendment and the Balanced Budget Amendment Task Force.

Other Americans have different concerns. In 2010, the Supreme Court struck down a wide range of campaign finance laws in *Citizens United v. Federal Election Commission*.[15] One result of this ruling was the "super PACs" that flooded television networks with attack advertisements during recent elections. A proposed constitutional amendment would overturn the *Citizens United* ruling. If getting the money out of politics is of interest to you, check out Move to Amend or Free Speech for People.

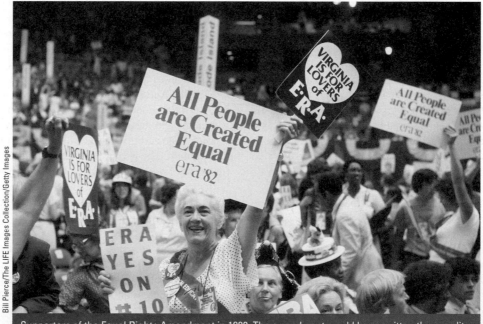

Bill Pierce/The LIFE Images Collection/Getty Images

Supporters of the Equal Rights Amendment in 1980. The amendment would have written the equality of women into the Constitution. It was not ratified by a large enough number of states, however, and so was not adopted. *Why is it so hard to amend the Constitution?*

15. 558 U.S. 310.

nominations for offices, run the campaigns, organize the members of Congress, and in fact change the election system from time to time.

In many ways, the Constitution has been adapted from a document serving the needs of a small, rural republic to one that provides a framework of government for an industrial giant with vast geographic, natural, and human resources.

Key Terms

Anti-Federalist 36
bicameral legislature 31
checks and balances 34
confederation 28
electoral college 34

Federalist 36
Great Compromise 32
judicial review 40
Madisonian model 33
natural rights 27

ratification 35
representative
   assembly 22
separation of powers 33
social contract 27

state 28
supremacy doctrine 32
unicameral
   legislature 28

Chapter Summary

>>> **LO1** The first permanent English colonies were established at Jamestown in 1607 and Plymouth in 1620. The Mayflower Compact created the first formal government in New England.

In the 1760s, the British began to impose on their increasingly independent-minded colonies a series of taxes and legislative acts. The colonists responded with protests and boycotts of British products. Representatives of the colonies formed the First Continental Congress in 1774. The Second Continental Congress established an army in 1775 to defend colonists against attacks by British soldiers.

>>> **LO2** On July 4, 1776, the Second Continental Congress approved the Declaration of Independence. Perhaps the most revolutionary aspects of the Declaration were its statements that people have natural rights to life, liberty, and the pursuit of happiness; that governments derive their power from the consent of the governed; and that people have a right to overthrow oppressive governments. During the Revolutionary War, the states signed the Articles of Confederation, creating a weak central government with few powers. The Articles proved to be unworkable because the national government had no way to ensure compliance by the states with such measures as securing tax revenues.

>>> **LO3** General dissatisfaction with the Articles of Confederation prompted the call for a convention in Philadelphia in 1787. Delegates focused on creating a constitution for a new form of government. The

Virginia Plan, which favored the larger states, and the New Jersey Plan, which favored small ones, did not garner sufficient support. The Great Compromise offered by Connecticut provided for a bicameral legislature and thus resolved the large-state/small-state dispute. The final version of the Constitution provided for the separation of powers, checks and balances, and a federal form of government.

>>> **LO4** The Anti-Federalists argued against adopting the Constitution, but supporters of the document won in the end. Fears of a strong central government prompted the addition of the Bill of Rights to the Constitution. The Bill of Rights, which includes the freedoms of religion, speech, and assembly, was initially applied only to the federal government, but amendments to the Constitution following the Civil War were interpreted to ensure that the Bill of Rights would apply to the states as well.

>>> **LO5** An amendment to the Constitution may be proposed either by a two-thirds vote in each chamber of Congress or by a national convention called by Congress at the request of two-thirds of the state legislatures. Ratification can occur either by the approval of three-fourths of the legislatures of the states or by special conventions called in the states for the purpose of ratifying the amendment and approval by three-fourths of these conventions. Informal methods of constitutional change include reinterpretation through congressional legislation, presidential actions, and judicial review.

Test Yourself

1. The Mayflower Compact, signed at Plymouth (Massachusetts) in 1620, was designed to:
   a. separate New England from the previously established colony of Virginia.
   b. require that all settlers obey the laws of the new colony.
   c. establish the Church of England in the new colony.

2. When the First Continental Congress convened in 1774, the British government:
   a. took no notice of it.
   b. agreed to allow the colonies to form a unified government.
   c. treated the meeting as an act of rebellion.

3. The Declaration of Independence established as unalienable rights those of:
   a. life, liberty, and property.
   b. life, liberty, and the pursuit of happiness.
   c. liberty, equality, and fraternity.

4. During the Revolutionary War era, those calling themselves *republicans* stood for:
   a. a strong central government.
   b. state legislatures unchecked by national or other authority.
   c. national unity to defeat the British.

5. A major defect in the Articles of Confederation was:
   a. the lack of power to raise funds for military forces.
   b. the lack of treaty-making power.
   c. the inability to easily communicate with citizens.

6. At the Constitutional Convention, the Great, or Connecticut, Compromise broke the deadlock between all of the following except:
   a. supporters of the Virginia and New Jersey plans.
   b. the large and small states.
   c. the northern and southern states.

7. Which of the following fundamental principles was not established by the Constitution of 1787?
   a. popular sovereignty, or control by the people.
   b. limited government with written laws.
   c. a requirement that state governments uphold the liberties listed in the Bill of Rights.

8. When no branch of government—executive, legislative, or judicial—is able to dominate the others, we call this:
   a. effective government.
   b. the separation of powers.
   c. limited government.

9. Those who opposed the ratification of the Constitution were called:
   a. Anti-Federalists.
   b. Federalists.
   c. Loyalists.

10. The major drafter of the Bill of Rights was:
    a. Washington.
    b. Jefferson.
    c. Madison.

11. The reason the U.S. Constitution has so few amendments is that:
    a. the formal amendment process is exceedingly difficult.
    b. the Constitution was written so well that it hasn't needed to be amended.
    c. Congress doesn't have time to consider new amendments.

12. When an amendment to the Constitution is sent to the state legislatures, how many must approve it if it is to be adopted?
    a. a majority of the states.
    b. two-thirds of the states.
    c. three-quarters of the states.

Essay Questions

1. Consider what might have happened if Georgia and the Carolinas had stayed out of the Union because of a desire to protect slavery. What would subsequent American history have been like? Would the eventual freedom of the slaves have been delayed—or advanced?

2. A result of the Great Compromise is that representation in the Senate dramatically departs from the one-person, one-vote rule. The 39 million people who live in California elect two senators, as do the almost 600,000 people living in Wyoming. What political results might occur when the citizens of small states are much better represented than the citizens of large ones?

Answers to multiple-choice questions: 1. b, 2. c, 3. b, 4. c, 5. a, 6. c, 7. c, 8. b, 9. a, 10. c, 11. a, 12. c.

3 | Federalism

ZUMA Press Inc / Alamy Stock Photo

Two-year-olds play ring-around-the-rosie in an Early Head Start class in Albuquerque, N.M. Head Start is a preschool program for low-income children. It is funded by the national government but administered by local agencies. *What benefits can follow from local administration?*

The five **Learning Outcomes (LOs)** below are designed to help improve your understanding of this chapter. After reading this chapter, you should be able to:

>>> **LO1** Explain some of the benefits of the federal system for the United States.

>>> **LO2** Describe how the various provisions of the U.S. Constitution provide a framework for federalism.

>>> **LO3** Discuss how, in the early years of the republic, the United States Supreme Court confirmed the authority of the national government, and how that authority was ratified by the Civil War.

>>> **LO4** Define the terms *dual federalism, cooperative federalism, categorical grants, block grants,* and *fiscal federalism*.

>>> **LO5** Detail recent Supreme Court rulings that affect the distribution of power between the national government and the states.

Check your understanding of the material with the Test Yourself section at the end of the chapter.

I n the United States, rights and powers are reserved to the states by the Tenth Amendment. In recent years, however, it may appear that the federal government, sometimes called the national or central government, has predominated. Nevertheless, that might be an exaggerated perception, for there are 89,528 separate governmental units in this nation. This number includes not just the national and state governments, but the governments of counties, municipalities, school districts, and a huge variety of special districts.

Visitors from France or Spain are often awestruck by the complexity of our system of government. Consider that a criminal action can be defined by state law, by national law, or by both. Thus, a criminal suspect can be prosecuted in the state court system or in the federal court system (or both). Often, economic regulation covering exactly the same issues exists at the local level, the state level, and the national level—generating multiple forms to be completed, multiple procedures to be followed, and multiple laws to be obeyed. Many programs are funded by the national government but administered by state and local governments.

Relations between central governments and local units can be structured in various ways. *Federalism* is one of these ways. Understanding federalism and how it differs from other forms of government is important in understanding the American political system. Indeed, many political issues today would not arise if we did not have a federal form of government in which governmental authority is divided between the central government and various subunits.

Federalism and Its Alternatives

>>> **LO1:** Explain some of the benefits of the federal system for the United States.

There are almost two hundred independent nations in the world today. Each of these nations has its own system of government. Generally, though, we can describe how nations structure relations between central governments and local units in terms of three models: (1) the unitary system, (2) the confederal system, and (3) the federal system. The most popular, both historically and today, is the unitary system.

A Unitary System

A **unitary system** of government is the easiest to define. Unitary systems place ultimate governmental authority in the hands of the national, or central, government. Consider a typical unitary system—France. The regions, departments, communes, and municipalities in France have elected and appointed officials.

So far, the French system appears to be very similar to the U.S. system, but the similarity is only superficial. Under the unitary French system, the decisions of the lower levels of government can be overruled by the national government. The national government also can cut off the funding for many local government activities. Moreover, in a unitary system such as that in France, all questions of education, police, the use of land, and welfare are handled by the national government. Britain, Egypt, Ghana, Israel, Japan, the Philippines, and Sweden—in fact, a majority of all nations—have unitary systems of government.[1]

A Confederal System

You were introduced to the elements of a **confederal system** of government earlier, when we examined the Articles of Confederation. A confederation is the opposite of a unitary governing system. It is a league of independent states in which a central government or administration handles only those matters of common concern expressly delegated to it by the member states. The central government has no ability to make laws directly applicable to member states unless the members explicitly support such laws. The United States under the Articles of Confederation was a confederal system.

Unitary System
A centralized governmental system in which ultimate governmental authority rests in the hands of the national, or central, government.

Confederal System
A system consisting of a league of independent states, in which the central government created by the league has only limited powers over the states.

---

1. Recent legislation has altered somewhat the unitary character of the French political system. In Britain, the unitary nature of the government has been modified by the creation of the Scottish Parliament.

Few, if any, confederations of this kind exist today. One possible exception is the European Union (EU), a league of countries that has developed a large body of Europe-wide laws that all members must observe. Many members even share a common currency, the euro. Not all members of the EU use the euro, however, which demonstrates the limits of a confederal system.

A Federal System

The federal system lies between the unitary and confederal forms of government. In a *federal system*, authority is divided, usually by a written constitution, between a central government and regional, or subdivisional, governments (often called *constituent governments*). The central government and the constituent governments both act directly on the people through laws and through the actions of elected and appointed governmental officials. Within each government's sphere of authority, each is supreme, in theory. Thus, a federal system differs from a unitary one, in which the central government is supreme and the constituent governments derive their authority from it. In addition to the United States, Australia, Brazil, Canada, Germany, India, and Mexico are examples of nations with federal systems. See Figure 3–1 for a comparison of the three systems.

Why Federalism?

Why did the United States develop in a federal direction? As you have learned, the historical basis of our federal system was established in Philadelphia at the Constitutional Convention, where advocates of a strong national government opposed states' rights advocates. This conflict continued through to the ratifying conventions in the several states. The resulting federal system was a compromise. The supporters of the new Constitution were political pragmatists—they realized that without a federal arrangement, there would be no ratification of the new Constitution. The appeal of federalism was that it retained state traditions and local power while establishing a strong national government capable of handling common problems.

FIGURE 3–1   **The Flow of Power in Three Systems of Government**

In a unitary system, power flows from the central government to the local and state governments. In a confederal system, power flows in the opposite direction—from the state governments to the central government. In a federal system, the flow of power, in principle, goes both ways. *Why do you think confederal systems are rare?*

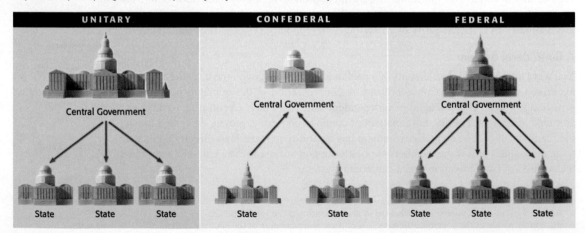

Large Geographical Areas. Even if the founders had agreed on the desirability of a unitary system, size and regional isolation would have made such a system difficult operationally. At the time of the Constitutional Convention, the thirteen states taken together were much larger geographically than England or France. Slow travel and communication, combined with geographic spread, contributed to the isolation of many regions within the states. It could take several weeks for all the states to be informed about a particular political decision.

Even with modern transportation and communications systems, the large area or population of some nations makes it impractical to locate all political authority in one place. Federalism brings government closer to the people. It allows more direct access to, and influence on, government agencies and policies, rather than leaving the population restive and dissatisfied with a remote, faceless, all-powerful central authority.

Mischa Richter/The New Yorker Collection/The Cartoon Bank

"They have very strict anti-pollution laws in this state."

Benefits for the United States. In the United States, federalism historically has yielded additional benefits. State governments have long been a training ground for future national leaders. Many presidents made their political mark as state governors. The states themselves have been testing grounds for new government initiatives. As United States Supreme Court justice Louis Brandeis once observed:

> It is one of the happy incidents of the federal system that a single courageous state may, if its citizens choose, serve as a laboratory and try novel social and economic experiments without risk to the rest of the country.[2]

Examples of programs pioneered at the state level include unemployment compensation, which began in Wisconsin, and air-pollution control, which was initiated in California. Same-sex marriage was first adopted in one state—Massachusetts. Recently, states have also tried new ways to manage marijuana. We take a closer look at these developments in the first of this chapter's *At Issue* features.

Allowance for Many Political Subcultures. The American way of life always has been characterized by a number of political subcultures, which divide along the lines of race and ethnic origin, region, wealth, education, and, more recently, degree of religious commitment and sexual preference. The existence of diverse political subcultures would appear to be incompatible with a political authority concentrated solely in a central government. Had the United States developed into a unitary system, various political subcultures certainly would have been less able to influence government behavior than they have been, and continue to be, in our federal system.

---

2. *New State Ice Co. v. Liebmann,* 285 U.S. 262 (1932).

AT ISSUE

Should Recreational Marijuana Be Legal?

Marijuana has been around for a long time. The earliest record we have of its use as a drug dates from the third millennium B.C.E. The drug was not criminalized in the United States until the twentieth century, however, beginning with restrictions in the District of Columbia in 1906. The Marijuana Tax Act of 1937 effectively banned the drug nationwide. Today, the federal government classifies marijuana as a substance with a high potential for abuse and no medical uses.

Yet twenty-one states have passed decriminalization laws, beginning in Oregon in 1973. As of 2016, forty-four states allow the sale and use of marijuana for medical purposes. In 2012, Colorado and Washington voters approved the sale and possession of marijuana for recreational use. Alaska, Oregon, and the District of Columbia joined them in 2014, and California, Maine, Massachusetts, and Nevada followed in 2016. So, should all states follow in the footsteps of these states? Should the federal government change its law similarly?

Don't Go the Alcohol and Tobacco Route

Some argue that legal recreational use of marijuana will generate huge costs to society, just like the recreational use of tobacco and alcoholic beverages. Abuse of alcohol and cigarettes leads to hundreds of thousands of premature deaths a year in this country. Why add marijuana to that list? For many—an estimated 6 million people—marijuana use is an addiction.

The American Medical Association claims that heavy marijuana use in adolescents causes impairments in neurocognitive performance and IQ. As one pundit put it, "The reason potheads appear stupid is because in fact they are becoming stupider." High school students who use marijuana tend to have lower grades and are less likely to get into college than nonsmokers.

Don't Fight Reality—Just Make It Legal

Cannabis has been illegal for decades, yet it is readily available just about everywhere. Why should we be hypocrites? The social cost of alcohol is vastly greater than that of marijuana. Indeed, marijuana is safer than alcohol. No one ever dies of a marijuana overdose, but alcohol poisoning kills about 2,250 Americans every year. More than 33 million Americans use marijuana, and a majority of them do so illegally. That is an absurd situation and fosters disrespect for the law in general. An additional problem is that the law is enforced more harshly against African Americans, who wind up in jail in large numbers. Finally, consider taxation—when pot is legal, state and local governments can obtain much needed tax revenues.

FOR CRITICAL ANALYSIS

What problems can arise when a state legalizes recreational marijuana, but the federal government continues to view it as illegal?

Arguments against Federalism

Not everyone thinks federalism is such a good idea. Some see it as a way for powerful state and local interests to block progress and impede national plans. Smaller political units are more likely to be dominated by a single political group. (This was essentially the argument that James Madison put forth in *Federalist Paper* No. 10, which you can read in Appendix C of this text.) In fact, the dominant groups in some cities and states have resisted implementing equal rights for minority groups. Members of various occupations have won state laws that limit competition through onerous licensing requirements. Cities often adopt anti-density zoning codes that drive up the value of existing housing and can force low-income residents out of the area. (Some argue, however, that the dominant factions in some states have been more progressive than the national government in many areas, such as environmental protection.)

Critics also feel that there is too much inequity among the states, so they call for increased federal oversight of various programs. Others, however, see dangers in the expansion of national powers at the expense of the states. President Ronald Reagan (1981–1989) said, "The Founding Fathers saw the federalist system as constructed something like a masonry wall. The states are the bricks, the national government is the mortar. . . . Unfortunately, over the years, many people have increasingly come to believe that Washington is the whole wall."[3]

The Constitutional Basis for American Federalism

>>> **LO2:** Describe how the various provisions of the U.S. Constitution provide a framework for federalism.

The term *federal system* cannot be found in the U.S. Constitution. Nor is it possible to find a systematic division of governmental authority between the national and state governments in that document. Rather, the Constitution sets out different types of powers. These powers can be classified as (1) the powers of the national government, (2) the powers of the states, and (3) prohibited powers. The Constitution also makes it clear that if a state or local law conflicts with a national law, the national law will prevail.

Powers of the National Government

The powers delegated to the national government include both expressed and implied powers, as well as the special category of inherent powers.

Enumerated Powers. Most of the powers expressly delegated to the national government are found in the first seventeen clauses of Article I, Section 8, of the Constitution. These **enumerated powers,** also called *expressed powers*, include coining money, setting standards for weights and measures, making uniform naturalization laws, admitting new states, establishing post offices and post roads, and declaring war. Another important enumerated power is the power to regulate commerce among the states—a topic we deal with later in this chapter.

The Necessary and Proper Clause. The implied powers of the national government are also based on Article I, Section 8, which states that the Congress shall have the power

> [t]o make all Laws which shall be necessary and proper for carrying into Execution the foregoing Powers, and all other Powers vested by this Constitution in the Government of the United States, or in any Department or Officer thereof.

This clause is sometimes called the **elastic clause,** or the **necessary and proper clause,** because it provides flexibility to our constitutional system. It gives Congress the power to do whatever is necessary to execute its specifically delegated powers. The clause was first used in the Supreme Court decision of *McCulloch v. Maryland*[4] (discussed later in this chapter) to develop the concept of implied powers. Through this concept, the national government has succeeded in strengthening the scope of its authority to meet the many problems that the framers of the Constitution did not, and could not, anticipate.

Enumerated Powers
Powers specifically granted to the national government by the Constitution. The first seventeen clauses of Article I, Section 8, specify most of the enumerated, or expressed, powers of the national government.

Elastic Clause, or Necessary and Proper Clause
The clause in Article I, Section 8, that grants Congress the power to do whatever is necessary to execute its specifically delegated powers.

Interact

This book refers to court cases, often decided by the United States Supreme Court. A good way to find out more about the American political system is to learn about key cases. Standard formats exist for citing cases. Consider *New State Ice Co. v. Liebmann* in footnote 2. The mysterious "285 U.S. 262" gives the location of this case in an official publication. Usually, you can just use the name of the case to search online for the ruling and articles that describe it. Sometimes, however, the name of the case is not enough. What if it is *United States v. Johnson?* There are at least twelve important cases by that name. To find this case, search for the full citation—for example, "*United States v. Johnson*, 457 U.S. 537 (1982)."

---

3. As quoted in Edward Millican, *One United People: The Federalist Papers and the National Idea* (Lexington: The University Press of Kentucky, 1990).
4. 17 U.S. 316 (1819).

Police Power
The authority to legislate for the protection of the health, morals, safety, and welfare of the people. In the United States, most police power is reserved to the states.

Inherent Powers. A special category of national powers that is not always implied by the necessary and proper clause consists of what have been labeled the *inherent powers* of the national government. These powers derive from the fact that the United States is a sovereign power among nations, and so its national government must be the only government that deals with other nations. Under international law, it is assumed that all nation-states, regardless of their size or power, have an inherent right to ensure their own survival. To do this, each nation must have the ability to act in its own interest among and with the community of nations—by, for instance, making treaties, waging war, seeking trade, and acquiring territory.

Note that no specific clause in the Constitution says anything about the acquisition of additional land. Nonetheless, the federal government's inherent powers allowed it to make the Louisiana Purchase in 1803 and then go on to acquire Florida, Texas, Oregon, California, Alaska, Hawaii, and other lands.

Powers of the State Governments

The Tenth Amendment states that the powers not delegated to the United States by the Constitution, nor prohibited by it to the states, are reserved to the states, or to the people. These are the *reserved powers* that the national government cannot deny to the states. Because these powers are not expressly listed, there is sometimes a question as to whether a certain power is delegated to the national government or reserved to the states.

State powers have been held to include each state's right to regulate commerce within its borders and to provide for a state militia. States also have the reserved power to make laws on all matters not prohibited to the states by the U.S. Constitution or state constitutions and not expressly, or by implication, delegated to the national government. Furthermore, the states have **police power**—the authority to legislate for the protection of the health, morals, safety, and welfare of the people. Their police power enables states to pass laws governing such activities as crimes, marriage, contracts, education, intrastate transportation, and land use. Because the states have these powers, laws can vary dramatically from one state to another. One topic on which state and local governments differ is how to handle new companies such as Uber and Lyft. We discuss that issue in the second of this chapter's *At Issue* features.

It is also worth noting that while the United States as a whole uses a federal system of government, each state has a unitary system. Hence, it is said that county, municipal, and other local governments are "creatures of the state." In principle, a state can alter or abolish a local government (though in some instances that might require an amendment to the state constitution). Such radical measures are rare. A more common exercise of state power is to prohibit local governments from passing various laws. For example, Colorado and Ohio do not let local governments ban *fracking* (a method of producing oil and natural gas).

A marijuana "grow" in Denver, Colo. Recreational marijuana is legal in that state but remains illegal under national law. *What do you think will happen under the Trump administration?*

Blaine Harrington III/Corbis Documentary/Getty Images

Should We Let Uber and Lyft Pick Up Passengers?

It was only a matter of time. Smartphone apps have become powerful and popular. Many people in big cities need to summon a taxicab or hire a car service. Why not create an app to let people order such services? That is exactly what has happened in major cities around the world. Uber was the first "transportation network company" to harness the power of mobile apps to arrange on-demand ridesharing. Lyft followed suit. Other competitors have joined this growing business.

To become an Uber or Lyft driver, you must pass a criminal background check and show that your car is safe and clean. To become a customer, all you have to do is download the app and furnish a credit-card number.

That is not the end of the story, however. Licensed taxis have been fighting Uber, Lyft, and their competitors, and in some cases winning. Many states, cities, and even countries have banned Uber altogether. Others have severely regulated it. So, should Uber, Lyft, and others be able to freely compete against traditional taxi companies and drivers?

It's the Twenty-First Century—Get Used to It

GPS is not going to go away. Smartphones are here to stay. Together, they can form the basis of a new transportation service. Whoever is providing this service, it can't be stopped. Drivers like it because they can earn extra money—provided they have a decent car, a pleasant demeanor, and free time to do the work. Drivers are rated by customers, so the bad ones are weeded out. Because payments are processed through a credit card, drivers are no longer sitting ducks for armed robbery.

True, Uber and Lyft pose a competitive threat to existing taxi companies. But the new companies are also expanding the size of the market. People are simply taking more rides. Taxicab company owners are the only people truly hurt by Uber and Lyft. Thousands of ordinary cabdrivers have found it makes sense to drive for the new firms instead of the old ones.

Unfair and Unsafe Competition

Uber, Lyft, and the like may provide a cool way to hail a cab. Taxicab companies, however, argue that this is not the real reason the new companies are successful. Rather, they are taking advantage of a new business model to escape regulations imposed on taxis. These regulations impose costs, but there are good reasons for them. Regulatory compliance is important to passenger safety. Too little is known about Uber drivers. There have actually been instances of drivers attacking passengers. Drivers can register online and pay off a shady mechanic to certify the safety of the cars. Drivers may also buy ordinary auto insurance. Doing so is a scam—commercial vehicle insurance is more expensive because claims are more frequent. Is it fair for Uber and Lyft to compete against licensed taxi services without paying these costs?

FOR CRITICAL ANALYSIS
At times, Uber and Lyft use "surge pricing" to balance supply and demand. On New Year's Eve, for example, ride prices are much higher than normal. Is this a problem? Why or why not?

The ambiguity of the Tenth Amendment has allowed the reserved powers of the states to be defined differently at different times in our history. When there is widespread support for increased regulation by the national government, the Tenth Amendment tends to recede into the background. When the tide turns the other way (in favor of states' rights), the Tenth Amendment is resurrected to justify arguments supporting the states.

Prohibited Powers

The Constitution prohibits or denies a number of powers to the national government. For example, the national government has expressly been denied the power to impose taxes on goods sold to other countries (exports). Moreover, any power not granted expressly or implicitly to the federal government by the Constitution is prohibited to it. For example, many legal experts believe that the national government could not create a national divorce law system without a constitutional amendment. The states are also denied certain powers. As one instance of this, no state is allowed to enter into a treaty on its own with another country.

Concurrent Powers

In certain areas, the states share **concurrent powers** with the national government. Most concurrent powers are not specifically listed in the Constitution but are only implied. An example of a concurrent power is the power to tax. The types of taxation are divided between the levels of government. For example, states may not levy a tariff (a set of taxes on imported goods). Only the national government may do this. Many scholars believe that the national government cannot impose real estate taxes. In contrast, both levels of government can and do collect taxes on income. Neither government may tax the facilities of the other. If the state governments did not have the power to tax, they would not be able to function independently of the national government.

Additional concurrent powers include the power to borrow funds, to establish courts, and to charter banks and corporations. To a limited extent, the national government exercises police power, and to the extent that it does, police power is also a concurrent power. Concurrent powers exercised by the states are normally limited to the geographic area of each state and to those functions not granted by the Constitution exclusively to the national government. Examples of functions exclusive to the national government are the coinage of money and the negotiation of treaties.

One concurrent power that has been the subject of recent controversy is the power to establish a *minimum wage*. A minimum wage is the lowest wage rate that an employer can legally pay. Currently, the national minimum wage is $7.25 per hour. Many states have adopted higher minimum wages. In some localities, the minimum wage is set to rise over time to as much as $15 per hour.

The Supremacy Clause

The supremacy of the national constitution over subnational laws and actions is established in the **supremacy clause** of the Constitution. The supremacy clause (Article VI, Clause 2) states the following:

> *This Constitution, and the Laws of the United States which shall be made in Pursuance thereof; and all Treaties made . . . under the Authority of the United States, shall be the supreme Law of the Land; and the Judges in every State shall be bound thereby, any Thing in the Constitution or Laws of any State to the Contrary notwithstanding.*

In other words, states cannot use their reserved or concurrent powers to thwart national policies. All national and state officers, including judges, must be bound by oath to support the Constitution. Hence, any legitimate exercise of national governmental power supersedes any conflicting state action. Of course, deciding whether a conflict actually exists is a judicial matter, as you will soon learn when we discuss the case of *McCulloch v. Maryland*.

The National Guard can serve as an example of how federal power supersedes that of the states. Normally, the National Guard functions as a state militia under the command of the governor. It is frequently called out to assist with recovery efforts after natural disasters such as hurricanes, floods, and earthquakes. The president can assume command of any National Guard unit at any time, however. Presidents George W. Bush and Barack Obama repeatedly "federalized" such units for deployment in Afghanistan and Iraq. In the conflicts in these countries, National Guard members and reservists made up a larger percentage of the forces on combat duty than during any previous war in U.S. history.

National government legislation in a concurrent area is said to preempt (take precedence over) conflicting state or local laws or regulations in that area. One of the ways in which the national government has extended its powers, particularly since 1900, is through

Concurrent Powers
Powers held jointly by the national and state governments.

Supremacy Clause
The constitutional provision that makes the Constitution and federal laws superior to all conflicting state and local laws.

the preemption of state and local laws by national legislation. In the first decade of the twentieth century, fewer than twenty national laws preempted laws and regulations issued by state and local governments. By the beginning of the twenty-first century, the number had grown into the hundreds.

Interstate Relations

So far, we have examined only the relationship between central and state governmental units. The states, however, have constant commercial, social, and other dealings among themselves. The national Constitution imposes certain "rules of the road" on interstate relations. These rules have had the effect of preventing any one state from setting itself apart from the other states. The three most important clauses governing interstate relations in the Constitution, all taken from the Articles of Confederation, require each state to do the following:

- Give full faith and credit to every other state's public acts, records, and judicial proceedings (Article IV, Section 1).
- Extend to every other state's citizens the privileges and immunities of its own citizens (Article IV, Section 2).
- Agree to return persons who are fleeing from justice in another state back to that state when requested to do so (Article IV, Section 2).

Additionally, states may enter into agreements with one another called **interstate compacts.** Congressional consent is necessary if such a compact increases the power of the contracting states relative to other states (or to the national government). An example is the Port Authority of New York and New Jersey, established by an agreement between those states in 1921.

Defining Constitutional Powers—The Early Years

>>> **LO3:** Discuss how, in the early years of the republic, the United States Supreme Court confirmed the authority of the national government, and how that authority was ratified by the Civil War.

Although political bodies at all levels of government play important roles in the process of settling disputes over the nature of our federal system, normally it is the United States Supreme Court that casts the final vote. As might be expected, the character of the referee will have an impact on the ultimate outcome of any dispute. From 1801 to 1835, the Supreme Court was headed by Chief Justice John Marshall, a Federalist who advocated a strong central government. We look here at two cases decided by the Marshall Court: *McCulloch v. Maryland*[5] and *Gibbons v. Ogden*.[6] Both cases are considered milestones in the movement toward national government supremacy.

McCulloch v. Maryland (1819)

The U.S. Constitution says nothing about establishing a national bank. Nonetheless, at different times Congress chartered two banks—the First and Second Banks of the United States— and provided part of their initial capital. Thus, they were national banks. The government of Maryland imposed a tax on the Second Bank's Baltimore branch in an attempt to put that branch out of business. The branch's cashier, James William McCulloch, refused to pay the Maryland tax. When Maryland took McCulloch to its state court, the state of Maryland won. The national government appealed the case to the Supreme Court.

---

5. 17 U.S. 316 (1819).
6. 22 U.S. 1 (1824).

Interstate Compact
An agreement between two or more states.

One of the issues before the Court was whether the national government had the implied power, under the necessary and proper clause, to charter a bank and contribute capital to it. The other important question before the Court was the following: If the bank was constitutional, could a state tax it? In other words, was a state action that conflicted with a national government action invalid under the supremacy clause?

Chief Justice Marshall held that if establishing a national bank aided the national government in the exercise of its designated powers, then the authority to set up such a bank could be implied. Having established this doctrine of implied powers, Marshall then answered the other question before the Court and established the doctrine of national supremacy. Marshall ruled that no state could use its taxing power to tax a part of the national government. If it could, "the declaration that the Constitution . . . shall be the supreme law of the land, is [an] empty and unmeaning [statement]."

Marshall's decision enabled the national government to grow and to meet problems that the Constitution's framers were unable to foresee. Today, practically every expressed power of the national government has been expanded in one way or another by use of the necessary and proper clause.

Gibbons v. Ogden (1824)

One of the most important parts of the Constitution, included in Article I, Section 8, is the **commerce clause,** in which Congress is given the power "[t]o regulate Commerce with foreign Nations, and among the several States, and with the Indian Tribes." The meaning of this clause was at issue in *Gibbons v. Ogden.*

The Background of the Case. Robert Fulton and Robert Livingston secured a monopoly on steam navigation on the waters in New York State from the New York legislature in 1803. They licensed Aaron Ogden to operate steam-powered ferryboats between New York and New Jersey. Thomas Gibbons, who had obtained a license from the U.S. government to operate boats in interstate waters, decided to compete with Ogden, but he did so without New York's permission. Ogden sued Gibbons. New York's state courts prohibited Gibbons from operating in New York waters. Gibbons appealed to the Supreme Court.

There were actually several issues before the Court in this case. The first issue was how the term *commerce* should be defined. New York's highest court had defined the term narrowly to mean only the shipment of goods, or the interchange of commodities, not navigation or the transport of people. The second issue was whether the national government's power to regulate interstate commerce extended to commerce within a state (*intrastate* commerce) or was limited strictly to commerce among the states (*interstate* commerce). The third issue was whether the power to regulate interstate commerce was a concurrent power (as the New York court had concluded) or an exclusive national power.

Marshall's Ruling. Marshall defined *commerce* as *all* commercial interactions—all business dealings—including navigation and the transport of people. Marshall also held that the commerce power of the national government could be exercised in state jurisdictions, even though it could not reach *solely* intrastate commerce. Finally, Marshall emphasized that the power to regulate interstate commerce was an *exclusive* national power. Marshall held that because Gibbons was duly authorized by the national government to navigate in interstate waters, he could not be prohibited from doing so by a state court.

Marshall's expansive interpretation of the commerce clause in *Gibbons v. Ogden* allowed the national government to exercise increasing authority over economic affairs

When John Marshall was chief justice of the United States Supreme Court (1801–1835), he championed the power of the federal government. *What are the most famous cases that the Marshall Court decided?*

Everett Historical/Shutterstock

Commerce Clause
The section of the Constitution in which Congress is given the power to regulate trade among the states and with foreign countries.

The National Archives

John Brown (1800–1859), an advocate of abolishing slavery, led an ill-fated raid on a federal arsenal at Harpers Ferry, Virginia. Brown had hoped to set off a slave uprising. He was executed on charges of treason and murder. Today, we would doubtless call him a terrorist. *Why do some people nevertheless consider him a hero?*

throughout the land. Congress did not immediately exploit this broad grant of power. In the 1930s and subsequent decades, however, the commerce clause became the primary constitutional basis for national government regulation—as you will read later in this chapter.

States' Rights and the Resort to Civil War

The controversy over slavery that led to the Civil War took the form of a dispute over national government supremacy versus the rights of the separate states. Essentially, the Civil War brought to an ultimate and violent climax the ideological debate begun by the Federalists and Anti-Federalists even before the Constitution was ratified.

The Shift Back to States' Rights. As we have seen, while John Marshall was chief justice of the Supreme Court, he did much to increase the power of the national government and to reduce that of the states. During the Jacksonian era (1829–1837), however, a shift back to states' rights began. The question of the regulation of commerce became one of the major issues in federal-state relations. When Congress passed a tariff in 1828, the state of South Carolina unsuccessfully attempted to nullify the tariff (render it void), claiming that in cases of conflict between a state and the national government, the state should have the ultimate authority over its citizens.

During the next three decades, the North and the South became even more sharply divided—especially over the slavery issue. On December 20, 1860, South Carolina formally repealed its ratification of the Constitution and withdrew from the Union. On February 4, 1861, representatives from six southern states met at Montgomery, Alabama, to form a new government called the Confederate States of America.

War and the Growth of the National Government. The ultimate defeat of the South in 1865 permanently ended the idea that a state could successfully claim the right to secede, or withdraw, from the Union. Ironically, the Civil War—brought about in large part because of the South's desire for increased states' rights—resulted in the opposite: an increase in the political power of the national government.

Thousands of new employees were hired to run the Union war effort and to deal with the social and economic problems that had to be handled in the aftermath of the war. A billion-dollar ($1.3 billion, which is close to $20 billion in today's dollars) national government budget was passed for the first time in 1865 to cover the increased government expenditures. The first (temporary) income tax was imposed on citizens to help pay for the war.

The Civil War Amendments. The expansion of the national government's authority during the Civil War was also reflected in the passage of the Civil War amendments to the Constitution. Before the war, it was a bedrock constitutional principle that the national government should not interfere with slavery in the states. The Thirteenth Amendment, ratified in 1865, did more than interfere with slavery—it abolished the institution altogether.

The Fourteenth Amendment, ratified in 1868, defined who was a citizen of each state. It sought to guarantee equal rights under state law with this language:

> *[No] State [shall] deprive any person of life, liberty, or property, without due process of law; nor deny to any person within its jurisdiction the equal protection of the laws.*

In time, the courts interpreted these words to mean that the national Bill of Rights applied to state governments, a development that we will examine later in this book. Finally, the Fifteenth Amendment (1870) gave African Americans the right to vote in all elections, including state elections—although a century would pass before that right was enforced in all states.

The Continuing Dispute over the Division of Power

>>> **LO4:** Define the terms *dual federalism, cooperative federalism, categorical grants, block grants,* and *fiscal federalism.*

Although the outcome of the Civil War firmly established the supremacy of the national government and put to rest the idea that a state could secede from the Union, the war by no means ended the debate over the division of powers between the national government and the states.

Dual Federalism

Dual Federalism
A model of federalism that looks on national and state governments as co-equal sovereign powers. Neither the state government nor the national government should interfere in the other's sphere.

During the decades following the Civil War, the prevailing model of federalism was what political scientists have called **dual federalism**—a doctrine that emphasizes a distinction between national and state spheres of government authority. Various images have been used to describe different configurations of federalism over time. Dual federalism is commonly depicted as a layer cake, because the state governments and the national government are viewed as separate entities, like separate layers of a cake. Under the doctrine of dual federalism, national and state governments are co-equal sovereign powers, and neither level of government should interfere in the other's sphere. The doctrine represented a revival of states' rights following the expansion of national authority during the Civil War. Many people viewed this change as a return to normal—that is, to the conditions that had existed before the war.

The Civil War crisis drastically reduced the influence of the United States Supreme Court, which had supported the institution of slavery in the years leading up to the war. Over time, however, the Court reestablished itself as the legitimate constitutional umpire. For the Court, dual federalism meant that the national government could intervene in state activities through grants and subsidies, but in most cases it was barred from regulating matters that the Court considered to be purely local.

The Court generally limited the exercise of police power to the states. For example, in 1918, the Court ruled that a 1916 national law banning child labor was unconstitutional because it attempted to regulate a local problem.[7] In effect, the Court placed severe limits on the ability of Congress to legislate under the commerce clause of the Constitution.

The New Deal and Cooperative Federalism

The doctrine of dual federalism receded into the background in the 1930s as the nation attempted to deal with the Great Depression. Franklin D. Roosevelt was inaugurated as president on March 4, 1933. In the previous year, nearly 1,500 banks had failed (and 4,000 more would fail in 1933). Thirty-two thousand businesses had closed down, and almost one-fourth of the labor force was unemployed. The public expected the national government to do something about the disastrous state of the economy. Yet for the first three years of the Great Depression (1930–1932), the national government did very little.

Child labor was still common in the early 1900s. *Why didn't the federal government simply ban it then?*

AP Images

Roosevelt, however, energetically intervened in the economy. Roosevelt's "New Deal" included large-scale emergency antipoverty programs and introduced major new laws regulating economic activity. Initially, the Supreme Court blocked many of Roosevelt's initiatives. Beginning in 1937, however, after a change in membership, the Court ceased to limit the federal government's actions. An expansive interpretation of the commerce clause became dominant.

Some political scientists have described national-state relations since 1937 as **cooperative federalism,** in which the states and the national government cooperate in solving complex common problems. Roosevelt's New Deal programs, for example, often involved joint action between the national government and the states. The pattern of national-state relationships during these years gave rise to a new metaphor for federalism—that of a marble cake. Unlike a layer cake, in a marble cake the two types of cake are intermingled, and any bite contains cake of both flavors.

The 1960s and 1970s were a time of even greater expansion of the national government's role in domestic policy. Today, few activities are beyond the reach of the regulatory arm of the national government.

Cooperative Federalism
A model of federalism in which the states and the national government cooperate in solving problems.

---

7. *Hammer v. Dagenhart*, 247 U.S. 251 (1918). This decision was overruled in *United States v. Darby*, 312 U.S. 100 (1940).

President Franklin D. Roosevelt (1933–1945). Roosevelt's national approach to addressing the effects of the Great Depression was overwhelmingly popular, although many of his specific initiatives were not. *How did the Great Depression change the political beliefs of many Americans?*

The Politics of Federalism

In determining the allocation of powers between the state and national governments, conservatives traditionally have favored the states, and liberals have favored the federal government. After all, national authority has been an agent of change throughout U.S. history. The expansion of national authority during the Civil War freed the slaves, and beginning in the 1960s, the federal government was likewise responsible for extending civil rights such as the right to vote to African Americans.

Republicans and Democrats. For much of American history, conservative southern Democrats were the major advocates of states' rights. Then, under Republican presidents Richard Nixon (1969–1974) and Ronald Reagan (1981–1989), **devolution,** or the transfer of power from the national government to state governments, became a major theme for the Republican Party. In recent decades, however, competing theories of federalism often appeared not to divide the two parties in practice. While the Republicans continued to advocate devolution in theory, they did not follow it in reality.

Consider that the passage of welfare reform legislation in 1996, which involved transferring significant control over welfare programs to the states, took place under Democratic president Bill Clinton (1993–2001). In contrast, under Republican president George W. Bush (2001–2009), Congress enacted the No Child Left Behind Act of 2001. This act increased federal control over education, which had traditionally been under the purview of state governments. In another example, the Bush administration prevented California from implementing its own tough new laws to regulate air pollution. Upon taking office, Obama reversed the Bush policies and allowed California to proceed.

Conservatives Look Again to the States. Beginning in 2009, conservative activists, especially from the Tea Party movement, began to rediscover states' rights. One reason may be that from January 2009 through January 2011, the Democrats were in control of the presidency, the U.S. House, and the U.S. Senate. Republicans were shut out at the national level, and many conservatives hoped that the states would be a counter-weight to the newly active national government. In fact, Republicans enjoyed considerable success in winning power at the state level in the midterm elections of 2010 and 2014. As a result of these victories, Republicans had many opportunities to implement conservative legislation at the state level.

Methods of Implementing Cooperative Federalism

One means of implementing cooperative federalism is through grants. Even before the Constitution was adopted, the national government gave grants to the states in the form of land to finance education. The national government also provided land grants for canals, railroads, and roads. In the twentieth century, federal grants increased significantly, especially during the Great Depression and again in the 1960s, when the dollar amount of these grants quadrupled. These funds were used for improvements in education, pollution control, recreation, and highways. With this increase in grants, however, came a bewildering number of restrictions and regulations.

Devolution
The transfer of powers from a national or central government to a state or local government.

Categorical Grant
A federal grant to a state or local government for a specific program or project.

Categorical Grants. By the 1980s, **categorical grants** were spread out across four hundred separate programs, but the largest five accounted for more than 50 percent of the revenues spent. These five programs were Medicaid (health care for the poor), highway construction, unemployment benefits, housing assistance, and welfare programs to assist mothers with dependent children and people with disabilities. For fiscal year 2017, the national government gave about $694 billion to the states.

Over the decades, federal grants to the states have increased significantly. One reason is that Congress has decided to off-load some programs to the states and provide a major part of the funding for them. Also, Congress continues to use grants to persuade states and cities to operate programs devised by the federal government. Finally, states often are happy to apply for grants because they are relatively "free," requiring only that the state match a small portion of each grant.

Block Grants. **Block grants** lessen the restrictions on federal grants given to state and local governments by grouping a number of categorical grants under one broad heading. Governors and mayors generally prefer block grants because such grants give state and local governments more flexibility in how the funds are spent. In contrast, Congress generally favors categorical grants because the expenditures can be targeted according to congressional priorities. Block grants, in reality, make up less than 10 percent of the funds transferred to the states by the federal government.

An example of a block grant program is the Surface Transportation Program, sponsored by the Federal Highway Administration. This program provides state and local authorities with considerable flexibility. Funds can be used to repair highways and bridges, or to support pedestrian, bicycle, or bus projects. Still, the program only amounts to about 16 percent of all federal transportation grants.

Fiscal Federalism and State Budgets. In discussions of government policy, you may have heard the word *fiscal*. This word simply means "having to do with government revenues and expenditures." **Fiscal** policy, therefore, is policy concerning taxing or borrowing— and then spending the revenues. When the federal government makes grants to state and local governments, funds raised through taxation or borrowing by one level of government (the national government) are spent by another level (state and local governments). We can speak of this process as **fiscal federalism.** With almost 20 percent of state and local revenues supplied by the federal government, fiscal federalism is clearly important.

The Great Recession had a devastating impact on state budgets, and in response the federal government substantially increased the amount of funding available to the states. From 2011 on, however, these extra funds were no longer available. State governments cut spending and employment substantially—so much so that total government spending as a share of the economy actually fell from 2010 through 2014.

Feeling the Pressure—the Strings Attached to Federal Grants. No dollars sent to the states are completely free of "strings." All funds come with requirements that must be met by the states. Often, through the use of grants, the national government has been able to exercise substantial control over matters that traditionally have been under the purview of state governments. When the federal government gives federal funds for highway improvements, for example, it may condition the funds on the state's cooperation with a federal policy. This is exactly what the federal government did in the 1980s to force the states to raise their minimum alcoholic-beverage drinking age to twenty-one.

Limits on the National Government's Power to Coerce the States The Supreme Court has generally supported the national government's attempts to pressure the states into adopting various policies through the use of grants. In the drinking-age case just mentioned, the Court held that the national government could push states to raise their drinking age by threatening

Block Grant
A federal grant that provides funds to a state or local government for a general functional area, such as criminal justice or mental-health programs.

Fiscal
Having to do with government revenues and expenditures.

Fiscal Federalism
A process by which funds raised through taxation or borrowing by one level of government (usually the national government) are spent by another level (typically, state or local governments).

A teacher high-fives an elementary school student in Miami. This teacher is funded by Teach for America, a nonprofit organization that places recent high-achieving college graduates in low-income community schools. The program receives federal grants. *Should the national government have a role in educational policy?*

to withhold 10 percent of their highway grants. A penalty of this size was not "coercive."[8] Provisions in the Affordable Care Act (Obamacare), however, penalized states that failed to expand their Medicaid programs by withholding 100 percent of their Medicaid funding. In 2015, the Court found that a penalty of that size was coercive in that it could seriously damage state budgets.[9] In other words, the Court's limit on how large a penalty the national government can impose lies somewhere between 10 and 100 percent.

The Court established another limit on national authority in 1997. The Brady Handgun Violence Prevention Act required local police officials to run background checks on persons purchasing firearms. The Court found that letting the Federal government "draft" state and local police officers into its service would be unconstitutional.[10] This ruling became relevant again in 2016 when president-elect Donald Trump threatened to revoke federal grants to "sanctuary cities." Such localities typically direct their police forces not to take down information on the immigration status of persons they stop or arrest. While Congress has passed a law that requires local law enforcement to share information with the national government, it seems likely that forcing local police to collect such information in the first place would violate the Brady Handgun ruling.

Federal Mandates.   Despite these limits, for years the federal government has passed legislation pressuring the states to improve environmental conditions or the civil rights of various groups. Since the 1970s, the national government has enacted hundreds of **federal mandates** demanding that the states take action in areas ranging from voter registration, to ocean-dumping restrictions, to the education of people with disabilities. The Unfunded Mandates Reform Act of 1995 requires the Congressional Budget Office to identify mandates that cost state and local governments more than $50 million to implement. Nonetheless, the federal government routinely continues to pass mandates for state and local governments that cost more than that to put into place.

Federal Mandate
A requirement in federal legislation that forces states and municipalities to comply with certain rules.

8. *South Dakota v. Dole*, 483 U.S. 203 (1987).
9. *National Federation of Independent Business v. Sebelius*, 132 S.Ct. 2566 (2012).
10. *Printz v. United States*, 521 U.S. 898 (1997).

Federalism and Today's Supreme Court

>>> **LO5:** Detail recent Supreme Court rulings that affect the distribution of power between the national government and the states.

The United States Supreme Court, which normally has the final say on constitutional issues, plays a major role in determining where the line is drawn between federal and state powers. Consider the decisions rendered by Chief Justice John Marshall in the cases discussed earlier in this chapter. Since the 1930s, Marshall's broad interpretation of the commerce clause has made it possible for the national government to justify its regulation of almost any activity, even when the activity appears to be completely local in character. In the 1990s and early 2000s, however, the Court evidenced a willingness to impose some limits on the national government's authority under the commerce clause and other constitutional provisions. As a result, it is difficult to predict how today's Court might rule on a particular case involving federalism.

A Trend toward States' Rights?

Since the mid-1990s, the Supreme Court has tended to give greater weight to states' rights than it did during previous decades. In a widely publicized 1995 case, the Supreme Court held that Congress had exceeded its constitutional authority under the commerce clause when it passed the Gun-Free School Zones Act in 1990.[11] The Court stated that the act, which banned the possession of guns within one thousand feet of any school, was unconstitutional because it attempted to regulate an area that had "nothing to do with commerce, or any sort of economic enterprise." This marked the first time in sixty years that the Supreme Court had placed a limit on the national government's authority under the commerce clause.

Although the Court has tended to favor states' rights in some decisions, in other decisions it has backed the federal government's position. For example, in 2005 the Court held that the federal government's power to declare various substances to be illegal drugs superseded California's law legalizing the use of marijuana for medical treatment.[12] Yet less than a year later, the Court favored states' rights when it upheld Oregon's controversial "death with dignity" law, which allows patients with terminal illnesses to choose to end their lives early and thus avoid suffering.[13]

Recent Decisions

In recent rulings, the Supreme Court has often shown sympathy for states' rights, even while avoiding revolutionary changes in relations between the state and federal governments.

Immigration. In one important opinion, the Court found that Arizona had gone too far in its attempt to subject unauthorized immigration to state authority. Under the ruling, Arizona cannot make it a crime when illegal immigrants fail to carry identification papers or when they attempt to find work. Arizona police cannot arrest individuals solely on suspicion of illegal status.[14]

Health-Care Reform. It was the Court's opinion on the Affordable Care Act (Obamacare) that was expected to be the most important states' rights ruling in decades. In the end, the Court's 2012 verdict was somewhat anticlimactic. It did not find that the *individual mandate*—a penalty imposed on those who do not buy health-care insurance—violated the police powers of the states. (The Court found that while the mandate could not be justified

---

11. *United States v. Lopez*, 514 U.S. 549 (1995).
12. *Gonzales v. Raich*, 545 U.S. 1 (2005).
13. *Gonzales v. Oregon*, 546 U.S. 243 (2006).
14. *Arizona v. United States*, 132 S.Ct. 2492 (2012).

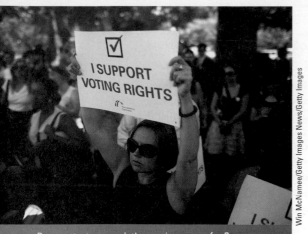

Demonstrators mark the anniversary of a Supreme Court ruling that destroyed the "preclearance" system. That system regulated changes in voting procedures in areas with a history of discrimination. *Why hasn't Congress updated the system to meet the Court's requirements?*

under the commerce clause, it was legitimate under the national government's power to tax.) Chief Justice John Roberts's ruling on Medicaid expansion did hearten states' rights advocates, however. By making Medicaid expansion optional for the states, the Court for the first time put limits on the ability of the federal government to coerce states by withholding grants.[15]

Same-Sex Marriage. Supreme Court rulings on same-sex marriage in 2013 also tended to enhance the authority of the states. In the most important of these, *United States v. Windsor*, the Court found that the federal government must recognize state-approved same-sex marriages. This was a victory for states' rights, as well as for same-sex couples in the affected states.[16]

Throughout 2014, federal district and appeals courts used arguments contained in the *Windsor* decision as justification for overturning bans on same-sex marriage in dozens of states. The Sixth Circuit Court of Appeals then broke ranks with the other courts by upholding bans on same-sex marriage. With different appeals courts handing down contradictory rulings, the Supreme Court was forced to act. In June 2015, in *Obergefell v. Hodges*, the Court effectively legalized same-sex marriage throughout the entire United States.[17] Earlier states' rights rulings were therefore capped by a decision that enhanced national authority.

The Voting Rights Act. A key Court ruling on the Voting Rights Act was a striking triumph for states' rights. The 1965 act imposed certain requirements on states and localities—mostly in the South—with a history of violating the voting rights of minority group members. Such areas had to obtain *preclearance* from the federal government to make changes in voting procedures or districts. In June 2013, the Court effectively destroyed the preclearance system when it ruled that the existing list of affected states and localities was based on obsolete data.[18]

In principle, Congress could update the method of identifying jurisdictions that need preclearance, but the chances of today's Congress passing such a law are low. Still, the Department of Justice continues to have the right to sue states and localities *after* they have changed their voting procedures or districts. Such suits, however, are likely to be much less effective than the preclearance system. It is also questionable whether President Trump's Department of Justice will have much interest in filing such suits.

Affirmative Action. In 2014, the Court provided an additional victory for states' rights when it ruled that Michigan was allowed to ban affirmative action in public university admissions.[19] Affirmative action programs attempt to assist groups who are victims of past discrimination—minority group members or women—by giving them limited privileges in college admissions or in employment. Several states ban such programs, and the number of states that do so is likely to grow.

15. *National Federation of Independent Business v. Sebelius*, 132 S.Ct. 2566 (2012).
16. 135 S.Ct. 2584.
17. *Obergefell v. Hodges*, 135 S.Ct. 2584 (2015).
18. *Shelby County v. Holder*, 133 S.Ct. 2612.
19. *Schuette v. Coalition to Defend Affirmative Action*, 134 S.Ct. 1623 (2014).

Writing E-mails and Letters to the Editor

Our federal system encourages debate over whether a particular issue should be a national, state, or local question. Many questions are, in fact, state or local ones.

Why Should You Care? Although the national government provides aid to educational programs, education is still primarily a state and local responsibility. Therefore, you can address this issue at the state or local level. Gambling laws are another state responsibility. Do you enjoy gambling—or do you believe that the effects of gambling make it a social disaster? State law—or state negotiations with Native American tribes—determines the availability of gambling.

What Can You Do? In our modern era, the number of ways in which you can communicate your opinion is vast. You can post a response on any of thousands of blogs. You could develop your own short video and post it on YouTube.

If you want to effect policy change at the state or local level, however, the local newspaper, in both its paper and online formats, continues to be essential. Blogs, YouTube, and other online venues tend to be nationally oriented. But most newspapers are resolutely local and the natural hub for discussions of local issues. Papers often allow responses and comments on their websites, and you can make a point by contributing in that fashion. Yet nothing will win you a wider audience than an old-fashioned letter to the editor, regardless of whether it appears online or is printed on paper. Use the following rules to compose an effective communication:

- Use a computer, and double-space the lines. Use a spelling checker and grammar checker.
- Include a lead topic sentence that is short, to the point, and powerful.
- Keep your thoughts on target—choose only one topic. Make sure it is newsworthy and timely.
- Make sure your communication is concise. Never let it exceed a page in length (double-spaced).
  - If you know that facts were misstated or left out in current news stories about your topic, supply the facts. The public wants to know.
  - Don't be afraid to express moral judgments. You can go a long way by appealing to the reader's sense of justice.
  - Personalize the communication by bringing in your own experiences, if possible.
  - If you are writing a letter, sign it and give your address (including your e-mail address) and your telephone number. Blogs and other communications may have their own rules for identifying yourself in posted comments. Follow these rules.
  - If writing a letter, send or e-mail it to the editorial office of the newspaper of your choice. Their websites usually give information on where you can send mail.

Rob Bartee / Alamy Stock Photo

A student reads a newspaper. *Why do so few students read newspapers any more?*

Key Terms

block grant 59	devolution 58	enumerated powers 49	police power 50
categorical grant 58	dual federalism 56	federal mandate 60	supremacy clause 52
commerce clause 54	elastic clause, or	fiscal 59	unitary system 45
concurrent powers 52	necessary and	fiscal federalism 59	
confederal system 45	proper clause 49	interstate compact 53	
cooperative federalism 57			

Chapter Summary

≫LO1 There are three basic models for ordering relations between central and local governments: (a) a unitary system (in which ultimate power is held by the national government), (b) a confederal system (in which ultimate power is retained by the states), and (c) a federal system (in which governmental powers are divided between the national government and the states).

≫LO2 The Constitution expressly grants certain powers to the national government. In addition to these enumerated powers, the national government has implied and inherent powers. Implied powers are those that are reasonably necessary to carry out the powers expressly given to the national government. Inherent powers are those that the national government holds by virtue of being a sovereign state with the right to preserve itself.

The Tenth Amendment to the Constitution states that powers not delegated to the United States by the Constitution, nor prohibited by it to the states, are reserved to the states, or to the people. In certain areas, the Constitution provides for concurrent powers (such as the power to tax), which are powers that are held jointly by the national and state governments.

The supremacy clause of the Constitution states that the Constitution, congressional laws, and national treaties are the supreme law of the land. States cannot use their reserved or concurrent powers to override national policies.

≫LO3 Chief Justice John Marshall's expansive interpretation of the necessary and proper clause of the Constitution in *McCulloch v. Maryland* (1819),

along with his affirmation of the supremacy clause, enhanced the power of the national government. Marshall's broad interpretation of the commerce clause in *Gibbons v. Ogden* (1824) further extended the powers of the national government.

The controversy over slavery that led to the Civil War took the form of a fight over national government supremacy versus the rights of the separate states.

≫LO4 Since the Civil War, federalism has evolved from dual federalism to cooperative federalism. In dual federalism, the states and the federal government remain supreme within their own spheres. The era since the Great Depression has been labeled one of cooperative federalism, in which states and the national government cooperate in solving complex problems.

Categorical grants from the federal government to state governments help finance specific projects. By attaching conditions to federal grants, the national government can effect policy changes in areas typically governed by the states. Block grants cover general functional areas and give state and local governments more flexibility. Federal mandates—laws pressuring states to implement certain policies—have generated controversy.

≫LO5 The United States Supreme Court plays a significant role in determining the line between state and federal powers. Since the mid-1990s, there has been a trend on the part of the Court to support states' rights. Yet the Court has also issued rulings in support of the federal government.

Test Yourself

1. The system of government in the United States that existed before the adoption of the Constitution was called a:
   a. federal system.
   b. unitary system.
   c. confederal system.
2. Reasons why the founders chose a federal system include all except:
   a. no other type of system would have been politically acceptable.
   b. the United States was large geographically, and it would have been difficult to govern just from the national capital.
   c. the thirteen states were geographically compact, so a federal system was appropriate.
3. When we say that state governments have police powers, we mean that:
   a. they have authority to legislate for the health, morals, safety, and welfare of their people.
   b. they have the right to establish law enforcement agencies.
   c. they have the right to exempt themselves from certain national laws.
4. When both the national government and the state governments share certain powers, we call them:
   a. prevailing powers.
   b. concurrent powers.
   c. constitutional powers.
5. One topic that has been addressed by both national and state legislation is:
   a. the taxation of real estate.
   b. defining who is a citizen.
   c. setting a minimum wage.
6. How must every state treat each others' public acts, records, and judicial proceedings?
   a. Accept them when they correspond to the state's own laws.
   b. Give them full faith and credit.
   c. Accept them when required to do so by the national government.

7. In the Supreme Court case of *McCulloch v. Maryland* (1819), the Court clearly established:
   a. that the Constitution is the supreme law of the land.
   b. that state governments can tax the national government.
   c. that the national government can tax the state governments.
8. The Supreme Court case of *Gibbons v. Ogden* (1824) involved regulation of:
   a. intrastate commerce.
   b. interstate commerce.
   c. foreign commerce.
9. The transfer of powers from a central or national government to a state or local one is called:
   a. devolution.
   b. cooperative federalism.
   c. states' rights.
10. When the federal (national) government sends dollars to state governments, those funds:
    a. are given without any restrictions.
    b. are to be returned to the federal government at a later date.
    c. come with many "strings" attached.
11. When funds raised by the national government are then spent by state governments, this is called:
    a. fiscal federalism.
    b. dual federalism.
    c. competitive federalism.

Essay Questions

1. Traditionally, conservatives have favored states' rights and liberals have favored national authority. Can you think of modern-day issues in which these long-standing preferences might be reversed, with conservatives favoring national authority and liberals favoring states' rights? Explain.
2. Some Tea Party activists wanted to repeal the Seventeenth Amendment. If the amendment were repealed, state legislatures would choose each state's U.S. senators. Advocates of repeal argue that it would strengthen the power of the states within the federal system. Would such a change have good or bad consequences? Explain.

Answers to multiple-choice questions: 1. c, 2. c, 3. a, 4. b, 5. c, 6. b, 7. a, 8. b, 9. a, 10. c, 11. a.

4 | Civil Liberties

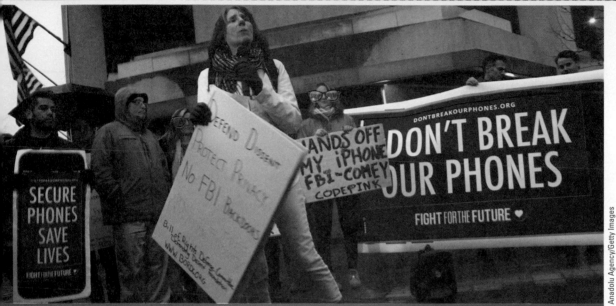

Apple supporters stage a protest in front of FBI headquarters in Washington, D.C. In 2016, the FBI sought to force Apple to "crack" the security on an iPhone that had been used by terrorists. Apple refused, arguing that such a step would undermine the privacy of all iPhone users. *What trade-offs are appropriate between civil liberties and the fight against terrorism?*

The five **Learning Outcomes (LOs)** below are designed to help improve your understanding of this chapter. After reading this chapter, you should be able to:

≫ LO1 Identify the rights listed in the original Constitution, describe the Bill of Rights, and discuss how it came to be applied to state governments as well as the national government.

≫ LO2 Explain how the First Amendment's establishment clause and free exercise clause guarantee our freedom of religion.

≫ LO3 Specify the limited circumstances in which the national and state governments may override the principles of free speech and freedom of the press.

≫ LO4 Provide the constitutional basis of the right to privacy, and explain how the principle has been applied to the abortion and right-to-die controversies.

≫ LO5 Identify the constitutional rights of those who are accused of a crime, describe the *Miranda* and exclusionary rules, and cite examples of how recent security concerns have affected our civil liberties.

Check your understanding of the material with the Test Yourself section at the end of the chapter.

"The land of the free." When asked what makes the United States distinctive, Americans will commonly say that it is a free country. Americans have long believed that limits on the power of government are an essential part of what makes this country free. Restraints on the actions of government against individuals generally are referred to as *civil liberties*. The first ten amendments to the U.S. Constitution—the Bill of Rights—place such restraints on the national government. Of these amendments, none is more famous than the First Amendment, which guarantees freedom of religion, speech, and the press, along with many additional rights.

Most other democratic nations have laws to protect these and other civil liberties, but none of the laws is quite like the First Amendment. Take the issue of "hate speech." What if someone makes statements that stir up hatred toward a particular race or other group of people? In Germany, where memories of Nazi anti-Semitism remain alive, such speech is unquestionably illegal. In the United States, the issue is not so clear. The courts have often extended constitutional protection to this kind of speech.

In this chapter, we describe the civil liberties provided by the Bill of Rights and some of the controversies that surround them. In addition to First Amendment liberties, we look at the right to privacy and the rights of defendants in criminal prosecutions.

The Constitutional Bases of Our Liberties

>>> **LO1:** Identify the rights listed in the original Constitution, describe the Bill of Rights, and discuss how it came to be applied to state governments as well as the national government.

As you read through this chapter, bear in mind that both the original Constitution and the Bill of Rights are relatively brief. The framers set forth broad guidelines, leaving it up to the courts to interpret these constitutional mandates and apply them to specific situations. Thus, judicial interpretations shape the true nature of the civil liberties and rights that we possess. Because judicial interpretations change over time, so do our liberties and rights. As you will read in the following pages, there have been many conflicts over the meaning of such simple phrases as *freedom of religion* and *freedom of the press*. To understand what freedoms we actually have, we need to examine how the courts—and particularly the United States Supreme Court—have resolved some of those conflicts.

Protections Listed in the Original Constitution

While Americans typically think of our civil liberties as guaranteed by the Bill of Rights, three important protections were written into the main body of the Constitution. In Article I, Section 9, we find this statement: "The privilege of the Writ of Habeas Corpus shall not be suspended, unless when in Cases of Rebellion or Invasion the public Safety may require it." The section goes on to state: "No Bill of Attainder or ex post facto Law shall be passed." What is meant by all this rather obscure legal language?

A **writ of *habeas corpus*** is a court order issued to any agency that is holding a prisoner. The writ requires the jailer to bring the prisoner before the court and explain why that person is being held. If the judge finds the imprisonment to be unlawful, he or she will order the jailer to rectify the situation. The prisoner may be brought to trial—or freed. It is *habeas corpus* that prevents the government from arbitrarily and indefinitely detaining political opponents or unpopular individuals. Following the terrorist attacks of September 11, 2001, the question of whether suspected terrorists had a right to *habeas corpus* became a major political and judicial issue.

During the early years of the republic, federal courts offered *habeas corpus* rights only to federal prisoners. Following the U.S. Civil War, however, federal courts began issuing writs on behalf of prisoners held by the states.

A **bill of attainder** is a law that inflicts punishment without a trial. An ***ex post facto*** **law** inflicts punishment for an act that was not illegal at the time it was committed. In Article I, Section 10, of the Constitution, the prohibition of both of these types of laws is explicitly extended to the states. In contrast, the Bill of Rights had a very different legal history.

Writ of *Habeas Corpus*
Habeas corpus means, literally, "you have the body." A writ of *habeas corpus* is an order that requires jailers to bring a prisoner before a court or judge and explain why the person is being held.

Bill of Attainder
A law that inflicts punishment without a trial.

***Ex Post Facto* Law**
A law that inflicts punishment for an act that was not illegal at the time it was committed.

Extending the Bill of Rights to State Governments

Many citizens do not realize that, as originally intended, the Bill of Rights limited the powers only of the national government. At the time the Bill of Rights was ratified, there was little concern over the potential of state governments to curb civil liberties. For one thing, state governments were closer to home and easier to control. For another, most state constitutions already had bills of rights. Rather, the fear was of the potential tyranny of the national government. The Bill of Rights begins with the words, "Congress shall make no law . . . ." It says nothing about states making laws that might abridge citizens' civil liberties. In 1833, the United States Supreme Court held that the Bill of Rights did not apply to state laws.[1]

We mentioned that most states had bills of rights. These bills of rights were similar to the national one, but there were some differences. Furthermore, each state's judicial system interpreted the rights differently. Citizens in different states, therefore, effectively had different sets of civil liberties. It was not until the Fourteenth Amendment was ratified in 1868 that civil liberties guaranteed by the national Constitution began to be applied to the states. Section 1 of that amendment provides, in part, as follows:

> *No State shall . . . deprive any person of life, liberty, or property, without due process of law. . . .*

Incorporation under the Fourteenth Amendment

There was no question that the Fourteenth Amendment applied to state governments. For decades, however, the courts were reluctant to define the liberties spelled out in the national Bill of Rights as constituting "due process of law," which was protected under the Fourteenth Amendment. Not until 1925, in *Gitlow v. New York*,[2] did the United States Supreme Court hold that the Fourteenth Amendment protected the freedom of speech guaranteed by the First Amendment to the Constitution from state infringement.

Only gradually did the Supreme Court accept **incorporation theory**—the view that the protections of the Bill of Rights are incorporated into the Fourteenth Amendment's protection against state government actions. Table 4–1 shows the rights that the Court has incorporated into the Fourteenth Amendment and the case in which it first applied each protection. As you can see in the table, in the fifteen years following the *Gitlow* decision, the Supreme Court incorporated into the Fourteenth Amendment the other basic freedoms (of the press, assembly, the right to petition, and religion) guaranteed by the First Amendment.

It took time for the Supreme Court to require the states to accept other liberties. Only in 2010 did the Court rule that the states were obligated under the Second Amendment to recognize an individual's right to bear arms. Even with that ruling, the national and state governments retain the power to regulate the ownership of firearms. The Third Amendment bars the government from quartering soldiers in private houses during peacetime, but the Court has never imposed this obligation on the states. The reason appears to be that the Court has never heard a case in which a state allegedly violated this right. In 1982, however, a U.S. appeals court ruled to incorporate the Third Amendment.[3]

Incorporation Theory
The view that the protections of the Bill of Rights apply to state governments through the Fourteenth Amendment's due process clause.

---

1. *Barron v. Baltimore*, 32 U.S. 243 (1833).
2. 268 U.S. 652 (1925).
3. *Engblom v. Carey*, 677 F.2d 957 (2d Cir. 1982).

TABLE 4–1	Incorporating the Bill of Rights into the Fourteenth Amendment		

Why would the Supreme Court have incorporated some of these rights many years before it incorporated others?

Year	Issue	Amendment Involved	Court Case
1925	Freedom of speech	I	*Gitlow v. New York,* 268 U.S. 652.
1931	Freedom of the press	I	*Near v. Minnesota,* 283 U.S. 697.
1932	Right to a lawyer in capital punishment cases	VI	*Powell v. Alabama,* 287 U.S. 45.
1937	Freedom of assembly and right to petition	I	*De Jonge v. Oregon,* 299 U.S. 353.
1940	Freedom of religion	I	*Cantwell v. Connecticut,* 310 U.S. 296.
1947	Separation of church and state	I	*Everson v. Board of Education,* 330 U.S. 1.
1948	Right to a public trial	VI	*In re Oliver,* 333 U.S. 257.
1949	No unreasonable searches and seizures	IV	*Wolf v. Colorado,* 338 U.S. 25.
1961	Exclusionary rule (see "The Great Balancing Act" later in this chapter)	IV	*Mapp v. Ohio,* 367 U.S. 643.
1962	No cruel and unusual punishment	VIII	*Robinson v. California,* 370 U.S. 660.
1963	Right to a lawyer in all criminal felony cases	VI	*Gideon v. Wainwright,* 372 U.S. 335.
1964	No compulsory self-incrimination	V	*Malloy v. Hogan,* 378 U.S. 1.
1965	Right to privacy	I, III, IV, V, IX	*Griswold v. Connecticut,* 381 U.S. 479.
1966	Right to an impartial jury	VI	*Parker v. Gladden,* 385 U.S. 363.
1967	Right to a speedy trial	VI	*Klopfer v. North Carolina,* 386 U.S. 213.
1969	No double jeopardy	V	*Benton v. Maryland,* 395 U.S. 784.
2010	Right to bear arms	II	*McDonald v. Chicago,* 561 U.S. 3025.

Freedom of Religion

>>> **LO2:** Explain how the First Amendment's establishment clause and free exercise clause guarantee our freedom of religion.

In the United States, freedom of religion consists of two principal rules that are presented in the First Amendment. The first rule guarantees the separation of church and state, and the second guarantees the free exercise of religion.

The Separation of Church and State—The Establishment Clause

The First Amendment to the Constitution states, in part, that "Congress shall make no law respecting an establishment of religion." In the words of Thomas Jefferson, the **establishment clause** was designed to create a "wall of separation of Church and State." As interpreted by the Supreme Court, the establishment clause in the First Amendment means at least the following:

> *Neither a state nor the federal government can set up a church. Neither can pass laws which aid one religion, aid all religions, or prefer one religion over another. Neither can force nor influence a person to go to or to remain away from church against his will or force him to profess a belief or disbelief in any religion. No person can be punished for entertaining or*

Establishment Clause
The part of the First Amendment prohibiting the establishment of a church officially supported by the national government.

professing religious beliefs or disbeliefs, for church attendance or nonattendance. No tax in any amount, large or small, can be levied to support any religious activities or institutions, whatever they may be called, or whatever form they may adopt to teach or practice religion. Neither a state nor the federal government can, openly or secretly, participate in the affairs of any religious organizations or groups and vice versa.[4]

The establishment clause covers such matters as the legality of giving state and local government aid to religious organizations and schools, allowing or requiring school prayers, teaching evolution versus creationist theories that reject evolution, placing religious displays in schools or public places, and discriminating against religious groups in publicly operated institutions.

Aid to Church-Related Schools. In the United States, almost 11 percent of school-age children attend private schools, of which about 80 percent have a religious affiliation. The United States Supreme Court has tried to draw a fine line between permissible public aid to students in church-related schools and impermissible public aid to religion.

In 1971, in *Lemon v. Kurtzman*,[5] the Court ruled that direct state aid could not be used to subsidize religious instruction. The Court in the *Lemon* case gave its most general pronouncement on the constitutionality of government aid to religious schools, stating that (1) the aid had to be secular (nonreligious) in aim, (2) it could not have the primary effect of advancing or inhibiting religion, and (3) the government must avoid "an excessive government entanglement with religion." All laws that raise issues under the establishment clause are now subject to the three-part *Lemon test*. How the test is applied, however, has varied over the years.

In a number of cases, the Supreme Court has held that state programs helping church-related schools are unconstitutional. In other cases, however, the Supreme Court has allowed states to use tax funds for lunches, textbooks, diagnostic services for speech and hearing problems, standardized tests, and special educational services for disadvantaged students attending religious schools.

School Vouchers. An ongoing controversy concerning the establishment clause has to do with school vouchers. Some people believe that the public schools are failing to educate our children adequately. One proposed solution to the problem has been for state and local governments to issue school vouchers. These vouchers represent state-issued funds that can be used to purchase education at any school, public or private. At issue is whether voucher programs violate the establishment clause.

In 2002, the United States Supreme Court held that a voucher program in Cleveland, Ohio, did not violate the establishment clause. The Court concluded that because the vouchers could be used for public as well as private schools, the program did not unconstitutionally entangle church and state.[6] The Court's 2002 decision was encouraging to those who support school choice, whether it takes the form of school vouchers or tuition tax credits to offset educational expenses in private schools.

Today, a variety of states allow public funds to be used for private school expenses. Some have small-scale voucher or scholarship programs for a limited number of students, frequently special-needs students. A growing number of states provide tax deductions for private school expenses.

---

4. *Everson v. Board of Education*, 330 U.S. 1 (1947).
5. 403 U.S. 602 (1971).
6. *Zelman v. Simmons-Harris*, 536 U.S. 639 (2002).

The Issue of School Prayer—*Engel v. Vitale.* Do the states have the right to promote religion in general, without making any attempt to establish a particular religion? That is the question raised in 1962 in *Engel v. Vitale*,[7] the so-called Regents' Prayer case in New York. The State Board of Regents of New York had suggested that a prayer be spoken aloud in the public schools at the beginning of each day. The recommended prayer was as follows:

> *Almighty God, we acknowledge our dependence upon Thee, And we beg Thy blessings upon us, our parents, our teachers, and our Country.*

Such a prayer was implemented in many New York public schools.

The parents of a number of students challenged the action of the regents, maintaining that it violated the establishment clause of the First

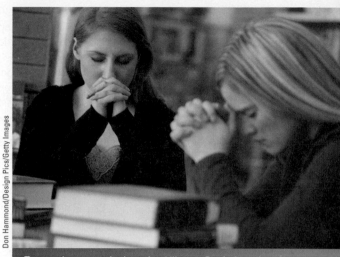

Two students pray in the school library. ***Do their actions violate the separation of church and state?***

Amendment. At trial, the parents lost. On appeal, however, the Supreme Court ruled that the regents' action was unconstitutional because "the constitutional prohibition against laws respecting an establishment of a religion must mean at least that in this country it is no part of the business of government to compose official prayers for any group of the American people to recite as part of a religious program carried on by any government."

Forbidding the Teaching of Evolution. For many decades, certain religious groups have opposed the teaching of evolution in the schools. To these groups, evolutionary theory directly counters their religious belief that human beings did not evolve but were created fully formed, as described in the biblical story of the creation. State and local attempts to forbid the teaching of evolution, however, have not passed constitutional muster in the eyes of the United States Supreme Court. For example, in 1968 the Supreme Court held that an Arkansas law prohibiting the teaching of evolution violated the establishment clause because it imposed religious beliefs on students.[8] Nonetheless, state and local groups around the country continue their efforts against the teaching of evolution.

The Issue of Intelligent Design. Some school districts have considered teaching the creationist theory of "intelligent design" as an alternative explanation of the origin of life. Proponents of intelligent design contend that evolutionary theory has "gaps" that can be explained only by the existence of an intelligent creative force (God).

The federal courts took up the issue of intelligent design in 2005. The previous year, the Dover Area Board of Education in Pennsylvania had voted to require the presentation of intelligent design as an explanation of the origin of life. In December 2005, a U.S. district court ruled that the Dover mandate was unconstitutional.[9] Subsequently, all of the school board members who endorsed the teaching of intelligent design were voted out of office.

---

7. 370 U.S. 421 (1962).
8. *Epperson v. Arkansas*, 393 U.S. 97 (1968).
9. *Kitzmiller v. Dover Area School District*, 400 F.Supp.2d 707 (M.D.Pa. 2005).

This nativity scene in front of the United States Supreme Court was part of a campaign to display nativity scenes on public property. *What rules govern such displays?*

Since 2005, advocates of intelligent design have made continued attempts to introduce their doctrine into the public schools. Intelligent design advocates have adopted the slogan "teach the controversy" as a way of introducing creationism alongside evolution. Opponents argue, however, that there *is* no controversy among biologists. Rather, the controversy is political and religious, and if it is taught at all, it should be covered in social science or politics classes.

Religious Displays on Public Property. On a regular basis, the courts are asked to determine whether religious symbols placed on public property violate the establishment clause. A frequent source of controversy is the placement of a crèche, or nativity scene, on public property during the Christmas season. The Supreme Court has allowed some displays but prohibited others. In general, a nativity scene is acceptable if it is part of a broader display that contains secular objects such as lights, Christmas trees, Santa Claus figures, and reindeer. A stand-alone crèche is not acceptable.[10]

The Free Exercise Clause

The First Amendment constrains Congress from prohibiting the free exercise of religion. Does this **free exercise clause** mean that no type of religious practice can be prohibited or restricted by government? Certainly, a person can hold any religious belief that he or she wants, or a person can have no religious belief. When, however, religious *practices* work against public policy and the public welfare, the government can act. For example, regardless of a child's or parent's religious beliefs, the government can require vaccinations. (Some states, such as Texas, allow philosophical exemption from vaccination requirements—but others, such as California, allow documented medical exemptions only.)

In other instances, the government can be relatively protective of actions based on personal beliefs. In one case, an Abercrombie & Fitch clothing store refused to hire a young Muslim woman who wore a head scarf for religious reasons. In 2015, the Court found this refusal to be illegal religious discrimination.[11]

Churches and other religious organizations are tax-exempt bodies, and as a result they are not allowed to endorse candidates for office or make contributions to candidates' campaigns. Churches are allowed to take positions on ballot proposals, however, and may contribute to referendum campaigns. For example, both the Latter-Day Saints (the Mormons) and the Roman Catholic Church were able to fund the campaign for California's 2008 Proposition 8, a measure to ban same-sex marriage.

The Internal Revenue Service (IRS) rarely bothers to threaten the tax-exempt status of a church based on simple candidate endorsements, however. In October 2012, about 1,400 ministers collectively endorsed Republican presidential candidate Mitt Romney in a deliberate challenge to the 1954 law that prohibits such endorsements. The IRS did not respond.

Free Exercise Clause
The provision of the First Amendment guaranteeing the free exercise of religion.

10. *Lynch v. Donnelly,* 465 U.S. 668 (1984).
11. *Equal Employment Opportunity Commission v. Abercrombie & Fitch Stores,* 575 U.S. ___ (2015).

In 1995, however, the IRS did revoke the tax-exempt status of Branch Ministries, Inc., and in 2000 a federal district court supported the revocation.[12] Branch Ministries went far beyond simply endorsing a candidate from the pulpit. The church had used tax-exempt income to buy newspaper advertisements denouncing Democratic presidential candidate Bill Clinton.

Freedom of Expression

>>> **LO3:** Specify the limited circumstances in which the national and state governments may override the principles of free speech and freedom of the press.

Perhaps the most frequently invoked freedom that Americans have is the right to free speech and a free press. For the most part, Americans can criticize public officials and their actions without fear of reprisal by any branch of our government.

No Prior Restraint

Restraining an activity before it has actually occurred is called **prior restraint.** When expression is involved, prior restraint means censorship, as opposed to subsequent punishment. Prior restraint of expression would require, for example, that a permit be obtained before a speech could be made, a newspaper published, or a movie or TV show exhibited. Most, if not all, Supreme Court justices have been very critical of any governmental action that imposes prior restraint on expression.

One of the most famous cases concerning prior restraint was *New York Times v. United States*[13] (1971), the so-called Pentagon Papers case. The *Times* and the *Washington Post* were about to publish the Pentagon Papers, a secret history of the U.S. government's involvement in the Vietnam War (1965–1975). The documents had been obtained illegally by a disillusioned former Pentagon official. The government wanted a court order to bar publication of the papers, arguing that national security was threatened and that the documents had been stolen. The newspapers argued that the public had a right to know the information contained in the papers and that the press had the right to inform the public. The Supreme Court ruled six to three in favor of the newspapers' right to publish the information. This case affirmed the no-prior-restraint doctrine.

The Protection of Symbolic Speech

Not all expression is in words or in writing. Articles of clothing, gestures, and other forms of nonverbal expressive conduct are considered **symbolic speech**. Such speech is given substantial protection today by our courts. For example, in a landmark decision issued in 1969, *Tinker v. Des Moines School District*,[14] the Supreme Court held that the wearing of black armbands by students in protest against the Vietnam War was a form of speech protected by the First Amendment.

Flag Burning. In 1989, the Supreme Court ruled that state laws that prohibited the burning of the American flag as part of a peaceful protest also violated the freedom of expression protected by the First Amendment.[15] Congress responded by passing the Flag Protection Act of 1989, which was ruled unconstitutional by the Supreme Court in 1990. Congress and

---

12. *Branch Ministries v. Rossetti*, 211 F.3d 137 (D.C.Cir. 2000).
13. 403 U.S. 713 (1971).
14. 393 U.S. 503 (1969).
15. *Texas v. Johnson*, 488 U.S. 884 (1989).

Prior Restraint
Restraining an activity before it has actually occurred. When expression is involved, this means censorship.

Symbolic Speech
Expression made through articles of clothing, gestures, and other forms of nonverbal conduct.

President George H. W. Bush immediately pledged to work for a constitutional amendment to "protect our flag"—an effort that has yet to be successful.

Cross Burning. In 2003, the Supreme Court concluded in a Virginia case that a state, consistent with the First Amendment, may ban cross burnings carried out with the intent to intimidate. The Court reasoned that historically, cross burning was a sign of impending violence, and a state has the right to ban threats of violence. The Court also ruled, however, that the state must prove intimidation and cannot infer it from the cross burnings themselves. In an impassioned dissent, Justice Clarence Thomas, who is African American and usually one of the Court's most conservative members, argued that cross burnings should be automatic evidence of intent to intimidate.[16]

The Protection of Commercial Speech

Commercial speech usually is defined as advertising statements. Can advertisers use their First Amendment rights to prevent restrictions on the content of commercial advertising? Until the 1970s, the Supreme Court held that such speech was not protected at all by the First Amendment. By the mid-1970s, however, more and more commercial speech had been brought under First Amendment protection. According to Justice Harry A. Blackmun, "Advertising, however tasteless and excessive it sometimes may seem, is nonetheless dissemination of information as to who is producing and selling what product for what reason and at what price."[17] Nevertheless, the Supreme Court will consider a restriction on commercial speech valid as long as it (1) seeks to implement a substantial government interest, (2) directly advances that interest, and (3) goes no further than necessary to accomplish its objective. In particular, a business engaging in commercial speech can be subject to liability for factual inaccuracies in ways that do not apply to noncommercial speech.

Attempts to Ban Subversive or Advocacy Speech

Over the past hundred years, the United States Supreme Court has established, in succession, a number of doctrines regarding language allegedly subversive to the public order.

The Clear and Present Danger Test. In 1919, the Supreme Court ruled that when a person's remarks present a clear and present danger to the peace or public order, they can be curtailed constitutionally. Justice Oliver Wendell Holmes used this reasoning when ratifying the conviction of a socialist who had been charged with violating the Espionage Act by distributing a leaflet that opposed the military draft. According to the *clear and present danger test*, expression may be restricted if evidence exists that such expression would cause a dangerous condition, actual or imminent, that Congress has the power to prevent.[18]

The Bad Tendency Rule. Over the course of the twentieth century, the Supreme Court modified the clear and present danger rule, limiting the constitutional protection of free speech in 1925 and 1951, and then broadening it substantially in 1969. In *Gitlow v. New York*, the Court reintroduced an earlier *bad tendency rule*, which placed greater restrictions on speech than are found in Justice Holmes's formulation.[19] According to this rule, speech may be curtailed if there is a possibility that such expression might lead to some "evil."

Commercial speech
Advertising statements, which increasingly have been given First Amendment protection.

16. *Virginia v. Black*, 538 U.S. 343 (2003).
17. *Virginia State Board of Pharmacy v. Virginia Citizens Consumer Council, Inc.*, 425 U.S. 748 (1976).
18. *Schenck v. United States*, 249 U.S. 47 (1919).
19. 268 U.S. 652 (1925).

In the *Gitlow* case, a member of a left-wing group was convicted of violating New York State's criminal anarchy statute when he published and distributed a pamphlet urging the violent overthrow of the U.S. government. In its majority opinion, the Supreme Court held that the First Amendment afforded protection against state incursions on freedom of expression—the first time that the First Amendment was ever invoked against a state government. Nevertheless, Gitlow could be punished legally because his expression would tend to bring about evils that the state had a right to prevent.

The Imminent Lawless Action Test. Some claim that the United States did not achieve true freedom of political speech until 1969. In that year, in *Brandenburg v. Ohio*, the Supreme Court overturned the conviction of a Ku Klux Klan leader for violating a state statute.[20] The statute prohibited anyone from advocating "the duty, necessity, or propriety of sabotage, violence, or unlawful methods of terrorism as a means of accomplishing industrial or political reform." The Court held that the guarantee of free speech does not permit a state "to forbid or proscribe [disallow] advocacy of the use of force or of law violation except where such advocacy is directed to inciting or producing imminent [immediate] lawless actions and is likely to incite or produce such action." The **imminent lawless action test** enunciated by the Court is a difficult one for prosecutors to meet. As a result, the Court's decision significantly broadened the protection given to advocacy speech.

An advertisement for Captain Morgan Long Island Iced Tea, an alcoholic beverage allegedly aimed at the college student market. *What rights do alcohol marketers have under the First Amendment?*

digitalreflections/Shutterstock

The Eclipse of Obscenity as a Legal Category

Traditionally, state and federal statutes made it a crime to disseminate obscene materials. But what is *obscenity*? Justice Potter Stewart once stated that even though he could not define obscenity, "I know it when I see it." The legal system needs a more precise definition than that, however.

The Rise and Fall of *Miller v. California*. In 1973, in *Miller v. California*, Chief Justice Warren Burger created a list of requirements that must be met for material to be legally obscene.[21] Material is obscene if (1) the average person finds that it violates contemporary community standards, (2) the work taken as a whole appeals to a *prurient interest* in sex, (3) the work shows patently offensive sexual conduct, and (4) the work lacks serious redeeming literary, artistic, political, or scientific merit. The definition of prurient interest would be determined by "community standards," thus leaving the definition to local and state authorities.

The Court's ruling came at a time when popular attitudes toward obscenity were undergoing a revolution. A few years earlier, literary works regarded as masterpieces by critics could be banned from the U.S. mail, from import, and from sale. Such works included

Imminent Lawless Action Test
The current standard established by the Supreme Court for evaluating the legality of advocacy speech. Such speech can be forbidden only when it is "directed to inciting . . . imminent lawless actions."

20. 395 U.S. 444 (1969).
21. 413 U.S. 5 (1973).

iStockphoto.com/Tom Nulens

Lady Chatterley's Lover by D. H. Lawrence and *Ulysses* by James Joyce. By the 1980s, however, it was possible in almost every corner of the country to buy or rent pornographic videotapes that left nothing to the imagination.

Internet Pornography. The rise of the Internet in the 1990s sealed the fate of obscenity as a useful legal category. Conventional pornography on the Internet was essentially impossible to police. Congress attempted to spare children from exposure to Internet pornography by laws passed in 1996 and 1998, but the Court found this legislation to be unconstitutional.[22] In 2000, Congress was more successful with the Children's Internet Protection Act, which penalizes public schools and libraries if they do not install filtering software to prevent children from viewing websites with "adult" content. This law was upheld.[23] Young people today, however, are not dependent on libraries for Internet access. Free Wi-Fi, for use by laptops, tablets, and smartphones, is available almost everywhere.

Remaining Restrictions. Pornography can still be limited by the private sector—for example, most mainstream movie theaters will not show a film that has received a "no [child] 17 and under admitted" (NC-17) rating from the Motion Picture Association of America. The government also retains the right to place restrictions on media that it controls, such as the broadcast spectrum. Therefore, restrictions on broadcast radio and television remain.

Pornography That Exploits Minors. The government has also successfully outlawed materials that show sexual performance by minors. In 1990, the Court ruled that states can criminalize the possession of child pornography. The Court reasoned that the ban on private possession is justified because owning the material constitutes a form of child abuse.[24] This legal reasoning, however, reveals just how barren the concept of obscenity had become. Child abuse was the crime—not obscenity. As a result, the law makes no attempt to ban depictions of sexual performance by children in literary works such as Vladimir Nabokov's *Lolita* or in obvious cartoons such as Japanese *hentai*. Novels and cartoons do not involve the exploitation of actual, identifiable children.

Unprotected Speech: Slander

Can you say anything you want about someone else? Not really. Individuals are protected from **defamation of character,** which is defined as wrongfully hurting a person's good reputation. The law imposes a general duty on all persons to refrain from making false, defamatory statements about others. Breaching this duty orally is the wrongdoing called **slander.** Breaching it in writing is the wrongdoing called *libel*, which we discuss later. The government itself does not bring charges of slander or libel. Rather, the defamed person may bring a civil suit (as opposed to a criminal action) for damages.

Legally, slander is the public uttering of a false statement that harms the good reputation of another. *Public uttering* means that the defamatory statement is made to, or within the

Defamation of Character
Wrongfully hurting a person's good reputation.

Slander
The public uttering of a false statement that harms the good reputation of another. The statement must be made to, or within the hearing of, someone other than the defamed party.

22. *Reno v. American Civil Liberties Union*, 521 U.S. 844 (1997); *American Civil Liberties Union v. Ashcroft*, 542 U.S. 646 (2004).
23. *United States v. American Library Association*, 539 U.S. 194 (2003).
24. *Osborne v. Ohio*, 495 U.S. 103 (1990).

hearing of, a person other than the defamed party. If one person calls another dishonest, manipulative, and incompetent to his or her face when no one else is around, that does not constitute slander. If, however, a third party accidentally overhears defamatory statements, the courts have generally held that this constitutes a public uttering and may therefore be slander.

Student Speech

In recent years, high school and university students at public institutions have faced a variety of free speech challenges. Court rulings on these issues have varied by the level of school involved. Elementary schools, in particular, have great latitude in determining what kinds of speech are appropriate for their students. High school students have more free speech rights than do elementary students, and college students have the most speech rights of all.

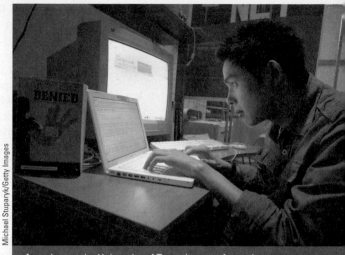

A student at the University of Texas is part of a project to track Internet censorship around the world. He and other concerned students then help people in various countries to bypass the censors. *Can the Internet be a force for freedom? Why or why not?*

Rights of Public School Students. High schools can impose restrictions on speech that would not be allowed in a college setting or in the general society. For example, high school officials may censor publications such as newspapers and yearbooks produced by the school's students. Courts have argued that a school newspaper is an extension of the school's educational mission and thus subject to control by the school administration.

One of the most striking rulings to illustrate the power of school officials was handed down by the United States Supreme Court in 2007. An Alaska high school student had displayed a banner reading "Bong Hits 4 Jesus" on private property across from the school as students on the school grounds watched the Winter Olympics torch relay. The school principal crossed the street, seized the banner, and suspended the student from school. The Supreme Court later held that the school had an "important— indeed, perhaps compelling— interest" in combating drug use, which allowed it to suppress the banner.[25] The Court's decision was widely criticized.

Campus Speech and Behavior Codes. Another free speech issue is the legitimacy of campus speech and behavior codes at some state universities. These codes prohibit so-called hate speech—abusive speech attacking persons on the basis of their ethnicity, race, or other criteria. For example, a University of Michigan code banned "any behavior, verbal or physical, that stigmatizes or victimizes an individual on the basis of race, ethnicity, religion, sex, sexual orientation, creed, national origin, ancestry, age, marital status, handicap," or Vietnam-veteran status. A federal court found that the code violated students' First Amendment rights.[26] Although the courts generally have held that campus speech codes are unconstitutional restrictions on the right to free speech, such codes continue to exist.

---

25. *Morse v. Frederick*, 551 U.S. 393 (2007).
26. *Doe v. University of Michigan*, 721 F.Supp. 852 (1989).

Soccer star David Beckham did not succeed in his libel suit against *In Touch* magazine. *Why would Beckham's celebrity status make it harder for him to win such a case?*

Photo Works/Shutterstock

"Political Correctness" on Campus. Free speech on campus becomes a somewhat more complicated issue when students, as opposed to the school administration, undertake controversial actions. At the University of Missouri, following a series of racially charged incidents, protesting students tried to prevent campus reporters from covering their activities. While journalists everywhere sided with the reporters, there are circumstances when citizens have a right to demand that reporters leave them alone. Students have also been accused of *political correctness* when they condemn language that may be insensitive or even racist. Of course, criticizing other people's speech is also a way to exercise one's own freedom of speech. In 2016, Donald Trump made opposition to political correctness a major theme of his presidential campaign.

Freedom of the Press

Freedom of the press can be regarded as a special instance of freedom of speech. Of course, at the time of the framing of the Constitution, *the press* meant only newspapers, pamphlets, magazines, and books. As technology has modified the ways in which we disseminate information, the laws touching on freedom of the press have been modified. What can and cannot be printed still occupies an important place in constitutional law, however.

Defamation in Writing. **Libel** is defamation in writing or in pictures, signs, films, or any other communication. As with slander, libel occurs only if the defamatory statements are observed by a third party. If Jane Smith sends a private communication to John Jones wrongfully accusing him of embezzling funds, that does not constitute libel.

The case of *New York Times Co. v. Sullivan* (1964) explored an important question regarding libelous statements made about public officials.[27] The Supreme Court held that only when a statement against a public official is made with **actual malice**—that is, with either knowledge of its falsity or a reckless disregard for the truth—can damages be obtained.

The standard set by the Court in the *New York Times* case has since been applied to **public figures** generally. Public figures include not only public officials but also any persons, such as movie stars, who are generally in the public limelight. Statements made about public figures usually are related to matters of general public interest. They are made about people who substantially affect all of us. Furthermore, public figures generally have some access to a public medium for answering disparaging falsehoods about themselves, whereas private individuals do not. For these reasons, public figures have a greater burden of proof in defamation cases than do private individuals.

The Internet has vastly expanded the number of published statements by the general citizenry, including anonymous comments. Today, as a result, libelous statements can be hard even to track down, much less prosecute.

Libel
A written defamation of a person's character or reputation. The defamatory statement must be observed by a third party.

Actual Malice
Either knowledge of a defamatory statement's falsity or a reckless disregard for the truth.

Public Figure
A public official, movie star, or other person known to the public because of his or her positions or activities.

27. 376 U.S. 254 (1964).

Films, Radio, and TV. As we have noted, in only a few cases has the Supreme Court upheld prior restraint of published materials. The Court's reluctance to accept prior restraint is less evident with respect to motion pictures. In the first half of the twentieth century, films were routinely submitted to local censorship boards. Only in 1952 did the Court find that motion pictures were covered by the First Amendment.[28] In contrast, the Court extended full protection to the Internet almost immediately by striking down provisions of the 1996 Telecommunications Act.[29] Cable TV received broad protection in 2000.[30]

While the Court has held that the First Amendment is relevant to broadcast radio and television, it has never extended full protection to these media. The Court has used a number of arguments to justify this stand—initially, the scarcity of broadcast frequencies. The Court later held that the government could restrict "indecent" programming based on the "pervasive" presence of broadcasting in the home.[31] On this basis, the Federal Communications Commission (FCC) has the authority to fine broadcasters for indecency or profanity.

The Right to Privacy

>>> **LO4:** Provide the constitutional basis of the right to privacy, and explain how the principle has been applied to the abortion and right-to-die controversies.

No explicit reference is made anywhere in the Constitution to a person's right to privacy. For many years, the courts did not take a very positive approach toward this right. In 1965, however, in *Griswold v. Connecticut*, the Supreme Court overthrew a Connecticut law that effectively prohibited the use of contraceptives, holding that the law violated the right to privacy.[32] Justice William O. Douglas formulated a unique way of reading this right into the Bill of Rights. He claimed that the First, Third, Fourth, Fifth, and Ninth Amendments created "penumbras formed by emanations [shadows, formed by the light], from those guarantees that help give them life and substance," and he went on to describe zones of privacy that are guaranteed by these rights.

When we read the Ninth Amendment, we can see the foundation for his reasoning: "The enumeration in the Constitution, of certain rights, shall not be construed to deny or disparage others retained by the people." In other words, the fact that the Constitution, including its amendments, does not specifically talk about the right to privacy does not mean that this right is denied to the people.

Privacy Rights and Abortion

Historically, abortion was not a criminal offense before the "quickening" of the fetus (the first movement of the fetus in the uterus, usually between the sixteenth and eighteenth weeks of pregnancy). During the last half of the nineteenth century, however, state laws became more severe. By 1973, performing an abortion at any time during pregnancy was a criminal offense in a majority of the states.

---

28. *Joseph Burstyn, Inc. v. Wilson*, 343 U.S. 495 (1952).
29. *Reno v. American Civil Liberties Union*, 521 U.S. 844 (1997).
30. *United States v. Playboy Entertainment Group*, 529 U.S. 803 (2000).
31. *FCC v. Pacifica Foundation*, 438 U.S. 726 (1978). In this case, the Court banned seven swear words (famously used by the late comedian George Carlin) during hours when children could hear them.
32. 381 U.S. 479 (1965).

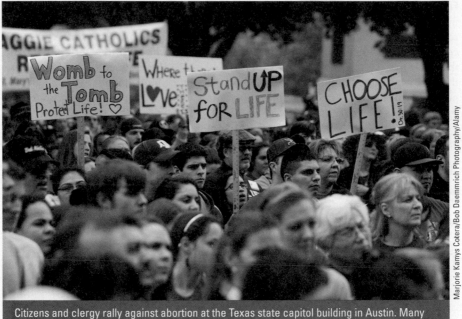

Citizens and clergy rally against abortion at the Texas state capitol building in Austin. Many devout Catholics oppose both abortion and the death penalty. *What arguments might others offer to distinguish between these two important issues?*

Roe v. Wade. In *Roe v. Wade* (1973), the Supreme Court accepted the argument that the laws against abortion violated "Jane Roe's" right to privacy under the Constitution.[33] The Court held that during the first trimester (three months) of pregnancy, abortion was an issue solely between a woman and her physician. The state could not limit abortions except to require that they be performed by licensed physicians. During the second trimester, to protect the health of the mother, the state was allowed to specify the conditions under which an abortion could be performed. During the final trimester, the state could regulate or even outlaw abortions except when they were necessary to preserve the life or health of the mother.

After the *Roe* case, the Supreme Court issued decisions in a number of cases defining and redefining the boundaries of state regulation of abortion. During the 1980s, the Court twice struck down laws that required a woman who wished to have an abortion to undergo counseling designed to discourage abortions. In the late 1980s and early 1990s, however, the Court took a more conservative approach. For example, in 1989 the Court upheld a Missouri statute that, among other things, banned the use of public hospitals or other taxpayer-supported facilities for performing abortions.[34] In 1992, the Court upheld a Pennsylvania law that required preabortion counseling, a waiting period of twenty-four hours, and for girls under the age of eighteen, parental or judicial permission.[35] As a result, abortions are more difficult to obtain in some states than in others.

33. 410 U.S. 113 (1973). Jane Roe was not the real name of the woman in this case. It is a common legal pseudonym used to protect a person's privacy.
34. *Webster v. Reproductive Health Services*, 492 U.S. 490 (1989).
35. *Planned Parenthood v. Casey*, 505 U.S. 833 (1992).

It is worth noting that while the Court has placed limits on what the national and state governments can do to restrict the availability of abortions, governments retain the right to discourage the procedure. Governments as well as individuals enjoy freedom of speech and have the right to condemn abortion. A state can issue "right-to-life" license plates without offering ones that support "freedom of choice." No level of government is required to fund abortions, and such government funding is in fact banned by the federal government and a majority of the states.

"Partial-Birth" Abortion. In 2000, the Supreme Court again addressed the abortion issue directly when it reviewed a Nebraska law banning "partial-birth" abortions. A partial-birth abortion, which physicians call intact dilation and extraction, is a procedure that can be used during the second trimester of pregnancy. Abortion rights advocates claim that in limited circumstances the procedure is the safest way to perform an abortion and that the government should never outlaw specific medical procedures. Opponents argue that the procedure has no medical merit and that it ends the life of a fetus that might be able to live outside the womb. The Supreme Court invalidated the Nebraska law on the ground that the law could be used to ban other abortion procedures and contained no provisions for protecting the health of the pregnant woman.[36]

In 2003, legislation similar to the Nebraska statute was passed by the U.S. Congress and signed into law by President George W. Bush. In 2007, the Supreme Court, with several changes in membership since the 2000 ruling, upheld the federal law in a five-to-four vote, effectively reversing its position on partial-birth abortions.[37]

The Controversy Continues. Abortion continues to be a divisive issue. Groups opposed to abortion continue to push for laws restricting abortion, to endorse political candidates who support their views, and to organize protests. Because of several episodes of violence during protests at abortion clinics, in 1994 Congress passed the Freedom of Access to Clinic Entrances Act. The act prohibits protesters from blocking entrances to such clinics. The Supreme Court has upheld laws requiring "buffer zones" around abortion clinics. In 2014, however, the Court ruled that a thirty-five-foot buffer zone established by Massachusetts was excessive.[38]

In recent years, abortion opponents have concentrated—often unsuccessfully—on state ballot proposals that could lay the groundwork for an eventual challenge to *Roe*. In one 2011 example, in Mississippi voters rejected a measure that would have outlawed all abortions and some forms of birth control. Abortion opponents have been more successful in winning new restrictions on abortion clinics. New state laws became especially common after the 2010 elections, when Republicans took over many state legislative chambers.

Subsequently, new laws restricting abortion in several states were struck down by federal district courts. In 2013, a new law in Texas required that physicians performing abortions have admitting privileges with a local hospital. (Hospitals are under no obligation to provide such privileges.) Further, abortion clinics had to follow extremely strict rules on their facilities, which in many cases would have required them to construct new (and expensive) buildings. The Texas law would have cut the number of abortion clinics in the state from an earlier forty-one to about ten. In June 2016, the Supreme Court

---

36. *Stenberg v. Carhart*, 530 U.S. 914 (2000).
37. *Gonzales v. Carhart*, 550 U.S. 124 (2007).
38. *McCullen v. Coakley*, 573 U.S ___ (2014).

struck down both the admitting privileges and the facilities provisions of the law.[39] This ruling effectively overturned laws in several other states, including Alabama, Mississippi, and Wisconsin.

Privacy Rights and the "Right to Die"

A 1976 case involving Karen Ann Quinlan was one of the first publicized right-to-die cases. The parents of Quinlan, a young woman who had been in a coma for nearly a year and who had been kept alive during that time by a respirator, wanted her respirator removed. The ruling of the New Jersey Supreme Court, *In re Quinlan*, stated that the right to privacy includes the right of a patient to refuse treatment and that patients unable to speak can exercise that right through a family member or guardian.[40] In 1990, the Supreme Court took up the issue. In *Cruzan v. Director, Missouri Department of Health*, the Court stated that a patient's life-sustaining treatment can be withdrawn at the request of a family member only if there is "clear and convincing evidence" that the patient did not want such treatment.[41]

What If There Is No Living Will? Since the 1976 *Quinlan* decision, most states have enacted laws permitting people to designate their wishes concerning life-sustaining procedures in "living wills" or durable health-care powers of attorney. These laws and the Supreme Court's *Cruzan* decision have resolved the right-to-die controversy for cases in which a living will has been drafted. Disputes are still possible if there is no living will.

An example is the case of Terri Schiavo. After the Florida woman had been in a persistent vegetative state for over a decade, her husband sought to have her feeding tube removed on the basis of oral statements that she would not want her life prolonged in such circumstances. Schiavo's parents fought this move in court but lost on the ground that a spouse, not a parent, is the appropriate legal guardian for a married person. Although the Florida legislature passed a law allowing then-governor Jeb Bush to overrule the courts, the state supreme court held that the law violated the state constitution.[42] The federal courts agreed with the Florida state courts, and Schiavo died shortly thereafter.

Physician-Assisted Suicide. In the 1990s, another issue surfaced: Do privacy rights include the right of terminally ill people to end their lives through physician-assisted suicide? Until 1996, the courts consistently upheld state laws that prohibited this practice. In 1996, after two federal appellate courts ruled that state laws banning assisted suicide were unconstitutional, the issue reached the Supreme Court. In 1997, the Court stated that the liberty interest protected by the Constitution does not include a right to commit suicide, with or without assistance.[43] The Court left the decision on whether to permit the practice in the hands of the states. Since then, assisted suicide has been allowed in California, Colorado, Montana, Oregon, Vermont, and Washington. In 2006, the Supreme Court upheld Oregon's physician-assisted suicide law against a challenge from the George W. Bush administration.[44]

---

39. *Whole Woman's Health v. Hellerstedt*, 136 S.Ct. 1001 (2016).
40. 70 N.J. 10 (1976).
41. 497 U.S. 261 (1990).
42. *Bush v. Schiavo*, 885 So.2d 321 (Fla. 2004).
43. *Washington v. Glucksberg*, 521 U.S. 702 (1997).
44. *Gonzales v. Oregon*, 546 U.S. 243 (2006).

The Great Balancing Act: The Rights of the Accused versus the Rights of Society

>>> **LO5:** Identify the constitutional rights of those who are accused of a crime, describe the *Miranda* and exclusionary rules, and cite examples of how recent security concerns have affected our civil liberties.

The United States has one of the highest murder rates in the industrialized world. It is also true that the murder rate—like the rates of other major crimes—has fallen substantially over the last two decades, as shown in Figure 4–1. Most Americans, however, are unaware of this fact. It is not surprising, therefore, that many citizens have extremely strong opinions about the rights of those accused of violent crimes.

Sometimes an accused person, even one who has confessed to some criminal act, is set free because of an apparent legal "technicality." In such cases, many people believe that the rights of the accused are being given more weight than the rights of potential or actual victims. Why, then, give criminal suspects rights? The answer is partly to avoid convicting innocent people, but mostly because due process of law and fair treatment benefit everyone who comes into contact with law enforcement or the courts.

The courts and the police must constantly engage in a balancing act of competing rights. The basis of all discussions about the appropriate balance is, of course, the U.S. Bill of Rights. The Fourth, Fifth, Sixth, and Eighth Amendments deal specifically with the rights of criminal defendants. Some people believe that despite the Constitution, minority group members often do not receive fair treatment from law enforcement. We discuss that question in this chapter's *At Issue* feature.

FIGURE 4–1   **Homicide Rates**

Despite an uptick in 2015, homicide rates have declined to levels last seen in the 1960s. (The 2001 rate does not include deaths attributed to the 9/11 terrorist attacks.) *Why might homicide rates have risen so high up through 1935? (Hint: check out the Eighteenth and Twenty-first Amendments to the Constitution.)*

Sources: U.S. Department of Justice; and National Center for Health Statistics, Vital Statistics.

AT ISSUE

Do Police Use Excessive Force against Black Men?

In recent years, police behavior toward minority group members—in particular, black men—has become a major political issue. Unarmed black men have died as a result of interactions with police officers in Baltimore, Chicago, Cleveland, and many other places. A loose alliance of activists opposed to the alleged excessive use of force has grown up under the label "Black Lives Matter." Are the activists responding to a real problem—or is the excessive use of force by police largely a myth?

Police Behavior Is Almost Always Appropriate

The first point when considering law enforcement behavior is that the United States is a relatively violent country. Americans have a constitutional right to bear arms for personal protection, and millions do just that. U.S. police know there is a good chance that anyone they stop or arrest may have a firearm—and may be prepared to use it. That is a problem that police in Europe or Japan simply don't face.

Supporters of the police contend that they use appropriate force given what they are up against. The greater use of force against African Americans simply reflects the disproportionate participation of that group in violent crime. Such participation may be caused by the disastrous conditions in which so many young black men grow up, but that does not change the culpability of participants. African Americans commit murder at almost eight times the rate of other races.

In *National Review*, David French states that the numbers back up the police. We have data from only a limited number of departments, but in 2015 police on those forces fatally shot 965 individuals. Of these, 564 were armed with a gun and 289 had another weapon. Only 90 were unarmed. In 75 percent of the shootings, the "police were under attack or defending someone

who was." Rogue officers exist, but for the most part the police are just doing their jobs.

Too Many Officers Are Quick on the Trigger

Writing in *Current Affairs*, Nathan Robinson finds French's statistical reasoning ludicrous. In effect, French argues that we have no problem if police shootings are justified, say, 96 percent of the time. But if the other 4 percent were murder, the fact that 96 percent "were *not* murder wouldn't make the slightest bit of difference." True, African Americans are disproportionately involved in violent crime. But black teens are over twenty times more likely to be killed by police than are white teens. It is not acceptable to kill black people simply because they may have committed a crime. Also, possession of a weapon is not in itself a crime. The Second Amendment applies to all citizens, regardless of race.

Further, police killings are only the tip of the iceberg. Three out of five black people report that they personally have been mistreated by police. This often takes place during investigatory stops—stops made without evidence of a crime. African Americans refer to these stops as the "crime of driving while black." Whites almost never experience these stops. According to Robinson, those who condemn Black Lives Matter seem to believe that "African Americans are delusional about their own first-person memories." Police personnel are rarely prosecuted and almost never convicted for excessive use of force. We need to change this system.

FOR CRITICAL ANALYSIS

If police behavior is sometimes abusive, how would that affect the willingness of African Americans to come forward with information about crimes they have witnessed?

Rights of the Accused

The basic rights of criminal defendants are outlined below. When appropriate, the specific constitutional provision or amendment on which a right is based is also given.

Limits on the Conduct of Police Officers and Prosecutors

- No unreasonable or unwarranted searches and seizures (Amendment IV).
- No arrest except on probable cause (Amendment IV).
- No coerced confessions or illegal interrogation (Amendment V).
- No entrapment.
- On questioning, following an arrest, a suspect must be informed of her or his rights.

Defendant's Pretrial Rights

- Writ of *habeas corpus* (Article I, Section 9).
- Prompt **arraignment** (Amendment VI).
- Legal counsel (Amendment VI).
- Reasonable bail (Amendment VIII).
- To be informed of charges (Amendment VI).
- To remain silent (Amendment V).

Trial Rights

- Speedy and public trial before a jury (Amendment VI).
- Impartial jury selected from a cross section of the community (Amendment VI).
- Trial atmosphere free of prejudice, fear, and outside interference.
- No compulsory self-incrimination (Amendment V).
- Adequate counsel (Amendment VI).
- No cruel and unusual punishment (Amendment VIII).
- Appeal of convictions.
- No double jeopardy (Amendment V).

Extending the Rights of the Accused

During the 1960s, the Supreme Court, under Chief Justice Earl Warren, significantly expanded the rights of accused persons. In a case decided in 1963, *Gideon v. Wainwright*,[45] the Court held that if a person is accused of a felony and cannot afford an attorney, an attorney must be made available to the accused person at the government's expense. Although the Sixth Amendment to the Constitution provides for the right to counsel, the Supreme Court had previously held that only criminal defendants in death-penalty cases automatically had a right to free legal counsel.

Miranda v. Arizona. In 1966, the Court issued its decision in *Miranda v. Arizona*.[46] The case involved Ernesto Miranda, who was charged with the kidnapping and rape of a young woman. After questioning, Miranda confessed and was later convicted. Miranda's lawyer appealed his conviction, arguing that the police had never informed Miranda that he had a right to remain silent and a right to be represented by counsel. The Court, in ruling in Miranda's favor, enunciated the now-familiar *Miranda* rights. Today, *Miranda* rights statements typically take the following form:

> You have the right to remain silent. Anything you say can and will be used against you in a court of law. You have the right to speak to an attorney. If you cannot afford an attorney, one will be appointed for you. Do you understand these rights as they have been read to you?

Exceptions to the *Miranda* Rule. As part of a continuing attempt to balance the rights of accused persons against the rights of society, the Supreme Court has made a number of exceptions to the *Miranda* rule. As one example, in an important 1991 decision, the Court stated that a suspect's conviction will not be automatically overturned if the suspect was coerced into making a confession. If the other evidence admitted at trial is strong enough to justify the conviction without the confession, then the fact that the confession was obtained illegally can be effectively ignored.[47]

Arraignment
The first act in a criminal proceeding, in which the defendant is brought before a court to hear the charges against him or her and enter a plea of guilty or not guilty.

---

45. 372 U.S. 335 (1963).
46. 384 U.S. 436 (1966).
47. *Arizona v. Fulminante*, 499 U.S. 279 (1991).

The Exclusionary Rule

At least since 1914, judicial policy has prohibited the admission of illegally seized evidence at trials in federal courts. This is the so-called **exclusionary rule.** Improperly obtained evidence, no matter how telling, cannot be used by prosecutors. This includes evidence obtained by police in violation of a suspect's *Miranda* rights or of the Fourth Amendment. The Fourth Amendment protects against unreasonable searches and seizures and provides that a judge may issue a search warrant to a police officer only on probable cause (a demonstration of facts that permit a reasonable belief that a crime has been committed). The courts must determine what constitutes an "unreasonable" search and seizure.

The reasoning behind the exclusionary rule is that it forces police officers to gather evidence properly, in which case their due diligence will be rewarded by a conviction. Nevertheless, the exclusionary rule has always had critics who argue that it permits guilty persons to be freed because of innocent procedural errors by the police.

Adjustments to the Exclusionary Rule. This rule was first extended to state court proceedings in a 1961 United States Supreme Court decision, *Mapp v. Ohio.*[48] In this case, the Court overturned the conviction of Dollree Mapp for the possession of obscene materials. Police found pornographic books in her apartment after searching it without a search warrant and despite her refusal to let them in. Under the Fourth Amendment, search warrants must describe the persons or things to be seized. However, officers are entitled to seize items not mentioned in the search warrant if the materials are in "plain view" and reasonably appear to be contraband or evidence of a crime.[49]

Recent Court Rulings. During the past several decades, the Supreme Court has diminished the scope of the exclusionary rule by creating exceptions to its applicability. For example, the Court has created a "good faith" exception to the exclusionary rule. In 2009, the Court found that the good faith exception applies when an officer makes an arrest based on an outstanding warrant in another jurisdiction, even if the warrant in question was based on a clerical error.[50]

The Supreme Court has also attempted to update the exclusionary rule to make it compatible with the latest technology. In 2014, a unanimous Court found it unconstitutional for officers to search and seize the digital contents of a cell phone without a search warrant. According to the Court, smartphones now contain such vast quantities of private data that they are "worthy of the protection for which the Founders fought."[51] A topic that is sure to reach the Court in the future is the use of drones for surveillance by law enforcement. Under what circumstances does the use of drones violate our Fourth Amendment protections?

Civil Liberties versus Security Issues

As former Supreme Court justice Thurgood Marshall once said, "Grave threats to liberty often come in times of urgency, when constitutional rights seem too extravagant to endure." Not surprisingly, antiterrorist legislation since the attacks on September 11, 2001, has eroded certain basic rights, in particular the Fourth Amendment protections against unreasonable searches and seizures.

Exclusionary Rule
A judicial policy prohibiting the admission at trial of illegally seized evidence.

48. 367 U.S. 643 (1961).
49. *Texas v. Brown,* 460 U.S. 730 (1983); and *Horton v. California,* 496 U.S. 128 (1990).
50. *Herring v. United States,* 555 U.S. 135 (2009).
51. *Riley v. California,* 134 S.Ct. 999 (2014).

The USA Patriot Act. The most significant piece of anti-terrorism legislation, the USA Patriot Act, was passed in 2001 and renewed in 2006. Many in government believed that a lack of cooperation among government agencies was a major reason for the failure to anticipate the 9/11 attacks. One goal of the Patriot Act was to lift such barriers to cooperation. Under the Patriot Act, law enforcement officials can also secretly search a suspect's home and monitor a suspect's Internet activities, phone conversations, and financial records. The government can even open a suspect's mail. While many believe that the Patriot Act is a necessary safety measure to prevent future terrorist attacks, others argue that it endangers civil liberties.

"Roving" Wiretaps. One civil liberties issue involves "roving" wiretaps. Previously, only specific telephone numbers, cell phone numbers, or computers could be tapped. Now a person under suspicion can be monitored electronically regardless of location or the technology in use. Such roving wiretaps appear to be inconsistent with the Fourth Amendment, which requires a judicial warrant to describe the *place* to be searched, not just the person. As an unavoidable side effect, the government has access to the conversations and e-mail of many innocent people.

National Security Agency Surveillance. In 2001, President Bush authorized the National Security Agency (NSA) to conduct secret surveillance without court warrants, even warrants from special security courts. The NSA was to monitor phone calls and other communications between foreign parties and persons within the United States when one of the parties had suspected links to terrorist organizations. When news of the program came out in 2005, it was criticized by civil liberties groups. In 2007 and 2008, however, Congress passed laws to authorize the NSA wiretaps.

Sergey Kohl/Shutterstock

A demonstrator holds a picture of Edward Snowden, the former NSA contractor who released vast amounts of information about the agency's surveillance activities. ***Should Snowden be tried or pardoned? In either case, why?***

Subsequent Revelations of NSA Activity

In June 2013, leaks provided by Edward Snowden, a federal contractor, revealed that NSA surveillance was far more extensive than previously assumed. Among the most striking revelations was that the NSA gathers information on *every* domestic landline phone call made in the United States and other countries. The NSA does not record the contents of the calls, but rather *"metadata,"* which includes time of call, the number of the caller, and the number of the phone that was called.

Collecting Actual Data. Under a second program, PRISM, the NSA has collected information from the websites of corporations, including Apple, Google, Facebook, Microsoft, Skype, and others. A third revelation was of NSA espionage actions against

European countries. These included bugging the offices of the European Union in advance of trade talks between the United States and that organization. The NSA also bugged the cell phones of a wide variety of world leaders, including Brazil's then-president Dilma Rousseff and Germany's chancellor Angela Merkel.

Consequences of the Revelations. Snowden fled to Russia. Meanwhile, the reports resulted in an outcry by U.S. civil libertarians and by European leaders. The Obama administration defended the programs, however, noting—correctly—that they had been authorized by secret courts. In addition, former NSA director Michael Hayden bluntly stated that the Fourth Amendment, which prohibits unreasonable searches, "is not an international treaty." Foreigners, in other words, had no privacy rights that the U.S. government was bound to respect.

As you might imagine, citizens of foreign countries, especially in Europe, found such statements to be alarming. Several nations announced initiatives aimed at protecting the privacy of data belonging to their own citizens. Such steps could cut into the sales of American high-tech firms. Currently, through "cloud-computing" services, U.S. companies such as Google and Microsoft store vast amounts of data belonging to people and corporations not just in America, but around the world. In the future, individuals and firms in Germany, for example, might limit their use of cloud computing to servers located in Germany.

Interact

The debate over civil liberties versus national security is a heated one. National Public Radio and Intelligence Squared U.S. have sponsored a debate on this topic. Search for "Spy on Me, I'd Rather Be Safe." to find a broadcast version of the debate or to download a transcript in PDF format. When you are done with the debate, decide who you think won. You can compare your verdict with the opinions of audience members.

Apple and Microsoft versus Government Surveillance. The question of whether government surveillance threatened high-tech businesses led to several confrontations. In 2015, domestic Islamist terrorists killed fourteen people in an attack in San Bernardino, California. They then died in a shootout with police, leaving behind a locked iPhone that the FBI sought to crack. In 2016, it obtained a court order demanding that Apple create a special version of the iPhone operating system that would bypass security. Apple refused, arguing that such a step would undermine the privacy of all iPhone users. Later, however, the FBI found a way to crack the iPhone without Apple's help.

One tool used by the government in the years since 9/11 has been national security orders (NSOs), subpoenas issued by the FBI without judicial oversight. Individuals, financial institutions, and Internet service providers are banned from speaking about NSOs with anyone. A U.S. district court has found NSOs to be unconstitutional, but thousands are still issued every year. In 2016, Microsoft sued the government, claiming that NSO "gag orders" violated the First and Fourth Amendments. In both the Apple and Microsoft cases, a serious concern existed that government powers first exercised in the war against terror would quickly be employed in general law enforcement.

MAKING A DIFFERENCE

Your Civil Liberties: Searches and Seizures

Our civil liberties include numerous protections of persons who are suspected of criminal activity. Among these are limits on how the police can conduct searches and seizures.

Why Should You Care? You may be the most law-abiding person in the world, but that does not guarantee that you will never be stopped, arrested, or searched by the police. Sooner or later, most citizens have some kind of interaction with the police. People who do not understand their rights or how to behave toward law enforcement officers can find themselves in serious trouble.

What Are Your Rights? How should you behave if you are stopped by police officers? Your civil liberties protect you from having to provide information other than your name and address. Normally, even if you have not been placed under arrest, the officers have the right to frisk you for weapons, and you must let them proceed. The officers cannot, however, lawfully check your person or your clothing further if, in their judgment, no weaponlike object is produced.

The officers may search you only if they have a search warrant or probable cause to believe that a search will likely produce incriminating evidence. What if the officers do not have probable cause or a warrant? Physically resisting their attempt to search you can lead to disastrous, even fatal, results. You can simply refuse orally to give permission for the search, if possible in the presence of a witness. Being polite is much better than acting out of anger and making the officers irritable.

If you are in your car and are stopped by the police, the same fundamental rules apply. Always be ready to show your driver's license and car registration. You may be asked to get out of the car. The officers may use a flashlight to peer inside if it is too dark to see otherwise. None of this constitutes a search. A true search requires either a warrant or a probable cause. No officer has the legal right to search your car simply to find out if you may have committed a crime.

If you are in your home and a police officer with a search warrant appears, you can ask to examine the warrant before granting entry. A warrant that is correctly made out will state the place or persons to be searched, the object sought, and the date of the warrant (which should be no more than ten days old). It will also bear the signature of a judge. If you believe the warrant to be invalid, or if no warrant is produced, you should make it clear orally that you have not consented to the search, if possible in the presence of a witness.

Officers who attempt to enter your home without a search warrant can lawfully do so only if they are pursuing a suspected felon into the house. Rarely is it advisable to give permission for a warrantless search. You, as the resident, must be the one to give permission if any evidence obtained is to be considered legal. A landlord, manager, or head of a college dormitory cannot give legal permission. A roommate, however, can give permission for a search of his or her room, which may allow the police to search areas where you have belongings.

To find out more about your rights and obligations under the laws of searches and seizures, you can contact the American Civil Liberties Union. Find its website by searching for "aclu."

AP Images/Sharon Cekada/Post-Crescent

This man was arrested on suspicion of shooting his estranged wife and his mother-in-law. *Can the police legally search him without a search warrant?*

Key Terms

actual malice 78	defamation of	free exercise clause 72	prior restraint 73
arraignment 85	character 76	imminent lawless	public figure 78
bill of attainder 67	establishment clause 69	action test 75	slander 76
commercial	exclusionary rule 86	incorporation theory 68	symbolic speech 73
speech 74	*ex post facto* law 67	libel 78	writ of *habeas corpus* 67

Chapter Summary

≫LO1 Protections included in the original Constitution include the right to a writ of *habeas corpus*, plus bans on bills of attainder and *ex post facto* laws. Originally, the Bill of Rights limited only the power of the national government, not that of the states. Gradually, however, the Supreme Court accepted incorporation theory, under which no state can violate most provisions of the Bill of Rights.

≫LO2 The First Amendment protects against government interference with freedom of religion by requiring a separation of church and state (under the establishment clause) and by guaranteeing the free exercise of religion. Controversial issues that arise under the establishment clause include aid to church-related schools, school vouchers, school prayer, the teaching of evolution, and religious displays on public property. The government can interfere with the free exercise of religion only when religious practices work against public policy or the public welfare.

≫LO3 The First Amendment protects against government interference with freedom of speech, which includes symbolic speech (expressive conduct). The Supreme Court has been especially critical of government actions that impose prior restraint on expression. Commercial speech (advertising) by businesses has received limited First Amendment protection. Restrictions on expression are permitted when the expression may incite imminent lawless action. Other speech that has not received First Amendment protection includes expression judged to be slanderous.

The First Amendment protects against government interference with the freedom of the press, which can be regarded as a special instance of freedom of speech. Speech by the press that does not receive protection includes libelous statements.

≫LO4 Under the Ninth Amendment, people's rights are not limited to those specifically mentioned in the Constitution. Among the unspecified rights protected by the courts is a right to privacy, which has been inferred from the First, Third, Fourth, Fifth, and Ninth Amendments. Whether an individual's privacy rights include a right to an abortion or a "right to die" continues to provoke controversy.

≫LO5 The Constitution includes protections for the rights of persons accused of crimes. Under the Fourth Amendment, no one may be subject to an unreasonable search or seizure or be arrested except on probable cause. Under the Fifth Amendment, an accused person has the right to remain silent. Under the Sixth Amendment, an accused person must be informed of the reason for his or her arrest. The accused also has the right to adequate counsel, even if he or she cannot afford an attorney, and the right to a prompt arraignment and a speedy and public trial before an impartial jury selected from a cross section of the community.

In *Miranda v. Arizona* (1966), the Supreme Court held that those arrested, before questioning by law enforcement personnel, must be informed of the right to remain silent and the right to counsel. The exclusionary rule forbids the admission in court of illegally obtained evidence.

Another major challenge concerns the extent to which we must forfeit civil liberties to control terrorism. Recent revelations of surveillance by the National Security Agency have fueled this debate.

Test Yourself

1. Since 1925, the Supreme Court, under the Fourteenth Amendment's due process clause, has gradually extended the Bill of Rights to cover state governments by using:
   a. incorporation theory.
   b. the establishment clause.
   c. the supremacy principle.

2. Only in this century have state governments been required to observe the right:
   a. to a writ of *habeas corpus*.
   b. to privacy.
   c. to bear arms.

3. The Supreme Court has held that any law prohibiting the teaching of evolution:
   a. violates the establishment clause because it imposes religious beliefs on students.
   b. violates the free exercise clause of the First Amendment because it bars the beliefs of atheists.
   c. violates both the establishment clause and the free exercise clause.

4. Religious displays on public property are:
   a. always acceptable.
   b. never acceptable.
   c. acceptable as part of a broader display that contains nonreligious elements.

5. Endorsements of candidates by a minister, priest, or rabbi:
   a. are protected under the First Amendment.
   b. could threaten a congregation's tax-exempt status, but the law is not enforced.
   c. automatically result in a loss of tax-exempt status by the congregation.

6. Clothing, gestures, and other forms of expressive conduct may be considered to be:
   a. symbolic speech.
   b. subversive speech.
   c. unprotected by the First Amendment.

7. If you utter a false statement that harms the good reputation of another, it is called slander, and such expression is:
   a. always protected under the First Amendment.
   b. unprotected speech and a potential basis for a lawsuit.
   c. prosecuted as a felony in most states.

8. The right to privacy:
   a. is explicitly guaranteed by the original text of the Constitution.
   b. is explicitly guaranteed by the Fifth Amendment to the Constitution.
   c. has been inferred from other rights by the Supreme Court.

9. The Supreme Court found that the right to an abortion is constitutionally protected in:
   a. *In re Quinlan*.
   b. *Roe v. Wade*.
   c. *Planned Parenthood v. Casey*.

10. The Supreme Court has ruled that the practice of assisted suicide is:
    a. constitutional.
    b. unconstitutional.
    c. an issue for the states to decide.

11. Illegally seized evidence is not admissible at trial because of the:
    a. exclusionary rule.
    b. *Miranda* rule.
    c. writ of *habeas corpus*.

12. A former head of the National Security Agency (NSA) has said that:
    a. the United States does not tap the phones of allied leaders.
    b. NSA surveillance should be exempt from judicial oversight.
    c. the Fourth Amendment, which prohibits unreasonable searches, "is not an international treaty."

Essay Questions

1. The courts have never held that the provision of military chaplains by the armed forces is unconstitutional, despite the fact that chaplains are religious leaders who are employed by and under the authority of the U.S. government. What arguments might the courts use to defend the military chaplain system?

2. In a surprisingly large number of cases, arrested individuals do not choose to exercise their right to remain silent. Why might a person not exercise his or her *Miranda* rights?

Answers to multiple-choice questions: 1. a, 2. c, 3. a, 4. c, 5. b, 6. a, 7. b, 8. c, 9. b, 10. c, 11. a, 12. c.

5 | Civil Rights

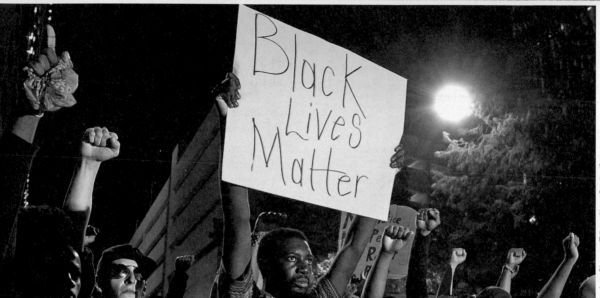

Protesters prepare to march through Charlotte, North Carolina, in 2016 following the death of a black man who was shot by police. *Why do many African Americans distrust their local police force?*

Charlotte Observer/Tribune News Service/Getty images

The five **Learning Outcomes (LOs)** below are designed to help improve your understanding of this chapter. After reading this chapter, you should be able to:

≫LO1 Summarize the historical experience of African Americans, state how the separate-but-equal doctrine was abolished, and describe the consequences of the civil rights movement.

≫LO2 Define the different levels of scrutiny used by the Supreme Court in civil rights cases, and describe recent rulings on affirmative action.

≫LO3 Discuss the history and current status of Latinos and American Indians.

≫LO4 Contrast the goals of the women's suffrage movement with the goals of modern feminism.

≫LO5 Summarize the recent revolution in the rights enjoyed by gay men and lesbians.

Check your understanding of the material with the Test Yourself section at the end of the chapter.

Civil Rights
Generally, all rights rooted in the Fourteenth Amendment's guarantee of equal protection under the law.

Equality is at the heart of the concept of civil rights. Generally, the term **civil rights** refers to the rights of all Americans to equal protection under the law, as provided by the Fourteenth Amendment to the Constitution. Although the terms *civil rights* and *civil liberties* are sometimes used interchangeably, scholars make a distinction between the two. Civil liberties are basically *limitations* on government. They specify what the government *cannot* do. Civil rights, in contrast, specify what the government *must* do to ensure equal protection and freedom from discrimination.

The history of civil rights in America is the story of the struggle of various groups to be free from discriminatory treatment. In this chapter, we look at several movements that had significant consequences for civil rights in America: the civil rights movement of the 1950s and 1960s, the women's movement, and the movement to gain equal rights for gay men and lesbians. Each of these movements resulted in legislation and court rulings that secured important basic rights for all Americans.

Note that most minorities in this nation have suffered—and some continue to suffer—from discrimination. These include such groups as Asian Americans, Muslim Americans, older Americans, and persons with disabilities. The fact that some groups are not singled out for special attention in the following pages should not be construed to mean that their struggle for equality is any less significant than the struggles of those groups that we do discuss.

One of the most obvious consequences of discrimination is high rates of poverty, as you can see in Figure 5–1.

The African American Experience and the Civil Rights Movement

>>>**LO1:** Summarize the historical experience of African Americans, state how the separate-but-equal doctrine was abolished, and describe the consequences of the civil rights movement.

Before 1863, the Constitution protected slavery and made equality impossible in the sense in which we use the word today. The system of slavery, however, did not survive the American Civil War (1861–1865).

Ending Servitude

With the emancipation of the slaves by President Lincoln's Emancipation Proclamation in 1863 and the passage of the Thirteenth, Fourteenth, and Fifteenth Amendments during the Reconstruction period (1865–1877) following the Civil War, constitutional inequality was ended.

Constitutional Amendments. The Thirteenth Amendment (1865) states that neither slavery nor involuntary servitude shall exist within the United States. The Fourteenth Amendment (1868) tells us that *all* persons born or naturalized in the United States are citizens of

FIGURE 5–1	Persons in Poverty in the United States by Race and Hispanic Origin

Why are children more likely to be poor?

Source: Bureau of the Census

Harriet Tubman was a leader of the "underground railroad" that smuggled slaves to freedom. During the Civil War, she served as a nurse, spy, and scout for the Union army. *Why has the Treasury Department decided to put her image on the twenty-dollar bill?*

Library of Congress Prints and Photographs Division Washington, D.C. [LC-USZ62-7816]

the United States. It states, furthermore, that "[n]o State shall make or enforce any law which shall abridge the privileges or immunities of citizens of the United States; nor shall any State deprive any person of life, liberty, or property, without due process of law; nor deny to any person within its jurisdiction the equal protection of the laws." Note the use of the terms *citizen* and *person* in this amendment. *Citizens* have political rights, such as the right to vote and run for political office. Citizens also have certain privileges or immunities. All *persons*, however, including noncitizen immigrants, have a right to due process of law and equal protection under the law.

Finally, the Fifteenth Amendment (1870) reads as follows: "The right of citizens of the United States to vote shall not be denied or abridged by the United States or by any State on account of race, color, or previous condition of servitude." The right to vote is also known as **suffrage,** or the franchise. Another term is *enfranchisement*, which means "granting the right to vote."

The Civil Rights Acts of 1865 to 1875. From 1865 to 1875, Congress passed a series of civil rights acts to enforce the Thirteenth, Fourteenth, and Fifteenth Amendments. The Civil Rights Act of 1866 implemented the extension of citizenship to anyone born in the United States and gave African Americans full equality under the law. The Enforcement Act of 1870 set out specific criminal penalties for interfering with the right to vote as protected by the Fifteenth Amendment and by the Civil Rights Act of 1866.

Equally important was the Civil Rights Act of 1872, known as the Anti–Ku Klux Klan Act. This act made it a federal crime for anyone to use law or custom to deprive an individual of rights, privileges, and immunities secured by the Constitution or by any federal law. The Second Civil Rights Act, passed in 1875, declared that everyone is entitled to full and equal enjoyment of public accommodations, theaters, and other places of public amusement, and it imposed penalties on violators.

The Ineffectiveness of the Early Civil Rights Laws

The civil rights acts ultimately did little to secure equality for African Americans. Both the *Civil Rights Cases* and the case of *Plessy v. Ferguson* (discussed next) effectively nullified these acts. Additionally, various barriers were erected that prevented African Americans from exercising their right to vote.

The *Civil Rights Cases*. The United States Supreme Court invalidated the 1875 Second Civil Rights Act when it held, in the *Civil Rights Cases* of 1883, that the enforcement clause of the Fourteenth Amendment (which states that "[n]o State shall make or enforce any law which shall abridge the privileges or immunities of citizens") was limited to correcting *official* actions taken by states. Thus, the discriminatory acts of private citizens were not illegal. ("Individual invasion of individual rights is not the subject matter of the Amendment.")[1]

The 1883 Supreme Court decision met with widespread approval by whites throughout most of the United States. Twenty years after the Civil War, the white majority was all too

Suffrage
The right to vote.

1. 109 U.S. 3 (1883).

willing to forget about the Civil War amendments to the U.S. Constitution and the civil rights legislation of the 1860s and 1870s. The other civil rights laws that the Court did not specifically invalidate became dead letters in the statute books, although they were never officially repealed by Congress.

Plessy v. Ferguson: **Separate but Equal.** A key decision during this period concerned Homer Plessy, who was one-eighth African American. In 1892, he boarded a train in New Orleans. The conductor made him leave the car, which was restricted to whites, and directed him to a car for nonwhites. At that time, Louisiana had a statute providing for separate railway cars for whites and African Americans.

Plessy went to court, claiming that such a statute was contrary to the Fourteenth Amendment's equal protection clause. In 1896, the United States Supreme Court rejected Plessy's contention in *Plessy v. Ferguson*.[2] The Court concluded that the Fourteenth Amendment "could not have been intended to abolish distinctions based upon color, or to enforce social . . . equality." The Court stated that segregation alone did not violate the Constitution: "Laws permitting, and even requiring, their separation in places where they are liable to be brought into contact do not necessarily imply the inferiority of either race to the other." So was born the **separate-but-equal doctrine.**

Plessy v. Ferguson became the judicial cornerstone of racial discrimination throughout the United States. The result was a system of racial segregation, particularly in the South, supported by state and local "Jim Crow" laws. (*Jim Crow* was an insulting term for African Americans derived from a song-and-dance show.) These laws required separate drinking fountains; separate seats in theaters, restaurants, and hotels; separate public toilets; and separate waiting rooms for the two races. "Separate" was indeed the rule, but "equal" was never enforced, nor was it a reality.

Voting Barriers. The brief voting enfranchisement of African Americans ended after 1877, when the federal troops that occupied the South during the Reconstruction era were withdrawn. White supremacist politicians regained control of state governments and, using everything except race as a formal criterion, passed laws that effectively deprived African Americans of the right to vote. By using the ruse that political parties were private entities, the Democratic Party managed to keep black voters from its primaries. The **white primary** was upheld by the Supreme Court until 1944, when the Court ruled it a violation of the Fifteenth Amendment.[3]

Another barrier to African American voting was the **grandfather clause,** which restricted voting to those who could prove that their ancestors had voted before 1867. **Poll taxes** required the payment of a fee to vote. Thus, poor African Americans—as well as poor whites—who could not afford to pay the tax were excluded from voting. Not until the Twenty-fourth Amendment to the Constitution was ratified in 1964 was the poll tax eliminated as a precondition to voting. **Literacy tests** were also used to deny the vote to African Americans. Such tests asked potential voters to read, recite, or interpret complicated texts, such as a section of the state constitution, to the satisfaction of local registrars—who were, of course, almost never satisfied with the responses of African Americans.

Extralegal Methods of Enforcing White Supremacy. The second-class status of African Americans was also a matter of social custom, especially in the South. In their interactions with southern whites, African Americans were expected to observe an informal but detailed code of behavior that confirmed their inferiority. The code was backed up by the common practice of

Separate-but-Equal Doctrine
The doctrine holding that separate-but-equal facilities do not violate the equal protection clause of the Fourteenth Amendment to the U.S. Constitution.

White Primary
A state primary election that restricted voting to whites only. Outlawed by the Supreme Court in 1944.

Grandfather Clause
A device used by southern states to disenfranchise African Americans. It restricted voting to those whose ancestors had voted before 1867.

Poll Tax
A special tax that had to be paid as a qualification for voting. The Twenty-fourth Amendment to the Constitution outlawed the poll tax in national elections, and in 1966, the Supreme Court declared it unconstitutional in state elections as well.

Literacy Test
A test administered as a precondition for voting, often used to prevent African Americans from exercising their right to vote.

2. 163 U.S. 537 (1896).
3. *Smith v. Allwright,* 321 U.S. 649 (1944).

Sisters Linda and Terry Lynn Brown sit on a fence outside of their racially segregated elementary school in Topeka, Kansas, in 1953. At that time, the Supreme Court had yet to decide *Brown v. Board of Education,* the landmark civil rights case that banned segregation in public schools. *What were the immediate results of this decision?*

Carl Iwasaki/Getty Images

lynching—mob action to murder an accused individual, usually by hanging and sometimes accompanied by torture. Of course, lynching was illegal, but southern authorities rarely prosecuted these cases, and white juries would not convict.

The End of the Separate-but-Equal Doctrine

As early as the 1930s, several court rulings began to chip away at the separate-but-equal doctrine. The United States Supreme Court did not explicitly overturn *Plessy v. Ferguson* until 1954, however, when it issued one of the most famous judicial decisions in U.S. history.

In 1951, Oliver Brown decided that his eight-year-old daughter, Linda Carol Brown, should not have to go to an all-nonwhite elementary school twenty-one blocks from her home, when there was a white school only seven blocks away. The National Association for the Advancement of Colored People (NAACP), formed in 1909, decided to support Oliver Brown.[4] The outcome would have a monumental impact on American society.

Brown v. Board of Education of Topeka. The 1954 unanimous decision of the Supreme Court in *Brown v. Board of Education of Topeka*[5] established that the segregation of races in the public schools violates the equal protection clause of the Fourteenth Amendment. Chief Justice Earl Warren said that separation implied inferiority, whereas the majority opinion in *Plessy v. Ferguson* had said the opposite.

The following year, in *Brown v. Board of Education* (sometimes called the second *Brown* decision), the Court declared that the lower courts needed to ensure that African Americans would be admitted to schools on a nondiscriminatory basis "with all deliberate speed."[6]

Reactions to School Integration. The white South did not let the Supreme Court ruling go unchallenged. Governor Orval Faubus of Arkansas used the state's National Guard to block the integration of Central High School in Little Rock in September 1957. President Dwight Eisenhower had to federalize the Arkansas National Guard and send in the Army's 101st Airborne Division to quell violent resistance. Central High became integrated.

Universities in the South remained segregated. When James Meredith, an African American student, attempted to enroll at the University of Mississippi in 1962, violence flared as it had in Little Rock. The riot by whites opposed to integration was so intense that President John Kennedy was forced to send in thirty thousand U.S. combat troops. Ultimately, peace was restored, and Meredith began attending classes.

De Jure and *De Facto* Segregation

The kind of segregation faced by Linda Carol Brown and James Meredith is called *de jure* **segregation,** because it is the result of discriminatory laws or government actions. (*De jure* is Latin for "by law.") A second kind of public school segregation was common in many northern

De Jure Segregation
Racial segregation that occurs because of laws or administrative decisions by public agencies.

4. *NAACP* is pronounced "N-double A-C-P."
5. 347 U.S. 483 (1954).
6. 349 U.S. 294 (1955).

communities—***de facto* segregation.** This term refers to segregation that is not due to an explicit law but results from other causes, such as residential patterns. Neighborhoods inhabited almost entirely by African Americans naturally led to *de facto* segregation of the public schools.

Discrimination was still a cause of the problem, however. In many communities, landlords would only rent to African Americans in specific districts, and realtors would not allow them to view houses for sale outside of these zones. In other words, nongovernmental discrimination confined African Americans to all-black districts, which became known as *ghettos*.[7]

The Civil Rights Movement

The *Brown* decisions applied only to public schools. Not much else in the structure of existing segregation was affected. In December 1955, an African American woman, Rosa Parks, boarded a public bus in Montgomery, Alabama. When the bus became crowded, Parks was asked to move to the rear of the bus, the "colored" section. She refused and was arrested. But that was not the end of the matter. For an entire year, African Americans boycotted the Montgomery bus system. The protest was headed by a twenty-seven-year-old Baptist minister, Dr. Martin Luther King, Jr. In 1956, a federal district court issued an injunction prohibiting the segregation of buses in Montgomery. The era of civil rights protests had begun.

King's Philosophy of Nonviolence. In the following year, 1957, King formed the Southern Christian Leadership Conference (SCLC). King advocated nonviolent **civil disobedience** as a means to achieve racial justice. The SCLC used tactics such as demonstrations and marches, as well as nonviolent, public disobedience of unjust laws. King's followers successfully used these methods to gain wider public acceptance of their cause.

For the next decade, African Americans and sympathetic whites engaged in sit-ins, freedom rides, and freedom marches. In the beginning, such demonstrations were often met with violence, and the contrasting image of nonviolent African Americans and violent, hostile whites created strong public support for the civil rights movement.

The March on Washington. In August 1963, African American leaders A. Philip Randolph and Bayard Rustin organized the massive March on Washington for Jobs and Freedom. Before nearly a quarter-million white and African American spectators and millions watching on television, Martin Luther King told the world: "I have a dream that my four little children will one day live in a nation where they will not be judged by the color of their skin but by the content of their character."

Modern Civil Rights Legislation

Attacks on demonstrators using police dogs, cattle prods, high-pressure water hoses, beatings, and bombings—plus the March on Washington—all led to an environment in which Congress felt compelled to act on behalf of African Americans. The second era of civil rights acts, sometimes referred to as the second Reconstruction period, was under way.

The Civil Rights Act of 1964. The Civil Rights Act of 1964, the most far-reaching bill on civil rights in modern times, banned discrimination on the basis of race, color, religion, gender, or national origin. The act's major provisions were as follows:

- It outlawed arbitrary discrimination in voter registration.
- It barred discrimination in public accommodations, such as hotels and restaurants, which have operations that affect interstate commerce.

De Facto Segregation
Racial segregation that occurs because of patterns of racial residence and similar social conditions.

Civil Disobedience
A nonviolent, public refusal to obey allegedly unjust laws.

---

7. *Ghetto* was originally the name of a district in Venice, Italy, in which Venetian Jews were required to live.

Martin Luther King, Jr.'s, speech at the Washington Monument in 1963 was watched by millions of Americans on television. *What were his most famous words?*

- It authorized the federal government to sue to desegregate public schools and facilities.
- It expanded the power of the Civil Rights Commission, which had been created in 1957, and extended its life.
- It provided for the withholding of federal funds from programs administered in a discriminatory manner.
- It established the right to equality of opportunity in employment.

Title VII of the Civil Rights Act of 1964 is the cornerstone of employment-discrimination law. It prohibits discrimination in employment based on race, color, religion, gender, or national origin. Under Title VII, executive orders were issued that banned employment discrimination by firms that received federal funding. The 1964 Civil Rights Act created the Equal Employment Opportunity Commission (EEOC) to administer Title VII. It was not until 1972, however, that Congress gave the EEOC the right to sue employers, unions, and employment agencies. Litigation then became an important EEOC activity.

The Voting Rights Act of 1965. As late as 1960, only 29 percent of African Americans of voting age were registered in the southern states, in stark contrast to 61 percent of whites. The Voting Rights Act of 1965 addressed this issue. The act had two major provisions. The first outlawed discriminatory voter-registration tests. The second authorized federal registration of voters and federally administered voting procedures in any political subdivision or state that discriminated electorally against a particular group. The act also provided that certain political subdivisions could not change their voting procedures and election laws without federal approval, a provision greatly weakened by the Supreme Court in 2013.

The act targeted counties, mostly in the South, in which fewer than 50 percent of the eligible population were registered to vote. Federal voter registrars were sent to those areas to register African Americans who had been kept from voting by local registrars. Within one week after the act was passed, forty-five federal examiners were sent to the South. A massive voter-registration drive covered the region.

The Civil Rights Act of 1968 and Other Housing Reform Legislation. The Civil Rights Act of 1968 banned discrimination in most housing and provided penalties for those attempting to interfere with individual civil rights (giving protection to civil rights workers, among others). Subsequent legislation added enforcement provisions to the federal government's rules against discriminatory mortgage-lending practices.

Consequences of Civil Rights Legislation. As a result of the Voting Rights Act of 1965 and its amendments, and the large-scale voter-registration drives in the South, the number of African Americans registered to vote climbed dramatically. By 1980, 55.8 percent of African Americans of voting age in the South were registered. In recent national elections, turnout by African American voters has come very close to the white turnout. In 2008, with an African American on the presidential ballot, African American turnout exceeded that of whites for the first time in history.[8]

Political Participation by African Americans. Today, there are more than ten thousand African American elected officials in the United States. After the 2016 elections, the U. S. Congress included fifty-one African Americans. The movement of African American citizens into high elected office has been sure, if exceedingly slow. Notably, recent polling data show that most Americans do not consider race a significant factor in choosing a president. In 1958, when a Gallup poll first asked whether respondents would be willing to vote for an African American as president, only 38 percent of the public said yes. By 2008, this number had reached 94 percent.

This high figure may have been attained, at least in part, because of the emergence of African Americans of presidential caliber. Of course, Barack Obama, first elected president in 2008 on the Democratic ticket, is African American. Republican African American presidential candidates have earned support in recent primary election seasons. These include businessman Herman Cain, who ran in the 2011–2012 cycle, and neurosurgeon Ben Carson, a candidate in 2016. Neither secured the Republican nomination.

Lingering Social and Economic Disparities. Social and economic disparities between whites and blacks (and other minorities) persist. The median household income for African Americans is about three-fifths of the white median. Consider also that the poverty rate for non-Hispanic whites in 2015 was 9.1 percent, compared with 24.1 percent for African Americans and 21.4 percent for Hispanics. The collapse in the housing market

Interact

Police shootings of suspects have attracted much attention recently. Often, the suspects who were killed were young black men. Officers in these cases typically reported threatening behavior. Community members, however, often saw the shootings as a perversion of justice. One solution is to equip police officers with video cameras, so that everyone can see exactly what happened in questionable interactions. Search online for "police cameras pro con" and read some of the articles that appear. Would wider use of such cameras be helpful? Given that many Americans are likely to accept an officer's explanation of what is shown in a video, would such recordings really affect police behavior?

---

8. A widely reported study claimed that African American turnout did not quite match that of whites, but this conclusion was based on an overestimate of the number of African Americans eligible to vote.

in 2008–2011 also hit minority households much harder than white ones. African American and Latino households lost more than half of their net assets.

Finally, race consciousness continues to divide black and white Americans. Whether we are talking about media stereotyping, racial profiling, or academic achievement, the black experience is different from the white one. One of the most troubling contrasts between the races is their differing experiences with the criminal justice system. African Americans, especially men, are far more likely to be arrested and imprisoned than whites, as you can see in Figure 5–2.

It is true that African Americans, young men especially, are disproportionately involved in violent crime. But they are also far more likely than whites to be arrested and convicted even when they do *not* commit a particular offense more often than whites. About the same number of blacks and whites admit to using illegal drugs. Yet African Americans are three times more likely than whites to be arrested on drug charges, and they wind up in prison far more frequently. Black youth in some urban neighborhoods report that they are stopped by police—for no particular reason—as often as once a month. Despite these long-standing problems, there is some good news. In recent years, the conviction rate for black and Latino youth has declined sharply. (There is also bad news: the conviction rate for middle-aged whites has gone up.)

| FIGURE 5–2 | Imprisonment Rates per 100,000 Persons for Selected U.S. Population Groups |

Why might the government want to report lower numbers?

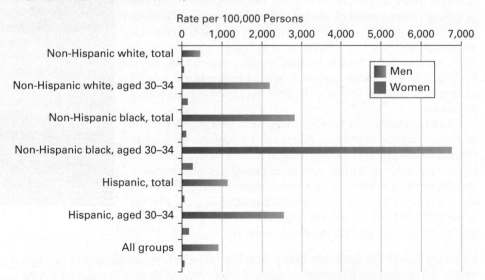

Source: E. Ann Carson, "Prisoners in 2013," *Bureau of Justice Statistics Bulletin,* U.S. Department of Justice (2014).

Note: The *imprisonment rate* measures only persons convicted of a crime and serving a sentence of at least one year. Through 2009, the government used the internationally recognized *incarceration rate,* which measures *all* persons held in custody, regardless of conviction status or period of confinement. Inevitably, the imprisonment rate yields smaller numbers—the total U.S. imprisonment rate was 478 per 100,000 persons in 2013, while the incarceration rate was 716. (Statistics are the latest available.)

Civil Rights and the Courts

>>>LO2: Define the different levels of scrutiny used by the Supreme Court in civil rights cases, and describe recent rulings on affirmative action.

The Fourteenth Amendment to the U.S. Constitution, adopted in 1869 following the Civil War, is the main constitutional basis for civil rights legislation and court decisions. Earlier we discussed the due process clause of the Fourteenth Amendment:

> *No State shall . . . deprive any person of life, liberty, or property, without due process of law . . . .*

This language mirrors that of the Fifth Amendment, which binds the federal government:

> *No person shall . . . be deprived of life, liberty, or property, without due process of law . . . .*

The due process clause was crucial to extending the civil liberties contained in the Bill of Rights to cover the actions of the individual states. The courts have made use of this clause in civil rights cases as well.

As a guarantee of civil rights, however, the next clause in the Fourteenth Amendment is at least as important:

> *. . . nor deny to any person within its jurisdiction the equal protection of the laws.*

The principal effect of *Plessy v. Ferguson*, described earlier, was to make this equal protection clause almost a dead letter in cases involving discrimination against individuals. Today, in contrast, the equal protection clause serves as the foundation of a sizable body of law.

Standards for Judicial Review

Federal courts use three standards when engaging in judicial review of laws or executive actions. The most exacting of these, **strict scrutiny,** is employed when fundamental rights are at stake, such as those guaranteed by the Bill of Rights. Strict scrutiny also comes into play when laws are based on a **suspect classification.** The original suspect class was race. As these terms suggest, the courts arc suspicious of, and will strictly scrutinize, any attempt by a government body to treat persons of different races in different ways. The Supreme Court has used this standard as a major tool in outlawing racial discrimination. Religion and national origin are also suspect classifications. To be acceptable under the strict scrutiny standard, a law must pass three tests:

- It must be justified by a compelling government interest.
- It must be narrowly tailored to meet that interest.
- It must be the least restrictive means of accomplishing the goal in question.

Intermediate, or Exacting, Scrutiny. The women's movement that arose in the 1960s led to suits claiming that various laws and government actions improperly discriminated against women. The courts were often sympathetic to such arguments. Still, the Supreme Court was reluctant to define gender as a suspect classification equivalent to race. The Court therefore established a new standard—**intermediate, or exacting, scrutiny.** To pass the intermediate scrutiny test, a law or government action "must further an important government interest by means that are substantially related to that interest." This standard is easier to meet than

Strict Scrutiny
A judicial standard for assessing the constitutionality of a law or government action when the law or action threatens to interfere with a fundamental right or potentially discriminates against members of a suspect classification.

Suspect Classification
A classification, such as race, religion, or national origin, that triggers strict scrutiny by the courts when a law or government action potentially discriminates against members of the class.

Intermediate, or Exacting, Scrutiny
A judicial standard used to determine whether a law or government action unconstitutionally discriminates against women.

the standard established for strict scrutiny. In later years, the Court tightened the test by requiring an "exceedingly persuasive justification" for gender-based discrimination.

Rational Basis Review. In cases in which neither strict scrutiny nor intermediate scrutiny are appropriate, the courts use **rational basis review** as a standard. This test requires that an action or law be "rationally related" to a "legitimate government interest." The legitimate interest does not have to be an interest cited by the government. If the courts can imagine a possible legitimate interest, the law stands. Rational basis review does not involve assessing the usefulness of laws. As Justice Thurgood Marshall observed on several occasions, "The Constitution does not prohibit legislatures from enacting stupid laws."[9] If a court can find no legitimate interest at all, however, a law or action can fail even this test. The courts have used rational basis review to strike down laws that discriminate against gay men and lesbians.

The Supreme Court Addresses Affirmative Action

As noted earlier in this chapter, the Civil Rights Act of 1964 prohibited discrimination against any person on the basis of race, color, national origin, religion, or gender. The act also established the right to equal opportunity in employment. A basic problem remained, however: minority groups and women, because of past discrimination, often lacked the education and skills to compete effectively in the marketplace. In 1965, the federal government attempted to remedy this problem by implementing the concept of affirmative action. **Affirmative action** policies attempt to "level the playing field" by giving special preferences in educational admissions and employment decisions to groups that have been discriminated against in the past. These policies go beyond a strict interpretation of the equal protection clause of the Fourteenth Amendment.

Implementing Affirmative Action. In 1965, President Lyndon Johnson issued an executive order mandating affirmative action policies to remedy the effects of past discrimination. All government agencies, including those of state and local governments, were required to implement such policies. Additionally, affirmative action requirements were imposed on companies that sell goods or services to the federal government and on institutions that receive federal funds, such as universities. Affirmative action policies were also required whenever an employer had been ordered to develop such a plan by a court or by the Equal Employment Opportunity Commission because of evidence of past discrimination. Finally, labor unions that had been found to discriminate against women or minorities in the past were required to establish and follow affirmative action plans.

Affirmative action programs have been controversial because they allegedly result in discrimination against "majority" groups, such as white males (or discrimination against other minority groups that may not be given preferential treatment under a particular affirmative action program). At issue in the current debate over affirmative action programs is whether such programs, because of their discriminatory nature, violate the equal protection clause of the Fourteenth Amendment to the Constitution.

The *Bakke* Case. The first Supreme Court case addressing the constitutionality of affirmative action examined a program at the University of California, Davis. Allan Bakke, a white student who had been turned down for medical school at the Davis campus, discovered that his academic record was better than those of some of the minority applicants who had been admitted to the program. He sued the University of California, alleging **reverse discrimination.** The UC Davis School of Medicine had held sixteen places out of one hundred for

Rational Basis Review
A judicial standard for assessing a law or government action that is employed when neither strict nor intermediate scrutiny apply.

Affirmative Action
A policy in educational admissions or job hiring that gives special attention or compensatory treatment to traditionally disadvantaged groups in an effort to overcome present effects of past discrimination.

Reverse Discrimination
Discrimination against individuals who are not members of a minority group.

---

9. As quoted in Justice John Paul Stevens's concurrence to *New York State Board of Elections v. Lopez Torres*, 552 U.S. 196 (2008).

educationally "disadvantaged students" each year, and administrators admitted to using race as a criterion for admission for these particular slots.

In 1978, the Supreme Court handed down its decision in *Regents of the University of California v. Bakke*.[10] The Court did not rule against affirmative action programs. Rather, it held that Bakke had to be admitted to the UC Davis School of Medicine because its admissions policy had used race as the sole criterion for the sixteen "minority" positions. Justice Lewis Powell, speaking for the Court, indicated that while race can be considered "as a factor" among others in admissions (and presumably hiring) decisions, race cannot be the sole factor. So affirmative action programs, but not specific quota systems, were upheld as constitutional.

Additional Limits on Affirmative Action. A number of cases decided during the 1980s and 1990s placed further limits on affirmative action programs. In a landmark decision in 1995, *Adarand Constructors, Inc. v. Peña*, the Supreme Court held that any federal, state, or local affirmative action program that uses racial or ethnic classifications as the basis for making decisions is subject to the strict scrutiny standard.[11] The Court's opinion in *Adarand* means that an affirmative action program cannot make use of quotas or preferences for unqualified persons. In addition, once the program has succeeded in achieving the purpose it was tailored to meet, the program must be changed or dropped.

In 2003, in two cases involving the University of Michigan, the Supreme Court indicated that limited affirmative action programs continued to be acceptable and that diversity was a legitimate goal. The Court struck down the affirmative action plan used for undergraduate admissions at the university, which automatically awarded a substantial number of points to applicants based on minority status.[12] At the same time, in *Grutter v. Bollinger*, it approved the admissions plan used by the law school, which took race into consideration as part of a complete examination of each applicant's background.[13]

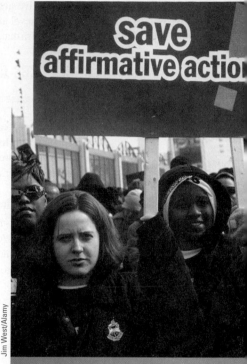

Demonstrators march in Detroit, Michigan, in support of affirmative action programs at the state's universities. The United States Supreme Court later ruled that the state had the power to ban such programs. *Should affirmative action to promote diversity in admissions be allowed?*

The End of Affirmative Action? Despite the position taken by the Supreme Court in the University of Michigan Law School case, affirmative action is subject to serious threats. In 2007, the Supreme Court tightened the guidelines for permissible affirmative action programs. In rejecting school integration plans in Seattle, Washington, and Louisville, Kentucky, the Court found that race could not be used as a "tiebreaker" when granting admission to a school.[14] Many observers thought that the Supreme Court might end affirmative action programs altogether in *Fisher v. University of Texas*, two cases with the same name heard in 2013 and 2016. In deciding the *Fisher* cases, however, the Court made no significant alterations to the law.[15]

---

10. 438 U.S. 265 (1978).
11. 515 U.S. 200 (1995).
12. *Gratz v. Bollinger*, 539 U.S. 244 (2003).
13. 539 U.S. 306 (2003).
14. *Parents Involved in Community Schools v. Seattle School District No. 1*, 551 U.S. 701 (2007).
15. 133 S.Ct. 2411 (2013) and 579 U.S. ___ (2016).

Affirmative action may face a greater danger from the states. Seven states have now banned state-level affirmative action programs. In 2014, the Supreme Court ruled in favor of Michigan's affirmative action ban, effectively upholding the law in six other states.[16]

Experiences of Other Minority Groups

>>>**LO3:** Discuss the history and current status of Latinos and American Indians.

In a brief textbook edition, it is not possible to describe the experiences of all groups of Americans who have had to struggle for civil rights. Still, two groups deserve mention: Hispanic Americans, or Latinos, are now the nation's largest minority group by population. American Indians are notable for their unusual and troubled history, and of course because they were here first.

Latinos and the Immigration Issue

The law recognizes that Latinos, or Hispanics, have been subjected to many of the same forms of ill treatment as African Americans. Therefore, Latinos are usually grouped with African Americans and American Indians in laws and programs that seek to protect minorities from discrimination or to address the results of past discrimination. To the U.S. Census Bureau, **Hispanics** can be of any race. The term *Hispanic* itself, although used by the government, is not universally popular, and some prefer the term **Latino** (in the feminine, *Latina*).

Immigration. The most striking characteristic of Latinos is that many of them are relatively recent immigrants. A century ago, most immigrants to the United States came from Europe. Today, most come from Latin America and Asia. Recently, immigrants from Asian nations have begun to outnumber Hispanic immigrants. This change is largely due to a drop in the number of Hispanics rather than an increase in the number of Asians. Table 5–1 shows the leading countries of origin for the foreign-born population in the United States.

TABLE 5–1	Top Ten Countries of Origin for the Foreign-Born U.S. Population

Hispanic countries are shown in red. *Why are there no European countries on this list?*

Mexico	11,585,000
China	2,384,000
India	2,035,000
Philippines	1,844,000
Vietnam	1,281,000
El Salvador	1,252,000
Cuba	1,144,000
Korea	1,070,000
Dominican Republic	991,000
Guatemala	902,000
ALL COUNTRIES	41,348,000

Source: U.S. Bureau of the Census. Figures are for 2013.

Hispanic
Someone who can claim a heritage from a Spanish-speaking country. Hispanics may be of any race.

Latino
An alternative to the term *Hispanic* that is preferred by many.

16. *Schuette v. Coalition to Defend Affirmative Action*, 572 U.S. ___ (2014).

The Changing Face of America. As a result of immigration, the ethnic makeup of the United States is changing. Yet immigration is not the only factor contributing to changes in the American ethnic mosaic. Another factor is ethnic differences in the *total fertility* rate. This rate measures the average number of children that women in a given group are expected to have over the course of a lifetime. A rate of 2.1 is the "long-term replacement rate." In other words, if a nation or group maintains a rate of 2.1, its population will eventually stabilize. This can take many years, however. On average, U.S. Hispanics have a higher total fertility rate than non-Hispanics, which adds to their future numbers.

Unauthorized Immigration. Illegal immigration—or unauthorized immigration, to use the language of the Department of Homeland Security—has been a major national issue for a long time. Naturally, the unauthorized population is hard to count, but it has probably stabilized at just over 11 million in recent years. We list the top ten countries of birth for unauthorized immigrants in the United States in Table 5–2.

Unauthorized immigrants often live in mixed households, in which one or more members of a family have lawful resident status, but others do not. Often, the parents in a family are unauthorized, while the children, who were born in the United States, possess American citizenship. Mixed families mean that deporting illegal immigrants may either break up a family or force one or more American citizens into exile. In some circumstances, though, immigrants actually choose to separate their families. In 2014 and 2015, large numbers of unaccompanied children from violence-torn Central American countries turned themselves in to U.S. authorities at the Mexican border. Because these children claimed the internationally recognized right of asylum, they could not be immediately deported.

Unauthorized immigrants typically come to the United States to work. Before the Immigration Reform and Control Act of 1986, there was no law against hiring foreign citizens who lacked proper papers. Until recently, laws penalizing employers were infrequently enforced. President Obama, however, stepped up enforcement of these laws substantially during his

TABLE 5–2	Top Ten Countries of Birth for Unauthorized Immigrants in the United States

Of necessity, these figures are rough estimates. Hispanic countries are shown in red. ***Given high rates of poverty in Africa, why don't more Africans come to the United States?***

Mexico	6,194,000
Guatemala	704,000
El Salvador	436,000
Honduras	317,000
China	285,000
India	284,000
Philippines	197,000
Korea	192,000
Ecuador	196,000
Colombia	137,000
ALL COUNTRIES	11,022,000

Source: Migration Policy Institute. Figures are for 2013.

first term. In the last years of his administration, Obama also sought to protect a substantial number of unauthorized immigrants from deportation by using executive orders. A 2012 order suspended deportations of unauthorized immigrants who were brought into the country as children and who were not otherwise in trouble with the law. A second order, in 2014, would have protected more than 4 million illegal immigrants. In 2015, a federal judge stayed (suspended) the second order. The Supreme Court confirmed the stay in 2016. Given Donald Trump's campaign promises, it is reasonable to assume that rates of deportation will rise sharply during the Trump administration. We examine that question in this chapter's *At Issue* feature.

Political Participation by Latinos. Latino political participation has increased in recent years, and they have gained political power in several states. Latinos do not vote at the same rate as African Americans, in large part because many Latinos are immigrants who are not yet citizens. Still, there are now about five thousand Latino elected officials in the United States.

National Security and the Rights of Immigrants

Legal immigrants who are not citizens have certain rights. The Fourteenth Amendment states that all persons (as opposed to all citizens) shall enjoy "due process of law." *Illegal* immigrants are subject to deportation. In 1903, however, the Supreme Court ruled that the government could not deport someone without a hearing that meets constitutional due process standards.[17] Today, most people facing deportation are entitled to a hearing before an immigration judge, to representation by a lawyer, and to the right to see the evidence presented against them. The government must prove that its grounds for deportation are valid.

Limits to the Rights of Deportees: Due Process. Despite the Fourteenth Amendment, the courts have often deferred to government assertions that noncitizens cannot make constitutional claims. The Antiterrorism and Effective Death Penalty Act of 1996 was especially restrictive. The government was given the right to deport noncitizens for alleged terrorism without any court review of the deportation order. Further, the government can deport noncitizens based on secret evidence that the deportee is not allowed to see.

Limits to the Rights of Deportees: Freedom of Association. A 1999 case involved a group of noncitizens associated with the Popular Front for the Liberation of Palestine (PFLP). PFLP members had carried out terrorist acts in Israel, but there was no evidence of criminal conduct by the group arrested in the United States. In this case, the Supreme Court ruled that noncitizens have no First Amendment rights to object to deportation, even if the deportation is based on their political associations.[18] This ruling also covers permanent residents—noncitizens with "green cards" that allow them to live and work in the United States on a long-term basis.

Limits to the Rights of Deportees: *Ex Post Facto* Laws. As you learned earlier, the Constitution prohibits *ex post facto* laws—laws that inflict punishments for acts that were not illegal when they were committed. This provision may not apply in deportation cases, however. The 1996 Antiterrorism and Effective Death Penalty Act, mentioned earlier, provided mandatory deportation for noncitizens convicted of an aggravated felony, even if the crime took place before 1996. In some jurisdictions, marijuana possession can be an aggravated felony. Under the 1996 law, permanent residents have been deported

---

17. *Yamataya v. Fisher*, 189 U.S. 86 (1903).
18. *Reno v. American-Arab Anti-Discrimination Committee*, 525 U.S. 471 (1999).

AT ISSUE

Should We Deport Unauthorized Immigrants?

Today, about 11 million unauthorized—or illegal—immigrants live in the United States. For years, Congress has failed to resolve this issue. Many proposals have involved programs to move illegal immigrants onto a path that ends in legal status or even citizenship. In contrast, during his presidential campaign, Donald Trump advocated the deportation of all 11 million.

Illegal Immigrants Should Be Deported

Those who oppose letting unauthorized immigrants regularize their status call such programs "amnesty." If we grant such individuals the legal right to stay in this country, we are rewarding people who have violated the law. That is unfair. Why should the unauthorized find it easier to stay in the United States than those who play by the rules? Amnesty would only encourage more individuals to enter the United States illegally. That, after all, is what happened in 1986, the last time Congress granted amnesty to a large number of illegal immigrants. After the law was passed, illegal immigration did not slow down at all.

Most illegal immigrants are low-skilled, low-wage workers. They compete against high school dropouts in America and drive down the wages of our poorest citizens. Illegal immigration can result in overcrowded schools and hospital emergency rooms. Immigration can also change the culture of the nation, especially when such a large share of it comes from a single region—Latin America. Ordinary citizens have never been asked whether they are willing to see fundamental changes to the very nature of the country. Conservatives also note that a majority of the immigrants who would benefit from amnesty would vote for Democrats if they became citizens. Even if we let such people stay, let's not support a Democratic Party power grab. These persons should not be allowed to become citizens and vote.

Mass Deportation Would Be a Disaster

Suppose that the federal government expanded its current deportation effort into a program aimed at identifying and deporting every last unauthorized immigrant. If this were a two-year project, as Trump initially proposed, we would need to deport more people every month than we now do in a year. We would need at least ten times as many immigration officers, ten times as many prison beds, and many more immigration courts and federal lawyers. Physically moving the deportees would require 84 buses and 47 chartered flights every day for two years. The total cost would be about $400 billion.

Deportation proponents argue that with fewer illegal immigrants, American citizens would have access to more jobs. Most economists disagree. The number of jobs in the economy is not fixed. When the economy grows, the number of jobs rises. Legal and illegal immigrants alike add to net employment because they not only work, they also spend. This spending adds to the demand for goods and services, which leads to more employment, not less. By one estimate, the reduction in economic activity resulting from mass deportation could exceed $1 trillion per year.

A successful mass deportation effort would require that police have the ability to "stop and ask." Everyone would have to produce proof of legal status. Latinos who are U.S. citizens would be singled out. Many non-Hispanic citizens might be caught in the net as well.

FOR CRITICAL ANALYSIS
If mass deportations were initiated, what might happen to the cost of farm produce?

to nations that they left when they were small children. In some cases, deported persons did not speak the language of the country to which they were deported.

The Agony of the American Indian

Whether living on rural reservations or in urban neighborhoods, American Indians have long experienced high rates of poverty. There is much history behind this problem. (In recent years, a majority of American Indians have come to prefer this description—or even, simply, Indian—to Native American. Still, both terms are in use.)

The Demographic Collapse. During the years after Columbus arrived in America, native population numbers—both in the future United States and in the Americas

This member of the Ute tribe attends a ceremony for Ute and Comanche leaders. *About how many Native Americans are there today?*

AP Photo/Rick Browne

generally—experienced one of the most catastrophic collapses in human history. The Europeans brought with them Old World diseases to which Native Americans had no immunity. A person who was able to resist one disease might die from another. By one estimate, 90 percent of the inhabitants of the New World died. For their part, the Europeans had no idea what caused diseases and did not understand what was happening. When the Pilgrims landed at Plymouth in 1620, the coast of New England was lined with empty Indian village sites. The villages had been abandoned because of an epidemic touched off by shipwrecked French sailors in 1616.

American Indians in the Nineteenth and Twentieth Centuries. In the United States, the American Indian population continued to decrease through the nineteenth century—a time when the European American and African American populations were experiencing explosive growth. The decrease was largely due to the concentration of Native Americans into ever-smaller territories. The U.S. Indian population bottomed out at 250,000 at the end of the nineteenth century. Since that time, however, it has recovered substantially. The number today is about 2.6 million, plus 2.8 million people of partial Indian ancestry. The total may exceed the number living here before Columbus.

American Indians faced additional challenges. A federal policy of "assimilation" adopted in the late 1880s resulted in further loss of territory and the suppression of traditional cultures. Indians did not become U.S. citizens until 1924.

In the late twentieth century, some native tribes hit upon a new strategy for economic development—gambling casinos on reservation lands. This strategy was possible because the U.S. Constitution grants the responsibility for Indian relations to the national government. As a result, reservations are not subject to the full authority of the states in which they are located.

Women's Struggle for Equal Rights

≫LO4: Contrast the goals of the women's suffrage movement with the goals of modern feminism.

Like African Americans and other minorities, women have had to struggle for equality. During the first phase of this struggle, the primary goal of women was to obtain *suffrage*, or the right to vote.

Early Women's Political Movements

In 1848, Lucretia Mott and Elizabeth Cady Stanton organized the first women's rights convention in Seneca Falls, New York. The three hundred people who attended approved a Declaration of Sentiments: "We hold these truths to be self-evident: that all men *and women* are created equal."

In 1869, after the Civil War, Susan B. Anthony and Stanton formed the National Woman Suffrage Association. In their view, women's suffrage was a means to achieve major improvements in the economic and social situation of women in the United States. In other words, the vote was to be used to seek broader goals. Lucy Stone, however, a key founder of the rival American Woman Suffrage Association, believed that the vote was the only major issue. In 1880, the two organizations joined forces. The resulting National American Woman Suffrage Association had just one goal—the enfranchisement of women—but it made little progress.

The Congressional Union for Woman Suffrage, founded in the early 1900s by Alice Paul, adopted a national strategy of obtaining an amendment to the U.S. Constitution. The Union employed militant tactics. It sponsored large-scale marches and civil disobedience—which resulted in hunger strikes, arrests, and jailings. Finally, in 1920, the Nineteenth Amendment was passed: "The right of citizens of the United States to vote shall not be denied or abridged by the United States or by any State on account of sex." (Today, the word *gender* is typically used instead of *sex*.)

The Modern Women's Movement

Historian Nancy Cott contends that the word *feminism* first began to be used around 1910. At that time **feminism** meant, as it does today, political, social, and economic equality for women—a radical notion that gained little support then.

After gaining the right to vote in 1920, women engaged in little independent political activity until the 1960s. The civil rights movement of that decade resulted in a growing awareness of rights for all groups, including women. Increased participation in the workforce gave many women greater self-confidence. Additionally, the publication of Betty Friedan's *The Feminine Mystique* in 1963 focused national attention on the unequal status of women in American life.

In 1966, Friedan and others formed the National Organization for Women (NOW). Many observers consider the founding of NOW to be the beginning of the modern women's movement—the feminist movement.

This woman, a senior airman in the U.S. Air Force, is stationed at a base used by the United States to resupply its forces in Afghanistan. Since 2013, women have been able to serve in combat units. *Is this a positive development?*

Feminism gained additional impetus from young women who entered politics to support the civil rights movement or to oppose the Vietnam War. In the late 1960s, "women's liberation" organizations began to spring up on college campuses. Women also began organizing independent "consciousness-raising groups," in which they discussed how gender issues affected their lives. The new women's movement experienced explosive growth, and by 1970 it had emerged as a major social force.

The Equal Rights Amendment. The initial focus of the modern women's movement was to eradicate gender inequality through a constitutional amendment. The proposed Equal Rights Amendment (ERA), which was first introduced in Congress in 1923, states as follows: "Equality of rights under the law shall not be denied or abridged by the United States or

Feminism
The movement that supports political, economic, and social equality for women.

by any state on account of sex." For years, the amendment was not even given a hearing in Congress, but finally it was approved by both chambers and sent to the state legislatures for ratification in 1972. The necessary thirty-eight states failed to ratify the ERA within the time specified by Congress, however. To date, efforts to reintroduce the amendment have failed.

Challenging Gender Discrimination in the Courts. When ratification of the ERA failed, women's rights organizations began a campaign to establish national and state laws that would guarantee the equality of women. This more limited campaign met with much success. Women's rights organizations also challenged discriminatory statutes and policies in the federal courts, contending that **gender discrimination** violated the Fourteenth Amendment's equal protection clause. Since the 1970s, the Supreme Court has employed intermediate, or exacting, scrutiny to invalidate many such statutes and policies. For example, in 1977 the Court held that police and firefighting units cannot establish arbitrary rules, such as height and weight requirements, that tend to keep women from participating in those occupations.[19] In 1983, the Court ruled that life insurance companies cannot charge different rates for women and men.[20]

Gender Equality on Campus. Congress sought to guarantee equality of treatment in education by passing Title IX of the Education Amendments of 1972, which states: "No person in the United States shall, on the basis of sex, be excluded from participation in, be denied the benefits of, or be subjected to discrimination under any education program or activity receiving Federal financial assistance." Title IX's best-known and most controversial impact has been on high school and collegiate athletics, although the original statute made no reference to sports.

In 2011, the Department of Education issued a statement clarifying that sexual harassment on campus, including rape, violated Title IX. Investigations by the Obama administration suggested that many schools were not taking such violations seriously. Dozens of schools were potentially subject to penalties. As a result, many colleges and universities launched efforts to address the issue.

Women in the Military. One of the most controversial issues involving women's rights has been the role of women in the armed forces. Many believe that the ERA failed because of the fear that women might be drafted (forced) into military service. Currently, no draft exists, but to this day young American men must register for it. Women do not face such a requirement.

A recent issue has been whether women should be allowed to serve in military combat units. In the past, women were not allowed to join such units. Due to the fluid nature of modern combat, however, women in support positions have often found themselves in firefights anyway. In January 2013, the Department of Defense lifted the Combat Exclusion Policy, and in the future women will be able to compete for assignment to combat units. Participation in such units is usually a requirement for promotion to top military positions.

Women in Politics Today

Although a "men's club" atmosphere still prevails in Congress, the number of women holding congressional seats has increased significantly in recent years. In 2001, for the first time, a woman was elected to a leadership post in Congress—Nancy Pelosi of California became the Democrats' minority whip in the U.S. House of Representatives. In 2002, Pelosi was elected

Gender Discrimination
Any practice, policy, or procedure that denies equality of treatment to an individual or to a group because of gender.

19. *Dothard v. Rawlinson*, 433 U.S. 321 (1977).
20. *Arizona v. Norris*, 463 U.S. 1073 (1983).

minority leader. In 2006, she became the first woman to be Speaker of the House, although she was forced to drop back to minority leader again in 2010 when the Republicans regained control of the House. The number of women in Congress after the 2016 elections was eighty-three women in the House and twenty-one in the Senate.

Recent Gallup polls show that close to 90 percent of Americans said they would vote for a qualified woman for president if she was nominated by their party. Increasing numbers of women are also being appointed to cabinet posts. More women are also sitting on federal judicial benches. These include Ruth Bader Ginsburg (appointed by President Bill Clinton), as well as Sonia Sotomayor and Elena Kagan (appointed by President Obama).

Nikki Haley addresses the Federalist Society, a group organized by conservative lawyers and law students. At the time, she was governor of South Carolina. In 2016, President-elect Trump named her to be his ambassador to the United Nations. *Why might it be that presidents of both parties have appointed women to top diplomatic posts?*

Gender-Based Discrimination in the Workplace

Traditional cultural beliefs concerning the proper role of women in society continue to be evident not only in the political arena but also in the workplace. Since the 1960s, however, women have gained substantial protection against discrimination through laws that require equal employment opportunities and equal pay.

Title VII of the Civil Rights Act of 1964. Title VII of the Civil Rights Act of 1964 prohibits gender discrimination in employment and has been used to strike down employment policies that discriminate against employees on the basis of gender. In 1978, Congress amended Title VII to expand the definition of *gender discrimination* to include discrimination based on pregnancy.

Sexual Harassment. The United States Supreme Court has also held that Title VII's prohibition of gender-based discrimination extends to **sexual harassment** in the workplace. One form of sexual harassment occurs when job opportunities, promotions, salary increases, and other benefits are given in return for sexual favors. Another form of sexual harassment is called *hostile-environment* harassment. It occurs when an employee is subjected to sexual conduct or comments that interfere with the employee's job performance or are so pervasive or severe as to create an intimidating, hostile, or offensive environment.

Wage Discrimination. Although Title VII and other legislation since the 1960s have mandated equal employment opportunities for men and women, women continue to earn less, on average, than men do. The Equal Pay Act, which was enacted in 1963, basically requires employers to provide equal pay for substantially equal work. In other words, males cannot legally be paid more than females who perform essentially the same job.

The Equal Pay Act did not address the fact that certain types of jobs traditionally held by women pay lower wages than the jobs usually held by men. For example, more women than men are salesclerks and nurses, whereas more men than women are construction

Sexual Harassment
Unwanted physical or verbal conduct or abuse of a sexual nature that interferes with a recipient's job performance, creates a hostile work environment, or carries with it an implicit or explicit threat of adverse employment consequences.

workers and truck drivers. Even if all clerks performing substantially similar jobs for a company earned the same salaries, they typically would still be earning less than the company's truck drivers.

The Rights and Status of Gay Males and Lesbians

>>>**LO5:** Summarize the recent revolution in the rights enjoyed by gay men and lesbians.

On June 27, 1969, patrons of the Stonewall Inn, a New York City bar popular with gay men and lesbians, responded to a police raid. They threw beer cans and bottles because they were angry at what they felt was unrelenting police harassment. In the ensuing riot, which lasted two nights, hundreds of gay men and lesbians fought with police. Before Stonewall, the stigma attached to homosexuality and the resulting fear of exposure had tended to prevent most gay men and lesbians from engaging in activism. In the months after Stonewall, however, the Gay Liberation Front and the Gay Activist Alliance were formed, and similar groups sprang up in other parts of the country.

Growth in the Gay Male and Lesbian Rights Movement

The Stonewall incident marked the beginning of the movement for gay and lesbian rights. Since then, gay men and lesbians have formed thousands of organizations to exert pressure on legislatures, the media, schools, churches, and other organizations to recognize their right to equal treatment.

To a great extent, lesbian and gay groups have succeeded in changing public opinion—and state and local laws that pertain to their status and rights. Nevertheless, they continue to struggle against age-old biases against homosexuality, often rooted in deeply held religious beliefs.

In time, the lesbian and gay rights movement came to include bisexuals and *transgender* people—that is, individuals who experience a gender identity at odds with their actual biology. The popular acronym *LGBT* signifies this broader movement.

State and Local Laws Targeting Gay Men and Lesbians

Before the Stonewall incident, forty-nine states had sodomy laws that made various kinds of sexual acts, including homosexual acts, illegal (Illinois, which had repealed its sodomy law in 1962, was the only exception). During the 1970s and 1980s, about half of these laws were either repealed or struck down by the courts.

Lawrence v. Texas. The states—mostly in the South—that resisted the movement to abolish sodomy laws received a boost in 1986 with the Supreme Court's decision in *Bowers v. Hardwick*.[21] In that case, the Court upheld, by a five-to-four vote, a Georgia law that made homosexual conduct between two adults a crime. But in 2003, the Court reversed its earlier position on sodomy with its decision in *Lawrence v. Texas*.[22] In this case, the Court held that laws against sodomy violate the due process clause of the Fourteenth Amendment. The Court stated: "The liberty protected by the Constitution allows homosexual persons the right to choose to enter upon relationships in the confines of their homes and their own private lives and still retain their dignity as free persons." As a result, *Lawrence v. Texas* invalidated the sodomy laws that remained on the books in fourteen states.

---

21. 478 U.S. 186 (1986).
22. 539 U.S. 558 (2003).

State Actions. Today, thirty-four states, the District of Columbia, and more than 180 cities and counties have enacted laws protecting lesbians and gay men from discrimination in employment in at least some workplaces. Many of these laws also ban discrimination in housing, in public accommodation, and in other contexts. Nineteen states extend private-sector employment rights to transgender individuals. It is a fact, however, that discrimination against LGBT individuals in housing, employment, and public accommodations remains legal in a majority of U.S. jurisdictions. Almost none of the discrimination laws and policies discussed earlier in this chapter were written to include LGBT persons.

"Don't Ask, Don't Tell"

Until recently, the armed forces have viewed homosexuality as incompatible with military service. In 1993, however, President Bill Clinton announced a new policy, described as "don't ask, don't tell." Enlistees would not be asked about their sexual orientation, and gay men and lesbians would be allowed to serve in the military so long as they did not declare that they were gay men or lesbians or commit homosexual acts. The new policy was a compromise— Clinton had promised during his presidential campaign to repeal outright the long-standing ban on gay male and lesbian military service. Despite the new policy, large numbers of gay men and lesbians were expelled from the military in subsequent years.

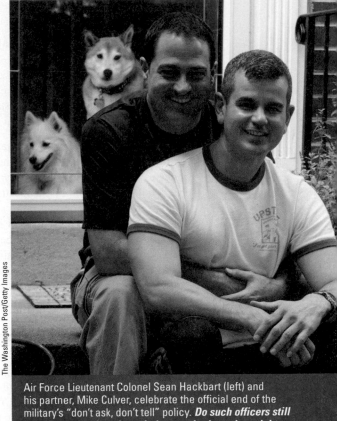

The Washington Post/Getty Images

Air Force Lieutenant Colonel Sean Hackbart (left) and his partner, Mike Culver, celebrate the official end of the military's "don't ask, don't tell" policy. *Do such officers still need to worry about how their sexual orientation might affect their careers?*

Barack Obama promised to repeal "don't ask, don't tell" and allow lesbians and gay men to serve openly, but Congress failed to act on legislation. Still, by December 2010, respondents in a public opinion poll supported the right of gay men and lesbians to serve openly by a margin of 77 to 21 percent. In September 2010, a U.S. district court judge ruled that the ban on open military service by gay men and lesbians was unconstitutional.[23] In December Congress finally passed repeal legislation. "Don't ask, don't tell" was phased out in mid-2011.

Same-Sex Marriage

Given the rampant hostility toward gay men and lesbians that existed throughout most of American history, legal same-sex marriage was beyond imagination for most Americans. Still, some same-sex couples celebrated their unions with private, unofficial ceremonies.

In 2015, however, the Supreme Court endorsed nationwide recognition of same-sex marriage. This landmark decision was part of one of the most rapid and profound

23. *Log Cabin Republicans v. United States*, 716 F.Supp.2d 884 (C.D.Cal. 2010).

extensions of civil rights in history—the recognition of equal rights regardless of sexual orientation.

The Defense of Marriage Act (DOMA). Controversy over this issue first flared up in 1993 when the Hawaii Supreme Court ruled that denying marriage licenses to gay couples might violate the equal protection clause of the Hawaii constitution.[24] In response, the U.S. Congress passed the Defense of Marriage Act of 1996, which banned federal recognition of lesbian and gay male couples and allowed state governments to ignore same-sex marriages performed in other states.

Recognition of Same-Sex Marriages. Massachusetts was the first state to recognize gay marriage. In November 2003, the Massachusetts Supreme Judicial Court ruled that same-sex couples have a right to civil marriage under the Massachusetts state constitution.[25] For four years, Massachusetts stood alone in approving such marriages. From 2008 on, however, more and more states began to accept same-sex marriage. In June 2013, the Supreme Court found, in *United States v. Windsor*, that the provision of the Defense of Marriage Act that banned federal recognition of same-sex marriages performed by the states was unconstitutional.[26] Ever-larger numbers of state and federal judges used the arguments in *United States v. Windsor* to overturn same-sex marriage bans. Finally, in June 2015, the Supreme Court overturned the remaining state-level prohibitions.[27]

The Rights of Transgender Individuals

The question of who is a woman and who is a man is not as open-and-shut as many people once assumed. Thousands of people grow up convinced that their bodies are lying to them. They may have been born with the physical characteristics of one sex, but in their hearts they know they belong to the other. The existence of such **transgender persons** has been known for many years and has led to the practice of reassigning gender through surgery. Not all transgender persons undergo such an invasive process, however. Indeed, some transgender persons find that they cannot identify as either men or women.

Forty-six states allow birth certificates to be amended to change a person's recorded sex. Twenty-eight states, however, allow such a change only following surgery. Discrimination against transgender individuals is widespread, and in recent years, such persons have increasingly come out into the open and demanded equal rights. In 2015 and 2016, however, various states and localities passed laws banning transgender persons from using public restrooms that did not accord with the sex listed on their birth certificates. A common argument was that trans women (born men) would use their access to women's restrooms to sexually harass women. (There is no recorded case of such an incident, and if it did happen it would be a felony under existing laws.) In response to North Carolina legislation, in 2016 the Obama administration announced that any such ban in a public school would threaten the school's access to federal funding. Eleven states sued the administration in an attempt to reverse this decision.

Transgender Persons
Persons who experience a mismatch between their gender identity and the gender assigned to them at birth.

24. *Baehr v. Lewin*, 852 P.2d 44 (Hawaii 1993).
25. *Goodridge v. Department of Public Health*, 798 N.E.2d 941 (Mass. 2003).
26. 133 S.Ct. 2675 (2013).
27. *Obergefell v. Hodges*, 135 S.Ct. 2584 (2015).

MAKING A DIFFERENCE

Dealing with Discrimination

Anyone applying for a job may be subjected to a variety of potentially discriminatory practices. The government continues to monitor the fairness and validity of criteria used in job-applicant screening, and as a result, there are ways of addressing the problem of discrimination.

Why Should You Care? Some people may think that discrimination is a problem only for members of racial or ethnic minorities. Actually, in some instances, white men have experienced "reverse discrimination"—and have obtained redress for it. Also, discrimination against women is common. Even if you are male, you probably have female friends and relatives whose well-being is of interest to you.

Chip Somodevilla/Getty Images

Members of the Council on American-Islamic Relations outside the Supreme Court building during oral arguments on *EEOC v. Abercrombie and Fitch.* The Court later ruled that the clothing retailer violated antidiscrimination laws when it refused to hire a young woman who wore a headscarf for religious reasons. *What limits, if any, should be placed on religious dress?*

What Can You Do? If you believe that you have been discriminated against by a potential employer, consider the following steps:

1. Evaluate your own capabilities, and determine if you are truly qualified for the position.
2. Analyze the reasons why you were turned down. Would others agree with you that you have been the object of discrimination?
3. If you still believe that you have been treated unfairly, you have recourse to several agencies and services.

You should first speak to the human resources director of the company and explain politely that you believe you have not been evaluated adequately. Explain your concerns clearly. If necessary, go into detail, and say that you may have been discriminated against.

If a second evaluation is not forthcoming, contact your local state employment agency. If you still do not obtain adequate help, contact one or more of the following state officials or agencies:

- If a government entity is involved, a state ombudsperson or citizen aide may be available to mediate.
- You can contact the state civil rights or human rights commission, which should at least give you advice, even if it does not wish to take up your case.
- The state attorney general's office may have a division dealing with discrimination and civil rights.
- There may be a special commission or department, such as a women's status commission or a commission on Hispanics or Asian Americans. If so, contact this commission.

Finally, at the national level, you can contact the Equal Employment Opportunity Commission at **www.eeoc.gov**.

Key Terms

affirmative action 102
civil disobedience 97
civil rights 92
de facto segregation 97
de jure segregation 96
feminism 109

gender discrimination 110
grandfather clause 95
Hispanic 104
intermediate, or
    exacting, scrutiny 101
Latino 104

literacy test 95
poll tax 95
rational basis review 102
reverse discrimination 102
separate-but-equal
    doctrine 95

sexual harassment 111
strict scrutiny 101
suffrage 94
suspect classification 101
transgender persons 114
white primary 95

Chapter Summary

≫LO1 Before the Civil War, slavery was protected by the Constitution. Constitutional amendments after the Civil War ended slavery, and African Americans gained citizenship, the right to vote, and other rights. This protection was largely a dead letter by the 1880s, however.

Segregation was declared unconstitutional by the Supreme Court in *Brown v. Board of Education of Topeka* (1954), in which the Court stated that separation implied inferiority. In 1955, the modern civil rights movement began. The Civil Rights Act of 1964 bans discrimination in employment and public accommodations on the basis of race, color, religion, gender, or national origin. The Voting Rights Act of 1965 outlawed discriminatory voter-registration tests and authorized federal voter registration.

≫LO2 The Supreme Court uses various standards when assessing the constitutionality of laws and government actions. Strict scrutiny applies to basic civil liberties and to the rights of racial, religious, and ethnic minorities. Intermediate, or exacting, scrutiny is used to consider claims of discrimination against women. Rational basis review is the easiest standard for the government to meet, but it has been used to protect gay men and lesbians.

Affirmative action programs are controversial because they could lead to reverse discrimination against majority groups or even other minority groups. Supreme Court decisions have limited affirmative action programs, and several states now ban state-sponsored affirmative action.

≫LO3 Today, most immigrants come from Asia and Latin America, especially Mexico. Many are unauthorized (or illegal) immigrants. Most came to find jobs, but their status is a major political issue.

The percentage of Latinos, or Hispanic Americans, in the population is growing rapidly. While Latinos who are citizens benefit from the same antidiscrimination protections as African Americans, immigrants who are not citizens have few civil rights.

Uniquely among minority groups, American Indians experienced demographic collapse upon the arrival of the Europeans in the New World. They continue to face high levels of poverty.

≫LO4 In the early history of the United States, women had no political rights. The first women's rights convention was held in 1848. Not until 1920, with the Nineteenth Amendment, did women finally obtain the right to vote in all states. The modern women's movement began in the 1960s in the wake of the civil rights and anti–Vietnam War movements. Efforts to secure the ratification of the Equal Rights Amendment failed, but the women's movement was successful in obtaining new laws, changes in social customs, and increased political representation.

Federal government efforts to eliminate gender discrimination in the workplace include Title VII of the Civil Rights Act of 1964, which prohibits gender-based discrimination, including sexual harassment on the job.

≫LO5 In 2003, a Supreme Court decision effectively invalidated all remaining sodomy laws which criminalized specific sexual practices. Many states, cities, and counties now have laws prohibiting at least some types of discrimination based on sexual orientation. Gay men and lesbians gained the right to serve openly in the military in 2011. In 2015, the Supreme Court established a constitutional right to same-sex marriage. Recently, the rights of transgender persons have become a major issue.

Test Yourself

1. The separate-but-equal doctrine was:
   a. addressed by the Supreme Court in *Plessy v. Ferguson*.
   b. addressed by the Supreme Court in *Roe v. Wade*.
   c. never addressed by the Supreme Court.

2. Barriers to African American voting established between the Civil War and the civil rights movement included all except:
   a. grandfather clauses.
   b. poll taxes.
   c. property qualifications.

3. Segregation that does not follow from discriminatory laws or government actions, but from other causes, is called:
   a. *de jure* segregation.
   b. *de facto* segregation.
   c. extralegal discrimination.

4. The Fourteenth Amendment requires that no state shall deprive any person of life, liberty, or property, without:
   a. due process of law.
   b. rational basis review.
   c. compensation.

5. The federal courts employ the following standard when evaluating differential treatment by race:
   a. rational basis review.
   b. intermediate, or exacting, scrutiny.
   c. strict scrutiny.

6. In educational admissions and employment, affirmative action programs have:
   a. awarded preferences to minority group members.
   b. relied on numerical quotas to improve outcomes.
   c. involved federal grants to complying institutions.

7. Currently, the largest immigrant group living in the United States comes from:
   a. China.
   b. Mexico.
   c. India.

8. The courts have placed serious restrictions on the rights of persons who are:
   a. living on Indian reservations.
   b. not fluent in English.
   c. subject to deportation.

9. In the years following the European discovery of America, the number of American Indians:
   a. rose because of the introduction of new foodstuffs.
   b. fell because of the introduction of new diseases.
   c. remained about the same for many years.

10. The Equal Rights Amendment today requires:
    a. that women be treated equally to men.
    b. that women be treated equally in the labor market.
    c. nothing at all, because the Equal Rights Amendment never passed.

11. Sexual harassment in the workplace can involve all except:
    a. rules that provide unequal pay for women.
    b. giving benefits in return for sexual favors.
    c. sexual conduct or comments that create a seriously hostile environment.

12. The Defense of Marriage Act (DOMA) provided for all of the following except:
    a. states were not required to recognize same-sex marriages conducted in other states.
    b. states were not required to recognize divorces obtained in other states.
    c. the federal government was barred from recognizing same-sex marriages when awarding benefits or collecting taxes.

Essay Questions

1. Not all African Americans agreed with the philosophy of nonviolence espoused by Dr. Martin Luther King, Jr. Advocates of black power called for a more militant approach. Can militancy make a movement more effective, or is it typically counterproductive? Either way, why?

2. The prevention of terrorist acts committed by adherents of radical Islamism is a major policy objective today. Can we defend ourselves against such acts without abridging the civil rights and liberties of American Muslims? Explain your reasoning.

Answers to multiple-choice questions: 1. a, 2. c, 3. b, 4. a, 5. c, 6. a, 7. b, 8. c, 9. b, 10. c, 11. a, 12. b.

6 | Public Opinion, Political Socialization, and the Media

A crowd of reporters surrounds Donald Trump as he arrives in Detroit for a debate among Republican presidential candidates. *Why are the debates leading up to the presidential primary elections important?*

Chip Somodevilla/Getty Images News/Getty Images

The six **Learning Outcomes (LOs)** below are designed to help improve your understanding of this chapter. After reading this chapter, you should be able to:

>>>**LO1** Define *public opinion*, *consensus*, and *divided opinion*, and discuss major sources of political socialization, including the family, the schools, the media, and political events.

>>>**LO2** Identify the effects of various influences on opinion, including education, income, religion, race/ethnicity, gender, and geography.

>>>**LO3** Describe the characteristics of a scientific opinion poll, and list some of the problems pollsters face in obtaining accurate results.

>>>**LO4** Consider the effect that public opinion may have on the political process.

>>>**LO5** Describe the different types of media and the changing roles they play in American society.

>>>**LO6** Summarize the impact of the media on political campaigns, and consider the issue of political bias in the media.

Check your understanding of the material with the Test Yourself section at the end of the chapter.

In a democracy, the ability of the people to freely express their opinions is fundamental. Americans can express their opinions in many ways. They can write letters to newspapers. They can share their ideas in online forums. They can organize politically. They can vote. They can respond to opinion polls.

Leaders of the Republican Party were reminded of the importance of public opinion during the 2016 Republican primary elections, won by businessman Donald Trump. Most Republican leaders supported a conservatism based on small government and free markets.

Tax-rate cuts for the richest Americans were the number-one issue. Spending on programs such as Social Security and Medicare should be controlled, if not cut. Foreign trade was a blessing, and quite a few believed that compromise on immigration was at least conceivable. These positions matched the preferences of the *donor class*—the multimillionaires who provide much Republican campaign funding. Many ordinary Republicans, however, had other ideas. Often, they depended on programs such as Social Security. Many believed, with some reason, that imports damaged the lives of American workers, despite the benefits to the overall economy. With less reason, they believed immigration was damaging as well. With Trump, these were the beliefs that won the primaries, to the shock of traditional small-government conservatives.

There is no doubt that public opinion can be powerful. The extent to which public opinion affects policymaking is not always so clear, however. For example, suppose that public opinion strongly supports a certain policy. If political leaders adopt that position, is it because they are responding to public opinion or because they share the public's beliefs? Also, political leaders themselves can shape public opinion to a degree.

Public Opinion
The aggregate of individual attitudes or beliefs shared by some portion of the population.

Consensus
General agreement among the citizenry on an issue.

Divided Opinion
Public opinion that is polarized between two different positions.

Public Opinion and Political Socialization

>>> **LO1:** Define *public opinion, consensus,* and *divided opinion*, and discuss major sources of political socialization, including the family, the schools, the media, and political events.

There is no single public opinion, because there are many different "publics." In a nation of 325 million people, there may be innumerable gradations of opinion on an issue. What we do is describe the distribution of opinions about a particular question. Thus, we define **public opinion** as the aggregate of individual attitudes or beliefs shared by some portion of the adult population.

Consensus and Divided Opinion

Typically, public opinion is distributed among several different positions, and the distribution of opinion can tell us how divided the public is on an issue and whether compromise is possible. When polls show that a large proportion of the respondents (those who respond to a poll) appears to express the same view on an issue, we say that a **consensus** exists, at least at the moment the poll was taken. Figure 6–1 shows a pattern of opinion that might be called consensual. Issues on which the public holds widely differing attitudes result in **divided opinion** (see Figure 6–2).

An interesting question arises as to when *private* opinion becomes *public* opinion. Everyone probably has a private opinion about the competence of the president, as well as about more personal concerns, such as the state of

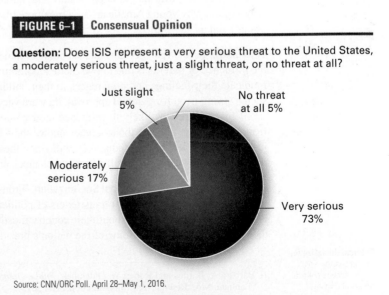

FIGURE 6–1   Consensual Opinion

Question: Does ISIS represent a very serious threat to the United States, a moderately serious threat, just a slight threat, or no threat at all?

Just slight 5%

No threat at all 5%

Moderately serious 17%

Very serious 73%

Source: CNN/ORC Poll. April 28–May 1, 2016.

FIGURE 6–2   Divided Opinion

Question: Do you favor or oppose the United States sending ground troops into combat operations against ISIS forces in Iraq or Syria?

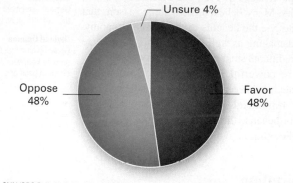

Unsure 4%

Oppose 48%

Favor 48%

Source: CNN/ORC Poll. April 28–May 1, 2016.

a neighbor's lawn. We say that private opinion becomes public opinion when the opinion is publicly expressed and concerns public issues. When someone's private opinion becomes so strong that the individual is willing to express it, then the opinion becomes public opinion.

Forming Public Opinion: Political Socialization

Most Americans are willing to express opinions on political issues when asked. How do people acquire these opinions and attitudes? Typically, views that are expressed as political opinions are acquired through the process of **political socialization**. By this, we mean that people acquire their political beliefs and values, often including their political party identification, through relationships with their families, friends, and co-workers.

The most important early sources of political socialization are the family and the schools. Individuals' basic political orientations are formed in the family if other family members hold strong views. When the adults in a family view politics as relatively unimportant and describe themselves as independent voters or disaffected from the political system, however, children may receive very little political socialization.

In the past few decades, more and more sources of information about politics have become available to all Americans, especially to young people through the Internet, and in particular through social media. Thus, although their basic outlook on the political system still may be formed by early family influences, young people are now exposed to many other sources of information about issues and values. This greater access to information may explain why young Americans are often more liberal than their parents on certain social issues such as gay rights.

The Family. How do parents transmit their political values to their offspring? Studies suggest that the influence of parents is due to two factors: communication and receptivity. Parents communicate their feelings and preferences to their children constantly. Because children have such a strong need for parental approval, they are very receptive to their parents' views.

Children are less likely to influence their parents, because parents expect deference from their children.[1] Nevertheless, other studies show that if children are exposed to political ideas at school and in the media, they will share these ideas with their parents, giving the parents what some scholars call a "second chance" at political socialization.

Education as a Source of Political Socialization. From the early days of the republic, schools were perceived to be important transmitters of political information and attitudes. Children in the primary grades learn about their country mostly in patriotic ways. They learn about the Pilgrims, the flag, and some of the nation's presidents. By high school, students have a

Political Socialization
The process by which people acquire political beliefs and values.

1. Barbara A. Bardes and Robert W. Oldendick, *Public Opinion: Measuring the American Mind*, 4th ed. (Lanham, Md.: Rowman & Littlefield Publishers, 2012).

more complex understanding of the political system. Generally, the more education a person receives, the more likely it is that the person will be interested in politics, be confident in his or her ability to understand political issues, and be an active participant in the political process.

Peers and Peer Group Influence. Once a child enters school, the child's friends become an important influence on behavior and attitudes. For children and for adults, friendships and associations in **peer groups** affect political attitudes. We must, however, separate the effects of peer group pressure on attitudes in general from the effects of peer group pressure on political opinions. For the most part, associations among peers are nonpolitical. Political attitudes are more likely to be shaped by peer groups when those groups are involved directly in political activities. For example, individuals who share an ethnic identity may find a common political bond through working for the group's civil liberties and rights.

Opinion Leaders' Influence. We are all influenced by those with whom we are closely associated or whom we hold in high regard—friends at school, family members and other relatives, and teachers. In a sense, these people are **opinion leaders,** but on an *informal* level. That is, their influence on our political views is not necessarily intentional or deliberate. We are also influenced by *formal* opinion leaders, such as presidents, lobbyists, congresspersons, news commentators, and religious leaders, who have as part of their jobs the task of swaying people's views.

The Media and Public Opinion

Clearly, the **media**—newspapers, television, radio, and Internet sources—strongly influence public opinion. This is because the media inform the public about the issues and events of our times and thus have an **agenda-setting** effect. Consider Bernard Cohen's classic statement about the media and public opinion: the media may not be successful in telling people what to think, but they are "stunningly successful in telling their audience what to think about."[2]

The Popularity of the Media. Today, many contend that the media's influence on public opinion has grown to equal that of the family. For example, in her analysis of the role played by the media in American politics,[3] media scholar Doris A. Graber points out that high school students, when asked where they obtain the information on which they base their views, mention the mass media far more than they mention their families, friends, and teachers.

The Impact of the New Media. The extent to which new forms of media have supplanted older ones—such as newspapers and the major broadcast networks—has been a major topic of discussion for several years. New forms include not only the Internet but also talk radio and cable television. Talk radio would seem to be a very dated medium, given that radio first became important early in the twentieth century. Between 1949 and 1987, however, the Federal Communications Commission (FCC) enforced the *Fairness Doctrine*, which required radio and television to present controversial issues in a manner that was (in the FCC's view) honest, equitable, and balanced. Modern conservative talk radio took off only after the Fairness Doctrine was abolished.

New Methods for Spreading Opinion. The impact of the various forms of new media appears to vary considerably. Talk radio and cable networks such as Fox News have given conservatives new methods for promoting their views and socializing their audiences. It is possible, however,

Peer Group
A group consisting of members who share common social characteristics. Such groups play an important part in the socialization process, helping to shape attitudes and beliefs.

Opinion Leader
One who is able to influence the opinions of others because of position, expertise, or personality.

Media
The channels of mass communication.

Agenda Setting
Determining which public-policy questions will be debated or considered.

---

2. Bernard C. Cohen, *The Press and Foreign Policy* (Princeton, N.J.: Princeton University Press, 1963; repr. 2016), p. 81.
3. Doris A. Graber, *On Media: Making Sense of Politics* (Boulder, Colo.: Paradigm Publishers, 2011).

His Holiness Pope Francis at the Cathedral Basilica of Saints Peter and Paul in Philadelphia. *Why might this pope be an opinion leader for many people who are not Catholic?*

that such media mostly strengthen the beliefs of those who are already conservative, rather than recruiting new members to the political right. Indeed, cable news and talk radio are widely blamed for the increased polarization that has characterized American politics in recent years. A similar observation is often made about political blogs on the Internet, although in this medium liberals may be better represented than conservatives.

Social Media. The impact of social-networking sites is more ambiguous. Facebook, for example, does have strongly political "pages" that, in effect, are political blogs. Many interactions on Facebook, however, are between members of peer groups, such as students who attend a particular school or individuals who work in the same profession. Members of such groups are more likely to hold a variety of views than are members of groups explicitly organized around a political viewpoint. Facebook, in other words, may enhance peer group influence.

Political Events and Public Opinion

Generally, older Americans tend to be somewhat more conservative than younger Americans—particularly on social issues but also, to some extent, on economic issues. This effect probably occurs because older adults are likely to retain the social values that they learned years ago when various kinds of inequality were more widely accepted. Nevertheless, a more important factor than a person's age may be the impact of momentous political events that shape the political attitudes of an entire generation. When events produce such a long-lasting result, we refer to it as a **generational effect** (also called the *cohort effect*).

Working-class voters who grew up in the 1930s during the Great Depression were likely to form lifelong attachments to the Democratic Party, the party of Franklin D. Roosevelt. In the 1960s and 1970s, the war in Vietnam, the Watergate break-in, and the subsequent presidential cover-up fostered widespread cynicism toward government. (The Watergate break-in was the 1972 illegal entry into Democratic National Committee offices by members of President Richard Nixon's reelection organization.) There is evidence that the years of economic prosperity under President Ronald Reagan during the 1980s led many young people to identify with the Republican Party. The high level of support that younger voters gave to Barack Obama may be good news for the Democratic Party in future years, although it was insufficient to propel the Democrats to victory in many recent elections.

Generational effects can be complicated by the widely recognized phenomenon of nostalgia. Throughout recorded history, older individuals have tended to view the world of their youth more positively than the world in which they currently live. As a presidential candidate, Donald Trump appealed to this tendency with the slogan "Make America Great Again."

Generational Effect
A long-lasting effect of the events of a particular time on the political opinions of those who came of political age at that time.

a katz/Shutterstock

The Influence of Demographic Factors

>>> **LO2:** Identify the effects of various influences on opinion, including education, income, religion, race/ethnicity, gender, and geography.

Demographic characteristics, such as education, income, religion, race/ethnicity, gender, and geographic location, are strongly correlated with political party preferences and political ideologies. Table 6–1 illustrates the impact of some of these variables on voting behavior.

Educational Achievement

In the past, having a college education tended to be associated with voting for Republicans. In recent years, however, this correlation has become weaker. In particular, individuals with a postgraduate education—more than a bachelor's degree—have become predominantly Democratic. Many people with postgraduate degrees are professionals, such as physicians, attorneys, and college instructors. In the 2016 primary and general elections, many observers remarked on the tendency of less-well-educated white voters to support Republican Donald Trump. Some even saw Trump as representing the white working class as a whole, using education as a marker for socioeconomic status. There are plenty of less-well-educated white Democrats, however. In the Democratic primaries, such persons often voted for Vermont senator Bernie Sanders.

Economic Status

Family income is a strong predictor of economic liberalism or conservatism. Those with low incomes tend to favor government action to benefit the poor or to promote economic equality. Those with high incomes tend to oppose government intervention in the economy or to support it only when it benefits business. The rich often tend toward the right and the poor often lean toward the left.

If we examine cultural as well as economic issues, however, the four-cornered ideological grid discussed at the beginning of this book becomes important. It happens that upper-class voters are more likely to endorse cultural liberalism, and lower-class individuals are more likely to favor cultural conservatism. Support for the right to have an abortion, for example, rises with income. It follows that libertarians—those who oppose government action on both economic and social issues—are concentrated among the wealthier members of the population. (Libertarians constitute the upper-right-hand corner of the four-cornered grid.) Those who favor government action both to promote traditional moral values and to promote economic equality—economic liberals, cultural conservatives—are concentrated among groups that are less well off. (This group fills up the lower-left-hand corner of the grid.) That said, it remains generally true that the higher a person's income, the more likely that person will be to vote Republican.

Religious Denomination

Traditionally, scholars have examined the impact of religion on political attitudes by dividing the population into such categories as Protestant, Catholic, and Jewish. In recent decades, however, such a breakdown has become less valuable as a means of predicting someone's political preferences. It is true that Jewish voters, as they were in the past, are notably more liberal than members of other groups on both economic and cultural issues. Persons reporting no religion are very liberal on social issues but have mixed economic views. White Protestants and non-Hispanic Catholics, however, have grown closer to each other politically

TABLE 6–1   Votes by Groups in Presidential Elections, 2000–2016 (in Percentages)

Why do African Americans and Hispanics tend to support Democrats?

	2000		2004		2008		2012		2016	
	Gore (Dem.)	Bush (Rep.)	Kerry (Dem.)	Bush (Rep.)	Obama (Dem.)	McCain (Rep.)	Obama (Dem.)	Romney (Rep.)	Clinton (Dem.)	Trump (Rep.)
Total vote	48	48	48	51	53	46	51	47	48	46
Gender										
Men	42	53	44	55	49	48	45	52	41	53
Women	54	43	51	48	56	43	55	44	54	42
Race or ethnicity										
White	42	54	41	58	43	55	39	59	37	58
Black	90	8	88	11	95	4	93	6	88	8
Hispanic	67	31	58	40[a]	67	31	71	27	65	29
Educational attainment										
Not a high school graduate	59	39	50	50	63	35	54	35	45	51[b]
High school only	48	49	47	52	52	46	51	48	43	52[c]
College graduate	45	51	46	52	50	48	47	51	49	45
Postgraduate education	52	44	54	45	58	40	55	42	58	37
Religion										
White Protestant	34	63	32	68	34	65	30	69[d]	37	60
Catholic	49	47	47	52	54	45	50	48	45	52
Jewish	79	19	75	24	78	21	69	30	71	24
White evangelical	NA	NA	21	79	24	74	21	78	16	81
Union status										
Union household	59	37	59	40	59	39	58	40	51	43
Family income										
Under $15,000	57	37	63	37	73	25	NA	NA	NA	NA
$15,000–29,000	54	41	57	41	60	37	63	35[e]	53	41
$30,000–49,000	49	48	50	49	55	43	57	42	51	42
Over $50,000	45	52	43	56	49	49	45	53	47	49
Size of place of residence										
Population over 500,000	71	26	60	40	70	28	69	29	59	35[f]
Population 50,000–500,000	57	40	50	50	59	39	58	40	45	50[g]
Population 10,000–50,000	38	59	48	51	45	53	42	56	NA	NA
Rural	37	59	39	60	45	53	37	61	34	62

NA = Not asked.

[a]The official figure reported by the National Election Pool was 44. Studies later proved that this figure was impossibly high. NBC News lowered it to 40, but even that figure may be somewhat too high. The 2016 figure for Trump had similar problems.

[b]In 2016, "high school or less."

[c]In 2016, "some college."

[d]In 2012 and 2016, Protestant or "other Christian."

[e]In 2012 and 2016, below $30,000.

[f]In 2016, "urban."

[g]In 2016, "suburban."

Sources: *New York Times;* Voter News Service; CBS News; and National Election Pool.

in recent years. This represents something of a change—in the late 1800s and early 1900s, northern Protestants were distinctly more likely to vote Republican, and northern Catholics were more likely to vote Democratic. Even now, in a few parts of the country, Protestants and Catholics tend to line up against each other when choosing a political party.

Religious Commitment and Beliefs

Today, two factors turn out to be major predictors of political attitudes among members of the various Christian denominations. One factor is the degree of religious commitment, as measured by such actions as regular churchgoing. The other is the degree to which the voter adheres to religious beliefs that (depending on the denomination) can be called conservative, evangelical, or fundamentalist. High scores on either factor are associated with cultural conservatism on political issues—that is, with beliefs that place a high value on social order.

In 2016, for example, 55 percent of those who attended services weekly voted for Republican candidate Donald Trump, compared with 46 percent of those who attended services a few times a year. Even though Trump's background revealed little evidence of religious commitment, many of the faithful expressed confidence that he would defend their interests. There is an exception to this trend—African Americans of all religious tendencies have been strongly supportive of Democrats.

The politics of white Protestant Americans who can be identified as holding evangelical or fundamentalist beliefs deserve special attention. Actually, a majority of American Protestants can be characterized as evangelical. Beliefs common to evangelicals include the ultimate authority of the Bible, the importance of a conversion experience (being "born again"), and that God's gift of salvation is limited to those who accept Christ. Not all evangelicals are politically conservative. Some are politically liberal, such as former Democratic presidents Jimmy Carter and Bill Clinton.

Fundamentalists are a subset of evangelicals who believe in a number of doctrines not held by all evangelicals. In particular, fundamentalists believe in biblical inerrancy—that is, that every word of the Bible is literally true. In politics, fundamentalists are notably more conservative than other evangelicals. Liberal fundamentalists are rare indeed.[4]

Race and Ethnicity

African Americans, on average, are somewhat conservative on certain cultural issues, such as gay rights and abortion. Yet they tend to be more liberal than whites on social-welfare matters, civil liberties, and even foreign policy. African Americans voted principally for Republicans until Democrat Franklin D. Roosevelt's New Deal in the 1930s. Since then, they have largely identified with the Democratic Party. Indeed, Democratic presidential candidates have received, on average, more than 80 percent of the African American vote since 1956. Of course, Barack Obama's support among African Americans was overwhelming.

Most Asian American groups lean toward the Democrats, although Vietnamese Americans tend to be Republican. Most Vietnamese Americans left Vietnam because of the Communist victory in the Vietnam War, and their strong anticommunism translates into conservative politics.

Muslim American immigrants and their descendants make up an interesting category.[5] In 2000, a majority of Muslim Americans of Middle Eastern ancestry voted for Republican

---

4. Douglas A. Sweeney, *The American Evangelical Story: A History of the Movement* (Grand Rapids, Mich.: Baker Academic, 2005).
5. About one-third of U.S. Muslims are actually African Americans whose ancestors have been in this country for a long time. In terms of political preferences, African American Muslims are more likely to resemble other African Americans than Muslim immigrants from the Middle East.

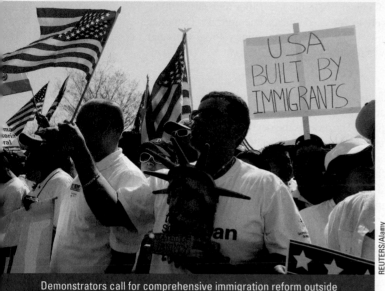

Demonstrators call for comprehensive immigration reform outside the Capitol building in Washington, D.C. *What kinds of changes to immigration policy are likely under President Donald Trump?*

REUTERS/Alamy

George W. Bush because they shared his cultural conservatism. By 2016, the issues of Muslim civil liberties and discrimination against Muslims had turned Islamic voters into one of the nation's most Democratic blocs.

The Hispanic Vote

The diversity among Hispanic Americans has resulted in differing political behavior. The majority of Hispanic Americans vote Democratic. Cuban Americans, however, are often Republican. Most Cuban Americans left Cuba because of Fidel Castro's Communist regime. As in the example of the Vietnamese, anticommunism leads to political conservatism. By 2016, however, increasing numbers of young Cuban Americans were supporting the Democrats.

In 2004, Republican presidential candidate George W. Bush may have received almost 40 percent of the Latino vote. In 2008, however, Barack Obama won more than two-thirds of the Latino vote. Why did Hispanic support for the Republicans fall so sharply? In a word: immigration. Bush favored a comprehensive immigration reform that would have granted unauthorized immigrants a path to citizenship. Most Republicans in Congress, however, refused to support Bush on this issue. The harsh rhetoric of some Republicans convinced many Latinos that the Republicans were hostile to Hispanic interests.

Following the 2012 elections, some Republicans advocated a more welcoming line toward unauthorized immigrants in hopes of winning Hispanic support. Most Republicans rejected this proposal, however. In 2016, Republicans nominated Donald Trump as their presidential candidate, and Trump's hostility toward immigrants may alienate Latinos from the Republicans for years to come.

The Gender Gap

Women won the right to vote in all states in 1920, and through the 1960 elections they gave somewhat more support to Republicans than men did. From 1964 through 1976, women did not demonstrate a clear partisan preference. Beginning in 1980, however, with the election of Ronald Reagan, scholars began to detect a **gender gap.** Women were now favoring the Democrats. In 2016, 54 percent of women voted for Democrat Hillary Clinton, compared with 41 percent of men, a gap of 13 percentage points. Clinton, of course, was the first female major-party candidate for president in U.S. history, and Republican Donald Trump was famous for his rude remarks about women.

Women's attitudes also appear to differ from those of their male counterparts on a range of issues other than presidential preferences. They are much more likely than men to oppose capital punishment and the use of force abroad. Studies also have shown that women are more concerned about risks to the environment, more supportive of social welfare, and more in agreement with extending civil rights to gay men and lesbians than are men.

Gender Gap
The difference between the percentage of women who vote for a particular candidate and the percentage of men who vote for the candidate.

Geographic Region

Finally, where you live can influence your political attitudes. In 2012, many commentators suggested that the white working class was hostile to Obama. This conclusion was not entirely accurate. Obama matched Romney's white working class vote in the East and West, and carried that vote in the Midwest. In the South, however, the overwhelming majority of all classes of whites voted Republican. That vote certainly included the white working class. Donald Trump, of course, improved considerably on Romney's performance among white working class voters in the three northern regions, especially in the Midwest. Opposition to Obama and to Clinton was strongest among those who saw themselves culturally as Southerners—that is, as persons who identified with the losing side in the American Civil War.

The split between the city and the countryside is almost as important as the one between the North and the South. Romney did much better than Obama—and Trump did much better than Clinton—in rural areas.

Measuring Public Opinion

>>> **LO3:** Describe the characteristics of a scientific opinion poll, and list some of the problems pollsters face in obtaining accurate results.

In a democracy, people express their opinions in a variety of ways, as mentioned in this chapter's introduction. One of the most common means of gathering and measuring public opinion on specific issues is through the use of **opinion polls.**

The History of Opinion Polls

During the 1800s, certain American newspapers and magazines spiced up their political coverage by conducting face-to-face polls or mail surveys of their readers' opinions. In the early twentieth century, the magazine *Literary Digest* mailed large numbers of questionnaires to individuals, many of whom were its own subscribers, to determine their political opinions. From 1916 to 1932, more than 70 percent of the magazine's election predictions were accurate.

In 1936, however, the magazine predicted that Republican Alfred Landon would defeat Democrat Franklin D. Roosevelt in the presidential race. Landon won in only two states. A major problem was that in 1936, several years into the Great Depression, the *Digest*'s subscribers were considerably wealthier than the average American. In other words, they did not accurately represent all the voters in the U.S. population.

Several newcomers to the public opinion poll industry accurately predicted Roosevelt's landslide victory. These newcomers are still active in the poll-taking industry today: the Gallup poll of George Gallup and the Roper poll, founded by Elmo Roper. Gallup and Roper, along with Archibald Crossley, developed the modern polling techniques of market research. Using personal interviews with small samples of selected voters (fewer than two thousand), they showed that they could predict with relative accuracy the behavior of the total voting population.

Sampling Techniques

How can interviewing fewer than two thousand voters tell us what tens of millions of voters will do? Clearly, it is necessary that the sample of individuals be representative of all voters in the population.

The most important principle in sampling is randomness. Every person should have a known chance, and in particular an *equal chance*, of being sampled. If sampling follows this principle, then a small sample should be representative of the whole group, both in

Opinion Poll
A method of systematically questioning a small, selected sample of respondents who are deemed representative of the total population.

Polling expert Nate Silver (center) with his colleagues Micah Cohen and Harry Enten. Silver was almost alone in saying that Trump could win despite the polls. His Fivethirtyeight blog is now sponsored by ESPN. *In what ways do politics resemble sports?*

Andrew Toth/Getty Images

demographic characteristics (age, religion, race, region, and the like) and in opinions. The ideal way to sample the voting population of the United States would be to put all voter names into a jar—or a computer file—and randomly sample, say, two thousand of them. Because this is too costly and inefficient, pollsters have developed other ways to obtain good samples. One technique is simply to randomly select telephone numbers and interview the respective households. This technique used to produce a relatively accurate sample at a low cost.

The Statistical Nature of Polling. Universally, when the results of an opinion poll are announced, the findings are reported as specific numbers. A poll might find, for example, that 10 percent of those surveyed approve of the job performance of Congress. Such precise figures can mislead you as to the essential nature of polling. In reality, it makes more sense to consider the results of a particular survey question as a range of numbers, not a single integer. That would mean that the question about Congress's job performance yielded an answer that fell somewhere between 7 percent and 13 percent. The figure of 10 percent is only the midpoint of the possible spread—the most probable result. If we had been able to question all members of the public, the chances that they would give Congress exactly a 10 percent rating are not high. Even if the pollster in this case employed the best possible practices, the odds are better than 50-50 that the true answer is not 10 percent, but some other number in the 7–13 percent range.

Sampling Error. Reputable polling firms report the margin of error associated with their results. The results of a carefully conducted poll that surveys a large number of respondents—say, two thousand people—might have a 95 percent chance of falling within a 3 point margin of error. The 95 percent figure is an industry standard. What this means, however, is that the pollster believes that any given poll result has a 5 percent chance of landing four or more percentage points away from the true answer, which we would get if we really could interview everyone. In the example of the question about Congress, there is a 5 percent chance—one chance in twenty—that the approval rating is actually below 7 percent or above 13 percent.

These variations are called **sampling error.** They follow from the fact that the poll taker is examining a sample and not the entire population. Sampling error is one reason that knowledgeable poll watchers disregard small variations in poll results. Gallup, for example, polls the public on its approval of the president's job performance every day. Such continuous polls are known as **tracking polls.** Suppose that on Monday, the tracking poll shows that the president has a 45 percent approval rating. On Tuesday, it is 47 percent; on Wednesday, 46 percent; and on Thursday, 43 percent. Was the president really more popular on Tuesday and Wednesday? Almost certainly not. These variations are simply so much "statistical noise."

Sampling Error
The difference between a sample result and the true result if the entire population had been interviewed.

Tracking Poll
A poll that is taken continuously—sometimes every day—to determine how support for an issue or candidate changes over time.

The Difficulty of Obtaining Accurate Results

Reputable polling organizations devote substantial effort to ensuring that their samples are truly random. If they succeed, then the accuracy of their results should be limited only by sampling error. Unfortunately, obtaining a completely random sample of the population is difficult. Women are more likely to answer the telephone than men. Some kinds of people, such as students and low-income individuals, are relatively hard to contact.

Many poll takers now rely on automated scripts—*"robocalls"*—rather than live interviewers. Under the law, however, robocallers are not allowed to dial cell phones. As a result, automated surveys are less accurate than traditional ones. Pollsters currently have no way at all to reach people who rely on Skype or similar systems for telephone service. Finally, more than 85 percent of households contacted by typical polls refuse to be interviewed.

Weighting the Sample. Polling firms address this problem of obtaining a true random sample by weighting their samples. That is, they correct for differences between the sample and the public by adding extra "weight" to the responses of underrepresented groups. For example, 20 percent of the respondents in a survey might state that they are evangelical Christians. Based on other sources of information, the poll taker believes that the true share of evangelicals in the target population is 25 percent. Therefore, the responses of the evangelical respondents receive extra weight so that they make up 25 percent of the reported result.

It is relatively easy to correct a sample for well-known demographic characteristics such as education, gender, race/ethnicity, religion, and geography. It is much harder—and more risky—to adjust for political ideology, partisan preference, or likelihood of voting. The formulas that firms use to weight their responses are typically trade secrets and are not disclosed to the public or the press.

House Effects. One consequence of the use of secret in-house weighting schemes is that the results reported by one polling firm may differ systematically from those reported by another. Pollster A might consistently rate the chances of Republican candidates as 2 percentage points higher than does pollster B. A consistent difference in polling results between firms is known as a **house effect**. (*House* here means the organization or firm, as when referring to casinos.) House effects are measured by comparing a firm's results with the average results of all other poll takers. A house effect does not mean that a firm's results are in error. It could be noticing something important that its rivals have missed.

How Accurate Are the Results? Despite all of the practical difficulties involved in poll taking, the major polling organizations have usually enjoyed a good record in predicting the outcome of presidential contests. (Predicting primary elections and state-level races is harder.) Some major poll takers, however, have reported presidential results that were embarrassingly inaccurate. In 2016, almost all poll takers predicted that Hillary Clinton would win the presidency. She did not. Of course, polls attempt to predict the national popular vote, which Clinton won by 2 percentage points. Most polls still overstated her support at the national level. In addition, polls in the states essential to Trump's victory—Michigan, Pennsylvania, and Wisconsin—should have signaled trouble for Clinton. They didn't. Figure 6–3 shows the 2016 presidential predictions of several prominent pollsters.

Additional Problems with Polls

Public opinion polls are snapshots of the opinions and preferences of the people at a specific moment in time and as expressed in response to a specific question. Given that definition, it is fairly easy to understand situations in which the polls are wrong. For example, opinion polls leading up to the 1980 presidential elections showed President Jimmy Carter defeating challenger Ronald Reagan. Only a few analysts noted the large number of

House Effect
In public opinion polling, an effect in which one polling organization's results consistently differ from those reported by other poll takers.

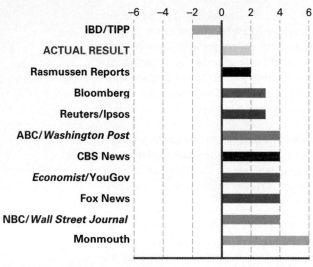

FIGURE 6–3 Hillary Clinton's Predicted Margin over Donald Trump

Normally, a 2-percentage-point margin in the popular vote will guarantee a presidential candidate a victory in the electoral college. That did not happen in 2016. Only IBD/TIPP correctly predicted Trump's win—yet its prediction was 4 points away from the true popular vote result, an error comparable to the one made by Monmouth. *Why is it hard for pollsters to factor in the effects of the electoral college on a presidential election?*

Source: RealClearPolitics blog.

"undecided" respondents a week before the election. Those voters shifted massively to Reagan at the last minute, and Reagan won the election.

A similar development helped elect Donald Trump in 2016. At the last minute, the share of the electorate swinging from "undecided" to Trump was about 2 percentage points larger than the share that swung to Clinton. The result was that most poll takers predicted that Clinton would do about 2 percentage points better in the popular vote than she actually did, as you can see in Figure 6–3.

Poll Questions. It makes sense to expect that the results of a poll will reflect the questions that are asked. Depending on what question is asked, voters could be said either to support a particular proposal or to oppose it. One of the problems with many polls is the yes/no answer format. For example, suppose that a poll question asks, "Do you favor arming the rebels in Syria?" A respondent who has a complicated view of these events, as many people do, has no way of indicating this view because "yes" and "no" are the only possible answers.

How a question is phrased can change the polling outcome dramatically. The Roper polling organization once asked a double-negative question that many people found hard to understand: "Does it seem possible or does it seem impossible to you that the Nazi extermination of the Jews never happened?" The survey results showed that 20 percent of Americans seemed to doubt that the Holocaust ever occurred. When the Roper organization rephrased the question more clearly, the percentage of doubters dropped to less than 1 percent.

Respondents' answers are also influenced by the order in which questions are asked and, in some cases, by their interactions with the interviewer. To a certain extent, people try to please the interviewer.

Unscientific and Fraudulent Polls. A perennial issue is the promotion of surveys that are unscientific or even fraudulent. All too often, a magazine or website asks its readers to respond to a question—and then publishes the answers as if they were based on a scientifically chosen random sample. Other news media may then publicize the survey as if it were a poll taken by such reliable teams as Gallup, CBS and the *New York Times*, or the *Wall Street Journal* and NBC. Critical consumers should watch out for surveys with self-selected respondents and other types of skewed samples. These so-called polls may be used to deliberately mislead the public. In addition, some campaigns have used *push polls*, in which the respondents are given misleading information in the questions, in an effort to persuade them to vote against a particular candidate.

Public Opinion and the Political Process

>>> **LO4:** Consider the effect that public opinion may have on the political process.

Public opinion affects the political process in many ways. Politicians see public opinion as important to their careers. The president, members of Congress, governors, and other elected officials realize that strong support by the public as expressed in opinion polls is a source of power in dealing with other politicians. It is more difficult for a senator to say no to the president if the president is immensely popular and if polls show approval of the president's policies. Public opinion also helps political candidates identify voters' most important concerns and may help them shape their campaigns successfully.

Political Culture and Public Opinion

Americans are divided into a multitude of ethnic, religious, regional, and political subgroups. Given the diversity of American society and the wide range of opinions contained within it, how is it that the political process continues to function without falling into chaos?

One explanation is rooted in the concept of the American political culture, which can be described as a set of attitudes and ideas about the nation and the government. As discussed earlier, our political culture is widely shared by Americans of many different backgrounds. To some extent, it consists of symbols, such as the American flag, the Liberty Bell, and the Statue of Liberty. The elements of our political culture also include certain shared beliefs about the most important values in the American political system, including liberty, equality, and property.

The political culture provides a general environment of support for the political system. If the people share certain beliefs about the system and a reservoir of good feeling exists toward the institutions of government, the nation will be better able to weather periods of crisis.

The political culture also helps Americans evaluate their government's performance. **Political trust,** the degree to which individuals express trust in political institutions, has been measured by a variety of polling questions. One of these is whether the respondent is satisfied with "the way things are going in the United States." As you can see in Figure 6–4, during the successful presidency of Republican Ronald Reagan (1981–1989), satisfaction levels rose from a fairly dismal 20 percent range to an average of around 50 percent. Republican George H. W. Bush (1989–1993) enjoyed high levels of satisfaction until 1992, when rates fell back to the 20 percent range. This fall reflected the economic problems and other difficulties that handed the presidency to Democrat Bill Clinton (1993–2001).

Clinton's two terms appear to have been mostly a success, as satisfaction levels rose as high as 70 percent. Under Republican George W. Bush (2001–2009), however, satisfaction levels slowly fell. In October 2008, at the peak of the crisis in the financial industry, satisfaction rates bottomed out at an unprecedented 7 percent. They have since recovered. Yet with more than two-thirds of Americans still saying that they were dissatisfied with "the way things are going," it is not surprising that outsiders such as Donald Trump and Bernie Sanders did well in the 2016 elections.

Policymaking and Public Opinion

Policymakers cannot always be guided by opinion polls. In the end, politicians must make their own choices, and those choices necessarily involve trade-offs. If politicians vote for increased spending to improve education, for example, by necessity fewer resources are

Political Trust
The degree to which individuals express trust in the government and political institutions, usually measured through a specific series of survey questions.

FIGURE 6–4 | Political Satisfaction Trend

Why have satisfaction rates been so slow to recover since 2008?

Question: In general, are you satisfied or dissatisfied with the way things are going in the United States at this time?

Sources: Gallup polls, 1979 through 2016.

available for other worthy projects. Individuals who are polled do not have to make such trade-offs when they respond to questions. Indeed, survey respondents usually are not even given a choice of trade-offs in their policy opinions. Moreover, to make an informed policy choice requires an understanding not only of the policy area but also of the consequences of any given choice. Public opinion polls rarely ensure that those polled have such information.

Finally, government decisions cannot be made simply by adding up individual desires. Politicians regularly engage in "horse trading" with each other. Politicians also know that they cannot satisfy every desire of every constituent. Therefore, each politician attempts to maximize the net benefits to his or her constituents, while keeping within the limits of whatever the politician believes the government can afford.

The Media in the United States

>>> **LO5:** Describe the different types of media and the changing roles they play in American society.

The study of people and politics must take into account the role played by the media. Historically, the print media played the most important role in informing public debate. The print media developed, for the most part, our understanding of how news is to be reported. Today, however, 55 percent of Americans use television news as their primary source of information.

In addition, the Internet has become a major source for news, political communication, and fund-raising. The Internet is now the second most widely used source of information—22 percent of all persons consider it their primary source of news. Only 9 percent of the public now relies on print publications as a primary news source.

The Roles of the Media

The mass media perform a number of different functions in any country. In the United States, we can list at least six media functions. Almost all of them can have political implications, and some are essential to the democratic process. These functions are as follows:

(1) entertaining the public, (2) reporting the news, (3) identifying public problems, (4) socializing new generations, (5) providing a political forum, and (6) making profits.

Entertaining the Public. By far the greatest number of radio and television hours are dedicated to entertaining the public. The battle for prime-time ratings indicates how important successful entertainment is to the survival of networks and individual stations. A number of network shows have a highly political content. Many younger people have reported that they get much of their political information from programs such as *The Daily Show*, formerly hosted by Jon Stewart and now by Trevor Noah. Another important personality is John Oliver, who hosts *Last Week Tonight* on HBO.

For many Americans, especially younger ones, the Internet is replacing television as a source of entertainment. While much time on the Internet may be spent chatting with friends on services such as Skype or watching television programs online, politics is often a topic. YouTube, in particular, offers a large number of politically oriented videos, many of which are satirical. Talk radio and television shows that feature personalities are another form of politically oriented entertainment—one that is dominated by the political right.

Reporting the News. A primary function of the mass media in all their forms is the reporting of news. The media provide words and pictures about events, facts, personalities, and ideas. The protections of the First Amendment are intended to keep the flow of news as free as possible, because it is an essential part of the democratic process. If citizens cannot obtain unbiased information about the state of their communities and their leaders' actions, how can they make voting decisions? One of the more incisive comments about the importance of the media was made by James Madison, who said, "A popular government without popular information or the means of acquiring it, is but a prologue to a farce or a tragedy or perhaps both."[6]

Identifying Public Problems. The power of the media is important not only in revealing what the government is doing but also in determining what the government ought to do—in other words, in setting the **public agenda.** As we noted earlier in this chapter, the mass media identify public issues. American journalists have a long tradition of uncovering public wrongdoing, corruption, and bribery, and of bringing such wrongdoing to the public's attention. For its part, the Internet offers an enormous collection of political sites, with policy proposals representing every point of view.

Agenda setting by the media is enhanced by the various ways in which they can present the news. One technique, called **priming,** involves reporting certain facts, but not others. Priming can shape the public's response to an issue. A similar concept is **framing,** that is, embedding the issue in a particular story line. Attitudes toward government spending on the poor, for example, can be altered by stories that present poor people who are victims of bad luck—or who are suffering mostly due to their own behavioral problems.

Public Agenda
Issues that are perceived by the political community as meriting public attention and governmental action.

Priming
In a media report, using only certain facts to shape the public's response to an issue.

Framing
In a media report, the technique of embedding an issue in particular examples or story lines to alter public perceptions of the issue.

Socializing New Generations. As mentioned earlier in this chapter, the media strongly influence the beliefs and opinions of Americans. Because of this influence, the media play a significant role in the political socialization of the younger generation and of immigrants to this country. Through the transmission of historical information (sometimes fictionalized), the presentation of American culture, and the portrayal of the diverse regions and groups in the United States, the media teach young people and immigrants about what it means to be an American. Many children's television shows are designed not only to entertain young

6. James Madison, "Letter to W. T. Barry," August 4, 1822, in Gaillard P. Hunt, ed., *The Writings of James Madison*, Vol. 9 (1910), p. 103.

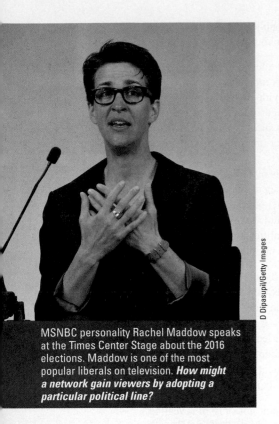

MSNBC personality Rachel Maddow speaks at the Times Center Stage about the 2016 elections. Maddow is one of the most popular liberals on television. *How might a network gain viewers by adopting a particular political line?*

D Dipasupil/Getty Images

viewers but also to instruct them in the moral values of American society. On the Internet, young Americans participate in political forums, obtain information for writing assignments, and, in general, acquire much of their political socialization.

Providing a Political Forum. As part of their news function, the media also provide a political forum for leaders and the public. Candidates for office use news reporting to sustain interest in their campaigns, while officeholders use the media to gain support for their policies or to present an image of leadership. Presidential trips abroad are one way for the chief executive to get colorful, positive, and exciting news coverage that makes the president look "presidential." The media also offer ways for citizens to participate in public debate through letters to the editor, blog posts, Twitter posts, and other channels.

Making Profits. Most of the news media in the United States are private, for-profit corporate enterprises. One of their goals is to make profits for expansion and for dividends to the stockholders who own the companies. In general, profits are made as a result of charging for advertising. Advertising revenues usually are related directly to circulation or to listener/viewer ratings.

Several well-known media outlets, in contrast, are publicly owned—public television stations in many communities and National Public Radio. These outlets operate without extensive commercials, are locally supported, and are often subsidized by the government and corporations.

For the most part, however, the media depend on advertisers for their revenues. Consequently, reporters may feel pressure from media owners and from advertisers. Media owners may take their cues from what advertisers want. If an important advertiser does not like the political bent of a particular newspaper reporter, for example, the reporter could be asked to alter his or her "style" of writing.

The Financial Crisis of the Press. Lately, newspapers have found it increasingly difficult to make a profit. Newspaper revenues have fallen because online services have taken over a greater share of classified advertising. The recent economic crisis, which depressed all forms of advertising spending, pushed many large daily newspapers over the edge. Newspapers in Chicago, Denver, and Seattle went out of business. Even some of the most famous papers, such as the *New York Times*, the *Chicago Tribune*, and the *Boston Globe*, were in serious financial trouble.

Although all major newspapers are now online, they have found it difficult to turn a profit on their online editions. News sites typically cannot sell enough advertising to meet their costs. In response to this problem, major newspapers have begun charging for online access, a process dubbed *retreating behind a paywall*. Access charges, however, reduce the number of users who are willing to view a site.

On the Internet, news organizations that employ reporters and create articles are known as *content providers*, because they provide original content. Unfortunately for the content providers, they collect only a small share of the total revenue from online advertising. Most ad revenue goes to *aggregators*, such as Google, that provide search and aggregation services, but generate little or no original content. Google alone collects more than half of all U.S. online ad revenue. Google's ad revenue is substantially greater than the total ad revenue, print and online, of every newspaper in the nation put together. In other words, there is no absolute shortage of ad revenue—the problem is that it does not go to the content providers. Of course, without content providers, there is nothing to aggregate.

Television versus the New Media

As we explained earlier, new forms of media are displacing older ones as sources of information on politics and society in general. Although it is only recently that newspapers have experienced severe economic difficulties, they were losing ground to television as early as the 1950s. Today, the Internet has begun to displace television.

New Patterns of Media Consumption. Not everyone, however, migrates to new media at the same rate. Among Americans older than sixty-five years of age, only 6 percent obtained the greatest amount of information about political campaigns in 2016 by going online. In this older generation, 11 percent still relied on a printed daily newspaper, although that is down from 58 percent in 2000.[7]

The media consumption patterns of *early adopters* of new technology are simply different from the past. Some older high-income persons are among the early adopters, but the new media are most popular among youth. Indeed, many younger people have abandoned e-mail, relying on Facebook, texting, and other systems for messages. Some have moved on from Facebook to newer, more innovative social-networking platforms. Television becomes something to watch only if you cannot find the program you want to see online.

Young early adopters may find much of the offline media irrelevant to their lives. Yet television news, cable networks, talk radio, and other forms of media are not irrelevant to American politics. Older voters outnumber younger ones by a wide margin. Older voters are more likely to make it to the polls—and many early adopters of new media technology are too young to vote. It follows that television remains essential to American politics.

The Continuing Influence of Television. Television's continuing influence on the political process is recognized by all who engage in that process. Television news is often criticized for being superficial, particularly compared with the detailed coverage available in newspapers, magazines, and online articles. In fact, television news is constrained by its technical characteristics, the most important being the limitations of time—stories must be reported in only a few minutes.

The most interesting aspect of television—and of online videos—is the fact that it relies on pictures rather than words to attract the viewer's attention. Therefore, video that is chosen for a particular political story has exaggerated importance. Viewers do not know what other videos may have been taken or what other events may have been recorded—they see only those appearing on their screens. Video clips, whether they appear on network news or YouTube, can also use well-constructed stories to exploit the potential for drama. Some critics suggest that there is pressure to produce television news that has a story line, like a novel or movie. The story should be short, with exciting pictures and a clear plot. In extreme cases, the news media are satisfied with a **sound bite,** a several-second comment selected or crafted for its immediate impact on the viewer.

Sound Bite
A brief, memorable comment that can easily be fit into news broadcasts.

---

7. Pew Research Center for the People & the Press, *"The 2016 Presidential Campaign—a News Event That's Hard to Miss,"* February 4, 2016.

It has been suggested that these formatting characteristics of video increase its influence on political events. As you are aware, real life is usually not dramatic, nor do all events have a plot that is neat or easily understood. Political campaigns are continuing events, lasting perhaps as long as two years. The significance of their daily turns and twists is only apparent later. The "drama" of Congress, with its 535 players and dozens of important committees and meetings, is also difficult for the media to present. Television requires, instead, dozens of daily three-minute stories.

Challenges Facing the Media

Media corporations can be large, and size usually translates into power. Have major media corporations used their power wisely? Two relevant issues are media consolidation and the net neutrality debate. A third issue is the possible impact of foreign governments on the administration of the Internet.

Media Consolidation. Many media outlets are now owned by corporate conglomerates. A single entity may own a television network. It may also own studios that produce shows, news, and movies. Finally, it may own the means to deliver that content to the home through cable, satellite, or the Internet. One concern advanced by observers of concentrated ownership is that media owners might use their power to steer the national agenda in a direction that they prefer. Indeed, several news organizations appear to have conservative or liberal viewpoints. Rupert Murdoch's Fox News clearly offers a conservative perspective. Some, however, believe that the great variety of Internet news sources provides an ample counterweight to the advocacy of media moguls.

Facebook founder Mark Zuckerberg supports his employees during San Francisco's gay pride parade. *How are leaders of the new media different from leaders of the old?*

Kobby Dagan/Shutterstock

The Unregulated Internet. The Internet is widely regarded as a triumph of unregulated enterprise, even though it is directly descended from ARPANET, a project of the Advanced Research Projects Agency within the Department of Defense. The federal government may have created the Internet, but Internet pioneers were remarkably successful in preventing the government from imposing regulations that might limit the freedom of users. Almost all Internet funding comes from the individuals and organizations that connect to it. An individual or organization can purchase connectivity from an **Internet service provider (ISP).**

Net Neutrality. The principle of **net neutrality** is that an ISP should treat all traffic equally. It should not block or degrade access to websites—for example, sites that compete with the ISP's own telephone or TV services. Nor should it create special "fast lanes" that allow favored content to load more quickly than the rest.

In the past, the structure of the Internet tended to enforce the network neutrality principle. If an ISP attempted to block access to a site, for example, angry users would switch to a different ISP. Today, however, for many customers, high-speed broadband service is available only from a cable TV company such as Comcast that has a local monopoly, and cell phone providers such as Verizon Wireless. Secure in the knowledge that it would be

Internet Service Provider (ISP)
A corporation or service that sells access to the Internet.

Net Neutrality
The principle that an ISP should treat all traffic equally.

difficult for their customers to switch to a different provider, large ISPs have explored the possibility of charging services such as Netflix for expedited transit. Such costs could be passed on to consumers.

As a result, net neutrality has recently become a public issue. Advocates of the principle contend that net neutrality has eased the creation of new services such as Facebook, YouTube, and Dropbox. Opponents argue that enforcing net neutrality will discourage investment in Internet infrastructure. Attempts by the FCC to issue regulations on this issue were frustrated by a court ruling that the commission would have to classify the Internet as a public utility before regulating it.[8] In February 2015, the FCC issued a proposal to do exactly that, proclaiming the Internet a public utility. In March, the commission issued specific rules. ISPs may not block content, slow transmissions, or create special fast lanes. In 2016, a U.S. appeals court upheld the FCC rules. Republicans have been supportive of cable and cell phone companies, however. In 2017, President Trump initiated the process of overturning the new rules.

Potential Problems with Foreign Governments. Could the actions of foreign governments impair Internet freedom? After all, every country with an authoritarian regime tries to control its citizens' Internet access. Witness China, home of the "Great Firewall of China." Many foreign websites are blocked. Bloggers and tweeters can be certain that government censors are analyzing their political statements.

The U.S. government, which sponsored the Internet, has kept some control of it. For example, the Internet Corporation for Assigned Names and Numbers (ICANN) has been responsible to the U.S. Commerce Department. ICANN oversees the system of assigning Internet domain names and addresses worldwide. In 2014, however, the Obama administration announced that it would end its control of ICANN. A controversy erupted. Some feared that if the U.S. government did not control ICANN, a United Nations (UN) body such as the International Telecommunication Union (ITU) might assume responsibility instead. The ITU, however, is run by governments, including authoritarian regimes such as China and Russia. These two nations have called for banning anonymity on the Internet and for taxing access to sites such as Google and Facebook.

In response to criticisms, the Obama administration postponed action. In 2016, however, ICANN finally adopted new governance rules. It is now controlled by a nongovernmental panel of technical experts located in Los Angeles. Governments will have little input into ICANN decisions. In particular, the ITU is frozen out.

The Media and Political Campaigns

>>> **LO6:** Summarize the impact of the media on political campaigns, and consider the issue of political bias in the media.

All forms of the media—television, newspapers, radio, magazines, and online services— have a significant political impact on American society. Although younger voters get a relatively small share of their news from television, it remains the primary news source for older voters. Therefore, candidates and their consultants spend much of their time devising strategies that use television to their benefit. Three types of TV coverage are generally employed in campaigns for the presidency and other offices: advertising, including negative ads; management of news coverage; and campaign debates.

---

8. *Verizon v. FCC*, 740 F.3d 623 (D.C. Cir. 2014).

Republican presidential candidate Donald Trump at a press conference in New York City in July 2016. *How did Trump's experience as host of a television reality show help him in his campaign?*

JStone/Shutterstock.com

Political Advertising

Political advertising has become increasingly important for the profitability of television station owners. Hearst Television, for example, obtains well over 10 percent of its revenues from political ads during an election year. During the 2012 presidential elections, total spending exceeded $7 billion. Among other expenses, candidates purchased more than 3 million campaign advertisements. At the presidential level, ad spending was down in 2016, but candidates in other races continued to increase their expenditures.

In recent elections, an ever-increasing share of political ads have been negative in nature. The public claims not to like negative advertising, but as one consultant put it, "Negative advertising works." Negative ads can backfire, though, when there are three or more candidates in the race, a typical state of affairs in the early presidential primaries. If one candidate attacks another, the attacker as well as the candidate who is attacked may come to be viewed negatively by the public. A candidate who "goes negative" may thus unintentionally boost the chances of a third candidate who is not part of the exchange. The 2016 Republican presidential primaries provided one example. New Jersey governor Chris Christie effectively criticized Florida senator Marco Rubio for repeating lines in an almost robotic fashion. While Christie's comment hurt Rubio, it did Christie himself no good at all.

Management of News Coverage

Using political advertising to get a message across to the public is a very expensive tactic. Coverage by the news media, however, is free. The campaign simply needs to ensure that coverage takes place. In recent years, campaign managers have shown increasing sophistication in creating newsworthy events for journalists to cover. Uniquely, in 2015 and 2016 Donald Trump had no need of a campaign manager to help him attract free media coverage. Trump's personal talent for winning media attention was unprecedented. Trump's abilities meant that he was able to succeed even though his advertising budget was far smaller than that of any major-party candidate in many years.

The campaign staff uses several methods to try to influence the quantity and type of coverage the campaign receives. First, with an understanding of the technical aspects of media coverage—camera angles, necessary equipment, timing, and deadlines—the staff plans political events to accommodate the press. Second, the campaign organization is aware that political reporters and their sponsors—networks, newspapers, or blogs—are in competition for the best stories and can be manipulated through the granting of favors, such as a personal interview with the candidate. Third, the scheduler in the campaign has the important task of planning events that will be photogenic and interesting enough for the evening news.

A related goal, although one that is more difficult to attain, is to convince reporters that a particular interpretation of an event is true. Today, the art of putting the appropriate **spin** on a story or event is highly developed. Press advisers, often referred to as **spin doctors,** try to convince journalists that the advisers' interpretations of political events are correct.

For example, the Obama administration and Republicans in Congress engaged in a major spinning duel over Obama's 2014 executive order on unauthorized immigrants. The order allowed certain classes of illegal immigrants to remain in the country. Republicans sought to portray the order as overreach by an imperial presidency. Republicans in the House tried—unsuccessfully—to overturn the order by refusing to fund the Department of Homeland Security. Democrats then argued that Republicans were acting irresponsibly and threatening our national security. (The order was blocked by the Supreme Court in 2016.)

Going for the Knockout Punch—Presidential Debates

In presidential elections, perhaps just as important as political advertisements and general news coverage is the performance of the candidates in televised presidential debates. In the first such debate in 1960, John Kennedy, the young senator from Massachusetts, took on the vice president of the United States, Richard Nixon. Many observers concluded that Kennedy's performance in these debates provided the edge he needed to win a very close contest. Thereafter, candidates became aware of the great potential of television for changing the momentum of a campaign. In general, challengers have much more to gain from debating than do incumbents. Challengers hope that the incumbent will make a mistake in the debate and undermine the "presidential" image. Incumbent presidents are loath to debate their challengers, because it puts their opponents on an equal footing with them, but the debates have become so widely anticipated that it is difficult for an incumbent to refuse to participate.

The 2015–2016 Primary Debates. Presidential candidates have often debated during primary election campaigns. In the past, such debates did not attract much interest, but the 2012 Republican presidential primary race marked a new departure. In both the 2012 and 2016 election cycles, primary debates drew large audiences. As a result, candidates could access the public without relying on expensive advertising. This circumstance tended to benefit Donald Trump, who spent little on ads. In the debates themselves, Trump was not exceptionally skillful, but he was able to get his message across to his supporters. The Democratic debates between Hillary Clinton and Vermont senator Bernie Sanders also attracted many viewers.

Clinton versus Trump. In 2016, the first debate between Hillary Clinton and Donald Trump was seen by an unprecedented 80 million viewers, not including people who watched on their computers or smartphones. Trump refused to prepare, and it showed. After an initial vigorous presentation on immigration, he lost steam. Clinton, in contrast, appeared calm and knowledgeable.

Going into the debates, Clinton's margin in the polls was very narrow. After all three debates, her margin approached 7 percentage points. By Election Day, however, most of her advantage had worn off. Some analysts suggested that the temporary bump in Clinton's support was an illusion. Recent studies suggest that good or bad news for a particular candidate can affect the willingness of the candidate's supporters to participate in polling. Clinton's 7-point advantage, in other words, was caused by discouraged Trump supporters who refused to talk to pollsters and by upbeat Clinton supporters who were more than happy to talk.

Spin
An interpretation of political events that is favorable to a candidate or officeholder

Spin Doctor
A political adviser who tries to convince journalists of the truth of a particular interpretation of events.

Political Campaigns and the Internet

Today, the campaign staff of almost every candidate running for a significant political office includes an Internet campaign strategist—a professional hired to create and maintain the campaign website, social media accounts, blogs, and podcasts. The work of this strategist includes designing a user-friendly and attractive website for the candidate and tracking campaign contributions made through the site. The strategist also manages the candidate's e-mail, Twitter, and Facebook communications. Finally, this staffer hires bloggers to promote the candidate's agenda on the Web and monitors websites for favorable or unfavorable comments or video clips about the candidate.

Blogosphere Politics

Within the past few years, politicians have also felt obligated to post regular blogs on their websites. The word **blog** comes from Web log, a regular updating of one's ideas at a specific website. Of course, many people besides politicians are also posting blogs. Most of the millions of blogs posted daily are not political. The ones that are can have a dramatic influence on events, giving rise to the term *blogosphere politics*.

Collective Blogs and Online Magazines. One development that has increasingly taken hold is the collective blog, in which writers—some of whom formerly had their own personal blogs—work together to produce the content. One example is Vox.com, a left-of-center news site. Another is RealClearPolitics, a right-of-center site that mostly aggregates articles from elsewhere (including from liberal sources). It is often hard to tell the difference between a collective blog and an online magazine. Among the sites we list in Table 6–2, only The Conscience of a Liberal is an old-fashioned, one-person blog. (Visiting it through Twitter will get you past the *New York Times* paywall.)

Trump's Use of Twitter. One characteristic of the 2016 elections was the enhanced role of Twitter. With 310 million active users in 2016, Twitter was not the largest social media service. Famously, "tweets" are limited to 140 characters. Still, Twitter proved to be an ideal platform for Donald Trump, who reveled in his ability to issue short, colorful statements. Trump's Twitter presence was backed up by a veritable army of supporters who retweeted

TABLE 6–2	Selected Political Blog Sites and Online Magazines
Progressive	
The Conscience of a Liberal	https://twitter.com/paulkrugman
Mother Jones	www.motherjones.com
Talking Points Memo	talkingpointsmemo.com
ThinkProgress	thinkprogress.org
Conservative	
American Thinker	www.americanthinker.com
Breitbart	www.breitbart.com
National Review Online	www.nationalreview.com
PJ Media	pjmedia.com

Blog
A regular updating of one's ideas on a specific Web site. The word comes from Web log.

each of his observations to thousands of additional people. These supporters were also quite willing to pile onto anyone who criticized their candidate. Trump's tweets often provoked controversy. His campaign devoted little time to screening sources that Trump quoted, some of which turned out to be highly questionable.

Bias in the Media

Traditionally, newspapers and other media have tried to separate opinion pieces from "straight news." In recent years, many media observers have worried that opinion is "taking over" and displacing news sources that try to be objective. Many blogs, for example, are almost pure opinion, even if they also provide some facts. Another media format in which opinion is dominant is talk radio.

Talk Radio. The most conspicuous characteristic of talk radio is that it is almost completely controlled by conservatives, many of whom are quite radical. None of the top talk show hosts are liberal. Talk show hosts do not pretend to be journalists. Rather, they are personalities who entertain their audiences with red-meat politics. Exaggeration for effect is typical, and language that would be unacceptable in other contexts is common. As you will learn shortly, many conservatives believe that liberals dominate the "mainstream media." Conservative control of talk radio, however, makes it harder to argue that the media as a whole have a liberal bias.

The Mainstream Media. For decades, the contention that the mainstream media have a liberal **bias** has been repeated time and again. A number of studies appear to back up this claim. For example, research at the University of Connecticut has shown that journalists consider themselves Democrats three times as often as they identify with the Republicans. A recent Gallup poll reports that 47 percent of the public think that the news media are too liberal, while 13 percent see the media as too conservative. These views are strongly associated with the politics of the respondent: 75 percent of Republicans believe the media are too liberal, while only 20 percent of Democrats think that is true.

Alternative Forms of Bias. Some writers have argued that the mainstream media are really biased in favor of stories that involve conflict and drama—the better to attract viewers. Still others contend the media are biased against "losers," and when a candidate falls behind in a race, his or her press quickly becomes negative. In the 2016 Republican presidential primaries, one candidate after another experienced dismissive news coverage as their poll numbers slipped. Of course, media coverage of Donald Trump was negative from the very start, but such coverage did not appear to hurt him much in the primaries. It is possible that most of Trump's voters had already written off the mainstream media as irredeemably hostile to their candidate.

Bias and Professionalism. While many journalists may be Democrats at heart, most operate under a code of professional ethics that dictates "objectivity" and a commitment to the truth. Journalists may not always succeed in living up to such a code, but it helps that it exists.

Interact

Many blogs—and also online newspapers and magazines—allow readers to comment on posts or articles. Comments can be a way to build a community around a small blog. Sites with a huge readership, however, experience problems with comments. They can quickly deteriorate into "flame wars," in which readers insult each other instead of entering useful observations. One solution is to publish only those comments approved by a moderator. For most sites, however, this procedure involves an unacceptable amount of effort. Visit at least one progressive and one conservative site listed in Table 6–2. Take the time to look at posted comments. What topics are most important to these sites? How much of what they report is news, and how much is opinion? What kinds of readers does the site appear to have?

Bias
An inclination or a preference that interferes with impartial judgment.

Rush Limbaugh is perhaps one of the most listened to talk radio hosts in America. At times, he has been considered the spokesperson for American conservatives. *Should the Federal Communications Commission be able to regulate what he says?*

George Gojkovich/Getty Images

To be sure, many media outlets have an explicit political point of view. This is especially common in the blogosphere, but it is true of some cable news channels as well. Fox News, for example, takes pride in avoiding what it sees as the liberal bias of the mainstream media.

Some progressives, however, have accused Fox and other conservative outlets of allowing politics to interfere with their objectivity. They argue that conservatives find liberal bias even in reporting that is scrupulously accurate. In the words of humorist Stephen Colbert, "Reality has a well-known liberal bias." Indeed, the professional commitment to objectivity among journalists can create problems when one party or candidate continually makes untrue statements. As liberal economist Paul Krugman put it, if one politician says that the earth is flat, the natural instinct of most journalists is to report that "opinions on the shape of the earth differ."

The Media in 2016: Trump. The behavior of the media during the 2016 presidential elections posed one of the greatest challenges in years to the theory of liberal bias in the mainstream media. To be sure, journalists did not pull their punches when reporting on Donald Trump. The media devoted ample resources to Trump's often questionable business dealings and his failure to release his income tax returns. Few voters could have remained ignorant of a tape in which Trump boasted that he had the ability to physically molest women.

Still, the media found it difficult to respond to Trump's constant disregard for whether his statements were actually true, as assessed by independent fact-checking organizations. Indeed, Trump's objective was never to report facts. Rather, he sought to assure his followers that he was *on their side*. There is evidence that many of his supporters understood this and did not mind. In the words of businessman and Trump supporter Peter Thiel, they took him "seriously but not literally."

The Media in 2016: Clinton. All journalists love a "scoop," that is, to be the first to report an exciting new development. The search for a scoop can be troubling, however, when the goal is to be the first to "bring down" a prominent politician. Unfortunately for Hillary Clinton, many reporters—and not just conservative ones—were highly interested in bringing her down. Clinton loathed the media, and many of its members hated her right back. Clinton's hostility was in part generated by a decades-long series of investigations into alleged scandals. None of these investigations revealed any significant wrongdoing, but they had a lethal impact on Clinton's relations with the media—and eventually, the public.

A major example was the controversy over Clinton's use of a private e-mail server while she was secretary of state. A lengthy investigation cleared her, though FBI director James Comey did take the unprecedented step of criticizing her use of the server. Clinton's e-mails were the number-one media event of 2016. According to the Tyndall Report, the three major networks devoted one hundred minutes to the e-mails—and thirty-two minutes to covering *all* policy issues taken together. As a result of this coverage, much of the media effectively supported Trump's contention that Clinton was a criminal who belonged in prison, not in the White House. Millions of Americans who had grave reservations about Trump concluded that they had no alternative but to vote for him. A vote for "crooked Hillary" was simply out of the question.

MAKING A DIFFERENCE

Being a Critical Consumer of the News

Television, print media, and the Internet provide a wide range of choices for Americans who want to stay informed. Still, critics of the media argue that a substantial amount of what you read and see is colored either by the subjectivity of editors and bloggers or by the demands of profit making. Few Americans take the time to become critical consumers of the news. Many people, in fact, get almost all of their information from partisan sources, from within their own political "bubble." Some of these sources are famous for running stories that are flatly not true.

Why Should You Care? Even if you do not plan to engage in political activism, you have a stake in ensuring that your beliefs are truly your own and that they represent your values and interests. To guarantee this result, you need to obtain accurate information from the media. If you do not take care, you could find yourself voting for a candidate who is opposed to what you believe in or voting against measures that are in your interest. After all, even when journalists themselves are successful at remaining objective, they will of necessity give publicity to politicians and interest group representatives who are far from impartial.

What Can You Do? To become a critical news consumer, you must develop a critical eye and ear. Sources such as blogs often have strong political preferences, and you should try to determine what these are. Does a blog merely give opinions, or does it back up its arguments with data? It is possible to select anecdotes to support almost any argument—does an anecdote represent typical circumstances, or is it a rare occurrence highlighted to make a point?

Watching the evening news can be far more rewarding if you look at how much the news depends on video effects. You will note that stories on the evening news tend to be no more than three minutes long, that stories with excellent video footage get more attention, and that considerable time is taken up with "happy talk" or human-interest stories.

Another way to critically evaluate news coverage is to compare how the news is covered by different outlets. Table 6–2 in this chapter provides online sources that you can compare. You might want to compare a conservative site such as the *National Review*—shown below highlighting an article on intelligence agencies—with one such as *Mother Jones*.

A variety of organizations try to monitor news sources for accuracy and bias. Consider visiting the following sites:

- Fairness & Accuracy in Reporting is a media watchdog with a strong liberal viewpoint.
- Accuracy in Media takes a combative conservative position on media issues.

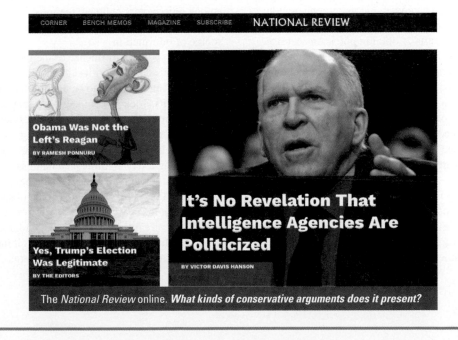

The *National Review* online. *What kinds of conservative arguments does it present?*

//

Key Terms

agenda setting 121	generational effect 122	opinion poll 127	public opinion 119
bias 141	house effect 129	peer group 121	sampling error 128
blog 140	Internet service	political	sound bite 135
consensus 119	provider (ISP) 136	socialization 120	spin 139
divided opinion 119	media 121	political trust 131	spin doctor 139
framing 133	net neutrality 136	priming 133	tracking poll 128
gender gap 126	opinion leader 121	public agenda 133	

//

Chapter Summary

》LO1 Public opinion is the aggregate of individual attitudes or beliefs shared by some portion of the adult population. A consensus exists when a large proportion of the public appears to express the same view on an issue. Divided opinion exists when the public holds widely differing attitudes on an issue.

People's opinions are formed through the political socialization process. Important factors in this process are the family, educational experiences, peer groups, opinion leaders, the media, and political events.

》LO2 Opinions are also influenced by demographic factors such as education, economic status, religion, race and ethnicity, gender, and geographic region.

》LO3 Most descriptions of public opinion are based on the results of opinion polls. An accurate poll includes a representative sample of the population being surveyed and ensures randomness in the selection of respondents.

Problems with polls include sampling error, the difficulty of persuading people to participate, badly weighted samples, and questions that are poorly worded. "Polls" that rely on self-selected respondents are inherently inaccurate and should be discounted.

》LO4 The political culture provides a general environment of support for the political system, allowing the nation to weather periods of crisis. The political culture also helps Americans to evaluate their government's performance.

Public opinion also plays an important role in policymaking. Politicians cannot always be guided by opinion polls, however. This is because respondents often do not understand the costs and consequences of policy decisions or the trade-offs involved in making such decisions.

》LO5 The media are enormously important in American politics today. They perform a number of functions, including (a) entertaining the public, (b) news reporting, (c) identifying public problems, (d) socializing new generations, (e) providing a political forum, and (f) making profits. Television remains the most important medium, in particular among older voters, who are the most likely to vote. Younger Americans are turning to the Internet as a source of information.

》LO6 The political influence of the media is most obvious during political campaigns. Negative advertisements continue to be a major feature of campaigns. Today's campaigns use expert management of news coverage. For presidential candidates, how they appear in campaign debates is of major importance. Internet resources are transforming today's political campaigns.

Frequently, the mainstream media have been accused of liberal bias, although some observers contend that these accusations result from true stories that offend conservatives. Talk radio, which is overwhelmingly conservative, makes it harder to claim that the media as a whole tilt liberal.

Test Yourself

1. We can best define *public opinion* as:
   a. beliefs held by moderate voters.
   b. beliefs shared by both Democrats and Republicans.
   c. the aggregate of individual beliefs shared by some portion of adults.

2. Friends and co-workers who may influence your political attitudes are called:
   a. opinion leaders.
   b. agents of socialization.
   c. a peer group.

3. The gender gap refers to:
   a. the difference in college attendance rates for males and females.
   b. the tendency for women to be more likely to vote for a particular candidate than men.
   c. the tendency for men to dominate the political process.

4. One way to compensate for underrepresented groups in a polling sample is to:
   a. eliminate all answers from those who are part of the underrepresented group.
   b. reduce the weight given to the underrepresented group so that it does not count excessively.
   c. add extra weight to the responses of the underrepresented group to correct for the underrepresentation.

5. When one polling organization's results consistently differ from those of other poll takers, we call this:
   a. sampling error.
   b. a house effect.
   c. statistical noise.

6. The same polling question can result in different responses depending on how that question is:
   a. phrased.
   b. weighted.
   c. averaged.

7. The trend in political satisfaction in this country has:
   a. always been very high.
   b. fallen since around 2001.
   c. risen since around 2001.

8. Television remains a key medium in American politics because:
   a. it is the number-one source of information for older voters, who dominate the electorate.
   b. young people are avoiding the Internet as a source of information.
   c. television advertisements are not that expensive to buy.

9. A major problem facing newspapers today is that they cannot collect enough online:
   a. clicks.
   b. advertising revenue.
   c. content.

10. A campaign press adviser who tries to convince reporters of a particular interpretation of an event is called a:
    a. campaign manager.
    b. media spokesperson.
    c. spin doctor.

11. The principle that all traffic on the Internet should be treated equally is called:
    a. net neutrality.
    b. the Fairness Doctrine.
    c. professionalism.

Essay Questions

1. Years ago, people with postgraduate degrees were more likely to vote for Republican than Democratic candidates, but in recent years, highly educated voters have been trending Democratic. Why might physicians and lawyers have become more likely to vote Democratic? For what reasons might college professors lean Democratic?

2. Individuals who respond to blog posts sometimes enter comments that are deliberately designed to foster disruption. (Such persons are commonly called *trolls*.) Consider also the prevalence of hostile and even threatening responses to posts by women on controversial topics. Why might people engage in such behaviors?

Answers to multiple-choice questions: 1. c, 2. c, 3. b, 4. c, 5. b, 6. a, 7. b, 8. a, 9. b, 10. c, 11. a.

7 Interest Groups and Political Parties

Members of environmental interest groups—and some politicians—gather to support windmills that generate electricity. The Long Island Power Authority in New York plans to erect such facilities off the shore of Long Island. *Why might other interest groups oppose offshore wind sites?*

The six **Learning Outcomes (LOs)** below are designed to help improve your understanding of this chapter. After reading this chapter, you should be able to:

>>> **LO1** Describe the basic characteristics of interest groups, and explain why Americans join them.

>>> **LO2** List the major types of interest groups, especially those with economic motivations.

>>> **LO3** Discuss direct and indirect interest group techniques, and describe the main ways in which lobbyists are regulated.

>>> **LO4** Cite some of the major activities of U.S. political parties, and discuss how they are organized.

>>> **LO5** Explain how the history of U.S. political parties has led to the two major parties that exist today.

>>> **LO6** Give reasons why the two-party system has endured in America, and evaluate the impact of third parties and independents on U.S. politics.

Check your understanding of the material with the Test Yourself section at the end of the chapter.

Interest Group
An organized group of individuals sharing common objectives who actively attempt to influence policymakers.

The structure of American government invites the participation of **interest groups** at various stages of the policymaking process. Americans can form groups in their neighborhoods or cities and lobby the city council or their state government. They can join statewide groups or national groups and try to influence government policy through Congress or through one of the executive agencies or cabinet departments. Representatives of large corporations may seek to influence members of Congress or the president personally at social events or fund-raisers. When attempts to influence government through the executive and legislative branches fail, interest groups can turn to the courts, filing suits in state or federal courts to achieve their political objectives.

Another way to influence policymaking is to become an active member of a political party and participate in the selection of political candidates, who, if elected, will hold government positions. A **political party** might be formally defined as a group of political activists who organize to win elections, operate the government, and determine public policy. This definition explains the difference between an interest group and a political party. Interest groups do not want to operate the government, and they do not put forth political candidates—even though they support candidates who will promote their interests if elected or reelected.

In this chapter, we define interest groups, describe how they try to affect the government, and summarize the legal restrictions on **lobbyists,** groups or individuals hired to affect legislation and government administrative decisions. We also describe the major political parties, their history, and their organization. Finally, we explain why the two-party system has prevailed in the United States.

A Nation of Joiners

>>> **LO1:** Describe the basic characteristics of interest groups, and explain why Americans join them.

Alexis de Tocqueville observed in the early 1830s that "in no country of the world has the principle of association been more successfully used or applied to a greater multitude of objectives than in America."[1] The French traveler was amazed at the degree to which Americans formed groups to solve civic problems, establish social relationships, and speak for their economic or political interests. Perhaps James Madison, when he wrote *Federalist Paper* No. 10 (see Appendix C), had already judged the character of his country's citizens similarly. He supported the creation of a large republic with many states to encourage the formation of multiple interests. The multitude of interests, in Madison's view, would work to discourage the formation of an oppressive majority interest.

Thousands of Groups

The large number of "pressure points" in American government helps to explain why there are so many—more than one hundred thousand—interest groups at work in our society. Another reason for the multitude of interest groups is that the right to join a group is protected by the First Amendment to the U.S. Constitution. Not only are all people guaranteed the right "peaceably to assemble," but they are also guaranteed the right "to petition the Government for a redress of grievances." This constitutional provision encourages Americans to form groups and to express their opinions to the government or to their elected representatives as group members.

Poll data show that more than two-thirds of all Americans belong to at least one group or association. Although the majority of these affiliations could not be classified as "interest groups" in the political sense, Americans certainly understand the principles of working in groups.

Today, interest groups range from the elementary school parent-teacher association to the statewide association of insurance agents. They include small groups such as local environmental organizations and national groups such as the American Civil Liberties Union, the National Education Association, and even the Association of Government Relations Professionals, formerly the American League of Lobbyists.

Political Party
A group of political activists who organize to win elections, operate the government, and determine public policy.

Lobbyist
An organization or individual who attempts to influence the passage, defeat, or content of legislation and the government's administrative decisions.

---

1. Alexis de Tocqueville, *Democracy in America*, Vol. 1 [1835], ed. Phillips Bradley (New York: Knopf, 1980), p. 191.

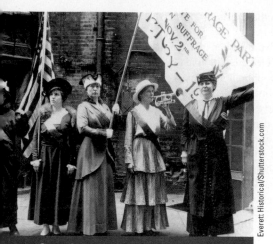

Campaigners for woman suffrage in San Francisco, 1915. *Did they have many supporters at that time?*

Interest Groups and Social Movements

Interest groups may be spawned by mass **social movements**. Such movements represent demands by a large segment of the population for change in the political, economic, or social system. A social movement is often the first expression of latent discontent with the existing system. It may be the authentic voice of weaker or oppressed groups in society that do not have the means or standing to organize as interest groups.

The civil rights movement of the 1950s and 1960s was clearly a social movement. To be sure, several formal organizations worked to support the movement—including the Southern Christian Leadership Conference, the National Association for the Advancement of Colored People, and the Urban League—but only a social movement could generate the kinds of civil disobedience that took place in hundreds of towns and cities across the country.

Social movements may generate interest groups with specific goals. In the example of the women's movement of the 1960s, the National Organization for Women was formed in part out of a demand to end gender-segregated job advertising in newspapers.

Reasons to Join—or Not Join

Individuals may join interest groups for a variety of reasons. We can identify three types of incentives for joining:

- People may join an interest group for companionship and the pleasure of associating with others who share their interests. We can call these benefits of association *solidarity incentives*.
- Some interest groups offer *material incentives*. For example, people may join the American Automobile Association (AAA) for emergency roadside assistance and trip planning. Members may not realize that the AAA is also an interest group seeking to shape laws that affect drivers.
- Finally, members may join interest groups precisely because they want to pursue political or economic goals through joint action. Such *purposive incentives* are important when individuals feel strongly about issues.

It can be rational for someone *not* to join an interest group even when that person stands to benefit from the group's activities. A dairy farmer, for example, will benefit from the lobbying of the American Dairy Association whether he or she joins the organization or not. The difficulty that interest groups face in recruiting members when benefits can be obtained without joining is referred to as the **free-rider problem.** This problem is especially acute for labor unions.

Social Movement
A movement that represents the demands of a large segment of the public for political, economic, or social change.

Free-Rider Problem
The difficulty that interest groups face in recruiting members when the benefits they achieve can be gained without joining the group.

Types of Interest Groups

>>> **LO2:** List the major types of interest groups, especially those with economic motivations.

Thousands of groups exist to influence government. Among the major types of interest groups are those that represent the main sectors of the economy. In addition, a number of environmental groups and public-interest organizations have been formed to protect the environment and represent the needs of the general citizenry. Other types of groups include single-issue groups, ideological groups, and groups based on race, sex, or sexual orientation. The interests of foreign governments and foreign businesses are represented in the American political arena as well.

This large number of interest groups would seem to support *pluralism* as a description of American politics. Pluralism views politics as a struggle among various interest groups to gain benefits. Yet if interest groups led by upper-class individuals are the dominant voices, then this reality would give as much support to *elite theory* as to pluralism. (We discussed pluralism and elite theory at the beginning of this book.)

Economic Interest Groups

More interest groups are formed to represent economic interests than any other set of interests. The variety of economic interest groups mirrors the complexity of the American economy.

Business Interest Groups. Thousands of business groups and trade associations work to influence government policies that affect their respective industries. "Umbrella groups" represent collections of businesses or other entities. For example, the National Association of Manufacturers is an umbrella group that represents manufacturing concerns. Some business groups are decidedly more powerful than others. Consider the U.S. Chamber of Commerce, which represents about 3 million member companies. It can bring constituent influence to bear on every member of Congress. Studies have shown that business groups—especially those representing specific industries such as banking or film-making—are exceptionally successful in winning beneficial legislation.

For example, drug companies and Hollywood have been enormously successful in winning protection for *intellectual property*. The Walt Disney Company has long fought to ensure that its rights to Mickey Mouse never expire. U.S. law now protects Disney's control of Mickey Mouse until at least 2036. Some economists have argued that lengthy copyright and patent protections discourage innovation and hurt the overall economy. Attempts to impose U.S. intellectual property standards on a variety of other nations located on the Pacific Rim were an essential part of the Trans-Pacific Partnership, a trade deal negotiated in 2016 by the Obama administration. This deal, however, was dead on arrival in the U.S. Congress even before the 2016 elections. Not only did Trump repudiate the agreement, but so did Clinton.

Agricultural Interest Groups. American farmers and their employees represent less than 1 percent of the U.S. population. In spite of this, farmers' influence on legislation beneficial to their interests has been significant. Farmers have very strong interest groups. For example, the American Farm Bureau Federation, or Farm Bureau, established in 1919, represents more than 5.5 million families (a majority of whom are not actually farm families).

Agricultural interest groups are among the most successful in obtaining subsidies from American taxpayers. The most recent "farm bill" was passed in 2014. This legislation provides $19 billion per year to the nation's farmers. The new bill did abolish *direct payments*— sums that formerly went to growers of corn, cotton, rice, soybeans, and wheat regardless of whether they actually planted the crops. Almost all of the funds saved were added back as crop insurance subsidies, however.

Labor Interest Groups. Interest groups representing the **labor movement** date back to at least 1886, when the American Federation of Labor (AFL) was formed. In 1955, the AFL joined forces with the Congress of Industrial Organizations (CIO). In 2005, however, four key

Labor Movement
The economic and political expression of working-class interests.

Service Sector
The sector of the economy that provides services—such as health care, banking, and education—in contrast to the sector that produces goods.

unions left the federation and formed the Change to Win Coalition. Today, Change to Win has a membership of about 4 million workers, while the AFL-CIO's membership is about 10 million.

The role of unions in American society has been waning, as witnessed by a decline in union membership (see Figure 7–1). Unions traditionally have been strongest in the manufacturing and construction sectors. In the age of automation and with the rise of the **service sector,** blue-collar workers in basic industries (auto, steel, and the like) represent a smaller and smaller percentage of the total working population. As a result, unions are looking to other areas for their membership, including migrant farmworkers, service workers, and, especially, public employees.

Public Employee Unions. The degree of unionization in the private sector has declined over the past fifty years, but this has been partially offset by growth in the unionization of public employees. With a total membership of more than 7 million, public-sector unions are a powerful force.

In recent years, conservatives have taken a strong stand against public employee unions, particularly teachers' unions such as the National Education Association and the American Federation of Teachers. In some states, mostly in the South, bargaining with public-sector unions is prohibited. Recently, Republican governors in several midwestern states—including Indiana, Michigan, Ohio, and Wisconsin—have attempted to restrict or abolish the bargaining rights of public employees.

FIGURE 7–1 **Decline in Union Membership, 1948 to Present**

The percentage of the total workforce that consists of labor union members has declined greatly over the past forty years. The percentage of government workers who are union members, however, increased significantly in the 1960s and 1970s and has remained stable since then. *Why might it be easier to organize a union among public-sector workers than workers in the private sector?*

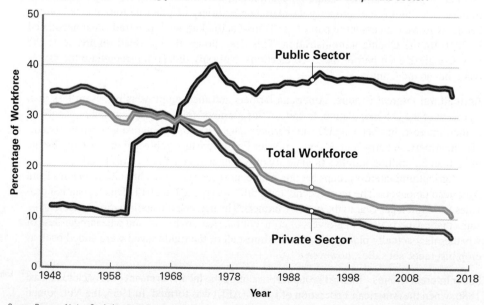

Source: Bureau of Labor Statistics.

The Political Environment Faced by Labor. The success or failure of attempts to form unions depends greatly on popular attitudes. Many business-oriented conservatives have never accepted unions as legitimate institutions. In states where this view is widely held, local laws and practices can make it hard for labor to organize. For example, only 3 percent of workers in North Carolina are union members. In New York, where voters are more sympathetic to labor, the unionization rate is 24.7 percent. One way a state can make it more difficult to form unions is by adopting *"right-to-work" laws.* Such legislation bans contracts that require all employees to pay union dues or fees. The result is a free-rider problem for the unions. Twenty-six states have such laws. Indiana, Michigan, West Virginia, and Wisconsin are the most recent states to adopt them.

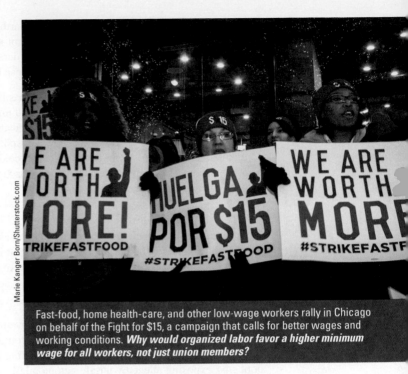

Marie Kanger Born/Shutterstock.com

Fast-food, home health-care, and other low-wage workers rally in Chicago on behalf of the Fight for $15, a campaign that calls for better wages and working conditions. *Why would organized labor favor a higher minimum wage for all workers, not just union members?*

Interest Groups of Professionals. Many professional organizations exist, including the American Bar Association, the Associated General Contractors of America, the Institute of Electrical and Electronics Engineers, and others. Some professional groups, such as those representing lawyers and physicians, are more influential than others because of their ability to restrict entry into their professions. Lawyers have a unique advantage—a large number of members of Congress share their profession.

The Unorganized Poor. Some have argued that the system of interest group politics leaves out poor Americans. If they are members of the working poor, they may hold two or more jobs just to survive, leaving them no time to participate in interest groups. Consequently, some scholars suggest that interest groups and lobbyists are the privilege of upper-middle-class Americans and those who belong to unions or other special groups.

Others, however, observe that the low-income population does obtain benefits from government. Without federal tax and spending programs aimed at low-income persons, as many as 25 percent of U.S. families would have incomes below the official poverty line. If you take into account all benefits that low-income families obtain, that number drops to about 10 percent. True, the poor cannot easily represent themselves. But for decades, liberal groups and, especially, religious groups have campaigned on behalf of those suffering from poverty. These interest groups have done for the poor what the poor cannot do for themselves.

Environmental Interest Groups

The National Audubon Society was founded in 1905 to protect the snowy egret from the commercial demand for hat decorations. The patron of the Sierra Club, John Muir, worked for the creation of national parks more than a century ago. But the blossoming of environmental groups with mass memberships did not occur until the 1970s.

Today's Environmental Groups. Since the first Earth Day, organized in 1972, many interest groups have sprung up to protect the environment in general or unique ecological niches. The groups range from the National Wildlife Federation, with a membership of more than 4 million, to the more elite Environmental Defense Fund, with a membership of 500,000.

Climate Change. The topic of climate change has become a major focus for environmental groups in recent years. This issue has pitted environmentalists against other interest groups—for example, interests representing industries that may promote global warming by releasing "greenhouse" gases into the atmosphere. Indeed, the reaction against environmentalism has been strong enough in such coal-producing states as West Virginia to transform them politically. Once a Democratic bastion, West Virginia now usually supports Republicans in national contests.

Public-Interest Groups

Public interest is a difficult term to define because, as we noted earlier in the book, there are many publics in our nation of about 325 million. It is almost impossible for one particular public policy to benefit everybody, which in turn makes it practically impossible to define the public interest. Nonetheless, over the past few decades, a variety of lobbying organizations have been formed "in the public interest."

The Consumer Movement. As an organized movement, consumerism began in 1936 with the founding of the Consumers Union, which continues to publish the popular magazine *Consumer Reports*. Consumerism took off during the 1960s. Ralph Nader, who gained notice by exposing allegedly unsafe automobiles, was a key figure in the new movement and a major sponsor of new organizations. These included Public Interest Research Groups (PIRGs)—campus organizations that emerged in the early 1970s and continue to provide students with platforms for civic engagement. Partly in response to a variety of consumer groups, several conservative public-interest legal foundations have sprung up that are often pitted against liberal groups in court.

Other Public-Interest Groups. One of the largest public-interest groups is Common Cause, founded in 1968. Its goal is to reorder national priorities toward "the public" and to make governmental institutions more responsive to the needs of the public. Another public-interest group is the League of Women Voters, founded in 1920. Although officially nonpartisan, it has lobbied for the Equal Rights Amendment and for government reform.

Additional Types of Interest Groups

A number of interest groups focus on just one issue. Single-interest groups, being narrowly focused, may be able to call attention to their causes because they have simple and straightforward goals and because their members tend to care intensely about the issues. Thus, such groups can easily motivate their members to contact legislators or to organize demonstrations in support of their policy goals.

The abortion debate has created groups opposed to abortion (such as the National Right to Life Committee) and groups in favor of abortion rights (such as NARAL Pro-Choice America). Further examples of single-issue groups are the National Rifle Association and the American Israel Public Affairs Committee (a pro-Israel group).

Public Interest
The best interests of the overall community. Also, the national good, rather than the narrow interests of a particular group.

Foreign Interest Groups. Homegrown interest groups are not the only players in the game. Washington, D.C., is also the center for lobbying by foreign governments, as well as private foreign interests. The governments of the largest U.S. trading partners, such as Japan, South Korea,

Canada, and the European Union (EU) countries, maintain substantial research and lobbying staffs. Even smaller nations, such as those in the Caribbean, engage lobbyists when vital legislation affecting their trade interests is considered.

Ideological Groups. Among the most important interest groups are those that unite citizens around a common ideological viewpoint. Americans for Democratic Action, for example, was founded in 1947 to represent liberals who were explicitly anti-Communist. On the political right, Americans for Tax Reform, organized by Grover Norquist, has been successful in persuading almost all leading Republicans to sign a pledge promising never to vote to raise taxes. The various organizations making up the Tea Party movement are widely seen as ideological interest groups.

Identity Groups. Still other groups represent Americans who share a common identity, such as membership in a particular race or ethnic group. The NAACP, founded in 1909 as the National Association for the Advancement of Colored People, represents African Americans. The National Organization for Women (NOW) has championed women's rights since 1966.

Elderly Americans can be considered to have a common identity. AARP (formerly the American Association of Retired Persons) is one of the most powerful interest groups in Washington, D.C. It is certainly the nation's largest interest group, with a membership of about 40 million. AARP played a significant role in the creation of Medicare and Medicaid, as well as in obtaining annual cost-of-living increases in Social Security payments. (Medicare pays for medical expenses incurred by those who are at least sixty-five years of age. Medicaid provides health-care support for the poor.) In 2009 and 2010, AARP strongly supported the Democratic health-care reform bills.

Interest Group Strategies

>>> **LO3:** Discuss direct and indirect interest group techniques, and describe the main ways in which lobbyists are regulated.

Interest groups employ a wide range of techniques and strategies to promote their policy goals. Although few groups are successful at persuading Congress and the president to endorse their programs completely, many are able to block—or at least weaken—legislation injurious to their members. The key to success for interest groups is access to legislators and executive branch officials. To gain such access, interest groups and their representatives try to cultivate long-term relationships with these officials. The best of these relationships are based on mutual respect and cooperation. The interest group provides the official with sources of information and assistance, and the official in turn gives the group opportunities to express its views.

The techniques used by interest groups can be divided into direct and indirect techniques. With **direct techniques,** the interest group and its lobbyists approach officials personally to present their case. With **indirect techniques,** in contrast, the interest group uses the general public or individual constituents to influence the government on behalf of the interest group.

Direct Technique
An interest group technique that uses direct interaction with government officials to further the group's goals.

Indirect Technique
An interest group technique that uses third parties to influence government officials.

Direct Techniques

Lobbying, publicizing ratings of legislative behavior, and providing campaign assistance are three main direct techniques used by interest groups.

AP Images/Jason Getz/Atlanta Journal-Constitution

Georgia governor Nathan Deal (on the left), meets with a lobbyist during a session of the state's legislature. *Why would a governor willingly be photographed with lobbyists?*

Lobbying Techniques. As you might have guessed, the term *lobbying* comes from the activities of private citizens regularly congregating in the lobbies of legislative chambers to petition legislators. In the latter part of the 1800s, railroad and industrial groups openly bribed state legislators to pass legislation beneficial to their interests, giving lobbying a well-deserved bad name. Today, in contrast, most lobbyists are professionals. They are either consultants to a company or interest group or members of one of the Washington, D.C., law firms that specialize in providing lobbying services. Such firms employ hundreds of former members of Congress and former government officials. Lobbyists are valued for their network of contacts in Washington.

Lobbyists engage in an array of activities to influence legislation and government policy. These include the following:

- Meeting privately with public officials. Although they are acting on behalf of their clients, lobbyists often furnish needed information to senators and representatives (and government agency appointees). It is to the lobbyists' advantage to provide useful information so that policymakers will rely on them in the future.
- Testifying before congressional committees for or against proposed legislation.
- Testifying before executive rulemaking agencies—such as the Federal Trade Commission or the Consumer Product Safety Commission—for or against proposed rules.
- Assisting legislators or bureaucrats in drafting legislation or regulations.
- Inviting legislators to social occasions, such as cocktail parties, boating expeditions, and other events, including conferences at exotic locations.
- Providing political information to legislators and other government officials. Sometimes, lobbyists have better information than the party leadership about how other legislators are going to vote.
- Suggesting nominations for federal appointments to the executive branch.

The Ratings Game. Many interest groups attempt to influence the overall behavior of legislators through their rating systems. Each year, these interest groups identify the legislation that they consider most important to their goals and then monitor how legislators vote on it. Legislators receive scores based on their votes. The usual ratings scheme ranges from 0 to 100 percent. In the scheme of the liberal Americans for Democratic Action, for example, a rating of 100 means that a member of Congress voted with the group on every issue and is, by that measure, very liberal.

Campaign Assistance. Groups recognize that the greatest concern of legislators is to be reelected, so they focus on the legislators' campaign needs. Associations with large memberships, such as labor unions, are able to provide workers for political campaigns, including precinct workers to get out the vote, volunteers to put up posters and pass out literature, and people to staff telephone banks at campaign headquarters.

Candidates vie for the groups' endorsements in a campaign. Gaining those endorsements may be automatic, or it may require that the candidates participate in debates or interviews with the interest groups. An interest group usually publicizes its choices in its membership publication, and the candidate can use the endorsement in her or his campaign literature.

Indirect Techniques

Interest groups can also try to influence government policy by working through others, who may be constituents or members of the general public. Indirect techniques mask an interest group's own activities and make the effort appear to be spontaneous. Furthermore, legislators and government officials are often more impressed by contacts from constituents than from an interest group's lobbyist.

Generating Public Pressure. In some instances, interest groups try to produce a "groundswell" of public pressure to influence the government. Such efforts may include advertisements online and in newspapers, mass e-mailings, television publicity, and demonstrations. The Internet and social media make communication efforts even more effective. Interest groups may commission polls to find out what the public's sentiments are and then publicize the results. The intent of this activity is to convince policymakers that public opinion supports the group's position.

Using Constituents as Lobbyists. An interest group may also use constituents of elected officials to lobby for the group's goals. In the "shotgun" approach, the interest group tries to mobilize large numbers of constituents to write, phone, or send e-mails and tweets to their legislators or to the president. Often, the group provides language that constituents can use in the communication, thus sparing people from the need of composing a message of their own. These efforts are effective on Capitol Hill only when the number of responses is very large, however. Legislators know that the voters did not initiate the communications on their own when many communications use exactly the same wording. Artificially manufactured grassroots activity has been aptly labeled *astroturf lobbying*.

A more powerful variation of this technique uses only important constituents. With this approach, known as the "rifle" technique or the "Utah plant manager theory," the interest group might, for example, ask the manager of a local plant in Utah to contact the senator from Utah. Because the constituent is seen as influential and responsible for many jobs, the legislator is more likely to listen carefully to the constituent's concerns about legislation than to a paid lobbyist.

Regulating Lobbyists

Congress made its first attempt to control lobbyists and lobbying activities through Federal Regulation of the Lobbying Act of 1946. The act proved to be ineffective, however.

A cartoon from 1889 contends that the United States Senate is dominated by corporate interests. The term *trust* refers to a type of monopoly. Prior to the 1914 elections, members of the Senate were elected by state legislatures. *Was such a body more likely to be corrupt than one elected directly by the people? Why or why not?*

The Lobbying Disclosure Act. The reform-minded Congress of 1995–1996 overhauled the lobbying legislation, fundamentally changing the ground rules for those who seek to influence the federal government. The Lobbying Disclosure Act passed in 1995 included the following provisions:

- A *lobbyist* is defined as anyone who spends at least 20 percent of his or her time lobbying members of Congress, their staffs, or executive-branch officials.
- Lobbyists must register with the clerk of the House and the secretary of the Senate.
- Semiannual reports must disclose the general nature of the lobbying effort.

Also in 1995, both the House and the Senate adopted new rules on gifts and travel expenses provided by lobbyists. The House adopted a flat ban on gifts, while the Senate established limits: senators were prohibited from accepting any gift with a value of more than $50 and from accepting gifts worth more than $100 from a single source in a given year. These gift rules stopped the broad practice of taking members of Congress to lunch or dinner at high-priced restaurants, but the various exemptions and exceptions have allowed much gift giving to continue.

Since 2007, under the Honest Leadership and Open Government Act, lobbyists must report quarterly, and the registration threshold is $10,000 in spending per quarter. Organizations must report coalition activities if they contribute more than $5,000 to a coalition. The House and the Senate must now post lobbying information in a searchable file on the Internet.

In a significant alteration to legislative practices, "earmarked" expenditures, commonly called "pork," must now be identified and made public. This last change has not always had its intended effect of reducing earmarks, however, because it turns out that many legislators are actually proud of their "pork" and are happy to tell the folks back home all about it.

The Impact of Lobbying. No matter how professional their conduct, lobbyists continue to have a poor reputation. It is widely believed that by benefiting special interests, their activities injure everyone else. One argument for this proposition is known as **concentrated benefits and dispersed costs.** If a special law, such as a tax break, helps a relatively small number of people, those who receive the benefit will fight hard to keep or enlarge it. Other citizens, who pay for the benefit, may have little motivation to oppose it. For the general public, after all, the cost to each individual is usually a matter of pennies. Still, when many interest groups are able to obtain benefits, the total impact can be very large.

Political Parties in the United States

>>> **LO4:** Cite some of the major activities of U.S. political parties, and discuss how they are organized.

Every two years, the media concentrate on the state of the political parties. Prior to an election, a typical poll usually asks the following question: "Do you consider yourself to be a Republican, a Democrat, or an independent?" For many years, Americans were divided fairly evenly among these three choices. Today, more than 40 percent of all voters call themselves **independents,** although in fact three-quarters or more of all independents lean toward either the Republicans or the Democrats.

In the United States, being a member of a political party does not require paying dues, passing an examination, or swearing an oath of allegiance. If nothing is really required to be a member of a political party, what, then, is a political party? As discussed earlier in this chapter, a political party is a group that seeks to win elections, operate the government, and determine public policy. Political parties are thus quite different from interest groups, which, as mentioned, seek to influence, not run, the government.

Functions of Political Parties in the United States

Political parties in the United States engage in a wide variety of activities, many of which are discussed in this chapter. Through these activities, parties perform a number of functions for the political system. These functions include the following:

1. *Recruiting candidates for public office.* Because it is the goal of parties to gain control of government, they must work to recruit candidates for all elective offices.
2. *Organizing and running elections.* Although elections are a government activity, political parties actually organize voter-registration drives, recruit volunteers to work at the polls, provide much of the campaign activity to stimulate interest in the election, and work to increase voter participation.
3. *Presenting alternative policies to the electorate.* Parties focus on a political program, which is typically detailed in the *party platform.* Party members, when elected, usually try to implement that program.
4. *Accepting responsibility for operating the government.* When a party elects the president or governor—or a majority of the members of a legislative body—it accepts responsibility for running the government. This includes developing linkages among elected officials in the various branches of government to gain support for policies and their implementation.

Concentrated Benefits and Dispersed Costs
The theory that a minority benefiting from a government program will make a stronger effort to keep it than the majority will ever make to abolish it.

Independent
A voter or candidate who does not identify with a political party.

Party Organization
The formal structure and leadership of a political party, including election committees; local, state, and national executives; and paid professional staff.

National Convention
The meeting held every four years by each major party to select presidential and vice-presidential candidates, write a platform, choose a national committee, and conduct party business.

Party Platform
A document drawn up at each national convention, outlining the policies, positions, and principles of the party.

National Committee
A standing committee of a national political party established to direct and coordinate party activities between national party conventions.

5. *Acting as the organized opposition to the party in power.* The "out" party, or the one that does not control the government, is expected to articulate its own policies and oppose the winning party when appropriate.

The major functions of American political parties are carried out by a small, relatively loose-knit nucleus of party activists. This arrangement is quite different from the more highly structured, mass-membership organization typical of many European parties. American parties concentrate on winning elections rather than on signing up large numbers of deeply committed, dues-paying members who believe passionately in the party's program.

The Party Organization

American political parties are sometimes seen as hierarchical, but this perception is not accurate. In reality, the formal structure of each party—the **party organization**—reflects a high degree of decentralization. The parties have a confederal structure, and each unit has substantial independence from the rest of the party.

The National Party Organization. Each party has a national organization, the most conspicuous part of which is the **national convention,** held every four years. The convention is used to officially nominate the presidential and vice-presidential candidates. In addition, the **party platform** is developed at the national convention. The platform sets forth the party's position on the issues and makes promises to initiate certain policies if the party wins control of the government.

After the convention, the platform sometimes is neglected or ignored when party candidates disagree with it. Still, once elected, the parties very often do try to carry out platform promises, and many of the promises eventually become law. Of course, some general goals, such as economic prosperity, are included in the platforms of both major parties.

Alex Wong/Getty Images

Thomas Perez is the chairperson of the Democratic National Committee. *What does his job involve?*

Convention Delegates. The party convention provides a striking illustration of the differences between the ordinary members of a party, or party identifiers, and party activists. Delegates to the Democratic National Convention are usually far more liberal than ordinary Democratic voters. Typically, delegates to the Republican National Convention are far more conservative than ordinary Republicans. Why does this happen? In part, it is because a person who wishes to become a delegate must be appointed by party leaders, or gather votes in a primary election from party members who care enough to vote in a primary. Voter turnout in primary elections is often quite low and those who do vote are likely to be among the most committed and ideological members of the party.

The National Committee. At the national convention, each of the parties formally chooses a national standing committee, elected by the individual state parties. This **national committee** directs and coordinates party activities during the following four years. One of the jobs of the national committee is to ratify the presidential nominee's choice of a national chairperson, who in principle acts as the spokesperson for the party. The national chairperson and the national committee plan the next campaign and the next convention, obtain financial contributions, and publicize the national party.

The State Party Organization. Every state party is unique. Nonetheless, state parties have several organizational features in common. Each state party has a chairperson, a committee, and a number of local organizations. In theory, the role of the **state central committee**—the principal organized structure of each political party within each state—is similar in the various states. The committee has responsibility for carrying out the policy decisions of the party's state convention. The committee also has control over the use of party campaign funds during political campaigns. Usually, the state central committee has little, if any, influence on party candidates once they are elected.

Local Party Machinery: The Grassroots. The lowest layer of party machinery is the local organization, supported by district leaders, precinct or ward captains, and party workers. In the 1800s, the institution of **patronage**—rewarding the party faithful with government jobs or contracts—held the local organization together. For immigrants and the poor, the political machine often furnished important services and protections.

The last big-city local political machine to exercise substantial power was run by Chicago mayor Richard J. Daley (1955–1976), who was also an important figure in national Democratic politics. City machines are now dead, mostly because their function of providing social services (and reaping the reward of votes) has been taken over by state and national agencies.

Local political organizations still provide the foot soldiers of politics—individuals who pass out literature and get out the vote on Election Day, which can be crucial in local elections. In many regions, local Democratic and Republican organizations still exercise some patronage, such as awarding courthouse jobs, contracts for street repair, and other construction contracts. The Supreme Court has ruled, however, that failing to hire or firing individuals because of their political affiliation is an infringement of these individuals' First Amendment rights to free expression.[2] Local party organizations are also the most important vehicles for recruiting young adults into political work.

Bloomberg/Getty Images

Ronna Romney McDaniel is the chairperson of the Republican National Committee. *Do all registered Republicans vote for this position?*

The Party-in-the-Electorate

The *party-in-the-electorate* consists of everyone who identifies with the party in question who is not an elected official or part of the formal party organization. The party-in-the-electorate does not just consist of ordinary Americans, however, but of elites—motivated interests, media personalities, fund-raisers, and prominent figures of all types. These are people who identify with a party but who are not part of its formal organization and are not elected officials.

In *The Party Decides*, a modern classic work, a team of political scientists has argued that **policy demanders** are a key part of any major party. Policy demanders are interest group members or other ideologically motivated individuals who participate in parties with the intent to see that certain policies are adopted, or at least specific groups favored.[3]

State Central Committee
The principal organized structure of each political party within each state. This committee is responsible for carrying out policy decisions of the party's state convention.

Patronage
The practice of rewarding faithful party workers and followers with government employment and contracts.

Policy Demanders
Individuals or interest group members who participate in political parties with the intent to see that certain policies are adopted or specific groups favored.

---

2. *Rutan v. Republican Party of Illinois*, 497 U.S. 62 (1990).
3. Marty Cohen et al., *The Party Decides: Presidential Nominations before and after Reform* (Chicago: University of Chicago Press, 2008).

In the Democratic Party, for example, teachers' unions are policy demanders who favor increased spending on education and policies that benefit teachers. Among Republicans, a variety of policy demanders oppose legislation that would grant legal status to unauthorized immigrants.

Another elite group is opinion leaders. Radio talk show host Rush Limbaugh, for example, holds no office in the government or the Republican Party, but his influence is substantial. Large-scale contributors such as the brothers Charles and David Koch certainly qualify as elites. Entertainment celebrities are an elite group that is heavily Democratic.

The Party-in-Government

After the election is over and the winners are announced, the focus of party activity shifts from getting out the vote to organizing and controlling the government—to the activities of the party-in-government. Party membership plays an important role in the day-to-day operations of Congress, with partisanship determining everything from office space to committee assignments and power on Capitol Hill. For the president, the political party furnishes a pool of qualified applicants for political appointments to run the government. Presidents can, and occasionally do, appoint executive personnel, such as cabinet members, from the opposition party, but it is uncommon to do so. Judicial appointments also offer a great opportunity to the winning party. For the most part, presidents are likely to appoint federal judges from their own party.

Divided Government. All of these party appointments suggest that the winning political party, whether at the national, state, or local level, has a great deal of control in the American system. Because of the checks and balances and the relative lack of cohesion in American parties, however, such control is the exception rather than the rule. One reason is that Americans have often seemed to prefer a **divided government,** with the executive and legislative branches controlled by different parties.

Party Polarization. In recent years, it has become increasingly difficult for legislators in either party to obtain support for legislation from members of the other party. More and more, voting takes place strictly along party lines. One reason for party-line voting is that political overlap between the two parties has vanished. Political scientists calculated that by 2009, the most conservative Democrat in the House was still more liberal than the most moderate Republican.

One effect of the new polarization is that interpersonal relationships between members of the two parties have deteriorated. A second effect is the growing tactic of blocking bills to make the other party appear ineffective, without any attempt to reach a compromise. Today, major changes to the legislative landscape may depend on one party obtaining control of both the presidency and Congress. This can happen—the Democrats had such control in 2009–2010 and the Republicans gained it in 2017, following the 2016 elections.

Divided Government
A situation in which one major political party controls the presidency and the other controls one or more chambers of Congress, or in which one party controls a state governorship and the other controls the state legislature.

Two-Party System
A political system in which only two parties have a reasonable chance of winning.

A History of Political Parties in the United States

>>> **LO5:** Explain how the history of U.S. political parties has led to the two major parties that exist today.

The United States has a **two-party system,** and that system has been around since before 1800. The function and character of the political parties, as well as the emergence of the two-party system itself, have much to do with the unique historical forces operating from this country's beginning as an independent nation.

Generally, we can divide the evolution of our nation's political parties into seven periods:

1. The formation of parties, from 1789 to 1816.
2. The era of one-party rule, from 1816 to 1828.
3. The period from Andrew Jackson's presidency to the eve of the Civil War, from 1828 to 1856.
4. The Civil War and post–Civil War period, from 1856 to 1896.
5. The Republican ascendancy and the progressive period, from 1896 to 1932.
6. The New Deal period, from 1932 to about 1968.
7. The modern period, from approximately 1968 to the present.

The Formative Years: Federalists and Anti-Federalists

The first political division in the United States occurred before the adoption of the Constitution. The Federalists pushed for the adoption of the Constitution, whereas the Anti-Federalists were against ratification.

In September 1796, George Washington, who had served as president for two terms, decided not to run again. In his farewell address, he made a somber assessment of the nation's future. Washington felt that the country might be destroyed by the "baneful [harmful] effects of the spirit of party." He viewed parties as a threat to both national unity and the concept of popular government. Nevertheless, in the years after the ratification of the Constitution, Americans came to realize that some permanent mechanism would be necessary to identify candidates for office and represent political differences among the people. The result was two political parties.

Library of Congress Prints and Photographs Division[LC-US262-387]

Thomas Jefferson, founder of the first Republican Party. His election to the presidency in 1800 was one of the world's first peaceful transfers of power from one party to another through a free election. *What did Jefferson's party stand for?*

Federalists and Republicans. One party was the Federalists, which included John Adams, the second president (1797–1801). The Federalists represented commercial interests such as merchants and large planters. They supported a strong national government.

Thomas Jefferson led the other party, which came to be called the Republicans. These Republicans should not be confused with the later Republican Party of Abraham Lincoln. (To avoid confusion, some scholars refer to Jefferson's party as the Democratic Republicans, but this name was never used during the time that the party existed.) Jefferson's Republicans represented artisans and farmers. They strongly supported states' rights. In 1800, when Jefferson defeated Adams in the presidential contest, one of the world's first peaceful transfers of power from one party to another was achieved.

The One-Party Interlude. From 1800 to 1820, a majority of U.S. voters regularly elected Jeffersonian Republicans to the presidency and to Congress. By 1816, the Federalist Party had nearly collapsed, and two-party competition did not really exist at the national level. Because there was no real political opposition to the Jeffersonian Republicans and thus little political debate, the administration of James Monroe (1817–1825) came to be known as the era of good feelings.

Library of Congress/Science Source

Andrew Jackson earned the name "Old Hickory" for exploits during the War of 1812. In 1828, Jackson was elected president as the candidate of the new Democratic Party. *Whom did this party seek to represent?*

Democratic Party
One of the two major American political parties evolving out of the Republican Party of Thomas Jefferson. It was formed in 1828.

Whig Party
A major party in the United States during the first half of the nineteenth century, formally established in 1836. The Whig Party was anti-Jackson and advocated spending on infrastructure.

Republican Party
One of the two major American political parties. It emerged in the 1850s as an antislavery party and consisted of former northern Whigs and antislavery Democrats.

GOP
A nickname for the Republican Party, which stands for "grand old party."

Democrats and Whigs

Organized two-party politics returned after 1824. Following the election of John Quincy Adams as president, the Republican Party split in two. The supporters of Adams called themselves National Republicans. The supporters of Andrew Jackson, who defeated Adams in 1828, formed the **Democratic Party.** Later, the National Republicans took the name **Whig Party,** which had been a traditional name for British liberals. The Whigs stood for, among other things, federal spending on "internal improvements," such as roads. The Democrats opposed this policy. The Democrats, who were the stronger of the two parties, favored personal liberty and opportunity for the "common man." It was understood implicitly that the "common man" was a white man—hostility toward African Americans was an important force holding the disparate Democratic groups together.[4]

The Civil War Crisis

In the 1850s, hostility between the North and the South over the issue of slavery divided both parties. The Whigs were the first to split in two. The Whigs had been the party of an active federal government, but white Southerners had come to believe that "a government strong enough to build roads is a government strong enough to free your slaves." The southern Whigs therefore ceased to exist as an organized party. In 1854, the northern Whigs united with antislavery Democrats and members of the radical antislavery Free Soil Party to found the modern **Republican Party.**

The Post–Civil War Period

After the Civil War, the Democratic Party was able to heal its divisions. Southern resentment of the Republicans' role in defeating the South and fears that the federal government would intervene on behalf of African Americans ensured that the Democrats would dominate the white South for the next century. It was in this period that the Republicans adopted the nickname **GOP,** which stands for "grand old party."

Cultural Politics. Northern Democrats feared a strong government for other reasons. The Republicans thought that the government should promote business and economic growth, but many Republicans also wanted to use the power of government to impose evangelical Protestant moral values on society. Democrats opposed what they saw as culturally coercive measures. Many Republicans wanted to limit or even prohibit the sale of alcoholic beverages. They favored the establishment of public schools—with a Protestant curriculum. As a result, Catholics were strongly Democratic. In this period, the parties were very evenly matched in strength.

The Triumph of the Republicans. In the 1890s, however, the Republicans gained a decisive edge. In that decade, the populist movement emerged in the West and South to champion the interests of small farmers, who were often greatly in debt. Populists supported inflation, which benefited

---

4. Edward Pessen, *Jacksonian America: Society, Personality, and Politics* (Homewood, Ill.: Dorsey Press, 1969). See especially pages 246-247. The small number of free blacks who could vote were overwhelmingly Whig.

debtors by reducing the real value of outstanding debts. In 1896, when William Jennings Bryan became the Democratic candidate for president, the Democrats embraced populism.

As it turned out, the few western farmers who were drawn to the Democrats by this step were greatly outnumbered by urban working class voters who believed that inflation would reduce the purchasing power of their paychecks and who therefore became Republicans. Political scientists use the term **realignment** to refer to this kind of large-scale change in support for the two major parties. From 1896 until 1932, the GOP was successful in presenting itself as the party that knew how to manage the economy.

Realignment
A large-scale, lasting change in the types of voters who support each of the major political parties.

The Progressive Interlude

In the early 1900s, a spirit of political reform arose in both major parties. Called *progressivism*, this spirit was compounded of a fear of the growing power of large corporations and a belief that honest, impartial government could regulate the economy effectively. In 1912, the Republican Party temporarily split as former Republican president Theodore Roosevelt campaigned for the presidency on a third-party Progressive ticket. The Republican split permitted the election of Woodrow Wilson, the Democratic candidate, along with a Democratic Congress.

Like Roosevelt, Wilson considered himself a progressive, although he and Roosevelt did not agree on how progressivism ought to be implemented. Wilson's progressivism marked the beginning of a radical change in Democratic policies. Dating back to its very foundation, the Democratic Party had been the party of limited government. Under Wilson, the Democrats became for the first time at least as receptive as the Republicans to government action in the economy. (Wilson's progressivism did not extend to race relations—African Americans found the Wilson administration to be unremittingly hostile to their interests.)

The New Deal Era

The Republican ascendancy resumed after Wilson left office. It ended with the election of 1932, in the depths of the Great Depression. Republican Herbert Hoover was president when the Depression began in 1929. While Hoover took some measures to fight the Depression, they fell far short of what the public demanded. Significantly, Hoover opposed federal relief for the unemployed and the destitute. In 1932, Democrat Franklin D. Roosevelt was elected president by an overwhelming margin. As with the election of 1896, the vote in 1932 constituted a major political realignment.

The Great Depression shattered the working-class belief in Republican economic competence. Under Roosevelt, the Democrats began to make major interventions in the economy in an attempt to combat the Depression and to relieve the suffering of the unemployed. Roosevelt's New Deal relief programs were open to all citizens, both black and white. As a result, African Americans began to support the Democratic Party in large numbers—a development that would have stunned any American politician of the 1800s.

Roosevelt's political coalition was broad enough to establish the Democrats as the new majority party, in place

Tom Williams/Getty Images

Governor Susana Martinez (R-N.M.) addresses the Republican National Convention in 2012.
Why do political parties often choose governors as presidential candidates?

of the GOP. In the 1950s, Republican Dwight D. Eisenhower, the leading U.S. general during World War II, won two terms as president. Otherwise, with minor interruptions, the Democratic ascendancy lasted until about 1968.

An Era of Divided Government

The New Deal coalition managed the unlikely feat of including both African Americans and whites who were hostile to African American advancement. This balancing act came to an end in the 1960s, a decade that was marked by the civil rights movement, by several years of "race riots" in major cities, and by increasingly heated protests against the Vietnam War (1965–1975). For many economically moderate, socially conservative voters, especially in the South, social issues had become more important than economic ones, and these individuals left the Democratic Party. These voters outnumbered the new voters who joined the Democrats—newly enfranchised African Americans and former liberal Republicans in New England and the upper Midwest.

The Parties in Balance. The result, after 1968, was a slow-motion realignment that left the nation almost evenly divided in politics. In presidential elections, the Republicans had more success than the Democrats. Until the 1990s, Congress remained Democratic, but official party labels can be misleading. Some of the Democrats were southern conservatives who normally voted with the Republicans on issues. As these conservative Democrats retired, they were largely replaced by Republicans. In 1994, Republicans were able to take control of both the House and the Senate for the first time in many years.

Red State, Blue State. Nothing demonstrated the nation's close political divisions more clearly than the 2000 presidential elections. Democratic presidential candidate Al Gore won the popular vote, but lost the electoral college by a narrow margin to Republican George W. Bush. The closeness of the vote in the electoral college led the press to repeatedly publish maps showing state-by-state results. Commentators discussed at length the supposed differences between the Republican "red states" and the Democratic "blue states."[5]

An interesting characteristic of the red state–blue state division is that it is an almost exact reversal of the results of the presidential elections of 1896, which established the Republican ascendancy that lasted until the Great Depression. Except for the state of Washington, every state that supported Democrat William Jennings Bryan in 1896 supported Republican George W. Bush in 2000 and 2004. This reversal parallels the transformation of the Democrats from an anti–civil rights to a pro–civil rights party and from a party that supported limited government to a party that favors positive government action.

The Parties Today

Not only was the presidential election of 2000 very close, but the partisan balance in the U.S. Congress was also very close in the opening years of the twenty-first century. It is true that from 1995 until the elections of 2006, the Republicans generally controlled Congress. Their margins of control, however, were very narrow.

From time to time, voters demonstrate that they are relatively dissatisfied with the performance of one or another of the major parties. This dissatisfaction can produce a "wave" of support for the other party. Unlike a realignment, the effects of a **wave election**

Wave Election
An election in which voters display dissatisfaction with one of the major parties through a "wave" of support for the other. In contrast to a realigning election, the results of a wave election are not permanent.

---

5. The use of red for Republicans and blue for Democrats is a twenty-first century development. It originated in the colors used by TV networks to display the results of presidential elections. This color scheme reverses the typical international pattern, which assigns red to the political left and blue to the right. Red is the traditional color of socialist and communist parties, and the U.S. color reversal was a deliberate attempt to avoid implying that Democrats were socialists.

are temporary. The first decade of the twenty-first century was marked by a series of wave elections, in which the voters punished first one party and then the other.

Wave Elections Sweep out the Republicans. By 2006, an ever-larger number of voters came to believe that U.S. intervention in Iraq had been a mistake. In the 2006 midterm elections, the Democrats took control of the U.S. House and Senate in a wave election. In September 2008, a worldwide financial panic turned what had been a modest recession into the greatest economic downturn since the Great Depression of the 1930s. The political consequences were inevitable. In November, Democratic presidential candidate Barack Obama was elected with one of the largest margins in recent years.

Republicans on the Upswing. In 2010, a wave election returned control of the House to the Republicans. Many voters were convinced that Democrats were expanding government to an unacceptable degree. The uncompromising politics of many of the new Republicans in Congress, however, may have helped President Obama win reelection in 2012. Still, the Republicans retained control of the House, even though Democratic House candidates won more votes nationwide than Republican candidates. In the 2014 elections, however, the Republicans did very well. In the House, their margin was now greater than any they had enjoyed since the 1920s.

While the Republican triumph in 2014 was undeniable, some observers questioned whether the result was in fact due to another wave election. Rather, the outcome may have been due to low voter turnout. In 2014, turnout was only 36.4 percent, lower than any year since the elections of 1942 (which were held in the middle of World War II). Many minority and youthful voters failed to vote in the midterms.

Two Electorates? One characteristic of the Obama years was a striking political divergence between the old and the young. As a result, the nation may be moving into a pattern in which the Democrats do better in presidential years, while the Republicans do best in the midterms. Although the Republicans won the 2016 elections, as you can see in Figure 7–2, the results still tended to confirm this pattern. After all, Democrat Hillary Clinton carried the popular vote by a margin of more than 2.8 million. The 2016 elections did reveal one trend that had been developing for several years. The continual rise in the number of Latino and Asian voters was counterbalanced by the growing popularity of Republicans among whites. The question for the future was whether the white Republican vote would continue to grow at least as fast as the number of young brown, black, and white Democratic voters.

Why Has the Two-Party System Endured?

>>> **LO6:** Give reasons why the two-party system has endured in America, and evaluate the impact of third parties and independents on U.S. politics.

There are several reasons why two major parties have dominated the political landscape in the United States for almost two centuries. These reasons have to do with

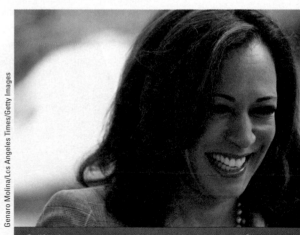

Genaro Molina/Los Angeles Times/Getty Images

California attorney general Kamala Harris won a U.S. Senate seat in 2016 running as a Democrat. Harris's parents were both immigrants—her mother from India and her father from Jamaica. *Why might a person with such a background be more likely to align with the Democrats than the Republicans?*

(1) the historical foundations of the system, (2) political socialization and practical considerations, (3) the winner-take-all electoral system, and (4) state and federal laws favoring the two-party system.

The Historical Foundations of the Two-Party System

As we have seen, at many times in American history one preeminent issue or dispute has divided the nation politically. In the beginning, Americans were at odds over ratifying the Constitution. After the Constitution went into effect, the power of the federal government became the major national issue. Thereafter, the dispute over slavery divided the nation, North versus South. At times—for example, in the North after the Civil War—cultural differences have been important. In that period, advocates of government-sponsored morality (such as banning alcoholic beverages) were pitted against advocates of personal liberty. During much of the twentieth century, economic differences were preeminent. In the New Deal period, the Democrats became known as the party of the working class, while the Republicans became known as the party of the middle and upper classes and commercial interests.

In situations like these, when politics is based on an argument between two opposing points of view, advocates of each viewpoint can mobilize most effectively by forming a single, unified party. The result is a two-party system. When such a system has been in existence for almost two centuries, it becomes difficult to imagine an alternative.

Political Socialization and Practical Considerations

Given that the majority of Americans identify with one of the two major political parties, it is not surprising that many children learn at a fairly young age to think of themselves as either Democrats or Republicans. This generates a built-in mechanism to perpetuate a

FIGURE 7–2   **The 2016 Presidential Election Results**

Donald Trump made major gains in the Midwest. (Maine awards two of its electoral votes by congressional district, and the pink square reflects Trump's victory in one of them.)

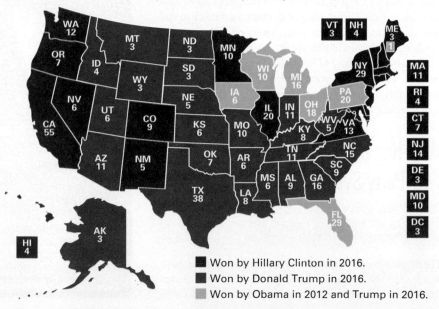

■ Won by Hillary Clinton in 2016.
■ Won by Donald Trump in 2016.
■ Won by Obama in 2012 and Trump in 2016.

two-party system. Also, most politically oriented people who aspire to work for change consider that the only realistic way to capture political power in this country is to be either a Republican or a Democrat.

The Winner-Take-All Electoral System

At almost every level of government in the United States, the outcome of elections is based on the **plurality,** winner-take-all principle. In a plurality system, the winner is the person who obtains the most votes, even if that person does not receive a majority (more than 50 percent) of the votes. Whoever gets the most votes gets everything. Most legislators in the United States are elected from single-member districts in which only one person represents the constituency, and the candidate who finishes second in such an election receives nothing for the effort.

Presidential Voting. The winner-take-all system also operates in the election of the U.S. president. Recall that the voters in each state do not vote for a president directly but vote for *electoral college* delegates who are committed to the various presidential candidates. These delegates are called *electors*.

In all but two states (Maine and Nebraska), if a presidential candidate wins a plurality in the state, then *all* of the state's electoral votes go to that candidate. This is known as the **unit rule.** For example, suppose that the electors pledged to a particular presidential candidate receive a plurality of 40 percent of the votes in a state. That presidential candidate will receive all of the state's votes in the electoral college. Minor parties have a difficult time competing under such a system. Because voters know that minor parties cannot win any electoral votes, they often will not vote for minor-party candidates, even if the candidates are in tune with them ideologically.

Popular Election of the Governors and the President. In most of Europe, the chief executive (usually called the prime minister) is elected by the legislature, or parliament. If the parliament contains three or more parties, as is usually the situation, two or more of the parties can join together in a coalition to choose the prime minister and the other leaders of the government. In the United States, however, the people elect the president and the governors of all fifty states. There is no opportunity for two or more parties to negotiate a coalition. Here, too, the winner-take-all principle discriminates powerfully against any third party.

Proportional Representation. Many other nations use a system of proportional representation with multimember districts. If, during the national election, party X obtains 12 percent of the vote, party Y gets 43 percent of the vote, and party Z gets the remaining 45 percent of the vote, then party X gets 12 percent of the seats in the legislature, party Y gets 43 percent of the seats, and party Z gets 45 percent of the seats. Because even a minor party may still obtain at least a few seats in the legislature, smaller parties have a greater incentive to organize under such electoral systems than they do in the United States.

State and Federal Laws Favoring the Two Parties

Many state and federal election laws offer a clear advantage to the two major parties. In some states, the established major parties need to gather fewer signatures to place their candidates on the ballot than minor parties or independent candidates do. The criterion

Interact

One of the most dangerous assumptions students can make is that something is true because they read it on the Internet. To be sure, some Internet sites are relatively reliable. Wikipedia, for example, receives much criticism. Yet studies have shown that its accuracy typically surpasses that of the *Encyclopedia Britannica* online. (Wikipedia does have the problem that its pages are occasionally subject to vandalism.) In contrast, statements made on the websites of political parties are utterly suspect. True facts that you can learn by visiting these sites may be limited to "What is the party trying to say?" and "Whom is it trying to say it to?" Anything that a party reports about another party is likely to be exaggerated, unfair, or flatly untrue. Try visiting the websites of the Republican and Democratic parties. Can you identify any statements that strike you as troublesome?

Plurality
A number of votes cast for a candidate that is greater than the number of votes for any other candidate but not necessarily a majority.

Unit Rule
A rule by which all of a state's electoral votes are cast for the presidential candidate who receives a plurality of the votes in that state.

Third Party
A political party other than the two major political parties (Republican and Democratic).

for determining how many signatures will be required is often based on the total party vote in the last general election, thus penalizing a new political party that did not compete in that election.

At the national level, minor parties face different obstacles. All of the rules and procedures of both chambers of Congress divide committee seats, staff members, and other privileges on the basis of party membership. A legislator who is elected on a minor-party ticket, such as the Conservative Party of New York, must choose to be counted with one of the major parties to obtain a committee assignment.

The Federal Election Commission (FEC) rules for campaign financing also place restrictions on minor-party candidates for president. Such candidates are not eligible for federal matching funds in either the primary or the general elections. In the 1980 elections, John Anderson, running for president as an independent, sued the FEC for campaign funds. The commission finally agreed to repay part of his campaign costs after Election Day in proportion to the votes he received. Giving funds to a candidate when the campaign is over is, of course, much less helpful than providing funds while the campaign is still under way.

The Role of Minor Parties in U.S. Politics

For the reasons just discussed, minor parties have a difficult, if not impossible, time competing within the American two-party political system. Still, minor parties have played an important role in our political life. Parties other than the Republicans or Democrats are usually called **third parties**. (Technically, of course, there could be fourth, fifth, or sixth parties as well, but we use the term *third party* because it has endured.) Third parties can come into existence in a number of ways. They may be founded from scratch by individuals or groups who are committed to a particular interest, issue, or ideology. They can split off from one of the major parties when a group becomes dissatisfied with the major party's policies. Finally, they can be organized around a particular charismatic leader and serve as that person's vehicle for contesting elections.

Frequently, third parties have acted as barometers of change in the political mood, forcing the major parties to recognize new issues or trends in the thinking of Americans. Political scientists also believe that third parties have acted as safety valves for dissident groups, preventing major confrontations and political unrest.

Ideological Third Parties. The longest-lived third parties have been those with strong ideological foundations that are typically

Library of Congress Prints and Photographs Division Washington, D.C. 20540 USA

Eugene V. Debs was the nation's most popular socialist ever—at least until Senator Bernie Sanders (D., Vt.). Debs ran for president five times from 1900 to 1920, the last time from a prison cell. He had been convicted of speaking out against World War I. *Why would such a conviction be impossible today?*

at odds with the majority mind-set. The Socialist Party is an example. The party was founded in 1901 and lasted until 1972, when it was finally dissolved. (A smaller party later took up the name.) The Socialists were never very popular in the United States. Conservatives recently revived the term *socialist* as an insult directed at President Obama. Given that, it was somewhat surprising that Bernie Sanders did so well as a presidential candidate in 2016 running as a democratic socialist.

Ideology has at least two functions in such parties. First, the members of the party regard themselves as outsiders and look to one another for support—ideology provides great psychological cohesiveness. Second, because the rewards of ideological commitment are partly psychological, these parties do not think in terms of immediate electoral success. A poor showing at the polls therefore does not dissuade either the leadership or the grassroots participants from continuing their quest for change in American government (and, ultimately, American society).

Today's active ideological parties include the Libertarian Party and the Green Party. The Libertarian Party supports a *laissez-faire* ("let it be") capitalist economic program, together with a hands-off policy on regulating matters of moral conduct. The Green Party began as a grassroots environmentalist organization with affiliated political parties across North America and Western Europe. It was established in the United States as a national party in 1996 and nominated Ralph Nader to run for president in 2000. Nader campaigned against what he called "corporate greed," advocated universal health insurance, and promoted environmental concerns. (He ran again for president as an independent in 2004 and 2008.)

Splinter Parties. Some of the more successful minor parties have been those that split from major parties. The impetus for these **splinter parties,** or factions, has usually been a situation in which a particular personality was at odds with the major party. The most successful of these splinter parties was the "Bull Moose" Progressive Party, formed in 1912 to support Theodore Roosevelt for president. The Republican national convention of that year denied Roosevelt the nomination, despite the fact that he had won most of the primaries. He therefore left the GOP and ran against Republican "regular" William Howard Taft in the general elections. Although Roosevelt did not win the elections, he did split the Republican vote so that Democrat Woodrow Wilson became president.

Third parties have also been formed to back individual candidates who were not rebelling against a particular party. H. Ross Perot, for example, who challenged Republican George H. W. Bush and Democrat Bill Clinton for the presidency in 1992, had not previously been active in a major party. Perot's supporters probably would have split their votes between Bush and Clinton had Perot not been in the race. In theory, Perot ran in 1992 as a nonparty independent. In practice, he had to create a campaign organization. By 1996, Perot's organization was formalized as the Reform Party.

The Impact of Minor Parties. Third parties have rarely been able to affect American politics by actually winning elections. (One exception is that third-party and independent candidates have occasionally won races for state governorships—for example, Jesse Ventura was elected governor of Minnesota on the Reform Party ticket in 1998.) Instead, the impact of third parties has taken two forms. First, third parties can influence one of the major parties to take up one or more issues. Second, third parties can determine the outcome of a particular election by pulling votes from one of the major-party candidates in what is called the "spoiler effect."

The presidential elections of 2000 were one instance in which a minor party may have altered the outcome. Green candidate Ralph Nader received almost one hundred thousand

Splinter Party
A new party formed by a dissident faction within a major political party. Often, splinter parties have emerged when a particular personality was at odds with the major party.

Party Identification
Linking oneself to a particular political party.

Straight-Ticket Voting
Voting exclusively for the candidates of one party.

votes in Florida, a majority of which would probably have gone to Democrat Al Gore if Nader had not been in the race. The real question, however, is not whether the Nader vote had an effect—clearly, it did—but whether the effect was important. The problem is that in elections as close as the presidential elections of 2000, *any* factor with an impact on the outcome can be said to have determined the results.

The Rise of the Independents

Polls that track **party identification** show increasing numbers of voters who identify themselves as independents. (See Figure 7–3.) Not only has the number of independents grown over the last half century, but voters also have been less willing to vote a straight ticket—that is, to vote for all the candidates of one party. In the early twentieth century, **straight-ticket voting** was nearly universal. By midcentury, 12 percent of voters engaged in split-ticket voting. By the 1970s and 1980s, 25 to 30 percent of all ballots cast in presidential election years were split-ticket. A major reason was that many voters, especially in the South, were pairing a Republican for president with a conservative Democrat for Congress. In recent years, however, conservative Democrats have become scarce, and the incidence of split-ticket voting has ranged only from 17 to 19 percent.

While the number of voters who identify as independents has never been greater, many voters who call themselves independents actually lean toward one or the other of the two major parties. In a poll taken in December 2016, for example, 42 percent of all voters reported either that they were Democrats or that they were independents who leaned toward the Democratic Party. The corresponding figure for the Republicans was 41 percent. Leaving aside respondents who were unable to answer the question, true independents were just 13 percent of the polling sample. The fact that many independents today are really party supporters— and the increased political polarization of recent years—means that straight-ticket voting is becoming more common again.

FIGURE 7–3   **Party Identification from 1945 to the Present**

Why would people who usually support one of the two major parties still call themselves independents?

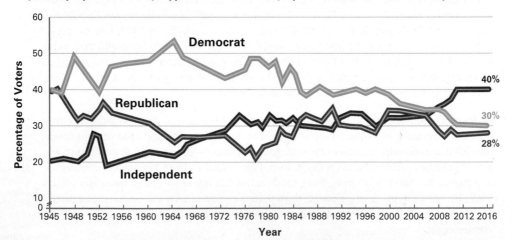

Sources: *Gallup Report*, August 1995; *New York Times*/CBS poll, June 1996; *Gallup Report*, February 1998; Pew Research Center for the People and the Press, November 2003; Gallup polls, 2004 through 2016. (Numbers do not add up to 100 due to undecided responses.)

MAKING A DIFFERENCE

You Can Be a Convention Delegate

The most exciting political party event, staged every four years, is the national convention. State conventions also take place on a regular basis. Surprising as it might seem, there are opportunities for the individual voter to become a delegate.

Why Should You Care? How would you like to exercise a small amount of real political power yourself—power that goes beyond simply voting in an election? You might be able to become a delegate to a county, district, or even state party convention. Many of these conventions nominate candidates for various offices. For example, in Michigan, the state party conventions nominate the candidates for the Board of Regents of the state's top three public universities.

In much of the country, there are more openings for party precinct delegates than there are people willing to serve. In such circumstances, almost anyone can become a delegate by collecting a handful of signatures on a nominating petition or by mounting a small-scale write-in campaign.

What Can You Do? When the parties choose delegates for the national convention, the process begins at the local level—either the congressional district or the state legislative district. District delegates may be elected in party primary elections or chosen in neighborhood or precinct caucuses. If the delegates are elected in a primary, persons who want to run for these positions may need to file petitions with the board of elections.

It is even easier to get involved in the grassroots politics of presidential caucuses. In some states—Iowa being the earliest and most famous one—delegates are first nominated at the local precinct caucus. These caucuses select delegates to the county conventions who are pledged to specific presidential candidates. This is the first step toward the national convention. At both the county caucus and the convention levels, the parties often try to find younger members to fill some of the seats.

For further information about these opportunities contact the state party office or your local state legislator.

Key Terms

concentrated benefits and dispersed costs 157
Democratic Party 162
direct technique 153
divided government 160
free-rider problem 148
GOP 162
independent 157
indirect technique 153

interest group 146
labor movement 149
lobbyist 147
national committee 158
national convention 158
party identification 170
party organization 158
party platform 158
patronage 159

plurality 167
policy demanders 159
political party 147
public interest 152
realignment 163
Republican Party 162
service sector 150
social movement 148
splinter party 169

state central committee 159
straight-ticket voting 170
third party 168
two-party system 160
unit rule 167
wave election 164
Whig Party 162

Chapter Summary

>>> **LO1** An interest group is an organization whose members share common objectives and actively attempt to influence government policy. Interest groups proliferate in the United States because they can influence government at many points in the political structure.

>>> **LO2** Major types of economic interest groups include business, agricultural, labor, and professional groups. Other important groups include environmental, public-interest, ideological, and identity groups.

>>> **LO3** Interest groups use direct and indirect techniques to influence government. Direct techniques include testifying before committees and rulemaking agencies, providing information to legislators, rating legislators' voting records, and aiding in political campaigns. Indirect techniques include conducting campaigns to rally public sentiment and using constituents to lobby for a group's interests.

In 1995, the Lobbying Disclosure Act defined lobbyists and their reporting requirements. In 2007, the Honest Leadership and Open Government Act increased the frequency of lobbyists' reports, required reports on coalition activity, and created a searchable Internet file on lobbying activity.

>>> **LO4** A political party is a group of political activists who organize to win elections, operate the government, and determine public policy. Functions of political parties include recruiting candidates for public office, organizing and running elections, presenting alternative policies to voters, assuming responsibility for operating the government, and acting as the opposition to the party in power.

A political party consists of those who identify with the party—the voters-in-the-electorate, the party organization, and the party-in-government. Each level of the party organization—local, state, and national—has considerable autonomy.

>>> **LO5** The evolution of our nation's political parties can be divided into seven periods: (a) the creation and formation of political parties, from 1789 to 1816; (b) the era of one-party rule from 1816 to 1828; (c) the period from Andrew Jackson's presidency to the eve of the Civil War, from 1828 to 1856; (d) the Civil War and post–Civil War period, from 1856 to 1896; (e) the Republican ascendancy and the progressive period, from 1896 to 1932; (f) the New Deal period, from 1932 to about 1968; and (g) the modern period, from approximately 1968 to the present. Throughout most of the modern period, the Republican and Democratic parties have been closely matched in strength.

>>> **LO6** Two major parties have dominated the political landscape in the United States for almost two centuries. The reasons for this include (a) the historical foundations of the system, (b) political socialization and practical considerations, (c) the winner-take-all electoral system, and (d) state and federal laws favoring the two-party system.

For these reasons, minor parties have found it extremely difficult to win elections. Still, third parties can affect the political process (even if they do not win) if major parties adopt their issues or if they help determine which major party wins an election.

From the 1940s to the present, independent voters have formed an increasing proportion of the electorate, with a consequent decline in Democratic and Republican party identification. Nevertheless, many independent voters lean toward one major party or the other.

Test Yourself

1. When individuals benefit from the actions of an interest group but do not support that group, they are:
   a. free riders.
   b. freeloaders.
   c. usually just waiting to join the group.

2. Union membership in the United States has:
   a. been growing, especially since 2000.
   b. stayed about the same since the Great Depression.
   c. been declining in recent years, except in the public sector.

3. There are many direct techniques that interest groups can use to affect legislation. They include:

   a. sending out large numbers of direct-mail advertising pieces.

   b. attempts at weakening other interest groups.

   c. hiring lobbyists to argue their positions with members of Congress.

4. Most lobbying is done by the following kind of people, who often work for Washington, D.C., law firms:

   a. constituents.

   b. professionals.

   c. activists.

5. Some interest groups try to organize campaigns that make it seem as if ordinary citizens are behind the effort. Such campaigns are called:

   a. astroturf lobbying.

   b. climate control.

   c. the rifle technique.

6. A difficulty in limiting the effect of lobbying is:

   a. opposition to new legislation by Democratic members of Congress.

   b. opposition to new legislation by Republican presidents.

   c. many legislators are proud of "pork" spending and are happy to tell their constituents all about it.

7. An American political party includes:

   a. the party-in-the-electorate, the party organization, and the members of the party.

   b. the party organization, the party-in-government, and the party-in-the-electorate.

   c. the party-in-government, the party-in-the-electorate, and the lobbyists for that party.

8. In the years following the adoption of the Constitution, the first two organized political parties in the United States were the:

   a. Democrats and Republicans.

   b. Whigs and Democrats.

   c. Federalists and Republicans.

9. The elections of 1896, in which the Republicans gained a lasting advantage, were an example of:

   a. political dealignment.

   b. a realigning election.

   c. the establishment of divided government.

10. The New Deal era under Democratic president Franklin D. Roosevelt began:

    a. at the beginning of the twentieth century.

    b. during the 1960s.

    c. during the Great Depression of the 1930s.

11. At almost every level of government in this country, the outcome of elections is based on the plurality voting system, which means that:

    a. the candidate with the largest number of votes wins, even if the winner does not receive 50 percent or more of the votes.

    b. when no one receives 50 percent of the vote, a runoff election is held.

    c. there is no need for everyone to vote in each election.

Essay Questions

1. About half of the paid lobbyists in Washington, D.C., are former government staff members or former members of Congress. Why would interest groups employ such people? Why might some reformers want to limit the ability of interest groups to employ them? On what basis might an interest group argue that such limits are unconstitutional?

2. Do you support (or lean toward) one of the major political parties today? If so, would you have supported the same party in the mid-to-late 1800s—or would you have supported a different party? Explain your reasoning.

Answers to multiple-choice questions: 1. a, 2. c, 3. c, 4. b, 5. a, 6. c, 7. b, 8. c, 9. b, 10. c, 11. a.

8 | Campaigns and Elections

Supporters of Republican presidential candidate Donald Trump in North Carolina shortly before the November elections.
What types of people were more likely to vote for Trump?

Chip Somodevilla/Getty Images News/Getty Images

The five **Learning Outcomes (LOs)** below are designed to help improve your understanding of this chapter. After reading this chapter, you should be able to:

>>>**LO1** Discuss who runs for office and how campaigns are managed.

>>>**LO2** Describe the current system of campaign finance.

>>>**LO3** Summarize the process of choosing a president of the United States.

>>>**LO4** Explain the mechanisms through which voting takes place on Election Day, and discuss voter turnout in the United States.

>>>**LO5** Provide some of the reasons why people vote in particular ways.

Check your understanding of the material with the Test Yourself section at the end of the chapter.

Free elections are the cornerstone of the American political system. By casting ballots in local, state, and federal elections, voters choose one candidate over another to hold political office. There are thousands of elective offices in the United States and, consequently, thousands of elections. Although the major political parties strive to provide a slate of candidates for every election, recruiting candidates is easier for some offices than for others. Political parties may have difficulty finding candidates for the board of the local water control district, for example, but they generally find a sufficient number of candidates for county commissioner or sheriff. The higher the office and the more prestige attached to it, the more candidates are likely to want to run. In many areas of the country, however, one major party may be considerably stronger than the other. In those situations, the minority party may have difficulty finding nominees for elections in which victory is unlikely.

The Twenty-First-Century Campaign

>>> **LO1:** Discuss who runs for office and how campaigns are managed.

The presidential campaign provides the most colorful and exciting look at candidates and how they prepare to compete for office—in this instance, the highest office in the land. The men and women who wanted to be their party's candidate in the 2016 presidential campaign faced a long and obstacle-filled path. First, they needed to tour the nation—particularly the states with early **presidential primaries**—to see if they had enough local supporters. They needed to create an organization and to win primary votes. Finally, when nominated as the party's candidate, the winner required funds to finance a successful campaign for president. Always, at every turn, there was the question of whether there were enough funds to effectively compete against primary opponents, and eventually against the candidate of the other party in the general election.

Who Is Eligible?

There are few constitutional restrictions on who can be elected to national office in the United States. As detailed in the Constitution, the formal requirements are as follows:

1. *President.* Must be a natural-born citizen, have attained the age of thirty-five years, and be a resident of the country for fourteen years by the time of inauguration.
2. *Vice president.* Must meet the same requirements as the president and also not be a resident of the same state as the president.[1]
3. *Senator.* Must be a citizen for at least nine years, have attained the age of thirty by the time of taking office, and be a resident of the state from which elected.
4. *Representative.* Must be a citizen for at least seven years, have attained the age of twenty-five by the time of taking office, and be a resident of the state from which elected.

The qualifications for state legislators are set by state constitutions and likewise include age, place of residence, and citizenship. (Usually, the requirements for the state senate are somewhat higher than those for the lower chamber of the state legislature.) The legal qualifications for serving as governor or in other state offices are similar.

Who Runs?

In spite of these minimal legal qualifications for office at both the national and the state levels, a quick look at the slate of candidates in any election—or at the current members of Congress—will reveal that not all segments of the population enjoy these opportunities equally. Holders of political office in the United States have been predominantly white and male. Until the twentieth century, presidential candidates were exclusively of northern European origin and of Protestant heritage.[2] Laws that effectively denied voting rights made it impossible to elect African American public officials in many areas in which African Americans constituted a significant portion of the population. As a result of the passage of major civil rights legislation in the 1960s, however, the number of African American public

Presidential Primary
A statewide primary election of delegates to a political party's national convention, held to determine a party's presidential nominee

---

1. Technically, a presidential and a vice-presidential candidate can be from the same state, but if they are, one of the two must forfeit the electoral votes of their home state.
2. A number of early presidents were Unitarian. The Unitarian Church is not Protestant, but it is historically rooted in the Protestant tradition.

Primary Election
An election in which political parties choose their candidates for the general election.

General Election
An election, normally held on the first Tuesday in November, that determines who will fill various elected positions.

officials has increased throughout the United States, and in a groundbreaking vote, the nation elected an African American president in 2008.

Women as Candidates. Until recently, women generally were considered to be appropriate candidates only for lower-level offices, such as state legislator or school board member. The past twenty-five years have seen a tremendous increase in the number of women who run for office, not only at the state level but for the U.S. Congress as well. In 2016, 174 women ran for Congress on major-party tickets, and 89 were elected. Today, a majority of Americans say they would vote for a qualified woman for president of the United States. Indeed, Hillary Clinton came close to winning the Democratic presidential nomination in 2008, a year in which the eventual Democratic nominee was favored to win the general election. Clinton did win the nomination in 2016, although she did not win the general election.

Professional Status. Political campaigning and officeholding are simply easier for some occupational groups than for others, and political involvement can make a valuable contribution to certain careers. Lawyers, for example, have more flexible schedules than do many other professionals, can take time off for campaigning, and can leave their jobs to hold public office full time. Furthermore, holding political office is good publicity for their professional practice. Perhaps most important, many jobs that lawyers aspire to—federal or state judgeships, state's attorney offices, or work in a federal agency—can be attained by political appointment.

Managing the Campaign

After the candidates have been nominated, typically through a **primary election,** the most exhausting and expensive part of the election process begins—the **general election** campaign, which actually fills the offices at stake. Political campaigns are becoming more complex and more sophisticated with every election. Even with the most appealing of candidates, today's campaigns require a strong organization with (1) expertise in political polling and marketing, (2) professional assistance in fund-raising and accounting, (3) financial management, and (4) technological capabilities in every aspect of the campaign.

Campaign Goals. The goal is the same for all campaigns—to convince voters to choose a candidate or a slate of candidates for office. In recent decades, the typical campaign for high office has no longer been centered on the party but on the candidate. The candidate-centered campaign emerged in response to changes in the electoral system,

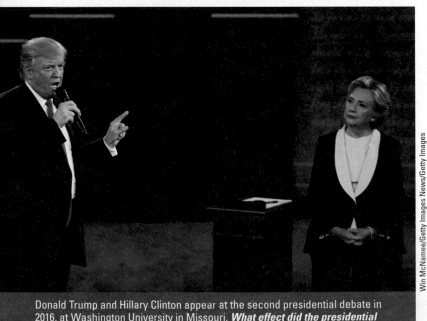

Donald Trump and Hillary Clinton appear at the second presidential debate in 2016, at Washington University in Missouri. *What effect did the presidential debates have on the race?*

Win McNamee/Getty Images News/Getty Images

the increased importance of television in campaigns, technological innovations such as the Internet, and the increased cost of campaigning.

To run a successful and persuasive campaign, the candidate's organization must be able to raise funds for the effort, produce and pay for political commercials and advertising, and obtain coverage from the media. In addition, the organization needs to schedule the candidate's time effectively, convey the candidate's position on the issues to the voters, and conduct research on the opposing candidate. Finally, the campaign must get the voters to go to the polls.

The Role of the Parties. When party identification was more widespread among voters and before the advent of television campaigning, a strong party organization at the local, state, or national level could furnish most of the services and expertise that the candidate needed. Parties used their precinct organizations to distribute literature, register voters, and get out the vote on Election Day. Less effort was spent on advertising each candidate's positions and character, because the party label presumably communicated that information to many voters.

Modern parties cannot provide the level of services that they did many years ago, but parties remain central to the elections system. The high levels of political polarization seen in recent years mean that each major party is a strong ideological rallying point. The party organization as such may be less significant, but for politicians, party identification is more important than ever. Also, the candidate-centered campaign does not change the fact that candidates for top national and state positions must normally win the support of their party in a primary election.

The Professional Campaign. Whether the candidate is running for the state legislature, for the governor's office, for the U.S. Congress, or for the presidency, every campaign has some fundamental tasks to accomplish. Today, in national elections, most of these tasks are handled by paid professionals rather than volunteers or amateur politicians.

The most sought-after and possibly the most criticized campaign expert is the **political consultant,** who, for a large fee, takes charge of the candidate's campaign. Paid political consultants began to displace volunteer campaign managers in the 1960s, about the same time that television became a force in campaigns. The paid consultant devises a campaign strategy and theme, oversees campaign advertising, and plans media appearances. Consultants and the firms they represent are not politically neutral. Most will work only for candidates from one party.

Opinion Polls. One of the major sources of information for both the media and the candidates is opinion polls. Poll taking is widespread during the primaries. Presidential hopefuls have private polls taken to make sure that there is at least some chance they could be nominated and, if nominated, elected. During the presidential campaign itself, polling is even more frequent. Polls are taken not only by the regular pollsters—Gallup, Mason-Dixon, Opinion Research, and others—but also privately by each candidate's campaign organization. These private polls are for the exclusive and confidential use of the candidate and his or her campaign organization. As the election approaches, many candidates use *tracking polls*, which are polls taken almost every day, to find out how well they are competing for votes. Tracking polls enable consultants to fine-tune advertising and the candidate's speeches in the last days of the campaign.

MANDEL NGAN/AFP/Getty Images

Steve Bannon was a political consultant to Donald Trump's campaign and then chief strategist in the Trump White House. Earlier, he ran Breitbart News, a website that serves as a platform for the *alt-right*. This online movement is known for antifeminism, white nationalism, and trolling its opponents. *Why might Trump have appointed Bannon to a position that does not require Senate confirmation?*

Political Consultant
A paid professional hired to devise a campaign strategy and manage a campaign.

Focus Groups. Another tactic used by campaign organizations to gain insights into public perceptions of the candidate is the **focus group.** The ten to fifteen ordinary citizens who comprise the group discuss the candidate or certain political issues. Professional consultants, who conduct the discussion, select focus group members from specific target groups in the population—for example, working women, blue-collar men, senior citizens, or young voters. Recent campaigns have tried to reach groups such as "soccer moms," "Walmart shoppers," or "NASCAR dads."[3]

The group may discuss personality traits of the candidate, political advertising, and other candidate-related issues. Focus groups can reveal more emotional responses to candidates or the deeper anxieties of voters—feelings that consultants believe often are not tapped by more impersonal telephone surveys. The campaign then can shape its messages to respond to those feelings and perceptions.

Financing the Campaign

>>> **LO2:** Describe the current system of campaign finance.

The connection between money and elections is a sensitive issue in American politics. The belief is widespread that large campaign contributions by special interests corrupt the political system. Indeed, spending on all campaigns taken together reached new heights during the 2015–2016 election cycle. Total spending on all candidates at all levels approached $6.6 billion. These funds had to be provided by the candidates and their families, borrowed, or raised by contributions from individuals, organizations, or *political action committees (PACs)*, which are set up under federal or state law for the express purpose of making political donations.

The way campaigns are financed has changed dramatically in the past several years. For decades, candidates and political parties had to operate within the constraints imposed by complicated laws regulating campaign financing. Some of these constraints still exist, but recent developments have opened up the process to a striking degree. Today, there are no limits on how much any person or institution can invest in the political process, and only modest limits on how this spending can take place.

The Evolution of the Campaign Finance System

Focus Group
A small group of individuals who are led in discussion by a professional consultant to gather opinions on, and responses to, candidates and issues.

Throughout much of early American history, campaign financing was unregulated. No limits existed on contributions, and no data were collected on campaign funding. During the twentieth century, however, a variety of federal corrupt practices acts were adopted to regulate campaign financing. The first of these acts, initially passed in 1910, contained many loopholes and proved to be ineffective. The **Hatch Act** (Political Activities Act) of 1939 is best known for restricting the political activities of civil servants. The act also made it unlawful for a political group to spend more than $3 million in any campaign and limited individual contributions to a campaign committee to $5,000. Of course, such restrictions were easily circumvented by creating additional political organizations.

Hatch Act
An act passed in 1939 that restricted the political activities of government employees. It also prohibited a political group from spending more than $3 million in any campaign and limited individual contributions to a campaign committee to $5,000.

The Federal Election Campaign Act. The Federal Election Campaign Act (FECA) of 1971, which became effective in 1972, replaced all previous laws. The act restricted the amount that could be spent on campaign advertising. It also limited the amount that candidates could contribute to their own campaigns and required disclosure of all contributions and

---

3. NASCAR stands for the National Association for Stock Car Auto Racing.

expenditures over $100. In principle, the FECA limited the role of labor unions and corporations in political campaigns.

Amendments to the FECA passed in 1974 created the **Federal Election Commission (FEC).** This commission consists of six bipartisan administrators whose duty is to enforce compliance with the requirements of the act. The 1974 amendments also placed limits on the sums that individuals and committees could contribute to candidates.

The principal role of the FEC today is to collect data on campaign contributions. Candidate committees must file periodic reports with the FEC listing who contributed, how much was spent, and for what it was spent. As an enforcement body, however, the FEC is conspicuously ineffective and typically does not determine that a campaign has violated the rules until an election is over, if then.

The original FECA of 1971 limited the amount that each individual could spend on his or her own behalf. The Supreme Court overturned the provision in 1976, in *Buckley v. Valeo*, stating that it was unconstitutional to restrict in any way the amount congressional candidates could spend on their own behalf.[4] The Court later extended this principle to state elections as well.

Political Action Committees. Changes to the FECA in 1974 and 1976 allowed corporations, labor unions, and other interest groups to set up **political action committees (PACs)** to raise funds for candidates. PACs can contribute up to $5,000 to each candidate in each election. Each corporation or each union is limited to one PAC. The number of PACs grew significantly after 1976, as did the amounts that they spent on elections. Since the 1990s, however, the number of traditional PACs has leveled off because interest groups and activists have found alternative mechanisms for funneling resources into campaigns.

Issue Advocacy Advertising. Business corporations, labor unions, and other interest groups have also developed ways of making independent expenditures that are not coordinated with those of a candidate or political party. A common tactic is **issue advocacy advertising,** which promotes positions on issues rather than candidates. Although promoting issue positions aligns very closely with promoting candidates who support those positions, the courts repeatedly have held that interest groups have a First Amendment right to advocate their positions.

Soft Money. Interest groups and PACs hit upon the additional strategy of generating **soft money**—that is, campaign contributions to political parties that escaped the limits of federal or state election law. No limits existed on contributions to political parties or party committees for activities such as voter education and voter-registration drives. This loophole enabled the parties to raise millions of dollars from corporations and individuals.

The Rise and Fall of the McCain-Feingold Act. The Bipartisan Campaign Reform Act of 2002, also known as the McCain-Feingold Act after its chief sponsors in the Senate, took effect on the day after the midterm elections of 2002. The law sought to regulate the new campaign-finance practices developed since the passage of the FECA. It banned soft money at the federal level, but it did not ban such contributions to state and local parties. It attempted to curb issue advocacy advertising, but also increased the sums that individuals could contribute directly to candidates.

Federal Election Commission (FEC)
The federal regulatory agency with the task of enforcing federal campaign laws. As a practical matter, the FEC's role is largely limited to collecting data on campaign contributions.

Political Action Committee (PAC)
A committee set up by and representing a corporation, labor union, or interest group. PACs raise campaign donations.

Issue Advocacy Advertising
Advertising paid for by interest groups that support or oppose a candidate's position on an issue without mentioning the candidate, voting, or elections.

Soft Money
Campaign contributions unregulated by federal or state law, usually given to parties and party committees to help fund general party activities.

---

4. 424 U.S. 1 (1976).

Interact

It has been said that if you want to understand what is happening in politics, you need to "follow the money." A number of online resources can help you do that. One is the OpenSecrets site maintained by the Center for Responsive Politics. If you don't know the name of your U.S. representative, Open-Secrets can search for that (or you can simply enter "find your representative" into a search engine). Now that you have the name, find this representative in OpenSecrets. Take note of the industries that contribute to this politician. Then, use OpenSecrets or Wikipedia to identify the House committees—and especially subcommittees—on which this member sits. Does the representative receive contributions from the industries that he or she oversees?

The constitutionality of the 2002 act was immediately challenged. In December 2003, the Supreme Court upheld almost all of the clauses of the act.[5] In 2007, however, the Court eased the act's restrictions on issue advocacy ads when it ruled that only those ads "susceptible of no reasonable interpretation other than as an appeal to vote for or against a specific candidate" could be restricted prior to an election.[6] Finally, in 2010, *Citizens United v. FEC* swept away almost all remaining restrictions on independent expenditures, leading to the system we have today.[7]

The Current Campaign Finance Environment

As of 2017, political campaigns are financed in two distinct ways. One of these is spending by the candidate's own committee. Contributions made directly to the candidate's committee are subject to limitations: an individual can donate no more than $2,500 to a candidate in a single election, and contributions by committees are limited as well. In exchange for these limits, candidates have almost complete control over how their own campaign money is spent.

Another way in which campaigns are financed is through **independent expenditures.** These funds may be spent on advertising and other political activities, but in theory the expenditures cannot be coordinated with those of a candidate. No limits exist on how much can be spent in this fashion. This two-part system is the direct result of the 2010 *Citizens United v. FEC* ruling by the Supreme Court.

Citizens United v. FEC. In January 2010, the Supreme Court ruled that corporations, unions, and nonprofits may spend funds to support or oppose candidates, so long as the expenditures are made independently and are not coordinated with candidate campaigns. (Political parties may also make independent expenditures on behalf of candidates.) These rulings overturned campaign-finance laws dating back decades. Democrats, plus many journalists and bloggers, accused the Court of granting corporations rights that ought to be exercised only by flesh-and-blood human beings. Republicans and others defended the ruling as protecting freedom of speech. Two months later, a federal court of appeals held that it was not possible to limit contributions to independent-expenditure groups based on the size of the contribution.[8] These rulings effectively abolished all limits on independent expenditures.

Independent Expenditures
Unregulated political expenditures by PACs, organizations, and individuals that are not coordinated with candidate campaigns or political parties.

Super PAC
A political organization that aggregates unlimited contributions by individuals and organizations to be spent independently of candidate committees.

Super PACs. These rulings led directly to a new type of political organization: the **super PAC.** Traditional PACs, which continue to exist, are set up to represent a corporation, labor union, or interest group. The super PAC, in contrast, is established to aggregate unlimited contributions by individuals and organizations and then funnel these sums into independent expenditures. By 2011, every major presidential candidate had a super PAC. It soon became clear that the supposed independence of these organizations is a fiction. Presidential super PACs are usually chaired by individuals who are closely associated with the

---

5. *McConnell v. FEC*, 540 U.S. 93 (2003).
6. *FEC v. Wisconsin Right to Life*, 551 U.S. 449 (2007).
7. 558 U.S. 310 (2010).
8. *SpeechNow.org v. FEC*, 599 F.3d 686 (D.C.Cir. 2010).

candidate. Frequently, the chair is a former top member of the candidate's campaign. A variety of other super PACs have been established as well. These groups are often oriented toward a party, rather than a candidate.

One interesting development has been the tendency for super PACs to be supported primarily by very wealthy individuals, rather than by corporations or other organizations. The Koch brothers provide a striking example of this phenomenon.[9] For years, Charles and David Koch have been famous for their large contributions to Republican campaigns. A political network overseen by the brothers spent almost $400 million during the 2012 election cycle, a huge sum at the time. For 2016, the network established a spending goal of almost $900 billion. That would almost match the sums raised by the candidate committees of Barack Obama or Mitt Romney in 2012.

This plan, however, ran into trouble when Donald Trump became the Republican presidential nominee. Trump was not acceptable to the libertarian-minded Koch brothers, who decided to devote whatever funds they could raise to the campaigns of "down-ticket" Republican candidates running for the Senate, House, and state-level positions. Trump's ability to win Republican primaries while spending very little money poses the question: just how important is campaign finance, really? We look at that question in this chapter's *At Issue* feature.

The 527 Organization. Well before *Citizens United*, interest groups realized that they could set up new organizations outside the parties to encourage voter registration and to run issue ads aimed at energizing supporters. So long as these committees did not endorse candidates, they faced no limits on fund-raising. These tax-exempt groups, called 527 organizations after the section of the tax code that provides for them, first had a major impact during the 2003–2004

Wichita Eagle/Getty Images

Charles Koch is head of Koch Industries. With his brother David, he runs one of the largest fund-raising operations in American politics. The brothers consider themselves libertarians and contribute to Republicans. *Are super PACs a problem with American politics? Why or why not?*

election cycle. Since then, they have largely been replaced by super PACs, but a number continue to be active to the present day.

The 501(c)4 Organization. In the 2007–2008 election cycle, campaign-finance lawyers began recommending a new type of independent group—the 501(c)4 organization, which, like the 527 organization, is named after the relevant provision of the tax code. A 501(c)4 is ostensibly a "social welfare" group and, unlike a 527, is not required to disclose the identity of its donors or to report spending to the FEC.

Lawyers then began suggesting that 501(c)4 organizations claim a special exemption that would allow the organization to ask people to vote for or against specific candidates as long as a majority of the group's effort was devoted to issues. Only those funds spent directly to support candidates had to be reported to the FEC, and the 501(c)4 could continue

9. The name is pronounced *coke.*

AT ISSUE

Can Money Buy Elections?

The 2010 Supreme Court decision *Citizens United v. FEC* allowed corporations, unions, and individuals to donate unlimited sums to entities that are "independent" of the candidates. So was born the super PAC. A super PAC can raise sums without limit. Some very rich people donated millions of dollars to various super PACs in the years following that decision. During the 2015–2016 election cycle, outside groups spent about $1.5 billion. Of course, the candidates' own campaign organizations themselves also raise large sums, which typically exceed what super PACs take in. Does all this money corrupt the political process?

Just Another Way for Big Money to Rule America

Those who are critical of the role of money in our elections argue that no one would give such large sums unless they expect to benefit in return. Candidates are perfectly well aware of who their largest contributors are. Often enough, they have spent time pleading with these people for donations. Super PACs are supposed to be independent, but in reality, most are run by candidates' former staff members. Hillary Clinton's super PAC, Priorities USA Action, was led by Guy Cecil, who was political director of Clinton's 2008 presidential campaign. Candidates are just as aware of who has donated to their super PACs as they are of donors to their actual campaigns.

Almost all the advertising purchased by super PACs is negative—the candidates can remain upbeat while their super PACs do the dirty work. These attack ads are themselves a corruption of the political process. Finally, due to the rise of 501(c)4 organizations, some super PACs manage to hide the identity of many of their donors. A number of public-interest groups have called for a constitutional amendment to overturn *Citizens United*. We need some such action to keep the United States from becoming a republic of the rich, by the rich, and for the rich.

Money Alone Can't Buy Elections

Those who support the current system argue that people should have the right to say whatever they want. Corporations and unions are made up of individuals, and so organizations as well as individuals should be able to express their views by donating to campaign organizations.

Does money buy elections? The dollars did not seem to have made that much difference in 2012. Casino owner Sheldon Adelson and his wife spent almost $100 million, including $20 million on Republican presidential candidate Newt Gingrich (he lost), and $20 million in the general election to support Mitt Romney (he lost, too).

Consider also Donald Trump's presidential campaign. In many key primary states, Trump ran no television ads at all, relying instead on social media and nonstop cable news coverage. In contrast, former Florida governor Jeb Bush raised about $130 million for his primary effort with almost nothing to show for it. (In the end, he gave much of this back to his donors.) Trump also spent relatively little on his general election campaign. The 2016 elections, therefore, were a test of how important campaign money really is. As it turned out, its impact was surprisingly small.

FOR CRITICAL ANALYSIS

Some have argued that limits on campaign spending violate First Amendment guarantees of freedom of speech. How strong is this argument?

to conceal its donors. One result, beginning with the 2008 elections, was to make it all but impossible to determine exactly how much was spent by independent groups. Critics claimed that 501(c)4s were being used illegally. The FEC has never ruled on their validity, however.

Candidate Committees. Despite the limits on contributions to candidate committees, these organizations continue to collect large sums. The committees of the 2012 major-party presidential nominees, Mitt Romney and Barack Obama, were able to amass more than $1 billion each, often from relatively small contributions. Major-party candidates were more frugal in 2016, however. Clinton collected about $500 million and Trump gathered only about $250 million.

Candidate committees at all levels received a boost in April 2014 as a result of the Supreme Court's latest ruling on campaign finance. The Court continued to hold that limits on the amount that any one individual could contribute to any one candidate were permissible. An overall cap on the total amount that an individual could contribute, however, was unconstitutional. In other words, there can be no limit on the number of different candidates a wealthy individual can support. A billionaire could, for example, give the $2,600 maximum contribution to every single candidate of a particular party running for the U.S. Congress. The ruling also freed up the amounts that individuals could give to the political parties.[10] The likely consequence will be to divert some funds away from super PACs and to candidate and party committees.

The Decline and Fall of Public Financing. From 1976 through 2004, most presidential candidates relied on a system of public funding financed by a checkoff on federal income tax forms. This system provided funds to match what a candidate could raise during the primary season. During the general election campaign, the system would pay for a candidate's entire campaign. Publicly funded candidates, however, could not raise funds independently for the general election or exceed the program's overall spending limits.

"Most of all, I want to thank the people of my district for their unflagging support and disturbingly short-term memories."

The system began to break down after 2000, when many candidates rejected public support during the primaries in the belief that they could raise larger sums privately. In 2008, Barack Obama became the first candidate since the program was founded to opt out of federal funding for the general elections as well. By 2012, the public financing system was essentially out of business. None of the major candidates in either party was willing to use it.

Running for President: The Longest Campaign

>>> **LO3:** Summarize the process of choosing a president of the United States.

The American presidential election is the culmination of two different campaigns: the presidential primary campaign and the general election campaign following the party's national convention. Traditionally, both the primary campaigns and the final campaigns take place during the first ten months of an election year. Increasingly, though, the states are holding their primaries earlier in the year, which has motivated the candidates to begin their campaigns earlier as well. Indeed, candidates in the 2016 presidential races began campaigning in early 2015, thus launching one of the longest presidential campaigns to date.

Primary elections were first organized for choosing state officials in 1904 in Wisconsin. The purpose of the primary was to open the nomination process to ordinary party members and to weaken the influence of party bosses. Until 1968, however, there were fewer than twenty primary elections for the presidency. They were often "beauty contests," in which the candidates competed for popular votes but the results did not control the selection of delegates to the national convention. National conventions were meetings of the party elite—legislators, mayors, county chairpersons, and loyal party workers—who were mostly

10. *McCutcheon v. FEC*, 134 S.Ct. 1434 (2014).

appointed to their delegations. The leaders of large blocs of delegates could direct their delegates to support a favorite candidate.

Reforming the Presidential Primaries

In recent decades, the character of the presidential primary process and the makeup of the national convention have changed dramatically. The public, rather than party elites, now generally controls the nomination process. After the disruptive riots outside the doors of the 1968 Democratic convention in Chicago, many party leaders pushed for serious reforms of the convention system.

The Power of Elected Delegates. The Democratic National Committee appointed a special commission to study the problems of the presidential primary system. During the next several years, the group—called the McGovern-Fraser Commission—formulated new rules for delegate selection that had to be followed by state Democratic parties beginning in 1972.

The reforms instituted by the Democratic Party, which were mostly imitated by the Republicans, revolutionized the nomination process for the presidency. The most important changes require that a majority of the convention delegates be elected by the voters in primary elections, in caucuses held by local parties, or at state conventions. Delegates are normally pledged to a particular candidate, although the pledge is not always formally binding at the convention. The delegation from each state must also include a proportion of women, younger party members, and representatives of the minority groups within the party. At first, almost no special privileges were given to party leaders and elected party officials, such as senators and governors. In 1984, however, many of these individuals returned to the Democratic convention as **superdelegates**.

The Role of the Superdelegates. The Democratic superdelegates became an issue in 2016, when most superdelegates with a preferred candidate lined up behind Hillary Clinton. Bernie Sanders claimed that the convention was therefore rigged against him. Of course, Clinton also outdid Sanders in electing regular delegates, so Sanders's charge was somewhat beside the point. Still, some Democrats recommended reducing the number of superdelegates in future years.

The Invisible Primary

Before the primary season even begins, presidential candidates must begin lining up as much support within their party as is possible. This process has been called the **invisible primary** because much of the action occurs behind closed doors. Potential candidates try to win support among elected officials, fund-raisers, interest groups, and opinion leaders. If a candidate can "win" the invisible primary, his or her chances in the actual primaries go way up. Historically, Republicans have been even more ready than Democrats to rally around the presumptive candidate. This process was described in *The Party Decides*, a widely acclaimed work of political science.[11]

As it happens, the 2015–2016 election cycle featured the primary election victories of Donald Trump, a candidate with almost no support among the party leaders who typically participate in the invisible primary. The resulting joke: "The party decides—except when it doesn't." Trump was not the first candidate ever to win a party's nomination after decisively losing the invisible primary, though such a result had not been seen in decades. Democratic candidates George McGovern and Jimmy Carter managed that feat in 1972 and 1976,

Superdelegate
A party leader or elected official who is given the right to vote at the party's national convention. Superdelegates are not elected at the state level.

Invisible Primary
The preprimary campaign to win supporters among elected officials, fund-raisers, interest groups, and opinion leaders.

11. Marty Cohen et al., *The Party Decides: Presidential Nominations before and after Reform* (Chicago: University of Chicago Press, 2008).

respectively. These were, however, the first two Democratic contests after the party reforms of 1972, and it may have taken that long for Democratic elders to adjust to the new system.

Primaries and Caucuses

Various types of primaries are used by the states. One notable difference is between proportional and winner-take-all primaries. Another important consideration is whether independent voters can take part in a primary. Some states also use caucuses and conventions to choose candidates for various offices.

Direct and Indirect Primaries. A **direct primary** is one in which voters decide party nominations by voting directly for candidates. In an **indirect primary,** voters instead choose convention delegates, and the delegates determine the party's candidate in the general election. Delegates may be pledged to a particular candidate. Indirect primaries are rare except when choosing a presidential candidate. Most candidates in state and local elections are chosen by direct primaries.

Proportional and Winner-Take-All Primaries. Most primaries are winner-take-all. Proportional primaries are used mostly to elect delegates to the national conventions of the two major parties—delegates who are pledged to one or another candidate for president. Under the proportional system, if one candidate for president wins 40 percent of the vote in a primary, that candidate receives about 40 percent of the pledged delegates.

In recent years, the Democrats have used the proportional system for all of their presidential primaries and caucuses. For the most part, the Republicans have relied on the winner-take-all principle. In 2012, however, the Republican National Committee began requiring that early primaries be proportional. Republicans made even greater use of proportional primaries in 2016. Following Trump's victories in that year, several members of the Republican National Committee recommended that all Republican primaries be proportional beginning in 2020.

Closed and Open Primaries. A closed primary is one of several types of primaries distinguished by how independent voters are handled. In a **closed primary,** only declared members of a party can vote in that party's primary. In other words, voters must declare their party affiliation, either when they register to vote or at the primary election. In a closed-primary system, voters cannot cross over into the other party's primary in order to nominate the weakest candidate of the opposing party or to affect the ideological direction of that party. In an **open primary,** any voter can vote in either party's primary without declaring a party affiliation. Basically, the voter makes the choice in the privacy of the voting booth. The voter must, however, choose one party's list from which to select candidates.

Blanket Primary. A *blanket primary* is one in which the voter can vote for candidates of more than one party. Until 2000, a few states, including Alaska, California, and Washington, had blanket primaries. In 2000, however, the United States Supreme Court abolished the blanket primary. The Court ruled that the blanket primary violated political parties' First Amendment right of association. Because the nominees represent the party, party members—not the general electorate—should have the right to choose the party's nominee.[12]

Run-Off Primary. Some states have a two-primary system. If no candidate receives a majority of the votes in the first primary, the top two candidates must compete in another primary, called a *run-off primary.*

---

12. *California Democratic Party v. Jones*, 530 U.S. 567 (2000).

Direct Primary
A primary election in which voters decide party nominations by voting directly for candidates.

Indirect Primary
A primary election in which voters choose convention delegates, and the delegates determine the party's candidate in the general election.

Closed Primary
A type of primary in which the voter is limited to choosing candidates of the party of which he or she is a member.

Open Primary
A primary in which any voter can vote in either party primary (but must vote for candidates of only one party).

The "final four" in the 2016 Republican presidential primaries. Left to right, Senator Marco Rubio of Florida, Donald Trump, Senator Ted Cruz of Texas, and Governor John Kasich of Ohio. Rubio and Cruz are both Cuban Americans. *How might the presidential campaign have been different if either of these senators had become the Republican candidate?*

Joe Raedle/Getty Images News/Getty Images

The "Top-Two" Primary. Louisiana has long used a special type of primary for filling some offices. Under the system, all candidates appear on a single ballot. A party cannot prevent a candidate from appearing on the primary ballot—an insurgent Republican, for example, could appear on the ballot alongside the party-supported Republican. The two candidates receiving the most votes, regardless of party, then move on to the general election. Following the abolition of the blanket primary, the state of Washington adopted this system. In 2008, the Supreme Court upheld the new plan.[13] In 2010, Californians voted to use this system beginning in 2012.

Conventions and Caucuses. In 2016, fifteen states relied at least in part on the **caucus system** for choosing delegates to the Republican and Democratic national conventions. Strictly speaking, the caucus system is a convention system. In North Dakota, for example, local citizens gather in party meetings, called caucuses, at the precinct level. They choose delegates to district conventions. The district conventions elect delegates to the state convention, and the state convention actually chooses the delegates to the national convention. The national delegates, however, are pledged to reflect the presidential preferences that voters expressed at the caucus level.

Front-Loading the Primaries

As soon as potential presidential candidates realized that winning as many primary elections as possible guaranteed them the party's nomination for president, their tactics changed dramatically. Candidates concentrated on building organizations in states that held early, important primary elections. By the 1970s, candidates recognized that the winner of an early contest, such as the Iowa caucuses or the New Hampshire primary election (both now held in January), would instantly become seen as the **front-runner,** increasing the candidate's media exposure and escalating the pace of contributions to his or her campaign.

The Rush to Be First. The state political parties began to see that early primaries had a much greater effect on the outcome of the presidential contest than did later ones. Accordingly, in every successive presidential election, more and more states moved their primaries into the first months of the year, a process known as **front-loading** the primaries. One result was a series of "Super Tuesdays," when multiple states held simultaneous primaries. In 2008, twenty-four states held their primaries or caucuses on February 5, making it the largest Super Tuesday ever. So many states were in play on February 5 that it was impossible for the candidates to campaign strongly in all of them. Rather than winning more attention, many Super Tuesday states found

Caucus System
A meeting of party members to select candidates and propose policies.

Front-Runner
The presidential candidate who appears to be ahead at a given time in the primary season.

Front-Loading
The practice of moving presidential primary elections to the early part of the campaign to maximize the impact of these primaries on the nomination.

---

13. *Washington State Grange v. Washington State Republican Party*, 552 U.S. 442 (2008).

that they were ignored. Because the Democratic race was not decided until the very end of the process in June 2008, the later Democratic primaries, such as those in Indiana, North Carolina, Ohio, Pennsylvania, and Texas, were hotly contested.

Front-loading, in short, had become counterproductive. As a result, in 2012 Super Tuesday was held on March 6, a month later than in 2008. Ten states participated instead of twenty-four. In 2016, Super Tuesday was on March 1, and twelve states participated.

The National Parties Seek to Regain Control. The process of front-loading the primaries alarmed many observers, who feared that a front-runner might wrap up the nomination before voters were able to make a thorough assessment of the candidates. In response, the national Democratic and Republican parties took steps to regain control of the primary schedule in 2012. Such steps included a requirement that states could not hold primaries or caucuses before a specified date. States would need special permission to choose delegates before that date. Traditional lead-off states such as Iowa and New Hampshire were allowed to go first, and a limited number of other states also received such permission. At first, a few states were unwilling to follow the official schedule, and as a result they were penalized by the national parties. By 2016, however, all states were obeying the rules.

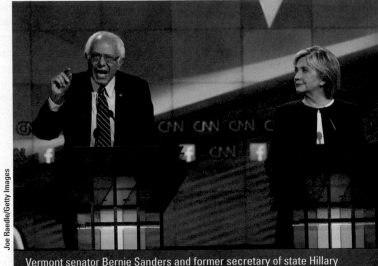

Joe Raedle/Getty Images

Vermont senator Bernie Sanders and former secretary of state Hillary Clinton at the first Democratic presidential primary debate in 2016. *How did the debates help Sanders gain national prominence?*

On to the National Convention

Presidential candidates have been nominated by the convention method in every election since 1832. Extra delegates are allowed from states won by the party in the preceding elections. Parties also accept delegates from the District of Columbia, the territories, and U.S. citizens living abroad.

Seating the Delegates. At the convention, each political party uses a **credentials committee** to determine which delegates may participate. Controversy may arise when rival groups claim to be the official party organization. The Mississippi Democratic Party split along racial lines in 1964 at the height of the civil rights movement. Two sets of delegates were selected at the state level—one made up of white delegates and the other including both whites and African Americans—and both factions showed up at the national convention. The committee decided to seat the pro–civil rights delegates and exclude those who represented the traditional "white" party.

Convention Activities. Most delegates arrive at the convention committed to a presidential candidate. No convention since 1952 has required more than one ballot to choose a nominee. Conventions normally last four days, but in both 2008 and 2012 the Republican convention was shortened to three days due to hurricanes. On each night, featured speakers seek to rally the party faithful and draw in uncommitted voters who are watching on television.

Credentials Committee
A committee used by political parties at their national conventions to determine which delegates may participate.

A major goal of the conventions is to unite each party around the winning candidate. Party members who supported losing candidates must be encouraged to switch their support to the winner. In 2016, both major party conventions were successful in this effort—ordinary party members largely rallied around the winners. The Democrats, however, were more successful in uniting their party. Most supporters of Bernie Sanders were willing to endorse Hillary Clinton. On the Republican side, a number of the party's officeholders failed even to attend the convention and some refused to back Donald Trump.

The Electoral College

Some people who vote for the president and vice president think that they are voting directly for a candidate. In actuality, they are voting for **electors** who will cast their ballots in the electoral college. Article II, Section 1, of the Constitution outlines in detail the method of choosing electors for president and vice president.

The Choice of Electors. Electors are selected during each presidential election year. The selection is governed by state laws. After the national party convention, the electors are pledged to the candidates chosen. Each state's number of electors equals that state's number of senators (two) plus its number of representatives. The total number of electors today is 538, equal to 100 senators, 435 members of the House, and 3 electors for the District of Columbia. (The Twenty-third Amendment, ratified in 1961, added electors for the District of Columbia.)

The Electors' Commitment. In all but two states, a *plurality* of voters in the state chooses a slate of electors. (A *plurality* is the largest number, but not necessarily a majority.) Those electors are pledged to cast their ballots on the first Monday after the second Wednesday in December in the state capital for the presidential and vice-presidential candidates of their party.[14] The Constitution does not, however, *require* the electors to cast their ballots for the candidates of their party, and on rare occasions so-called *faithless electors* have voted for a candidate to whom they were not pledged. The 2016 presidential elections were marked by an unusual number of faithless electors. Five Clinton electors refused to vote for her, and two Trump electors jumped ship as well. Apparently, most of the faithless Clinton electors were promoting a scheme under which electors from both parties would vote for a moderate Republican such as Ohio governor John Kasich. Such votes are illegal in twenty-nine states, but no faithless elector has ever been prosecuted.

The ballots are counted and certified before a joint session of Congress early in January. The candidates who receive a majority (270) of the electoral votes are certified as president-elect and vice president–elect. According to the Constitution, if no candidate receives a majority of the electoral votes, the election of the president is decided in the House of Representatives from among the candidates with the three highest numbers of votes, with each state having one vote (decided by a plurality of each state delegation). The selection of the vice president is determined by the Senate in a choice between the two candidates with the most votes, each senator having one vote. The House was required to choose the president in 1801 (Thomas Jefferson), and again in 1825 (John Quincy Adams).

Problems with the Electoral College System. It is possible for a candidate to become president without obtaining a majority of the popular vote. There have been many presidents in our history who did not win such a majority. Such an event becomes more likely when there are important

Elector
A member of the electoral college, which selects the president and vice president. Each state's electors are chosen in each presidential election year according to state laws.

---

14. In Maine and Nebraska, electoral votes are based in part on congressional districts. Each district chooses one elector. The remaining two electors are chosen by a plurality of all votes cast statewide.

third-party candidates. Perhaps more distressing is the possibility of a candidate's being elected when an opposing candidate receives a plurality of the popular vote. This has occurred on five occasions—in the elections of John Quincy Adams in 1824, Rutherford B. Hayes in 1876, Benjamin Harrison in 1888, George W. Bush in 2000, and Donald Trump in 2016. All of these candidates won elections in which an opponent received more popular votes than they did.

The 2016 elections were particularly troublesome because the gap between the popular vote and the electoral vote was so large. Hillary Clinton's popular vote margin over Donald Trump exceeded 2.8 million votes, or about 2.1 percent. In previous cases when the winner lost the popular vote, the margin was very close. This was not so in 2016. Trump won because he carried his states by smaller margins than Clinton carried hers. Three states determined the outcome. In Pennsylvania, Trump's margin was approximately 44,000 votes. In Michigan, his margin was about 11,000. In Wisconsin, it was roughly 23,000. The national outcome was decided, therefore, by fewer than 80,000 votes. In contrast, Clinton carried California by the largest margin that a Democrat has ever enjoyed in the history of that state. Those extra California votes were wasted—Clinton was going to win the state anyway.

Clinton's loss was the second time in sixteen years that the Democratic presidential candidate won the popular vote but lost in the electoral college. Inevitably, many Democrats have become hostile to this system. Replacing it seems almost impossible, however. Doing so might require a constitutional amendment. Republicans, however, would never support an amendment so contrary to their political interests.

How Are Elections Conducted?

>>> **LO4:** Explain the mechanisms through which voting takes place on Election Day, and discuss voter turnout in the United States.

The United States uses the **Australian ballot**—a secret ballot that is prepared, distributed, and counted by government officials at public expense. Since 1888, all states have used the Australian ballot. Before that, many states used oral voting or differently colored ballots prepared by the parties. Obviously, knowing which way a person was voting made it easy to apply pressure on the person to change his or her vote, and vote buying was common.

Voting by Mail

Voting by mail has been accepted for absentee ballots for many decades (for example, for individuals who are doing business away from home or for members of the armed forces). Recently, several states have offered mail ballots to all of their voters. The rationale for using the mail ballot is to make voting easier and increase turnout. Oregon has gone one step further: since 1998, that state has employed postal ballots exclusively, and there are no polling places. (Voters who do not prepare their ballots in time for the U.S. Postal Service to deliver them can drop off their ballots at drop boxes on Election Day.) In addition, Colorado and Washington now use mail ballots exclusively. By national standards, voter turnout in those three states has been high, especially in midterm elections when turnout in most states is substantially reduced.

Voting Fraud and Voter ID Laws

Voting fraud is something regularly suspected but seldom proved. Voting in the 1800s, when secret ballots were rare and people had a cavalier attitude toward the open buying of votes, was probably much more conducive to fraud than modern elections are. Still, some observers claim that the potential for voting fraud is high in many states, particularly through the

Australian Ballot
A secret ballot prepared, distributed, and tabulated by government officials at public expense. Since 1888, all states have used the Australian ballot rather than an open, public ballot.

use of phony voter registrations and absentee ballots. Other observers claim, however, that errors due to fraud are trivial in number and that a few mistakes are inevitable in a system involving millions of voters. These people argue that an excessive concern with voting fraud makes it harder for minorities and poor people to vote.

Voter ID Requirements. In recent years, many states have adopted laws requiring enhanced proof of identity before voters can cast their ballots. Indiana imposed what was then the nation's toughest voter identification (ID) law in 2005. Indiana legislators claimed that they were motivated by a desire to prevent voting fraud, but critics argued that they were really trying to suppress voter turnout among minority group members and the poor—the individuals least likely to possess adequate identification. In 2008, the United States Supreme Court upheld the Indiana voter ID law.[15]

Voting Restrictions. Since 2008, dozens of states have moved to tighten voter ID requirements. Republicans provided almost all of the support for the new ID laws. By Election Day 2016, twenty-one states had enacted new laws that made it harder to vote. Cumbersome voter ID rules were the most common, but other laws limited early voting or absentee ballots. In some states, however, state or federal courts overturned the new laws. In a few states, they were repealed by the voters. Also, twenty states passed laws making it easier to vote.

In Texas, acceptable forms of ID included concealed carry permits for guns, but not student IDs. Persons without acceptable forms of ID could obtain free Texas ID cards, but only through an in-person application at a limited number of state offices during normal

Senator Charles Schumer (D., N.Y.) points to a blowup of a flyer with misleading voting information. Schumer cosponsored a bill to make the distribution of fraudulent election material a federal offense. *How likely is it that a voter would be misled by such a flyer?*

Tom Williams/Getty Images

---

15. *Crawford v. Marion County Election Board*, 553 U.S. 181 (2008).

business hours. In July 2016, however, the Texas ID law was ruled unconstitutional by a U.S. appeals court. That same month, a second appeals court struck down a North Carolina law, finding that it targeted African American voters "with almost surgical precision."

Until 2013, most southern states with a history of racial discrimination had to obtain preclearance from the federal government for any significant change to their voting laws and procedures under the 1965 Voting Rights Act. The Department of Justice refused to preclear voter ID laws in South Carolina and Texas on the ground that the laws impose a greater burden on minority voters than on whites. In 2013, however, the Supreme Court effectively suspended the preclearance procedure. As a result, many southern states were able to implement strict voter ID laws in time for the 2014 elections.

The Impact of Restrictive Voting Laws on Voter Turnout. In any election, the number of Americans who fail to vote is very large. Any factor that affects voter turnout, therefore, can have a major impact on election results. In 2012, a belief by minority group members that their voting rights were at risk seems to have increased minority turnout measurably. If the new voting laws really were meant to reduce the Democratic vote in 2012, they apparently backfired. In the 2014 and 2016 elections, however, several jurisdictions with new restrictive laws reported substantial drops in turnout compared with earlier elections.

Turning Out to Vote

In 2016, the number of Americans eligible to vote was about 231.6 million people. Of that number, about 138.9 million, or 60.0 percent of the eligible population, actually cast a ballot. When voter turnout is this low, it means, among other things, that the winner of a close election may be voted in by a very small share of those eligible to vote.

Figure 8–1 shows **voter turnout** for presidential and **midterm elections** from 1910 to 2016. Each of the peaks in the figure represents voter turnout in a presidential election. Thus, we can also see that turnout for congressional elections is influenced greatly by whether there is a presidential election in the same year. Whereas voter turnout during the presidential elections of 2012 was 58.6 percent, it was only 35.9 percent in the midterm elections of 2014.

The same is true at the state level. When there is a race for governor, more voters participate in the elections than when only state legislators are on the ballot. Voter participation rates in gubernatorial elections are also greater in presidential election years. The average turnout in state elections is about 14 percentage points higher when a presidential election is held.

Now consider local elections. In races for mayor, city council, county auditor, and the like, it is fairly common for only 25 percent or less of the electorate to vote. Is something amiss here? It would seem that people should be more likely to vote in elections that directly affect them. At the local level, each person's vote counts more (because there are fewer voters). Furthermore, the issues—crime control, school bonds, sewer bonds, and the like—touch the immediate interests of the voters. In reality, however, potential voters are most interested in national elections, when a presidential choice is involved. Otherwise, voter participation in our representative government is very low (and, as we have seen, it is not overwhelmingly high even in presidential elections).

The Effect of Low Voter Turnout. There are two schools of thought concerning low voter turnout. Some view low voter participation as a threat to our democratic republic. Too few individuals are deciding who wields political power in our society. In addition, low voter participation presumably signals apathy about our political system in general.

Others are less concerned about low voter participation. They contend that low participation simply indicates relative acceptance of the status quo. Also, they believe that

Voter Turnout
The percentage of citizens taking part in the election process. Also, the number of eligible voters who actually "turn out" to cast their ballots.

Midterm Elections
National elections in which candidates for president are not on the ballot. In midterm elections, voters choose all members of the U.S. House of Representatives and one-third of the members of the U.S. Senate.

FIGURE 8–1   Voter Turnout for Presidential and Midterm Elections, 1912–2016

The peaks represent voter turnout in presidential election years. The troughs represent voter turnout in midterm years with no presidential elections. *Why might turnout have been higher in 2016 than in 2012?*

Sources: Historical Data Archive, Inter-university Consortium for Political and Social Research; Michael P. McDonald and Samuel L. Popkin, "The Myth of the Vanishing Voter," *American Political Science Review,* Vol. 95, No. 4 (December 2001), p. 966; and the United States Elections Project.

Note: Prior to 1948, the voting-age population is used as a proxy for the population eligible to vote.

representative democracy is a reality even if a small percentage of eligible voters vote. It is enough that these people could vote if they were sufficiently moved.

The Voting-Age Population and the Vote-Eligible Population. In the past, the press and even many political scientists calculated voter turnout by taking the number of people who vote as a percentage of the nation's **voting-age population.** Until about 1972, this was a reasonable way to obtain an approximate figure for turnout. In recent decades, however, turnout figures based on the voting-age population have become less and less reliable. The problem is that the voting-age population is not the same as the population of eligible voters, the **vote-eligible population.** The figure for the voting-age population includes felons and ex-felons who have lost the right to vote. Above all, it includes a large number of new immigrants who are not yet citizens. Finally, it does not include Americans living abroad, who can cast absentee ballots.

In 2016, the voting-age population included 3.2 million ineligible felons and ex-felons and an estimated 21.0 million noncitizens. It did not include 4.7 million Americans abroad who could cast absentee ballots. The voting-age population in 2016 was 251.1 million people. The number of eligible voters, however, was only 231.6 million. If we calculated 2016 voter turnout based on the larger voting-age population, turnout would appear to be 55.3 percent, not 60.0 percent.

Legal Restrictions on Voting

Legal restrictions on voter registration have existed since the founding of our nation. Most groups in the United States have been concerned with the suffrage (voting) issue at one time or another. The writers of the Constitution allowed the states to decide who could vote. Thus, women were allowed to vote in Wyoming in 1870 but not in the entire nation until the Nineteenth Amendment was ratified in 1920.

Voting-Age Population
The number of people of voting age living in the country at a given time, regardless of whether they have the right to vote.

Vote-Eligible Population
The number of people who, at a given time, enjoy the right to vote in national elections.

Property Requirements. Many government functions concern property rights and the distribution of income and wealth, and some of the founders believed it was appropriate that only people who had an interest in property should vote. In colonial times, therefore, only white males who owned property with a certain minimum value were eligible to vote, leaving more Americans ineligible to take part in elections than were eligible. By about 1850, however, most white adult males in almost all the states could vote without any property qualification.

Further Extensions of the Franchise. Extension of the *franchise* (the right to vote) to black males occurred with the passage of the Fifteenth Amendment in 1870. This enfranchisement was short lived, however, as the "redemption" of the South by white supremacists had rolled back those gains by the end of the century. It was not until the 1960s that African Americans, both male and female, were able to participate in the electoral process in all states. The most recent extension of the franchise occurred when the voting age was reduced from twenty-one to eighteen by the Twenty-sixth Amendment in 1971. One result of lowering the voting age was to depress voter turnout for several decades beginning in 1972, as you can see in Figure 8–1. Young people are less likely to vote than older citizens.

Is the Franchise Still Too Restrictive?

There continue to be certain classes of people who do not have the right to vote. These include noncitizens and, in many states, convicted felons who have been released from prison. Also, no one under the age of eighteen can vote. A number of political activists have argued that some of these groups should be allowed to vote. Most other democracies do not prevent convicts from voting after they have completed their sentences.

According to the American Civil Liberties Union, ten states currently prevent felons from voting after they have completed their sentences. (The number used to be higher, but recently some states have relaxed their laws.) The Sentencing Project reports that several states prohibit 6 to 11 percent of their electorate from voting. In three states—Florida, Kentucky, and Virginia—more than 20 percent of African Americans of voting age have lost the right to vote. Barring felons from the polls injures minority groups because they make up a disproportionate share of former prison inmates.

Current Eligibility and Registration Requirements. Voting generally requires **registration,** and to register, a person must meet the following legal requirements: (1) citizenship, (2) age (eighteen or older), and (3) residency. Since 1972, states cannot impose residency requirements of more than thirty days.

Each state has different laws for voting and registration. In 1993, Congress passed the "motor voter" bill, which requires that states provide voter-registration materials when people receive or renew driver's licenses, that all states allow voters to register by mail, and that voter-registration forms be made available at a wider variety of public places and agencies.

In 2015, Oregon passed a law under which any citizen who obtains an Oregon driver's license is automatically registered to vote. Anyone who does not want to be registered can opt out, but doing so requires an explicit act by the nonvoter. Automatic voter registration quickly took off around the country. California, Vermont, and West Virginia adopted similar legislation. By mid-2016, twenty-five additional states and the District of Columbia were considering such laws, though few were in place in time for the 2016 elections.

In general, a person must register well in advance of an election, although voters in eleven states are allowed to register up to, or even on, Election Day. North Dakota has no voter registration at all. Some argue that registration requirements are responsible for much of the nonparticipation in our political process. There also is a partisan dimension

Registration
The entry of a person's name onto the list of registered voters for elections. To register, a person must meet certain legal requirements of age, citizenship, and residency.

to the debate over registration and nonvoting. Republicans generally fear that an expanded electorate would help to elect more Democrats—because more Democrats than Republicans are the kinds of persons who have trouble registering.

The Voting Rights Act. The Voting Rights Act was enacted in 1965 to ensure that African Americans had equal access to the polls. Section 5 of the act requires that new voting practices or procedures in jurisdictions with a history of discrimination in voting be approved by the national government before being implemented.

In June 2013, in *Shelby County v. Holder*, the Supreme Court effectively invalidated the requirement that changes to voting procedures in covered states and districts receive preclearance.[16] The Court did not throw out Section 5. Rather, it overturned Section 4, which determined those states and localities that should be covered by Section 5. The Court contended that Section 4, which dated back to the 1960s, was obsolete. In principle, Congress could adopt a new set of Section 4 formulas based on more current conditions. The chances of such legislation making its way through today's Congress, however, seemed slight.

Even with the suspension of the preclearance system, the federal government retained the power under the Voting Rights Act to sue states and localities *after* a change to voting procedures was implemented. Such suits are far less effective than preclearance. Then–Attorney General Eric Holder announced that the Department of Justice would sponsor such lawsuits whenever necessary. The chances that Trump's attorney general would pursue such suits, however, appear low.

How Do Voters Decide?

≫ LO5: Provide some of the reasons why people vote in particular ways.

A variety of factors appear to influence political preferences. Party identification is among the most important. Other factors include the perception of the candidates and issue preferences. Various demographic factors influence political preferences as well.

Party Identification

With the possible exception of race, party identification is the most important determinant of voting behavior in national elections. Party affiliation is influenced by family and peer groups, by generational effects, by the media, and by the voter's assessment of candidates and issues.

As we have observed on more than one occasion, the number of independent voters has grown over the years. While party identification may have little effect on the voting behavior of true independents, it remains a crucial determinant for the majority of the voters, who have established party preferences.

Other Political Factors

Factors such as perception of the candidates and issue preferences also affect how people vote. While most people do not change their party identification from year to year, candidates and issues can change greatly, and voting behavior can therefore change as well.

Perception of the Candidates. The image of the candidate seems to be important in a voter's choice, especially of a president. To some extent, voter attitudes toward candidates are based on emotions (such as trust) rather than on any judgment about experience or policy.

---

16. 133 S.Ct. 2612 (2013).

In some years, voters have been attracted to a candidate who appeared to share their concerns and worries. In other years, voters have sought a candidate who appeared to have high integrity and honesty.

Perceptions of candidates were especially important in 2016. In that year, Hillary Clinton suffered from a strong perception that she was untrustworthy. For his part, Donald Trump's negative ratings in polls set new records. It appeared that many voters would have to decide which candidate they disliked the least.

Issue Preferences. Issues make a difference in presidential and congressional elections. Although personality or image factors may be very persuasive, most voters have some notion of how the candidates differ on basic issues or at least know which candidates want a change in the direction of government policy.

Historically, economic concerns have been among the most powerful influences on public opinion. When the economy is doing well, it is very difficult for a challenger, especially at the presidential level, to defeat the incumbent. In contrast, inflation, unemployment, or high interest rates are likely to work to the disadvantage of the incumbent.

These young voters—all Haitian immigrants—sport t-shirts from Citizen Change, a get-out-the-vote group backed by musician P. Diddy along with Mary J. Blige, Mariah Carey, and 50 Cent. *Why are young people often less likely to vote?*

RosalreneBetancourt 11 / Alamy

While true swing voters may be influenced by the issues when picking a candidate, issue preferences may have little influence on strong party loyalists. In fact, much evidence suggests that such persons often change their issue preferences to match those of their party. One example occurred when President Obama, after a long delay, finally endorsed same-sex marriage. Some conservatives hoped that this stand would alienate conservative African Americans who opposed such unions. Nothing of the sort happened. Instead, opinion polls reported a marked increase in black support for gay marriage.

Another example was the startling drop in Republican hostility toward Russian president Vladimir Putin following the nomination of Donald Trump. From July 2014 to December 2016, Putin's net approval rate among Republicans rose from –66 to –10, an improvement of 56 percentage points. (Among Democrats it fell from –54 to –62.) The reason for the change appears to be Trump's well-known friendly attitude toward Putin.

Demographic Characteristics

Demographic characteristics that influence political preferences include race, religion, education, income and **socioeconomic status,** and similar traits. People who share the same religion or any other demographic trait are likely to influence one another and may also have common political concerns that follow from the common characteristic. We examined these factors, such as race and religion, earlier in this book as part of the discussion of political socialization.

Demographic influences reflect an individual's personal background and place in society. Some factors have to do with the family into which a person was born: race and (for most people) religion. Others may be the result in large part of choices made throughout an individual's life. They include place of residence, educational achievement, and profession.

Many of these factors are interrelated. People who have more education are likely to have higher incomes and to hold professional jobs. Similarly, children born into wealthier

Socioeconomic Status
The value assigned to a person due to occupation or income. A professional person with a substantial income, for example, has high socioeconomic status.

families are far more likely to complete college than children from poor families. A number of other interrelationships are not so immediately obvious. For example, many people might not realize that 75 percent of African Americans report that religion is very important in their lives, compared with only 49 percent of whites.[17]

MAKING A DIFFERENCE

Registering and Voting

Very close elections, such as the 2008 Minnesota Senate race, demonstrate that your vote can make a difference. In local races, elections have sometimes been decided by one or two votes. In nearly every state, before you are allowed to cast a vote in an election, you must first register. Registration laws vary considerably from state to state.

Residency and Age Requirements What do you have to do to register and cast a vote? In general, you must be a citizen of the United States, at least eighteen years old on or before Election Day, and a resident of the state in which you intend to register. A number of states require that you meet a minimum-residency requirement. The minimum-residency requirement is

very short in some states— for example, ten days in Wisconsin. No state requires more than thirty days. Thirty states do not have any minimum-residency requirement.

Time Limits Nearly every state also specifies a closing date by which you must be registered before an election. You may not be able to vote if you register too close to the day of the election. The closing date for registration varies from Election Day itself to thirty days before the election. In North Dakota, no registration is necessary.

In most states, your registration can be revoked if you do not vote within a certain number of years or do not report a change of address. Federal regulations place limits on how purges are conducted, but Democrats have frequently accused Republican state officials of violating the rules. The belief is that those who move frequently or who often fail to vote— and who are therefore purged—tend to be Democrats. For their part, Republicans contend that aggressive purges limit voter fraud.

An Example Let us look at voter registration in Texas as an example. If you live in Texas, you may have registered to vote when you obtained your Texas driver's license. If not, you can find a voter registration form online by searching on "texas vrapp." You must mail the application to the voter registrar in your county. (The registrar's address appears on the form after you finish filling it out.) Applications are also available at post offices, libraries, Texas Department of Public Safety offices, and Texas Department of Human Services offices. Your application must be postmarked thirty days before Election Day.

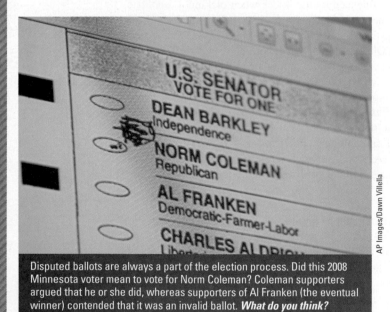

AP Images/Dawn Villella

Disputed ballots are always a part of the election process. Did this 2008 Minnesota voter mean to vote for Norm Coleman? Coleman supporters argued that he or she did, whereas supporters of Al Franken (the eventual winner) contended that it was an invalid ballot. *What do you think?*

---

17. The Pew Forum on Religion and Public Life, "U.S. Public Becoming Less Religious," November 3, 2015, p. 46.

Key Terms

Australian ballot 189
caucus system 186
closed primary 185
credentials
    committee 187
direct primary 185
elector 188
Federal Election
    Commission
    (FEC) 179
focus group 178

front-loading 186
front-runner 186
general election 176
Hatch Act 178
independent
    expenditures 180
indirect primary 185
invisible primary 184
issue advocacy
    advertising 179
midterm elections 191

open primary 185
political action
    committee
    (PAC) 179
political consultant 177
presidential primary 175
primary election 176
registration 193
socioeconomic
    status 195
soft money 179

superdelegate 184
super PAC 180
vote-eligible
    population 192
voter turnout 191
voting-age
    population 192

Chapter Summary

≫ LO1 The legal qualifications for holding political office are minimal at the national, state, and local levels, but holders of political office still are predominantly white and male and are likely to have professional status.

American political campaigns are lengthy and extremely expensive. In recent decades, they have become more candidate centered rather than party centered in response to a relative decline in party resources.

≫ LO2 Interest groups are major sources of campaign funds. The contributions are often made through political action committees, or PACs. Other methods of contributing include issue advocacy advertising. The McCain-Feingold Act of 2002 imposed significant restrictions on campaign finance, but in 2010 these restrictions were largely swept away by the Supreme Court in its ruling *Citizens United v. FEC*.

Campaign finance today is largely based on two types of committees. Super PACs can raise unlimited funds from any source, but supposedly are not allowed to coordinate with candidate campaigns. Candidate committees face restrictions on contributions but are not limited in how they may spend their funds to support a campaign.

≫ LO3 After the Democratic convention of 1968, the McGovern-Fraser Commission formulated new rules for primaries, most of which were also adopted by Republicans. These reforms opened up the nomination process for the presidency to all voters.

A presidential primary is a statewide election to help a political party determine its presidential nominee at the national convention. Some states use the caucus system of choosing convention delegates.

In the general elections, a voter technically does not vote directly for president but chooses between slates of presidential electors. In most states, the slate that wins the most popular votes throughout the state gets to cast all the electoral votes for the state. The candidate receiving a majority (270) of the electoral votes wins the election.

≫ LO4 The United States uses the Australian ballot, a secret ballot that is prepared, distributed, and counted by government officials. Voter participation in the United States is often considered to be low, especially in elections that do not feature a presidential contest. Turnout is lower when measured as a percentage of the voting-age population than it is when measured as a percentage of the population actually eligible to vote.

In colonial times, only white males who owned property were eligible to vote. The suffrage issue has concerned, at one time or another, most groups in the United States. Today, to be eligible to vote, a person must satisfy registration, citizenship, age, and residency requirements. Each state has different qualifications.

≫ LO5 The two most important determinants of voting behavior are party identification and race. Perceptions of candidates' characters and their stand on the issues are also important, as are the demographic characteristics described earlier in this book.

Test Yourself

1. The most sought-after (and most criticized) campaign expert, who for a large fee takes over the candidate's campaign, is the:
   a. spin doctor.
   b. political consultant.
   c. campaign organizer.

2. The Supreme Court ruling that was most important in creating our current campaign finance system was:
   a. *McConnell v. FEC.*
   b. *Citizens United v. FEC.*
   c. *California Democratic Party v. Jones.*

3. Today, presidential candidates do not accept matching public funds because:
   a. candidates can raise far more outside of the public system than they would receive if they participated in it.
   b. once candidates accept public funds for the primaries, they must match public funds in a ratio of two to one for the general elections.
   c. public funds are no longer available.

4. In an indirect primary:
   a. voters decide party nominations by voting directly for candidates.
   b. voters make no decisions directly about convention delegates.
   c. voters choose convention delegates, and those delegates determine the party's candidate in the general elections.

5. Any voter can vote in either party primary without declaring a party affiliation in:
   a. an open primary.
   b. a closed primary.
   c. a "top-two" primary.

6. The practice of moving presidential primary elections to the early part of the campaign is called:
   a. the strategy of winning.
   b. front-running.
   c. front-loading.

7. The electoral college has become controversial because:
   a. it can award the presidency to a candidate who did not receive a plurality of the popular vote.

b. "faithless electors" have changed the outcome of presidential elections.
   c. it discriminates against residents of small states.

8. In the United States today, all states use secret ballots that are prepared, distributed, and counted by government officials at public expense. This system is called:
   a. the Australian ballot.
   b. the Massachusetts ballot.
   c. the open ballot.

9. In statistics on voter participation, the voting-age population is typically larger than the:
   a. total population.
   b. vote-eligible population.
   c. adult population.

10. In colonial times, the right to vote was typically limited to persons who were:
    a. of English ancestry.
    b. adult white males.
    c. adult white males who owned some property.

11. Perhaps the two most important factors in determining how voters cast their ballots are:
    a. perception of the candidates and issue preferences.
    b. party identification and race.
    c. level of education and gender.

Essay Questions

1. Some have argued that limits on campaign spending violate First Amendment guarantees of freedom of speech. How strong is this argument? Can such spending be seen as a form of protected expression? Under what circumstances can contributions be seen instead as a method of bribing elected officials?

2. Some people are more likely to vote than others. Older persons vote more frequently than younger people. Wealthy voters make it to the polls more often than poor voters. What might cause older and wealthier individuals to exhibit greater turnout?

Answers to multiple-choice questions: 1. b, 2. b, 3. a, 4. c, 5. a, 6. c, 7. a, 8. a, 9. b, 10. c, 11. b.

9 | Congress

Zach Gibson/Getty Images

Speaker of the House Paul Ryan (R., Wisc.), center, meets the press after his reelection as Speaker in November 2016. Republican colleagues stand around him. *What does the Constitution say about the role of political parties?*

The five **Learning Outcomes (LOs)** below are designed to help improve your understanding of this chapter. After reading this chapter, you should be able to:

LO1≫ Describe the various roles played by Congress and the constitutional basis of its powers.

LO2≫ Explain some of the differences between the House and the Senate, and some of the privileges enjoyed by members of Congress.

LO3≫ Examine the implications of apportioning House seats.

LO4≫ Describe the committee structure of the House and the Senate, and specify the key leadership positions in each chamber.

LO5≫ Discuss the process by which a bill becomes law and how the federal government establishes its budget.

Check your understanding of the material with the Test Yourself section at the end of the chapter.

Most Americans view Congress in a less-than-flattering light. In recent years, Congress has appeared to be deeply split, highly partisan in its conduct, and not very responsive to public needs. Polls show that the share of the public with a favorable opinion of Congress as a whole has at times fallen as low as 7 percent. In one poll, respondents rated traffic jams, root canal operations, and cockroaches more favorably than Congress. (Congress did beat North Korea, meth labs, and gonorrhea.) Yet individual members of Congress often receive much higher approval ratings from the voters in their districts. This is one of the paradoxes of the relationship between the people and Congress. Members of the public hold the institution in relatively low regard compared with the satisfaction they express with their individual representatives.

Part of the explanation for these seemingly contradictory appraisals is that members of Congress spend considerable time and effort serving their **constituents.** If the federal bureaucracy makes a mistake that affects a legislator's constituent, the office of that senator or representative tries to resolve the issue. On a personal level, what most Americans see, therefore, is the work of these local representatives in their home states. Congress, however, was created to work not just for local constituents but also for the nation as a whole. Understanding the nature of the institution and the process of lawmaking is an important part of understanding how the policies that shape our lives are made.

The Nature and Functions of Congress

>>> **LO1:** Describe the various roles played by Congress and the constitutional basis of its powers.

The founders of the American republic believed that the bulk of the power that would be exercised by a national government should be in the hands of the legislature. The leading role envisioned for Congress in the new government is apparent from its primacy in the Constitution. Article I deals with the structure, the powers, and the operation of Congress.

Bicameralism

The **bicameralism** of Congress—its division into two legislative houses—was in part the result of the Connecticut Compromise, which tried to balance the large-state population advantage, reflected in the House, and the small-state demand for equality in policymaking, which was satisfied in the Senate. Beyond that, the two chambers of Congress also reflected the social class biases of the founders. They wished to balance the interests and the numerical superiority of the common citizens with the property interests of the less numerous landowners, bankers, and merchants.

They achieved this goal by providing that members of the House of Representatives should be elected directly by "the People," whereas members of the Senate were to be chosen by the elected representatives sitting in state legislatures, who were more likely to be members of the elite. (The latter provision was changed in 1913 by the passage of the Seventeenth Amendment, which provides that senators are also to be elected directly by the people.)

The logic of the bicameral Congress was reinforced by differences in length of tenure. Members of the House are required to face the electorate every two years, whereas senators can serve for a much more secure term of six years—even longer than the four-year term provided for the president. Furthermore, the senators' terms are staggered so that only one-third of the senators face the electorate every two years, along with all of the House members.

The bicameral Congress was designed to perform certain functions for the political system. These functions include lawmaking, representation, service to constituents, oversight (regulatory supervision), public education, and conflict resolution. Of these, the two most important and the ones that most often interfere with each other are lawmaking and representation.

Constituent
One of the persons represented by a legislator or other elected or appointed official.

Bicameralism
The division of a legislature into two separate assemblies.

The Lawmaking Function

The principal and most obvious function of any legislature is **lawmaking.** Congress is the highest elected body in the country, charged with making binding rules for all Americans. This does not mean, however, that Congress initiates most of the ideas for legislation that it eventually considers. A majority of the bills that Congress acts on originate in the executive branch. Many other bills are traceable to interest groups and political party organizations. In dealing with legislation, members engage in compromise and *logrolling* (offering to support a fellow member's bill in exchange for that member's promise to support your bill in the future). Through such tactics, as well as debate and discussion, backers of legislation attempt to fashion a winning majority coalition.

Traditionally, logrolling often involved agreements to support another member's legislative **earmarks,** also known as pork. Earmarks are special provisions in legislation to set aside funds for projects that have not passed an impartial evaluation by agencies of the executive branch. (Normal spending projects pass through such evaluations.) Recent attempts to curtail pork have not eliminated the process altogether but have substantially reduced its frequency.

The Representation Function

Representation includes both representing the desires and demands of the constituents in the member's home district or state and representing larger national interests, such as the nation's security. Because the interests of constituents in a specific district may be at odds with the demands of national policy, the representation function is often a source of conflict for lawmakers. For example, although it may be in the interest of the nation to reduce defense spending by closing certain military bases, such closures are not in the interest of the states and districts that will lose jobs and local spending. Every legislator faces votes that set local representational issues against lawmaking realities.

How should the legislators fulfill the representation function? There are several views on how this task should be accomplished.

The Trustee View of Representation. One approach to the question of how representation should be achieved is that legislators should act as **trustees** of the broad interests of the entire society. They should vote against the narrow interests of their constituents if their conscience and their perception of national needs so dictate. For example, in 2011 Congress approved trade agreements with Colombia, Panama, and South Korea, despite the widely held belief that such agreements cost specific Americans their jobs.

The Instructed-Delegate View of Representation. Directly opposed to the trustee view of representation is the notion that members of Congress should behave as

Lawmaking
The process of establishing the legal rules that govern society.

Earmarks
Special provisions in legislation to set aside funds for projects that have not passed an impartial evaluation by agencies of the executive branch. Also known as *pork.*

Representation
The function of members of Congress as elected officials representing the views of their constituents as well as larger national interests.

Trustee
A legislator who acts according to her or his conscience and the broad interests of the entire society.

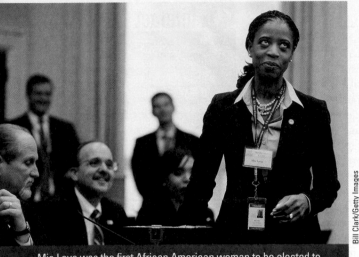

Mia Love was the first African American woman to be elected to the House as a Republican. Love is from Utah and is a member of the Latter Day Saints. Her parents were born in Haiti. Here she participates in a lottery to determine the location of her new office. *Why might she have won in an overwhelmingly white district?*

Bill Clark/Getty Images

instructed delegates—that is, they should mirror the views of the majority of the constituents who elected them.

Generally, most legislators hold neither a pure trustee view nor a pure instructed-delegate view. Typically, they combine both perspectives in a pragmatic mix.

Service to Constituents

Constituents expect individual members of Congress to act as brokers between private citizens and the federal government. This function of providing service to constituents usually takes the form of **casework**. The legislator and her or his staff spend a considerable portion of their time in casework activities, such as explaining the meaning of particular bills to people who may be affected by them, promoting a local business interest, or interceding with a regulatory agency on behalf of constituents who disagree with proposed agency regulations.

This **ombudsperson** role strongly benefits the members of Congress. A government characterized by a large, confusing bureaucracy and complex public programs offers innumerable opportunities for legislators to come to the assistance of (usually) grateful constituents.

The Oversight Function

Instructed Delegate
A legislator who is an agent of the voters who elected him or her and who votes according to the views of constituents, regardless of personal beliefs.

Casework
Personal work for constituents by members of Congress.

Ombudsperson
A person who hears and investigates complaints by private individuals against public officials or agencies (from the Swedish word *ombudsman*, meaning "representative").

Oversight
The process by which Congress follows up on laws it has enacted to ensure that they are being enforced and administered in the way Congress intended.

Oversight of the bureaucracy is essential if the decisions made by Congress are to have any force. **Oversight** is the process by which Congress follows up on the laws it has enacted to ensure that they are being enforced and administered in the way Congress intended. This is done by holding committee hearings and investigations, changing the size of an agency's budget, or cross-examining high-level presidential nominees to head major agencies.

A problem with oversight is that it has become entangled in partisan politics. Members of Congress have tended to ease up on oversight whenever the president is of their political party. During the transition from the Obama to the Trump administrations, the Office of Government Ethics (OGE) became alarmed at the actions of the Trump team. Normally, incoming administrations work with the OGE to ensure new appointees stay on the right side of ethics laws. Trump's people ignored the OGE altogether, and the head of the agency complained on Twitter. In response, Jason Chaffetz (R., Utah), the head of the House Committee on Oversight and Government Reform, threatened to investigate the OGE itself.

In contrast, oversight can become intense, and even excessive, when the president faces a chamber of Congress that is controlled by the other party. For example, in 2015 and 2016 the Republicans launched a series of investigations of former secretary of state Hillary Clinton. The thinly disguised reason was that she was expected to be the Democratic candidate for president in 2016. A committee unsuccessfully tried to find improper conduct by Clinton during and after an attack on the U.S. consulate in Benghazi, Libya. A more promising line of questioning opened up after the FBI criticized Clinton for using a private e-mail server instead of a federal computer system while she was secretary of state.

The Public-Education Function

Educating the public is a function that Congress performs whenever it holds public hearings, exercises oversight of the bureaucracy, or engages in committee and floor debate on such major issues and topics as immigration, oil pipelines, and the concerns of small businesses. In so doing, Congress presents a range of viewpoints on pressing national questions. Congress also decides what issues will come up for discussion and decision. This **agenda setting** is a major facet of its public-education function.

The Conflict-Resolution Function

Congress is commonly seen as an institution for resolving conflicts within American society. Organized interest groups and spokespersons for different racial, religious, economic, and ideological interests look on Congress as an access point for airing their grievances and seeking help. This view of Congress puts it in the position of trying to resolve the differences among competing points of view by passing laws to accommodate as many interested parties as possible. To the extent that Congress meets pluralist expectations in accommodating competing interests, it tends to build support for the entire political process. Its failure to do so, however, tends to bring the political process into disrepute.

The Powers of Congress

The Constitution is both highly specific and extremely vague about the powers that Congress may exercise. The first seventeen clauses of Article I, Section 8, specify most of the **enumerated powers** of Congress—that is, powers expressly given to that body.

Enumerated Powers. The enumerated, or expressed, powers of Congress include the right to:

- Impose a variety of taxes, including tariffs on imports.
- Borrow funds.
- Regulate interstate commerce and international trade.
- Establish procedures for naturalizing citizens.
- Make laws regulating bankruptcies.
- Coin money and regulate its value.
- Establish standards of weights and measures.
- Punish counterfeiters.
- Establish post offices and post roads.
- Regulate copyrights and patents.
- Establish the federal court system.
- Punish illegal acts on the high seas.
- Declare war.
- Raise and regulate an army and a navy.
- Call up and regulate the state militias to enforce laws, to suppress insurrections, and to repel invasions.
- Govern the District of Columbia.

The most important of the domestic powers of Congress, listed in Article I, Section 8, are the rights to impose taxes, to spend, and to regulate commerce. The most important foreign policy power is the power to declare war. Other sections of the Constitution allow Congress to establish rules for its own members, to regulate congressional elections, and to override a presidential veto. Congress may also regulate the extent of the Supreme Court's authority to review cases decided by the lower courts, regulate relations among states, and propose amendments to the Constitution.

Agenda Setting
Determining which public-policy questions will be debated or considered.

Enumerated Powers
Powers specifically granted to the national government by the Constitution. The first seventeen clauses of Article I, Section 8, specify most of the enumerated powers of Congress.

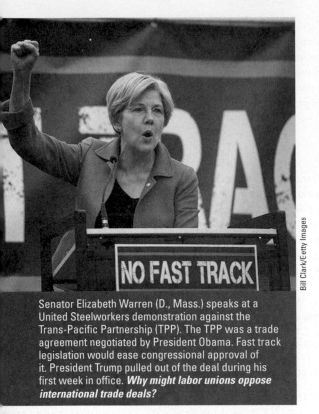

Senator Elizabeth Warren (D., Mass.) speaks at a United Steelworkers demonstration against the Trans-Pacific Partnership (TPP). The TPP was a trade agreement negotiated by President Obama. Fast track legislation would ease congressional approval of it. President Trump pulled out of the deal during his first week in office. *Why might labor unions oppose international trade deals?*

Bill Clark/Getty Images

Powers of the Senate. Some functions are restricted to one chamber. The Senate must advise on, and consent to, the ratification of treaties and must accept or reject presidential nominations of ambassadors, Supreme Court justices, other federal judges, and "all other Officers of the United States." But the Senate may delegate to the president or lesser officials the power to make lower-level appointments.

Constitutional Amendments. Amendments to the Constitution provide for other congressional powers. Congress must certify the election of a president and a vice president or itself choose those officers if no candidate has a majority of the electoral vote (Twelfth Amendment). It may levy an income tax (Sixteenth Amendment) and determine who will be acting president in case of the death or incapacity of the president or vice president (Twentieth Amendment and Twenty-fifth Amendment).

The Necessary and Proper Clause. Beyond these numerous specific powers, Congress enjoys the right under clause 18 of Article I, Section 8 (the elastic, or "necessary and proper," clause), "to make all Laws which shall be necessary and proper for carrying into Execution the foregoing Powers [of Article I], and all other Powers vested by this Constitution in the Government of the United States, or in any Department or Officer thereof." This vague statement of congressional responsibilities has provided, over time, the basis for a greatly expanded national government. It has also constituted, at least in theory, a check on the expansion of presidential powers.

House-Senate Differences and Congressional Perks

>>> **LO2:** Explain some of the differences between the House and the Senate, and some of the privileges enjoyed by members of Congress.

Congress is composed of two markedly different—but co-equal—chambers. Although the Senate and the House of Representatives exist within the same legislative institution, each has developed certain distinctive features that distinguish one from the other.

Size and Rules

The central difference between the House and the Senate is simply that the House is much larger than the Senate. The House has 435 voting representatives, plus delegates from the District of Columbia, Puerto Rico, Guam, American Samoa, and the Virgin Islands, compared with just 100 senators. This size difference means that a greater number of formal rules are needed to govern activity in the House, whereas correspondingly looser procedures can be followed in the less-crowded Senate. This difference is most obvious in the rules governing debate on the floors of the two chambers.

The Senate usually permits extended debate on all issues that arise before it. In contrast, the House generally operates with an elaborate system in which its **Rules Committee** proposes time limitations on debate for any bill, and a majority of the entire body accepts or modifies those suggested time limits. As a consequence of its stricter time limits on debate, the House, despite its greater size, often is able to act on legislation more quickly than the Senate.

Debate and Filibustering

The Senate tradition of the **filibuster,** or the use of unlimited debate as a blocking tactic, dates back to 1790.[1] In that year, a proposal to move the U.S. capital from New York to Philadelphia was stalled by such time-wasting maneuvers. This unlimited-debate tradition—which also existed in the House until 1811—is not absolute, however.

Cloture. Under Senate Rule 22, debate may be ended by invoking *cloture*. Cloture shuts off discussion on a bill. Amended in 1975 and 1979, Rule 22 states that debate may be closed off on a bill if sixteen senators sign a petition requesting it and if, after two days have elapsed, three-fifths of the entire membership (sixty votes, assuming no vacancies) vote for cloture. After cloture is invoked, each senator may speak on a bill for a maximum of one hour before a vote is taken.

Increased Use of the Filibuster. Traditionally, filibusters were rare, and the tactic was employed only on issues of principle. Filibustering senators spoke for many hours, sometimes reading names from a telephone book. By the twenty-first century, however, filibusters could be invoked without such speeches, and senators were threatening to filibuster almost every significant piece of legislation to come before the body. The threats were sufficient to create a new, ad hoc rule that important legislation needed the support of sixty senators, not fifty. As a result of the increased use of the filibuster, some senators have called for its abolition. We discuss that topic in this chapter's *At Issue* feature.

Reconciliation. An additional way of bypassing the filibuster is known as **reconciliation.** Budget bills sent from the House of Representatives to the Senate can be handled under special reconciliation rules that do not permit filibusters. Under the rules, reconciliation can be used *only* to handle budgetary matters. Also, in principle, the procedure is to be invoked only for measures that would have the net effect of reducing the federal deficit. This last restriction, however, has frequently been avoided by the use of misleading bookkeeping.

The Democrats used reconciliation in 2010 to tidy up some of the loose ends in the Affordable Care Act, also known as Obamacare. (This step was necessary because the Democrats lost their sixty-vote supermajority in January after a special election.) In 2017, Republicans planned to use reconciliation to repeal Obamacare, even though they had only fifty-two votes in the Senate. Such action might change the nature of reconciliation completely, making it applicable to almost any legislation. In the end, however, Republicans were unable to find even fifty votes for repeal.

Rules Committee
A standing committee of the House of Representatives that provides special rules under which specific bills can be debated, amended, and considered by the House.

Filibuster
The use of the Senate's tradition of unlimited debate as a delaying tactic to block bills or nominations.

Reconciliation
A special rule that can be applied to budget bills sent from the House of Representatives to the Senate. Reconciliation measures cannot be filibustered.

Chip Somodevilla/Getty Images

Orrin Hatch of Utah is the Republican with the longest continuous term of service in the U.S. Senate. Therefore, when Republicans took control of the Senate in January 2015, Hatch became the president pro tempore of the Senate. *How can long service make a senator more influential?*

---

1. *Filibuster* comes from a Spanish word for pirate, which in turn came from the Dutch term *vrijbuiter*, or freebooter. The word was first used in 1851 to accuse senators of pirating or hijacking debate.

AT ISSUE

Is It Time to Get Rid of the Filibuster?

It is not in the Constitution, but it is an important institution. It is the filibuster, and it follows from Senate Rule 22, which allows for unlimited debate. Throughout American history, senators could tie up the Senate's business by talking indefinitely. In 1975, Rule 22 was revised. Since that year, a vote by sixty senators is required to stop floor debate (instead of the previous sixty-seven). A second significant change in Senate practice developed, however—today, senators don't actually have to *talk* to hold a filibuster. All they have to do to maintain a filibuster is to announce that a filibuster exists. Some want the filibuster abolished. Others do not agree.

The Filibuster Is Not Even Constitutional

Critics of the filibuster argue that it has no constitutional basis and implicitly violates many actual provisions of the Constitution. After all, the Constitution requires a *supermajority*—more than a simple majority—only for special situations such as ratifying treaties, proposing constitutional amendments, overriding presidential vetoes, and convicting impeached officials.

Consider this statement by Alexander Hamilton in *Federalist Paper* No. 75: "All provisions which require more than a majority of any [legislative] body to its resolutions have a direct tendency to embarrass the operations of the government and an indirect one to subject the sense of the majority to that of the minority." Hamilton was writing about a proposal to require that more than half of a chamber's members be present to convene a session, but his argument certainly applies to whether a body should need more than a majority of its members to take a vote.

The Filibuster as Damage Control

True, filibusters today are not as colorful as they were before 1975, when senators were forced to read out of a telephone book or even wear diapers to keep a filibuster going. Yet supporters of the current filibuster system argue that it continues to provide an important protection for minority rights. Why shouldn't Congress be forced to obtain broad support for important legislation? It would be dangerous to allow major taxation and spending measures to be decided by a bare majority. Polling has shown that the filibuster is quite popular among the public at large. Clearly, Americans see the importance of slowing down legislation created by only a single party in Congress. The filibuster still serves a useful purpose, so let's keep it.

FOR CRITICAL ANALYSIS
What would be likely to happen if the filibuster were abolished?

The Nuclear Option. It takes sixty senators to invoke cloture. Senate rules, however, can be changed by a simple majority vote. It is possible, therefore, to limit or abolish the filibuster by a majority vote. Such an act has been dubbed the *nuclear option*, in comparison to the most extreme option in warfare. In the past, such a procedure would have been considered an unthinkable violation of Senate tradition. In the polarized Congress of the twenty-first century, however, very few tricks are still unthinkable.

In 2005, after Democratic senators blocked a vote on a series of Republican judicial candidates, the Republican leadership threatened to employ the nuclear option. A bipartisan group arranged a compromise. Filibusters of nominees were to be reserved for "extraordinary circumstances." In 2013, Democrats contended that Republicans had violated this understanding. No compromise was reached, and so Democrats voted to abolish filibusters against all executive branch nominees and judicial nominees other than to the Supreme Court. (Court nominations were added in 2017.) The rules change did not affect use of the filibuster against proposed legislation. It is quite possible, however, that future changes to the rules may put additional limits on the filibuster—or even abolish it altogether.

The Hastert Rule. Speakers of the House from the Republican Party have used another procedure that can prevent action on a bill. Under the Hastert Rule, a Republican Speaker will only allow a bill to reach the floor of the House for a vote if it has the support of a majority of the Republican members. In other words, no bill is allowed to pass with the support of a minority of the Republicans plus some Democrats. Of course, Democratic Speakers have also employed this tactic, but they have never formalized it as a rule. In 2011 through 2015, however, then–Republican Speaker John Boehner violated the rule on several occasions. Had he not done so, tax cuts would have expired or portions of the federal government would have been forced to shut down.

Congresspersons and the Citizenry: A Comparison

Members of the Senate and the House of Representatives are not typical American citizens. Members of Congress are older than most Americans, partly because of constitutional age requirements and partly because a good deal of political experience normally is an advantage in running for national office. Members of Congress are also disproportionately white, male, and trained in high-status occupations. Lawyers are by far the largest occupational group among congresspersons, although the proportion of lawyers in the House is lower now than it was in the past.

Compared with the average American citizen, members of Congress are well paid. Annual congressional salaries are now $174,000. Increasingly, members of Congress are also much wealthier than the average citizen. Table 9–1 summarizes selected characteristics of the members of Congress.

Perks and Privileges

Legislators have many benefits. Among the most important of these is a team of staff members. More than thirty thousand people are employed on Capitol Hill. About half of them are personal and committee staff members. The personal staff includes office clerks and assistants; professionals who deal with media relations, draft legislation, and satisfy constituency requests for service; and staffers who maintain local offices in the member's home district or state.

The average Senate office on Capitol Hill employs about thirty staff members, and twice that number work on the personal staffs of senators from the most populous states. House office staffs typically are about half as large as those of the Senate.

Members of Congress also benefit from a number of special constitutional protections. Under Article I, Section 6, of the Constitution, for example, "for any Speech or Debate in either House, they shall not be questioned in any other Place." The "speech or debate" clause means that a member may make any allegations

TABLE 9–1	Characteristics of the 115th Congress, 2017–2018		
Why might it be difficult to determine the wealth of a member of Congress?			
Characteristic	**U.S. Population**	**House**	**Senate**
Age (median)*	36.8	57.0	61.0
Percentage minority	34.9	20.7	10
Religion			
Percentage church or synagogue members	66.4	88.5	88
Percentage Roman Catholic	23.9	30.8	24
Percentage Protestant	51.3	48.2	55
Percentage Jewish	1.7	5.1	9
Percentage female	50.7	19.1	21
Percentage with advanced degrees (persons age 25 or above only)	10.1	61.3	74
Occupation			
Percentage lawyers of those employed	0.8	35.9	54
Family income			
Percentage of families earning more than $50,000 annually	44.9	100.0	100
Median net worth			
Excluding principal residence	$45,000	$860,000	$2,900,000

Data applies to members immediately after the 2016 elections. Thereafter, congressional membership changes slowly due to resignation, death, and other factors.
*114th Congress.

Sources: *CIA Factbook;* Census Bureau; and authors' updates.

or other statements he or she wishes in connection with official duties and normally not be sued for defamation (libel or slander) or otherwise be subject to legal action.

Congressional Elections and Apportionment

>>> **LO3:** Examine the implications of apportioning House seats.

The process of electing members of Congress is decentralized. Congressional elections are conducted by the individual state governments. The states, however, must conform to the rules established by the U.S. Constitution and federal statutes. The Constitution states that representatives are to be elected every second year by popular ballot, and the number of seats awarded to each state is to be determined every ten years by the results of the census. Each state has at least one representative, with most congressional districts having almost 750,000 residents. Senators are elected by popular vote every six years. Approximately one-third of the seats are chosen every two years. Each state has two senators. Under Article I, Section 4, of the Constitution, state legislatures are given control over "[t]he Times, Places and Manner of holding Elections for Senators and Representatives," although "the Congress may at any time by Law make or alter such Regulations."

Candidates for Congressional Elections

Congressional campaigns have changed considerably in the past two decades. Like all other campaigns, they are much more expensive, with the average cost of a winning Senate campaign now $10.5 million and a winning House campaign almost $1.7 million. In addition, large sums are spent on congressional campaigns by independent committees. Once in office, legislators spend time almost every day raising funds for their next campaign.

Presidential Effects. When a party has a popular candidate at the top of the ballot, party members further down may benefit as well. This is called the *coattail effect*. Congressional candidates are always hopeful that a strong presidential candidate will sweep in other members of their party. (In fact, in some presidential elections coattail effects have not materialized at all.) One way to measure the coattail effect is to look at the subsequent midterm elections, held in the even-numbered years following the presidential contests. In these years, voter turnout falls sharply. The party controlling the White House frequently loses seats in Congress in the midterm elections, in part because the coattail effect ceases to apply. Table 9–2 shows the pattern for midterm elections since 1946.

The Power of Incumbency. The power of incumbency in the outcome of congressional elections cannot be overemphasized. Figure 9–1 shows that a sizable majority of representatives and senators who decide to run for reelection are successful. This conclusion holds for both presidential-year and midterm elections. Even in 2010, when the Republicans made very large gains, most incumbents were safe.

TABLE 9–2	Midterm Gains and Losses by the Party of the President, 1946–2014

Does it appear that Obama had coattails in 2008? How about 2012?

Seats Gained or Lost by the Party of the President in the House of Representatives		
Year	President's Party	Outcome
1946	D.	−55
1950	D.	−29
1954	R.	−18
1958	R.	−47
1962	D.	−4
1966	D.	−47
1970	R.	−12
1974	R.	−48
1978	D.	−15
1982	R.	−26
1986	R.	−5
1990	R.	−8
1994	D.	−52
1998	D.	+5
2002	R.	+5
2006	R.	−30
2010	D.	−63
2014	D.	−16

FIGURE 9–1 The Power of Incumbency

Senators and members of the House taken together. *Why did so many incumbents lose in 2010?*

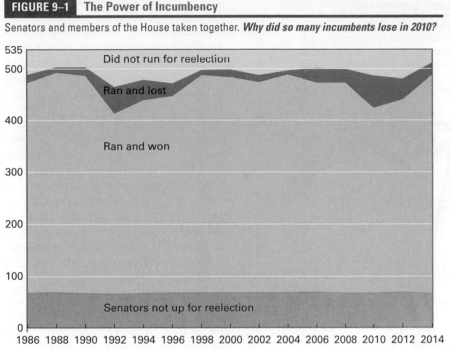

Apportionment of the House

Two of the more complicated aspects of congressional elections are apportionment issues—
reapportionment (the allocation of seats in the House to each state after a census) and
redistricting (the redrawing of the boundaries of the districts within each state). In a landmark
six-to-two vote in 1962, the United States Supreme Court made the redistricting of state legislative seats a *justiciable* (that is, a reviewable) *question.*[2] The Court did so by invoking the Fourteenth Amendment principle that no state can deny to any person "the equal protection of the
laws." In 1964, the Court held that both chambers of a state legislature must be designed so that
all districts are equal in population.[3] Later that year, the Court applied this "one person, one vote"
principle to U.S. congressional districts on the basis of Article I, Section 2, of the Constitution,
which requires that members of the House be chosen "by the People of the several States."[4]

As a result of severe malapportionment of congressional districts before 1964, some
districts contained two or three times the population of other districts in the same state,
thereby diluting the effect of a vote cast in the more populous districts. This system generally benefited the conservative residents of rural areas and small towns and harmed the
interests of the more heavily populated and liberal cities.

Gerrymandering

Although the general issue of apportionment has been dealt with fairly successfully by
the one person, one vote principle, the **gerrymandering** issue has not yet been resolved.

Reapportionment
The allocation of
seats in the House of
Representatives to each
state after a census.

Redistricting
The redrawing of
the boundaries of the
congressional districts
within each state.

Gerrymandering
The drawing of legislative
district boundary lines for
the purpose of obtaining
partisan advantage.
A district is said to be
gerrymandered when
its shape is altered
substantially to determine
which party will win it.

---

2. *Baker v. Carr*, 369 U.S. 186 (1962). The term *justiciable* is pronounced juhs-*tish*-a-buhl.
3. *Reynolds v. Sims*, 377 U.S. 533 (1964).
4. *Wesberry v. Sanders*, 376 U.S. 1 (1964).

FIGURE 9–2	The Original Gerrymander

In 1812 the Massachusetts legislature carved out a misshapen district in Essex County. The cartoon likening the district to a mythical salamander was probably drawn by Elkanah Tisdale, a Boston painter and engraver. Editor Nathan Hale is credited with naming the creature a "gerrymander" (after Elbridge Gerry, then-governor of Massachusetts).

Source: Boston's *Columbian Centinel*, 1812.

Congressional Quarterly's Guide to Congress, 3d ed. (Washington, D.C. Congressional Quarterly Press, 1982), p. 695.

This term refers to the tactics that were used under Elbridge Gerry, the governor of Massachusetts, in the 1812 elections to draw legislative boundaries (see Figure 9–2). A district is said to have been gerrymandered when its shape is altered substantially to determine which party will win it.

In 1986, the Supreme Court heard a case that challenged gerrymandered congressional districts in Indiana. The Court ruled for the first time that redistricting for the political benefit of one group could be challenged on constitutional grounds.[5] In this specific case, however, the Court did not agree that the districts had been drawn unfairly. According to the Court, it could not be proved that a group of voters would consistently be deprived of influence at the polls as a result of the new districts.

Independent Redistricting Commissions. A number of states have attempted to resolve the problem of gerrymandering by taking the power to set district lines away from the state legislature. Instead, an independent or bipartisan commission draws the lines. The Arizona legislature challenged the constitutionality of such commissions, but in 2015 the Supreme Court ruled that they were constitutional.[6]

How Gerrymandering Works. Congressional and state legislative redistricting decisions are often made by a small group of political leaders within a state legislature. Typically, their goal is to shape voting districts in such a way as to maximize their party's chances of winning state legislative seats, as well as seats in Congress. Two of the techniques in use are called **packing** and **cracking.** By employing powerful computers and software, voters supporting the opposing party are "packed" into as few districts as possible or the opposing party's supporters are "cracked" into different districts.

Figure 9–3 illustrates the redistricting process. In these three examples, sixty-four individuals must be distributed among four districts, each of which has a population of sixteen. Two political parties are involved: the O Party and the X Party.

In Example 1, supporters of the two parties are sorted so that each district contains only one kind of voter. Such a pattern sometimes appears when the members of a state legislature are most interested in preserving the seats of incumbents, regardless of party. In this example, it would be almost impossible to dislodge a sitting member in a general election. Example 2 is the reverse case. Every district is divided evenly between the parties, and even a very slight swing toward one of the parties could give that party all four seats.

Packing
In gerrymandering, packing as many voters as possible of the opposing party into a single district.

Cracking
In gerrymandering, splitting the opposing party's voters into many different districts.

---

5. *Davis v. Bandemer*, 478 U.S. 109 (1986).
6. *Arizona State Legislature v. Arizona Independent Redistricting Commission*, 576 U.S. ___ (2015).

FIGURE 9–3 Examples of Districting

Why might a nonpartisan redistricting board tend to favor solutions such as Example 2?

Example 1. A "bipartisan gerrymander" aimed at protecting incumbents in both the O Party and the X Party.

Example 2. An unstable system. All districts have the same number of supporters in each party.

Example 3. A classic partisan gerrymander. The X Party is almost guaranteed to carry three districts.

Example 3 is a classic partisan gerrymander benefiting the X Party. The district in the lower right is an example of packing—the maximum possible number of supporters of the O Party are packed into that district. The other three districts are examples of cracking. The O Party supporters are cracked so that they do not have a majority in any of the three districts. In these districts, the X Party has majorities of eleven to five, ten to six, and eleven to five.

Redistricting after the 2010 Census. As we have observed repeatedly, 2010 was a very good year for the Republican Party—and 2010 was also a census year. Republicans, therefore, controlled an unusually large number of the state legislatures responsible for redistricting. As you might expect, gerrymandering in 2012 favored the Republicans. Consider Pennsylvania. In 2012, Democratic candidates for the U.S. House of Representatives in that state received a total of 2.72 million votes. Republican candidates did slightly less well with 2.65 million votes. Nonetheless, with these votes, Pennsylvania elected five Democrats and thirteen Republicans.

Democrats also face a problem that is not due to deliberate gerrymandering. Many Democrats are "packed" into large cities that are heavily Democratic. Unless a legislature deliberately draws lines to connect inner-city neighborhoods with suburban and rural ones, Democrats face a "natural" gerrymander. Also, linking inner-city neighborhoods with surrounding conservative ones is not feasible in very large metro areas such as Chicago.

"Minority-Majority" Districts

Under the mandate of the Voting Rights Act of 1965, the Justice Department issued directives to states after the 1990 census instructing them to create congressional districts that would maximize the voting power of minority groups—that is, create districts in which minority group voters were the majority. The result was a number of creatively drawn congressional districts—see, for example, the depiction of Illinois's Fourth Congressional District in Figure 9–4, which is commonly described as "a pair of earmuffs."

These districts were challenged in a number of lawsuits. Plaintiffs claimed that district boundaries based on race alone violate the equal protection clause of the Constitution. Consider North Carolina's Twelfth District. In 1996, the district was 165 miles long, following Interstate 85 for the most part. In that year, the Supreme Court held that the district was unconstitutional because race was the dominant factor in drawing the district's boundaries. The district was redrawn, and in 2001, the Court accepted the new boundaries.

FIGURE 9–4 The Fourth Congressional District of Illinois

This district, which is mostly within Chicago's city limits, was drawn to connect two Hispanic neighborhoods separated by an African American majority district. *Given that Democrats are in the majority in every central Chicago district, why might Illinois's Democratic legislature have bothered to shape this district as they did?*

Source: *National Atlas of the United States,* U.S. Department of the Interior.

In 2017, however, the Court rejected both the North Carolina Twelfth and First districts as racially biased.[7] It seems that the Court is now willing to take accusations of bias in redistricting more seriously than in the recent past. The Court also made it clear, however, that it has no current objections to gerrymanders that are purely partisan.

How Congress Is Organized

>>> **LO4:** Describe the committee structure of the House and the Senate, and specify the key leadership positions in each chamber.

The limited amount of centralized power that exists in Congress is exercised through party-based mechanisms. Congress is organized by party. When the Republican Party, for example, wins a majority of seats in either the House or the Senate, Republicans control the official positions of power in that chamber, and every important committee has a Republican chairperson and a majority of Republican members. The same process holds when Democrats are in the majority.

In each chamber of Congress, members of the two major political parties meet separately in *caucuses*. In these meetings, members elect leaders who coordinate party action and negotiate with the other chamber and with the president. Still, much of the actual work of legislating is performed by the committees and subcommittees within Congress.

Thousands of bills are introduced in every session of Congress, and no single member can possibly be adequately informed on all the issues that arise. The committee system is a

7. *Cooper v. Harris,* ___ U.S. ___ (2017).

way to provide for specialization, or a division of the legislative labor. Members of a committee can concentrate on just one area or topic—such as taxation or energy—and develop sufficient expertise to draft appropriate legislation when needed. The flow of legislation through both the House and the Senate is determined largely by the speed with which the members of these committees act on bills and resolutions.

The Power of Committees

Sometimes called "little legislatures," committees usually have the final say on pieces of legislation.[8] Committee actions may be overturned on the floor by the House or Senate, but this rarely happens. Legislators normally defer to the expertise of the chairperson and other members of the committee who speak on the floor in defense of a committee decision. Chairpersons of committees exercise control over the scheduling of hearings and formal actions on bills. They also decide which subcommittee will act on legislation falling within their committee's jurisdiction. Committees normally have the power to kill proposed legislation by refusing to act on it—that is, by never sending it to the entire chamber for a vote.

Committees only very rarely are deprived of control over bills—although this kind of action is provided for in the rules of each chamber. In the House, if a bill has been considered by a standing committee for thirty days, the signatures of a majority (218) of the House membership on a **discharge petition** can pry a bill out of an uncooperative committee's hands. From 1909 to 2016, more than nine hundred such petitions were initiated, but only slightly more than two dozen resulted in successful discharge efforts. Of those, twenty resulted in bills that passed the House.[9]

Types of Congressional Committees

Over the past two centuries, Congress has created several types of committees, each of which serves particular needs of the institution.

Standing Committees. By far, the most important committees in Congress are the **standing committees**—permanent bodies that are established by the rules of each chamber and that continue from session to session. We present a list of the standing committees of the 115th Congress in Table 9–3. In addition, most of the standing committees have created subcommittees to carry out their work. For example, the 115th Congress has 73 subcommittees in the Senate and 104 in the House. Each standing committee is given a specific area of legislative policy jurisdiction, and almost all legislative measures are considered by the appropriate standing committees.

Because of the importance of their work and the traditional influence of their members in Congress, certain committees are considered to be more prestigious than others. Seats on standing committees that handle

Discharge Petition
A procedure by which a bill in the House of Representatives may be forced (discharged) out of a committee that has refused to report it for consideration by the House.

Standing Committee
A permanent committee in the House or Senate that considers bills within a certain subject area.

Rex Tillerson was confirmed by the Senate as the new secretary of state in February 2017. Previously he had been the chief executive officer of Exxon Mobil, an oil company. Exxon Mobil has business interests in Russia, and Tillerson is a personal friend of Russian president Vladimir Putin. *Why might some senators have considered that to be a reason not to confirm him?*

Bloomberg/Getty Images

8. The term *little legislatures* is from Woodrow Wilson, *Congressional Government* (New York: Meridian Books, 1956 [first published in 1885]).
9. *Congressional Quarterly's Guide to Congress*, 6th ed. (Washington, D.C.: Congressional Quarterly Press, 2007); and authors' updates.

| TABLE 9–3 | Standing Committees of the 115th Congress, 2017–2018 |

In 2011, House Republicans changed the name of the Committee on Education and Labor to the Committee on Education and the Workforce. "Labor" often refers to unions. *Why might Republicans have a problem with labor unions?*

House Committees	Senate Committees
Agriculture	Agriculture, Nutrition, and Forestry
Appropriations	Appropriations
Armed Services	Armed Services
Budget	Banking, Housing, and Urban Affairs
Education and the Workforce	Budget
Energy and Commerce	Commerce, Science, and Transportation
Ethics	Energy and Natural Resources
Financial Services	Environment and Public Works
Foreign Affairs	Finance
Homeland Security	Foreign Relations
House Administration	Health, Education, Labor, and Pensions
Judiciary	Homeland Security and Governmental Affairs
Natural Resources	Judiciary
Oversight and Government Reform	Rules and Administration
Rules	Small Business and Entrepreneurship
Science, Space, and Technology	Veterans' Affairs
Small Business	
Transportation and Infrastructure	
Veterans' Affairs	
Ways and Means	

spending issues are especially sought after because members can use these positions to benefit their constituents. Committees that control spending include the Appropriations Committee in either chamber and the Ways and Means Committee in the House. Members also normally seek seats on committees that handle matters of special interest to their constituents. A member of the House from an agricultural district, for example, will have an interest in joining the House Agriculture Committee.

Select Committee
A temporary legislative committee established for a limited time period and for a special purpose.

Select Committees. In principle, a **select committee** is created for a limited time and for a specific legislative purpose. For example, a select committee may be formed to investigate a public problem, such as child nutrition or aging. In practice, a select committee, such as the Select Committee on Intelligence in each chamber, may continue indefinitely. Select committees rarely create original legislation.

Joint Committee
A legislative committee composed of members from both chambers of Congress.

Joint Committees. A **joint committee** is formed by the concurrent action of both chambers of Congress and consists of members from each chamber. Joint committees, which may be permanent or temporary, have dealt with the economy, taxation, and the Library of Congress.

Conference Committee
A special joint committee appointed to reconcile differences when bills pass the two chambers of Congress in different forms.

Conference Committees. Special joint committees—**conference committees**—are formed for the purpose of achieving agreement between the House and the Senate on the exact wording of legislative acts when the two chambers pass legislative proposals in different forms. No bill can be sent to the White House to be signed into law unless it first passes both chambers in identical form. Conference committees are in a position to make significant alterations to legislation and frequently become the focal point of policy debates.

The House Rules Committee. Due to its special "gatekeeping" power over the terms on which legislation will reach the floor of the House of Representatives, the House Rules Committee holds a uniquely powerful position. For each bill, the committee passes a special rule that sets the time limit on debate and determines whether and how a bill may be amended. The Rules Committee has the unusual power to convene while the House is meeting as a whole, to have its resolutions considered immediately on the floor, and to initiate legislation on its own.

The Selection of Committee Members

In both chambers, members are appointed to standing committees by the steering committee of their party. The majority-party member with the longest term of continuous service on a standing committee is given preference when the committee selects its chairperson. The most senior member of the minority party is called the *ranking committee member* for that party. This **seniority system** is not required by law but is an informal, traditional process, and it applies to other significant posts in Congress as well. The system provides a predictable means of assigning positions of power within Congress.

The general pattern until the 1970s was that members of the House or Senate who represented safe seats would be reelected repeatedly and eventually could accumulate enough years of continuous committee service to enable them to become the chairpersons of their committees. In the 1970s, reforms to the chairperson selection process somewhat modified the seniority system in the House. The reforms introduced the use of a secret ballot in electing House committee chairpersons and allowed for the possibility of choosing a chairperson on a basis other than seniority. The Democrats immediately replaced three senior chairpersons who were out of step with the rest of their party. In 1995, the Republicans chose relatively junior House members as chairpersons of several key committees, thus ensuring conservative control of the committees. The Republicans also passed a rule limiting the term of a chairperson to six years.

Leadership in the House

The House leadership is made up of the Speaker, the majority and minority leaders, and the party whips.

The Speaker. The foremost power holder in the House of Representatives is the **Speaker of the House.** The Speaker's position is technically a nonpartisan one, but in fact, for the better part of two centuries, the Speaker has been the official leader of the majority party in the House. When a new Congress convenes in January of odd-numbered years, each party nominates a candidate for Speaker. All Republican members of the House are expected to vote for their party's nominee, and all Democrats are expected

Seniority System
A custom followed in both chambers of Congress specifying that the member of the majority party with the longest term of continuous service will be given preference when a committee chairperson (or a holder of some other significant post) is selected.

Speaker of the House
The presiding officer in the House of Representatives. The Speaker is chosen by the majority party and is the most powerful and influential member of the House.

Senator John McCain (R., Ariz.) is chair of the Senate Armed Services Committee. (He was also the Republican candidate for president in 2008.) McCain has been more critical of the Trump administration than most Republicans. *Why is it important to the administration to have good relations with him?*

Alan Freed/Shutterstock.com

Majority Leader of the House
A leader elected by the majority party in the House to assist the Speaker and foster party cohesion.

to support their candidate. The vote to organize the House is the one vote in which representatives are strongly expected to vote with their party. In a sense, this vote defines a member's partisan status.

The major formal powers of the Speaker include the following:

- Presiding over meetings of the House.
- Appointing members of joint committees and conference committees.
- Scheduling legislation for floor action.
- Deciding points of order and interpreting the rules with the advice of the House parliamentarian.
- Referring bills and resolutions to the appropriate standing committees of the House.

A Speaker may take part in floor debate and vote, as can any other member of Congress, but recent Speakers usually have voted only to break a tie.

In the years since 2011, when the Republicans took control of the House, the Speaker's job has often been difficult. Speaker John Boehner was forced to confront insurgent conservatives who were willing to shut down the government if that was what it took to attain their policy goals. In October 2015, Boehner decided that enough was enough, and he resigned. After a brief period of political turbulence, Republicans settled on Paul Ryan of Wisconsin as his replacement.

The Majority Leader. The **majority leader of the House** is elected by the caucus of the majority party to foster cohesion among party members and to act as a spokesperson for the party. The majority leader influences the scheduling of debate and acts as the chief supporter of the Speaker. The majority leader cooperates with the Speaker and other party leaders, both inside and outside Congress, to formulate the party's legislative program and to guide that program through the legislative process in the House. The parties have often recruited future Speakers from those who hold the position of majority leader.

From left to right: Win McNamee/Getty Images, Chip Somodevilla/Getty Images, Photo Courtesy of the U.S. Congress

Speaker of the House Republican Paul Ryan of Wisconsin (left) was elected in 2015 along with House majority leader Kevin McCarthy of California (center). Minority leader Nancy Pelosi (right), a California Democrat, was Speaker until the Republicans took control of the House in the 2010 elections. *What problems might a Speaker have in leading his or her own party members?*

The Minority Leader. The **minority leader of the House** is the candidate nominated for Speaker by the caucus of the minority party. Like the majority leader, the leader of the minority party has as her or his primary responsibility the maintaining of cohesion within the party's ranks. The minority leader speaks on behalf of the president if the minority party controls the White House. In relations with the majority party, the minority leader consults with both the Speaker and the majority leader on recognizing members who wish to speak on the floor, on House rules and procedures, and on the scheduling of legislation. Minority leaders have no actual power in these areas, however.

Whips. The leadership of each party includes assistants to the majority and minority leaders known as **whips.**[10]

After Republicans took control of the U.S. Senate in the 2014 elections, Republican senator Mitch McConnell of Kentucky, left, was elected Senate majority leader. Democratic senator Chuck Schumer of New York, right, was elected minority leader in November 2016. It is rare for a congressional leader to become president. *How might a congressional leadership position interfere with presidential aspirations?*

The whips are members of Congress who assist the party leaders by passing information down from the leadership to party members and by ensuring that members show up for floor debate and cast their votes on important issues. Whips conduct polls among party members about the members' views on legislation, inform the leaders about whose vote is doubtful and whose is certain, and may exert pressure on members to support the leaders' positions.

Leadership in the Senate

The Senate is less than one-fourth the size of the House. This fact alone probably explains why a formal, complex, and centralized leadership structure is not as necessary in the Senate as it is in the House.

The two highest-ranking formal leadership positions in the Senate are essentially ceremonial in nature. Under the Constitution, the vice president of the United States is the president (that is, the presiding officer) of the Senate and may vote to break a tie. The vice president, however, is only rarely present for a meeting of the Senate. The Senate elects instead a **president pro tempore** ("pro tem") to preside over the Senate in the vice president's absence. Ordinarily, the president pro tem is the member of the majority party with the longest continuous term of service in the Senate. As mentioned, the president pro tem is mostly a ceremonial position. More junior senators take turns actually presiding over the sessions of the Senate.

The real leadership power in the Senate rests in the hands of the **Senate majority leader,** the **Senate minority leader,** and their respective whips. The Senate majority and minority leaders have the right to be recognized first in debate on the floor and generally exercise the same powers available to the House majority and minority leaders. They control the

Minority Leader of the House
The party leader elected by members of the minority party in the House.

Whip
A member of Congress who aids the majority or minority leader of the House or the Senate.

President pro tempore
The senator who presides over the Senate in the absence of the vice president.

Senate Majority Leader
The chief spokesperson of the majority party in the Senate, who directs the legislative program and party strategy.

Senate Minority Leader
The party officer in the Senate who commands the minority party's opposition to the policies of the majority party and directs the legislative program and strategy of his or her party.

---

10. *Whip* comes from "whipper-in," a fox-hunting term for someone who keeps the hunting dogs from straying.

scheduling of debate on the floor in conjunction with the majority party's policy committee, influence the allocation of committee assignments for new members or for senators attempting to transfer to a new committee, influence the selection of other party officials, and participate in selecting members of conference committees.

The leaders are expected to mobilize support for partisan legislative or presidential initiatives. They act as liaisons with the White House when the president is of their party, try to obtain the cooperation of committee chairpersons, and seek to facilitate the smooth functioning of the Senate through the senators' unanimous consent to various procedural motions. The majority and minority leaders are elected by their respective party caucuses.

Senate party whips, like their House counterparts, maintain communication within the party on platform positions and try to ensure that party colleagues are present for floor debate and important votes. The Senate whip system is far less elaborate than its counterpart in the House, because there are fewer members to track and senators have a greater tradition of independence.

Lawmaking and Budgeting

>>> **LO5:** Discuss the process by which a bill becomes law and how the federal government establishes its budget.

Each year, Congress and the president propose and approve many laws. Some are budget and appropriation laws that require extensive bargaining but must be passed for the government to continue to function. Other laws are relatively free of controversy and are passed with little dissension. Still other proposed legislation is extremely controversial and reaches to the roots of differences between Republicans and Democrats.

Figure 9–5 shows that each law begins as a bill, which must be introduced in either the House or the Senate. Often, similar bills are introduced in both chambers. A budget bill, however, must start in the House. In each chamber, the bill follows similar steps. It is referred to a committee and its subcommittees for study, discussion, hearings, and markup (rewriting). When the bill is reported out to the full chamber, it must be scheduled for debate (by the Rules Committee in the House and by the leadership in the Senate). After the bill has been passed in each chamber, if the two versions of the bill contain different provisions, a conference committee is formed to write a compromise bill, which must be approved by both chambers before it is sent to the president to sign or veto.

How Much Will the Government Spend?

The Constitution is very clear about where the power of the purse lies in the national government: all taxing or spending bills must originate in the House of Representatives. Much of the business of Congress is concerned with approving government expenditures through the budget process and with raising the revenues to pay for government programs.

From 1922 until 1974, Congress required the president to prepare and present to the legislature an **executive budget.** Still, the congressional budget process was so disjointed that it was difficult to visualize the total picture of government finances. The president presented the executive budget to Congress in January. It was broken down into thirteen or more appropriations bills. Some time later, after all of the bills had been debated, amended, and passed, it was more or less possible to estimate total government spending for the next year.

Frustrated by the president's ability to impound, or withhold, funds and dissatisfied with the entire budget process, Congress passed the Budget and Impoundment Control Act of 1974 to regain some control over the nation's spending. The act required the president to spend

Executive Budget
The budget prepared and submitted by the president to Congress.

FIGURE 9–5   **How a Bill Becomes Law**

This illustration shows the most typical way in which proposed legislation is enacted into law. Most legislation begins as similar bills introduced into the House and the Senate. The process is illustrated here with two hypothetical bills, House Bill No. 100 (HR 100) and Senate Bill No. 200 (S 200). The path of HR 100 is shown on the left and that of S 200 on the right. *Where does the filibuster fit into this process?*

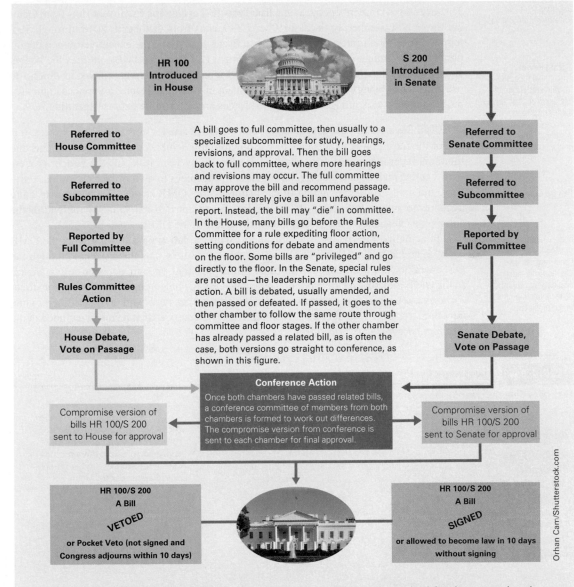

HR 100 Introduced in House

S 200 Introduced in Senate

Referred to House Committee

Referred to Subcommittee

Reported by Full Committee

Rules Committee Action

House Debate, Vote on Passage

Referred to Senate Committee

Referred to Subcommittee

Reported by Full Committee

Senate Debate, Vote on Passage

A bill goes to full committee, then usually to a specialized subcommittee for study, hearings, revisions, and approval. Then the bill goes back to full committee, where more hearings and revisions may occur. The full committee may approve the bill and recommend passage. Committees rarely give a bill an unfavorable report. Instead, the bill may "die" in committee. In the House, many bills go before the Rules Committee for a rule expediting floor action, setting conditions for debate and amendments on the floor. Some bills are "privileged" and go directly to the floor. In the Senate, special rules are not used—the leadership normally schedules action. A bill is debated, usually amended, and then passed or defeated. If passed, it goes to the other chamber to follow the same route through committee and floor stages. If the other chamber has already passed a related bill, as is often the case, both versions go straight to conference, as shown in this figure.

Conference Action
Once both chambers have passed related bills, a conference committee of members from both chambers is formed to work out differences. The compromise version from conference is sent to each chamber for final approval.

Compromise version of bills HR 100/S 200 sent to House for approval

Compromise version of bills HR 100/S 200 sent to Senate for approval

HR 100/S 200 A Bill
VETOED
or Pocket Veto (not signed and Congress adjourns within 10 days)

HR 100/S 200 A Bill
SIGNED
or allowed to become law in 10 days without signing

Orhan Cam/Shutterstock.com

A compromise bill approved by both chambers is sent to the president, who can sign it into law or veto it and return it to Congress. Congress may override a veto by a two-thirds majority vote in both chambers. The bill then becomes law without the president's approval.

Fiscal Year (FY)
A twelve-month period that is used for bookkeeping or accounting purposes. Usually, the fiscal year does not coincide with the calendar year. For example, the federal government's fiscal year runs from October 1 through September 30.

Spring Review
The annual process in which the Office of Management and Budget (OMB) requires federal agencies to review their programs, activities, and goals, and submit their requests for funding for the next fiscal year.

Fall Review
The annual process in which the OMB, after receiving formal federal agency requests for funding for the next fiscal year, reviews the requests, makes changes, and submits its recommendations to the president.

the funds that Congress had appropriated, ending the president's ability to kill programs by withholding funds. The other major result of the act was to force Congress to examine total national taxing and spending at least twice in each budget cycle. (See Figure 9–6 for a graphic illustration of the budget cycle.)

Preparing the Budget

The federal government operates on a **fiscal year (FY)** cycle. The fiscal year runs from October through September, so fiscal 2019, or FY19, runs from October 1, 2018, through September 30, 2019. Eighteen months before a fiscal year starts, the executive branch begins preparing the budget. The Office of Management and Budget (OMB) outlines the budget and then sends it to the various departments and agencies. Bargaining follows, in which—to use only two of many examples—the Department of Health and Human Services argues for more antipoverty spending, and the armed forces argue for more defense spending.

The OMB Reviews the Budget. Even though the OMB has fewer than 550 employees, it is one of the most powerful agencies in Washington. It assembles the budget documents and monitors federal agencies throughout each year. Every year, it begins the budget process with a **spring review,** in which it requires all of the agencies to review their programs, activities, and goals. At the beginning of each summer, the OMB sends out a letter instructing agencies to submit their requests for funding for the next fiscal year. By the end of the summer, each agency must submit a formal request to the OMB.

In actuality, the "budget season" begins with the **fall review.** At this time, the OMB looks at budget requests and, in almost all cases, routinely cuts them back. Although the OMB works within guidelines established by the president, specific decisions often are left to the OMB director and the director's associates. By the beginning of November, the director's review begins. The director meets with cabinet secretaries and budget officers. Time becomes crucial. The budget must be completed by January so that it can be included in the *Economic Report of the President*.

FIGURE 9–6 **The Budget Cycle**

Why does Congress require the president to spend appropriated funds?

Executive Budgeting Process	**Executive agency requests:** about twelve to eighteen months before the start of the fiscal year, or in March to September	**Office of Management and Budget (OMB) review and presidential approval:** nine to twelve months before the start of the fiscal year, or in September to December
Legislative Budgeting Process	**Second budget resolution:** by October 1 ← **First budget resolution:** by May 15	**Executive branch submits a budget to Congress:** eight to nine months before the start of the fiscal year, at the end of January
Execution	**Start of fiscal year:** October 1 → **Outlays and obligations:** October 1 to September 30	**Audit of fiscal year outlays:** on a selective basis by the Government Accountability Office (GAO)

Tad Denson/Shutterstock.com

The Election-Year Budget. The schedule just described cannot apply to a year in which the voters elect a new president or to a year in which a new president is inaugurated. In 2016, Barack Obama did not engage in a fall review of the FY 2018 budget, because he would no longer be in office when the budget went into effect in October 2017. Donald Trump could hardly have undertaken the fall review either, given that he was still campaigning for the presidency. Following the election of a new president, the budget process is compressed into the first months of the new administration.

Congress Faces the Budget

In January, nine months before the fiscal year starts, the president takes the OMB's proposed budget, approves it, and submits it to Congress. Then the congressional budgeting process takes over. The budgeting process involves two steps: authorization and appropriation.

The Authorization Process. First, Congress must authorize funds to be spent. The **authorization** is a formal declaration by the appropriate congressional committee that a certain amount of funding may be available to an agency. Congressional committees and subcommittees look at the proposals from the executive branch and the Congressional Budget Office in making the decision to authorize funds.

The Appropriation Process. After the funds have been authorized, they must be appropriated by Congress. The appropriations committees of both the House and the Senate forward spending bills to their respective bodies. The **appropriation** of funds occurs when the final bill is passed. In this process, large sums are in play. Representatives and senators, especially those who chair key committees, have traditionally found it easy to slip earmarks, or pork, into a variety of bills. These proposals may have nothing to do with the explicitly stated purpose of the bill.

Evading the Ban on Earmarks. In March 2010, the Republican-controlled House implemented rules designed to eliminate earmarks benefiting individuals or corporations. The new rules have substantially reduced the amount of pork inserted into appropriations bills, but lawmakers have been creative in attempting to circumvent the ban. In some instances, legislators have simply denied that a particular funding request is actually an earmark. More commonly, members have lobbied the various executive agencies to include projects that benefit their districts. According to the OMB definition, spending requested by executive agencies is not pork. Further, the White House itself frequently inserts special requests into the executive budget, thus making the president the biggest "porkmeister" of all.

Budget Resolutions and Crises

The **first budget resolution** by Congress is due in May. It sets overall revenue goals and spending targets. Spending and tax laws that are drawn up over the summer are supposed to be guided by the first budget resolution. By September, Congress is scheduled to pass its **second budget resolution,** one that will set binding limits on taxes and spending for the fiscal year beginning October 1.

The Continuing Resolution. In actuality, Congress has finished the budget on time in only three years since 1977. As mentioned earlier, the budget is usually broken into a series of appropriations bills. If Congress has not passed one of these bills by October 1, it normally passes a **continuing resolution** that allows the affected agencies to keep on doing whatever they were doing the previous year with the same amount of funding.

Authorization
A formal declaration by a legislative committee that a certain amount of funding may be available to an agency. Some authorizations terminate in a year. Others are renewable automatically without further congressional action.

Appropriation
The passage, by Congress, of a spending bill specifying the amount of authorized funds that actually will be allocated for an agency's use.

First Budget Resolution
A resolution passed by Congress in May that sets overall revenue goals and spending targets for the following fiscal year.

Second Budget Resolution
A resolution passed by Congress in September that sets binding limits on taxes and spending for the following fiscal year.

Continuing Resolution
A temporary funding law that Congress passes when an appropriations bill has not been passed by the beginning of the new fiscal year on October 1.

Senator Al Franken (D., Minn.), left, talks with Senate Foreign Relations Committee chair Bob Corker (R., Tenn.) as they head for a closed-door briefing by U.S. intelligence agencies in January 2017. *Why might closed-door meetings be less partisan than open ones?*

Chip Somodevilla/Getty Images

The Federal Debt Ceiling. If the federal government runs a budget deficit—if it spends more than it takes in—it must issue new debt. The government has, in fact, run a deficit in most years. Current law limits the amount of debt the government can issue. If the federal debt approaches the *debt ceiling*, Congress must raise the ceiling to allow additional debt. Many people mistakenly believe that raising the ceiling is a prerequisite for new, future spending, but that is not the case. If the debt ceiling is not raised as needed, the government might be forced to default on its existing obligations.

Traditionally, members of Congress often "grandstanded" by voting against the debt ceiling hike, even though passage was never in doubt. In 2011, however, House Republicans successfully used the ceiling vote to force Democrats to accept spending cuts. Republicans tried this tactic again in 2013, but this time the Democrats refused to negotiate, and the effort collapsed. It would be surprising if the tactic were revived any time soon, given that the Republicans now control both chambers of Congress and the presidency.

MAKING A DIFFERENCE

Learning About Your Representatives

Do you know the names of your senators and your representative in Congress? A surprising number of Americans do not. Even if you know the names and parties of your elected delegates, there is still much more you could learn about them that would be useful.

Why Should You Care? The legislation that Congress passes can directly affect your life. Consider, for example, the Affordable Care Act, commonly known as Obamacare. The Republican Congress elected in 2016 along with President Donald Trump has pledged to "repeal and replace" this program. To do so, the Republicans will have to unite almost completely around a legislative package and also find a way to bypass a Democratic filibuster in the Senate. If they succeed, your access to health-care insurance could undergo major changes.

You can make a difference on major legislation simply by voting for the candidates you prefer. In between elections, you can lobby your senators or your representative and ask that they support legislation that meets your approval. To do so effectively, however, you need to know what positions these officials are currently advocating.

What Can You Do? To contact a member of Congress, start by going to the websites of the U.S. House of Representatives and the U.S. Senate.

Although you can communicate easily with your representatives by e-mail, using it has some drawbacks. Representatives and senators now receive large volumes of e-mail from constituents, which they rarely read themselves. They have staff members who read and respond to e-mail instead. Many interest groups argue that U.S. mail, or even express mail or a phone call, is more likely to capture the attention of a representative than e-mail. You can contact your representative and senators by using one of the following addresses or phone numbers:

United States House of Representatives
Washington, DC 20515
202-224-3121

United States Senate
Washington, DC 20510
202-224-3121

Key Terms

agenda setting 203
appropriation 221
authorization 221
bicameralism 200
casework 202
conference committee 214
constituent 200
continuing resolution 221
cracking 210
discharge petition 213
earmarks 201
enumerated powers 203

executive budget 218
fall review 220
filibuster 205
first budget
   resolution 221
fiscal year (FY) 220
gerrymandering 209
instructed delegate 202
joint committee 214
lawmaking 201
majority leader
   of the House 216

minority leader
   of the House 217
ombudsperson 202
oversight 202
packing 210
president pro
   tempore 217
reapportionment 209
reconciliation 205
redistricting 209
representation 201
Rules Committee 205

second budget
   resolution 221
select committee 214
Senate majority
   leader 217
Senate minority leader 217
seniority system 215
Speaker of the House 215
spring review 220
standing committee 213
trustee 201
whip 217

Chapter Summary

≫LO1 The authors of the U.S. Constitution believed that the bulk of national power should be in the legislature. The Connecticut Compromise established the House of Representatives with a membership based on population, and the Senate based on the equality of states.

The functions of Congress include (a) lawmaking, (b) representation, (c) service to constituents, (d) oversight, (e) public education, and (f) conflict resolution.

The Constitution specifies the enumerated, or expressed, powers of Congress, including the rights to impose taxes, to borrow funds, to regulate commerce, and to declare war. In addition, Congress enjoys the right, under the elastic, or "necessary and proper," clause, to make all laws necessary and proper for executing the various powers of the national government.

≫LO2 There are 435 members of the House of Representatives and 100 members of the Senate. Owing to its larger size, the House has a greater number of formal rules. The Senate tradition of unlimited debate, expressed in the filibuster, has been used over the years to frustrate the passage of bills. Budget bills can be exempt from a filibuster, and by 2017 most presidential nominations were exempt as well.

Members of Congress are older and wealthier than most Americans, disproportionately white and male, and more likely to be lawyers.

≫LO3 Most incumbent representatives and senators who run for reelection are successful. The Supreme Court's "one person, one vote" rule means that the populations of congressional and state legislative districts must be effectively equal. Still, district boundaries are frequently drawn to benefit one of the parties by gerrymandering.

≫LO4 Most of the work of legislating is performed by committees and subcommittees within Congress. Legislation introduced into the House or Senate is assigned to standing committees. Joint committees are formed by the action of both chambers and consist of members from each. Conference committees are joint committees set up to achieve agreement between the House and the Senate on the wording of legislative acts that were passed by the chambers in different forms. The seniority rule, which is usually followed, specifies that the longest-serving member of the majority party will be the chair of a committee.

The foremost power in the House is the Speaker of the House. Other leaders are the House majority leader, the House minority leader, and the majority and minority whips. Formally, the vice president is the presiding officer of the Senate. Actual Senate leadership rests with the majority leader, the minority leader, and their whips.

>>>**LO5** A bill becomes law by progressing through both chambers of Congress and their appropriate committees before submission to the president.

The budget process for a fiscal year begins with the preparation of an executive budget by the president. This is reviewed by the Office of Management and Budget and then sent to Congress, which is supposed to pass a final budget by the end of September. Since 1977, Congress generally has not followed its own time rules.

Test Yourself

1. The bicameralism of Congress means that:
   a. every district has two members.
   b. every state has two senators.
   c. Congress is divided into two legislative bodies.

2. The process of compromise in which members of Congress support each other's bills is called:
   a. agenda setting.
   b. logrolling.
   c. reconciliation.

3. The central difference between the House and the Senate is that:
   a. the House is much larger than the Senate.
   b. the Senate is much larger than the House.
   c. the Senate meets only occasionally, but the House meets all of the time.

4. In contrast to the House, only the Senate has the power to accept or reject:
   a. treaties with foreign nations.
   b. executive agreements with foreign governments.
   c. the recognition of foreign governments.

5. A high percentage of senators and representatives are reelected, and we describe this as due to:
   a. coattail effects.
   b. presidential effects.
   c. the power of incumbency.

6. Congressional redistricting often involves gerrymandering, which means that the redistricting:
   a. results in an equal number of Democratic and Republican districts.
   b. results in strange-shaped districts designed to favor one party.
   c. results in districts that have almost no representation.

7. Gerrymandering can be accomplished by:
   a. cracking and packing.
   b. varying the population of districts.
   c. more frequent redistricting.

8. The typical method of appointing committee chairpersons in Congress is based on:
   a. rotation.
   b. presidential appointment.
   c. the seniority system.

9. The leader of the majority party in the House of Representatives is the:
   a. House majority leader.
   b. Speaker of the House.
   c. president pro tempore.

10. When an appropriations bill has not been passed by the beginning of the new fiscal year, Congress may pass a temporary funding law called:
    a. a continuing resolution.
    b. a second budget resolution.
    c. a temporary authorization.

Essay Questions

1. The District of Columbia is not represented in the Senate and has a single, nonvoting delegate to the House. Should the District of Columbia be represented in Congress by voting legislators? Why or why not?

2. Identify some advantages to the nation that might follow when one party controls the House, the Senate, and the presidency. Identify some of the disadvantages that might follow from such a situation.

Answers to multiple-choice questions: 1. c, 2. b, 3. a, 4. a, 5. c, 6. b, 7. a, 8. c, 9. b, 10. a.

President Donald Trump in New York during his election campaign. *How effective has Trump been during his first year in office?*

JStone/Shutterstock.com

The five **Learning Outcomes (LOs)** below are designed to help improve your understanding of this chapter. After reading this chapter, you should be able to:

LO1》》》 Identify the types of people who typically undertake serious campaigns for the presidency.

LO2》》》 Distinguish among the major roles of the president, including head of state, chief executive, commander in chief, chief diplomat, chief legislator, party chief, and politician.

LO3》》》 Describe some of the special powers of the president, and tell how a president can be removed from office.

LO4》》》 Explain the organization of the executive branch and, in particular, the executive office of the president.

LO5》》》 Evaluate the role of the vice president, and describe what happens if the presidency becomes vacant.

Check your understanding of the material with the Test Yourself section at the end of the chapter.

The writers of the Constitution had no models to follow when they created the presidency of the United States. Nowhere else in the world was there an elected head of state. What the founders did not want was a king. The two initial plans considered by the founders—the Virginia and New Jersey plans—both called for a relatively weak executive elected by Congress. Other delegates, especially those who had witnessed the need for a strong leader in the Revolutionary Army, believed a powerful executive would be necessary for the new republic. The delegates, after much debate, created a chief executive who had enough powers granted in the Constitution to balance those of Congress.

Who Can Become President?

>>> **LO1:** Identify the types of people who typically undertake serious campaigns for the presidency.

The requirements for becoming president, as outlined in Article II, Section 1, of the Constitution, are not overwhelmingly strict:

> *No person except a natural born Citizen, or a Citizen of the United States, at the time of the Adoption of this Constitution, shall be eligible to the Office of President; neither shall any Person be eligible to that Office who shall not have attained to the Age of thirty-five Years, and been fourteen Years a Resident within the United States.*

The president receives a salary of $400,000, plus $169,000 for expenses and a vast array of free services, beginning with residence in the White House.

Birthplace and Age

The only question that arises about these constitutional requirements relates to the term *natural born Citizen*. Does that mean only citizens born in the United States and its territories? What about a child born to U.S. citizens visiting or living in another country? Although the question has not been dealt with directly by the United States Supreme Court, it is reasonable to expect that someone would be eligible if her or his parents were Americans.

Birth Controversies. These questions were debated when opponents of President Barack Obama claimed that Obama was not a natural born citizen. In fact, Obama was born in Honolulu, Hawaii, in 1961. Those who disputed Obama's birth—notably Donald Trump—claimed that his birth certificate was a forgery, even though Obama's birth was also recorded by two Honolulu newspapers.

The Age and Background of the President. Although the Constitution states that the minimum-age requirement for the presidency is thirty-five years, most presidents have been much older than that when they assumed office. John F. Kennedy (1961–1963), at the age of forty-three, was the youngest elected president, and the oldest was Donald Trump, at age seventy. The average age at initial inauguration has been fifty-five. There has clearly been a demographic bias in the selection of presidents. All have been male, white, and from the Protestant tradition, except for John F. Kennedy, a Roman Catholic, and Barack Obama, an African American.

The Process of Becoming President

Major and minor political parties nominate candidates for president and vice president at national conventions every four years. The nation's voters do not elect a president and vice president directly but rather cast ballots for presidential electors, who then vote for president and vice president in the electoral college.

The Electoral College. Because victory goes to the candidate with a majority in the electoral

AP Images

President Ronald Reagan (1981–1989) was the oldest person ever elected before Donald Trump, who was older than Reagan by a few months. *What problems might result if presidents serve while in their seventies or eighties?*

college, it is conceivable that someone could be elected to the office of the presidency without having a plurality of the popular vote cast. In elections in which more than two candidates were running for office, many presidential candidates have won with less than 50 percent of the total popular votes cast for all candidates—including Abraham Lincoln, Woodrow Wilson, Harry Truman, John F. Kennedy, Richard Nixon, and Bill Clinton. It is even possible for a presidential candidate to win when another candidate has received more popular votes. Does this fact mean that the electoral college should be bypassed or abolished? We examine that question in the first *At Issue* feature in this chapter.

When the Electoral College Fails to Choose a President. Thus far, on two occasions the electoral college has failed to give any candidate a majority. At that point, the House of Representatives takes over, and the president is then chosen from among the three candidates having the most electoral college votes. In 1800, Thomas Jefferson and Aaron Burr tied in the electoral college. This happened

In 1960, John F. Kennedy became the youngest person elected president of the United States. Despite his youth, Kennedy had serious health problems that he kept secret. *Could a presidential candidate do such a thing today?*

because the Constitution had not been explicit in indicating which of the two electoral votes was for president and which was for vice president. In 1804, the **Twelfth Amendment** clarified the matter by requiring that the president and the vice president be chosen separately. In 1824, the House again had to make a choice, this time among John Quincy Adams, William H. Crawford, and Andrew Jackson. It chose Adams, even though Jackson had more electoral and popular votes.

The Many Roles of the President

>>> **LO2:** Distinguish among of the major roles of the president, including head of state, chief executive, commander in chief, chief diplomat, chief legislator, party chief, and politician.

The Constitution speaks briefly about the duties and obligations of the president. Based on this brief list of powers and on the precedents of history, the presidency has grown into a very complicated job that requires fulfilling at least five constitutional roles. These are (1) head of state, (2) chief executive, (3) commander in chief of the armed forces, (4) chief diplomat, and (5) chief legislator of the United States. In addition to these constitutional roles, the president serves as the leader of his or her political party. Of course, the president is also the nation's most prominent and successful politician. Here we examine each of these significant presidential functions, or roles. It is worth noting that one person plays all these roles simultaneously and that the needs of the roles may at times come into conflict.

Head of State

Every nation has at least one person who is the ceremonial head of state. In most democratic nations, the role of **head of state** is given to someone other than the chief executive, who leads the executive branch of government. In Britain, for example, the head of state is the

Twelfth Amendment
An amendment to the Constitution, adopted in 1804, that specifies the separate election of the president and the vice president by the electoral college.

Head of State
The role of the president as ceremonial head of the government.

AT ISSUE

Should We Elect the President by Popular Vote?

It is possible for a presidential candidate to be elected when an opposing candidate receives a plurality of the popular vote. This has occurred on five occasions. Most recently, it happened in the elections of George W. Bush in 2000 and Donald Trump in 2016. These candidates won elections in which an opponent received more popular votes than they did. In 2000, Democrat Al Gore received 547,000 more votes than George W. Bush, the Republican. Still, Bush won enough electoral college votes to become president. In 2016, Hillary Clinton won 2,865,000 more votes than Donald Trump. This was by far the largest popular vote margin ever won by a candidate who lost in the electoral college. Such results have led to calls for replacing the electoral college with a popular-vote system.

Abolishing the college would require a constitutional amendment, however, and the likelihood that such an amendment would be ratified is remote. As an alternative, the National Popular Vote movement advocates an interstate compact to bypass the existing system. This proposal would require each participating state to cast all of its electoral votes for the candidate who receives the most popular votes nationwide. The plan will go into effect if the number of participating states grows to the point at which these states can elect a majority of the electoral college. As of 2018, ten states and the District of Columbia had joined the compact. Is bypassing the electoral college a good idea?

We Should Keep the Existing System

Supporters of the electoral college argue that without it, small states would be ignored. Candidates would concentrate on large states with plenty of voters. Also, the current system typically encourages certainty in elections by exaggerating the winner's margin of victory. Under the existing system, if the election is close and votes must be recounted, the recounts will take place in only a few jurisdictions. If the popular vote determined the winner, votes might have to be recounted in every corner of the country. Finally, we have a federal system in this country, and the electoral college reflects that. If you leave aside Clinton's huge margin in California, Trump won the popular vote in the rest of the country. Why should we let California choose the president?

Let's Bypass the Electoral College

In contrast, supporters of the interstate compact say that it is unfair and undemocratic for a president to be elected without winning the popular vote. Further, the existing system tends to disenfranchise voters in much of the nation. Presidential candidates have little reason to campaign in states where they are certain either to win or to lose by a large margin. During recent presidential elections, major campaigns took place in only a few swing states. If presidential candidates had to win the popular vote, they would be forced to campaign in every state. And as to the California argument just made, you can change the outcome of any election if you don't count the votes of one or more states. Exactly when did California cease to be part of the Union?

FOR CRITICAL ANALYSIS

All of the states that have recently joined the interstate compact are solidly Democratic. Why might that be?

---

queen. In much of Europe, the head of state is a relatively powerless president, and the prime minister is the chief executive. But in the United States, the president is both chief executive and head of state.

Some observers of the American political system believe that having the president serve as both the chief executive and the head of state limits the time available to do "real" work. Most presidents have not agreed with this conclusion, however—particularly those presidents who have skillfully blended these two roles with their role as politician. Being head of state gives the president much public exposure. When that exposure is positive, it helps the president deal with Congress over proposed legislation and increases the chances of being reelected—or getting the candidates of the president's party elected.

Chief Executive

According to the Constitution, "The executive Power shall be vested in a President of the United States of America. . . . [H]e may require the Opinion, in writing, of the principal Officer in each of the executive Departments, upon any Subject relating to the Duties of their respective Offices . . . and he shall nominate, and by and with the Advice and Consent of the Senate, shall appoint . . . Officers of the United States. . . . [H]e shall take Care that the Laws be faithfully executed." As **chief executive,** the president is constitutionally bound to enforce the acts of Congress, the judgments of federal courts, and treaties signed by the United States.

The Powers of Appointment and Removal. To assist in the various tasks of the chief executive, the president has a federal bureaucracy, which currently consists of 2.0 million federal civilian employees, not counting the U.S. Postal Service (493,000 employees). You might think that the president, as head of the largest bureaucracy in the United States, wields enormous power. The president, however, only nominally runs the executive bureaucracy. Most government positions are filled by **civil service** employees, who generally gain government employment through a merit system rather than presidential appointment. Therefore, even though the president has important **appointment power,** that power is limited to cabinet and subcabinet jobs, federal judgeships, agency heads, and several thousand lesser jobs—about eight thousand positions in total. This means that most of the 2.5 million employees of the executive branch (USPS included) owe no political allegiance to the president. They are more likely to owe loyalty to congressional committees or to interest groups representing the sector of society that they serve.

The president's power to remove from office those officials who are not doing a good job or who do not agree with the president is not explicitly granted by the Constitution and has been limited. In 1926, however, a Supreme Court decision prevented Congress from interfering with the president's ability to fire those executive-branch officials whom the president had appointed with Senate approval.[1]

Harry Truman (1945–1953) spoke candidly of the difficulties a president faces in trying to control the executive bureaucracy. On leaving office, he referred to the problems that Dwight Eisenhower (1953–1961), as a former general of the army, was going to have: "He'll sit here and he'll say do this! do that! and nothing will happen. Poor Ike—it won't be a bit like the Army. He'll find it very frustrating."[2]

The Power to Grant Reprieves and Pardons. Section 2 of Article II of the Constitution gives the president the power to grant **reprieves** and **pardons** for offenses against the United States except in cases of impeachment. All pardons are administered by the Office of the Pardon Attorney in the Department of Justice.

The Supreme Court upheld the president's power to grant reprieves and pardons in a 1925 case concerning a pardon granted by the president to an individual convicted of contempt of court. A federal circuit court had contended that only judges had the authority to convict individuals for contempt of court when court orders were violated and that the courts should be free from interference by the executive branch. The Supreme Court simply stated that the president could grant reprieves or pardons for all offenses "either before trial, during

Chief Executive
The role of the president as head of the executive branch of the government.

Civil Service
A collective term for employees of the government. Generally, *civil service* is understood to apply to all those who gain government employment through a merit system.

Appointment Power
The president's authority to fill a government office or position.

Reprieve
A formal postponement of the execution of a sentence imposed by a court of law.

Pardon
A release from the punishment for, or legal consequences of, a crime. A pardon can be granted by the president before or after a conviction.

---

1. *Meyers v. United States*, 272 U.S. 52 (1926).
2. Quoted in Richard E. Neustadt, *Presidential Power: The Politics of Leadership* (New York: Wiley, 1960), p. 9. Note that Truman may not have considered the amount of politics involved in decision making in the upper reaches of the army.

Commander in Chief
The role of the president as supreme commander of the military forces of the United States and of the state National Guard units when they are called into federal service.

trial, or after trial, by individuals, or by classes, conditionally or absolutely, and this without modification or regulation by Congress."[3]

Commander in Chief

The president, according to the Constitution, "shall be Commander in Chief of the Army and Navy of the United States, and of the Militia of the several States, when called into the actual Service of the United States." In other words, the armed forces are under civilian, rather than military, control.

Wartime Powers. Those who wrote the Constitution had George Washington (1789–1797) in mind when they made the president the **commander in chief.** Although we do not expect our president to lead the troops into battle, presidents as commanders in chief have wielded dramatic power.

- Harry Truman made the fateful decision to drop atomic bombs on Hiroshima and Nagasaki in 1945 with the goal of forcing Japan to surrender and thus bring World War II to an end.
- Lyndon Johnson (1963–1969) ordered bombing missions against North Vietnam in the 1960s, and he personally selected some of the targets.
- Richard Nixon (1969–1974) decided to invade Cambodia in 1970.
  - Ronald Reagan sent troops to Lebanon and Grenada in 1983 and ordered U.S. fighter planes to attack Libya in 1986.
  - George H. W. Bush (1989–1993) sent troops to Panama in 1989 and to the Middle East in 1990.
  - Bill Clinton (1993–2001) sent troops to Haiti in 1994 and to Bosnia in 1995, ordered missile attacks on alleged terrorist bases in 1998, and sent American planes to bomb Serbia in 1999.
  - George W. Bush (2001–2009) ordered the invasion of Afghanistan in 2002 and of Iraq in 2003.
  - Barack Obama ordered more troops into Afghanistan in 2009, authorized air strikes in Libya in 2011, and increased U.S. troop strength in Iraq back up to 5,000 in as attempt to combat ISIS.

The president is the ultimate decision maker in military matters. Everywhere the president goes, so too goes the "football"—a briefcase filled with all of the codes necessary to order a nuclear attack. Only the president has the power to order the use of nuclear force.

As commander in chief, the president exercises more authority than in any other role. Constitutionally, Congress has the sole power to declare war, but the president can send the armed forces into situations that are certainly the equivalent of war. Harry Truman dispatched troops to Korea in 1950. Johnson and Nixon waged an undeclared war in Southeast Asia, where more than 58,000 Americans were killed and 300,000 were wounded. In neither of these

President Harry Truman (1945–1953, at right), stands with General Dwight Eisenhower in 1951. A year later, Eisenhower successfully ran for president. *Why might a general make a good president?*

George Skadding/Getty Images

---

3. Ex parte *Grossman*, 267 U.S. 87 (1925).

AT ISSUE

Should President Trump Send U.S. Ground Forces to Syria?

Compared with other presidents, Barack Obama was somewhat reluctant to commit the United States military to foreign interventions. That does not mean that America was at peace in the Obama years. U.S. troops continued to fight in Afghanistan. Obama employed U.S. air power in Iraq, Libya, and Syria. Military drones took out terrorist targets in Pakistan, Yemen, and elsewhere. Still, Obama won the 2008 Democratic presidential primaries in part because he opposed George W. Bush's war in Iraq. Donald Trump's positions on the use of military power are not so clear. At times, he has spoken of utterly destroying ISIS. At other times, he has opposed sending U.S. ground troops to Syria. What exactly should the new president do?

ISIS Must Be Destroyed

Hawks say that whether it is called ISIS, ISIL, the Islamic State, or by the Arabic term Daesh, we are confronting a major threat to world peace. ISIS has tried to carve out a new country uniting Iraq and Syria. It terrorizes the people under its control. Women who belong to the wrong religion or even the wrong Islamic denomination are enslaved. ISIS propagates a world view of unprecedented viciousness. It delights in posting videos in which its soldiers chop off the heads of Christians and other "infidels." It has begun sponsoring major terrorist attacks in Western nations.

U.S. air power can do a lot in Syria, but every war in recent memory has proved that victory requires the famous "boots on the ground." What this term really means is the *infantry*. We already have about 500 members of the special forces in Syria

and almost 5,000 soldiers of various types in Iraq. That is a help, but victory requires more. Further, Trump's surprisingly friendly relationship with Russian president Vladimir Putin opens the possibility that the United States and Russia might collaborate in Syria.

This Is Not Our Fight

Those who oppose additional military action ask why we should take responsibility for what happens in Syria—or for that matter Iraq. The troubles in Syria, where almost half a million people have died and millions have been driven from their homes, have led to massive refugee flows into Turkey and Europe. If Syria needs straightening out, why should the United States do it—and not these other countries? To be sure, our armed forces are powerful enough that we could quickly take over all ISIS-held territory. We would then be foreign occupiers, hated by every Syrian patriot. We don't need that.

Furthermore, current policies are showing signs of success. ISIS has lost territory in both Syria and Iraq, and it will lose more. Its finances have been cut in half. The terrorist attacks ISIS organized in Paris, Brussels, Baghdad, and Ankara, Turkey—and the ones it inspired in San Bernardino, Orlando, and Nice—are signs of weakness. ISIS is reverting to terrorism because it cannot hold real estate. Sooner or later, ISIS will fall.

FOR CRITICAL ANALYSIS

Should we cooperate with Syrian dictator Bashar al-Assad against ISIS? Why or why not?

---

situations had Congress declared war. Should President Trump deploy U.S. ground forces in Syria to fight ISIS? We discuss that question in the second of this chapter's *At Issue* feature.

The War Powers Resolution. In an attempt to gain more control over such military activities, in 1973 Congress passed the **War Powers Resolution** over President Nixon's veto. The act requires that the president consult with Congress when sending American forces into action. Once they are sent, the president must report to Congress within forty-eight hours. Unless Congress approves the use of troops within sixty days or extends the sixty-day time limit, the forces must be withdrawn. In spite of the War Powers Resolution, the effective powers of the president as commander in chief are more extensive today than they were in the past.

Chief Diplomat

The Constitution gives the president the power to recognize foreign governments and to make treaties with the **advice and consent** of the Senate. The president also nominates U.S.

War Powers Resolution
A law passed in 1973 spelling out the conditions under which the president can commit troops without congressional approval.

Advice and Consent
Terms in the Constitution describing the U.S. Senate's power to review and approve treaties and presidential appointments.

President George H.W. Bush meets with the foreign minister of Saudi Arabia in 1990. George H.W. Bush is the father of George W. Bush, making the Bush family a true political dynasty. *Is it common for the children of elected officials to go into politics?*

Barry Thumma/AP Images

ambassadors to other countries. As **chief diplomat,** the president dominates American foreign policy, a role that has been supported many times by the Supreme Court.

Diplomatic Recognition. An important power of the president as chief diplomat is that of **diplomatic recognition,** or the power to recognize—or refuse to recognize— foreign governments as legitimate. In the role of ceremonial head of state, the president has always received foreign diplomats. In modern times, the simple act of receiving a foreign diplomat has been equivalent to accrediting the diplomat and officially recognizing his or her government. Such recognition of the legitimacy of another country's government is a prerequisite to diplomatic relations or treaties between that country and the United States.

Deciding when to recognize a foreign power is not always simple. The United States, for example, did not recognize the Soviet Union until 1933—sixteen years after the Russian Revolution of 1917. All attempts to reverse the effects of that revolution—including military invasion of Russia and diplomatic isolation—proved futile. Only then did Franklin D. Roosevelt (1933–1945) extend recognition to the Soviet government. In December 1978, long after the Communist victory in China in 1949, President Jimmy Carter (1977–1981) granted official recognition to the People's Republic of China.[4]

Proposal and Ratification of Treaties. The president has the sole power to negotiate treaties with other nations. These treaties must be presented to the Senate. A two-thirds vote in the Senate is required for approval, or *ratification.* After ratification, the president can approve the treaty as adopted by the Senate. Approval poses a problem when the Senate has added substantive amendments or reservations to a treaty, particularly when such changes may require reopening negotiations with the other signatory governments. Sometimes, a president may decide to withdraw a treaty if the senatorial changes are too extensive—as Woodrow Wilson (1913–1921) did with the Versailles Treaty in 1919 that concluded World War I. Wilson believed that the senatorial reservations would weaken the treaty so much that it would be ineffective.

Ratifying a treaty may be a difficult process, but revoking a treaty appears to be easier. The Constitution says nothing about how a treaty can be terminated, and on at least two occasions presidents have revoked treaties unilaterally, without the approval of Congress.

Chief Diplomat
The role of the president in recognizing foreign governments, making treaties, and effecting executive agreements.

Diplomatic Recognition
The formal acknowledgment of a foreign government as legitimate.

4. The Nixon administration first encouraged new relations with the People's Republic of China by allowing a cultural exchange of table tennis teams. Nixon subsequently traveled to China.

One of these terminations was challenged by a lawsuit. Ultimately, the Supreme Court refused to overrule the president's decision.[5]

The president's ability to revoke treaties may become an issue again under President Trump. He has made no secret of his desire to either rewrite or tear up many of the nation's trade agreements with other nations. Some of these agreements, such as the North American Free Trade Agreement (NAFTA) contain clauses describing how a nation may terminate its participation. Other treaties, however, could conceivably be revoked simply through the president's inherent powers. If that were to happen, Trump's opponents might sue, hoping for a new and different Supreme Court ruling on the issue.

Executive Agreements. Presidential power in foreign affairs is enhanced greatly by the use of **executive agreements** made between the president and other heads of state. Such agreements do not require Senate approval, although the House and Senate may refuse to appropriate the funds necessary to implement them. Whereas treaties are normally binding on succeeding administrations, executive agreements require each new president's consent to remain in effect.

Among the advantages of executive agreements are speed and secrecy. The former is essential during a crisis. The latter is important when the administration fears that open senatorial debate may be detrimental to the best interests of the United States or to the interests of the president.[6] There have been far more executive agreements (about nine thousand) than treaties (about thirteen hundred). Many executive agreements contain secret provisions calling for American military assistance or other support.

The Constitution makes no mention—explicit or implicit—of executive agreements. The Supreme Court, however, has given executive agreements the same legal weight as formal treaties.[7] This conclusion follows from earlier cases in which the Court found the president's powers in the international realm to be "plenary and exclusive." Executive agreements are clearly an attractive way for a president to bypass Congress when making foreign policy. President Obama used an executive agreement when endorsing the nuclear arms deal with Iran and five other world powers in 2015. Some have argued, however, that even if the president can bypass Congress, doing so is not good practice.

Chief Legislator

Constitutionally, presidents must recommend to Congress legislation that they judge necessary and expedient. Not all presidents have wielded their power as **chief legislator** in the same manner. Some presidents have been almost completely unsuccessful in getting their legislative programs implemented by Congress. Presidents Franklin D. Roosevelt and Lyndon Johnson, however, saw much of their proposed legislation put into effect.

Creating the Congressional Agenda. In modern times, the president has played a dominant role in creating the congressional agenda. In the president's annual **State of the Union message,** which is required by the Constitution (Article II, Section 3) and is usually given in late January shortly after Congress reconvenes, the president presents a legislative program. The message gives a broad, comprehensive view of what the president wishes the legislature to accomplish during its session. It is as much a message to the American people

Executive Agreement
An international agreement made by the president, without senatorial ratification, with the head of a foreign state.

Chief Legislator
The role of the president in influencing the making of laws.

State of the Union Message
An annual message to Congress in which the president proposes a legislative program. The message is addressed not only to Congress but also to the American people and to the world.

---

5. *Goldwater v. Carter*, 444 U.S. 996 (1979).
6. The Case Act of 1972 requires that all executive agreements be transmitted to Congress within sixty days after taking effect. Secret agreements are transmitted to the foreign relations committees as classified information.
7. *United States v. Belmont*, 301 U.S. 324 (1937); and *United States v. Pink*, 315 U. S. 203 (1942).

and to the world as it is to Congress. Its impact on public opinion can determine the way in which Congress responds to the president's agenda.

Since 1913, the president has delivered the State of the Union message in a formal address to Congress. Today, this address is one of the great ceremonies of American governance, and many customs have grown up around it. For example, one cabinet member, the "designated survivor," stays away to ensure that the country will always have a president even if someone manages to blow up the Capitol building. Everyone gives the president an initial standing ovation out of respect for the office, but this applause does not necessarily represent support for the individual who holds the office. During the speech, senators and House members either applaud or remain silent to indicate their opinion of the policies that the president announces.

Getting Legislation Passed. The president can propose legislation, but Congress is not required to pass—or even introduce—any of the administration's bills. How, then, does the president get those proposals made into law? One way is by exercising the power of persuasion. The president writes to, telephones, and meets with various congressional leaders. He or she makes public announcements to influence public opinion. Finally, as head of a party, the president exercises leadership over the party's members in Congress. A president whose party holds a majority in both chambers of Congress usually has an easier time getting legislation passed than does a president who faces a hostile Congress.

Saying No to Legislation. The president has the power to say no to legislation through use of the veto, by which the White House returns a bill unsigned to Congress with a **veto message** attached.[8] Because the Constitution requires that every bill passed by the House and the Senate be sent to the president before it becomes law, the president must act on each bill:

1. If the bill is signed, it becomes law.
2. If the bill is not sent back to Congress after ten congressional working days, it becomes law without the president's signature.
3. The president can reject the bill and send it back to Congress with a veto message setting forth objections. Congress then can change the bill, hoping to secure presidential approval, and repass it. Or Congress can simply reject the president's objections by overriding the veto with a two-thirds roll-call vote of the members present in both the House and the Senate.
4. If the president refuses to sign the bill and Congress adjourns within ten working days after the bill has been submitted to the president, the bill is killed for that session of Congress. This is called a **pocket veto.** If Congress wishes the bill to be reconsidered, the bill must be reintroduced during the following session.

Presidents employed the veto power infrequently until after the Civil War, but it has been used with increasing vigor since then. Presidents George W. Bush and Barack Obama, however, made little or no use of the veto during the periods when their parties controlled Congress.

Congress's Power to Override Presidential Vetoes. A veto is a clear-cut indication of the president's dissatisfaction with congressional legislation. Congress, however, can override a presidential veto, although it rarely exercises this power. Consider that two-thirds of the members of each chamber who are present must vote to override the president's veto in a

Veto Message
The president's formal explanation of a veto, which accompanies the vetoed legislation when it is returned to Congress.

Pocket Veto
A special veto exercised by the chief executive after a legislative body has adjourned. Bills not signed by the chief executive die after a specified period of time.

---

8. *Veto* in Latin means "I forbid."

roll-call vote. This means that if only one-third plus one of the members voting in one of the chambers of Congress do not agree to override the veto, the veto holds. In American history, only about 4 percent of all vetoes have been overridden.

Party Chief and Politician

Presidents are by no means above political partisanship, and one of their many roles is that of chief of party. Although the Constitution says nothing about the function of the president within a political party (the mere concept of political parties was abhorrent to most of the authors of the Constitution), today presidents are the actual leaders of their parties.

The President as Chief of Party. As party leader, the president chooses the national committee chairperson and can try to discipline party members who fail to support presidential policies. One way of exerting political power within the party is through **patronage**—rewarding the faithful by appointing them to government or public jobs. This power was more extensive in the past, before the establishment of the civil service in 1883, but the president still retains important patronage power. As we noted earlier, the president can appoint several thousand individuals to jobs in the cabinet, the White House, and the federal regulatory agencies.

Perhaps the most important partisan role that the president has played in the late 1900s and early 2000s has been that of fund-raiser. The president is able to raise large sums for the party through appearances at dinners, speaking engagements, and other social occasions. President Clinton may have raised more than half a billion dollars for the Democratic Party during his two terms. President Bush was even more successful than Clinton. Barack Obama carried on this fund-raising tradition.

Presidents have a number of other ways of exerting influence as party chief. The president may make it known that a particular congressperson's choice for federal judge will not be appointed unless that member of Congress is more supportive of the president's legislative program. The president may agree to campaign for a particular program or for a particular candidate. Presidents also reward loyal members of Congress with support for the funding of local projects, tax breaks for regional industries, and other forms of "pork."

Presidential Constituencies. Presidents have many constituencies. In principle, they are beholden to the entire electorate—the public of the United States—even those who did not vote. Presidents are certainly beholden to their party, because its members helped to put them in office. The president's constituencies also include members of the opposing party whose cooperation the president needs. Finally, the president must take into consideration a constituency that has come to be called the *Washington community*, also known as those "inside the beltway."[9] This community consists of individuals who—whether in or out of political office—are intimately familiar with the workings of government, thrive on gossip, and measure on a daily basis the political power of the president.

Public Approval. All of these constituencies are impressed by presidents who maintain a high level of public approval, partly because doing so is very difficult to accomplish. Presidential popularity, as measured by national polls, gives the president an extra political resource to use in persuading legislators to pass legislation. A president who suffers a dramatic loss of popularity will have trouble getting legislation through Congress. In such circumstances, a president can even fail to be reelected. That was the fate of President Jimmy Carter, who lost to Ronald Reagan after a disastrous collapse in popular support.

Patronage
The practice of rewarding faithful party workers and followers with government employment and contracts.

9. Here, the *beltway* refers to I-495, the interstate highway that completely encircles the District of Columbia as well as many close-in Washington suburbs.

President Barack Obama at one of his last news conferences. Obama was more popular at the end of his presidency than he had been for much of his time in office. *Why might he have left office on a high note?*

Anadolu Agency/Getty Images

Recent Presidents and the Public Opinion Polls. Immediately after 9/11, President George W. Bush had the highest job-approval ratings ever recorded. By the time he left office, however, only 25 percent of the public approved of his performance as president.

Obama's popularity figures were also very high when he took office. Some of that initial popularity came from Republicans, however, and could not survive the partisan battles that began in 2009. Thereafter, Obama's job-approval ratings fluctuated, usually falling between 40 and 50 percent. He was more popular toward the end of his administration, however, with ratings consistently above 50 percent.

At the time of his inauguration, President Trump's approval ratings were about 40 percent in most polls. These are the lowest numbers for an incoming president since polling was first developed. Such low numbers may not stand in the way of Trump's ability to "change the system," however, because upon election he had the support of a Republican House and Senate. Still, such low ratings suggested that Republicans needed to take care. Any further decline in the president's popularity could have negative consequences in the elections of 2018 and 2020. A silver lining for Trump: according to polls, the public was relatively optimistic about his ability to improve the economy.

"Going Public." Since the early 1900s, presidents have spoken more to the public and less to Congress. In the 1800s, only 7 percent of presidential speeches were addressed to the public. Since 1900, 50 percent have been addressed to the public. Presidents frequently go over the heads of Congress and the political elites, taking their cases directly to the people. This strategy, dubbed "going public," gives the president additional power through the ability to persuade and manipulate public opinion. By identifying their own positions so clearly, presidents can weaken the legislators' positions. In times when the major political parties are highly polarized, however, the possibility of compromise with the opposition party may actually be reduced if the president openly takes a strong position. Legislation that might have won bipartisan support can fail if it comes to be seen as a partisan issue. As a result, going public is not as effective as it once was.

Presidential Powers

>>> **LO3:** Describe some of the special powers of the president, and tell how a president can be removed from office.

Presidents have at their disposal a variety of special powers and privileges not available in the other branches of the U.S. government. Most of the powers of the president discussed earlier in this chapter in the section on the roles of the president are called **constitutional powers,** because their basis lies in the Constitution. In addition, Congress has established by law, or statute, numerous other presidential powers—such as the ability to declare

Constitutional Power
A power vested in the president by Article II of the Constitution.

national emergencies. These are called **statutory powers**. Both constitutional and statutory powers have been labeled the **expressed powers** of the president, because they are expressly written into the Constitution or into law.

Presidents also have what have come to be known as **inherent powers**. These depend on the statements in the Constitution that "the executive Power shall be vested in a President" and that the president should "take Care that the Laws be faithfully executed." The most common example of inherent powers are those emergency powers invoked by the president during wartime. Franklin D. Roosevelt, for example, used his inherent powers to move Japanese Americans living on the West Coast into internment camps for the duration of World War II. President George W. Bush often justified expanding the powers of the presidency by saying that such powers were necessary to fight the war on terrorism.

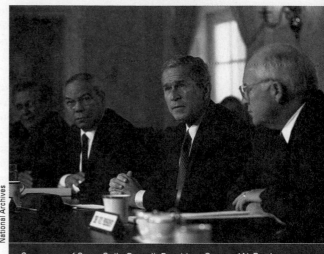

National Archives

Secretary of State Colin Powell, President George W. Bush, and Vice President Dick Cheney at a National Security Council meeting held the day after the 9/11 terrorist attacks. *What effect did that crisis have on the powers of the president?*

Emergency Powers

If you read the Constitution, you will find no mention of the additional powers that the executive office may exercise during national emergencies. Indeed, the Supreme Court has stated that an "emergency does not create power."[10] But it is clear that presidents have made strong use of their inherent powers during times of emergency, particularly in the realm of foreign affairs. The **emergency powers** of the president were first enunciated in the Supreme Court's decision in *United States v. Curtiss-Wright Export Corp.*[11] In that case, President Franklin Roosevelt, without authorization by Congress, ordered an embargo on the shipment of weapons to two warring South American countries. The Court recognized that the president may exercise inherent powers in foreign affairs and that the national government has primacy in these affairs.

Examples of emergency powers are abundant, coinciding with crises in domestic and foreign affairs. Abraham Lincoln suspended certain civil liberties at the beginning of the Civil War (1861–1865) and called the state militias into national service. These actions and his subsequent governance of conquered areas—and even of areas of northern states— were justified by claims that they were essential to preserve the Union. Franklin Roosevelt declared an "unlimited national emergency" following the fall of France in World War II (1939–1945) and took steps to ready the federal budget and the economy for war.

President Harry Truman authorized the federal seizure of steel plants and their operation by the national government in 1952 during the Korean War. Truman claimed that he was using his inherent emergency power as chief executive and commander in chief to safeguard the nation's security, as an ongoing steel mill strike threatened the supply of weapons to the armed forces. The Supreme Court did not agree, holding that the president

Statutory Power
A power created for the president through laws enacted by Congress.

Expressed Power
A power of the president that is expressly written into the Constitution or into statutory law.

Inherent Power
A power of the president derived from the statements in the Constitution that "the executive Power shall be vested in a President" and that the president should "take Care that the Laws be faithfully executed."

Emergency Power
An inherent power exercised by the president during a period of national crisis.

10. *Home Building and Loan Association v. Blaisdell*, 290 U.S. 398 (1934).
11. 299 U.S. 304 (1936).

had no authority under the Constitution to seize private property or to legislate such action.[12] According to legal scholars, this was the first time a limit had been placed on the exercise of the president's emergency powers.

Executive Orders

Congress allows the president (as well as administrative agencies) to issue **executive orders** that have the force of law. These executive orders can do the following: (1) enforce legislative statutes, (2) enforce the Constitution or treaties with foreign nations, and (3) establish or modify rules and practices of executive administrative agencies.

An executive order, then, represents the president's legislative power. The only apparent requirement is that under the Administrative Procedure Act of 1946, all executive orders must be published in the *Federal Register,* a daily publication of the U.S. government. Executive orders have been used to implement national affirmative action regulations, to restructure the White House bureaucracy, and to establish military tribunals for suspected terrorists. In recent years, presidents have also accomplished such goals with *presidential memoranda.* In practice, these are identical to executive orders except for a politically motivated change in name.

Executive orders can be controversial. President Obama, recognizing that he could expect little from the Republicans in Congress, repeatedly used executive orders in an attempt to implement his policies. By the time Obama left office, however, some of his most controversial orders were tied up in the courts. One was an order deferring the deportation of several million unauthorized immigrants, most of whom had children who are citizens. Regardless of whether the courts agreed that Obama had a right to issue this order, President Trump planned to revoke it. Trump's action revealed a problem with executive orders—they can be reversed by the next president. Reversing legislation passed by Congress and signed by the president is much harder.

Executive Privilege

Another inherent executive power that has been claimed by presidents concerns the right of the president and the president's executive officials to withhold information from, or refuse to appear before, Congress or the courts. This is called **executive privilege,** and it relies on the constitutional separation of powers for its basis.

Invoking Executive Privilege. Presidents have frequently invoked executive privilege to avoid having to disclose information to Congress about actions of the executive branch. Executive privilege rests on the assumption that a certain degree of secrecy is essential to national security. Critics of executive privilege believe that it can be used to shield from public scrutiny actions of the executive branch that should be open to Congress and to the American citizenry.

Limiting Executive Privilege. Limits to executive privilege went untested until the Watergate affair in the early 1970s. Five men had broken into the headquarters of the Democratic National Committee and were caught searching for documents that might damage the candidacy of the Democratic nominee, George McGovern. Later investigation showed that the break-in had been planned by members of Richard Nixon's campaign committee and that Nixon and his closest advisers had devised a strategy for impeding the investigation of the crime. After it became known that all conversations held in the Oval Office had been

Executive Order
A rule or regulation issued by the president that has the effect of law.

Federal Register
A daily publication of the U.S. government that prints executive orders, rules, and regulations.

Executive Privilege
The right of executive officials to withhold information from, or to refuse to appear before, a legislative committee or a court.

---

12. *Youngstown Sheet and Tube Co. v. Sawyer,* 343 U.S. 579 (1952).

recorded on a secret system, Nixon was ordered to turn over the tapes to the special prosecutor in charge of the investigation.

Nixon refused to do so, claiming executive privilege. He argued that "no president could function if the private papers of his office, prepared by his personal staff, were open to public scrutiny." In 1974, in one of the Supreme Court's most famous cases, *United States v. Nixon*, the justices unanimously ruled that Nixon had to hand over the tapes.[13] The Court held that executive privilege could not be used to prevent evidence from being heard in criminal proceedings.

Signing Statements

Is the president allowed to refuse to enforce certain parts of legislation if he or she believes that they are unconstitutional? This question came to the forefront in recent years because of President George W. Bush's extensive use of signing statements. A **signing statement** is a written declaration that a president may make when signing a bill into law regarding the law's enforcement.

Presidents have been using such statements for decades, but President Bush used 161 statements to invalidate more than one thousand provisions of federal law. No previous president used signing statements to make such sweeping claims on behalf of presidential power. Earlier presidents often employed statements to serve notice that parts of bills might be unconstitutional, but they were just as likely to issue statements that were purely rhetorical. That is, statements might praise Congress and the measure just passed—or denounce the opposition party. During his first presidential campaign, Barack Obama criticized Bush's use of signing statements. As president, Obama's statements were more in line with tradition.

Abuses of Executive Power and Impeachment

Presidents normally leave office in one of two ways. It may be that their first term has expired and they have not sought (or won) reelection. They may leave because, having served two full terms, they are not allowed to be elected for a third term (owing to the Twenty-second Amendment, passed in 1951). Eight presidents have died in office. But there is still another way for a president to leave office—by **impeachment** and conviction. Articles I and II of the Constitution authorize the House and Senate to remove the president, the vice president, or other civil officers of the United States for committing "Treason, Bribery, or other high Crimes and Misdemeanors." According to the Constitution, the impeachment process begins in the House, which impeaches (accuses) the federal officer involved. If the House votes to impeach the officer, it draws up articles of impeachment and submits them to the Senate, which conducts the actual trial.

Presidents Andrew Johnson and Richard Nixon. In the history of the United States, no president has ever actually been impeached and also convicted—and thus removed from office—by means of this process. President Andrew Johnson (1865–1869), who succeeded to the office after the assassination of Abraham Lincoln, was impeached by the House but acquitted by the Senate. More than a century later, the House Judiciary Committee approved articles of impeachment against President Richard Nixon for his involvement in the cover-up of the Watergate break-in of 1972. Informed by members of his own party that he had no hope of surviving the trial in the Senate, Nixon resigned

Signing Statement
A written declaration that the president may make when signing a bill into law. It may contain instructions to the bureaucracy on how to administer the law or point to sections of the law that the president considers unconstitutional or contrary to national security interests.

Impeachment
An action by the House of Representatives to accuse the president, vice president, or other civil officers of the United States of committing "Treason, Bribery, or other high Crimes and Misdemeanors."

---

13. 318 U.S. 683 (1974).

President Bill Clinton announces the first federal budget surplus in twenty-nine years at the White House in 1998. The economy boomed while Clinton was president. *What effect does the state of the economy have on a president's popularity?*

Richard Ellis / Alemy

on August 9, 1974, before the full House voted on the articles. Nixon is the only president to have resigned from office.

President Bill Clinton. The second president to be impeached by the House but not convicted by the Senate was President Bill Clinton. In 1998, the Republican House approved two charges against Clinton: lying to a grand jury about his affair with White House intern Monica Lewinsky and obstruction of justice. The articles of impeachment were then sent to the Senate, which acquitted Clinton. The attempt to remove Clinton was very unpopular, although the allegations against him did damage his popularity as well. Part of the problem for Clinton's Republican opponents was that the charges against the president essentially boiled down to his lying about sex. As one observer put it, "Everyone lies about sex." Of course, not everyone lies about sex when under oath.

The Executive Organization

>>> **LO4:** Explain the organization of the executive branch and, in particular, the executive office of the president.

Gone are the days when presidents answered their own mail, as George Washington did. It was not until 1857 that Congress authorized a private secretary for the president, to be paid by the federal government. Woodrow Wilson typed most of his correspondence, even though he did have several secretaries. At the beginning of Franklin Roosevelt's long tenure in the White House, the entire staff consisted of thirty-seven employees. With the New Deal and World War II, however, the presidential staff became a sizable organization.

The Cabinet

Although the Constitution does not include the word *cabinet*, it does state that the president "may require the Opinion, in writing, of the principal Officer in each of the executive Departments." Since the time of George Washington, these officers have formed an advisory group, or **cabinet,** to which the president turns for counsel.

Cabinet
An advisory group selected by the president to aid in making decisions. The cabinet includes the heads of fifteen executive departments and others named by the president.

Members of the Cabinet. Originally, the cabinet consisted of only four officials—the secretaries of state, treasury, and war and the attorney general. Today, the cabinet numbers fourteen department secretaries and the attorney general. The cabinet may include others as well. The president at his or her discretion can, for example, ascribe cabinet rank to the vice president, the head of the Office of Management and Budget, the national security adviser, or additional officials. Under President Donald Trump, the additional members of the cabinet are the following:

- The vice president
- The White House chief of staff

- The administrator of the Environmental Protection Agency
- The director of the Office of Management and Budget
- The U.S. trade representative
- The U.S. ambassador to the United Nations
- The chair of the Council of Economic Advisers
- The administrator of the Small Business Administration

Often, a president will use a **kitchen cabinet** to replace the formal cabinet as a major source of advice. The term *kitchen cabinet* originated during the presidency of Andrew Jackson (1829–1837), who relied on the counsel of close friends who allegedly met with him in the kitchen of the White House. A kitchen cabinet is a very informal group of advisers. Usually, they are friends with whom the president worked before being elected.

Presidential Use of Cabinets. Because neither the Constitution nor statutory law requires the president to consult with the cabinet, its use is purely discretionary. Some presidents have relied on the counsel of their cabinets more than others. Dwight Eisenhower was used to the team approach to solving problems from his experience as supreme allied commander during World War II, and therefore he frequently turned to his cabinet for advice on a wide range of issues. More often, presidents have solicited the opinions of their cabinets and then have done what they wanted to do. Lincoln supposedly said—after a cabinet meeting in which a vote was seven nays against his one aye—"Seven nays and one aye; the ayes have it." President Trump's cabinet may present some significant issues. Many of Trump's cabinet selections have voiced opinions that differ substantially from those of the president. It remains to be seen how such differences will be worked out.

It is not surprising that presidents tend to disregard their cabinet members' advice. Often, the departmental heads are more responsive to the wishes of their own staffs or to their own political ambitions than they are to the president. They may be more concerned with obtaining resources for their departments than with achieving the president's goals. So there is often a strong conflict of interest between presidents and their cabinet members. How can the president keep cabinet members and other agency heads from putting the goals of their departments above those of the president? One technique that Trump has used is to appoint leaders who are fundamentally at odds with the goals of their own agencies. For example, Scott Pruitt, Trump's Environmental Protection Agency administrator, has a long history of suing the agency.

The Executive Office of the President

When President Franklin Roosevelt appointed a special committee on administrative management, he knew that the committee would conclude that the president needed help. Indeed, the committee proposed a major reorganization of the executive branch. Congress did not approve the entire reorganization, but it did create the **Executive Office of the President (EOP)** to provide staff assistance for the chief executive and to help coordinate the executive bureaucracy. Since that time, a number of agencies have been

Interact

The president has a website at whitehouse.gov. It is designed both to entertain and to provide information about the president's programs. One of the most entertaining parts of the site is "We the People," accessible from the White House home page. We the People lets you create and sign petitions addressed to the government. At any time, there may be up to one hundred open petitions on topics ranging from student loans to the protection of African elephants. Almost every topic of the day will have an associated petition. Visit We the People and try to locate a petition you can support. You should have no trouble finding one.

Kitchen Cabinet
The informal advisers to the president.

Executive Office of the President (EOP)
An organization established by President Franklin Roosevelt to assist the president in carrying out major duties.

created within the EOP to supply the president with advice and staff help. Presidents reorganize the EOP and the White House Office constantly, and any table of organization is therefore temporary. As of 2017, however, the EOP agencies under Donald Trump were the following:

- Council of Economic Advisers
- Council on Environmental Quality
- Executive Residence
- National Security Council
- Office of Administration
- Office of Management and Budget
- Office of National Drug Control Policy
- Office of Science and Technology Policy
- Office of the United States Trade Representative
- Office of the Vice President
- President's Intelligence Advisory Board
- White House Office

Several of the offices within the EOP are especially important, including the White House Office and the Office of Management and Budget.

The White House Office. The **White House Office** includes most of the key personal and political advisers to the president. Among the jobs held by these aides are those of secretary, press secretary, appointments secretary, and legal counsel to the president. Often, the individuals who hold these positions are recruited from the president's campaign staff. Their duties—mainly protecting the president's political interests—are similar to campaign functions. In 2017, the White House Office was made up of the following units:

- Domestic Policy Council
- National Economic Council
- Office of Cabinet Affairs
- Office of the Chief of Staff
- Office of Communications
- Office of Digital Strategy
- Office of the First Lady
- Office of Information Technology
- Office of Intergovernmental Affairs
- Office of Legislative Affairs
- Office of Management and Administration
- Office of the National Security Adviser
- Office of Political Affairs
- Oval Office Operations
- Office of Presidential Personnel
- Office of Public Liaison
- Office of Scheduling and Advance
- Office of the Staff Secretary
- Office of Trade and Manufacturing Policy
- Office of the White House Counsel
- White House Fellows
- White House Military Office

White House Office
The personal office of the president, which tends to presidential political needs and manages the media.

Chief of Staff
The person who is named to direct the White House Office and advise the president.

Key White House Staff. In all recent administrations, one member of the White House Office has been named **chief of staff.** This person, who is responsible for coordinating the office, is also one of the president's chief advisers. In addition to civilian advisers, the president is supported by a large number of military personnel, who are organized under the White House Military Office. These members of the military provide communications, transportation, medical care, and food services to the president and the White House staff.

White House staff members are closest to the president and may have considerable influence over the administration's decisions. Often, when presidents are under fire for their decisions, the staff is accused of keeping the chief executive too isolated from criticism or help. Presidents insist that they will not allow the staff to become too powerful, but given the difficulty of the office, each president eventually turns to staff members for loyal assistance and protection.

The Office of Management and Budget.   The **Office of Management and Budget (OMB)** was originally the Bureau of the Budget, which was created in 1921 within the Department of the Treasury. Recognizing the importance of this agency, Franklin Roosevelt moved it into the White House Office in 1939. Richard Nixon reorganized the Bureau of the Budget in 1970 and changed its name to reflect its new managerial function. It is headed by a director, who drafts the annual federal budget that the president presents to Congress each January for approval. In principle, the director of the OMB has broad fiscal powers in planning and estimating various parts of the federal budget, because all agencies must submit their proposed budget to the OMB for approval. In reality, it is not so clear that the OMB truly can affect the greater scope of the federal budget. The OMB may be more important as a clearinghouse for legislative proposals initiated in the executive agencies.

Office of Management and Budget (OMB)
A division of the Executive Office of the President. The OMB assists the president in preparing the annual budget, clearing and coordinating departmental agency budgets, and supervising the administration of the federal budget.

Archive Image / Alamy

Members of the national security team receive an update on the mission against Osama bin Laden in the Situation Room of the White House on May 1, 2011. Those present included Vice President Joe Biden (left), President Barack Obama (second left), Secretary of State Hillary Clinton (second right), and Secretary of Defense Robert Gates (right). *What happened to bin Laden?*

The National Security Council. The **National Security Council (NSC)** is a link between the president's key foreign and military advisers and the president. Its members consist of the president, the vice president, and the secretaries of state and defense, plus other informal members. The NSC is managed by the president's assistant for national security affairs, also known as the national security adviser.

The Vice President

>>> **LO5:** Evaluate the role of the vice president, and describe what happens if the presidency becomes vacant.

The Constitution does not give much power to the vice president. The only formal duty is to preside over the Senate—which is rarely necessary. This obligation is fulfilled when the Senate organizes and adopts its rules and also when the vice president is needed to decide a tie vote. In all other cases, the president pro tem manages parliamentary procedures in the Senate. The vice president is expected to participate only informally in senatorial deliberations, if at all.

The Vice President's Job

Vice presidents have traditionally been chosen by presidential nominees to balance the ticket by attracting groups of voters or appeasing party factions. If a presidential nominee is from the North, it is not a bad idea to have a vice-presidential nominee who is from the South. If the presidential nominee is from a rural state, perhaps someone with an urban background would be most suitable as a running mate. Presidential nominees who are strongly conservative or strongly liberal would do well to have vice-presidential nominees whose views lie more in the middle of the political road.

In recent presidential elections, however, vice-presidential candidates have often been selected for other reasons. Barack Obama picked Joe Biden to be his running mate in 2008 to add gravitas (seriousness) and foreign policy experience to the ticket. In 2012, Republican presidential candidate Mitt Romney chose Representative Paul Ryan of Wisconsin as his running mate. Ryan, the author of conservative House budget proposals, was greeted with enthusiasm by Republicans who were skeptical of Romney's conservative credentials.

In 2016, Republican candidate Donald Trump picked Indiana governor Mike Pence to be his running mate. Pence was a fairly conventional conservative Republican. By choosing him, Trump sought to rally Republicans who were uncomfortable with Trump's insurgent politics. For her part, Democrat Hillary Clinton selected Virginia senator Tim Kaine, a moderate from a vital swing state. Kaine was also fluent in Spanish. The apparent plan was that Kaine could help with independent voters.

Traditionally, the job of the vice president has not been very demanding. In recent years, however, presidents have granted their running mates increased responsibilities and power. President Jimmy Carter was the first modern president to rely on his vice president—Walter Mondale—as a major adviser. Under President George W. Bush, Dick Cheney became the most powerful vice president in history. Cheney was able to place his supporters throughout the bureaucracy and exert influence on a wide range of issues. He could exercise this degree of power, however, only because he had the support of the president. In contrast, Vice President Biden's relationship to President Obama was more conventional. For his part, Vice President Pence may prove to be a vital link between President Trump and the Republicans in Congress.

National Security Council (NSC)
An agency in the Executive Office of the President that advises the president on national security.

Presidential Succession

Eight vice presidents have become president because of the death of the president. John Tyler, the first to do so, took over William Henry Harrison's position in 1841 after Harrison had served for only one month. No one knew whether Tyler should simply be a caretaker until a new president could be elected three and a half years later or whether he actually should be president. Tyler assumed that he was supposed to be the chief executive, and he acted as such—although his political opponents referred to him as "His Accidency." Since then, vice presidents taking over the position of the presidency because of the incumbent's death have assumed the presidential powers.

But what should a vice president do if a president becomes incapable of carrying out necessary duties while in office? This question was not addressed in the original Constitution. Article II, Section 1, says only that "[i]n Case of the Removal of the President from Office, or of his Death, Resignation, or Inability to discharge the Powers and Duties of the said Office, the same shall devolve on [the same powers shall be exercised by] the Vice President." In October 1919, President Woodrow Wilson was incapacitated by a stroke. He had seventeen months left in his term of office. No one was willing to take responsibility for certifying that Wilson was unable "to discharge the powers and duties" of the presidency. In fact, most of his duties were assumed by cabinet members and even by the First Lady.

When Dwight Eisenhower became ill for a second time in 1958, he entered into a pact with Richard Nixon specifying that the vice president could determine whether the president was incapable of carrying out his duties if the president could not communicate. John F. Kennedy and Lyndon Johnson entered into similar agreements with their vice presidents.

Vice President Mike Pence was formerly the governor of Indiana. Here, he speaks at a rally in Missouri during his election campaign. *What is the vice president's main job?*

Gino Santa Maria/Shutterstock.com

Finally, in 1967, the **Twenty-fifth Amendment** was passed, establishing procedures in the event of presidential incapacity, death, or resignation.

When the President Becomes Incapacitated. According to the Twenty-fifth Amendment, when a president believes that he or she is incapable of performing the duties of office, the president must inform Congress in writing. Then the vice president serves as acting president until the president can resume normal duties. When the president is unable to communicate, a majority of the cabinet, including the vice president, can declare that fact to Congress. Then the vice president serves as acting president until the president resumes normal duties. If a dispute arises over the return of the president's ability, a two-thirds vote of both chambers of Congress is required to allow the vice president to remain acting president. Otherwise, the president resumes normal duties.

When the Vice Presidency Becomes Vacant. The Twenty-fifth Amendment also addresses the issue of how the president should fill a vacant vice presidency. Section 2 of the amendment states, "Whenever there is a vacancy in the office of the Vice President, the President shall nominate a Vice President who shall take office upon confirmation by a majority vote of both Houses of Congress."

Twenty-fifth Amendment
A 1967 amendment to the Constitution that establishes procedures for filling presidential and vice-presidential vacancies and makes provisions for presidential incapacity.

The question of who shall be president if both the president and the vice president die is answered by the Presidential Succession Act of 1947. If the president and vice president die, resign, or are disabled, the Speaker of the House will become president, after resigning from Congress. Next in line is the president pro tem of the Senate, followed by the cabinet officers in the order of the initial creation of their departments (see Table 10–1).

TABLE 10–1   **Line of Succession to the Presidency of the United States**

How might the public react if the Speaker of the House became president—and was of a different political party than the deceased president?

1. Vice president
2. Speaker of the House of Representatives
3. Senate president pro tempore
4. Secretary of State
5. Secretary of the Treasury
6. Secretary of Defense
7. Attorney general (head of the Justice Department)
8. Secretary of Interior
9. Secretary of Agriculture
10. Secretary of Commerce
11. Secretary of Labor
12. Secretary of Health and Human Services
13. Secretary of Housing and Urban Development
14. Secretary of Transportation
15. Secretary of Energy
16. Secretary of Education
17. Secretary of Veterans Affairs
18. Secretary of Homeland Security

Communicating with the White House

When it comes to caring about the presidency, most people do not need much encouragement. Many people, however, believe the president is such a remote figure that nothing they can do will affect what he or she does. That is not always true. On many issues, your voice—combined, of course, with the voices of many others—can have an impact. Writing to the president is a traditional way for citizens to express their opinions.

Why Should You Care? The president makes many decisions that directly influence your life. For example, in recent years many voices began to raise the question of changing the nation's immigration policies. If changes to immigration policies succeed, they will need strong support from the president. Immigration might be a subject on which you have firm opinions.

What Can You Do? The most traditional way to communicate with the White House is by letter. Letters to the president should be addressed to:

The President of the United States
The White House
1600 Pennsylvania Avenue NW
Washington, DC 20500

Will you get an answer? Almost certainly. The White House mail room is staffed by volunteers and paid employees who sort the mail for the president and tally the public's concerns. You may receive a standard response to your comments or a more personal, detailed response.

You can also send your comments and ideas to the White House using e-mail: comments@whitehouse.gov. According to the Obama administration, e-mail is the fastest way to communicate with the president, and that should remain true under Trump. Despite Trump's extensive use of Twitter, that platform is not an effective way of sending messages to the president.

The White House has an active Web presence. Here, you see its home page. You can find information on just about all aspects of the federal government through this particular portal. Additionally, you can go to the "contact" section to e-mail your comments to the president and to the vice president. *Even though both of those top officials are unlikely to personally read your e-mails, why is it important to communicate with them?*

Key Terms

advice and consent 231
appointment power 229
cabinet 240
chief diplomat 232
chief executive 229
chief legislator 233
chief of staff 242
civil service 229
commander in
   chief 230
constitutional
   power 236

diplomatic
   recognition 232
emergency power 237
executive agreement 233
Executive Office of the
   President (EOP) 241
executive order 238
executive privilege 238
expressed power 237
Federal Register 238
head of state 227
impeachment 239

inherent power 237
kitchen cabinet 241
National Security
   Council (NSC) 244
Office of Management
   and Budget (OMB)
   243
pardon 229
patronage 235
pocket veto 234
reprieve 229
signing statement 239

State of the Union
   message 233
statutory power 237
Twelfth Amendment 227
Twenty-fifth
   Amendment 246
veto message 234
War Powers
   Resolution 231
White House Office 242

Chapter Summary

≫ LO1 The office of the president of the United States, combining as it does the functions of chief of state and chief executive, was unique at the time of its creation. The framers of the Constitution were divided over whether the president should be a weak or a strong executive. The requirements for the office of the presidency are outlined in Article II, Section 1, of the Constitution.

≫ LO2 The president's roles include both formal and informal duties. These roles include head of state, chief executive, commander in chief, chief diplomat, chief legislator, party chief, and politician.

As head of state, the president is ceremonial leader of the government. As chief executive, the president is bound to enforce the acts of Congress, the judgments of the federal courts, and treaties. The chief executive has the power of appointment and the power to grant reprieves and pardons.

As commander in chief, the president is the ultimate decision maker in military matters. As chief diplomat, the president recognizes foreign governments, negotiates treaties, signs agreements, and nominates and receives ambassadors.

The role of chief legislator includes recommending legislation to Congress, lobbying for the legislation, approving laws, and exercising the veto power. Presidents are also politicians and

leaders of their political parties. Presidents rely on their personal popularity to help them fulfill these functions.

≫ LO3 In addition to constitutional and inherent powers, the president has statutory powers written into law by Congress. Presidents also have a variety of special powers not available to other branches of the government. These include emergency powers and the power to issue executive orders, to invoke executive privilege, and to issue signing statements.

Abuses of executive power are dealt with by Articles I and II of the Constitution, which authorize the House and Senate to impeach and remove the president, vice president, or other officers of the federal government for committing "Treason, Bribery, or other high Crimes and Misdemeanors."

≫ LO4 The president receives assistance from the cabinet and from the Executive Office of the President (including the White House Office).

≫ LO5 The vice president is the constitutional officer assigned to preside over the Senate and to assume the presidency in case of the death, resignation, removal, or disability of the president. The Twenty-fifth Amendment, passed in 1967, established procedures to be followed in case of presidential incapacity, death, or resignation, and when filling a vacant vice presidency.

Test Yourself

1. **Anyone can become president of the United States, as long as she or he:**
   a. is at least 35 years old.
   b. is at least 35 years old and a natural born citizen.
   c. is at least 40 years old and a natural born citizen.

2. **To date, only one president has been a Roman Catholic, and that person was:**
   a. George W. Bush.
   b. Ronald Reagan.
   c. John F. Kennedy.

3. **If no presidential candidate has a majority in the electoral college, the question of who should become president is decided by the:**
   a. U .S. House.
   b. U .S. Senate.
   c. United States Supreme Court.

4. **Our president is both head of state and chief executive, which means that the president:**
   a. engages in ceremonial activities both at home and abroad, and faithfully ensures that the acts of Congress are enforced.
   b. designates the vice president to represent the United States in public ceremonies abroad.
   c. makes sure that treaties are upheld but delegates other actions to the cabinet.

5. **The president may grant reprieves and pardons:**
   a. with the advice and consent of the Senate.
   b. with the approval of the attorney general.
   c. without modification or regulation by Congress.

6. **When the president issues an executive order, such action represents the president's:**
   a. constitutional powers.
   b. legislative powers.
   c. emergency powers.

7. **A president who disagrees with a part of legislation that he or she has signed into law can make a written declaration regarding the law's enforcement. This declaration is called:**
   a. a signing statement.
   b. a veto message.
   c. executive privilege.

8. **Upon impeachment by the House of Representatives, the president:**
   a. must leave office immediately.
   b. cannot run for reelection.
   c. is tried by the Senate.

9. **The White House chief of staff, the ambassador to the United Nations, and the head of the Environmental Protection Agency:**
   a. have at different times been named members of the president's cabinet.
   b. are all part of the Executive Office of the President (EOP).
   c. are not subject to presidential appointment.

10. **The only formal duty imposed on the vice president by the Constitution is to preside over the:**
    a. U.S. House.
    b. U.S. Senate.
    c. cabinet.

Essay Questions

1. What characteristics do you think voters look for when choosing a president? Might these characteristics change as a result of changes in the political environment and the specific problems facing the nation? If you believe voters almost always look for the same characteristics, why do they do so? If voters seek somewhat different people as president, which circumstances favor which kinds of leaders?

2. Many presidents have been lawyers, though George W. Bush was a businessman, Ronald Reagan was an actor, and Jimmy Carter was a naval officer and owned a peanut warehouse. What advantages might these three presidents have gained from their career backgrounds? In particular, what benefits might Ronald Reagan have derived from his experience as an actor?

Answers to multiple-choice questions: 1. b, 2. c, 3. a, 4. a, 5. c, 6. b, 7. a, 8. c, 9. a, 10. b.

11 | The Executive Branch

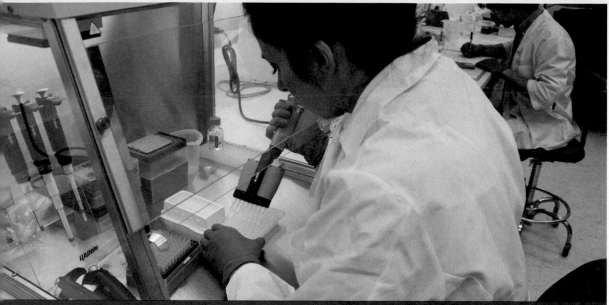

A scientist with the federal Food and Drug Administration studies stem cells at the campus of the National Institutes of Health in Maryland. *Could basic research be funded adequately by the private sector? Why or why not?*

US Food and Drug Administration

The five **Learning Outcomes (LOs)** below are designed to help improve your understanding of this chapter. After reading this chapter, you should be able to:

>>>**LO1** Discuss the nature of the federal bureaucracy, and identify the largest federal spending programs.

>>>**LO2** Describe the various types of agencies and organizations that make up the federal executive branch.

>>>**LO3** Explain how government employees are hired and how the civil service is administered.

>>>**LO4** Evaluate different methods that have been put into place to reform bureaucracies and make them more efficient.

>>>**LO5** Discuss how federal agencies make rules and what the role of Congress is in this process.

Check your understanding of the material with the Test Yourself section at the end of the chapter.

aceless bureaucrats—this is how many Americans visualize the civil servants and political appointees who make up the executive branch of the federal government. Polls consistently report that the majority of Americans support "less government." The same polls, however, report that the majority of Americans support almost every specific program that the government undertakes. The conflict between the desire for small government and the desire for the benefits that only a large government can provide has been a constant feature of American politics. For example, the goal of preserving endangered species has widespread support. At the same time, many people believe that restrictions imposed under the Endangered Species Act violate the rights of landowners. Helping the elderly pay their medical bills is a popular objective, but hardly anyone enjoys paying the Medicare tax that supports this effort.

In this chapter, we describe the size, organization, and staffing of the federal executive branch. We review modern attempts at bureaucratic reform and the process by which Congress exerts ultimate control over the bureaucracy. We also discuss the bureaucracy's role in making rules and setting policy.

The Nature and Scope of the Federal Bureaucracy

>>> **LO1:** Discuss the nature of the federal bureaucracy, and identify the largest federal spending programs.

Bureaucracy is the name given to an organization that is structured hierarchically to carry out specific functions. Generally, bureaucracies are characterized by an organization chart. The units of the organization are divided according to the specialization and expertise of the employees.

Public and Private Bureaucracies

We should not think of bureaucracy as unique to government. Any large corporation or university can be considered a bureaucratic organization, even though the term bureaucracy is most often applied to government agencies. The fact is that the handling of complex problems requires a division of labor. Individuals must concentrate their skills on specific, well-defined aspects of a problem and depend on others to solve the rest of it.

Public or government bureaucracies differ from private organizations in some important ways, however. A private corporation has a single leader—its chief executive officer (CEO). Public bureaucracies do not have a single leader. Although the president is the chief administrator of the federal system, all agencies are subject to the dictates of Congress for their funding, staffing, and, indeed, their continued existence. Public bureaucracies supposedly serve all citizens, while private ones serve private interests.

One other important difference between private corporations and government bureaucracies is that government bureaucracies are not organized to make a profit. Rather, they are supposed to perform their functions as efficiently as possible to conserve taxpayers' dollars.

The Size of the Bureaucracy

In 1789, the new government's executive branch was tiny. There were three departments—State (with nine employees), War (with two employees), and Treasury (with thirty-nine employees)—and the Office of the Attorney General (which later became the Department of Justice). The bureaucracy was still small in 1798. At that time, the secretary of state had seven clerks and spent a total of $500 (about $10,500 in 2018 dollars) on stationery and printing. In that same year, an appropriations act allocated $1.4 million, or $29.4 million in 2018 dollars, to the War Department.

Government Employment Today. Times have changed. Excluding 1.3 million military service members, but including employees of Congress, the courts, and the U.S. Postal Service, the federal bureaucracy includes approximately 2.8 million employees. That number has remained relatively stable for the past several decades. It is somewhat deceiving, however, because many other individuals work directly or indirectly for the federal government as subcontractors or consultants and in other capacities.

Figure 11–1 shows the combined growth in government employment at the federal, state, and local levels. Since 1960, this growth has been mainly at the state and local levels.

Bureaucracy
A large organization that is structured hierarchically to carry out specific functions.

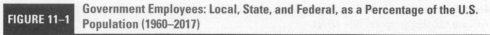

FIGURE 11–1   Government Employees: Local, State, and Federal, as a Percentage of the U.S. Population (1960–2017)

Why might a majority of government workers be employed by local government?

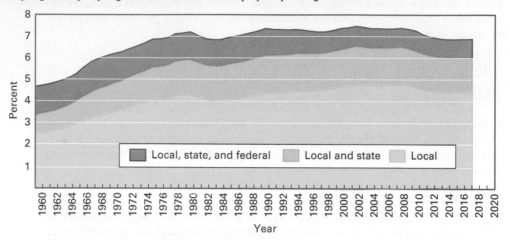

Source: The Federal Reserve Economic Data (FRED) service of the St. Louis Federal Reserve.

If all government employees are included, more than 15 percent of civilian employment is accounted for by government.

The Impact of Ronald Reagan. Notice in Figure 11–1 that government employment as a share of the total U.S. population grew rapidly until 1980. In that year, Republican Ronald Reagan was elected president. Under Reagan, government employment actually fell, in large part because of the elimination of revenue sharing, a program through which the federal government transferred large sums to state and local governments. While government employment picked up later in Reagan's administration, it never resumed the constant upward course characteristic of the 1960s and 1970s. In short, Reagan's "conservative revolution" had a genuine impact on the trajectory of government.

The Federal Budget

In 1929, spending by all levels of government was equivalent to only about 11 percent of the nation's gross domestic product (GDP). For fiscal year 2017, it was about 36.5 percent. One factor that drove the rate of government spending recently was the Great Recession that began in December 2007. Increased spending enacted in an attempt to combat the recession—plus a fall in federal revenues—dramatically increased the size of the federal budget deficit. In 2009, the deficit peaked at $1,400 billion, or almost 10 percent of GDP. The deficit then fell as the nation slowly recovered. By fiscal year 2017, it was $325 billion, or about 2.6 percent of GDP.

Social Spending. Studies repeatedly show that most Americans have a very inaccurate idea of how the federal budget is spent. The first pie chart in Appendix D of this book can help. This pie chart demonstrates that almost 40 percent of all federal spending goes to two programs that benefit older Americans—Social Security and Medicare. Additional social programs, many aimed at low-income individuals and families, push the total amount of social spending to the 60 percent mark. Because of these additional social programs, the federal government spends much more on the poor than many people realize. Medicaid, a joint federal-state program that provides health-care services, is the largest of these programs. These programs also include the Children's Health Insurance Program (CHIP) and the Supplementary Nutrition Assistance Program (SNAP), previously known as food stamps. In contrast, traditional cash welfare—Temporary Assistance for Needy Families (TANF)—accounts for only 0.4 percent of the budget ($17 billion) and is buried in the "Miscellaneous low-income support" slice.

Defense and All the Rest. Military defense and veterans' benefits are almost 20 percent of the whole. Interest payments on the national debt are above 7 percent. All other functions amount to only about 13 percent of the budget. Foreign aid, which is included in the "Everything else" slice, is 1.4 percent, or $59 billion. This is a substantial sum, but it is much smaller than many people imagine.

Revenue Sources. Where does the federal government get the funds that support its spending? The second pie chart in Appendix D of this book can help answer this question. As you might expect, the personal income tax provides the largest share of federal revenues, about 43 percent. Revenue from the Social Security trust funds is about 20 percent. About 12 percent is borrowed externally—this pie slice represents the sale of new U.S. debt obligations, such as bonds. Many people believe the tax system is too complicated and should be simplified. We look at that issue in this chapter's *At Issue* feature.

The Organization of the Executive Branch

>>> **LO2:** Describe the various types of agencies and organizations that make up the federal executive branch.

Within the federal bureaucracy are a number of different types of government agencies and organizations. Figure 11–2 outlines the several bodies within the executive branch, as well as the separate organizations that provide services to Congress, to the courts, and directly to the president. The executive branch, which employs most of the government's staff, has four major types of structures. They are (1) cabinet departments, (2) independent executive agencies, (3) independent regulatory agencies, and (4) government corporations. Each has a distinctive relationship to the president, and some have unusual internal structures, overall goals, and grants of power.

Cabinet Departments

The fifteen **cabinet departments** are the major service organizations of the federal government. They can also be described in management terms as **line organizations.** This means that they are directly accountable to the president and are responsible for performing government functions, such as printing money and training troops. These cabinet departments were created by Congress when the need for each department arose. The first department to be created was State, and the most recent one was Homeland Security, established in 2003. A president might ask that a new department be created or an old one abolished, but the president has no power to do so without legislative approval from Congress.

Each department is headed by a secretary (except for the Justice Department, which is headed by the attorney general). Each department also has several levels of undersecretaries, assistant secretaries, and other personnel.

Presidents theoretically have considerable control over the cabinet departments, because presidents are able to appoint or fire all of the top officials. Even cabinet departments do not

Cabinet Department
One of the fifteen major departments of the executive branch.

Line Organization
In the federal government, an administrative unit that is directly accountable to the president.

AT ISSUE

Should We Simplify the Income Tax System?

In 1913, the Sixteenth Amendment to the Constitution let Congress levy an income tax. In that year, not even 1 percent of Americans paid this tax, and rates were low. Today, the top rate is 39.6 percent. Filing consumes huge amounts of time and money. As a result, every few years someone proposes simplifying our tax system.

Different income tax rates are not really what make the system complicated. After all, a table that fully defines the various personal income tax brackets can easily fit on a postcard. A major source of complication is the vast collection of rules on what "income" even means. Such rules rarely trouble people whose income consists of wages or salaries—they are an issue, rather, for investors and businesspeople. For the middle class, complications are typically due to the huge number of possible tax deductions and credits. The deductions and credits available to businesses are even more numerous.

The IRS itself has estimated that individuals and businesses spend more than 6 billion hours each year to prepare their taxes. So, should Congress try to simplify this system?

The Country Would Benefit from a Simpler Tax Code

Those who favor a simpler tax system gain support from economists who argue that special tax breaks distort the economy. If economic efficiency is the measure, we spend too much on goods and services that receive tax breaks—and too little on items that receive no such breaks. The best tax code is one in which there are few or no exemptions. The government can then raise the same amount of revenue by charging lower tax rates. Lower rates are a second reason that a simpler code is more efficient: high rates themselves tend to distort the economy. A deduction from income such as the one for interest on home mortgages means that we will invest too much in houses and

not enough in other goods and services. And of course it doesn't hurt at all if citizens and businesses do not have to spend so much time and money in filling out their forms. Back in 1986, Congress was able to greatly simplify our taxes and lower rates. Since then, year by year the tax code has become more complicated. It's time for another simplification effort.

Messing with the Tax Code Is Dangerous—and a Waste of Time

Democrats in Congress currently oppose changes to the tax system—and with good reason. With both chambers of Congress and the presidency in Republican hands, any "reform" passed now would surely help Republican interests at the expense of Democratic ones. In 1986, the reform effort was bipartisan and still required a tremendous effort to succeed. Those who benefit from any specific tax break will fight like tigers to protect it, and today's Congress is in no position to respond. Under current circumstances, tax reform is a waste of time.

Reform can also be dangerous. Major changes to the system would be disruptive. Consider that mortgage interest deduction. For most people, a house is the largest investment they will ever have an opportunity to make. Taxing interest payments will not only reduce these people's income—it will reduce house values and cut into their wealth. If we plan on a major economic disruption, the benefits must be great, and provisions must be made for those who lose out. None of the tax reform plans recently discussed meet those tests.

FOR CRITICAL ANALYSIS
What would happen if middle- and upper-income people could no longer deduct charitable contributions from their taxable income?

always respond to the president's wishes, though. One reason why presidents are frequently unhappy with their departments is that the entire bureaucratic structure below the top political levels is staffed by permanent employees. Many of these employees are committed to established programs or procedures and resist change. Table 11–1 shows each cabinet department. The table also describes some of the functions of each of the departments.

Independent Executive Agency
A federal agency that is not part of a cabinet department but reports directly to the president.

Independent Executive Agencies

Independent executive agencies are bureaucratic organizations that are not located within a department but report directly to the president, who appoints their chief officials. When a new federal agency is created—the Environmental Protection Agency, for example—Congress

FIGURE 11–2   **Organization Chart of the Federal Government, 2018**

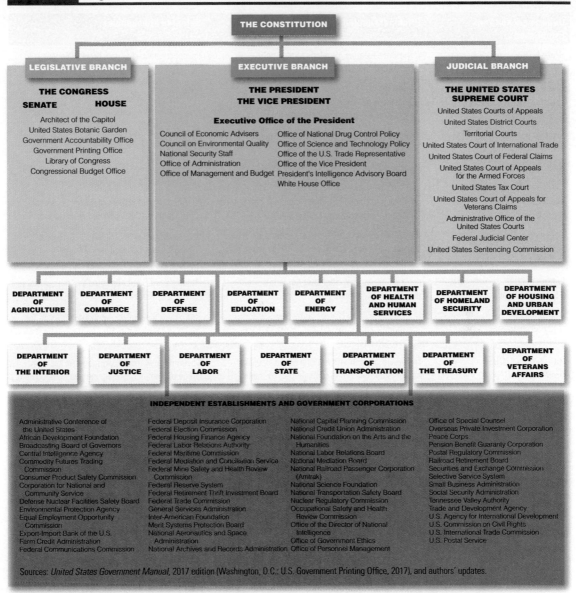

THE CONSTITUTION

LEGISLATIVE BRANCH

THE CONGRESS

SENATE   HOUSE

Architect of the Capitol
United States Botanic Garden
Government Accountability Office
Government Printing Office
Library of Congress
Congressional Budget Office

EXECUTIVE BRANCH

**THE PRESIDENT
THE VICE PRESIDENT**

Executive Office of the President

Council of Economic Advisers   Office of National Drug Control Policy
Council on Environmental Quality   Office of Science and Technology Policy
National Security Staff   Office of the U.S. Trade Representative
Office of Administration   Office of the Vice President
Office of Management and Budget   President's Intelligence Advisory Board
                                       White House Office

JUDICIAL BRANCH

**THE UNITED STATES
SUPREME COURT**

United States Courts of Appeals
United States District Courts
Territorial Courts
United States Court of International Trade
United States Court of Federal Claims
United States Court of Appeals
for the Armed Forces
United States Tax Court
United States Court of Appeals for
Veterans Claims
Administrative Office of the
United States Courts
Federal Judicial Center
United States Sentencing Commission

DEPARTMENT OF AGRICULTURE | **DEPARTMENT OF COMMERCE** | **DEPARTMENT OF DEFENSE** | **DEPARTMENT OF EDUCATION** | **DEPARTMENT OF ENERGY** | **DEPARTMENT OF HEALTH AND HUMAN SERVICES** | **DEPARTMENT OF HOMELAND SECURITY** | **DEPARTMENT OF HOUSING AND URBAN DEVELOPMENT**

DEPARTMENT OF THE INTERIOR | **DEPARTMENT OF JUSTICE** | **DEPARTMENT OF LABOR** | **DEPARTMENT OF STATE** | **DEPARTMENT OF TRANSPORTATION** | **DEPARTMENT OF THE TREASURY** | **DEPARTMENT OF VETERANS AFFAIRS**

INDEPENDENT ESTABLISHMENTS AND GOVERNMENT CORPORATIONS

Administrative Conference of
the United States
African Development Foundation
Broadcasting Board of Governors
Central Intelligence Agency
Commodity Futures Trading
Commission
Consumer Product Safety Commission
Corporation for National and
Community Service
Defense Nuclear Facilities Safety Board
Environmental Protection Agency
Equal Employment Opportunity
Commission
Export-Import Bank of the U.S.
Farm Credit Administration
Federal Communications Commission

Federal Deposit Insurance Corporation
Federal Election Commission
Federal Housing Finance Agency
Federal Labor Relations Authority
Federal Maritime Commission
Federal Mediation and Conciliation Service
Federal Mine Safety and Health Review
Commission
Federal Reserve System
Federal Retirement Thrift Investment Board
Federal Trade Commission
General Services Administration
Inter-American Foundation
Merit Systems Protection Board
National Aeronautics and Space
Administration
National Archives and Records Administration

National Capital Planning Commission
National Credit Union Administration
National Foundation on the Arts and the
Humanities
National Labor Relations Board
National Mediation Board
National Railroad Passenger Corporation
(Amtrak)
National Science Foundation
National Transportation Safety Board
Nuclear Regulatory Commission
Occupational Safety and Health
Review Commission
Office of the Director of National
Intelligence
Office of Government Ethics
Office of Personnel Management

Office of Special Counsel
Overseas Private Investment Corporation
Peace Corps
Pension Benefit Guaranty Corporation
Postal Regulatory Commission
Railroad Retirement Board
Securities and Exchange Commission
Selective Service System
Small Business Administration
Social Security Administration
Tennessee Valley Authority
Trade and Development Agency
U.S. Agency for International Development
U.S. Commission on Civil Rights
U.S. International Trade Commission
U.S. Postal Service

Sources: *United States Government Manual*, 2017 edition (Washington, D.C.: U.S. Government Printing Office, 2017), and authors' updates.

decides where it will be located in the bureaucracy. In recent decades, presidents often have asked that a new organization be kept separate or independent rather than added to an existing department, particularly if a department may be hostile to the agency's creation.

Independent Regulatory Agencies

Typically, an **independent regulatory agency** is responsible for a specific type of public policy. Its function is to make and implement rules and regulations in a particular sphere of action to protect the public interest. The earliest such agency was the Interstate Commerce

**Independent
Regulatory Agency**
An agency outside
the major executive
departments charged with
making and implementing
rules and regulations
within a specific area.

TABLE 11-1 Cabinet Departments

Department and Year Established	Principal Functions	Selected Subagencies
State (1789) (13,138 employees)	Negotiates treaties, develops foreign policy, protects citizens abroad.	Passport Services Office, Foreign Service.
Treasury (1789) (94,459 employees)	Pays all federal bills, borrows money, collects federal taxes, mints coins and prints paper currency, supervises national banks.	Internal Revenue Service, U.S. Mint.
Interior (1849) (64,054 employees)	Supervises federally owned lands and parks, supervises Native American affairs.	National Park Service, Bureau of Indian Affairs.
Justice (1870)[a] (116,530 employees)	Furnishes legal advice to the president, enforces federal criminal laws, supervises federal prisons.	Federal Bureau of Investigation, Drug Enforcement Administration, Bureau of Prisons.
Agriculture (1889) (87,460 employees)	Provides assistance to farmers and ranchers, conducts agricultural research, works to protect forests.	Food Safety and Inspection Service, Federal Crop Insurance Corporation, Forest Service.
Commerce (1913)[b] (46,012 employees)	Grants patents and trademarks, conducts a national census, monitors the weather, protects the interests of businesses.	Bureau of the Census, Patent and Trademark Office, National Oceanic and Atmospheric Administration.
Labor (1913)[b] (15,749 employees	Administers federal labor laws, promotes the interests of workers.	Occupational Safety and Health Administration, Bureau of Labor Statistics.
Defense (1947)[c] (740,633 employees)	Manages the armed forces (army, navy, air force, and marines), operates military bases, is responsible for civil defense.	National Security Agency; Departments of the Air Force, Navy, Army.
Housing and Urban Development (1965) (8,000 employees)	Deals with the nation's housing needs, develops and rehabilitates urban communities, oversees resale of mortgages.	Government National Mortgage Association, Office of Community Planning and Development.
Transportation (1967) (55,508 employees)	Finances improvements in mass transit; develops and administers programs for highways, railroads, and aviation.	Federal Aviation Administration, National Highway Traffic Safety Administration.
Energy (1977) (15,217 employees)	Promotes the conservation of energy and resources, analyzes energy data, conducts research and development.	Federal Energy Regulatory Commission, National Nuclear Security Administration.
Health and Human Services (1979)[d] (87,020 employees)	Promotes public health, enforces pure food and drug laws, conducts and sponsors health-related research.	Food and Drug Administration, Centers for Disease Control and Prevention, Centers for Medicare and Medicaid Services.
Education (1979)[d] (4,411 employees)	Coordinates federal programs and policies for education, administers aid to education, promotes educational research.	Office of Elementary and Secondary Education, Office of Federal Student Aid.
Veterans Affairs (1988) (376,100 employees)	Promotes the welfare of veterans of the U.S. armed forces.	Veterans Health Administration, Veterans Benefits Administration.
Homeland Security (2003) (194,802 employees)	Attempts to prevent terrorist attacks within the United States, control America's borders, and minimize the damage from natural disasters.	U.S. Coast Guard, Secret Service, Federal Emergency Management Agency, U.S. Immigration and Customs Enforcement.

[a]Formed from the Office of the Attorney General (created in 1789).

[b]Formed from the Department of Commerce and Labor (created in 1903).

[c]Formed from the Department of War (created in 1789) and the Department of the Navy (created in 1798).

[d]Formed from the Department of Health, Education, and Welfare (created in 1953).

Commission (ICC), which was established in 1887 when Americans began to seek some form of government control over the rapidly growing business and industrial sector. This new form of organization, the independent regulatory agency, was supposed to make technical, nonpolitical decisions about rates, profits, and rules that would be for the benefit of all and that did not require congressional legislation. In the years that followed the creation of the ICC, other agencies were formed to regulate communication (the Federal Communications Commission) and nuclear power (the Nuclear Regulatory Commission). (The ICC was abolished in 1995.)

The Purpose and Nature of Regulatory Agencies. In practice, regulatory agencies are administered independently of all three branches of government. They were set up because Congress felt it was unable to handle the complexities and technicalities required to carry out specific laws. Regulatory agencies and commissions combine some functions of all three branches of government—legislative, executive, and judicial. They are legislative in that they make rules that have the force of law. They are executive in that they provide for the enforcement of those rules. They are judicial in that they decide disputes involving the rules they have made.

David R. Frazier Photolibrary, Inc. / Alamy

Even at $0.49 for the one-ounce first-class rate, postage in the United States is a bargain by international standards. First-class rates are $0.74 in Japan, $0.78 in France, and $0.84 in Britain. *Why has the U.S. Postal Service experienced financial difficulties?*

Heads of regulatory agencies and members of agency boards or commissions are appointed by the president with the consent of the Senate, although they do not report to the president. When an agency is headed by a board rather than an individual, the members of the board cannot, by law, all be from the same political party. Presidents can influence regulatory agency behavior by appointing people of their own parties or individuals who share their political views when vacancies occur, in particular when the chair is vacant. Members may be removed by the president only for causes specified in the law creating the agency.

Agency Capture. Over the last several decades, some observers have concluded that regulatory agencies, although nominally independent, may in fact not always be so. They contend that many agencies have been captured by the very industries and firms that they were supposed to regulate and therefore make decisions based on the interests of the industry, not the general public. The results of **agency capture** have been less competition rather than more competition, higher prices rather than lower prices, and fewer choices rather than more choices for consumers.

Deregulation and Reregulation. During the presidency of Jimmy Carter (1977–1981), significant deregulation (the removal of regulatory restraints—the opposite of regulation) was initiated. For example, Carter appointed a chairperson of the Civil Aeronautics Board (CAB) who gradually eliminated regulation of airline fares and routes. Deregulation continued under President Ronald Reagan (1981–1989). During the administration of George H. W. Bush (1989–1993), however, calls for reregulation of many businesses increased, and several new regulatory acts were passed.

Agency Capture
The act by which an industry being regulated by a government agency gains direct or indirect control over agency personnel and decision makers.

Interact

In this modern age, many government agencies have developed attractive and entertaining websites. The NASA site is enormously popular, especially for its striking photos of celestial objects. The page you can find by searching on "nasa benefits to you" shows the practical benefits of space exploration. An all-time favorite, however, has to be the zombie apocalypse comic written by the Centers for Disease Control (CDC). When you've finished reading it, consider whether it does a good job of providing useful information on disaster preparedness. You can find it by searching for "cdc zombie comic."

Under President Bill Clinton (1993–2001), the Interstate Commerce Commission was eliminated, and the banking and telecommunications industries, along with many other sectors of the economy, were deregulated. At the same time, there was extensive regulation to protect the environment, a trend somewhat attenuated by the George W. Bush administration.

Regulation Today. After the financial crisis of September 2008, many people saw inadequate regulation of the financial industry as a major cause of the nation's economic difficulties. During President Barack Obama's administration, therefore, reregulation of that industry became a major objective. After intense debate, Congress passed a comprehensive financial industry regulation plan in 2010.

Americans have had conflicting views about the amount of regulation that is appropriate for various industries ever since the government began to undertake serious regulatory activities. Many people find regulation to be contrary to the spirit of free enterprise and the American tradition of individualism. Yet in cases such as BP's Deepwater Horizon oil spill disaster in the Gulf of Mexico in April 2010, citizens of all political stripes were outraged to learn that the relevant regulatory agency at the time, the Minerals Management Service, had failed to do its job.

Government and Government-Controlled Corporations

Another form of bureaucratic organization in the United States is the **government corporation**. Although the concept is borrowed from the world of business, there are important differences between public and private corporations.

A private corporation has shareholders (stockholders) who in principle elect a board of directors, who in turn choose the corporate officers, such as the chief executive officer (CEO). When a private corporation makes a profit, it must pay taxes (unless it avoids them through various legal loopholes). It distributes the after-tax profits to shareholders as dividends or plows the profits back into the corporation to make new investments, or both.

A government corporation has a board of directors and managers, but it does not usually have any stockholders. The public cannot buy shares of stock in a typical government corporation, and if the entity makes a profit, it does not distribute the profit as dividends. Nor does it have to pay taxes on profits—the profits remain in the corporation. The largest and most famous government corporation is the U.S. Postal Service, with 509,000 employees. Another well-known example is Amtrak, the passenger railway service, with a staff of more than 20,000.

Government Corporation
An agency of government that administers a quasi-business enterprise. These corporations are used when government activities are primarily commercial.

Bankruptcy. The federal government can also take effective control of a private corporation in a number of different circumstances. One is bankruptcy. When a company files for bankruptcy, it asks a federal judge for relief from its creditors. The judge, operating under bankruptcy laws established by Congress (as specified in the Constitution), is ultimately responsible for the fate of the enterprise. When a bank fails, the government has a special interest in protecting customers who have deposited funds with the bank. For that reason, the failing institution is taken over by the Federal Deposit Insurance Corporation (FDIC), which ensures continuity of service to bank customers.

Government Ownership of Private Enterprises. The federal government can also obtain partial or complete ownership of a private corporation by purchasing its stock. Before 2008, such takeovers were rare, although they occasionally happened. When Continental Illinois, then the nation's seventh-largest bank, failed in 1984, the FDIC wound up in control of the institution for ten years before it could find a buyer.

The Continental Illinois rescue provided a blueprint for the massive bank bailout initiated in October 2008. The government made investments in more than eight hundred businesses, including banks, automobile companies, and the giant insurance company AIG. The bailout program was tremendously unpopular. Still, by 2014, the government had recovered all of its investments and even turned a small profit.

The Government-Sponsored Enterprise. An additional type of corporation is the government-sponsored enterprise, a business created by the federal government itself, which then sells part or all of the corporation's stock to private investors. Until 2008, the leading examples of this kind of company were the Federal Home Loan Mortgage Corporation, known as Freddie Mac, and the Federal National Mortgage Association, commonly known as Fannie Mae. Both of these firms buy mortgages from banks and bundle them into securities that can be sold to investors. When the housing market collapsed, so—eventually—did Freddie Mac and Fannie Mae.

Investors had always assumed that the federal government backed the obligations of the two enterprises, even though the government had never issued an explicit guarantee. In September 2008, the implicit guarantee became real when the government seized the two companies in what was effectively a bankruptcy. Freddie Mac and Fannie Mae became government-owned corporations. Eventually, they returned to profitability, and today all profits go to the U.S. Treasury.

Staffing the Bureaucracy

>>> **LO3:** Explain how government employees are hired and how the civil service is administered.

There are two categories of executive branch employees: political appointees and civil servants. As noted earlier, the president can make political appointments to most of the top jobs in the federal bureaucracy. The president also can appoint ambassadors to foreign posts. All of the jobs that are considered "political plums" and that usually go to the politically well connected are listed in *Policy and Supporting Positions*, a book published by the Government Printing Office after each presidential election. Informally (and appropriately), this has been called the "Plum Book." The rest of the national government's employees belong to the civil service and obtain their jobs through a much more formal process.

Political Appointees

To fill the positions listed in the Plum Book, the president and the president's advisers solicit suggestions from politicians, businesspersons, and other prominent individuals. Appointments to these positions offer the president a way to pay off outstanding political debts. Presidents often use ambassadorships to reward individuals for their campaign contributions. But the president must also take into consideration such things as the candidate's ability to actually do the job.

The Aristocracy of the Federal Government. Political appointees are in some sense the aristocracy of the federal government. But their powers, although they appear formidable

Spoils System
The awarding of government jobs to political supporters and friends.

on paper, are often exaggerated. Like the president, a political appointee will occupy her or his position for a comparatively brief time. Political appointees often leave office before the president's term ends. In fact, the average term of service for political appointees is less than two years. As a result, most appointees have little background for their positions and may be mere figureheads. Often, they only respond to the paperwork that flows up from below. Additionally, the professional civil servants who make up the permanent executive branch workforce may not feel compelled to carry out their current chief's directives quickly, because they know that he or she will not be around for very long.

The Difficulty in Firing Civil Servants. This inertia is compounded by the fact that it is very difficult to discharge civil servants. In recent years, fewer than 0.1 percent of federal employees have been fired for incompetence. Because discharged employees may appeal their dismissals, many months or even years can pass before the issue is resolved conclusively. This occupational rigidity helps to ensure that most political appointees, no matter how competent or driven, may not be able to exert much meaningful influence over their subordinates, let alone implement dramatic changes in the bureaucracy itself.

History of the Federal Civil Service

When the federal government was formed in 1789, it had no career public servants but rather consisted of amateurs who were almost all Federalists. When Thomas Jefferson took over as president, few federal administrative jobs were held by members of his party, so he fired more than one hundred officials and replaced them with his own supporters. Then, for the next twenty-five years, a growing body of federal administrators gained experience and expertise, becoming in the process professional public servants. These administrators stayed in office regardless of who was elected president. The bureaucracy had become a self-maintaining, long-term element within government.

Library of Congress, Prints & Photographs Division, Reproduction number [LC-US262-7622]

President James A. Garfield was assassinated in 1881 by a disappointed office seeker. The long-term effect of this crime was to replace the spoils system with a permanent career civil service. *What kinds of problems would result today if we relied, even in part, on the spoils system?*

To the Victors Belong the Spoils. When Andrew Jackson took over the White House in 1828, he could not believe how many appointed officials (appointed before he became president, that is) were overtly hostile toward him and his Democratic Party. Because the bureaucracy was reluctant to carry out his programs, Jackson did the obvious: he fired federal officials—more than all his predecessors combined. The **spoils system**—an application of the principle that to the victors belong the spoils— became the standard method of filling federal positions. Whenever a new president was elected from a party different from the party of the previous president, there would be an almost complete turnover in the staffing of the federal government.

The Civil Service Reform Act of 1883. Jackson's spoils system survived for a number of years, but it became increasingly corrupt. In addition, the size of the bureaucracy increased by 300 percent between 1851 and 1881. As the bureaucracy grew larger, the cry for civil service reform became louder. Reformers began to look to the example of several European countries—in particular, Germany. That country had established a professional civil service that operated under a **merit system,** in which job appointments were based on competitive examinations.

In 1883, the **Pendleton Act**—or **Civil Service Reform Act**—was passed, placing the first limits on the spoils system. The act established the principle of employment on the basis of open, competitive examinations and created the **Civil Service Commission** to administer the personnel service. Only 10 percent of federal employees were covered by the merit system initially. Later laws and executive orders, however, increased the coverage to more than 90 percent of federal employees. The effects of these reforms were felt at all levels of government.

The Supreme Court strengthened the civil service system in 1976 and in 1980.[1] In those two cases, the Court used the First Amendment to forbid government officials from discharging or threatening to discharge public employees solely for not being supporters of the political party in power unless party affiliation is an appropriate requirement for the position. A 1990 ruling added further enhancements to the civil service system.[2] The Court's ruling in that year effectively prevented the use of partisan political considerations as the basis for hiring, promoting, or transferring most public employees. An exception was permitted, however, for senior policymaking positions, which usually go to officials who will support the programs of the elected leaders.

The Civil Service Reform Act of 1978. In 1978, the Civil Service Reform Act abolished the Civil Service Commission and created two new federal agencies to perform its duties. To administer the civil service laws, rules, and regulations, the act created the Office of Personnel Management (OPM). The OPM is empowered to recruit, interview, and test potential government workers and determine who should be hired. The OPM makes recommendations to the individual agencies as to which persons meet the standards (typically, the top three applicants for a position), and the agencies then decide whom to hire. To oversee promotions, employees' rights, and other employment matters, the act created the Merit Systems Protection Board (MSPB). The MSPB evaluates charges of wrongdoing, hears employee appeals of agency decisions, and can order corrective action against agencies and employees.

Federal Employees and Political Campaigns. In 1933, when President Franklin D. Roosevelt set up his New Deal, a veritable army of civil servants was hired to staff the many new agencies that were created. Because the individuals who worked in these agencies owed their jobs to the Democratic Party, it seemed natural for them to campaign for Democratic candidates. The Democrats who controlled Congress in the mid-1930s did not object. But in 1938, a coalition of conservative Democrats and Republicans took control of Congress and forced through the Hatch Act—or Political Activities Act—of 1939. The act prohibited federal employees from actively participating in the political management of campaigns. It also forbade the use of federal authority to influence nominations and elections, and it outlawed the use of bureaucratic rank to pressure federal employees to make political contributions.

Hatch Act Controversies. The Hatch Act created controversies that lasted for decades. Many contended that the act deprived federal employees of their First Amendment freedoms of speech and association. In 1972, a federal district court declared the act unconstitutional.

Merit System
The selection, retention, and promotion of government employees on the basis of competitive examinations.

Pendleton Act (Civil Service Reform Act)
An act that established the principle of federal government employment based on merit and created the Civil Service Commission to administer the personnel service.

Civil Service Commission
The initial central personnel agency of the national government, created in 1883.

1. *Elrod v. Burns*, 427 U.S. 347 (1976); and *Branti v. Finkel*, 445 U.S. 507 (1980).
2. *Rutan v. Republican Party of Illinois*, 497 U.S. 62 (1990).

The United States Supreme Court, however, reaffirmed the challenged portion of the act in 1973, stating that the government's interest in preserving a nonpartisan civil service was so great that the prohibitions should remain.[3] Twenty years later, Congress addressed the criticisms of the Hatch Act by passing the Federal Employees Political Activities Act of 1993. This act, which amended the Hatch Act, lessened the harshness of the 1939 act in several ways. Among other things, the 1993 act allowed federal employees to run for office in nonpartisan elections, participate in voter-registration drives, make campaign contributions to political organizations, and campaign for candidates in partisan elections.

Modern Attempts at Bureaucratic Reform

>>> **LO4:** Evaluate different methods that have been put into place to reform bureaucracies and make them more efficient.

As long as the federal bureaucracy exists, attempts to make it more open, efficient, and responsive to the needs of U.S. citizens will continue. The most important reforms in the last several decades include sunshine laws, privatization, and attempts to protect so-called whistleblowers.

Sunshine Laws before and after 9/11

In 1976, Congress enacted the **Government in the Sunshine Act.** It required for the first time that all multiheaded federal agencies—agencies headed by a committee instead of an individual—hold their meetings regularly in public session. The bill defined *meeting* as almost any gathering, formal or informal, of agency members, including a conference telephone call. The only exceptions to this rule of openness are discussions of matters such as court proceedings or personnel problems, and these exceptions are specifically listed in the bill. Sunshine laws now exist at all levels of government.

Information Disclosure. In 1966, the federal government passed the Freedom of Information Act (FOIA), which required federal government agencies, with certain exceptions, to disclose to individuals information contained in government files. FOIA requests are helpful not just to individuals. Indeed, the major beneficiaries of the act have been news organizations, which have used it to uncover government waste, scandals, and incompetence.

As one example, in 2014 the Associated Press obtained records that revealed police efforts to restrict airspace to keep away news helicopters during violent street protests in Ferguson, Missouri. In recent years, however, news organizations have found it more difficult to use the FOIA. In particular, the Obama administration set new records for censoring government files, denying access to information, and failing to address FOIA requests in a timely fashion.

Curbs on Information Disclosure. Since the terrorist attacks of September 11, 2001, the trend toward open government has been reversed at both the federal and the state levels. Within weeks after September 11, 2001, federal agencies removed hundreds, if not thousands, of documents from Internet sites, public libraries, and the reading rooms found in various federal government departments. Information contained in some of the documents included diagrams of power plants and pipelines, structural details on dams, and safety plans for chemical plants. The military also immediately began restricting information about its current and planned activities, as did the Federal Bureau of Investigation. These agencies were concerned that terrorists could make use of this information to plan attacks.

Government in the Sunshine Act
A law that requires all committee-directed federal agencies to conduct their business regularly in public sessions.

---

3. *United States Civil Service Commission v. National Association of Letter Carriers*, 413 U.S. 548 (1973).

Privatization, or Contracting Out

Another approach to bureaucratic reform is **privatization**, which occurs when government services are replaced by services from the private sector. For example, the government has contracted with private firms to operate prisons. Supporters of privatization argue that some services can be provided more efficiently by the private sector. A similar scheme involves furnishing vouchers to government "clients" in lieu of services. Instead of supplying housing, the government could offer vouchers that recipients could use to "pay" for housing in privately owned buildings.

The privatization, or contracting-out, strategy has been most successful on the local level. Some municipalities have contracted with private companies for such services as trash collection. This approach is not a cure-all, however, because many functions, particularly on the national level, cannot be contracted out in any meaningful way.

The increase in the amount of government work being contracted out to the private sector has led to significant controversy in recent years. Some have criticized the lack of competitive bidding for many contracts that the government has awarded. Another concern is the perceived lack of federal government oversight over the work done by private contractors.

A park ranger at the Upper Delaware Scenic and Recreational River, a national park on the New York–Pennsylvania border. *Why might the national parks be popular with most citizens?*

The Issue of Whistleblowers

A **whistleblower** is someone who "blows the whistle" on gross governmental inefficiency or illegal action. Whistleblowers may be clerical workers, managers, or specialists, such as scientists.

Laws Protecting Whistleblowers. The 1978 Civil Service Reform Act prohibits reprisals against whistleblowers by their superiors, and it set up the Merit Systems Protection Board as part of this protection. Many federal agencies also have toll-free hotlines that employees can use anonymously to report bureaucratic waste and inappropriate behavior. About 35 percent of all calls result in agency action or follow-up.

Further protection for whistleblowers was provided in 1989, when Congress passed the Whistleblower Protection Act. That act established an independent agency, the Office of Special Counsel (OSC), to investigate complaints brought by government employees who have been demoted, fired, or otherwise punished for reporting government fraud or waste.

Some state and federal laws encourage employees to blow the whistle on their employers' wrongful actions by providing monetary incentives to the whistleblowers. At the federal level, the False Claims Act of 1986 allows a whistleblower who has disclosed information about a fraud against the U.S. government to receive a monetary award. If the government chooses to prosecute the case and wins, the whistleblower receives between 15 and 25 percent of the proceeds. If the government declines to intervene, the whistleblower can bring a suit on behalf of the government and, if the suit is successful, will receive between 25 and 30 percent of the proceeds.

The Problem Continues. Despite these efforts to help whistleblowers, there is little evidence that they truly receive much protection. According to a survey, more than 41 percent of the employees who turned to the OSC for assistance stated that they were no longer employees

Privatization
The replacement of government services with services provided by private firms.

Whistleblower
In the context of government, someone who brings gross governmental inefficiency or an illegal action to the public's attention.

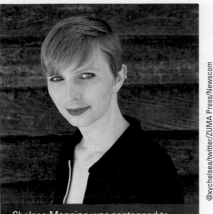

@xychelsea/twitter/ZUMA Press/Newscom

Chelsea Manning was sentenced to thirty-five years in prison for giving classified U.S. government information to website WikiLeaks. She was later pardoned by President Obama and released from prison in May 2017. *Is Manning a criminal, a hero—or both?*

of the government agencies on which they had blown the whistle. The government's difficulty in dismissing employees seems to magically disappear when the employee is a whistleblower.

Whistleblowers under President Obama. During his 2008 campaign, Obama promised to protect whistleblowers. Many observers believe, however, that in fact the Obama administration's record on whistleblowers was one of the worst ever. This conclusion is based, in large part, on the administration's use of the Espionage Act of 1917 to prosecute persons who leaked national security information to the press. By 2013, the administration had launched seven such prosecutions. The Espionage Act has been used regularly against persons spying for foreign governments. Not since 1984, however, had the government initiated such a case based on leaks to the press.

The most recent—and most dramatic—case involved Edward Snowden, a National Security Agency (NSA) contractor. Snowden delivered a vast collection of information on NSA surveillance to journalists Glenn Greenwald and Laura Poitras. Snowden was aware of how the government had treated Private First Class Chelsea (formerly Bradley) Manning, an earlier leaker. Manning had been held in solitary confinement in ways that some critics saw as abusive. Snowden therefore relocated to Hong Kong, hoping that the Chinese government would grant him asylum. On learning that asylum would not be granted, Snowden fled to Russia.

Whistleblowers, Leakers, and President Trump. As a presidential candidate, Donald Trump had no complaints about leaks, including ones that had little in common with traditional whistleblowing. When Russian hackers broke into the e-mail system of John Podesta, Hillary Clinton's campaign chair, Trump applauded. As president, however, Trump's attitude was very different. That should come as no surprise: Trump was in charge of what was possibly the most leak-prone administration in U.S. history.

Many of the leaks revealed questionable conversations with Russian authorities by members of the Trump campaign and transition teams. In particular, it appears that National Security Adviser Mike Flynn lied to other members of the administration about his contacts with Russian officials. (Flynn was also an agent of the Turkish government right up to the time when he took office.) Trump eventually fired Flynn. Trump loyalists spoke darkly of a conspiracy against the president by the intelligence community—a conspiracy that they labeled the "deep state." It does not appear, however, that the leakers were acting in concert.

Indeed, the most leak-prone institution in Washington may have been the White House itself. Almost every top adviser seemed to be spreading stories to embellish his or her own reputation and to damage the reputations of other staff members.

In May 2017, it became clear that FBI Director James Comey was mounting a serious investigation into relations between Trump staff and the Russian government. Trump fired Comey. The resulting storm of criticism was great enough that the Justice Department felt compelled to appoint a *special counsel* to investigate. The counsel was Robert Mueller, a respected former director of the FBI. The bureaucrats responsible for setting this chain of events in motion may be called anonymous whistleblowers or national security leakers, but in either case they managed to land the White House in serious hot water.

Bureaucrats as Politicians and Policymakers

>>> **LO5:** Discuss how federal agencies make rules and what the role of Congress is in this process.

Because Congress is unable to oversee the day-to-day administration of its programs, it must delegate certain powers to administrative agencies. Congress delegates power to agencies through **enabling legislation.** For example, the Federal Trade Commission was created by the Federal Trade Commission Act of 1914, the Equal Employment Opportunity Commission was created by the Civil Rights Act of 1964, and the Occupational Safety and Health Administration was created by the Occupational Safety and Health Act of 1970. The enabling legislation generally specifies the name, purpose, composition, functions, and powers of the agency.

In theory, the agencies should put into effect laws passed by Congress. Laws are often drafted in such vague and general terms, however, that they provide limited guidance to agency administrators as to how they should be implemented. This means that the agencies themselves must decide how best to carry out the wishes of Congress.

The discretion given to administrative agencies is not accidental. Congress has long realized that it lacks the technical expertise and the resources to monitor the implementation of its laws. Hence, administrative agencies are created to fill the gaps. This gap-filling role requires an agency to formulate administrative rules (regulations) to put flesh on the bones of the law. But it also forces the agency itself to become an unelected policymaker.

The Rulemaking Environment

Rulemaking does not occur in a vacuum. Suppose that Congress passes a new air-pollution law. The Environmental Protection Agency (EPA) might decide to implement the new law through a technical regulation on power-plant emissions. This proposed regulation would be published in the *Federal Register*, a daily government publication, so that interested parties would have an opportunity to comment on it. Individuals and companies that oppose parts or all of the rule might then try to convince the EPA to revise or redraft the regulation. Some parties might try to persuade the agency to withdraw the proposed regulation altogether. In any event, the EPA would consider these comments in drafting the final version of the regulation.

Waiting Periods and Court Challenges. Once the final regulation has been published in the *Federal Register*, there is a sixty-day waiting period before the rule can be enforced. During that period, businesses, individuals, and state and local governments can ask Congress to overturn the regulation. After the sixty-day period has lapsed, the regulation can still be challenged in court by a party having a direct interest in the rule, such as a company that expects to incur significant costs in complying with it. The company could argue that the rule misinterprets the applicable law or goes beyond the agency's legal authority. An allegation by the company that the EPA made a mistake in judgment probably would not be enough to convince the court to throw out the rule. The company instead would have to demonstrate that the rule itself was "arbitrary and capricious."

Controversies. How agencies implement, administer, and enforce legislation has resulted in controversy. For example, decisions made by agencies charged with administering the Endangered Species Act have led to protests from farmers, ranchers, and others whose economic interests have been harmed.

At times, a controversy may arise when an agency *refuses* to issue regulations to implement a particular law. During the George W. Bush administration, the EPA refused to issue

Enabling Legislation
A statute enacted by Congress that authorizes the creation of an administrative agency and specifies the name, purpose, composition, functions, and powers of the agency being created.

regulations designed to curb the emission of carbon dioxide and other greenhouse gases. State and local governments, as well as a number of environmental groups, then sued the agency. Those bringing the suit claimed that the EPA was not fulfilling its obligation to implement the provisions of the Clean Air Act. Ultimately, the Supreme Court held that the EPA had the authority to—and should—regulate such gases.[4]

Revoking an Existing Rule. One goal of the Trump administration was a massive cutback in regulation. In particular, the administration wanted to reverse a number of specific rules long opposed by Republicans. One was the Clean Power Plan (CPP) advanced by the Environmental Protection Agency (EPA) that would have made it much harder to use coal to generate electrical power. True, the CPP was in substantial danger of being struck down by the Supreme Court. But the president could also simply direct the EPA to withdraw the CPP. That step is not as easy as it sounds, however. The rulemaking process just described applies not only to creating new rules, but to revoking existing ones as well. The agency responsible for the rule must prepare a justification for the revocation. Comments and waiting periods are required. Lawsuits are possible. The process of making a rule can take years, and unmaking one can take just as long.

Negotiated Rulemaking

Since the end of World War II in 1945, companies, environmentalists, and other special interest groups have challenged government regulations in court. In the 1980s, however, the sheer wastefulness of attempting to regulate through litigation became increasingly apparent. Today, a growing number of federal agencies encourage businesses and public-interest groups to become directly involved in drafting regulations. Agencies hope that such participation may help to prevent later courtroom battles over the regulations.

Congress formally approved such a process, which is called *negotiated rulemaking*, in the Negotiated Rulemaking Act of 1990. The act authorizes agencies to allow those who will be affected by a new rule to participate in the rule-drafting process. If an agency chooses to engage in negotiated rulemaking, it must publish in the *Federal Register* the subject and scope of the rule to be developed, the names of the parties that will be affected significantly by the rule, and other information. Representatives of the affected groups and other interested parties then may apply to be members of the negotiating committee.

The agency is represented on the committee, but a trained public policy mediator from the private sector presides over the proceedings. Once the committee members have reached agreement on the terms of the proposed rule, a notice is published in the *Federal Register*, followed by a period for comments by any person or organization interested in the proposed rule. Negotiated rulemaking often is conducted under the condition that the participants promise not to challenge in court the outcome of any agreement to which they were a party.

Bureaucrats as Policymakers

Theories of public administration once assumed that bureaucrats do not make policy decisions but only implement the laws and policies developed by the president and legislative bodies. A more realistic view is that the agencies and departments of government play important roles in policymaking. The bureaucracy often initiates regulations and programs based on its expertise and on scientific studies. The views and beliefs of the bureaucrats themselves may also influence the results. How a law passed by Congress eventually is

---

4. *Massachusetts v. EPA*, 549 U.S. 497 (2007).

translated into action—from the forms to be filled out to decisions about who gets what benefits—usually is determined within each agency or department. Even the evaluation of whether a policy has achieved its purpose usually is based on studies that are commissioned and interpreted by the agency administering the program.

The bureaucracy's policymaking role often has been depicted as an *iron triangle*. Recently, many political scientists have come to see the concept of an *issue network* as a more accurate description of the typical policymaking process.

Iron Triangles. In the past, scholars often described the bureaucracy's role in the policymaking process by using the concept of an **iron triangle**—a three-way alliance among legislators in Congress, bureaucrats, and interest groups. Consider as an example the development of agricultural policy. Congress, as one component of the triangle, includes two major committees concerned with agricultural policy, the House Committee on Agriculture and the Senate Committee on Agriculture, Nutrition, and Forestry. The Department of Agriculture, the second component of the triangle, has more than 85,000 employees, plus thousands of contractors and consultants. Agricultural interest groups, the third component of the triangle, include many large and powerful associations, such as the American Farm Bureau Federation, the National Cattlemen's Beef Association, and the National Corn Growers Association. These three components of the iron triangle work together, formally or informally, to create policy.

For example, the various agricultural interest groups lobby Congress to develop policies that benefit their groups' economic welfare. Members of Congress cannot afford to ignore the wishes of interest groups because those groups are potential sources of voter support and campaign contributions. The legislators in Congress also work closely with the Department of Agriculture, which, in implementing a policy, can develop rules that benefit—or at least do not hurt—various industries or groups. The Department of Agriculture, in turn, supports policies that enhance the department's budget and powers. In this way, according to theory, agricultural policy is created that benefits all three components of the iron triangle.

Issue Networks. With the growth in the complexity of government, policymaking also has become more complicated. The bureaucracy is larger, Congress has more committees and subcommittees, and interest groups are more powerful than ever. Although iron triangles still exist, often they are inadequate as descriptions of how policy is made today. Frequently, different interest groups concerned about a certain area of policy have conflicting demands, which makes agency decision making difficult. Additionally, during periods of divided government, departments are pressured by the president to take one approach and by Congress to take another.

Many scholars now use the term *issue network* to describe the policymaking process. An **issue network** consists of individuals or organizations that support a particular policy position on the environment, taxation, consumer safety, or some other issue. Typically, an issue network includes legislators and/or their staff members, interest group leaders, bureaucrats, scholars and other experts, and representatives from the media. Members of a particular issue network work together to influence the president, members of Congress, administrative agencies, and the courts to affect public policy on a specific issue. Each policy issue may involve conflicting positions taken by two or more issue networks.

Congressional Control of the Bureaucracy

Many political pundits doubt whether Congress can meaningfully control the federal bureaucracy. These commentators forget that Congress specifies in an agency's enabling legislation the powers of the agency and the parameters within which it can operate. Additionally, Congress has

Iron Triangle
A three-way alliance among legislators in Congress, bureaucrats, and interest groups to make or preserve policies that benefit their respective interests.

Issue Network
A group of individuals or organizations—which may consist of legislators and legislative staff members, interest group leaders, bureaucrats, scholars and other experts, and media representatives—that supports a particular policy position on a given issue.

Two farmers walking together near their cattle. *What part do farmers play in agricultural policymaking at the federal level?*

Bloomberg/Getty Images

"the power of the purse" and theoretically could refuse to authorize or appropriate funds for a particular agency. Whether Congress would actually take such a drastic measure would depend on the circumstances. It is clear, however, that Congress does have the legal authority to decide whether or not to fund administrative agencies.

Congress also can exercise oversight over agencies. Congressional committees conduct investigations and hold hearings to oversee an agency's actions, reviewing them to ensure compliance with congressional intentions. The agency's officers and employees can be ordered to testify before a committee about the details of various actions. Through the questions and comments of members of the House or Senate during the hearings, Congress indicates its positions on specific programs and issues. The views expressed in any investigations and hearings are taken seriously by agency officials, who often act on them.

MAKING A DIFFERENCE

What the Government Knows about You

The federal government collects billions of pieces of information on tens of millions of Americans each year. You are probably the subject of several federal records (for example, in the Social Security Administration, the Internal Revenue Service, and, if you are male, the Selective Service).

Why Should You Care? Verifying the information that the government has about you can be important. On several occasions, the records of two people with similar names have become confused. Sometimes innocent persons have had the criminal records of other persons erroneously inserted into their files. Such disasters are not always caused by bureaucratic error. One of the most common crimes in today's world is "identity theft," in which one person makes use of another individual's personal identifiers (such as a Social Security number) to commit fraud.

What Can You Do? The 1966 Freedom of Information Act (FOIA) requires that the federal government release, at your request, any identifiable information it has about you or about

any other subject. (Some categories of material are exempted, however.) To request material, write directly to the Freedom of Information Act officer at the agency in question. You must have a relatively specific idea about the document or information you want to obtain.

A second law, the Privacy Act of 1974, gives you access specifically to information the government may have collected about you. This law allows you to review records on file with federal agencies and to check those records for possible inaccuracies.

If you want to look at any records or find out if an agency has a record on you, write to the agency head or Privacy Act officer, and address your letter to the specific agency. State that "under the provisions of the Privacy Act of 1974, 5 U.S.C. 522a, I hereby request a copy of (or access to)." Then describe the record that you wish to investigate.

The General Services Administration (GSA) has published a citizen's guide, *Your Right to Federal Records*. You can locate this manual by entering its name into your favorite search engine.

Key Terms

agency capture 257
bureaucracy 251
cabinet department 253
Civil Service
    Commission 261
enabling legislation 265

government
    corporation 258
Government in the
    Sunshine Act 262
independent executive
    agency 254

independent regulatory
    agency 255
iron triangle 267
issue network 267
line organization 253
merit system 261

Pendleton Act
    (Civil Service
    Reform Act) 261
privatization 263
spoils system 260
whistleblower 263

Chapter Summary

≫ LO1 Bureaucracies are hierarchical organizations characterized by division of labor and extensive procedural rules. Bureaucracy is the primary form of organization of most major corporations and universities, as well as governments.

Since the founding of the United States, the federal bureaucracy has grown from a few employees to about 2.5 million (including the U.S. Postal Service but excluding the military). Federal, state, and local employees together make up more than 15 percent of the nation's civilian labor force. Social Security, Medicare, Medicaid, and military defense are the largest components of federal spending. Major sources of federal revenue include the individual and corporate income taxes, Social Security and Medicare payroll taxes, and borrowing.

≫ LO2 The executive branch consists of fifteen cabinet departments, as well as a large number of independent executive agencies, independent regulatory agencies, and government corporations. These entities enjoy varying degrees of autonomy, visibility, and political support.

≫ LO3 A federal bureaucracy of career civil servants was formed during Thomas Jefferson's presidency. Andrew Jackson implemented a spoils system through which he appointed his own political supporters. A civil service based on professionalism and merit was the goal of the Civil Service Reform Act of 1883. Concerns that the civil service be

freed from the pressures of politics prompted the passage of the Hatch Act in 1939. The Civil Service Reform Act of 1978 made significant changes in the administration of the civil service by creating the Office of Personnel Management and the Merit Systems Protection Board.

≫ LO4 There have been many attempts to make the federal bureaucracy more open, efficient, and responsive to the needs of U.S. citizens. The most important reforms have included sunshine laws, privatization, and protection for whistleblowers, who are often subject to severe reprisals.

≫ LO5 Congress delegates much of its authority to federal agencies when it creates new laws. The bureaucrats who run these agencies may become important policymakers, because Congress has neither the time nor the technical expertise to oversee the administration of its laws. The agency rulemaking process begins when a proposed regulation is published. A comment period follows, during which interested parties may offer suggestions for changes.

Congress exerts ultimate control over all federal agencies, because it controls the federal government's purse strings. The appropriations process provides a way to send messages of approval or disapproval to particular agencies, as do congressional hearings and investigations of agency actions.

Test Yourself

1. In terms of federal dollars spent, the most important programs are:
   a. social programs, including Social Security and Medicare.
   b. the military and subsidies for corporations.
   c. foreign aid.

2. After the individual income tax, the next two largest sources of funds to support the federal government are:
   a. the Social Security payroll tax and the Medicare payroll tax.
   b. the corporate income tax and the Social Security payroll tax.
   c. the Social Security payroll tax and the sale of federal debt obligations.

3. When a federal agency's function is to make and implement rules and regulations to protect the public interest, it is called:
   a. an independent executive agency.
   b. an independent regulatory agency.
   c. a government corporation.

4. The heads of federal regulatory agencies and members of agency boards and commissions are appointed by:
   a. the president acting alone.
   b. the president with the consent of the Senate.
   c. the Supreme Court.

5. When an agency serves the industry it is meant to regulate, rather than serving the general public, we call this:
   a. agency capture.
   b. deregulation.
   c. an iron triangle.

6. In the early days of this country, when a new president was of a different party than the outgoing president, government employees were often fired and replaced with supporters of the incoming president's party. This was called the:
   a. civil service system.
   b. spoils system.
   c. patronage system.

7. The first significant legislation aimed at making the federal civil service nonpartisan and independent was:
   a. the Civil Service Act of 1978.
   b. the Hatch Act.
   c. the Pendleton Act of 1883.

8. *Privatization* means that:
   a. the government must provide individuals with the information it has on them.
   b. private companies replace members of the civil service in providing a government service.
   c. bonuses are awarded for efficient work.

9. Under the Obama administration, whistleblowers:
   a. received increased protection from reprisals.
   b. became less active.
   c. faced criminal charges with unprecedented frequency.

10. Because Congress cannot oversee the daily administration of its many programs, it delegates power to agencies through:
    a. enabling legislation.
    b. negotiated rulemaking.
    c. congressional oversight.

11. An issue network consists of individuals or organizations that support a particular policy position. A typical issue network includes:
    a. Congress, the president's cabinet, and the Supreme Court.
    b. federal judges, congressional staff, and the heads of certain private corporations.
    c. legislators (or their staff), interest group leaders, bureaucrats, scholars and other experts, and the media.

Essay Questions

1. The U.S. attorney general, head of the Justice Department, is appointed by the president and is frequently the president's close political ally. Should the attorney general and other U.S. attorneys be appointed on a partisan basis? Why or why not?

2. If Congress tried to make civil servants easier to fire, what political forces might stand in the way?

Answers to multiple-choice questions: 1. a, 2. c, 3. b, 4. b, 5. a, 6. b, 7. c, 8. b, 9. c, 10. a, 11. c.

12 | The Courts

Pro-choice and pro-life activists await a Supreme Court ruling in June 2016 on whether a Texas law on abortion clinics is unconstitutionally restrictive. *What did the Court decide about abortion in its famous decision* Roe v. Wade?

The five **Learning Outcomes (LOs)** below are designed to help improve your understanding of this chapter. After reading this chapter, you should be able to:

>>>**LO1** Explain the main sources of American law, including constitutions, statutes and regulations, and the common law tradition.

>>>**LO2** Describe the structure of the federal court system and such basic judicial requirements as jurisdiction and standing to sue.

>>>**LO3** Discuss the procedures used by the United States Supreme Court and the various types of opinions it hands down.

>>>**LO4** Evaluate the manner in which federal judges are selected.

>>>**LO5** Consider the ways in which the Supreme Court makes policy, and explain the forces that limit the activism of the courts.

Check your understanding of the material with the Test Yourself section at the end of the chapter.

A s Alexis de Tocqueville, a French commentator on American society in the 1800s, noted, "scarcely any political question arises in the United States that is not resolved, sooner or later, into a judicial question."[1] Our judiciary forms part of our political process. The instant that judges interpret the law, they become actors in the political arena—policymakers working within a political institution. The most important

---

1. Alexis de Tocqueville, *Democracy in America*, trans. George Lawrence (New York: Harper & Row, 1966), p. 248.

political force within our judiciary is the United States Supreme Court. The justices of the Supreme Court are not elected but are appointed by the president and confirmed by the Senate, as are all other federal court judges.

How do courts make policy? Why do the federal courts play such an important role in American government? The answers to these questions lie, in part, in our colonial heritage. Most of American law is based on the English system, particularly the English *common law tradition*. In that tradition, the decisions made by judges constitute an important source of law. We open this chapter with an examination of this tradition and of the various other sources of American law. We then look at the federal court system—how it is organized, how its judges are selected, how these judges affect policy, and how they are restrained by our system of checks and balances.

Sources of American Law

>>> **LO1:** Explain the main sources of American law, including constitutions, statutes and regulations, and the common law tradition.

The body of American law includes the federal and state constitutions, statutes passed by legislative bodies, administrative law, and case law—the legal principles expressed in court decisions. Case law is based in part on the common law tradition, which dates to the earliest English settlements in North America.

The Common Law Tradition

In 1066, the Normans conquered England, and William the Conqueror and his successors began the process of unifying the country under their rule. One of the ways in which they did this was to establish king's courts. Before the conquest, disputes had been settled according to local custom. The king's courts sought to establish a common, or uniform, set of rules for the whole country. As the number of courts and cases increased, portions of the most important decisions of each year were gathered together and recorded in Year Books. Judges who were settling disputes similar to ones that had been decided before used the Year Books as the basis for their decisions. If a case was unique, judges had to create new rules, but they based their decisions on the general principles suggested by earlier cases. The body of judge-made law that developed under this system is still used today and is known as the **common law.**

Common Law
The body of law developed from judicial decisions in English and U.S. courts, not attributable to a legislature.

Precedent
A court ruling bearing on subsequent legal decisions in similar cases. Judges rely on precedents in deciding cases.

Stare Decisis
To stand on decided cases—the judicial policy of following precedents established by past decisions.

Stare Decisis. The practice of deciding new cases with reference to former decisions—that is, according to **precedent**—became a cornerstone of the English and American judicial systems. It is embodied in the doctrine of ***stare decisis*** (pronounced *ster*-ay dih-*si*-ses), a Latin phrase that means "to stand on decided cases." The doctrine of *stare decisis* obligates judges to follow the precedents set previously by their own courts or by higher courts that have authority over them.

Examples of Precedents. *Stare decisis* means that a lower state court in California would be obligated to follow a precedent set by the California Supreme Court. That lower court, however, would not be obligated to follow a precedent set by the supreme court of another state, because each state court system is independent. Of course, when the United States Supreme Court decides an issue, all of the nation's other courts are obligated to abide by the Court's decision, because the Supreme Court is the highest court in the land.

The doctrine of *stare decisis* provides a basis for judicial decision making in all countries that have common law systems. Today, the United States, Britain, and several dozen other countries have common law systems. Generally, those countries that were once colonies of Britain, including Australia, Canada, India, New Zealand, and others, have retained their English common law heritage.

Constitutions

The constitutions of the federal government and the states set forth the general organization, powers, and limits of government. The U.S. Constitution is the supreme law of the land. A law in violation of the Constitution, no matter what its source, may be declared unconstitutional and thereafter cannot be enforced. Similarly, the state constitutions are supreme within their respective borders (unless they conflict with the U.S. Constitution or federal laws and treaties made in accordance with it). The Constitution thus defines the political playing field on which state and federal powers are reconciled.

A law student looks up cases in a law library. *Would it be easier to find cases online? Why or why not?*

Statutes and Administrative Regulations

Although the English common law provides the basis for both our civil and our criminal legal systems, statutes (laws enacted by legislatures) have become increasingly important in defining the rights and obligations of individuals. Federal statutes may relate to any subject that is a concern of the federal government and may apply to areas ranging from hazardous waste to federal taxation. State statutes include criminal codes, commercial laws, and laws covering a variety of other matters. Cities, counties, and other local political bodies also pass statutes, which are called *ordinances*. These ordinances may be adopted to deal with such issues as real estate zoning and public safety.

Rules and regulations issued by administrative agencies are another source of law. Today, much of the work of the courts consists of interpreting these laws and regulations and applying them to the specific circumstances of the cases that come before the courts.

Case Law

Because we have a common law tradition, in which the doctrine of *stare decisis* plays an important role, the decisions rendered by the courts also form an important body of law, collectively referred to as **case law.** Case law includes judicial interpretations of common law principles and doctrines, as well as interpretations of constitutional provisions, statutes, and administrative agency regulations. As you learned in previous chapters, it is up to the courts—and ultimately, if necessary, the Supreme Court—to decide what a constitutional provision or a statutory phrase means. In doing so, the courts, in effect, establish law.

The Federal Court System

>>> **LO2:** Describe the structure of the federal court system and such basic judicial requirements as jurisdiction and standing to sue.

The United States has a dual court system, with state courts and federal courts. Each of the fifty states, as well as the District of Columbia, has its own independent system of courts. This means that there are fifty-two court systems in total. Here we focus on the federal courts.

Case Law
Judicial interpretations of common law principles and doctrines, as well as interpretations of constitutional law, statutory law, and administrative law.

Basic Judicial Requirements

In any court system, state or federal, certain requirements must be met before a case can be brought. Two important requirements are *jurisdiction* and *standing to sue*.

Jurisdiction. A state court can exercise **jurisdiction** (the authority of the court to hear and decide a case) over the residents of a particular geographic area, such as a county or district. A state's highest court, or supreme court, has jurisdictional authority over all residents within the state.

Because the Constitution established a federal government with limited powers, federal jurisdiction is also limited. Article III, Section 1, of the U.S. Constitution limits the jurisdiction of the federal courts to cases that involve either a federal question or diversity of citizenship. A **federal question** arises when a case is based, at least in part, on the U.S. Constitution, a treaty, or a federal law. A person who claims that her or his rights under the Constitution, such as the right to free speech, have been violated could bring a case in a federal court. **Diversity of citizenship** exists when the parties to a lawsuit are from different states or (more rarely) when the suit involves a U.S. citizen and a government or citizen of a foreign country. The amount in controversy must be at least $75,000 before a federal court can take jurisdiction in a diversity case, however.

Given the significant limits on federal jurisdiction, most lawsuits and criminal cases are heard in state, rather than federal, courts. A defendant or a party to a dispute handled by a state court may file an appeal with a state appeals court, or even the state's supreme court. Appeals cannot be taken to a federal court, however, unless a federal question is involved.

Standing to Sue. Another basic judicial requirement is *standing to sue*, or a sufficient "stake" in a matter to justify bringing suit. The party bringing a lawsuit must have suffered a harm, or have been threatened by a harm, as a result of the action that led to the dispute in question. Standing to sue also requires that the controversy at issue be a justiciable (pronounced just-*tish*-a-bul) controversy. A **justiciable controversy** is a controversy that is real and substantial, as opposed to hypothetical or academic. In other words, a court will not give advisory opinions on hypothetical questions.

Parties to Lawsuits

In most lawsuits, the parties are the *plaintiff* (the person or organization that initiates the lawsuit) and the *defendant* (the person or organization against whom the lawsuit is brought). There may be a number of plaintiffs and defendants in a single lawsuit. Many lawsuits are brought by interest groups. Interest groups play an important role in our judicial system, because they **litigate**—bring to trial—or assist in litigating most cases of racial or gender-based discrimination, virtually all civil liberties cases, and more than one-third of the cases involving business matters. Interest groups also file **amicus curiae** (pronounced ah-*mee*-kous *kur*-ee-eye) **briefs,** or "friend of the court" briefs, in more than 50 percent of these kinds of cases.

Sometimes, interest groups or other plaintiffs will bring a **class-action suit,** in which whatever the court decides will affect all members of a class similarly situated (such as users of a particular product manufactured by the defendant in the lawsuit). The strategy of class-action lawsuits was pioneered by such groups as the National Association for the Advancement of Colored People (NAACP), the Legal Defense Fund, and the Sierra Club.

Procedural Rules

Both the federal and the state courts have established procedural rules that shape the litigation process. These rules are designed to protect the rights and interests of the parties and

Jurisdiction
The authority of a court to decide certain cases. Not all courts have the authority to decide all cases. Where a case arises and what its subject matter is are two jurisdictional issues.

Federal Question
A question that has to do with the U.S. Constitution, acts of Congress, or treaties. A federal question provides a basis for federal jurisdiction.

Diversity of Citizenship
The condition that exists when the parties to a lawsuit are from different states or when the suit involves a U.S. citizen and a government or citizen of a foreign country. Diversity of citizenship can provide a basis for federal jurisdiction.

Justiciable Controversy
A controversy that is real and substantial, as opposed to hypothetical or academic.

Litigate
To engage in a legal proceeding or seek relief in a court of law. To carry on a lawsuit.

Amicus Curiae Brief
A written legal argument filed by a third party, or *amicus curiae* (Latin for "friend of the court"), who is not directly involved in the litigation but who has an interest in the outcome of the case.

Class-Action Suit
A lawsuit filed by an individual seeking damages for "all persons similarly situated."

to ensure that the litigation proceeds in a fair and orderly manner. The rules also serve to identify the issues that must be decided by the court—thus saving court time and expense. Court decisions may also apply to trial procedures. For example, the Supreme Court has held that the parties' attorneys cannot discriminate against prospective jurors on the basis of race or gender. Some lower courts have also held that people cannot be excluded from juries because of their sexual orientation or religion.

The parties must comply with procedural rules and with any orders given by the judge during the course of the litigation. When a party does not follow a court's order, the court can cite that person for contempt. A party who commits civil contempt (failing to comply with a court's order for the benefit of another party to the proceeding) can be taken into custody, fined, or both, until that party complies with the court's order. A party who commits *criminal* contempt (obstructing the administration of justice or disrespecting the rules of the court) also can be taken into custody and fined but cannot avoid punishment by complying with a previous order.

Trial Court
The court in which most cases begin.

General Jurisdiction
A court's authority to hear cases that Is not significantly restricted. A court of general jurisdiction normally can hear a broad range of cases.

Limited Jurisdiction
A court's authority to hear cases that is restricted to certain types of claims, such as tax claims or bankruptcy petitions.

Types of Federal Courts

As you can see in Figure 12–1, the federal court system is basically a three-tiered model consisting of (1) U.S. district courts and various specialized courts of limited jurisdiction (not all of the latter arc shown in the figure), (2) intermediate U.S. courts of appeals, and (3) the United States Supreme Court.

U.S. District Courts. The U.S. district courts are trial courts. A **trial court** is what the name implies—a court in which trials are held and testimony is taken. The U.S. district courts are courts of **general jurisdiction,** meaning that they can hear cases involving a broad array of issues. Federal cases involving most matters typically are heard in district courts. The other courts on the lower tier of the model shown in Figure 12–1 are courts of **limited jurisdiction,**

FIGURE 12–1 The Federal Court System

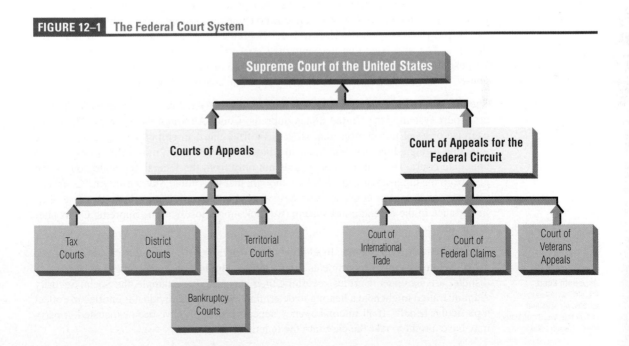

meaning that they can try cases involving only certain types of claims, such as tax claims or bankruptcy petitions.

There is at least one federal district court in every state. The number of judicial districts has varied historically owing to population changes and corresponding caseloads, but no entirely new district has been created since California was redivided in 1966. Today, there are ninety-four federal judicial districts and 678 authorized district court judgeships. The Southern District of New York has the largest number of judges—44. The Central District of California is second with 30.

A party who is dissatisfied with the decision of a district court can appeal the case to the appropriate U.S. court of appeals, or federal **appellate court**. Figure 12–2 shows the jurisdictional boundaries of the district courts (which are state boundaries, unless otherwise indicated by dotted lines within a state) and of the U.S. courts of appeals.

U.S. Courts of Appeals. There are thirteen U.S. courts of appeals—also referred to as U.S. circuit courts of appeals. Twelve of these courts, including the U.S. Court of Appeals for the District of Columbia, hear appeals from the federal district courts located within their respective judicial circuits (geographic areas over which they exercise jurisdiction). The Court of Appeals for the Thirteenth Circuit, called the Federal Circuit, has national appellate jurisdiction over certain types of cases, such as cases involving patent law and those in which the U.S. government is a defendant.

Note that when an appellate court reviews a case decided in a district court, the appellate court does not conduct another trial. Rather, a panel of three or more judges reviews the record of the case on appeal, which includes a transcript of the trial proceedings. The panel determines whether the trial court committed an error. Usually, appellate courts do not look at questions of *fact* (such as whether a party did commit a certain action, such as burning a flag). Instead, they look at questions of *law* (such as whether the act of flag-burning is a form of speech protected by the First Amendment to the Constitution). An appellate court will challenge a trial court's finding of fact only when the finding is clearly contrary to the evidence presented at trial or when there is no evidence to support the finding.

A party can petition the United States Supreme Court to review an appellate court's decision. The likelihood that the Supreme Court will grant the petition is slim, however, because the Court reviews only a small percentage of the cases decided by the appellate courts. This means that decisions made by appellate courts usually are final.

The United States Supreme Court. The highest level of the three-tiered model of the federal court system is the United States Supreme Court. Although the Supreme Court can exercise original jurisdiction (that is, act as a trial court) in certain cases, such as those affecting foreign diplomats and those in which a state is a party, most of its work is as an appellate court. The Court hears appeals not only from the federal appellate courts, but also from the highest state courts. Note, though, that the United States Supreme Court can review a state supreme court decision only if a federal question is involved. Because of its importance in the federal court system, we look more closely at the Supreme Court later in this chapter.

Administrative Law Tribunals. In addition to the federal court system, federal administrative agencies and executive departments often employ administrative law judges, who resolve disputes arising under the rules governing their agencies. For example, the Social Security Administration might hold a hearing to determine whether an individual is entitled to collect a particular benefit. If all internal agency appeals processes have been exhausted, a party may have a right to take the case into the federal court system.

Appellate Court
A court having jurisdiction to review cases and issues that were originally tried in lower courts.

Federal Courts and the War on Terrorism

As noted, the federal court system includes a variety of trial courts of limited jurisdiction, dealing with matters such as tax claims or international trade. The government's attempts to combat terrorism have drawn attention to certain specialized courts that meet in secret. We look next at these courts, as well as at the role of the federal courts with respect to the detainees accused of terrorism.

The FISA Court. The federal government created the first secret court in 1978. In that year, Congress passed the Foreign Intelligence Surveillance Act (FISA), which established a court to hear requests for warrants for the surveillance of suspected spies. Officials can request a warrant without having to reveal to the suspect or to the public the information used to justify the warrant or even that the warrant exists. The FISA court has approved almost all of the thousands of requests for warrants that officials have submitted. There is no public access to the court's proceedings or records. All FISA court judges are appointed by the chief justice of the Supreme Court without review by any other authority.

In the aftermath of the terrorist attacks on September 11, 2001, the Bush administration expanded the powers of the FISA court. Previously, the FISA had allowed secret domestic surveillance only if the purpose was to combat intelligence gathering by foreign powers. Amendments to the FISA enacted after 9/11 changed this wording to "a significant purpose"—meaning that warrants may now be requested to obtain evidence that can be used in criminal trials.

FIGURE 12–2   The Federal Court System

Suspected terrorists detained at the Guantánamo Bay naval base prison in Cuba. *Should such detainees have rights under the law?*

SHANE T. MCCOY/MCT/Newscom

The FISA Court and the National Security Agency. Some of the National Security Agency (NSA) material that Edward Snowden leaked to the press in 2013 dealt with the FISA court. One of the first stories described a FISA court order that required Verizon to provide a daily, ongoing feed of all landline *metadata* (data about data) to the NSA. Metadata, in this case, include information about calls, such as time, who called, and who was called. They do not include the content of actual conversations. It soon came out that the FISA court had effectively granted the NSA the right to collect metadata on all phone calls, regardless of carrier.

The FISA court apparently justified the massive data collection through a "special needs" exception to the Fourth Amendment's requirement of a warrant for searches and seizures. It would seem that under this exception the Fourth Amendment does not apply to national security surveillance. These revelations touched off a massive debate between advocates of civil liberties and those concerned about national security.

Many of the actions authorized by the FISA court were based on the USA Patriot Act, which was passed in 2001 in the wake of the 9/11 terrorist attacks. In 2015, Congress passed the USA Freedom Act. This law reauthorized some of the actions permitted under the Patriot Act, but curbed others. The new law placed several new limits on surveillance authorized by the FISA court. In addition, the court was now required to release any new precedents that it might set, as well as any new guidance the court might issue on surveillance activities.

Alien "Removal Courts." In 1996, Congress passed the Anti-Terrorism and Effective Death Penalty Act. The new law was a response to the bombing of a federal building in 1995 in Oklahoma City, which killed 168 people. Even though the perpetrators of this crime were white U.S. citizens whose motives were entirely domestic, the new law focused on noncitizens. For example, the act created an alien "removal court" to hear evidence against suspected "alien terrorists." The judges in this court rule on whether there is probable cause for deportation. If so, a public deportation proceeding is held in a U.S. district court. The prosecution does not need to follow procedures that normally apply in criminal cases. In addition, the defendant cannot see the evidence that the prosecution used to secure the hearing.

The Federal Courts and Suspected Terrorists. After the 9/11 attacks, the U.S. military took custody of hundreds of suspected terrorists seized in Afghanistan and elsewhere and held them at Guantánamo Bay, Cuba. According to the Bush administration, they could be held indefinitely. The handling of the prisoners at Guantánamo has been a source of ongoing controversy. The Supreme Court held, first in 2004 and then in 2006, that the Bush administration's treatment of these detainees violated the U.S. Constitution.[2]

---

2. *Hamdi v. Rumsfeld,* 542 U.S. 507 (2004); *Hamdan v. Rumsfeld,* 548 U.S. 557 (2006).

In response to the Court's 2006 decision, Congress passed an act that eliminated federal court jurisdiction over challenges by these detainees based on *habeas corpus*. (This term refers to the right of a detained person to challenge the legality of his or her detention before a judge.) In 2008, in *Boumediene v. Bush*, the Court ruled that the provisions restricting the federal courts' jurisdictional authority over detainees' *habeas corpus* challenges were illegal.[3] The decision gave Guantánamo detainees the right to challenge their detention in federal civil courts. In 2010, however, a federal appeals court ruled that the administration had the right to detain prisoners indefinitely at Bagram Air Force Base in Afghanistan because the prison is located on foreign soil and within a war zone.[4]

The Supreme Court at Work

>>> **LO3:** Discuss the procedures used by the United States Supreme Court and the various types of opinions it hands down.

The Supreme Court begins its regular annual term on the first Monday in October and usually adjourns in late June or early July of the next year. Special sessions may be held after the regular term ends, but only a few cases are decided in this way. More commonly, cases are carried over until the next regular session.

Of the total number of cases that are decided each year in U.S. courts, those reviewed by the Supreme Court represent less than one in four thousand. Included in these, however, are decisions that profoundly affect our lives. In recent years, the United States Supreme Court has decided issues involving the right to bear arms, health-care reform, and campaign finance. Other cases have involved affirmative action programs, religious freedom, abortion, and many other matters with significant consequences for the nation.

Because the Supreme Court exercises a great deal of discretion over the types of cases it hears, it can influence the nation's policies by issuing decisions in some types of cases and refusing to hear appeals in others, thereby allowing lower court decisions to stand. Indeed, the fact that George W. Bush assumed the presidency in 2001 instead of Al Gore, his Democratic opponent, was largely due to a Supreme Court decision to review a Florida court's ruling. In *Bush v. Gore*, the Supreme Court reversed the Florida court's order to recount manually the votes in selected Florida counties—a decision that effectively handed the presidency to Bush.[5]

David Hume Kennerly/Getty Images

Justice Clarence Thomas with his clerks. *Why is a Supreme Court clerkship a desirable position for a young attorney?*

---

3. 553 U.S. 723 (2008).

4. *Maqaleh v. Gates,* 605 F.3d 84 (D.C.Cir. 2010).

5. 531 U.S. 98 (2000).

Which Cases Reach the Supreme Court?

Many people are surprised to learn that in a typical case, there is no absolute right of appeal to the Supreme Court. The Court's appellate jurisdiction is almost entirely discretionary—the Court chooses which cases it will decide. The justices never explain their reasons for hearing certain cases and not others, so it is difficult to predict which case or type of case the Court might select.

Factors That Bear on the Decision. A number of factors bear on the decision to accept a case. If a legal question has been decided differently by various lower courts, it may need resolution by the highest court. A ruling may be necessary if a lower court's decision conflicts with an existing Supreme Court ruling. In general, the Court considers whether the issue could have significance beyond the parties to the dispute. Another factor is whether the solicitor general is asking the Court to take a case. The solicitor general, a high-ranking presidential appointee within the Justice Department, represents the national government before the Supreme Court and promotes presidential policies in the federal courts. He or she decides what cases the government should request the Supreme Court to review and what position the government should take in cases before the Court.

Granting Petitions for Review. If the Court decides to grant a petition for review, it issues a **writ of** *certiorari* (pronounced sur-shee-uh-*rah*-ree). The writ orders a lower court to send the Supreme Court a record of the case for review. The vast majority of the petitions for review are denied. A denial is not a decision on the merits of a case, nor does it indicate agreement with the lower court's opinion. (The judgment of the lower court remains in force, however.) Therefore, denial of the writ has no value as a precedent. The Court will not issue a writ unless at least four justices approve of it. This is called the **rule of four.**[6]

Court Procedures

Once the Supreme Court grants *certiorari* in a particular case, the justices do extensive research on the legal issues and facts involved in the case. (Of course, some preliminary research is necessary before deciding to grant the petition for review.) Each justice is entitled to four law clerks, who undertake much of the research and preliminary drafting necessary for the justice to form an opinion.

The Court normally does not hear any evidence, as is true with all appeals courts. The Court's consideration of a case is based on the abstracts, the record, and the briefs. The attorneys are permitted to present **oral arguments.** Unlike the practice in most courts, lawyers addressing the Supreme Court can be (and often are) questioned by the justices at any time during oral arguments. All statements and the justices' questions during oral arguments are recorded.

Writ of *Certiorari*
An order issued by a higher court to a lower court to send up the record of a case for review.

Rule of Four
A United States Supreme Court procedure by which four justices must vote to grant a petition for review if a case is to come before the full court.

Oral Arguments
The arguments presented in person by attorneys to an appellate court.

---

6. The "rule of four" is modified when seven or fewer justices participate, which occurs from time to time. When that happens, as few as three justices can grant *certiorari*.

The justices meet to discuss and vote on cases in conferences held throughout the term. In these conferences, in addition to deciding cases already before the Court, the justices determine which new petitions for *certiorari* to grant. These conferences are strictly private—no stenographers, audio recorders, or video cameras are allowed.

Decisions and Opinions

When the Court has reached a decision, its opinion is written. The **opinion** contains the Court's ruling on the issue or issues presented, the reasons for its decision, the rules of law that apply, and other information. In many cases, the decision of the lower court is **affirmed,** resulting in the enforcement of that court's judgment or decree. If the Supreme Court believes that the lower court made the wrong decision, however, the decision will be **reversed**. Sometimes, the case will be **remanded** (sent back to the court that originally heard the case) for a new trial or other proceeding. For example, a lower court might have held that a party was not entitled to bring a lawsuit under a particular law. If the Supreme Court holds to the contrary, it will remand (send back) the case to the trial court with instructions that the trial go forward.

The Court's written opinion sometimes is unsigned. This is called an opinion *per curiam* ("by the court"). Typically, the Court's opinion is signed by all the justices who agree with it. When in the majority, the chief justice decides who writes the opinion and may write it personally. When the chief justice is in the minority, the senior justice on the majority side assigns the opinion.

Types of Opinions. When all justices unanimously agree on an opinion, the opinion is written for the entire Court (all the justices) and can be deemed a **unanimous opinion.** When there is not a unanimous opinion, a **majority opinion** is written, outlining the views of the majority of the justices involved in the case. Often, one or more justices who feel strongly about making or emphasizing a particular point that is not made or emphasized in the majority written opinion will write a **concurring opinion.** That means the justice writing the concurring opinion agrees (concurs) with the conclusion given in the majority written opinion but wants to make or clarify a particular point or to voice disapproval of the grounds on which the decision was made.

Note that it is also possible for a group of justices to issue a **plurality opinion.** Such an opinion does not represent a majority of the Court, but it will still decide the case because one or more concurring opinions agrees with its verdict.

Finally, in other than unanimous opinions, one or more dissenting opinions are usually written by those justices who do not agree with the majority. The **dissenting opinion** is important because it often forms the basis of the arguments used years later if the Court reverses the previous decision and establishes a new precedent.

Publishing Opinions. Shortly after opinions are written, the Supreme Court announces its decision from the bench. The clerk of the Court also releases opinions for online publication. Ultimately, the opinions are published in the *United States Reports*, which is the official printed record of the Court's decisions.

The Court's Dwindling Caseload. Some have complained that the Court reviews too few cases each term, thus giving the lower courts insufficient guidance on important issues. Indeed, the number of signed opinions issued by the Court has dwindled notably since the 1980s. For example, in its 1982–1983 term, the Court issued signed opinions in 151 cases. By the early 2000s, this number had dropped to between 70 and 80 per term. In the term ending in June 2017, the number was 70.

Opinion
A statement by a judge or a court of the decision reached in a case. An opinion sets forth the applicable law and details the reasoning on which the ruling was based.

Affirm
To declare that a court ruling is valid and must stand.

Reverse
To annul or make void a court ruling on account of some error or irregularity.

Remand
To send a case back to the court that originally heard it.

Unanimous Opinion
A court opinion or determination on which all judges agree.

Majority Opinion
A court opinion reflecting the views of the majority of the judges.

Concurring Opinion
A separate opinion prepared by a judge who supports the decision of the majority of the court but for different reasons.

Plurality Opinion
An opinion by a minority of the Court that decides a case because it is supported by one or more concurring opinions.

Dissenting Opinion
A separate opinion in which a judge dissents from (disagrees with) the conclusion reached by the majority of the court and expounds his or her own views about the case.

The Selection of Federal Judges

>>> **LO4:** Evaluate the manner in which federal judges are selected.

All federal judges are appointed. The Constitution, in Article II, Section 2, states that the president is to appoint the justices of the Supreme Court with the advice and consent of the Senate. Congress has established the same procedure for staffing other federal courts. This means that the Senate and the president jointly decide who shall fill every vacant judicial position, no matter what the level.

There are currently 874 federal judicial posts at all levels, although at any given time many of these positions are vacant. Once appointed to a federal judgeship, a person holds that job for life. Judges serve until they resign, retire voluntarily, or die. Federal judges who engage in blatantly illegal conduct may be removed through impeachment and conviction, although such action is rare. In contrast to federal judges, many state judges—including the judges who sit on state supreme courts—are chosen by the voters in elections. What arguments favor the election of judges? What problems can such a system create? We examine such questions in this chapter's *At Issue* feature.

Judicial Appointments

Candidates for federal judgeships are suggested to the president by the Department of Justice, senators, other judges, the candidates themselves, and lawyers' associations and other interest groups. In selecting a candidate to nominate for a judgeship, the president considers not only the person's competence but also other factors, including the person's political philosophy (as will be discussed shortly), ethnicity, and gender.

The nomination process—no matter how the nominees are obtained—always works the same way. The president makes the actual nomination, submitting the name to the Senate. To reach a conclusion, the Senate Judiciary Committee (operating through subcommittees) invites testimony, both written and oral, at its various hearings. The Senate then either confirms or rejects the nomination.

Federal District Court Judgeship Nominations. Although the president officially nominates federal judges, in the past the nomination of federal district court judges actually originated with a senator or senators of the president's party from the state in which there was a vacancy (if such a senator existed). In effect, judicial appointments were a form of political patronage. President Jimmy Carter (1977–1981) ended this tradition by establishing independent commissions to oversee the initial nomination process. President Ronald Reagan (1981–1989) abolished Carter's nominating commissions and established complete presidential control of nominations.

A practice used in the Senate, called **senatorial courtesy,** is a constraint on the president's freedom to appoint federal district judges. Senatorial courtesy allows a senator of the president's political party to veto a judicial appointment in her or his state. During much of American history, senators from the "opposition" party (the party to which the president does not belong) have also enjoyed the right of senatorial courtesy, although their veto power has varied over time.

Senatorial Courtesy
In federal district court judgeship nominations, a tradition allowing a senator to veto a judicial appointment in her or his state.

In 2000, Orrin Hatch, Republican chair of the Senate Judiciary Committee, announced that the opposition party (at that point, the Democrats) would no longer be allowed to invoke senatorial courtesy. When the Democrats took over the Senate following the elections of 2006, Senator Patrick J. Leahy (D., Vt.), chair of the Judiciary Committee, let it be known that the old bipartisan system of senatorial courtesy would return.

Should State Judges Be Elected?

The nation's founders sought to insulate the courts from popular passions, and as a result, all of the judges and justices in the federal court system are appointed by the president and confirmed by the Senate. Federal judges and justices are appointed for life. In thirty-nine states, in contrast, some or all state judges must face election and reelection.

The question of whether state judges should be elected or whether they should be appointed has proved to be very divisive. Many in the legal community agreed with a former Oregon Supreme Court justice, Hans A. Linde, when he pointed out that "to the rest of the world, American adherence to judicial elections is as incomprehensible as our rejection of the metric system." Public opinion polls, however, regularly show strong public support for electing judges.

The People's Will Should Prevail

Those who advocate the election of state judges see the issue as a simple matter of democracy. Judges cannot be insulated from politics. Governors who appoint judges are highly political creatures and are likely to appoint members of their own party. If politics is going to play a role, the people ought to have their say directly. In addition, researchers at the University of Chicago School of Law found that elected judges write more opinions than do appointed judges.

We let ordinary people participate in the legal process through the jury system, and they ought to be able to choose judges as well. That way, the people can be confident that judges will respond to popular concerns, such as the fear of crime. Without elections, judges living in safe, upscale neighborhoods may fail to appreciate what it is like to fear for your safety on an everyday basis.

Electing Judges Leads to Corruption

Former United States Supreme Court justice Sandra Day O'Connor condemned the practice of electing judges: "No other nation in the world does that because they realize you are not going to get fair and impartial judges that way." Opponents of judicial elections observe that most voters do not have enough information to make sensible choices when they vote for judicial candidates.

Judicial candidates raise considerable funds from the lawyers who will appear before them if they win. Additional campaign funds are raised by special interest groups. People in favor of electing judges think that the candidates they vote for will, for example, be "tough on crime." Often, they are. But those who oppose judicial elections contend that elected judges will also tilt toward the wealthy groups that put them in office, and away from the interests of ordinary people.

FOR CRITICAL ANALYSIS

In some states, judicial candidates are nominated by political parties. What consequences can follow from such explicit partisan identification?

Federal Courts of Appeals Appointments. There are many fewer federal courts of appeals appointments than federal district court appointments, but they are more influential. Federal appellate judges handle more important matters, and therefore presidents take a keener interest in the nomination process for such judgeships. Also, the U.S. courts of appeals have become "stepping-stones" to the Supreme Court.

Supreme Court Appointments. As you can see in Table 12–1, which summarizes the background of all Supreme Court justices to 2018, the most common occupational background of the justices at the time of their appointment has been private legal practice or state or federal judgeship. Those nine justices who were in federal executive posts at the time of their appointment held the high offices of secretary of state, comptroller of the treasury, secretary of the navy, postmaster general, secretary of the interior, chairman of the Securities and Exchange Commission, and secretary of labor. In the "Other" category under "Occupational Position before Appointment" in Table 12–1 are two justices who were professors of law (including William H. Taft, a former president) and one justice who was a North Carolina state employee with responsibility for organizing and revising the state's statutes.

TABLE 12–1	Background of Supreme Court Justices to 2018		
	Number of Justices (113 = Total)		**Number of Justices (113 = Total)**
Occupational Position before Appointment		**Political Party Affiliation**	
Federal judgeship	32	Federalist (to 1835)	13
Private legal practice	25	Jeffersonian Republican (to 1828)	7
State judgeship	21	Whig (to 1861)	1
U.S. attorney general	7	Democrat	46
Deputy or assistant U.S. attorney general	2	Republican	45
U.S. solicitor general	3	Independent	1
U.S. senator	6	**Age on Appointment**	
U.S. representative	2	Under 40	5
State governor	3	41–50	34
Federal executive post	9	51–60	60
Other	3	61–70	14
Religious Background		**Gender**	
Protestant	84	Male	109
Roman Catholic	14	Female	4
Jewish	7	**Race**	
Unitarian	7	White (non-Hispanic)	110
No religious affiliation	1	African American	2
Educational Background		Hispanic	1
College graduate	97		
Not a college graduate	16		

Sources: Congressional Quarterly, *Congressional Quarterly's Guide to the U.S. Supreme Court* (Washington, D.C.: Congressional Quarterly Press, 1996); and authors' updates.

Partisanship and Judicial Appointments

In most circumstances, the president appoints judges or justices who belong to the president's own political party. Presidents see their federal judiciary appointments as the one sure way to institutionalize their political views long after they have left office. By 1993, for example, Presidents Ronald Reagan and George H. W. Bush together had appointed nearly three-quarters of all federal court judges. This preponderance of Republican-appointed federal judges strengthened the legal moorings of the conservative social agenda on a variety of issues, ranging from abortion to civil rights. President Bill Clinton, a Democrat, had the opportunity to appoint 371 federal district and appeals court judges, thereby shifting the ideological makeup of the federal judiciary. George W. Bush appointed 322 federal district and appeals court judges, again ensuring a majority of Republican-appointed judges in the federal courts. Barack Obama then appointed a total of 329 judges, and the balance shifted again.

Supreme Court Appointments by Bush. President George W. Bush also had the opportunity to fill two Supreme Court vacancies, those left by the death of Chief Justice William Rehnquist and by the retirement of Justice Sandra Day O'Connor. Bush appointed two conservatives to these positions—John G. Roberts, Jr., who became chief justice, and Samuel Alito, Jr., who replaced O'Connor. The appointment of Alito, in particular, strengthened the rightward movement of the Court that had begun years before with the appointment of Rehnquist as chief justice. This was because Alito was a reliable member of the Court's conservative wing, whereas O'Connor had been a "swing voter."

Supreme Court Appointments by Obama. President Barack Obama had two opportunities to fill Supreme Court vacancies in the first two years of his term. The vacancies resulted from the retirement of justices David Souter and John Paul Stevens. Both had been members of the Court's so-called liberal wing, so Obama's appointments did not change the ideological balance of the Court. Obama chose two women: Sonia Sotomayor, who had been an appeals court judge and is the Court's first Hispanic member, and Elena Kagan, who had been Obama's solicitor general.

The Senate's Role

Ideology also plays a large role in the Senate's confirmation hearings, and presidential nominees to the Supreme Court have not always been confirmed. In fact, almost 20 percent of presidential nominations to the Supreme Court have either been rejected or not been acted on by the Senate.

Controversial Supreme Court Appointments. One of the most memorable of these rejections was the Senate's refusal to confirm Robert Bork—an unusually conservative nominee—in 1987. Many observers saw the Bork confirmation battle as a turning point after which confirmations became much more partisan. Another controversial appointment was that of Clarence Thomas, who underwent a volatile and acrimonious confirmation hearing in 1991, replete with charges against him of sexual harassment. He was ultimately confirmed by the Senate, nonetheless.

President Clinton had little trouble gaining approval for both of his nominees to the Supreme Court: Ruth Bader Ginsburg and Stephen G. Breyer. President George W. Bush's nominees faced hostile grilling in their confirmation hearings, however, and Bush was forced to withdraw the nomination of White House counsel Harriet Miers when it became clear she would not be confirmed.

The Controversy Following the Death of Justice Scalia. In February 2016, Justice Antonin Scalia died unexpectedly. Scalia had been the lion of the Court's conservative wing. (It is a sign of the Court's collegiality that Scalia was also a close personal friend of liberal Justice Ruth Ginsburg.) President Obama then nominated as Scalia's replacement Merrick Garland, a respected appeals court judge. Garland was as moderate a judge as Obama could be expected to name. By replacing Scalia, however, Garland would inevitably swing the Court to the left.

The nomination was issued in the middle of the 2016 presidential primaries. Republicans in the Senate recognized that if they could postpone action on Scalia's replacement until 2017, there was a chance that a new Republican president might make the nomination. Senate Republicans therefore announced that they would not even hold hearings on Garland's nomination. While not unprecedented, this was a relatively unusual and unpopular step, and it showed how thoroughly political the nomination process had become.

Republican Donald Trump was in fact elected president. As one of his first acts following his inauguration, he nominated Neil Gorsuch to the Court. An appeals court judge, Gorsuch was widely respected and also quite conservative. Democrats, angered over the treatment of

Garland, filibustered the appointment. Republicans then abolished the filibuster as it applies to Supreme Court appointments. Gorsuch was confirmed and took office in April 2017.

Lower Court Appointment Battles. Presidents have often had great trouble with appointments to district and appeals courts. For an extended period during the presidency of Bill Clinton, the Republican majority in Congress adopted a strategy of trying to block almost every action taken by the administration—including judicial appointments.

The modern understanding that sixty votes are required before the Senate will consider a major measure has given the minority party significant power as well. After 2000, the Democratic minority in the Senate was able to hold up many of George W. Bush's more controversial judicial appointments. Frustrated Republican senators threatened to use the "nuclear option," under which Senate rules would be revised to disallow filibusters against judicial nominees. In the end, a bipartisan group engineered a compromise to preserve the filibuster.

President Obama also had considerable difficulty in getting his judicial candidates approved by the Senate. This was especially true after the 2010 elections, when a number of newly elected Republicans replaced Democratic senators. Democratic frustration with Republican blocking tactics came to a head in 2013. In that year, Democrats exercised the "nuclear option," abolishing filibusters against executive branch nominees and all judicial nominees other than to the Supreme Court. As noted, in 2017 the abolition of the filibuster was extended to Supreme Court nominees.

Policymaking and the Courts

>>> **LO5:** Consider the ways in which the Supreme Court makes policy, and explain the forces that limit the activism of the courts.

The partisan battles over judicial appointments reflect an important reality in today's American government: the importance of the judiciary in national politics. Because appointments to the federal bench are for life, the ideology of judicial appointees can affect national policy for years to come. Although the primary function of judges in our system of government is to interpret and apply the laws, inevitably judges make policy when carrying out this task. One of the major policymaking tools of the federal courts is their power of judicial review.

Judicial Review

The power of the courts to determine whether a law or action by the other branches of government is constitutional is known as the power of *judicial review*. This power enables the judicial branch to act as a check on the other two branches of government, in line with the system of checks and balances established by the U.S. Constitution.

The power of judicial review is not mentioned in the Constitution, however. Rather, it was established by the United States Supreme Court's decision in *Marbury v. Madison*.[7] In that case, in which the Court declared that a law passed by Congress violated the Constitution, the Court claimed such a power for the judiciary:

> *It is emphatically the province and duty of the Judicial Department to say what the law is. Those who apply the rule to a particular case must of necessity expound and interpret that rule. If two laws conflict with each other, the courts must decide on the operation of each.*

---

7. 5 U.S. 137 (1803).

If a federal court declares that a federal or state law or policy is unconstitutional, the court's decision affects the application of the law or policy only within that court's jurisdiction. For this reason, the higher the level of the court, the greater the impact of the decision on society. Because of the Supreme Court's national jurisdiction, its decisions have the greatest impact. For example, when the Supreme Court held that an Arkansas state constitutional amendment limiting the terms of congresspersons was unconstitutional, laws establishing term limits in twenty-three other states also were invalidated.[8]

Judicial Activism and Judicial Restraint

Judicial scholars like to characterize judges and justices as being either "activist" or "restraintist."

Judicial Activism. The doctrine of **judicial activism** rests on the conviction that the federal judiciary should take an active role by using its powers to check the activities of Congress, state legislatures, and administrative agencies when those governmental bodies exceed their authority. One of the Supreme Court's most activist eras was the period from 1953 to 1969, when the Court was headed by Chief Justice Earl Warren. The Warren Court propelled the civil rights movement forward by holding, among other things, that laws permitting racial segregation violated the equal protection clause.

Chief Justice John Roberts. *Which president nominated Roberts to be chief justice?*

Judicial Restraint. In contrast, the doctrine of **judicial restraint** rests on the assumption that the courts should defer to the decisions made by the legislative and executive branches, because members of Congress and the president are elected by the people, whereas members of the federal judiciary are not. Because administrative agency personnel normally have more expertise than the courts do in the areas regulated by the agencies, the courts likewise should defer to agency rules and decisions. In other words, under the doctrine of judicial restraint, the courts should not thwart the implementation of legislative acts and agency rules unless they are clearly unconstitutional.

Political Implications. In the past, judicial activism was often linked with liberalism, and judicial restraint with conservatism. In fact, though, a conservative judge can be activist, just as a liberal judge can be restraintist. In the 1950s and 1960s, the Supreme Court was activist and liberal. Some observers believe that the Roberts Court, with its conservative majority, has become increasingly activist over time.

The *Citizens United v. Federal Election Commission* decision, in which the Court struck down long-standing campaign finance laws, lends credence to this view. Some believed that the Court was stepping back from conservative judicial activism when it upheld most of Obama's health-care reform legislation in June 2012. In fact, however, the Court's decision was mostly based on precedent. In one major departure from precedent, the Court set new limits on the commerce clause, a conservative goal. These limits did not change the outcome of the case, however.

Other terms that are often used to describe a justice's philosophy are *strict construction* and *broad construction*. Justices who believe in strict construction look to the "letter of the law" when they attempt to interpret the Constitution or a particular statute. Those who favor broad construction try to determine the context and purpose of the law.

Judicial Activism
A doctrine holding that the federal judiciary should take an active role by using its powers to check the activities of governmental bodies when those bodies exceed their authority.

Judicial Restraint
A doctrine holding that courts should defer to the decisions made by the elected representatives of the people in the legislative and executive branches when possible.

8. *U.S. Term Limits, Inc. v. Thornton*, 514 U.S. 779 (1995).

The Roberts Court

John Roberts became chief justice in 2005, following the death of Chief Justice William H. Rehnquist. Replacing one conservative chief justice with another did not immediately change the Court's ideological balance. The real change came in January 2006, when Samuel Alito replaced Sandra Day O'Connor. Unlike O'Connor, Alito was firmly in the conservative camp. This fact had consequences. In a 2007 case, for example, the Court upheld a 2003 federal law banning partial birth abortion, by a close (five-to-four) vote.[9] The Supreme Court's conservative drift continued in the following years. In 2008, for example, the Court established the right of individuals to own guns for private use.[10] It also upheld lethal injection as an execution method.[11]

The Nature of the Court's Conservatism. Although the Roberts Court is widely characterized as conservative, its philosophy is not identical to the conservatism of the Republicans in

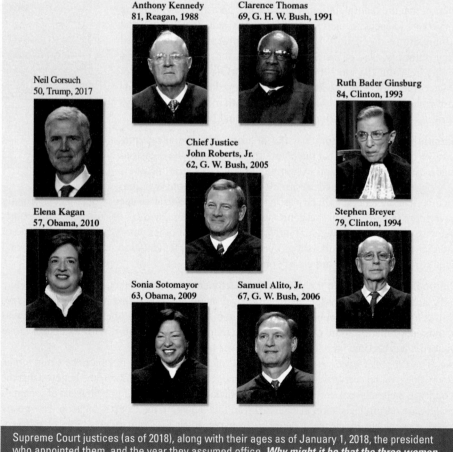

Neil Gorsuch
50, Trump, 2017

Anthony Kennedy
81, Reagan, 1988

Clarence Thomas
69, G. H. W. Bush, 1991

Ruth Bader Ginsburg
84, Clinton, 1993

Chief Justice
John Roberts, Jr.
62, G. W. Bush, 2005

Elena Kagan
57, Obama, 2010

Stephen Breyer
79, Clinton, 1994

Sonia Sotomayor
63, Obama, 2009

Samuel Alito, Jr.
67, G. W. Bush, 2006

United States Supreme Court; Alex Wong/Getty Images News/Getty Images

Supreme Court justices (as of 2018), along with their ages as of January 1, 2018, the president who appointed them, and the year they assumed office. *Why might it be that the three women were all appointed by Democratic presidents?*

9. *Gonzales v. Carhart*, 550 U.S. 124 (2007).
10. *District of Columbia v. Heller*, 554 U.S. 570 (2008).
11. *Baze v. Rees*, 553 U.S. 35 (2008).

Congress or the broader conservative movement. True, justices such as Thomas could rightly be characterized as in full agreement with the conservative movement. Justice Kennedy and even Chief Justice Roberts, however, clearly "march to their own drummer." As one example, the Court has shown a degree of sympathy for the rights of gay men and lesbians that cannot be found in the Republican Party platform. It was Justice Kennedy, after all, who in 2003 wrote the opinion in *Lawrence v. Texas* striking down laws that ban gay sex nationwide.[12] Chief Justice Roberts demonstrated his independence in 2012 by authoring the opinion that affirmed the constitutionality of Obamacare.[13]

The Supreme Court expanded upon those rulings in the following years. In *King v. Burwell*, the Court turned back another challenge to the Affordable Care Act.[14] In *Obergefell v. Hodges*, the Court established a nationwide constitutional right to same-sex marriage.[15] Both of these rulings were liberal victories. Not all of the term's rulings were liberal, however. The Court refused to block Oklahoma's use of a controversial drug in executing condemned prisoners.[16]

Recent Court Rulings. The death of Justice Scalia in February 2016 left the Court with a four-to-four split between conservative and liberal justices. For the next fourteen months, the Court was at least somewhat more liberal than before. The four-to-four split also raised the possibility of tie votes. When that happens, the decision of the lower court is sustained. The Court's action does not, however, serve as a precedent. Chief Justice Roberts sought consensus on the Court, but a few four-to-four deadlocks did occur. For example, a four-to-four split sustained a lower court ruling that allowed teachers' unions to collect service fees from nonmembers.[17]

The Court decided few important cases in the term ending in 2017. Still, conservatives were pleased when the Court found that Missouri cannot deny a grant to upgrade a playground solely because the playground belonged to a church.[18] The Court also determined that Muslims subject to illegal treatment by federal officials in the months following 9/11 cannot sue those officials for monetary damages.[19] Liberals were heartened by a ruling that a North Carolina redistricting plan amounted to unlawful racial gerrymandering.[20] With Justice Gorsuch now on board, the Court was poised to issue a large number of crucial decisions in the 2017–2018 term.

What Checks Our Courts?

Our judicial system is one of the most independent in the world. But the courts do not have absolute independence, for they are part of the political process. Political checks limit the extent to which courts can exercise judicial review and engage in an activist policy. These checks are exercised by the executive branch, the legislature, the public, and, finally, the judiciary itself.

Executive Checks. President Andrew Jackson was once supposed to have said, after Chief Justice John Marshall made an unpopular decision, "John Marshall has made his decision; now let him enforce it."[21] This purported remark goes to the heart of **judicial implementation**—the

Judicial Implementation
The way in which court decisions are translated into action.

12. 539 U.S. 558 (2003).
13. *National Federation of Independent Business v. Sebelius*, 132 S.Ct. 2566 (2012).
14. 576 U.S. ___ (2015).
15. 576 U.S. ___ (2015).
16. *Glossip v. Gross*, 576 U.S. ___ (2015).
17. *Friedrichs v. California Teachers Association*, 578 U.S. ___ (2016).
18. *Trinity Lutheran Church v. Comer*, ___ U.S. ___ (2017).
19. *Ziglar v. Abbasi*, ___ U.S. ___ (2017).
20. *Cooper v. Harris*, ___ U.S. ___ (2017).
21. The decision that Jackson was referring to was *Cherokee Nation v. Georgia*, 30 U.S. 1 (1831).

The late Justice Antonin Scalia, who died in 2016. *What was Scalia's judicial philosophy?*

Tim Sloan/AFP/Getty Images

enforcement of judicial decisions in such a way that those decisions are translated into policy. The Supreme Court simply does not have any enforcement powers, and whether a decision will be implemented depends on the cooperation of the other two branches of government. Rarely, though, will a president refuse to enforce a Supreme Court decision, as President Jackson did.

Executives at the state level may also refuse to implement court decisions with which they disagree. A notable example of such a refusal occurred in Arkansas after the Supreme Court ordered schools to desegregate "with all deliberate speed" in 1955.[22] Arkansas governor Orval Faubus refused to cooperate with the decision and used the state's National Guard to block the integration of Central High School in Little Rock. Ultimately, President Dwight Eisenhower had to federalize the Arkansas National Guard to force it to stand down and also send federal troops to Little Rock to quell the violence that had erupted.

Legislative Checks. Courts may make rulings, but often the legislatures at local, state, and federal levels are required to appropriate funds to carry out the courts' rulings. A court, for example, may decide that prison conditions must be improved, but it is up to the legislature to authorize the funds necessary to carry out the ruling. When such funds are not appropriated, the court that made the ruling, in effect, has been checked.

Courts' rulings can be overturned by constitutional amendments at both the federal and the state levels. For example, the Sixteenth Amendment to the U.S. Constitution, ratified in 1913, overturned a United States Supreme Court ruling that found the income tax to be unconstitutional.

Finally, Congress or a state legislature can rewrite (amend) old laws or enact new ones to overturn a court's rulings if the legislature concludes that the court is interpreting laws or legislative intentions erroneously. For example, in 2009 Congress passed (and President Obama signed) the Lilly Ledbetter Fair Pay Act, which resets the statute of limitations for filing an equal-pay lawsuit each time an employer issues a discriminatory paycheck. The law was a direct answer to *Ledbetter v. Goodyear*, in which the Supreme Court held that the statute of limitations begins at the date the pay was agreed upon, not at the date of the most recent paycheck.[23] The new legislation made it much easier for employees to win pay discrimination lawsuits.

Public Opinion. Public opinion plays a significant role in shaping government policy, and certainly the judiciary is not excepted from this rule. One problem is that persons affected by a Supreme Court decision that is contrary to their views may simply ignore it. Officially sponsored prayers were banned in public schools in 1962, yet it was widely known that the ban was (and still is) ignored in many southern and rural districts. What can the courts do in this situation? Unless someone complains about the prayers and initiates a lawsuit, the courts can do nothing.

Naturally, liberal and conservative justices may look to different strands of public opinion. With conservative majorities, the Court tended to reflect conservative opinion. Two cases on states' rights illustrate this tendency. In 1995, the Court held, for the first time in

---

22. *Brown v. Board of Education*, 349 U.S. 294 (1955)—referred to as the second *Brown* decision.
23. 550 U.S. 618 (2007).

sixty years, that Congress had overreached its powers under the commerce clause when it attempted to regulate the possession of guns in school zones. According to the Court, the possession of guns in school zones had nothing to do with the commerce clause.[24] Yet in a 2005 case, the Court ruled that Congress's power to regulate commerce allowed it to ban marijuana use even when a state law permitted such use, and the growing and use of the drug were strictly local in nature.[25] What these two rulings had in common was that they supported policies generally considered to be conservative—the right to possess firearms on the one hand, and strict laws against marijuana on the other.

Judicial Traditions and Doctrines. Supreme Court justices (and other federal judges) typically exercise self-restraint in fashioning their decisions. To a large degree, this restraint is mandated by various judicially established traditions and doctrines. For example, in exercising its discretion to hear appeals, the Supreme Court will not hear a meritless appeal just so it can rule on the issue.

Also, when reviewing a case, the Supreme Court frequently narrows its focus to just one issue involved in the case. In the past, the court has rarely made broad, sweeping decisions on issues. Furthermore, the doctrine of *stare decisis* acts as a restraint because it obligates the courts, including the Supreme Court, to follow established precedents when deciding cases. Only rarely will courts overrule a precedent.

Hypothetical and Political Questions. As already mentioned, the courts will hear only what are called justiciable disputes—disputes that arise out of actual cases. In other words, a court will not hear a case that involves a merely hypothetical issue.

Additionally, if a political question is involved, the Supreme Court often will exercise judicial restraint and refuse to rule on the matter. A **political question** is one that the Supreme Court declares should be decided by the elected branches of government—the executive branch, the legislative branch, or those two branches acting together. For example, the Supreme Court has refused to rule on whether women in the military should be allowed to serve in combat units, preferring instead to defer to the executive branch's decisions on the matter. (In January 2013, the Department of Defense lifted the ban on women serving in combat units.) Generally, though, fewer questions are deemed political questions by the Supreme Court today than in the past.

The Impact of the Lower Courts. Higher courts can reverse the decisions of lower courts. Lower courts can act as a check on higher courts, too. Lower courts can ignore—and have ignored—Supreme Court decisions. Usually, they do so indirectly. A lower court might conclude, for example, that the precedent set by the Supreme Court does not apply to the exact circumstances in the case before the court. Alternatively, the lower court may decide that the Supreme Court's decision was ambiguous with respect to the issue before the lower court. The fact that the Supreme Court rarely makes broad and clear-cut statements makes it easier for lower courts to interpret the Supreme Court's decisions in different ways.

Mario Tama/Getty Images News/Getty Images

Justice Neil Gorsuch became the latest member of the Supreme Court in 2017, replacing the late Justice Antonin Scalia. *Why was the nomination of Gorsuch controversial?*

Political Question
An issue that a court believes should be decided by the executive or legislative branch, or both.

---

24. *United States v. Lopez*, 514 U.S. 549 (1995).
25. *Gonzales v. Raich*, 545 U.S. 1 (2005).

Changing the Legal System

The U.S. legal system may seem too complex to be influenced by one individual, but its power nonetheless depends on the support of individuals. The public has many ways of resisting, modifying, or overturning statutes and rulings of the courts.

Why Should You Care? You may find it worthwhile to attend one or more court sessions to see how the law works. Legislation is given its practical form by court rulings. Therefore, if you care about the effects of a particular law, pay attention to how the courts are interpreting it. For example, do you believe that sentences handed down for certain crimes are too lenient—or too strict?

What Can You Do? Public opinion can have an effect on judicial policies. There is probably an organization that pursues lawsuits to benefit whichever causes that you support. A prime example is the modern women's movement, which undertook long series of lawsuits to change the way women are treated in American life. The courts only rule on cases that are brought before them, and the women's movement changed American law by filing— and winning—case after case.

- In 1965, a federal circuit court opened a wide range of jobs for women by overturning laws that kept women out of work that was "too hard" for them.
- In 1974, the Court ruled that employers could not use the "going market rate" to justify lower wages for women.
- In 1978, an Oregon court became the first of many to find that a man could be prosecuted for raping his wife.

Today, groups such as the National Organization for Women continue to support lawsuits to advance women's rights.

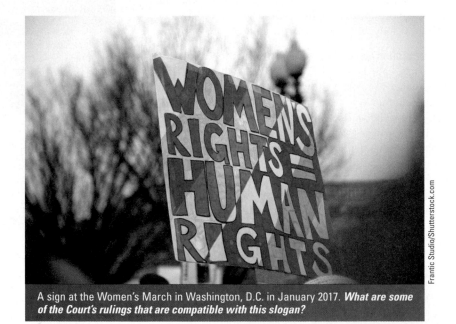

Frantic Studio/Shutterstock.com

A sign at the Women's March in Washington, D.C. in January 2017. *What are some of the Court's rulings that are compatible with this slogan?*

Key Terms

affirm 281	federal question 274	litigate 274	senatorial courtesy 282
amicus curiae brief 274	general jurisdiction 275	majority opinion 281	*stare decisis* 272
appellate court 276	judicial activism 287	opinion 281	trial court 275
case law 273	judicial	oral arguments 280	unanimous opinion 281
class-action suit 274	implementation 289	plurality opinion 281	writ of *certiorari* 280
common law 272	judicial restraint 287	political question 291	
concurring opinion 281	jurisdiction 274	precedent 272	
dissenting opinion 281	justiciable	remand 281	
diversity of	controversy 274	reverse 281	
citizenship 274	limited jurisdiction 275	rule of four 280	

Chapter Summary

»»LO1 American law is rooted in the common law tradition. The common law doctrine of *stare decisis* (which means "to stand on decided cases") obligates judges to follow precedents established previously by their own courts or by higher courts that have authority over them. Precedents established by the United States Supreme Court, the highest court in the land, are binding on all lower courts. Fundamental sources of American law include the U.S. Constitution and state constitutions, statutes enacted by legislative bodies, regulations issued by administrative agencies, and case law.

»»LO2 Article III, Section 1, of the U.S. Constitution limits the jurisdiction of the federal courts to cases involving (a) a federal question, which is a question based, at least in part, on the U.S. Constitution, a treaty, or a federal law, or (b) diversity of citizenship, which arises when parties to a lawsuit are from different states or when the lawsuit involves a foreign citizen or government.

The federal court system is a three-tiered model consisting of (a) U.S. district (trial) courts and various lower courts of limited jurisdiction, (b) intermediate U.S. courts of appeals, and (c) the United States Supreme Court. Cases may be appealed from the district courts to the appellate courts. In most cases, the decisions of the federal appellate courts are final because the Supreme Court hears relatively few cases.

»»LO3 The Supreme Court's decision to review a case is influenced by many factors, including the significance of the issues involved and whether the solicitor general is asking the Court to take the case. After a case is accepted, the justices undertake research (with the help of their law clerks) on the issues involved in the case, hear oral arguments from the parties, meet in conference to discuss and vote on the issues, and announce one or more opinions, which are then released for publication. Types of opinions include unanimous, majority, plurality, concurring, and dissenting opinions.

»»LO4 Federal judges are nominated by the president and confirmed by the Senate. Once appointed, they hold office for life, barring gross misconduct. The nomination and confirmation process, particularly for Supreme Court justices, is often extremely politicized. Democrats and Republicans alike realize that justices may occupy seats on the Court for decades and want to have persons appointed who share their views. Nearly 20 percent of all presidential nominations to the Supreme Court have either been rejected or not acted on by the Senate.

»»LO5 In interpreting and applying the law, judges inevitably become policymakers. The most important policymaking tool of the federal courts is the power of judicial review. This power was not mentioned specifically in the Constitution, but the Supreme Court claimed this power for the federal courts in its 1803 decision in *Marbury v. Madison*.

Judges who take an active role in checking the activities of the other branches of government sometimes are characterized as "activist" judges, and judges who defer to the decisions of the other branches sometimes are regarded as "restraintist" judges. The Warren Court of the 1950s and 1960s was activist in a liberal direction, whereas the Roberts Court has become increasingly activist in a conservative direction.

Checks on the powers of the federal courts include executive checks, legislative checks, public opinion, and judicial traditions and doctrines.

Test Yourself

1. One important source of American law is:
   a. the rights and duties of workers as expressed in employment agreements.
   b. case law based in part on the common law tradition.
   c. case law based in part on the federal tradition.

2. The supreme law of the land in the United States is:
   a. the Bible.
   b. the Declaration of Independence.
   c. the United States Constitution.

3. To bring a lawsuit, a party must show that he or she suffered an actual harm or is threatened by an actual harm as a result of the action that led to the dispute. If so, then that party has:
   a. a federal question.
   b. standing to sue.
   c. jurisdiction.

4. The distinction between federal district courts and federal appellate courts can be summarized by the following statement:
   a. federal district courts are trial courts that hear evidence, but federal appellate courts do not hear evidence.
   b. federal district courts only hear appeals from federal appellate courts.
   c. federal appellate courts only accept cases involving state constitutions.

5. The secret court set up to issue warrants in national security cases is called:
   a. the FISA court.
   b. the Court of Federal Claims.
   c. an administrative law tribunal.

6. "I'll take it all the way to the Supreme Court." A lawyer cannot truthfully promise this because:
   a. the Supreme Court may be too far away from the state in which the controversy occurred.
   b. the Supreme Court hears only a limited number of cases in which a federal question is involved.
   c. the Supreme Court is not in session for a full twelve months each year.

7. Supreme Court justices who do not agree with the majority opinion of the Court often write a:
   a. concurring opinion.
   b. dissenting opinion.
   c. plurality opinion.

8. U.S. senators have considerable power over federal judicial appointments in each senator's own state due to the tradition of:
   a. senatorial courtesy.
   b. seniority.
   c. presidential restraint.

9. The most common occupational position held by a Supreme Court justice before appointment has been:
   a. U.S. senator.
   b. state governor.
   c. federal judgeship.

10. When a federal court declares that a federal or state law or policy is unconstitutional, that court is engaging in:
    a. judicial review.
    b. congressional condemnation.
    c. administrative oversight.

11. **The belief that the federal judiciary should actively use its powers to check the laws passed by Congress and state legislatures is called:**
    a. broad construction.
    b. judicial restraint.
    c. judicial activism.

2. In "Public Opinion" in the section "What Checks Our Courts," we described how the Supreme Court ruled in favor of states' rights in a gun-control case and against states' rights in a marijuana case. Why do you think the justices might have come to different conclusions in these two cases?

Essay Questions

1. What are the benefits of having lifetime appointments to the United States Supreme Court? What problems might such appointments cause? What would be the likely result if Supreme Court justices faced term limits?

Domestic and Economic Policy

A Texas worker unloads a mixture of oil, sediment, and water generated during hydraulic fracturing (fracking). Components of the mixture will be separated and either recycled or eliminated. *Why is fracking controversial?*

Bloomberg/Getty Images

The five **Learning Outcomes (LOs)** below are designed to help improve your understanding of this chapter. After reading this chapter, you should be able to:

>>> **LO1** Describe the five steps of the policymaking process, using the Affordable Care Act as an example.

>>> **LO2** Explain why illegal immigration is seen as a problem, and cite some of the steps that have been taken in response to it.

>>> **LO3** Evaluate how the nation has reacted to its reliance on foreign oil and the controversy over climate change.

>>> **LO4** Define *unemployment, inflation, fiscal policy, public debt*, and *monetary policy*.

>>> **LO5** Describe the various taxes that Americans pay, and discuss some of the controversies surrounding taxation.

Check your understanding of the material with the Test Yourself section at the end of the chapter.

Domestic Policy
All government laws, planning, and actions that concern internal issues of national importance, such as health care, the environment, and the economy.

art of the public-policy debate in our nation involves domestic problems. **Domestic policy** can be defined as all laws, government planning, and government actions that concern internal issues of national importance. Consequently, the span of such policies is enormous. Domestic policies range from relatively simple issues, such as what the speed limit should be on interstate highways, to more complex ones, such as how best to protect our environment. Many of our domestic policies are formulated and implemented by the federal government, but a number of others are the result of the combined efforts of federal, state, and local governments.

We can define several types of domestic policy. *Regulatory policy* seeks to define what is and is not legal. Setting speed limits is obviously regulatory policy. *Redistributive policy* transfers income from certain individuals or groups to others, often based on the belief that these transfers enhance fairness. Social Security is an example. *Promotional policy* seeks to foster or discourage various economic or social activities, typically through subsidies and tax breaks. A tax credit for buying a fuel-efficient car would qualify as promotional. Typically, whenever a policy decision is made, some groups will be better off and some groups will be hurt. All policymaking generally involves such a dilemma.

In this chapter, we look at domestic policy issues involving health care, immigration, and energy and the environment. This chapter's *At Issue* feature looks at how state governments have handled the minimum wage issue. We also examine national

AT ISSUE

Should States Raise the Minimum Wage?

A minimum wage is the lowest wage rate that an employer can legally pay. The national minimum wage is set by Congress. Currently, it is $7.25 per hour. Australia has the world's highest such wage—$13.21 in U.S. dollars.

Thirty-one states now have a minimum wage higher than the national rate. The New Mexico rate is only 25 cents more than the national minimum. As of January 2017, Massachusetts and Washington had the highest state minimum wages at $11.00 per hour. A national movement has grown up around raising the minimum wage to $15.00 per hour, and a number of state and local governments have backed this effort. California, the District of Columbia, New York, and the city of Seattle are phasing in a $15.00 minimum wage over a period of years.

Minimum-wage laws are generally popular with voters. In a recent poll, 90 percent of Democrats and 53 percent of Republicans supported a higher minimum wage. Economists, however, are much less likely to favor such laws than are average voters.

Higher Minimum Wages Kill Jobs

Most conservative politicians—and many economists who aren't necessarily that conservative—oppose minimum-wage laws. Obviously, hiking the minimum wage raises the pay of the lowest-paid workers. These workers become more expensive to hire. It is basic economics that in normal circumstances, if something costs more, people will buy less of it. A higher minimum wage should therefore reduce the number of low-wage jobs.

Many minimum-wage workers are employed by fast-food restaurants and retail stores that cater to the poor. If minimum wages continue to rise, these businesses may need to raise their prices to recoup lost profits. The result: more expensive food and clothing for other low-income workers. Ultimately, no businessperson will consistently pay a worker a wage rate that exceeds the value of that worker's output. Teenagers—especially minorities—who cannot find a minimum-wage job would lose out on the opportunity to learn basic work skills that could help them find better jobs later.

Higher Minimum Wages Are Good Policy

Advocates of raising minimum wages accept that higher wages would reduce employment if they were set very high. Advocates also argue, however, that the modest increases in the minimum wage seen in many states do not in fact have such a result—the employment effect of these wage increases is so small we can't reliably measure it. For example, at the Idaho–Washington border, there appears to be no tendency to shift fast-food employment to the Idaho side, even though Idaho has no state minimum wage and the Washington rate is relatively high.

Higher minimum wages can lift many of the working poor out of poverty. We can also predict that with a higher minimum wage, there would be less turnover—workers would stay longer in low-wage jobs. Finally, it's worth noting that the stereotype of a minimum-wage worker as a teenager is not accurate. The average age of minimum-wage workers is thirty-five, and 88 percent are at least twenty years old. Paying workers a living wage is only fair.

FOR CRITICAL ANALYSIS

If a San Francisco bookstore closes because it can't afford to pay its clerks the California minimum wage, would you blame the minimum-wage law—or Amazon?

economic policies undertaken by the federal government—for example, the issue of the federal budget deficit. As we analyze the first of these issues, health care, we consider how public policy is made.

The Policymaking Process: Health Care as an Example

>>> **LO1:** Describe the five steps of the policymaking process, using the Affordable Care Act as an example.

How does any issue get resolved? First, of course, the issue must be identified as a problem. Often, policymakers have only to open their local newspapers or letters from their constituents to discover that a problem is brewing. On rare occasions, a crisis—such as that brought about by the terrorist attacks of September 11, 2001—creates the need to formulate policy. Like most Americans, however, policymakers receive much of their information from the national media. Finally, various lobbying groups provide information to members of Congress.

No matter how simple or how complex the problem, those who make policy follow a number of steps. We can divide the process of policymaking into five steps: (1) agenda building, (2) policy formulation, (3) policy adoption, (4) policy implementation, and (5) policy evaluation. The health-care legislation passed in 2010 can be used to illustrate this process. Although this legislation passed several years ago, it remains a major political issue to this day.

In March 2010, President Barack Obama signed into law the **Affordable Care Act (ACA)**, a massive overhaul of the nation's health-care funding system. A few days later, Obama signed the Health Care and Education Reconciliation Act, a series of adjustments to the main legislative package. These measures constitute the most important legislative package in the United States since 2010. They have become known by the nickname *Obamacare*.

Health Care: Agenda Building

First of all, an issue must get on the agenda. In other words, Congress must become aware that a problem requires congressional action. Agenda building may occur as the result of a crisis, a technological change, or a mass media campaign, as well as through the efforts of strong political personalities and effective lobbying groups. To understand how health care came to be an important issue and how health-care reform became part of the national agenda, we need to examine the background of the issue.

Health Care's Role in the American Economy. Spending for health care is now estimated to account for almost 18 percent of the total U.S. economy. In 1965, about 6 percent of our national income was spent on health care, but that percentage has been increasing ever since, as you can see in Figure 13-1. Per capita spending on health care is greater in the United States than almost anywhere else in the world. Measured by the percentage of the **gross domestic product (GDP)** devoted to health care, America spends about 70 percent more than Britain or Canada. (The GDP is the dollar value of all final goods and services produced in a one-year period.)

As of 2010, before the reform legislation was implemented, government spending on health care constituted about 50 percent of total health-care spending. Private insurance accounted for more than 30 percent of payments for health care. The remainder—less than 20 percent—was paid directly by individuals or by charities. The government programs **Medicare** and **Medicaid** are the main sources of hospital and other medical

---

Affordable Care Act (ACA)
A law passed in 2010 that seeks, among other things, to provide health-care insurance to all American citizens. The act has been nicknamed "Obamacare."

Gross Domestic Product (GDP)
The dollar value of all final goods and services produced in a one-year period.

Medicare
A federal health-insurance program that covers U.S. residents over the age of sixty-five. The costs are met in part, by a tax on wages and salaries.

Medicaid
A joint state-federal program that provides medical care to the poor (including indigent elderly persons in nursing homes). The program is funded out of general government revenues.

FIGURE 13–1	Percentage of Total National Income Spent on Health Care in the United States

The portion of total national income spent on health care has risen steadily since 1965.

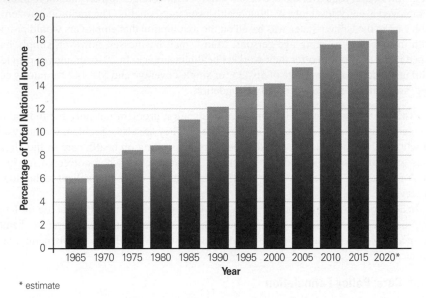

* estimate

Sources: U.S. Department of Commerce; U.S. Department of Health and Human Services; Deloitte and Touche LLP; VHA, Inc.; and Centers for Medicare and Medicaid Services.

benefits for about 120 million Americans—more than one-third of the nation's population. Many of these people are elderly. Like Social Security, Medicare and Medicaid are **entitlement programs.** Anyone who meets specific requirements is *entitled* to benefits under such programs.

Medicare. The Medicare program, which was created in 1965 under President Lyndon Johnson, pays hospital and physician bills for U.S. residents over the age of sixty-five. Since 2006, Medicare has also paid for at least part of the prescription drug expenses of the elderly. In return for paying a tax on their earnings (for most people currently set at 2.9 percent of wages and salaries), retirees are assured that the majority of their hospital and physician bills will be paid for with public funds.

Medicaid. In recent decades, the joint federal-state, taxpayer-funded Medicaid program for the "working poor" has generated a major expansion of government entitlements. In 1990, federal Medicaid spending was about $41 billion. By 2017, spending on Medicaid, the Children's Health Insurance Program, and allied functions was $738 billion. By 2000, 34 million people were enrolled in the programs. Today, there are about 75 million enrolled.

Currently, the federal government pays more than 70 percent of Medicaid's total cost. The states pay the rest. Wealthy states must pick up a greater share of the tab than poor states. As you will learn later in this section, the ACA (Obamacare) expanded considerably the share of the population that is eligible for Medicaid. The federal government's share of the cost also rose substantially.

Entitlement Program
A government program that entitles a defined class of people to obtain benefits. Entitlements operate under open-ended budget authorizations that do not limit how much can be spent.

The Problem of the Uninsured. In 2013, before Obamacare was fully implemented, about 42 million Americans—more than 18 percent of the population—did not have health insurance. The uninsured population has been relatively young, in part due to Medicare, which covers almost everyone over the age of sixty-five. Also, younger workers are more likely to be employed in entry-level jobs without health-insurance benefits. The traditional system of health care in the United States was based on the assumption that employers would provide health insurance to working-age persons. Many small businesses, however, simply have not been able to afford to offer their workers health insurance. In 2016, employer-provided health insurance cost an average of $6,435 for single coverage and $18,142 for family coverage, according to the Kaiser Family Foundation.

The Problem of High Costs. High medical costs are a problem not only for individuals with inadequate or nonexistent insurance coverage. They are also a problem for the system as a whole. Over the last four decades, per capita spending on health care in the United States grew at an average rate of 4.9 percent per year, even when corrected for inflation. A main driver of the growth in health-care spending was new medical technologies and services.

In addition, people over the age of sixty-five run up health-care bills that are far larger than those incurred by the rest of the population. As a federal problem, therefore, health-care spending growth remains chiefly a Medicare issue, even after the implementation of Obamacare.

Health Care: Policy Formulation

During the next step in the policymaking process, various policy proposals are discussed among government officials and the public. Such discussions may take place in the media and in the halls of Congress. Congress holds hearings, the president voices the administration's views, and the topic may even become a campaign issue.

For more than half a century, liberals have sought to establish a universal health-insurance system in this country. All attempts went nowhere. After the 2008 elections, however, the Democrats were in complete control of Congress and the presidency. Universal health insurance now appeared to be politically possible.

Under Democratic plans, universal coverage would result from a mandate that all citizens must obtain health insurance from some source—an employer, Medicare or Medicaid, or a new plan sponsored by the federal government or a state government. Low-income families would receive a subsidy to help them pay their insurance premiums.

Health Care: Policy Adoption

The third step in the policymaking process involves choosing a specific policy from among the proposals that have been discussed.

One key element of the proposed health-care legislation was the *individual mandate*, a requirement to obtain insurance coverage. Congressional Democrats adopted the individual mandate because without it, there was no way that the numbers would add up. Universal coverage was impossible unless everyone—healthy and sick alike—chipped in. Unfortunately for the Democrats, the individual mandate allowed the Republicans to accuse the Democrats of "forcing" people to do something, never a popular position in America.

Funding the legislation required additional taxes. Democrats in the House called for heavier taxes on the rich, while the Senate proposed taxes on drug and insurance companies. In the end, the two chambers compromised on some of each.

Initially, popular support for health-care reform, as reported by opinion polls, was relatively high. Support eroded quickly, however, as Congress took up the actual legislation.

Passage. The House and Senate passed different versions of the Affordable Care Act (ACA) in late 2009. After a special election cost the Democrats a Senate seat, the Republicans had the votes to filibuster any compromise written by a conference committee. Democrats, however, assembled enough support in the House to pass the Senate bill unaltered in March 2010, thus eliminating the need for a conference committee. The new law did not receive the vote of even a single Republican.

Details of the Legislation. Most of the major provisions of the new legislation did not go into effect until 2014. Some provisions took effect quickly, however. Young adults were allowed to stay on their parents' health plans until they turned twenty-six, and insurance companies could not drop people when they became sick.

In 2014, most of the program kicked in, including the following:

- A ban on excluding people with preexisting conditions from insurance plans.
- A requirement that most people obtain insurance or pay an income tax penalty.
- State health-insurance exchanges where individuals and small businesses can buy insurance.
- Subsidies to help persons with incomes up to four times the federal poverty level purchase coverage on the exchanges.
- Medicaid coverage for individuals with incomes up to 133 percent of the poverty level (but only in participating states).

Health Care: Policy Implementation

The fourth step in the policymaking process involves the implementation of the policy alternative chosen by Congress. Government action must be implemented by bureaucrats, the courts, police, and individual citizens.

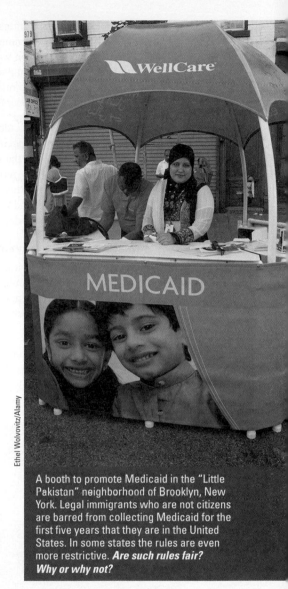

Ethel Wolvovitz/Alamy

A booth to promote Medicaid in the "Little Pakistan" neighborhood of Brooklyn, New York. Legal immigrants who are not citizens are barred from collecting Medicaid for the first five years that they are in the United States. In some states the rules are even more restrictive. *Are such rules fair? Why or why not?*

Congressional Opposition. Implementation would not occur, of course, if Obamacare could be repealed. Complete repeal of the legislation, however, was difficult. Repeal would have to pass both chambers of Congress and survive a presidential veto.

Also, much of the ACA took the form of an entitlement program. Funding for entitlement programs continues on a year-to-year basis unless it is explicitly altered or abolished. Therefore, even if Republicans in Congress were able to "defund" certain aspects of the reforms, most of the new policies would survive.

Opposition in the Courts and in the States. Many conservative state officials challenged the constitutionality of the ACA in court. In 2012, however, the Supreme Court ruled that most of the act was constitutional. The one exception: the Court threw out the mechanism by which the federal government could force states to expand their Medicaid programs.[1]

Medicaid expansion was fully funded by the federal government for the first six years and funded at 90 percent thereafter. Still, a large number of conservative state governments exercised their option to refuse expansion. As a result, several million low-income persons were not eligible for coverage.

Rollout Problems. In October 2013, the federal website, healthcare.gov, opened for business. Millions were expected to use the site to purchase individual health-care insurance plans. As it turned out, the site was so badly designed as to be unusable. The government launched an emergency repair operation. Still, the site was not completely fixed until the end of the year. Many state websites were better designed, but a few were so unworkable that they had to be abandoned in favor of the federal site. Despite these problems, by May 2014 enrollments exceeded forecasts by the Congressional Budget Office.

Health Care: Policy Evaluation

After a policy has been implemented, it is evaluated. When a policy has been in place for a given period of time, groups inside and outside the government conduct studies to determine how the program has actually worked. Based on this feedback and the perceived success or failure of the policy, a new round of policymaking initiatives may be undertaken to improve on the effort.

Popular Opinion. For many years, Obamacare remained unpopular, although a majority of those polled would rather improve it than abolish it. The ACA was favored by Democrats, but Republicans strongly opposed it. Democratic leaders assumed that when people saw Obamacare in action, they would warm to it. That did not immediately happen. One reason

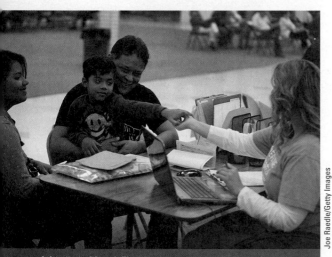

is that few people got their health-care insurance through the individual marketplaces. Most continued to depend on Medicare, Medicaid, or employer-provided insurance. Without direct experience of the programs, many people obtained their information from politicized sources.

A family in Miami, Florida, discusses health-care insurance options with an insurance agent. The family is eligible for coverage under the Affordable Care Act. *Why does Obamacare remain unpopular with many people?*

Joe Raedle/Getty Images

The Impact of the Reforms. Despite the claims of many conservatives, by 2016 the reforms were, for the most part, meeting anticipated goals. With more people insured, the nation's total health-care bill was larger than in the past. Surprisingly, the rate of increase in total costs fell. For example, annual Medicare costs per person are about $1,000 below the sums projected earlier. One reason is that the ACA contained a variety of measures that pressure physicians and hospitals to curb expenses.

According to a Gallup poll, the share of uninsured adults dropped from 18 percent in 2013 to 11 percent in 2016. Clearly, although millions

---

1. *National Federation of Independent Business v. Sebelius*, 132 S.Ct. 2566 (2012).

gained insurance, Obamacare was not truly universal. Low-income persons in states that did not expand Medicaid lost out. Some people refused to participate. (The income tax penalties for nonparticipation were low.) Finally, illegal immigrants were simply not allowed to participate in the programs.

Will Obamacare Be Replaced? By 2017, a widespread consensus had developed over the ACA. Those who purchased insurance policies through the online exchanges were pleased that they could obtain coverage. Still, many believed that their policies were too stingy. Those buying less expensive policies faced large out-of-pocket expenses for *co-pays* (the patient's share of an expense) and *deductibles* (the sums charged before insurance kicks in). The minority of persons with incomes too high for them to receive subsidies often found their *premiums* (monthly bills) to be uncomfortably large.

Repeal and Replace? These common criticisms were picked up by Republican leaders. Republican legislation to replace the ACA, however, revealed that the true conservative problem with the program was the taxes necessary to fund it. Replacements for the ACA uniformly reduced taxes on upper-income individuals by cutting the funds available for coverage—the opposite of what many people wanted. Initial attempts to replace the ACA in the House failed to win enough Republican votes to pass. (Democrats were united in opposition.) In May 2017, however, the House passed—by the narrowest of margins—the American Health Care Act (AHCA).

The House leadership was so eager to pass this legislation that it did not wait for an evaluation by the Congressional Budget Office (CBO). When the CBO report did arrive, it estimated that under the AHCA, 23 million people would lose coverage in the next few years. Most of the lost coverage would result from large cuts to Medicaid benefits. In addition, low-income persons in their sixties could be charged premiums that exceeded half of their total income.

The bill then went to the Senate, where the Republican margin of control was smaller than in the House. Senate Republicans drafted a new bill, but it had many of the same features as the House bill. The leadership also prepared alternative bills to repeal the ACA without replacement. In July, Senate Republicans failed to find fifty votes for any of these bills, and they failed to pass. The ACA, in other words, was proving to be very hard to kill. In 2017, for the first time, a majority of respondents supported the ACA in opinion polls. Support for the AHCA, in contrast, was in the 20-percent range, depending on the poll.

Immigration

>>> **LO2:** Explain why illegal immigration is seen as a problem, and cite some of the steps that have been taken in response to it.

In recent years, immigration rates in the United States have been among the highest since their peak in the early twentieth century. Every year, more than 1 million people immigrate to this country legally, a figure that does not include the large number of unauthorized immigrants. Those who were born on foreign soil now constitute about 13 percent of the U.S. population—more than twice the percentage of thirty years ago.

Since 1977, four out of five immigrants have come from Latin America or Asia. Hispanics have overtaken African Americans as the nation's largest minority. If current immigration rates continue, by 2050 minority groups collectively will constitute the majority of Americans. If such groups were to form coalitions, they could increase their political power dramatically.

The Issue of Unauthorized Immigration

Illegal immigration—or unauthorized immigration, to use the terminology of the Department of Homeland Security—has been a major national issue for many years. Latin Americans, especially those migrating from Mexico, have constituted the majority of individuals entering the United States without permission. In addition, many unauthorized immigrants have entered the country legally, often as tourists or students, and then failed to return home when their visa status expired. Naturally, the unauthorized population is hard to count, but recent estimates have put the number of such persons at about 11 million, down from about 12 million in 2007. Today, 66 percent of all unauthorized immigrants have been in the United States for more than a decade. This is up from 41 percent in 2005.

A major complication in addressing the issue of unauthorized immigrants is that they frequently live in mixed households, in which one or more members of a family have lawful resident status, but others do not. A woman from Guatemala with permanent resident status, for example, might be married to a Guatemalan man who is in the country illegally. Often, the parents in a family are unauthorized, whereas the children, who were born in the United States, possess American citizenship. Mixed families mean that deporting the unauthorized immigrant will either break up a family or force one or more American citizens into exile.

The Immigration Debate

Some people regard the high rate of immigration as a plus for America because it offsets the low birthrate and aging population. Immigrants expand the workforce and help to support, through their taxes, government programs that benefit older Americans, such as Medicare and Social Security. Critics, though, fear that immigrants may take jobs away from American workers and alter the nature of American culture.

The split in the public's attitudes has been reflected in differences among the nation's leaders over how to handle the issue of illegal immigration. Most Republicans in Congress have favored a harder line toward illegal immigrants than have most Democrats.

State Immigration Laws. In April 2010, Arizona's governor signed the nation's toughest-ever bill on illegal immigration. The law criminalized the failure to carry immigration documents, and it required police to stop and question anyone suspected of being in the country illegally. Opponents contended that the act would lead to harassment of Latinos regardless of their citizenship status.

In June 2012, the United States Supreme Court ruled that Arizona could not make an immigrant's failure to register under federal law a state crime, could not make it a felony for illegal immigrants to work, and could not arrest people without warrants if they might be deportable under federal law. The Court did not block police from investigating the immigration status of anyone they might stop. It left the door open, however, to future challenges to this law if police were shown to engage in discrimination when making stops.[2]

In 2011, Alabama adopted a new law aimed at illegal immigration that was in many respects even tougher than the Arizona legislation. Much of the law was blocked as a result of federal court rulings, however. Since 2010, Georgia, Indiana, South Carolina, and Utah have also passed laws similar to the ones in Arizona and Alabama. These laws also face court challenges.

---

2. *Arizona v. United States*, 567 U.S. ___ (2012).

Immigration and the Obama Administration.
During his 2008 campaign, Barack Obama supported reforms that would give illegal immigrants a path toward citizenship. Reform was put off to allow Congress to concentrate on health-care issues, however. Obama focused instead on border security and rounding up deportable persons. In fact, in Obama's first term, his administration deported 1.5 million illegal immigrants, an all-time record.

The resulting Latino dissatisfaction with the administration raised the question of whether Hispanics would turn out to vote for Democratic candidates in forthcoming elections. The 2012 Republican presidential candidates, however, took a hard line against illegal immigration. Also, in June 2012, Obama announced a new policy under which immigration authorities would suspend deportations of unauthorized immigrants who were brought into the country as children and who were not otherwise in trouble with the law. In the end, Latinos and Asian Americans turned out for the Democrats in large numbers during the 2012 elections.

A twelve-year-old unauthorized immigrant wipes tears as she tells her story of escaping from violence in her home country of Honduras. She is testifying before the Congressional Progressive Caucus. *Should young people fleeing from violence be granted asylum in the United States? Why or why not?*

Following the elections, some Republicans announced that they were open to changing their positions on immigration. By 2014, however, that party was again blocking new legislation. One reason was opposition to an executive order issued by President Obama in 2014. Under the order, more than 4 million additional unauthorized immigrants were protected from deportation and allowed to obtain work permits. In 2015, a district court judge suspended the order. The Supreme Court may make the final decision on its legality—provided that President Trump's attempt to reverse Obama's order does not make the issue irrelevant.

Immigration and President Trump. A tough line on illegal immigration was Donald Trump's signature campaign issue. With Trump as president, any attempt to grant legal status to unauthorized immigrants was impossible. The only question was how far Trump would go in deporting those currently in the country. Congress appeared willing to authorize additional funds for Immigration and Customs Enforcement (ICE). By mid-2017, it was clear that rates of deportation had risen. ICE was now able to deport unauthorized immigrants who were not otherwise in trouble with the law—a reversal of Obama's policies. Deporting all 11 million unauthorized immigrants, however, remained an impossibly daunting project.

One Trump proposal was partially blocked by the courts—his attempt, through two successive executive orders, to halt altogether the admission of persons from several Muslim-majority nations. U.S. district and appeals courts ruled that this plan amounted to unconstitutional discrimination on the basis of religion. In June 2017, however, the Supreme Court reinstated the ban for persons with no "bona fide relationship with any person or entity in the United States." That blocked the arrival of new asylum seekers while allowing most others to enter.

Energy and the Environment

>>> **LO3:** Evaluate how the nation has reacted to its reliance on foreign oil and the controversy over climate change.

Energy policy addresses two major problems: (1) America's reliance on foreign oil, much of which is produced by unfriendly regimes, and (2) climate change, purportedly caused by increased emissions of carbon dioxide (CO_2) and other greenhouse gases.

Energy Independence—A Strategic Issue

In 2017, America's net imports of petroleum were about one-quarter of total consumption. We relied on foreign oil much more heavily only a few years ago. In 2006, almost 60 percent of our oil came from abroad. Today, Canada, a friendly neighbor, supplies three-fifths of our remaining net imports. Still, the world's largest oil exporters include nations that are not our friends. Russia is the world's second-largest oil exporter, after Saudi Arabia. Other major exporters include Venezuela and Iran, both openly hostile to the United States.

While the United States has not yet attained the goal of energy independence, the nation has taken significant steps in that direction. What changes were responsible for this turnaround?

High Prices and New Production. If the price of a commodity goes up, producers of that commodity have an incentive to produce more of it. The price of gasoline has certainly risen in recent years. In the summer of 2008, the price of gasoline exceeded $4 for the first time. Clearly, petroleum producers had an incentive to extract more crude oil, if possible. The question was, could they?

Some experts doubted that enough new oil could be extracted to keep prices from rising indefinitely. They underestimated the impact of increased applications of technology in the form of hydraulic fracturing, or **fracking.** This process involves injecting water, sand, and chemicals under high pressure into hydrocarbon-bearing rocks, releasing oil or natural gas. Expensive oil made fracking profitable.

Fracking has had an even greater impact on the supply of natural gas. A decade ago, it seemed likely that the United States would need to import natural gas. By 2012, however, so much natural gas was available domestically that the nation had run out of storage space. Low natural gas prices plus new air-pollution regulations made coal uncompetitive as a source of electricity. As a result, plans for 168 new coal-based power plants were abandoned, and about 100 existing plants were scheduled for retirement. Despite concerns that fracking might harm drinking-water supplies or otherwise damage the environment, use of the process continues to grow in importance.

Fracking
Also called hydraulic fracturing, the injection of a high-pressure solution of water, sand, and chemicals into hydrocarbon-bearing rocks, releasing oil or natural gas.

The Politics of Energy. In the summer of 2014, a barrel of crude oil cost more than $100. By the end of the year, the price was cut in half and seemed set to remain around $50 for years to come. The cause was clear—fracking had done its work. The United States, not Saudi Arabia, was now the "swing producer" that would determine the price of oil. By the end of 2015, gasoline was $2.50 per gallon in most of the country.

The government has also taken steps to curb the consumption—and hence the price—of gasoline. President Obama issued higher fuel-efficiency standards for vehicles in 2009 and 2012. As of 2016, the requirement was 39 miles per gallon for cars and 30 miles per gallon for light trucks. By 2025, the nation's combined fleet of new cars and light trucks must have an average fuel efficiency of 54.5 miles per gallon.

The federal government also subsidizes the development of alternative fuels. Subsidies to encourage the production of ethanol from corn are controversial. Critics charge that ethanol production is an inefficient method of producing energy and makes food more expensive. Subsidies for renewable energy sources, such as windmills and solar power panels, have also attracted criticism. A problem with wind and especially solar power has been high costs. Prices have fallen rapidly, however, and use of these technologies has risen quickly. Still, they are a small fraction of the nation's power supply.

Unlike many Democrats, Obama also favored building new energy plants that would use nuclear power. Electric utilities planned several new nuclear plants, but most of these plans were shelved almost immediately. The major problem was that nuclear power could not compete with the falling costs of natural gas. A second problem was safety. In March 2011, a giant tsunami struck northeast Japan and severely damaged four nuclear reactors located on the coast. The resulting radiation leaks convinced many people that new nuclear power plants would be dangerous.

travellinglight / Alamy

A Tesla Roadster plugged into a recharging station in Santa Cruz, California. The Roadster can travel 244 miles on a single charge of its battery pack. *Do electric cars represent the future? Why or why not?*

Climate Change

In the 1990s, many scientists working on climate issues began to conclude that average world temperatures would rise significantly in the twenty-first century. Gases released by human activity, principally carbon dioxide (CO_2), may be producing a "greenhouse effect," trapping the sun's heat and slowing its release into outer space.

The Climate Change Debate. Most scientists who perform research on the world's climate believe that climate change will be significant, but there is considerable disagreement as to how much warming will actually occur. It is generally accepted that world temperatures have already increased by about 0.74 degrees Celsius over the last century. The United Nations' Intergovernmental Panel on Climate Change predicts increases ranging from 1.0 to 4.8 degrees Celsius by 2100. This range of estimates is rather wide and reflects the uncertainties involved in predicting the world's climate.

Climate change has become a major political football to be kicked back and forth by conservatives and liberals. Environmental groups and others have been pressing the federal government to take action now to avert a planet-threatening crisis.

Their efforts are complicated by the fact that a major share of the American electorate does not believe that global warming is happening or, if it is happening, that it is caused by human activities. Disbelief in man-made climate change is a partisan phenomenon.

Interact

One Internet trick for bringing up both sides of a controversial issue is to search using "pro con." For example, try searching for "fracking pro con." You will find a variety of pages that purport to give both sides of the debate on fracking. Not all actually do. Some pro-con pieces may only pretend to represent both sides. One recent article considered the impact of fracking only on local employment and property values, with the emphasis on property values. The national interest was not considered. Not surprisingly, the author opposed fracking. Try locating some pages that really try to present both sides of the issue, and evaluate the arguments. Who seems to you to have the most convincing case?

According to one poll, skepticism about climate change among Republicans rose by 11 percentage points from 2008 to 2009, and a majority of Republicans now believe that man-made climate change does not exist. The opinions of Democrats have not changed—about four-fifths of them accept that climate change is a problem. If there is no global warming, of course, there would be no reason to limit emissions of CO_2 and other greenhouse gases. By 2013, in the wake of superstorms and droughts, skepticism about climate change among Republicans and independents had eased somewhat—but opposition to CO_2 restrictions remained strong.

Addressing the Issue. In 2009, Democrats made an initial attempt to legislate on CO_2 emissions. The bill sank without a trace in the Senate. With Republicans in control of the House beginning in 2011, no further legislation was possible. Despite the lack of government action, by 2011 CO_2 emissions in the United States were actually down from 2008 levels. The most important cause was new power plants that used natural gas instead of coal. (Gas does release some CO_2, but less than half as much as coal.) More fuel-efficient cars also contributed to the reduction.

It was also possible that the Environmental Protection Agency (EPA) might act without new legislation. In 2007, the Supreme Court found that the EPA had the authority to regulate the emission of CO_2 and other greenhouse gases under the Clean Air Act.[3] In 2009, the EPA issued a finding that greenhouse gases did in fact threaten the public health and welfare. In 2013, it issued rules covering new power plants. Coal-based power plants were already suffering serious price competition from natural gas, and the EPA's rules made the construction of new coal-based plants almost impossible.

In June 2014, the EPA proposed rules covering existing power plants. The rules sought to cut emissions from such plants by 30 percent by 2030. In 2014, several states sued the EPA in an attempt to overturn the rules. As a result, federal courts stayed (suspended) the new rules pending a decision by the Supreme Court. In 2016, the Court split four-to-four over the case, which meant the stays remained in place. It was likely that with the addition of conservative justice Neil Gorsuch, the Court would decide the issue against the EPA if, as is probable, the case returned to the Court at a later date. In March 2017, however, President Trump ordered the EPA to revoke the rules covering new power plants.

An additional controversy centered on the proposed Keystone XL pipeline. This project would carry petroleum from the Alberta oil sands (and also from North Dakota) to refineries on the Gulf Coast. Opponents of the pipeline claimed that the oil sands were one of the world's most pollution-intense sources of oil. Proponents argued for the economic benefits of greater supply. Republicans in Congress tried to force President Obama to approve the project. In 2015, he canceled the pipeline instead. Upon taking office, however, President Trump announced plans to revive the project.

The Politics of Economic Decision Making

>>> **LO4:** Define *unemployment, inflation, fiscal policy, public debt,* and *monetary policy.*

Nowhere are the principles of public policymaking more obvious than in the economic decisions made by the federal government. The president and Congress are constantly faced with questions of economic policy. Economic policy becomes especially important when the nation enters a recession.

---

3. *Massachusetts v. EPA*, 549 U.S. 497 (2007).

Good Times, Bad Times

Like any economy that is fundamentally capitalist, the U.S. economy experiences ups and downs. Good times—booms—are followed by lean years. If a slowdown is severe enough, it is called a **recession**. Recessions are characterized by increased **unemployment**, the inability of those who are in the workforce to find a job. The government tries to moderate the effects of such downturns. In contrast, booms are historically associated with another economic problem that the government must address—rising prices, or **inflation**.

Unemployment. Some psychologists say that unemployment is one of the most traumatizing events in a person's life. Certainly, unemployment imposes costs on the entire economy, not just on the unemployed individuals. Since the Great Depression of the 1930s, fighting unemployment has been a major goal of the federal government. The federal government also provides unemployment insurance. Not all unemployed workers are eligible, however. In fact, only about one-third of the unemployed receive benefits. Benefits are not available to employees who quit their jobs voluntarily or are fired for cause. They are also not paid to workers who are entering the labor force for the first time but cannot find a job.

Measuring Unemployment. Estimates of the number of unemployed are prepared by the U.S. Department of Labor. The Bureau of the Census also generates estimates using survey research data. Critics of the published unemployment rate calculated by the federal government believe that it fails to reflect the true numbers of discouraged workers and "hidden unemployed." There is no exact way to measure discouraged workers, but the Department of Labor defines them as people who have dropped out of the labor force and are no longer looking for a job because they believe that the job market has little to offer them. As a result, some economists believe that a better way to look at the unemployment issue is to calculate the share of the population that is actually working.

Inflation. Rising prices, or inflation, can also be a serious economic and political problem. Inflation is a sustained upward movement in the average level of prices. Another way of defining inflation is as a decline in the purchasing power of money over time. The government measures inflation using the *consumer price index*, or CPI. The Bureau of Labor Statistics identifies a market basket of goods and services purchased by the typical consumer and regularly checks the price of that basket. Over a period of many years, inflation can add up. For example, today's dollar is worth (very roughly) about a twentieth of what it was worth a century ago. In effect, today's dollar is a pre–World War I nickel.

The Business Cycle. Economists refer to the regular succession of economic expansions and contractions as the *business cycle*. An extremely severe recession is called a *depression*, as in the example of the Great Depression of the 1930s. By 1933, actual output was 35 percent below the nation's productive capacity. Unemployment reached 25 percent. Compared with this catastrophe, recessions since 1945 have usually been mild. Nevertheless, the United States has experienced recessions with some regularity. Recession years since 1960 have included 1970, 1974, 1980, 1982, 1990, 2001, and 2008–2009.

To try to control the ups and downs of the national economy, the government has several policy options. One is to change the level of taxes or government spending. The other possibility involves influencing interest rates and the money side of the economy. We will examine taxing and spending, or fiscal policy, first.

Recession
An economic downturn, usually characterized by a fall in the GDP and rising unemployment.

Unemployment
The inability of those who are in the labor force to find a job.

Inflation
A sustained rise in the general price level of goods and services.

Walter Stoneman/Getty Images

John Maynard Keynes (1883–1946) argued in favor of government intervention to smooth out economic booms and busts. *What interventions did he propose?*

Fiscal Policy

Fiscal policy is the domain of Congress. A fiscal policy approach to stabilizing the economy is often associated with the twentieth-century economist John Maynard Keynes (1883–1946). This British economist originated the school of thought that today is called **Keynesian economics,** which supports the use of government spending and taxing to help stabilize the economy. (*Keynesian* is pronounced *kayn-zee-un*.) Keynes believed that there was a need for government intervention in the economy, in part because after falling into a recession or depression, a modern economy may become trapped in an ongoing state of less-than-full employment.

Government Spending and Borrowing. Keynes developed his fiscal policy theories during the Great Depression of the 1930s. He believed that the forces of supply and demand operated too slowly on their own in such a serious recession. Unemployment meant people had less to spend, and because they could not buy things, more businesses failed, creating additional unemployment. It was a vicious cycle. Keynes's idea was simple: in such circumstances, the government should step in and engineer the spending that is needed to return the economy to a more normal state.[4]

The spending promoted by the government could take either of two forms. The government could increase its own spending, or it could cut taxes, allowing the taxpayer to undertake the spending instead. To have the effect Keynes wanted, however, it was essential that the spending be financed by borrowing. In other words, the government should run a **budget deficit**—it should spend more than it receives.

Discretionary Fiscal Policy. As mentioned, Keynes originally developed his fiscal theories as a way of lifting an economy out of a major disaster such as the Great Depression. Beginning with the presidency of John F. Kennedy (1961–1963), however, policymakers have attempted to use Keynesian methods to "fine-tune" the economy. This is discretionary fiscal policy—*discretionary* meaning left to the judgment, or discretion, of a policymaker.

The Timing Problem. Attempts to fine-tune the economy encounter a timing problem. Fiscal policy time lags are long and variable, so a policy designed to combat a recession may not produce results until the economy is already out of the recession.

Because of the timing problem, attempts by the government to employ fiscal policy in the last fifty years have typically taken the form of tax cuts or increases. Tax changes can take effect more quickly than government spending. In 2009, therefore, the Obama administration was employing an exceptional approach when it secured from Congress a roughly $900 billion package consisting largely of economic stimulus spending.

Criticisms of Keynes. Following World War II (1939–1945), Keynes's theories were integrated into the mainstream of economic thinking. There have always been economic schools of thought, however, that consider Keynesian economics to be fatally flawed. These schools argue either that fiscal policy has no effect or that it has negative side effects that outweigh any benefits. Some opponents of fiscal policy believe that the federal government should limit itself to monetary policy, which we will discuss shortly. Others believe that it is best for the government to do nothing at all.

Fiscal Policy
The federal government's use of taxation and spending policies to affect overall business activity.

Keynesian Economics
A school of economic thought that favors active federal government policymaking to stabilize economy-wide fluctuations, including the use of discretionary fiscal policy.

Budget Deficit
Government expenditures that exceed receipts.

---

4. Robert Skidelsky, *Keynes: The Return of the Master* (New York: PublicAffairs, 2010).

The Eclipse of Fiscal Policy. It is worth noting that most voters have neither understood nor accepted Keynesian economics. Despite popular attitudes, politicians of both parties accepted Keynesian ideas for many years. Democratic president John F. Kennedy was perhaps the first Keynesian in the White House. Republican president Richard Nixon (1969–1974) is alleged to have said, "We are all Keynesians now." Even George W. Bush justified many of his policies using Keynesian language. During the first years of Obama's presidency, however, Keynesian thinking among Republicans in Congress vanished almost completely. Some members adopted the ideas of anti-Keynesian economists. The majority simply rejected "countercyclical" policies, reflecting the popular belief that during a recession the government should "tighten its belt."

It did not help the Keynesian cause that Obama's stimulus package failed to end high rates of unemployment—Keynesian economists argued that the stimulus was less than half of what was needed to accomplish such a goal. When Obama, in his 2010 State of the Union address, employed the belt-tightening metaphor, Keynesians realized that they had lost control of the political discourse. By the time of the 2016 elections, the size of the federal budget deficit was no longer a top political issue, in part because economic recovery had reduced the size of the deficit substantially. As a result, legislators from both major parties were more receptive to proposals that might have the side effect of increasing the deficit.

The Public Debt and Deficit Spending

The government typically borrows by selling U.S. Treasury bills, notes, and bonds, known collectively as *Treasury securities* and informally as **treasuries.** The sale of these federal obligations to corporations, private individuals, pension plans, foreign governments, foreign businesses, and foreign individuals adds to this nation's **public debt,** or **national debt.** In the last few years, foreign governments, especially those of China and Japan, have come to own about half of the U.S. public debt. Thirty years ago, the share of the U.S. public debt held by foreigners was only 15 percent.

The Public Debt. There are two types of public debt—gross and net. The *gross public debt* includes all federal government interagency borrowings, which really do not matter. This is similar to your taking an IOU ("I owe you") out of your left pocket and putting it into your right pocket. What is important is the *net public debt*—the public debt that does not include interagency borrowing. The best way to examine the relative importance of the public debt is to compare it with the gross domestic product (GDP), as is done in Figure 13-2. (As noted earlier in this chapter, the gross domestic product is the dollar value of all final goods and services produced in a one-year period.) In the figure, you see that the public debt reached its peak during World War II and fell until 1975. From about 1960 to 2008, the net public debt as a percentage of GDP ranged between 25 and 50 percent. Thereafter, deficits incurred during the Great Recession drove the debt up rapidly.

Note that the net public debt as a percentage of GDP can fall even when the federal government is still running a budget deficit. If the economy is growing faster than the debt, then the debt as a share of the economy will fall even if it is still rising slowly. For example, the government never actually paid off the sums it borrowed to finance World War II. Rather, the economy grew fast enough that, over time, the wartime debt ceased to be important.

The Public Debt in Perspective. From 1960 until 1998, the federal government spent more than it received in all but two years. Some observers considered those ongoing budget deficits to be the negative result of Keynesian policies. Others argued that the deficits actually

Treasuries
U.S. Treasury securities—bills, notes, and bonds. Debt issued by the federal government.

Public, or National, Debt
The total amount of debt carried by the federal government.

FIGURE 13–2   Net Public Debt as a Percentage of the Gross Domestic Product

During World War II, the net public debt grew dramatically. It fell thereafter but rose again from 1975 to 1995. The percentage fell after 1995, only to rise dramatically after 2008 and then level off from 2014 on.

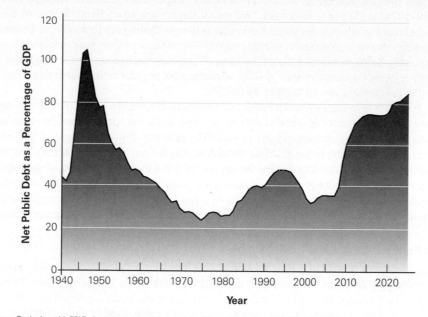

Source: Beginning with 2017, the percentages are projections. Office of Management and Budget; FRED, the Federal Reserve Bank of St. Louis; and the Congressional Budget Office.

resulted from the abuse of Keynesianism. Politicians have been more than happy to run budget deficits in recessions. They have sometimes refused to implement the other side of Keynes's recommendations—to run a *budget surplus* during boom times, or at least to keep the percentage growth of the debt well below the growth of GDP.

In 1993, however, President Bill Clinton (1993–2001) obtained a tax increase as the nation emerged from a mild recession. Between the tax increase and the "dot-com boom," the United States had a budget surplus each year from 1998 to 2002. Some commentators predicted that we would be running federal government surpluses for years to come.

Back to Deficit Spending. All of those projections went by the wayside because of several events. One event was the "dot-com bust," followed by the 2001–2002 recession, which lowered the rate of growth of not only the economy but also federal government tax receipts. Another event was a series of large tax cuts passed by Congress in 2001 and 2003 at the urging of President George W. Bush. A third event took place on September 11, 2001. As a result of the terrorist attacks, the federal government spent much more than it had planned to spend on security against terrorism. The government also had to pay for the war in Iraq in 2003 and the occupation of that country thereafter. Finally, Congress authorized major increases in spending on discretionary programs.

The Great Recession dramatically increased the budget deficit and the level of public debt. Tax revenues collapsed, and spending on such items as unemployment compensation rose automatically. In addition, immediately upon taking office, President Obama obtained legislation from Congress that helped push the public debt to levels not seen since World

War II. Such high levels of debt became a major political issue. As noted, however, the budget deficit then fell as the economy slowly recovered. As a result, the public debt leveled off.

Dangers of Deficit Spending. Can high levels of deficit spending go on forever? Before the onset of the Great Recession, many economists feared that if high levels of deficit spending went on long enough, the rest of the world—which owns about 50 percent of all treasuries—might lose faith in our government. So far, however, there has been little sign of such a problem. On the contrary, following the financial crisis that struck on September 15, 2008, panicked investors bought large amounts of treasuries in the belief that they were the safest instruments in existence. These developments have convinced some economists that as long as the dollar remains the world's dominant currency, "runs" on the dollar are not actually possible. Still, the larger the national debt, the more interest the federal government must pay to sustain it. If interest rates—now very low—go back up, the burden becomes greater. This poses the question of whether paying interest to the holders of U.S. treasuries is a desirable use of our tax dollars.

Monetary Policy

Controlling the rate of growth of the money supply is called **monetary policy.** This policy is the domain of the **Federal Reserve System,** also known simply as **the Fed.** The Fed is the most important regulatory agency in the U.S. monetary system.

The Fed performs a number of important functions. Perhaps the Fed's most important task is regulating the amount of money in circulation, which can be defined loosely as checking account balances and currency. The Fed also provides a system for transferring checks from one bank to another. In addition, it holds reserves deposited by most of the nation's banks, savings and loan associations, savings banks, and credit unions. Finally, it plays a role in supervising the banking industry.

Organization of the Federal Reserve System. A board of governors manages the Fed. This board consists of seven full-time members appointed by the president with the approval of the Senate. There are twelve Federal Reserve district banks. The most important unit within the Fed is the **Federal Open Market Committee.** This is the body that actually determines the future growth of the money supply and other important economy-wide financial variables. This committee is composed of the members of the Board of Governors, the president of the New York Federal Reserve Bank, and presidents of four other Federal Reserve banks, rotated periodically.

The Board of Governors of the Federal Reserve System is independent. The president can attempt to influence the board, and Congress can threaten to merge the Fed into the Treasury Department, but as long as the Fed retains its independence, its chairperson and governors can do what they please. Hence, any talk about "the president's monetary policy" or "Congress's monetary policy" is inaccurate. The Fed remains an independent entity.

Loose and Tight Monetary Policies. The Federal Reserve System seeks to stabilize nation-wide economic activity by controlling the amount of money in circulation. Credit, like any good or service, has a cost. The cost of borrowing—the interest rate—is similar to the cost of any other aspect of doing business. When the cost of borrowing falls, businesspersons can undertake more investment projects. When it rises, businesspersons undertake fewer projects. Consumers also react to interest rates when deciding whether to borrow funds to buy houses, cars, or other "big-ticket" items.

Monetary Policy
The use of changes in the amount of money in circulation to alter credit markets, employment, and the rate of inflation.

Federal Reserve System (the Fed)
The system created by Congress in 1913 to serve as the nation's central banking organization.

Federal Open Market Committee
The most important body within the Federal Reserve System. The Federal Open Market Committee decides how monetary policy should be carried out.

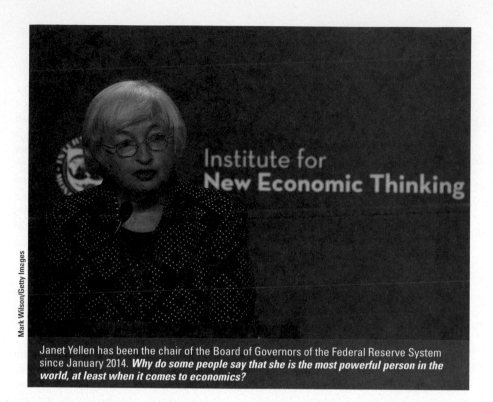

Mark Wilson/Getty Images

Janet Yellen has been the chair of the Board of Governors of the Federal Reserve System since January 2014. *Why do some people say that she is the most powerful person in the world, at least when it comes to economics?*

If the Fed implements a *loose monetary policy* (often called an "expansionary" policy), the supply of credit increases and its cost falls. If the Fed implements a *tight monetary policy* (often called a "contractionary" policy), the supply of credit falls (or fails to grow) and its cost increases. A loose money policy is often implemented as an attempt to encourage economic growth. You may be wondering why any nation would want a tight monetary policy. The answer is to control inflation.

Monetary Policy during Recessions. A tight monetary policy is a powerful tool for taming inflation. (Some would argue that it is the *only* way that inflation can be stopped.) If interest rates go high enough, people *will* stop borrowing. How effective, though, is a loose monetary policy at ending a recession? Under normal conditions, it is very effective. A loose monetary policy will spur an expansion in economic activity.

To combat the Great Recession, however, the Fed reduced its interest rate almost to zero. The rate could not go any lower. Yet when consumers had credit, they were still reluctant to make major purchases. Many businesses found that they had little need to borrow to invest in new activities—and no need to hire new staff. Overall demand for goods and services was so low that companies could produce all they needed with their existing capacity and workforce. Monetary policy had run out of steam—using it was like "pushing on a string." Even if the Fed created large amounts of new money, banks would not loan out these funds. Instead, they would pile up as unused reserves that banks leave on deposit with the Fed. After all, the government has little power to force banks to lend, and it certainly has no power to make people borrow and spend. As a result, the Obama administration placed its bets on fiscal policy.

The Fed and the Great Recession. During 2008 and 2009, the Fed developed a new way to respond to the failure of banks to lend. Relying on its ability to create money, it began to make loans itself, without turning to Congress for appropriations. The Fed bought debt issued by corporations. It bought securities that were based on student loans and credit-card debt. By 2009, the Fed had loaned out close to $2 trillion in fresh credit. In 2010 and 2011, the Fed implemented yet another innovative policy, called *quantitative easing*, in an attempt to make monetary policy more effective. Quantitative easing essentially means buying quantities of long-term treasuries and mortgage-backed securities to hold down long-term interest rates.

In 2013, the Fed began a policy of *tapering*. Under this plan, the Fed slowly reduced the size of its quantitative easing purchases. (The purchases were ended altogether in October 2015.) The Fed also developed a program of *forward guidance*. Under this policy, the Fed made it clear that interest rates would remain low for a long time to come. In 2015, however, for the first time since the onset of the Great Recession, the Fed began to contemplate the possibility of raising interest rates. The Fed in fact raised rates incrementally in December 2015, December 2016, and then several times in 2017. It also hinted that it might sell some of the securities it bought under the quantitative easing program. In short, the special measures that the Fed had used in an attempt to fight the Great Recession were coming to an end.

The Politics of Taxation

>>> **LO5:** Describe the various taxes that Americans pay, and discuss some of the controversies surrounding taxation.

Congress enacts tax laws at the federal level. The Internal Revenue Code, which is the federal tax code, encompasses thousands of pages, thousands of sections, and thousands of subsections—our tax system is not very simple.

Americans pay a variety of taxes. At the federal level, the income tax is levied on most sources of income. Social Security and Medicare taxes are assessed on wages and salaries. There is an income tax for corporations, which has an indirect effect on many individuals. The estate tax is collected from property left behind by wealthy persons who have died. You can see the size of the most important federal taxes in the second pie chart in Appendix D. State and local governments also assess taxes on income, sales, and land. Altogether, the value of all taxes collected by the federal government and by state and local governments is about 30 percent of the gross domestic product. This is a substantial sum, but it is less than what many other countries collect.

Federal Income Tax Rates

Individuals and businesses pay income taxes based on tax rates. Not all of your income is taxed at the same rate. The first few dollars of income that you earn are not taxed at all. The highest rate is imposed on the "last" dollar of income that you make. This highest rate is the *marginal* tax rate. Table 13-1 shows the 2018 marginal tax rates for individuals and married couples (which apply to income earned in the previous year, 2017). The higher the tax rate, the greater the public's reaction to that tax rate. If the highest tax rate you pay on the income you make is 15 percent, then any method you can use to reduce your taxable income by one dollar saves you fifteen cents in tax liabilities that you owe the federal government.

Individuals paying a 15 percent rate have a relatively small incentive to avoid paying taxes, but consider individuals who were faced with a tax rate of 94 percent in the 1940s during World War II. They had a tremendous incentive to find legal ways to reduce their taxable incomes. For every dollar of income that was somehow deemed nontaxable, the tax liabilities of these taxpayers would be reduced by ninety-four cents.

Income Tax Loopholes and Other Types of Taxes

Individuals and corporations facing high tax rates will adjust their earning and spending behavior to reduce their taxes. They will also make concerted attempts to get Congress to add **loopholes** to the tax law that allow them to reduce their taxable incomes. When Congress imposed very high tax rates on high incomes, it also provided more loopholes than it does today. For example, special provisions enabled investors in oil and gas wells to reduce their taxable incomes.

Progressive and Regressive Taxation. As Table 13–1 shows, the greater your taxable income, the higher the marginal tax rate. Persons with large incomes pay a larger share of their income in income tax. A tax system in which rates go up with income is called a **progressive tax** system. The federal income tax is clearly progressive.

The income tax is not the only tax you must pay. For example, the federal Social Security tax is levied on all wage and salary income at a flat rate of 6.2 percent. (Employers pay another 6.2 percent, making the total effective rate 12.4 percent.) In 2017, however, there was no Social Security tax on wages and salaries in excess of $127,200. (This "cap" changes from year to year.) Persons with very high salaries, therefore, pay no Social Security tax on much of their wages.

In addition, the tax is currently not levied on investment income (including capital gains, rents, royalties, interest, dividends, or profits from a business). The wealthy receive a much greater share of their income from these sources than others do. As a result, the wealthy pay a much smaller portion of their income in Social Security taxes than do the working poor. The Social Security tax is therefore a **regressive tax**.

To fund Medicare, a combined employer/employee 2.9 percent tax is also assessed on all wage income. The income of individuals that exceeds $200,000, however, is subject to a rate of 3.8 percent. For married couples filing jointly, the threshold is $250,000. Note that three-quarters of all taxpayers owe more in payroll taxes, such as Social Security and Medicare taxes, than they do in income taxes.

Capital Gains. Finally, as part of the income tax system, the federal government also taxes *capital gains*, that is, increases in the value of property over time. If you own stocks, for example, and sell them for a higher price than you bought them, the difference is a capital gain. The tax rate on long-term capital gains is lower than the rate for wage or salary income, on the theory that such a lower rate encourages investment. Taxpayers in the 10 and 15 percent tax brackets pay no tax on most capital gains. Taxpayers in the 25 to 35 percent brackets pay a

Loophole
A legal method by which individuals and businesses are allowed to reduce the tax liabilities they owe to the government.

Progressive Tax
A tax that rises in percentage terms as incomes rise.

Regressive Tax
A tax that falls in percentage terms as incomes rise.

TABLE 13–1	Marginal Tax Rates for Single Persons and Married Couples (Filed in 2018 for Income Earned in 2017)		
Single Persons		**Married Filing Jointly**	
Marginal Tax Bracket	**Marginal Tax Rate**	**Marginal Tax Bracket**	**Marginal Tax Rate**
0–$9,325	10%	0–$18,650	10%
$9,326–$37,950	15%	$18,651–$75,900	15%
$37,951–$91,900	25%	$75,901–$153,100	25%
$91,901–$191,650	28%	$153,101–233,350	28%
$191,651–$416,700	33%	$233,351–$416,700	33%
$416,701–$418,400	35%	$416,701–$470,700	35%
$418,401 and higher	39.6%	$470,701 and higher	39.6%

15 percent rate. For those in the top 39.6 percent bracket, the rate is 20 percent. A special capital gains tax of 3.8 percent is also levied on upper-income persons to help fund the Affordable Care Act. Because long-term capital gains are taxed at a lower rate than ordinary income, taxpayers have an interest in defining as much of their income as possible as capital gains.

What Kind of Tax System Do We Have? The various taxes Americans pay pull in different directions. The federal estate tax is extremely progressive, because it is not imposed at all on smaller estates. Sales taxes are regressive, because the wealthy spend a relatively smaller portion of their income on items subject to the sales tax. Add everything up, and the tax system as a whole is slightly progressive.

MAKING A DIFFERENCE

Learning about Entitlement Reform

As discussed earlier in the chapter, programs such as Medicare, Medicaid, Social Security, unemployment compensation, and several others are known as entitlement programs. They are called entitlements because if you meet certain qualifications—of age or income, for example—you are entitled to specified benefits. The federal government can estimate how much it will have to pay out in entitlements but cannot set an exact figure in advance. In this way, entitlement spending differs from other government spending. When Congress decides what it will give to the national park system, for example, it allocates an exact sum, and the park system cannot exceed that budget. Along with national defense, entitlements make up by far the greatest share of the federal budget. This fact led a Bush administration staff member to joke, "It helps to think of the government as an insurance company with an army."

Why Should You Care? What happens to entitlement programs will affect your life in two major ways. Entitlement spending will largely determine how much you pay in taxes throughout your working lifetime. Entitlement policy will also determine how much support you receive from the federal government when you grow old. Because entitlements make up such a large share of the federal budget, it is not possible to address the issue of budget deficits without considering entitlement spending. Further, under current policies, spending on Medicare will rise in future years, placing ever-greater pressure on the federal budget. Sooner or later, entitlement reform will be impossible to avoid. However these programs are changed, you will feel the effects in your wallet throughout your life.

What Can You Do? Should Medicare and Social Security benefits be high, with the understanding that taxes must therefore go up? Should these programs be cut back in the hope of avoiding deficits and tax increases? Do entitlements mean that the old are fleecing the young—or is that argument irrelevant because we will all grow old someday? Progressives and conservatives disagree strongly about these questions. You can develop your own opinions by learning more about entitlement reform. The following organizations take a conservative position on entitlements:

- National Center for Policy Analysis. Find its webpage on entitlement reform by searching for "ncpa retirement."
- The Heritage Foundation. See what it has to say by searching for "heritage entitlements."

The following organizations take a liberal stand on entitlements:

- National Committee to Preserve Social Security and Medicare. You can locate the home page of this organization by typing in "ncpssm."
- AARP (formerly the American Association of Retired Persons). To learn this group's position on entitlements, enter "aarp advocacy."

Medicare.gov

Who is entitled to Medicare?

///

Key Terms

Affordable Care
   Act (ACA) 298
budget deficit 310
domestic policy 296
entitlement program 299
Federal Open Market
   Committee 313

Federal Reserve System
   (the Fed) 313
fiscal policy 310
fracking 306
gross domestic product
   (GDP) 298
inflation 309

Keynesian
   economics 310
loophole 316
Medicaid 298
Medicare 298
monetary policy 313
progressive tax 316

public, or national,
   debt 311
recession 309
regressive tax 316
treasuries 311
unemployment 309

///

Chapter Summary

≫ LO1 Domestic policy consists of laws, government planning, and government actions that concern internal issues of national importance. The policymaking process is initiated when policymakers become aware—through the media or from their constituents—of a problem that needs to be addressed. The process of policymaking includes agenda building, policy formulation, policy adoption, policy implementation, and policy evaluation.

Health-care spending accounts for almost 18 percent of the U.S. economy. A major source of funding is Medicare, the federal program that pays health-care expenses of U.S. residents over the age of sixty-five.

Much of the population has lacked health insurance—a major political issue. In the past, individual health-insurance policies (not obtained through an employer) were expensive and often unobtainable at any price. In 2010, Congress passed the Affordable Care Act (ACA, or Obamacare), which was designed to greatly increase coverage in the United States. It requires residents not already covered to purchase coverage, which is subsidized for low-income persons.

≫ LO2 Today, more than 1 million immigrants enter the United States each year, and foreign-born persons make up about 13 percent of the U.S. population. The status of illegal immigrants, who may number 11 million, is a major political issue. Some people wish to give such persons a legally recognized status and allow them someday to become citizens. Others call for tougher laws against illegal immigration and against hiring undocumented workers.

≫ LO3 Issues concerning energy and the environment are on the nation's agenda. One problem is our reliance on petroleum imports,

given that many petroleum exporters are hostile to American interests. In recent years, however, production techniques such as fracking have increased the domestic supply of crude oil (thereby lowering its cost) and especially of natural gas. Climate change, caused by the emission of CO_2 and other greenhouse gases, is a second major problem, although some dispute how serious it is.

≫ LO4 Fiscal policy is the use of taxes and spending to affect the overall economy. Lower taxes or higher spending can increase the budget deficit, which some believe can stimulate the economy.

The federal government has run a deficit in most years since 1960. The deficit is met by U.S. Treasury borrowing. This adds to the public debt of the U.S. government. Although the budget was temporarily in surplus from 1998 to 2002, large deficits now seem likely for many years to come.

Monetary policy is controlled by the Federal Reserve System, or the Fed. Monetary policy consists of changing the rate of growth of the money supply in an attempt to either stimulate or cool the economy. A loose monetary policy, in which more money is created, encourages economic growth. A tight monetary policy, in which less money is created, may be the only effective way of ending an inflationary spiral.

≫ LO5 U.S. taxes amount to about 30 percent of the gross domestic product. The federal individual income tax is progressive, that is, higher earners pay a larger share of their income. Individuals and corporations that pay taxes at the highest rates will try to pressure Congress into creating exemptions and tax loopholes. Loopholes allow high-income earners to reduce their taxable incomes.

Test Yourself

1. The policymaking process includes, but is not limited to:
   a. agenda building, policy formulation, and judicial approval.
   b. agenda building, policy formulation, and policy adoption.
   c. agenda building, policy formulation, and state referendums.

2. Entitlement programs include:
   a. Social Security and unemployment insurance.
   b. welfare and foreign aid.
   c. highway construction and veterans' benefits.

3. The last two phases of the policymaking process involve policy:
   a. formulation and adoption.
   b. adoption and implementation.
   c. implementation and evaluation.

4. Within U.S. borders, there are many illegal immigrants, numbering as many as:
   a. 3 million.
   b. 23 million.
   c. 11 million.

5. Latino citizens have tended to vote:
   a. for the Republican Party.
   b. for the Democratic Party.
   c. by absentee ballot in elections in their home countries.

6. A major new source of increased energy supplies within the United States comes from:
   a. running existing wells at a faster pace.
   b. fracking (hydraulic fracturing).
   c. the new oil boom in Alaska.

7. Emissions of carbon dioxide (CO_2) have fallen since 2008 in part because of the increased use in power plants of:
   a. natural gas.
   b. uranium.
   c. hydrogen.

8. When an economic slowdown is severe enough, it is officially called a:
   a. depression.
   b. recession.
   c. contraction.

9. Economic boom times are sometimes accompanied by:
   a. inflation.
   b. unemployment.
   c. lower taxes.

10. Fiscal policy involves:
    a. government spending and changes in the money supply in circulation.
    b. government taxation and the changes in the money supply in circulation.
    c. government taxing and spending policies.

11. The federal personal income tax system can be called:
    a. a progressive tax.
    b. a regressive tax.
    c. a degressive tax.

12. Americans who work for a salary typically pay federal income taxes, as well as payroll taxes that fund:
    a. Social Security and Medicaid.
    b. Medicare and Medicaid.
    c. Social Security and Medicare.

Essay Questions

1. Just how serious an offense should illegal immigration be? Construct arguments in favor of considering it a felony and arguments for viewing it as a mere civil infraction.

2. Until recently, Congress always opposed the establishment of a universal health-insurance system for the United States. What could the reasons for this stance have been? Are the reasons compelling? What political interests might oppose a universal system, and why?

Answers to multiple-choice questions: 1. b, 2. a, 3. c, 4. c, 5. b, 6. b, 7. a, 8. b, 9. a, 10. c, 11. a, 12. c.

14 | Foreign Policy

Pool/ABACA/Newscom

French president Emmanuel Macron meets with U.S. president Donald Trump in May 2017. Macron, a moderate, had just decisively beaten Marine Le Pen of the National Front in the French presidential elections. Le Pen is a radical nationalist. **Why might Trump have expressed support for Le Pen during the elections?**

The five **Learning Outcomes (LOs)** below are designed to help improve your understanding of this chapter. After reading this chapter, you should be able to:

≫**LO1** Define *foreign policy*, and discuss moral idealism versus political realism in foreign policy.

≫**LO2** Describe recent foreign policy challenges that involve the use of force.

≫**LO3** Discuss the use of diplomacy in addressing such issues as nuclear proliferation, the rise of China, and the confrontation between Israel and the Palestinians.

≫**LO4** Explain the roles of the president, executive agencies, and Congress in making U.S. foreign policy.

≫**LO5** Cite the main themes in the history of U.S. foreign policy.

Check your understanding of the material with the Test Yourself section at the end of the chapter.

O n September 11, 2001, Americans were forced to change their view of national security and of their relations with the rest of the world—literally overnight. No longer could citizens of the United States believe that national security issues involved only threats overseas or that the American homeland could not be attacked.

Within a few days, it became known that the 9/11 attacks on the World Trade Center and on the Pentagon had been planned and carried out by a terrorist network named al Qaeda, which was directed by the radical Islamist leader Osama bin Laden. The network was closely linked to the Taliban government of Afghanistan, which had ruled that nation since 1996.

Americans were shocked by the success of the attacks. They wondered how our airport security systems could have failed so drastically. Shouldn't our intelligence community have known about, and defended against, this terrorist network? How could our foreign policy have been so blind to the anger of Islamist groups throughout the world?

In this chapter, we examine the tools of foreign policy and national security policy in the light of the many challenges facing the United States. One such challenge for U.S. foreign policymakers today is how best to respond to the threat of terrorism. We also review the history of American foreign policy.

Facing the World: Foreign and Defense Policies

>>> **LO1:** Define *foreign policy*, and discuss moral idealism versus political realism in foreign policy.

The United States is only one nation in a world with almost two hundred independent countries, many located in regions where armed conflict is ongoing. What tools does our nation have to deal with the many challenges to its peace and prosperity? One tool is **foreign policy.** By this term, we mean both the goals the government wants to achieve in the world and the techniques and strategies used to achieve them. These techniques and strategies include **diplomacy, economic aid,** and military intervention.

As you will read later in this chapter, in the United States the *foreign policy process* usually originates with the president and those agencies that provide advice on foreign policy matters. Congressional action and national public debate often affect foreign policy formulation as well.

Aspects of Foreign Policy

As one aspect of overall foreign policy, **national security policy** is designed primarily to protect the independence and the political integrity of the United States. It concerns itself with the defense of the United States against actual or potential enemies.

U.S. national security policy is based on determinations made by the Department of Defense, the Department of State, and a number of other federal agencies, including the National Security Council (NSC). The NSC acts as an advisory body to the president, and it has often been a rival of the State Department in influencing the foreign policy process.

Defense policy is a subset of national security policy. Generally, defense policy refers to the set of policies that direct the nature and activities of the U.S. armed forces. Defense policies are proposed by the leaders of the nation's military forces and the secretary of Defense, and are greatly influenced by congressional decision makers.

Diplomacy refers to the settling of disputes and conflicts among nations by peaceful methods. Diplomacy is also the set of negotiating techniques by which a nation attempts to carry out its foreign policy. Of course, diplomacy can be successful only if the parties involved are willing to negotiate.

Idealism versus Realism in Foreign Policy

Since the earliest years of the republic, Americans have felt that their nation has a special destiny. The American experiment in political and economic liberty, it was thought, would provide the best possible life for its citizens and be a model for other nations. As the United States became a power in world politics, Americans came to believe that the nation's actions in the world should be guided by American political and moral principles.

Foreign Policy
A nation's external goals and the techniques and strategies used to achieve them.

Diplomacy
The process by which states carry on political relations with each other. Also, the process of settling conflicts among nations by peaceful means.

Economic Aid
Assistance to other nations in the form of grants, loans, or credits to buy the assisting nation's products.

National Security Policy
Foreign and domestic policy designed to protect the nation's independence and political integrity. Policy that is concerned with the safety and defense of the nation.

Defense Policy
A subset of national security policy concerning the U.S. armed forces.

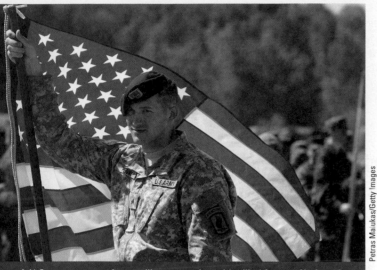

A U.S. paratrooper after a military exercise with allied forces. *Under what circumstances is it appropriate for the United States to intervene abroad using ground forces?*

Petras Malukas/Getty Images

Moral Idealism. This view of America's mission has led to the adoption of many foreign policy initiatives that are rooted in **moral idealism.** This philosophy views the world as fundamentally benign and assumes that most nations can be persuaded to take moral considerations into account when setting their policies.[1] In this perspective, nations should come together and agree to keep the peace, as President Woodrow Wilson (1913–1921) proposed for the League of Nations. Many foreign policy initiatives taken by the United States have been based on this idealistic view of the world. These include humanitarian relief efforts following great natural disasters. For example, the United States provided aid to West Africa in response to an outbreak of the Ebola virus in 2014.

Political Realism. In opposition to the moral perspective is **political realism.** Realists see the world as a dangerous place in which each nation strives for its own survival and interests, regardless of moral considerations. The United States must therefore base its foreign policy decisions on cold calculations, without regard to morality. Realists believe that other nations are, by definition, dangerous. A strong defense will show the world that the United States is willing to protect its interests.

Donald Trump has been a strikingly forthright advocate of political realism—his doctrine of "America first" is as far away from moral idealism as we have ever seen in an American president. Trump has explicitly rejected the policy—endorsed by most recent U.S. presidents—of promoting human rights in his meetings with foreign leaders. He has also exhibited a surprisingly warm attitude toward authoritarian rulers such as Russia's Vladimir Putin and Rodrigo Duterte of the Philippines. Trump's foreign policy has been described as "transactional." That is, he has emphasized exchanging favors with individual nations. Trump has also shown profound skepticism toward collective international organizations such as the North Atlantic Treaty Organization (NATO), a military alliance that includes the United States, Canada, and most of the nations of Europe.

American Foreign Policy—A Mixture of Both. It is important to note that the United States has rarely been guided by only one of these principles. Typically, both moral idealism and political realism affect foreign policymaking. At times, idealism and realism can pull in different directions, making it difficult to establish a coherent policy. The so-called Arab Spring serves as an example of such cross-currents in American foreign policy.

Acting on the basis of political realism, the United States built up long-standing relationships with various dictators in the Arab world, such as Hosni Mubarak of Egypt. Given

Moral Idealism
A philosophy that views nations as normally willing to cooperate and to agree on moral standards for conduct.

Political Realism
A philosophy that views each nation as acting principally in its own interest.

---

1. James M. McCormick, *American Foreign Policy and Process*, 6th ed. (Independence, Ky.: Cengage Learning, 2013).

such alliances, the United States had to determine whether to support existing governments when they came under attack by popular rebellions.

President Obama and then Secretary of State Hillary Clinton, however, did not believe that realism and idealism were necessarily in conflict. The United States could support democratic movements and remain true to its values. Initially, this course of action appeared to be workable, because in Egypt and Tunisia, at least, the democratic rebels were winning. In 2013, however, the military seized power in Egypt, ending its experiment with democracy. In 2014, speaking at the graduation ceremony for the U.S. Military Academy, Obama was blunt: American relations with Egypt were again based on political realism.

As it turned out, Tunisia was the only nation in which the Arab Spring rebellions were a success. In Libya, rebels were initially successful in taking power only in the eastern region. The United States and its European allies then intervened with air strikes to assist the rebels. The Libyan dictator, Muammar Gaddafi, was overthrown and killed. Libya was unable to establish a coherent national government in subsequent years, however, and the country wound up divided between rival regimes. Critics accused idealists of supporting an irresponsible intervention.

Terrorism and Warfare

>>> **LO2:** Describe recent foreign policy challenges that involve the use of force.

The foreign policy of the United States—whether idealist, realist, or both—must be formulated to deal with world conditions. In some instances, these policies have involved the use of force.

The Emergence of Terrorism

Terrorism is a systematic attempt to inspire fear to gain political ends. Typically, terrorism involves the indiscriminate use of violence against noncombatants. In the past, terrorism was a strategy generally employed by radicals who wanted to change the status of a particular nation or province. For example, over many years the Irish Republican Army undertook terrorist attacks in the British province of Northern Ireland with the aim of driving out the British and uniting the province with the Republic of Ireland. In the twenty-first century, however, the United States has confronted a new form of terrorism that is not associated with such clear-cut aims.

September 11. In 2001, nineteen terrorists hijacked four airplanes and crashed three of them into buildings—two into the World Trade Center towers in New York City and one into the Pentagon in Washington, D.C. The fourth airplane crashed in a field in Pennsylvania, after the passengers fought the hijackers.

Why did the al Qaeda network plan and launch attacks on the United States? In part, the attacks were intended to frighten and demoralize America so that it would withdraw its troops from the Middle East.

Al Qaeda's Aims. Al Qaeda's ultimate goals, however, were not limited to forcing the United States to withdraw from the Middle East. Al Qaeda envisioned worldwide revolutionary change, with all nations brought under the theocratic rule of an Islamist empire. Governments have successfully negotiated with terrorists who profess limited aims—today, radicals associated with the Irish Republican Army are part of a coalition government in Northern Ireland. There is no way to negotiate with an organization such as al Qaeda.

Terrorism
A systematic attempt to inspire fear to gain political ends, typically involving the indiscriminate use of violence against noncombatants.

Thousands of Syrian refugees walk back into Syria from Turkey to celebrate the Eid festival in June 2017. *Why has the United States been reluctant to intervene in the Syrian civil war?*

Dha/ZUMA Press/Newscom

Domestic Terrorism in the United States. Al Qaeda is not the only group ever to launch a terrorist attack on U.S. soil. Radicals opposed to the U.S. war in Vietnam set off bombs in the 1960s and 1970s (usually without fatalities). Right-wing terrorists were an issue in the 1990s—notably, a bomb set off at a federal office building in Oklahoma City killed 168 people.

In more recent years, however, attacks by domestic Islamists have been the major concern. Such individuals are typically "self-radicalized" through the Internet and are not controlled by a foreign organization. A bombing at the Boston Marathon in 2013 killed three people and cost fourteen victims at least one of their legs. The alleged perpetrators were two self-radicalized Muslim brothers, one of them a U.S. citizen. A husband-and-wife team killed fourteen people in San Bernardino, California, in 2015. A lone gunman murdered forty-nine people at a nightclub in Orlando, Florida, in 2016. Other nations have experienced devastating incidents. In 2015, terrorists murdered 130 people in Paris, France. In a 2016 atrocity in the French city of Nice, eighty-six were killed, and an additional 434 were injured. A suicide bombing in Manchester, England, in 2017 claimed twenty-three lives.

The War on Terrorism. After 9/11, President George W. Bush implemented stronger security measures, including heightened airport security, new laws allowing greater domestic surveillance of potential terrorists, and increased funding for the military. In addition, Bush launched two military efforts abroad. The first was to attack al Qaeda's bases in Afghanistan, as well as the Taliban government of that country, which was allied with the terrorists. The second, which began in 2003, was a war against the dictatorial regime in Iraq.

Wars in Iraq

In 1990, the Persian Gulf became the setting for a major challenge to the international system set up after World War II (1939–1945). President Saddam Hussein of Iraq sent troops into the neighboring oil sheikdom of Kuwait, occupying that country. This was the most clear-cut case of aggression against an independent nation in half a century. In January 1991, U.S.-led coalition forces retook Kuwait, and the First Gulf War ended.

As part of the cease-fire that ended the First Gulf War, Iraq agreed to allow United Nations (UN) weapons inspectors to oversee the destruction of its missiles and all chemical and nuclear weapons development. In 1999, though, Iraq placed so many obstacles in the path of the UN inspectors that they withdrew from the country.

The Second Gulf War—The Iraq War. In 2002 and early 2003, President Bush began assembling an international coalition that might support further military action in Iraq. Bush was unable to convince the UN Security Council that military force was necessary in Iraq, so the United States took the initiative. In March 2003, U.S. and British forces invaded Iraq and within a month had toppled Hussein's dictatorship. The process of establishing order in Iraq turned out to be very difficult, however.

Occupied Iraq.   The people of Iraq are divided into three principal ethnic groups. The Kurdish-speaking people of the north were overjoyed by the invasion. The Arabs adhering to the Shiite branch of Islam live principally in the south and constitute a majority of the population. They were deeply skeptical of U.S. intentions. The Arabs belonging to the Sunni branch of Islam live mainly to the west of Baghdad. Many Sunnis considered the occupation to be a disaster.

In short order, a Sunni guerrilla insurgency arose and launched attacks against the coalition forces. A newly organized al Qaeda in Iraq sponsored suicide bombings and other attacks against coalition troops and the forces of the new Iraqi government. Al Qaeda also attacked Iraqi Shiites. The major bloodletting in the country now took place between Sunnis and Shiites. By late 2006, polls indicated that about two-thirds of Americans wanted to see an end to the Iraq War—a sentiment expressed in the 2006 elections.

Iraqi Endgame?   In January 2007, President Bush announced a major increase, or "surge," in U.S. troop strength. Skeptics doubted that the new troop levels would have much effect on the outcome. In April 2007, however, Sunni tribal leaders rose up against al Qaeda and called in U.S. troops to help them. Al Qaeda, it seems, had badly overplayed its hand by terrorizing the Sunni population.

During subsequent months, the Iraqi government gained substantial control over its own territory. Still, American attitudes toward the war remained negative. In 2008, President Bush and Iraqi prime minister Nouri al-Maliki negotiated a deadline for withdrawing U.S. troops. U.S. combat forces left Iraq in August 2010. The rest of the American troops were out by the end of 2011.

Afghanistan

The Iraq War was not the only military effort launched by the Bush administration as part of the war on terrorism. The first military effort was directed against al Qaeda camps in Afghanistan and the Taliban regime, which had ruled most of Afghanistan since 1996. In late 2001, after building a coalition of international allies and anti-Taliban rebels within Afghanistan, the United States began an air campaign against the Taliban regime. The anti-Taliban rebels, known as the Northern Alliance, were able to take Kabul, the capital, and oust the Taliban from power.

The Return of the Taliban.   The Taliban were defeated, but not destroyed. The Taliban and al Qaeda both retreated to the rugged mountains between Afghanistan and Pakistan, where they were able to establish bases on the Pakistani side of the border. In 2003, the Taliban began to launch attacks against Afghan soldiers, foreign aid workers, and American troops. Through 2008 and 2009, the Taliban were able to take over a number of Pakistani districts, even as the United States began attacking suspected Taliban and al Qaeda targets in Pakistan using small unmanned aircraft.

During 2009 and 2010, President Obama almost doubled the number of U.S. troops stationed in Afghanistan. At the same time, he announced that he would begin making troop withdrawals in 2011. By 2015, the number of troops was down to about 10,000.

The Death of bin Laden.   In 2011, intelligence agencies obtained evidence that bin Laden might be living in a residential compound in Abbottabad, Pakistan, possibly under the protection of members of Pakistan's military. On May 1, 2011, U.S. Navy SEALs launched a helicopter raid that killed bin Laden and four others.

Female soldiers of the Peshmerga, the militia of Iraq's autonomous Kurdish region. They will join the fight against ISIS in Iraq. *Why might most Arab armies be men-only?*

dpa picture alliance/Alamy Stock Photo

The Civil War in Syria and the Rise of ISIS

In 2011, Syrians rebelled against their dictator, Bashar al-Assad. The rebellion soon turned into a stalemate. Assad's forces inflicted horrifying casualties on the civilian population. By 2017, the death toll was well over 400,000, and almost half the country's people had been driven from their homes. The rebels were also fighting among themselves and were increasingly dominated by radical Islamists who held beliefs similar to those of al Qaeda. With few attractive forces that America could back, political realism left the Obama administration reluctant to intervene.

The Rise of ISIS. The most hard-line Islamist group in Syria was the Islamic State in Iraq and Greater Syria (ISIS), also known as the Islamic State in Iraq and the Levant (ISIL) and as *Daesh*, an Arabic acronym. This group was a reorganized version of al Qaeda in Iraq, but in 2014, the al Qaeda movement expelled ISIS due to its vicious tactics.

As its name implies, ISIS was active in both Syria and Iraq. In June 2014, ISIS launched a major offensive in Iraq that soon left it in control of Mosul, Iraq's second largest city. ISIS was aided in its advance by the acquiescence of various Sunni groups that had grievances against the Shiite-led government of Iraq. At the end of June, ISIS changed its name to simply the "Islamic State" (IS). It announced that it sought to rule not only the Middle East, but the entire world.

The Islamic State in Iraq. IS soon began expelling, killing, and even enslaving religious minorities in the lands it controlled. These included Christians and members of the small Yazidi faith. IS also clashed with the Peshmerga, the militia of Iraq's autonomous Kurdish region. In August 2014, President Obama authorized air strikes to support the Peshmerga. After a reorganization of the Iraqi government to push out anti-Sunni leaders, the United States began to provide air support to the Iraqi government as well. In 2017, Iraqi forces retook Mosul. By that point, U.S. forces in Iraq were back up to almost 5,000 soldiers.

The Ongoing Catastrophe in Syria. By 2015, the civil war in Syria had developed into a three-way conflict among the government, IS, and more moderate rebel factions. Syrian Kurds located along the Turkish border constituted a fourth element. IS conquests in Iraq resulted in U.S. intervention in Syria for the first time. This included the bombing of IS targets and also support for the small number of Syrian rebels who were not Islamist radicals. President Obama was opposed to any additional U.S. involvement, arguing that such a step would not have positive results. Many foreign policy experts disagreed with that calculation, however. President Trump's attitude toward the conflict in Syria has been ambiguous, though in practice Trump's actions have not been greatly different from those undertaken by Obama.

At the request of the Syrian government, in 2015 the Russian air force began air strikes against both IS and the more moderate rebels. Russia claimed to be attacking IS, but the majority of its strikes actually hit moderate targets. It appeared that the Syrian civil war was developing into an international war by proxy. Iran and Russia were in support of the Assad government, while the United States and Saudi Arabia supported various rebel factions. Turkey's position was ambiguous, though it is nominally a U.S. NATO ally. In 2015, more than a million Syrian refugees poured into Europe through Turkey, precipitating a crisis in that continent.

U.S. Diplomatic Efforts

>>>**LO3:** Discuss the use of diplomacy in addressing such issues as nuclear proliferation, the rise of China, and the confrontation between Israel and the Palestinians.

The United States has dealt with many international problems through diplomacy, rather than the use of armed force. Some of these issues include the proliferation of nuclear weapons, the confrontation between Israel and the Palestinians, the growing power of China, and ongoing economic problems in Europe.

Nuclear Weapons

In 1945, the United States was the only nation to possess nuclear weapons. Several nations quickly joined the "nuclear club," however, including the Soviet Union in 1949, Britain in 1952, France in 1960, and China in 1964. India and Pakistan were among the most recent nations to do so, detonating nuclear devices within a few weeks of each other in 1998. North Korea conducted an underground nuclear explosive test in October 2006. Several other nations, Israel in particular, are believed to possess nuclear weapons or the capability to produce them in a short time.

About 15,000 nuclear warheads are known to be stocked worldwide, though the exact number is uncertain. The United States and Russia dismantled some of their nuclear weapons systems after the end of the **Cold War** and the breakup of the Soviet Union in 1991 (discussed later in this chapter). Still, both retain sizable nuclear arsenals.

Nuclear Proliferation: Iran. For years, the United States, the European Union (EU), and the UN have tried to prevent Iran from becoming a nuclear power. In spite of these efforts, many observers believed that Iran was in the process of developing nuclear weapons. The group of nations trying to negotiate with Iran included Britain, China, France, Germany, Russia, and the United States. By 2009, the UN Security Council had voted three rounds of penalties called *sanctions* against Iran in reaction to its nuclear program. By 2012, it was clear that the sanctions were beginning to damage Iran's economy. In 2012, it was disclosed that the United States had successfully destroyed many of Iran's nuclear enrichment centrifuges by deploying a specially designed computer virus. Threats that Israel or the United States might bomb Iran's nuclear sites added to the pressure.

Before 2013, talks between Iran and the six nations just mentioned went nowhere. In 2013, however, Iran elected a new president, Hassan Rouhani, who initiated a "charm offensive" directed at the West. It appeared that for the first time, Iran was prepared to negotiate seriously.

Reaching a Deal. In July 2015, Iran reached a deal with the six world powers and the European Union. The agreement lifted most sanctions in exchange for substantial restrictions on Iran's nuclear program. Until 2030, Iran may produce only limited amounts of low-enriched uranium. The International Atomic Energy Agency will be able to inspect all Iranian nuclear facilities.

Cold War
The ideological, political, and economic confrontation between the United States and the Soviet Union following World War II.

Advocates of the deal contended that even if Iran were to drop out of it, the country would still be at least a year away from building a usable nuclear bomb. In that time, other nations would be able to impose pressure on Iran to change course. Opponents of the deal included most Republicans in Congress and Israeli leader Benjamin Netanyahu. Donald Trump promised to withdraw from the deal if elected. Given that the world's other major powers were part of it, however, it was not certain what would follow from an American withdrawal. In the end, Trump took no action.

Nuclear Proliferation: North Korea. North Korea tested a nuclear device in 2006. An agreement reached in February 2007 provided that North Korea would start disabling its nuclear facilities and allow UN inspectors into the country. In July 2007, North Korea dismantled one of its nuclear reactors and admitted UN inspectors.

By 2009, however, North Korea was pulling back from its treaty obligations. In April, the country tested a long-range missile capable of delivering a nuclear warhead. After the UN Security Council issued a statement condemning the test, North Korea ordered UN inspectors out of the country, broke off negotiations, and conducted a second nuclear test. North Korea has continued to engage in tests since that time. In 2017, it began testing a medium-range rocket capable of reaching South Korea, Japan, the U.S. island of Guam, and most of China.

The United States and other parties have sought to persuade China to take the lead in bringing North Korea back to the negotiating table—China is the one nation that has significant economic leverage over North Korea. China has participated in UN sanctions aimed at bringing North Korea back to the negotiating table. At the same time, China has been reluctant to push that country too far. China is concerned over the consequences that could follow if sanctions or other measures were to lead to a collapse of the North Korean regime.

Chemical Weapons in Syria. Most nations have signed treaties banning the use of chemical weapons. In 2013, however, Bashar al-Assad's regime in Syria used nerve gas against districts under rebel control, with massive fatalities. President Obama proposed to respond to this act by launching air strikes and asked Congress for approval. Russia then announced that Syria would sign a treaty banning chemical weapons and yield up its weapons.

To the surprise of many, the Assad regime cooperated with international inspectors. The weapons were moved to a U.S. ship equipped with decontamination systems. In 2014, President Obama announced that the destruction of the weapons was complete. That same year, however, Assad allegedly used chlorine gas against rebels. Chlorine is not a controlled substance, but its use as a weapon is banned.

In April 2017, the Assad regime employed nerve gas against a rebel-held town in northern Syria, killing up to one hundred civilians. Clearly, either Assad had failed to yield up all of his chemical weapon stocks, or he had managed to obtain

Iranian president Hassan Rouhani. *How successful has Rouhani been in nuclear negotiations with major world powers?*

Itar-Tass Photo Agency/Alamy

a new supply. In response to this attack, President Trump ordered the bombing of the airbase from which the attack was launched. This strike appeared to be a one-time response to a violation, however. Trump did not follow it up with further actions against Syria.

Israel and the Palestinians

As a longtime supporter of the state of Israel, the United States has undertaken to persuade the Israelis to negotiate with the Palestinian Arabs who live in the territories occupied by Israel. The conflict between Israel and the Palestinians, which began in 1948, has been extremely hard to resolve. The internationally recognized solution is for Israel to yield the West Bank and the Gaza Strip to the Palestinians in return for effective security commitments and abandonment by the Palestinians of any right of return to Israel proper. The Palestinians, however, have been unwilling to stop terrorist attacks on Israel, and Israel has been unwilling to dismantle its settlements in the occupied territories. Further, the two parties have been unable to come to an agreement on how much of the West Bank should go to the Palestinians and what compensation (if any) the Palestinians should receive for abandoning all claims to settlement in Israel proper. Although it is clear that any peace deal would require that Palestinians give up the right of return to Israel, the Palestinians have not yet abandoned that claim.

Talks with the PLO. In 1991, under pressure from the United States, the Israelis opened talks with the Palestine Liberation Organization (PLO). In 1993, the PLO and Israel agreed to set up Palestinian self-government—the Palestinian Authority—in the West Bank and the Gaza Strip.

Further, the agreements were rejected by Palestinian radicals, who began a campaign of suicide bombings in Israeli cities. In 2002, the Israeli government moved tanks and troops into Palestinian towns to kill or capture the terrorists. One result of the Israeli reoccupation was an almost complete—if temporary—collapse of the Palestinian Authority.

In February 2004, Israeli prime minister Ariel Sharon announced a plan under which Israel would withdraw from the Gaza Strip, regardless of whether a deal could be reached with the Palestinians.

The Rise of Hamas. In January 2006, the militant group Hamas won a majority of the seats in the Palestinian legislature. American and European politicians refused to talk to Hamas until it agreed to rescind its avowed desire to destroy Israel. In 2007, after fighting between Hamas and the PLO, Hamas wound up in complete control of the Gaza Strip, and the PLO retained exclusive power in the West Bank.

Israel sought to pressure the Hamas regime in the Gaza Strip to relinquish power through an economic blockade. Hamas retaliated by firing a series of rockets into Israel. In January 2009, Israel temporarily reoccupied the Gaza Strip. In June 2014, fighting again broke out between Israel and the Hamas regime in the Gaza Strip.

Xinhua/Alamy Stock Photo

President Trump meets with Israeli prime minister Benjamin Netanyahu in May 2017. *Why has the Israeli-Palestinian dispute been so hard to resolve?*

Normal Trade Relations (NTR) Status
A status granted through an international treaty by which each member nation must treat other members as well as it treats the country that receives its most favorable treatment. This status was formerly known as *most-favored-nation status*.

A cease-fire was finally established in August. By that time, Gaza had suffered massive destruction and loss of life.

Talks Fail Again. In 2013, the United States attempted to restart negotiations between Israel and the Palestinians. By 2014, however, the talks had collapsed again. One obstacle to peace was the tough positions taken by Prime Minister Benjamin Netanyahu, who was elected in 2009. Despite opposition from the Obama administration, Netanyahu accelerated the growth of Israeli settlements in the West Bank. In May 2017, President Trump visited the region and announced his desire to restart the peace talks. Such a step, however, would require an investment of time and energy that the Trump administration might not be able to maintain.

The New Power: China

An important factor in U.S.-Chinese relations has been the large and growing trade ties between the two countries. In 1980, China was granted **normal trade relations (NTR) status** on a year-to-year basis. In 2000, Congress approved a permanent grant of NTR status to China.

While officially Communist, China permits a striking degree of free enterprise. China has become substantially integrated into the world economic system, and it exports considerably more goods and services to the United States than it imports. As a result, China's *current account surplus* (the most comprehensive measurement of excess exports) has been very large, though it has fallen since 2011.

As a presidential candidate, Donald Trump made such trade imbalances a major issue. He threatened major economic retaliation against China, which might take the form of tariffs (taxes) on imports from China and other nations running a surplus in their trade with the United States. After his inauguration, however, Trump dialed back such rhetoric substantially. Trump admitted that he needed China's help in addressing issues such as North Korea's nuclear program. Trade disputes, in other words, were less important than national security.

China's Explosive Economic Growth. The growth of the Chinese economy during the last thirty-five years is one of the most important developments in world history. For the past several decades, the Chinese economy has grown at a rate of about 10 percent annually, a long-term growth rate previously unknown in human history. Never have so many escaped poverty so quickly.

China now produces more steel than America and Japan combined. It generates more than 40 percent of the world's output of cement. Skyscrapers fill the skyline of every major Chinese city.

In 2007, for the first time, China manufactured more passenger automobiles than did the United States. China is building a limited-access highway system that, when complete, will be longer than the U.S. interstate highway system. The economy of China may already be larger than that of the United States. China, in short, is becoming the world's second superpower.

The Issue of Taiwan. Inevitably, economic power translates into military potential. Is this a problem? It could be if China had territorial ambitions. At this time, China does not appear to have an appetite for non-Chinese territory. China's leaders, however, seem to have

Interact

One way to learn more about foreign affairs is to consult news sources from countries that are either not allied with the United States or actively hostile toward it. You can find English-language news reports from China by searching online for "cctv news." Find news from Russia simply by entering "rt." Both websites are controlled by their governments. As you scan these sites, ask yourself these questions:

- How does the site report on its own national leaders?
- According to the site, what appear to be the most important issues?
- What attitudes does the site project toward the United States?
- Do the reports from either nation suggest that it might pose a threat to world peace?

a rather expansive concept of what is meant by "Chinese territory." For example, China has always considered the island of Taiwan to be Chinese. In principle, Taiwan agrees. Taiwan calls itself the "Republic of China" and officially considers its government to be the legitimate ruler of the entire country—both Taiwan and mainland China. This diplomatic fiction has remained in effect since 1949, when the Chinese Communist Party won a civil war and drove the anti-Communist forces off the mainland.

China's position is that sooner or later, Taiwan must rejoin the rest of China. The position of the United States is that this reunification must not come about by force. Is peaceful reunification possible? China holds up Hong Kong as an example. Hong Kong came under Chinese sovereignty peacefully in 1997. The people of Taiwan, however, are far from considering Hong Kong to be an acceptable precedent.

Chinese Nationalism. Growing expressions of Chinese nationalism have raised concern in some of China's neighbors. China has recently engaged in disputes with Japan, the Philippines, Vietnam, and other Asian nations over the ownership of uninhabited islands in the East China and South China seas. In 2011, President Obama visited Australia and promised to establish a new U.S. force at Darwin, on Australia's north coast. This development was widely perceived as an attempt to reassure nations in the area that were concerned about potential

Chinese president Xi Jinping and his wife, Peng Liyuan, visit Mexico. Peng Liyuan, a People's Liberation Army folksinger, was nationally famous years before her husband became China's leader. *What has happened with China's economy in recent years?*

Chinese pressure. In one arena—cyberspace—Chinese-American relations were already quite heated. In 2014 and 2015, the United States accused the Chinese military of sponsoring cyberattacks on U.S. computer networks.

Economic Troubles in Europe

Many Europeans consider the European Union (EU) to be one of their most important achievements. The EU, which grew out of the earlier European Economic Community, has been seen as guaranteeing a permanent peace in Europe. Given that Europe was home to World Wars I and II—arguably the two greatest disasters in human history—such a peace is of the utmost importance to the United States and the world. In 2000, a majority of EU members sought to deepen their union through a common currency, the euro.

The Debt Crisis. The seventeen nations that shared the euro were hit hard by the worldwide financial panic of 2008. In Greece and, to a lesser extent, Portugal, governments had borrowed irresponsibly. In Ireland and Spain, many real estate loans went sour, and these countries found themselves in danger when their governments assumed the debts of the threatened banks.

These nations began running out of funds to service their debts, and they faced ruinous interest rates if they attempted to borrow in the financial markets. If a nation such as Britain, Japan, or the United States faced such a crisis, it could rely on its central bank—in America, the Fed—to serve as *lender of last resort* and simply "print" the necessary money. But the "Eurozone" nations did not control their own money supplies, and the European Central Bank (ECB) was barred from acting as lender of last resort. Investors began pulling funds out of the troubled nations, reducing their money supplies further. The panic threatened to spread to Italy. Eventually, Eurozone nations did come up with bailout plans for Greece, Ireland, Portugal, and Spain. Perhaps of even more importance, the ECB developed indirect methods of functioning as a lender of last resort.

The German Question. A major response of the ECB to the crisis was to demand that troubled governments follow policies of fiscal austerity, in which they would meet their debts by major reductions in spending and increases in taxes. Such a policy directly contradicted the advice of Keynesian economics. Keynesians argued that austerity would push the periphery further into recession, thus making the debt crisis even harder to resolve. Leaders of key nations such as Germany, however, were profoundly hostile to Keynesianism.

An additional problem has been Germany's tremendous trade surplus. In 2011, Germany's current account surplus passed that of China to become the largest in the world. According to most economists, the size of a nation's current account balance has little to do with trade agreements. For any country, the current account balance is actually a function of the nation's own economic policy. If America as a whole consumes more than it produces, it will have to make up the difference through imports from abroad. In other words, it will run a current account deficit. Attempts to reduce imports from one nation will simply result in more imports from somewhere else. The same principle applies—in reverse—to Germany. If Germany as a whole consumes *less* than it produces, it will run a surplus. Many economists, therefore, argue that Germany should encourage its own citizens to consume more, through lower taxes or more spending on infrastructure. The result would be a more balanced German economy and greater economic growth throughout Europe and the world.

Given President Trump's hostility toward trade surpluses that other nations have with the United States, it was inevitable that he would pay attention to the German surplus. During a May 2017 visit to Europe, Trump stated: "The Germans are bad, very bad. See the millions of cars they are selling in the U.S.? Terrible. We will stop this." Such language was not likely to persuade the Germans to trim their current account surplus by easing their austerity policies. Further, Trump appeared not to understand that under the EU, Germany simply did not have an independent trade policy. All trade issues are handled by the EU itself.

Greece at the Breaking Point. In 2015, having experienced average wage cuts of 25 percent plus 30 percent unemployment, the Greek electorate rebelled against austerity. In January of that year, voters threw out a multiparty coalition and gave Syriza—a seriously left-wing party—control of the government. Syriza, however, was unable to obtain any better terms from its European creditors. The question of whether Greece could actually repay its obligations in full was postponed.

Brexit. A major concern during the Greek crisis was that Greece might be forced to exit from the Eurozone—or even from the EU as a whole. "Grexit" never happened. In 2013, however, for domestic political reasons, British prime minister David Cameron promised a referendum on U.K. membership in the EU if his Conservative Party won the 2015 elections. The Conservatives won, and the referendum was duly held in June 2016. The United States, almost every other world power, and all major U.K. institutions backed "remain." (Donald Trump was a major exception in endorsing "leave.") Still, the "leave" campaign won by a narrow margin. Cameron was forced to resign.

The number-one issue for those endorsing "Brexit"—Britain's exit from the EU— was immigration. The vote was held in the wake of massive refugee flows into continental Europe from Syria and other troubled nations. Britain faced little pressure to accept Syrian refugees. Under EU law, however, all members are required to accept "three freedoms"—the free movement not only of goods and services, but also of investment capital and of labor. By 2016, thousands of Eastern Europeans had entered Britain seeking work. In 2017, the new Conservative prime minister, Theresa May, began talks with her continental counterparts.

Who Makes Foreign Policy?

>>> **LO4:** Explain the roles of the president, executive agencies, and Congress in making U.S. foreign policy.

Given the vast array of challenges in the world, developing a comprehensive U.S. foreign policy is a demanding task. Does this responsibility fall to the president, to Congress, or to both acting jointly? There is no easy answer to this question because, as constitutional authority Edwin S. Corwin once observed, the U.S. Constitution created an "invitation to struggle" between the president and Congress for control over the foreign policy process. Let us look first at the powers given to the president by the Constitution.

Constitutional Powers of the President

The Constitution confers broad powers on the president. Article II vests the executive power of the government in the president. The presidential oath of office, given in Article II, Section 1, requires that the president "solemnly swear" to "preserve, protect and defend the Constitution of the United States."

War Powers. In addition, and perhaps more important, Article II, Section 2, designates the president as "Commander in Chief of the Army and Navy of the United States." Starting with Abraham Lincoln, all presidents have interpreted this authority broadly. Indeed, since George Washington's administration, the United States has been involved in at least 125 undeclared wars that were conducted under presidential authority. For example, in 1950 Harry Truman ordered U.S. armed forces in the Pacific to counter North Korea's invasion of South Korea. Bill Clinton sent troops to Haiti and Bosnia. George W. Bush initiated wars in Afghanistan and Iraq, and Barack Obama undertook air strikes to support rebels in Libya.

Treaties and Executive Agreements. Article II, Section 2, of the Constitution also gives the president the power to make treaties, provided that the Senate concurs. In addition to this formal treaty-making power, the president makes use of executive agreements. Since World War II (1939–1945), executive agreements have accounted for almost 95 percent of the understandings reached between the United States and other nations.

Other Constitutional Powers. An additional power conferred on the president in Article II, Section 2, is the right to appoint ambassadors, other public ministers, and consuls. In Section 3 of that article, the president is given the power to recognize foreign governments by receiving their ambassadors.

The Executive Branch and Foreign Policymaking

There are at least four foreign policymaking sources within the executive branch, in addition to the president. These are the (1) Department of State, (2) National Security Council, (3) intelligence community, and (4) Department of Defense.

The Department of State. In principle, the State Department is the executive agency that has primary authority over foreign affairs. It supervises U.S. relations with the nearly two hundred independent nations around the world and with the United Nations and other multinational groups. It staffs embassies and consulates throughout the world. It does this with one of the smallest budgets of the cabinet departments.

The National Security Council. The National Security Council (NSC) is managed by the national security adviser. Other members are the president, the vice president, the secretaries of State and Defense, and often the chairperson of the Joint Chiefs of Staff and the director of the Central Intelligence Agency (CIA). The role of national security adviser has changed from president to president. National Security Adviser Henry Kissinger was President Nixon's most important confidant. Under President Obama, however, the adviser was relatively unimportant.

The role of national security adviser has regained some of its former importance under President Trump. It has also been a source of political difficulties, however. Trump's first adviser was retired Army lieutenant general Michael Flynn, who had been forced out of an intelligence position in the Obama administration for what was in effect insubordination. Flynn served under Trump for less than a month. He was fired for lying to Vice President Mike Pence about contacts with Russian officials before Trump took office. Flynn was at the center of an investigation undertaken by Special Counsel Robert Mueller into Russian interference in the 2016 elections. In contrast, Flynn's replacement, Lieutenant General H. R. McMaster, had a sterling reputation. He soon became known for for giving Trump advice that the president did not want to hear.

Doug Mills/AP Images

President George W. Bush, fourth from the right, with his National Security Council (NSC) the day after the terrorist attacks on September 11, 2001. Secretary of State Colin Powell is to the left of the president. Vice President Dick Cheney is to the right. National Security Adviser Condoleezza Rice is at the far end of the table. *What is the NSC's role in determining U.S. foreign policy?*

The Intelligence Community. The **intelligence community** consists of the forty or more government agencies and bureaus that are involved in intelligence activities. The CIA, created as part of the National Security Act of 1947, is the key official member of the intelligence community.

Intelligence activities consist mostly of overt information gathering, but covert actions also are undertaken. Covert actions, as the name implies, are carried out in secret, and the American public rarely finds out about them. The CIA covertly aided in the overthrow of the Mossadegh regime in Iran in 1953 and was instrumental in destabilizing the Allende government in Chile from 1970 to 1973.

The Intelligence Community and the War on Terrorism. With the rise of terrorism as a threat, the intelligence agencies have received more funding and enhanced surveillance powers, but these moves have also provoked fears of civil liberties violations. Legislation enacted in 2004 established the Office of the Director of National Intelligence to oversee the intelligence community.

A simmering controversy that came to a boil in 2009 concerned the CIA's use of a technique called *waterboarding* while interrogating several prisoners in the years immediately following 9/11. In May 2009, President Obama, even as he denounced waterboarding, assured CIA employees that no member of the agency would be penalized for following Justice Department rulings that had legitimized harsh interrogation methods. As a candidate, Trump advocated methods that would be "worse than waterboarding." As president, he accepted advice from his secretary of defense not to restore such tactics.

The Department of Defense. The Department of Defense (DOD) was created in 1947 to bring all of the various activities of the American military establishment under the jurisdiction of a single department headed by a civilian secretary of Defense. At the same time, the Joint Chiefs of Staff, consisting of the commanders of the various military branches and a chairperson, was created to formulate a unified military strategy.

Although the Department of Defense is larger than any other federal department, it declined in size after the fall of the Soviet Union in 1991. In the subsequent ten years, the total number of civilian employees was reduced by about 400,000, to approximately 665,000. Military personnel were also reduced in number. The wars in Afghanistan and Iraq forced increases in funding and civilian staff. Attempts in 2012 to reduce federal spending, however, meant cuts in the military budget from 2013 on.

Congress Balances the Presidency

A new interest in the balance of power between Congress and the president on foreign policy questions developed during the Vietnam War (1965–1975). Sensitive to public frustration over the long and costly war and angry at Richard Nixon for some of his other actions as president, Congress attempted to establish limits on the power of the president in setting foreign and defense policy.

The War Powers Resolution. In 1973, Congress passed the War Powers Resolution over President Nixon's veto. The act limited the president's use of troops in military action without congressional consultation and approval. Most presidents, however, have not interpreted the "consultation" provisions of the act as meaning that Congress should be involved before military action is taken. Instead, Presidents Ford, Carter, Reagan, George H. W. Bush, Clinton, and Obama undertook military actions and then informed congressional leaders.

Intelligence Community
The government agencies that gather information about the capabilities and intentions of foreign governments or that engage in covert actions.

The Pentagon takes its name from its unusual shape. When the media refer to "the Pentagon," they are making reference to the Department of Defense. *What does it say about American self-confidence that its military headquarters is so obvious from the air?*

Hisham Ibrahim/Getty Images

The Power of the Purse. One of Congress's most significant constitutional powers is the so-called power of the purse. The president may order that a certain action be taken, but that order cannot be executed unless Congress funds it. When the Democrats took control of Congress in January 2007, many asked whether the new Congress would use its power of the purse to bring an end to the Iraq War, in view of strong public opposition to the war. Congress's decision was to add conditions to an emergency war-funding request submitted by the president. The conditions required the president to establish a series of timelines for the removal of American troops from Iraq. President George W. Bush immediately threatened to veto any bill that imposed such conditions on the funding. His threat carried the day. The Democrats simply did not have a large enough majority to override a veto.

The Major Foreign Policy Themes

>>> **LO5:** Cite the main themes in the history of U.S. foreign policy.

In the early years of the nation, presidents and the people generally agreed that the United States should avoid foreign entanglements and concentrate instead on its own development. From the beginning of the twentieth century until the present, however, a major theme has been increasing global involvement. The theme of the post–World War II years was the containment of communism. A theme for at least the first part of the twenty-first century is combating terrorism.

The Formative Years: Avoiding Entanglements

Monroe Doctrine
A policy statement made by President James Monroe in 1823. The United States would not accept any new European intervention in the Western Hemisphere. In return, the United States would not meddle in European affairs.

Isolationist Foreign Policy
A policy of abstaining from an active role in international affairs or alliances, which characterized U.S. foreign policy toward Europe during most of the 1800s.

The founders of the United States had a basic mistrust of European governments. This was a logical position at a time when the United States was so weak militarily that it could not influence European developments directly. Moreover, being protected by oceans that took weeks to cross certainly allowed the nation to avoid foreign entanglements. During the 1800s, therefore, the United States generally stayed out of European conflicts and politics. In the Western Hemisphere, however, the United States pursued an active policy of expansion. The nation purchased Louisiana in 1803, annexed Texas in 1845, gained substantial territory from Mexico in 1848, purchased Alaska in 1867, and annexed Hawaii in 1898.

The Monroe Doctrine. President James Monroe, in his message to Congress in 1823, set out three principles: (1) European nations should not establish new colonies in the Western Hemisphere, (2) European nations should not intervene in the affairs of independent nations of the Western Hemisphere, and (3) the United States would not interfere in the affairs of European nations. The **Monroe Doctrine** was the underpinning of the U.S. **isolationist foreign policy** toward Europe, which continued throughout the 1800s.

The Spanish-American War and World War I. The end of the isolationist policy started with the Spanish-American War in 1898. Winning the war gave the United States possession of Guam, Puerto Rico, and the Philippines (which gained independence in 1946). On the heels of that war came World War I (1914–1918). The United States declared war on Germany in 1917 because that country refused to give up its campaign of sinking all ships headed for Britain, including passenger ships from America.

In the 1920s, the United States went "back to normalcy," as President Warren G. Harding urged it to do. U.S. military forces were largely disbanded, and the nation returned to a period of isolationism.

The Era of Internationalism

Isolationism was permanently shattered by the bombing of the U.S. naval base at Pearl Harbor, Hawaii, on December 7, 1941. The surprise attack by the Japanese caused the deaths of 2,403 American servicemen. President Franklin Roosevelt asked Congress to declare war on Japan immediately, and the United States entered World War II. Germany then declared war on the United States.

At the conclusion of the war, the United States was the only major participating country to emerge with its economy intact, and even strengthened. The United States was also the only country to have control over operational nuclear weapons. President Harry Truman had made the decision to use two atomic bombs in August 1945 to end the war with Japan. (Historians still argue over the necessity of this action, which ultimately killed more than 100,000 Japanese and left an equal number permanently injured.) The United States truly had become the world's superpower.

The Cold War. The United States had become an uncomfortable ally of the Soviet Union after Adolf Hitler's invasion of that country. Soon after World War II ended, relations between the Soviet Union and the West deteriorated. The Soviet Union wanted a weakened Germany, and to achieve this, it insisted that Germany be divided in two, with East Germany becoming a buffer against the West. Little by little, the Soviet Union helped to install Communist governments in Eastern European countries, which were soon referred to collectively as the **Soviet bloc.** In response, the United States encouraged the rearming of Western Europe. The Cold War had begun.

Containment Policy. In 1947, a remarkable article was published in *Foreign Affairs* magazine, signed by "X." The actual author was George F. Kennan, chief of the policy-planning staff for the State Department. The doctrine of **containment** set forth in the article became—according to many—the bible of Western foreign policy. "X" argued that whenever and wherever the Soviet Union could successfully challenge the West, it would do so. He recommended that our policy toward the Soviet Union be "firm and vigilant containment of Russian expansive tendencies."[2]

The containment theory was expressed clearly in the **Truman Doctrine,** which was enunciated by President Harry Truman in 1947. Truman held that the United States must help countries in which a Communist takeover seemed likely. Later that year, he backed the Marshall Plan, an economic assistance plan for Europe that was intended to prevent the expansion of Communist influence there. In 1949, the United States, along with several European

Soviet Bloc
The Soviet Union and the Eastern European countries that installed Communist regimes after World War II and that were dominated by the Soviet Union.

Containment
A U.S. diplomatic policy adopted by the Truman administration to contain Communist power within its existing boundaries.

Truman Doctrine
The policy adopted by President Harry Truman in 1947 to halt Communist expansion.

Photo courtesy of U.S. Air Force

President Truman ordered two atomic bomb attacks on Japan in 1945. *Was his decision justified?*

---

2. X, "The Sources of Soviet Conduct," *Foreign Affairs*, July 1947, p. 575.

nations, entered into a military alliance called the North Atlantic Treaty Organization, or NATO, to offer a credible response to any Soviet military attack.

Superpower Relations

During the Cold War, there was never any direct military conflict between the United States and the Soviet Union. Only on occasion did the United States enter a conflict with any Communist-led country. Two such occasions were in Korea and in Vietnam.

The Korean War. After the end of World War II, northern Korea was occupied by the Soviet Union, and southern Korea was occupied by the United States. The result was two rival Korean governments. In 1950, North Korea invaded South Korea. Under UN authority, the United States entered the war, which prevented an almost certain South Korean defeat. When U.S. forces were on the brink of conquering North Korea, however, China joined the war on the side of the North, resulting in a stalemate. An armistice signed in 1953 led to the two Koreas that exist today. U.S. forces have remained in South Korea since that time.

The Vietnam War. The Vietnam War (1965–1975) also involved the United States in a civil war between a Communist north and pro-Western south. When the French army in Indochina was defeated by the Communist forces of Ho Chi Minh in 1954 and the two Vietnams were created, the United States assumed the role of supporting the South Vietnamese government against North Vietnam. American forces in Vietnam at the height of the U.S. involvement totaled more than 500,000 troops. In excess of 58,000 Americans were killed in the conflict. A peace agreement in 1973 allowed U.S. troops to leave the country, and in 1975, North Vietnam easily occupied Saigon (the South Vietnamese capital) and unified the nation.

Over the course of the Vietnam War, the debate concerning U.S. involvement became extremely heated and, as mentioned previously, spurred congressional efforts to limit the ability of the president to commit forces to armed combat. The military draft was also a major source of contention during the Vietnam War.

In a famous meeting in Yalta in February 1945, British prime minister Winston Churchill (left), U.S. president Franklin Roosevelt (center), and Soviet leader Joseph Stalin (right) decided the fate of several nations in Europe, including Germany. *What happened to Germany immediately after World War II?*

Library of Congress Prints & Photographs Division, Washington, D.C.

The Cuban Missile Crisis. Perhaps the closest the two superpowers came to a nuclear confrontation was the Cuban missile crisis in 1962. The Soviets placed missiles in Cuba, ninety miles off the U.S. coast, in response to Cuban fears of an American invasion and to try to balance an American nuclear advantage. President John F. Kennedy and his advisers rejected the option of invading Cuba, setting up a naval blockade around the island instead. In October, the Soviet Union announced the withdrawal of its missile operations from Cuba. In exchange, the United States agreed not to invade Cuba in the future.

Still, the United States maintained a comprehensive economic embargo of Cuba following this crisis. The relationship between the

United States and Cuba did not substantially improve until 2015, when President Obama announced plans to establish diplomatic relations with the Cuban government.

A Period of Détente. The French word **détente** means a relaxation of tensions. By the end of the 1960s, it was clear that some efforts had to be made to reduce the threat of nuclear war between the United States and the Soviet Union. The Soviet Union had gradually begun to catch up in the building of bombers and missiles, thus balancing the nuclear scales between the two countries. Each nation had acquired the military capacity to destroy the other.

As the result of lengthy negotiations under Secretary of State Henry Kissinger and President Richard Nixon, the United States and the Soviet Union signed the Strategic Arms Limitation Treaty (SALT I) in May 1972. That treaty limited the number of offensive missiles each country could deploy.

The policy of détente was not limited to the U.S. relationship with the Soviet Union. Seeing an opportunity to capitalize on increasing friction between the Soviet Union and the People's Republic of China, Kissinger secretly began negotiations to establish a new relationship with China. President Nixon eventually visited that nation in 1972. The visit set the stage for the formal diplomatic recognition of that country, which occurred during the Carter administration (1977–1981).

Nuclear Arms Agreements with the Soviet Union and Russia. In subsequent years, several American presidents negotiated and signed arms control agreements with the Soviet Union (and later, with Russia). These presidents included Republicans Ronald Reagan (1981–1989) and George H. W. Bush (1989–1993). The most recent such treaty, New START, was signed in 2010 by President Obama and Dmitry Medvedev, who was then president of Russia. New START reduced the number of permitted warheads to 1,550 for each side, a drop of about 30 percent from previous agreements. After some delays, the Senate ratified the treaty.

The Dissolution of the Soviet Union. In 1989, the fall of the Berlin Wall that had divided that city into eastern and western sectors marked the first step in the reunification of Germany. By then, it was clear that the Soviet Union had relinquished much of its political and military control over the states of Eastern Europe that formerly had been part of the Soviet bloc. No one expected the Soviet Union to dissolve into separate states as quickly as it did, however. Demands for political, ethnic, and religious autonomy grew, and on the day after Christmas in 1991, the Soviet Union was officially dissolved into fifteen independent nations.

Russia after the Soviet Union. Vladimir Putin became Russia's second president in 2000, following Boris Yeltsin. Putin chipped away at Russia's democratic institutions, slowly turning the country into what was, in essence, an elected autocracy.

In recent years, the United States has become concerned over Russia's aggressive attitude toward its neighbors. For example, in 2008,

Détente
A French word meaning a relaxation of tensions. The term characterized U.S.-Soviet relations as they developed under President Richard Nixon and Secretary of State Henry Kissinger.

A roadblock set up by pro-Russian militias in the eastern Ukraine to control traffic between rebel-held areas and the rest of the country. *Why is Russia so hostile to the Ukrainian government?*

Russian troops entered Georgia to prevent that nation from retaking an autonomous region that was under Russian protection.

Crisis in Ukraine. In November 2013, Ukraine's pro-Russian president Viktor Yanukovych abruptly broke off economic talks with the European Union, apparently under pressure from Putin. The resulting tumult was so intense that Yanukovych fled the country in February 2014. Parliament assumed power and began steering the country back toward Europe.

Putin denounced the new government as "fascist." Claiming the right to protect Russian-speaking populations in Ukraine, Putin annexed the Crimean Peninsula, which has an ethnic-Russian majority. Pro-Russian militias, with Russian support, forceably took control of parts of two eastern provinces. Western nations responded with a series of sanctions. Attempts to obtain a cease-fire in eastern Ukraine had mixed results. The annexation of Crimea, however, appeared to be irreversible. How much of a problem is Putin's belligerence? This chapter's *At Issue* feature addresses that question.

AT ISSUE

How Dangerous Is Putin's Russia?

More than fifteen years ago, the former head of the Soviet Union's secret police, Vladimir Putin, took over as the leader of the Russian government. Many hoped he would support integration with the West and the rule of law. Today, few believe that Putin ever agreed with these goals. Rather, they see an autocrat, chosen through corrupt elections, who rules his country with an iron fist. Putin has called the collapse of the Soviet Union "the greatest geopolitical catastrophe of the century." His actions indicate that he wants to reverse it and dominate all the nations that were once part of the Soviet Union. He has occupied several disputed districts in neighboring countries. He has also invaded and annexed Ukraine's Crimea province. Almost all journalists who have opposed him have either fled Russia or are dead. The free press in Russia is almost extinct.

Putin Is a Very Dangerous Leader

Some believe that Putin is not going to stop after his takeover of Crimea. He continues to provide weapons and even Russian troops to support rebels in eastern Ukraine, in spite of many cease-fires. He is sending sophisticated air defense systems to Iran. He has tried to lure China into an anti-Western alliance, though China does not appear to be greatly interested.

Putin has threatened all of the small Baltic countries—Estonia, Latvia, and Lithuania. Russia's air force has begun flying nuclear-armed bombers around the world on an ongoing basis. Russian jets have constantly violated the air-space of the Scandinavian and Baltic nations. Some of Putin's government officials have casually mentioned in off-the-record discussions that Russia was prepared to use its nuclear weapons.

What, then, is to be done? Enhanced military support for NATO's easternmost members has been one response. Those in Congress who are most alarmed by Putin's behavior also advocate supplying U.S. arms to the Ukrainian government.

Russia Presents a Problem, but One We Can Handle

Others believe that providing Ukraine with arms would be a mistake. Unless NATO is prepared for all-out war in Ukraine, Putin can always provide his minions with more military support than we can offer the Ukrainian government.

Unfortunately, the problem with Russia is not just Putin. Most Russians do not accept that their country should be one nation among many, playing by universal rules. They believe Russia is a great power that deserves special respect. In particular, it must have a "sphere of influence" over neighboring countries, which cannot be allowed to pursue policies that conflict with Russian interests. After all, aren't Western European nations mere puppets of the Americans?

We need to resurrect the policy of containment once used against the Soviet Union. We must be firm, but not reckless. Containment can succeed. Russia is fundamentally weak. It has few real friends. Its economy and its military power are puny compared to ours. In time, Russians will realize that belligerence is self-defeating.

For Critical Analysis

How can a country with a small economy still be a threat to the United States?

Russia's Future. Even as Russia reasserts itself as a great power, its future is in doubt. Its population is dropping and may fall as low as 138 million by 2050, down from 150 million. Russia has not only a low birthrate but also a very high death rate—Russian life expectancy for men is below that of India, despite the widespread poverty in that country. If Russia's population continues to fall, its ability to project power will decline as well.

MAKING A DIFFERENCE

Working for Human Rights

In many countries throughout the world, human rights are not protected. In some nations, people are imprisoned, tortured, or killed because they oppose the current regime. In other nations, certain ethnic or racial groups are oppressed by the majority population.

Why Should You Care? The defense of human rights is unlikely to put a single dollar in your pocket, so why get involved? The strongest reason for involving yourself with human rights issues in other countries is simple moral altruism—unselfish regard for the welfare of others.

What Can You Do? How can you work for the improvement of human rights in other nations? One way is to join an organization that attempts to keep watch over human rights violations. By publicizing human rights violations, such groups try to pressure nations into changing their practices. Sometimes, they are able to apply enough pressure and cause enough embarrassment that victims may be freed from prison or allowed to emigrate.

If you want to obtain general information about the position of the United States on human rights violations, enter "state human rights" into a search engine.

Amnesty International U.S.A. and the American Friends Service Committee (AFSC) are well known for their watchdog efforts in countries that violate human rights for political reasons. To find Amnesty International, go to www.amnestyusa.org. For the AFSC, type "afsc" into a search engine.

Amnesty International members in front of the White House protest America's use of drone strikes in the war on terrorism. Activists claim that too many innocent civilians die in drone attacks against terrorists. *Are such deaths something that Americans should worry about?*

Ann Little/Alamy

Key Terms

Chapter Summary

≫LO1 *Foreign policy* includes the nation's external goals and the techniques and strategies used to achieve them. *Diplomacy* involves the nation's external relationships and is an attempt to resolve conflict without resort to arms. U.S. foreign policy is based both on moral idealism and on political realism.

≫LO2 Terrorism is the attempt to create fear to gain political ends by violence against noncombatants. It has become a major challenge facing the United States and other nations. The United States waged war on terrorism after the attacks of September 11, 2001.

In 1991 and again in 2003, the United States sent combat troops to Iraq. The second war in Iraq, begun in 2003, succeeded in toppling the dictatorship of Saddam Hussein, but led to a long, grinding conflict with insurgent forces. The United States also went to war in Afghanistan to track down al Qaeda, which was responsible for the 9/11 attacks, and to expel the Taliban government that had supported the terrorists. In the last several years, the growth of the terrorist group ISIS has drawn the United States back into Iraq and, to an extent, into Syria as well.

≫LO3 Recent diplomatic efforts by the United States include containing the nuclear ambitions of Iran and North Korea. The rise of China as a superpower raises a series of issues, including trade concerns. American efforts to promote the peace process between Israel and the Palestinians have had limited success. Economic issues, such as European economic problems, demand U.S. attention.

≫LO4 The U.S. Constitution designates the president as commander in chief of the army and navy. Presidents have interpreted this authority broadly. They also have the power to make treaties and executive agreements. The State Department is the executive agency with primary authority over foreign affairs. The National Security Council also plays a major role. The intelligence community engages in information gathering and covert operations. To establish some limits on the power of the president to intervene abroad, Congress passed the War Powers Resolution in 1973.

≫LO5 In the early years of the nation, isolationism was the foreign policy strategy. With the start of the twentieth century, isolationism gave way to global involvement. The end of the policy of isolationism toward Europe started with the Spanish-American War of 1898. U.S. involvement in Europe became more extensive when the United States entered World War I. The United States was the only major country to emerge from World War II with its economy intact and with operating nuclear weapons.

After World War II, the Cold War began. A policy of containment of the Soviet Union was enunciated in the Truman Doctrine.

The United States signed nuclear arms control agreements with the Soviet Union under several presidents. After the fall of the Soviet Union, Russia emerged as a less threatening state. Under President Vladimir Putin, however, Russia has moved away from democracy and begun threatening its neighbors.

Test Yourself

1. As part of foreign policy, national security policy is designed to:
   a. provide economic assistance to other nations.
   b. ensure that all other countries respect each other's borders.
   c. protect the independence and political integrity of the United States.

2. In foreign policy, U.S. support for disaster relief is sometimes an example of:
   a. moral idealism.
   b. political realism.
   c. strategic balancing.

3. Acts of terrorism are:
   a. the result of governments' attempts to gain new territory.
   b. attempts to inspire fear to gain political ends.
   c. due to governments that failed in diplomacy.

4. The three major groups in Iraq are:
   a. the Arabs, the Kurds, and the Christians.
   b. the Sunni Arabs, the Shiite Arabs, and the Taliban.
   c. the Sunni Arabs, the Shiite Arabs, and the Kurds.

5. The two countries that today represent the most serious problems with nuclear proliferation are:
   a. Iran and North Korea.
   b. Japan and Germany.
   c. China and Brazil.

6. China considers the following to be part of its territory:
   a. Vietnam.
   b. Taiwan.
   c. Mongolia.

7. The Palestinian territories are made up of:
   a. Judea and Samaria.
   b. The West Bank and the Golan Heights.
   c. The West Bank and the Gaza Strip.

8. The intelligence community is involved in foreign policy and consists of:
   a. the CIA and the Department of Defense.
   b. more than forty government agencies and bureaus involved in intelligence activities.
   c. the CIA and the National Security Council.

9. In the 1820s, the United States proclaimed that it would not accept any new European intervention in the Western Hemisphere, and in turn it would not intervene in European affairs. This was the:
   a. Monroe Doctrine.
   b. Jackson Doctrine.
   c. policy of détente.

10. After World War II, President Harry Truman vowed that the United States must help countries in which a Communist takeover seemed likely. This became known as the:
    a. rollback policy.
    b. Marshall Plan.
    c. Truman Doctrine.

11. The Cold War refers to a period during which:
    a. the Soviet Union and the United States faced off throughout the world.
    b. the United States reverted back to isolationist policies.
    c. the United States engaged in economic conflict with many Asian countries.

12. Russia has recently annexed:
    a. Armenia.
    b. Kiev.
    c. Crimea.

Essay Questions

1. Some people believe that if no U.S. military personnel were stationed abroad, terrorists would have less desire to harm Americans or the United States. Do you agree? Why or why not?

2. Why do you think that North Korea and Iran might want to possess nuclear weapons, even though they can never hope to match the nuclear arsenals of the original nuclear powers?

Answers to multiple-choice questions: 1. c, 2. a, 3. b, 4. c, 5. a, 6. b, 7. c, 8. b, 9. a, 10. c, 11. a, 12. c.

Appendix A

The Declaration of Independence

In Congress, July 4, 1776

A Declaration by the Representatives of the United States of America, in General Congress assembled. When in the Course of human Events, it becomes necessary for one People to dissolve the Political Bands which have connected them with another, and to assume among the Powers of the Earth, the separate and equal Station to which the Laws of Nature and of Nature's God entitle them, a decent Respect to the Opinions of Mankind requires that they should declare the causes which impel them to the Separation.

We hold these Truths to be self-evident, that all Men are created equal, that they are endowed by their Creator with certain unalienable Rights, that among these are Life, Liberty, and the Pursuit of Happiness— That to secure these Rights, Governments are instituted among Men, deriving their just Powers from the Consent of the Governed, that whenever any Form of Government becomes destructive of these Ends, it is the Right of the People to alter or to abolish it, and to institute new Government, laying its Foundation on such Principles, and organizing its Powers in such Forms, as to them shall seem most likely to effect their Safety and Happiness. Prudence, indeed, will dictate that Governments long established should not be changed for light and transient Causes; and accordingly all Experience hath shewn, that Mankind are more disposed to suffer, while Evils are sufferable, than to right themselves by abolishing the Forms to which they are accustomed. But when a long Train of Abuses and Usurpations, pursuing invariably the same Object, evinces a Design to reduce them under absolute Despotism, it is their Right, it is their Duty, to throw off such Government, and to provide new Guards for their future Security. Such has been the patient Sufferance of these Colonies; and such is now the Necessity which constrains them to alter their former Systems of Government. The History of the present King of Great-Britain is a History of repeated Injuries and Usurpations, all having in direct Object the Establishment of an absolute Tyranny over these States. To prove this, let Facts be submitted to a candid World.

He has refused his Assent to Laws, the most wholesome and necessary for the public Good.

He has forbidden his Governors to pass Laws of immediate and pressing Importance, unless suspended in their Operation till his Assent should be obtained; and when so suspended, he has utterly neglected to attend to them.

He has refused to pass other Laws for the Accommodation of large Districts of People, unless those People would relinquish the Right of Representation in the Legislature, a Right inestimable to them, and formidable to Tyrants only.

He has called together Legislative Bodies at Places unusual, uncomfortable, and distant from the Depository of their Public Records, for the sole Purpose of fatiguing them into Compliance with his Measures.

He has dissolved Representative Houses repeatedly, for opposing with manly Firmness his Invasions on the Rights of the People.

He has refused for a long Time, after such Dissolutions, to cause others to be elected; whereby the Legislative Powers, incapable of Annihilation, have returned to the People at large for their exercise; the State remaining in the mean time exposed to all the Dangers of Invasion from without, and Convulsions within.

He has endeavoured to prevent the Population of these States; for that Purpose obstructing the Laws for Naturalization of Foreigners; refusing to pass others to encourage their Migrations hither, and raising the Conditions of new Appropriations of Lands.

He has obstructed the Administration of Justice, by refusing his Assent to Laws for establishing Judiciary Powers.

He has made Judges dependent on his Will alone, for the Tenure of their offices, and the Amount and payment of their Salaries.

He has erected a Multitude of new Offices, and sent hither Swarms of Officers to harrass our People, and eat out their Substance.

He has kept among us, in Times of Peace, Standing Armies, without the consent of our Legislatures.

He has affected to render the Military independent of, and superior to the Civil Power.

He has combined with others to subject us to a Jurisdiction foreign to our Constitution, and unacknowledged by our Laws; giving his Assent to their Acts of pretended Legislation:

For quartering large Bodies of Armed Troops among us:

For protecting them, by a mock Trial, from Punishment for any Murders which they should commit on the Inhabitants of these States:

For cutting off our Trade with all Parts of the World: For imposing Taxes on us without our Consent:

For depriving us, in many cases, of the Benefits of Trial by Jury:

For transporting us beyond Seas to be tried for pretended Offences:

For abolishing the free System of English Laws in a neighbouring Province, establishing therein an arbitrary Government, and enlarging its Boundaries, so as to render it at once an Example and fit Instrument for introducing the same absolute Rule into these Colonies:

For taking away our Charters, abolishing our most valuable Laws, and altering fundamentally the Forms of our Governments:

For suspending our own Legislatures, and declaring themselves invested with Power to legislate for us in all Cases whatsoever.

He has abdicated Government here, by declaring us out of his Protection and waging War against us.

He has plundered our Seas, ravaged our Coasts, burnt our towns, and destroyed the Lives of our People.

He is, at this Time, transporting large Armies of foreign Mercenaries to compleat the works of Death, Desolation, and Tyranny, already begun with circumstances of Cruelty and Perfidy, scarcely paralleled in the most barbarous Ages, and totally unworthy the Head of a civilized Nation.

He has constrained our fellow Citizens taken Captive on the high Seas to bear Arms against their Country, to become the Executioners of their Friends and Brethren, or to fall themselves by their Hands.

He has excited domestic Insurrections amongst us, and has endeavoured to bring on the Inhabitants of our Frontiers, the merciless Indian Savages, whose known Rule of Warfare, is an undistinguished Destruction, of all Ages, Sexes and Conditions.

In every state of these Oppressions we have Petitioned for Redress in the most humble Terms: Our repeated Petitions have been answered only by repeated Injury. A Prince, whose Character is thus marked by every act which may define a Tyrant, is unfit to be the Ruler of a free People.

Nor have we been wanting in Attentions to our British Brethren. We have warned them from Time to Time of Attempts by their Legislature to extend an unwarrantable Jurisdiction over us. We have reminded them of the Circumstances of our Emigration and Settlement here. We have appealed to their native Justice and Magnanimity, and we have conjured them by the Ties of our common Kindred to disavow these Usurpations, which, would inevitably interrupt our Connections and Correspondence. They too have been deaf to the Voice of Justice and of Consanguinity. We must, therefore, acquiesce in the Necessity, which denounces our Separation, and hold them, as we hold the rest of Mankind, Enemies in War, in Peace, Friends.

We, therefore, the Representatives of the UNITED STATES OF AMERICA, in General Congress Assembled, appealing to the Supreme Judge of the World for the Rectitude of our Intentions, do, in the Name, and by the Authority of the good People of these Colonies, solemnly Publish and Declare, That these United Colonies are, and of Right ought to be, Free and Independent States; that they are absolved from all Allegiance to the British Crown, and that all political Connection between them and the State of Great Britain, is and ought to be totally dissolved; and that as Free and Independent States, they have full Power to levy War, conclude Peace, contract Alliances, establish Commerce, and to do all other Acts and Things which Independent States may of right do. And for the support of this declaration, with a firm Reliance on the Protection of divine Providence, we mutually pledge to each other our lives, our Fortunes, and our sacred Honor.

Appendix B

The Constitution of the United States*

The Preamble

We the People of the United States, in Order to form a more perfect Union, establish Justice, insure domestic Tranquility, provide for the common defence, promote the general Welfare, and secure the Blessings of Liberty to ourselves and our Posterity, do ordain and establish this Constitution for the United States of America.

The Preamble declares that "We the People" are the authority for the Constitution (unlike the Articles of Confederation, which derived their authority from the states). The Preamble also sets out the purposes of the Constitution.

Article I. (Legislative Branch)

The first part of the Constitution, Article 1, deals with the organization and powers of the lawmaking branch of the national government, the Congress.

Section 1. Legislative Powers

All legislative Powers herein granted shall be vested in a Congress of the United States, which shall consist of a Senate and House of Representatives.

Section 2. House of Representatives

Clause 1: Composition and Election of Members. The House of Representatives shall be composed of Members chosen every second Year by the People of the several States, and the Electors in each State shall have the Qualifications requisite for Electors of the most numerous Branch of the State Legislature.

Each state has the power to decide who may vote for members of Congress. Within each state, those who may vote for state legislators may also vote for members of the House of Representatives (and, under the Seventeenth Amendment, for U.S. senators). When the Constitution was written, nearly all states limited voting rights to white male property owners or taxpayers at least twenty-one years old. Subsequent amendments

---

* The spelling, capitalization, and punctuation of the original have been retained here. Brackets indicate passages that have been altered by amendments to the Constitution. We have added article titles (in parentheses), section titles, and clause designations. We have also inserted annotations in blue italic type.

---

granted voting power to African American men, all women, and eighteen-year-olds.

Clause 2: Qualifications. No Person shall be a Representative who shall not have attained to the Age of twenty five Years, and been seven Years a Citizen of the United States, and who shall not, when elected, be an Inhabitant of that State in which he shall be chosen.

Each member of the House must be at least twenty-five years old, a citizen of the United States for at least seven years, and a resident of the state in which she or he is elected.

Clause 3: Apportionment of Representatives and Direct Taxes. Representatives [and direct Taxes][1] shall be apportioned among the several States which may be included within this Union, according to their respective Numbers [which shall be determined by adding to the whole Number of free Persons, including those bound to Service for a Term of Years, and excluding Indians not taxed, three fifths of all other Persons].[2] The actual Enumeration shall be made within three Years after the first Meeting of the Congress of the United States, and within every subsequent Term of ten Years, in such Manner as they shall by Law direct. The Number of Representatives shall not exceed one for every thirty Thousand, but each State shall have at Least one Representative; and until such enumeration shall be made, the State of New Hampshire shall be entitled to chuse three, Massachusetts eight, Rhode Island and Providence Plantations one, Connecticut five, New York six, New Jersey four, Pennsylvania eight, Delaware one, Maryland six, Virginia ten, North Carolina five, South Carolina five, and Georgia three.

A state's representation in the House is based on the size of its population. Population is counted in each decade's census, after which Congress reapportions House seats. Since early in the twentieth century, the number of seats has been limited to 435.

Clause 4: Vacancies. When vacancies happen in the Representation from any State, the Executive

---

1. Modified by the Sixteenth Amendment.
2. Modified by the Fourteenth Amendment.

Authority thereof shall issue Writs of Election to fill such Vacancies.

The "Executive Authority" is the state's governor. When a vacancy occurs in the House, the governor calls a special election to fill it.

Clause 5: *Officers and Impeachment.* The House of Representatives shall chuse their Speaker and other Officers; and shall have the sole Power of Impeachment.

The power to impeach is the power to accuse. In this case, it is the power to accuse members of the executive or judicial branch of wrongdoing or abuse of power. Once a bill of impeachment is issued, the Senate holds the trial.

Section 3. The Senate

Clause 1: *Term and Number of Members.* The Senate of the United States shall be composed of two Senators from each State [chosen by the Legislature thereof],[3] for six Years; and each Senator shall have one Vote.

Every state has two senators, each of whom serves for six years and has one vote in the upper chamber. Since the Seventeenth Amendment in 1913, all senators have been elected directly by voters of the state during the regular election.

Clause 2: *Classification of Senators.* Immediately after they shall be assembled in Consequence of the first Election, they shall be divided as equally as may be into three Classes. The Seats of the Senators of the first Class shall be vacated at the Expiration of the second Year, of the second Class at the Expiration of the fourth Year, and of the third Class at the Expiration of the sixth Year, so that one third may be chosen every second Year; [and if Vacancies happen by Resignation, or otherwise, during the Recess of the Legislature of any State, the Executive thereof may make temporary Appointments until the next Meeting of the Legislature, which shall then fill such Vacancies].[4]

One-third of the Senate's seats are open to election every two years (in contrast, all members of the House are elected simultaneously).

Clause 3: *Qualifications.* No Person shall be a Senator who shall not have attained to the Age of thirty Years, and been nine Years a Citizen of the United States, and who shall not, when elected, be an Inhabitant of that State for which he shall be chosen.

Every senator must be at least thirty years old, a citizen of the United States for a minimum of nine years, and a resident of the state in which he or she is elected.

Clause 4: *The Role of the Vice President.* The Vice President of the United States shall be President of the Senate, but shall have no Vote, unless they be equally divided.

The vice president presides over meetings of the Senate but cannot vote unless there is a tie. The Constitution gives no other official duties to the vice president.

Clause 5: *Other Officers.* The Senate shall chuse their other Officers, and also a President pro tempore, in the Absence of the Vice President, or when he shall exercise the Office of President of the United States.

The Senate votes for one of its members to preside when the vice president is absent. This person is usually called the president pro tempore because of the temporary nature of the position.

Clause 6: *Impeachment Trials.* The Senate shall have the sole Power to try all Impeachments. When sitting for that Purpose, they shall be on Oath or Affirmation. When the President of the United States is tried, the Chief Justice shall preside: And no Person shall be convicted without the Concurrence of two thirds of the Members present.

The Senate conducts trials of officials that the House impeaches. The Senate sits as a jury, with the vice president presiding if the president is not on trial.

Clause 7: *Penalties for Conviction.* Judgment in Cases of Impeachment shall not extend further than to removal from Office, and disqualification to hold and enjoy any Office of honor, Trust, or Profit under the United States: but the Party convicted shall nevertheless be liable and subject to Indictment, Trial, Judgment, and Punishment, according to Law.

On conviction of impeachment charges, the Senate can only force an official to leave office and prevent him or her from holding another office in the federal government. The individual, however, can still be tried in a regular court.

Section 4. Congressional Elections: Times, Manner, and Places

Clause 1: *Elections.* The Times, Places and Manner of holding Elections for Senators and Representatives, shall be prescribed in each State by the Legislature thereof; but the Congress may at any time by Law make or alter such Regulations, except as to the Places of chusing Senators.

---

3. Repealed by the Seventeenth Amendment.
4. Modified by the Seventeenth Amendment.

Congress set the Tuesday after the first Monday in November in even-numbered years as the date for congressional elections. In states with more than one seat in the House, Congress requires that representatives be elected from districts within each state. Under the Seventeenth Amendment, senators are elected at the same places as other officials.

Clause 2: Sessions of Congress. [The Congress shall assemble at least once in every Year, and such Meeting shall be on the first Monday in December, unless they shall by Law appoint a different Day.]⁵

Congress has to meet every year at least once. The regular session now begins at noon on January 3 of each year, subsequent to the Twentieth Amendment, unless Congress passes a law to fix a different date. Congress stays in session until its members vote to adjourn. Additionally, the president may call a special session.

Section 5. Powers and Duties of the Houses
Clause 1: Admitting Members and Quorum. Each House shall be the Judge of the Elections, Returns, and Qualifications of its own Members, and a Majority of each shall constitute a Quorum to do Business; but a smaller Number may adjourn from day to day, and may be authorized to compel the Attendance of absent Members, in such Manner, and under such Penalties as each House may provide.

Each chamber may exclude or refuse to seat a member-elect.

The quorum rule requires that 218 members of the House and 51 members of the Senate be present to conduct business. This rule normally is not enforced in the handling of routine matters.

Clause 2: Rules and Discipline of Members. Each House may determine the Rules of its Proceedings, punish its Members for disorderly Behaviour, and, with the Concurrence of two thirds, expel a Member.

The House and the Senate may adopt their own rules to guide their proceedings. Each may also discipline its members for conduct that is deemed unacceptable. No member may be expelled without a two-thirds majority vote in favor of expulsion.

Clause 3: Keeping a Record. Each House shall keep a Journal of its Proceedings, and from time to time publish the same, excepting such Parts as may in their Judgment require Secrecy; and the Yeas and Nays of the Members of either House on any question shall, at the Desire of one fifth of those Present, be entered on the Journal.

---

5. Changed by the Twentieth Amendment.

The journals of the two chambers are published at the end of each session of Congress.

Clause 4: Adjournment. Neither House, during the Session of Congress, shall, without the Consent of the other, adjourn for more than three days, nor to any other Place than that in which the two Houses shall be sitting.

Congress has the power to determine when and where to meet, provided, however, that both chambers meet in the same city. Neither chamber may recess for more than three days without the consent of the other.

Section 6. Rights of Members
Clause 1: Compensation and Privileges. The Senators and Representatives shall receive a Compensation for their services, to be ascertained by Law, and paid out of the Treasury of the United States. They shall in all Cases, except Treason, Felony and Breach of the Peace, be privileged from Arrest during their Attendance at the Session of their respective Houses, and in going to and returning from the same; and for any Speech or Debate in either House, they shall not be questioned in any other Place.

Congressional salaries are to be paid by the U.S. Treasury rather than by the members' respective states. The original salaries were $6 per day; in 1857 they were $3,000 per year. Both representatives and senators were paid $165,200 in 2007.

Treason is defined in Article III, Section 3. A felony is any serious crime. A breach of the peace is any indictable offense less than treason or a felony. Members cannot be arrested for things they say during speeches and debates in Congress. This immunity applies to the Capitol Building itself and not to their private lives.

Clause 2: Restrictions. No Senator or Representative shall, during the Time for which he was elected, be appointed to any civil Office under the Authority of the United States, which shall have been created, or the Emoluments whereof shall have been increased during such time; and no Person holding any Office under the United States, shall be a Member of either House during his Continuance in Office.

During the term for which a member was elected, he or she cannot concurrently accept another federal government position.

Section 7. Legislative Powers: Bills and Resolutions
Clause 1: Revenue Bills. All Bills for raising Revenue shall originate in the House of Representatives; but the Senate may propose or concur with Amendments as on other Bills.

All tax and appropriation bills for raising money have to originate in the House of Representatives. The Senate, though, often amends such bills and may even substitute an entirely different bill.

Clause 2: The Presidential Veto. Every Bill which shall have passed the House of Representatives and the Senate, shall, before it becomes a Law, be presented to the President of the United States; If he approve he shall sign it, but if not he shall return it, with his Objections to the House in which it shall have originated, who shall enter the Objections at large on their Journal, and proceed to reconsider it. If after such Reconsideration two thirds of that House shall agree to pass the Bill, it shall be sent together with the Objections, to the other House, by which it shall likewise be reconsidered, and if approved by two thirds of that House, it shall become a Law. But in all such Cases the Votes of both Houses shall be determined by Yeas and Nays, and the Names of the Persons voting for and against the Bill shall be entered on the Journal of each House respectively. If any Bill shall not be returned by the President within ten Days (Sundays excepted) after it shall have been presented to him, the Same shall be a Law, in like Manner as if he had signed it, unless the Congress by their Adjournment prevent its Return in which Case it shall not be a Law.

When Congress sends the president a bill, he or she can sign it (in which case it becomes law) or send it back to the chamber in which it originated. If it is sent back, a two-thirds majority of each chamber must pass it again for it to become law. If the president neither signs it nor sends it back within ten days, it becomes law anyway, unless Congress adjourns in the meantime.

Clause 3: Actions on Other Matters. Every Order, Resolution, or Vote to which the Concurrence of the Senate and House of Representatives may be necessary (except on a question of Adjournment) shall be presented to the President of the United States; and before the Same shall take Effect, shall be approved by him, or being disapproved by him, shall be repassed by two thirds of the Senate and House of Representatives, according to the Rules and Limitations prescribed in the Case of a Bill.

The president must have the opportunity to either sign or veto everything that Congress passes, except votes to adjourn and resolutions not having the force of law.

Section 8. The Powers of Congress
Clause 1: Taxing. The Congress shall have Power To lay and collect Taxes, Duties, Imposts and Excises, to pay the Debts and provide for the common Defence and general Welfare of the United States; but all Duties, Imposts and Excises shall be uniform throughout the United States;

Duties are taxes on imports and exports. Impost is a generic term for tax. Excises are taxes on the manufacture, sale, or use of goods.

Clause 2: Borrowing. To borrow Money on the credit of the United States;

Congress has the power to borrow money, which is normally carried out through the sale of U.S. treasury bonds on which interest is paid. Note that the Constitution places no limit on the amount of government borrowing.

Clause 3: Regulation of Commerce. To regulate Commerce with foreign Nations, and among the several States, and with the Indian Tribes;

This is the commerce clause, which gives to Congress the power to regulate interstate and foreign trade. Much of the activity of Congress is based on this clause.

Clause 4: Naturalization and Bankruptcy. To establish an uniform Rule of Naturalization, and uniform Laws on the subject of Bankruptcies throughout the United States;

Only Congress may determine how aliens can become citizens of the United States. Congress may make laws with respect to bankruptcy.

Clause 5: Money and Standards. To coin Money, regulate the Value thereof, and of foreign Coin, and fix the Standard of Weights and Measures;

Congress mints coins and prints and circulates paper money. Congress can establish uniform measures of time, distance, weight, and so on. In 1838, Congress adopted the English system of weights and measurements as our national standard.

Clause 6: Punishing Counterfeiters. To provide for the Punishment of counterfeiting the Securities and current Coin of the United States;

Congress has the power to punish those who copy American money and pass it off as real. Currently, the punishment is a fine up to $5,000 and/or imprisonment for up to fifteen years.

Clause 7: Roads and Post Offices. To establish Post Offices and post Roads;

Post roads include all routes over which mail is carried— highways, railways, waterways, and airways.

Clause 8: Patents and Copyrights. To promote the Progress of Science and useful Arts, by securing for limited Times to Authors and Inventors the exclusive Right to their respective Writings and Discoveries;

Authors' and composers' works are protected by copyrights established by copyright law, which currently is the Copyright Act of 1976, as amended. Copyrights are valid for the life of the author or composer plus seventy years. Inventors' works are protected by patents, which vary in length of protection from fourteen to twenty years. A patent gives a person the exclusive right to control the manufacture or sale of her or his invention.

Clause 9: Lower Courts. To constitute Tribunals inferior to the supreme Court;

Congress has the authority to set up all federal courts, except the Supreme Court, and to decide what cases those courts will hear.

Clause 10: Punishment for Piracy. To define and punish Piracies and Felonies committed on the high Seas, and Offences against the Law of Nations;

Congress has the authority to prohibit the commission of certain acts outside U.S. territory and to punish certain violations of international law.

Clause 11: Declaration of War. To declare War, grant Letters of Marque and Reprisal, and make Rules concerning Captures on Land and Water;

Only Congress can declare war, although the president, as commander in chief, can make war without Congress's formal declaration. Letters of marque and reprisal authorized private parties to capture and destroy enemy ships in wartime. Since the middle of the nineteenth century, international law has prohibited letters of marque and reprisal, and the United States has honored the ban.

Clause 12: The Army. To raise and support Armies, but no Appropriation of Money to that Use shall be for a longer Term than two Years;

Congress has the power to create an army; the money used to pay for it must be appropriated for no more than two-year intervals. This latter restriction gives ultimate control of the army to civilians.

Clause 13: Creation of a Navy. To provide and maintain a Navy;

This clause allows for the maintenance of a navy. In 1947, Congress created the U.S. Air Force.

Clause 14: Regulation of the Armed Forces. To make Rules for the Government and Regulation of the land and naval Forces;

Congress sets the rules for the military mainly by way of the Uniform Code of Military Justice, which was enacted in 1950 by Congress.

Clause 15: The Militia. To provide for calling forth the Militia to execute the Laws of the Union, suppress Insurrections and repel Invasions;

The militia is known today as the National Guard. Both Congress and the president have the authority to call the National Guard into federal service.

Clause 16: How the Militia Is Organized. To provide for organizing, arming, and disciplining the Militia, and for governing such Part of them as may be employed in the Service of the United States, reserving to the States respectively, the Appointment of the Officers, and the Authority of training the Militia according to the discipline prescribed by Congress;

This clause gives Congress the power to "federalize" state militia (National Guard). When called into such service, the National Guard is subject to the same rules that Congress has set forth for the regular armed services.

Clause 17: Creation of the District of Columbia. To exercise exclusive Legislation in all Cases whatsoever, over such District (not exceeding ten Miles square) as may, by Cession of particular States, and the Acceptance of Congress, become the Seat of the Government of the United States, and to exercise like Authority over all Places purchased by the Consent of the Legislature of the State in which the Same shall be, for the Erection of Forts, Magazines, Arsenals, dock-Yards, and other needful Buildings;—And

Congress established the District of Columbia as the national capital in 1791. Virginia and Maryland had granted land for the District, but Virginia's grant was returned because it was believed it would not be needed. Today, the District covers sixty-nine square miles.

Clause 18: The Elastic Clause. To make all Laws which shall be necessary and proper for carrying into Execution the foregoing Powers, and all other Powers vested by this Constitution in the Government of the United States, or in any Department or Officer thereof.

This clause—the necessary and proper clause, or the elastic clause—grants no specific powers, and thus it can be stretched to fit different circumstances. It has allowed Congress to adapt the government to changing needs and times.

Section 9. The Powers Denied to Congress

Clause 1: Question of Slavery. The Migration or Importation of such Persons as any of the States now existing shall think proper to admit, shall not be prohibited by the Congress prior to the Year one thousand eight hundred and eight, but a Tax or duty may be imposed on such Importation, not exceeding ten dollars for each Person.

"Persons" referred to slaves. Congress outlawed the slave trade in 1808.

Clause 2: Habeas Corpus. The privilege of the Writ of Habeas Corpus shall not be suspended, unless when in Cases of Rebellion or Invasion the public Safety may require it.

A writ of habeas corpus is a court order directing a sheriff or other public officer who is detaining another person to "produce the body" of the detainee so the court can assess the legality of the detention.

Clause 3: Special Bills. No Bill of Attainder or ex post facto Law shall be passed.

A bill of attainder is a law that inflicts punishment without a trial. An ex post facto law is a law that inflicts punishment for an act that was not illegal when it was committed.

Clause 4: Direct Taxes. [No Capitation, or other direct, Tax shall be laid, unless in Proportion to the Census or Enumeration herein before directed to be taken.][6]

A capitation is a tax on a person. A direct tax is a tax paid directly to the government, such as a property tax. This clause was intended to prevent Congress from levying a tax on slaves per person and thereby taxing slavery out of existence.

Clause 5: Export Taxes. No Tax or Duty shall be laid on Articles exported from any State.

Congress may not tax any goods sold from one state to another or from one state to a foreign country. (Congress does have the power to tax goods that are bought from other countries, however.)

Clause 6: Interstate Commerce. No Preference shall be given by any Regulation of Commerce or Revenue to the Ports of one State over those of another: nor shall Vessels bound to, or from, one State, be obliged to enter, clear, or pay Duties in another.

Congress may not treat different ports within the United States differently in terms of taxing and commerce powers. Congress may not give one state's port a legal advantage over the ports of another state.

Clause 7: Treasury Withdrawals. No Money shall be drawn from the Treasury, but in Consequence of Appropriations made by Law; and a regular Statement and Account of the Receipts and Expenditures of all public Money shall be published from time to time.

Federal funds can be spent only as Congress authorizes. This is a significant check on the president's power.

Clause 8: Titles of Nobility. No Title of Nobility shall be granted by the United States: And no Person holding any Office of Profit or Trust under them, shall, without the Consent of the Congress, accept of any present, Emolument, Office, or Title, of any kind whatever, from any King, Prince, or foreign State.

No person in the United States may hold a title of nobility, such as duke or duchess. This clause also discourages bribery of American officials by foreign governments.

Section 10. Those Powers Denied to the States

Clause 1: Treaties and Coinage. No State shall enter into any Treaty, Alliance, or Confederation; grant Letters of Marque and Reprisal; coin Money; emit Bills of Credit; make any Thing but gold and silver Coin a Tender in Payment of Debts; pass any Bill of Attainder, ex post facto Law, or Law impairing the Obligation of Contracts, or grant any Title of Nobility.

Prohibiting state laws "impairing the Obligation of Contracts" was intended to protect creditors. (Shays' Rebellion—an attempt to prevent courts from giving effect to creditors' legal actions against debtors—occurred only one year before the Constitution was written.)

Clause 2: Duties and Imposts. No State shall, without the Consent of the Congress, lay any Imports or Duties on Imports or Exports, except what may be absolutely necessary for executing its inspection Laws; and the net Produce of all Duties and Imposts, laid by any State on Imports or Exports, shall be for the Use of the Treasury of the United States; and all such Laws shall be subject to the Revision and Controul of the Congress.

Only Congress can tax imports. Further, the states cannot tax exports.

Clause 3: War. No State shall, without the Consent of Congress, lay any Duty of Tonnage, keep Troops, or Ships of War in time of Peace, enter into any Agreement or Compact with another State, or with a foreign Power or engage in War, unless actually invaded, or in such imminent Danger as will not admit of delay.

A duty of tonnage is a tax on ships according to their cargo capacity. No states may tax ships according to their cargo unless Congress agrees. Additionally, this clause forbids any state to keep troops or warships during peacetime or to make a compact with another state or foreign nation unless Congress so agrees. A state, in contrast, can maintain a militia, but its use has to be limited to disorders that occur within the state—unless, of course, the militia is called into federal service.

---

6. Modified by the Sixteenth Amendment.

Article II. (Executive Branch)

Section 1. The Nature and Scope of Presidential Power

Clause 1: Four-Year Term. The executive Power shall be vested in a President of the United States of America. He shall hold his Office during the Term of four Years, and, together with the Vice President, chosen for the same Term, be elected, as follows.

The president has the power to carry out laws made by Congress, called the executive power. He or she serves in office for a four-year term after election. The Twenty-second Amendment limits the number of times a person may be elected president.

Clause 2: Choosing Electors from Each State. Each State shall appoint, in such Manner as the Legislature thereof may direct, a Number of Electors, equal to the whole Number of Senators and Representatives to which the State may be entitled in the Congress; but no Senator or Representative, or Person holding an Office of Trust or Profit under the United States, shall be appointed an Elector.

The "Electors" are known more commonly as the "electoral college." The president is elected by electors—that is, representatives chosen by the people—rather than by the people directly.

Clause 3: The Former System of Elections. [The Electors shall meet in their respective States, and vote by Ballot for two Persons, of whom one at least shall not be an Inhabitant of the same State with themselves. And they shall make a List of all the Persons voted for, and of the Number of Votes for each; which List they shall sign and certify, and transmit sealed to the Seat of the Government of the United States, directed to the President of the Senate. The President of the Senate shall, in the Presence of the Senate and House of Representatives, open all the Certificates, and the Votes shall then be counted. The Person having the greatest Number of Votes shall be the President, if such Number be a Majority of the whole Number of Electors appointed; and if there be more than one who have such Majority, and have an equal Number of Votes, then the House of Representatives shall immediately chuse by Ballot one of them for President; and if no Person have a Majority, then from the five highest on the List the said House shall in like Manner chuse the President. But in chusing the President, the Votes shall be taken by States, the Representation from each State having one Vote; A quorum for this Purpose shall consist of a Member or Members from two thirds of the States, and a Majority of all the States shall be necessary to a Choice. In every Case, after the Choice of the President, the Person having the greater Number of Votes of the Electors shall be the Vice President. But if there should remain two or more who have equal Votes, the Senate shall chuse from them by Ballot the Vice President.][7]

The original method of selecting the president and vice president was replaced by the Twelfth Amendment. Apparently, the framers did not anticipate the rise of political parties and the development of primaries and conventions.

Clause 4: The Time of Elections. The Congress may determine the Time of chusing the Electors, and the Day on which they shall give their Votes; which Day shall be the same throughout the United States.

Congress set the Tuesday after the first Monday in November every fourth year as the date for choosing electors. The electors cast their votes on the Monday after the second Wednesday in December of that year.

Clause 5: Qualifications for President. No person except a natural born Citizen, or a Citizen of the United States, at the time of the Adoption of this Constitution, shall be eligible to the Office of President; neither shall any Person be eligible to that Office who shall not have attained to the Age of thirty five Years, and been fourteen Years a Resident within the United States.

The president must be a natural-born citizen, be at least thirty-five years of age when taking office, and have been a resident within the United States for at least fourteen years.

Clause 6: Succession of the Vice President. [In Case of the Removal of the President from Office, or of his Death, Resignation or Inability to discharge the Powers and Duties of the said Office, the same shall devolve on the Vice President, and the Congress may by Law provide for the Case of Removal, Death, Resignation or Inability, both of the President and Vice President, declaring what Officer shall then act as President, and such Officer shall act accordingly, until the Disability be removed, or a President shall be elected.][8]

This section provided for the method by which the vice president was to succeed to the presidency, but its wording is ambiguous. It was replaced by the Twenty-fifth Amendment.

---

7. Changed by the Twelfth Amendment.
8. Modified by the Twenty-fifth Amendment.

Clause 7: The President's Salary. The President shall, at stated Times, receive for his Services, a Compensation, which shall neither be encreased nor diminished during the Period for which he shall have been elected, and he shall not receive within that Period any other Emolument from the United States, or any of them.

The president maintains the same salary during each four-year term. Moreover, she or he may not receive additional cash payments from the government. Originally set at $25,000 per year, the salary is currently $400,000 a year plus a $50,000 nontaxable expense account.

Clause 8: The Oath of Office. Before he enter on the Execution of his Office, he shall take the following Oath or Affirmation: "I do solemnly swear (or affirm) that I will faithfully execute the Office of President of the United States, and will to the best of my Ability, preserve, protect and defend the Constitution of the United States."

The president is "sworn in" prior to beginning the duties of the office. Currently, the taking of the oath of office occurs on January 20, following the November election. The ceremony is called the inauguration. The oath of office is administered by the chief justice of the United States Supreme Court.

Section 2. Powers of the President
Clause 1: Commander in Chief. The President shall be Commander in Chief of the Army and Navy of the United States, and of the Militia of the several States, when called into the actual Service of the United States; he may require the Opinion, in writing, of the principal Officer in each of the executive Departments, upon any Subject relating to the Duties of their respective Offices, and he shall have Power to grant Reprieves and Pardons for Offences against the United States, except in Cases of Impeachment.

The armed forces are placed under civilian control because the president is a civilian but still commander in chief of the military. The president may ask for the help of the head of each of the executive departments (thereby creating the cabinet). The cabinet members are chosen by the president with the consent of the Senate, but they can be removed without Senate approval.

The president's clemency powers extend only to federal cases. In those cases, he or she may grant a full or conditional pardon, or reduce a prison term or fine.

Clause 2: Treaties and Appointment. He shall have Power, by and with the Advice and Consent of the Senate, to make Treaties, provided two thirds of the Senators present concur; and he shall nominate, and by and with the Advice and Consent of the Senate, shall appoint Ambassadors, other public Ministers and Consuls, Judges of the supreme Court, and all other Officers of the United States, whose Appointments are not herein otherwise provided for, and which shall be established by Law; but the Congress may by Law vest the Appointment of such inferior Officers, as they think proper, in the President alone, in the Courts of Law, or in the Heads of Departments.

Many of the major powers of the president are identified in this clause, including the power to make treaties with foreign governments (with the approval of the Senate by a two-thirds vote) and the power to appoint ambassadors, Supreme Court justices, and other government officials. Most such appointments require Senate approval.

Clause 3: Vacancies. The President shall have Power to fill up all Vacancies that may happen during the Recess of the Senate, by granting Commissions which shall expire at the end of their next Session.

The president has the power to appoint temporary officials to fill vacant federal offices without Senate approval if the Congress is not in session. Such appointments expire automatically at the end of Congress's next term.

Section 3. Duties of the President
He shall from time to time give to the Congress Information of the State of the Union, and recommend to their Consideration such Measures as he shall judge necessary and expedient; he may, on extraordinary Occasions, convene both Houses, or either of them, and in Case of Disagreement between them, with Respect to the Time of Adjournment, he may adjourn them to such Time as he shall think proper; he shall receive Ambassadors and other public Ministers; he shall take Care that the Laws be faithfully executed, and shall Commission all the Officers of the United States.

Annually, the president reports on the state of the union to Congress, recommends legislative measures, and proposes a federal budget. The State of the Union speech is a statement not only to Congress but also to the American people. After it is given, the president proposes a federal budget and presents an economic report. At any time, the president may send special messages to Congress while it is in session. The president has the power to call special sessions, to adjourn Congress when its two chambers do not agree on when to adjourn, to receive diplomatic representatives of other governments, and to ensure the proper execution of all federal laws. The president further has the ability to empower federal officers to hold their positions and to perform their duties.

Section 4. Impeachment

The President, Vice President and all civil Officers of the United States, shall be removed from Office on Impeachment for, and Conviction of, Treason, Bribery, or other high Crimes and Misdemeanors.

Treason denotes giving aid to the nation's enemies. The definition of high crimes and misdemeanors is usually given as serious abuses of political power. In either case, the president or vice president may be accused by the House (called an impeachment) and then removed from office if convicted by the Senate. (Note that impeachment does not mean removal but rather refers to an accusation of treason or high crimes and misdemeanors.)

Article III. (Judicial Branch)

Section 1. Judicial Powers, Courts, and Judges

The judicial Power of the United States, shall be vested in one supreme Court, and in such inferior Courts as the Congress may from time to time ordain and establish. The Judges, both of the supreme and inferior Courts, shall hold their Offices during good Behaviour, and shall, at stated Times, receive for their Services a Compensation, which shall not be diminished during their Continuance in Office.

The Supreme Court is vested with judicial power, as are the lower federal courts that Congress creates. Federal judges serve in their offices for life unless they are impeached and convicted by Congress. The payment of federal judges may not be reduced during their time in office.

Section 2. Jurisdiction

Clause 1: Cases under Federal Jurisdiction. The judicial Power shall extend to all Cases, in Law and Equity, arising under this Constitution, the Laws of the United States, and Treaties made, or which shall be made, under their Authority;—to all Cases affecting Ambassadors, other public Ministers and Consuls;—to all Cases of admiralty and maritime Jurisdiction;—to Controversies to which the United States shall be a Party;—to Controversies between two or more States; [—between a State and Citizens of another State;—][9] between Citizens of different States;—between Citizens of the same State claiming Lands under Grants of different States, [and between a State, or the Citizens thereof, and foreign States, Citizens or Subjects.][10]

The federal courts take on cases that concern the meaning of the U.S. Constitution, all federal laws, and treaties. They also can take on cases involving citizens of different states and citizens of foreign nations.

Clause 2: Cases for the Supreme Court. In all Cases affecting Ambassadors, other public Ministers and Consuls, and those in which a State shall be a Party, the supreme Court shall have original Jurisdiction. In all the other Cases before mentioned, the supreme Court shall have appellate Jurisdiction, both as to Law and Fact, with such Exceptions, and under such Regulations as the Congress shall make.

In a limited number of situations, the Supreme Court acts as a trial court and has original jurisdiction. These cases involve a representative from another country or involve a state. In all other situations, the cases must first be tried in the lower courts and then can be appealed to the Supreme Court. Congress may, however, make exceptions. Today, the Supreme Court acts as a trial court of first instance on rare occasions.

Clause 3: The Conduct of Trials. The Trial of all Crimes, except in Cases of Impeachment, shall be by Jury; and such Trial shall be held in the State where the said Crimes shall have been committed; but when not committed within any State, the Trial shall be at such Place or Places as the Congress may by Law have directed.

Any person accused of a federal crime is granted the right to a trial by jury in a federal court in that state in which the crime was committed. Trials of impeachment are an exception.

Section 3. Treason

Clause 1: The Definition of Treason. Treason against the United States, shall consist only in levying War against them, or, in adhering to their Enemies, giving them Aid and Comfort. No Person shall be convicted of Treason unless on the Testimony of two Witnesses to the same overt Act, or on Confession in open Court.

Treason is the making of war against the United States or giving aid to its enemies.

Clause 2: Punishment. The Congress shall have Power to declare the Punishment of Treason, but no Attainder of Treason shall work Corruption of Blood, or Forfeiture except during the Life of the Person attainted.

Congress has provided that the punishment for treason ranges from a minimum of five years in prison and/or a $10,000 fine to a maximum of death. "No Attainder of Treason shall work Corruption of Blood" prohibits punishment of the traitor's heirs.

9. Modified by the Eleventh Amendment.
10. Modified by the Eleventh Amendment.

Article IV. (Relations among the States)

Section 1. Full Faith and Credit

Full Faith and Credit shall be given in each State to the public Acts, Records, and judicial Proceedings of every other State. And the Congress may by general Laws prescribe the Manner in which such Acts, Records and Proceedings shall be proved, and the Effect thereof.

All states are required to respect one another's laws, records, and lawful decisions. There are exceptions, however. A state does not have to enforce another state's criminal code. Nor does it have to recognize another state's grant of a divorce if the person obtaining the divorce did not establish legal residence in the state in which it was given.

Section 2. Treatment of Citizens

Clause 1: Privileges and Immunities. The Citizens of each State shall be entitled to all Privileges and Immunities of Citizens in the several States.

A citizen of a state has the same rights and privileges as the citizens of another state in which he or she happens to be.

Clause 2: Extradition. A Person charged in any State with Treason, Felony, or other Crime, who shall flee from Justice, and be found in another State, shall on Demand of the executive Authority of the State from which he fled, be delivered up, to be removed to the State having Jurisdiction of the Crime.

Any person accused of a crime who flees to another state must be returned to the state in which the crime occurred.

Clause 3: Fugitive Slaves. [No Person held to Service or Labour in one State, under the Laws thereof, escaping into another, shall, in Consequence of any Law or Regulation therein, be discharged from such Service or Labour, but shall be delivered up on Claim of the Party to whom such Service or Labour may be due.][11]

This clause was struck down by the Thirteenth Amendment, which abolished slavery in 1865.

Section 3. Admission of States

Clause 1: The Process. New States may be admitted by the Congress into this Union; but no new State shall be formed or erected within the Jurisdiction of any other State; nor any State be formed by the Junction of two or more States, or Parts of States, without the Consent of the Legislatures of the States concerned as well as of the Congress.

Only Congress has the power to admit new states to the union. No state may be created by taking territory from an existing state unless the state's legislature so consents.

Clause 2: Public Land. The Congress shall have Power to dispose of and make all needful Rules and Regulations respecting the Territory or other Property belonging to the United States; and nothing in this Constitution shall be so construed as to Prejudice any Claims of the United States, or of any particular State.

The federal government has the exclusive right to administer federal government public lands.

Section 4. Republican Form of Government

The United States shall guarantee to every State in this Union a Republican Form of Government, and shall protect each of them against Invasion; and on Application of the Legislature, or of the Executive (when the Legislature cannot be convened) against domestic Violence.

Each state is promised a republican form of government—that is, one in which the people elect their representatives. The federal government is bound to protect states against any attack by foreigners or during times of trouble within a state.

Article V. (Methods of Amendment)

The Congress, whenever two thirds of both Houses shall deem it necessary, shall propose Amendments to this Constitution, or on the Application of the Legislatures of two thirds of the several States, shall call a Convention for proposing Amendments, which, in either Case, shall be valid to all Intents and Purposes, as Part of this Constitution, when ratified by the Legislatures of three fourths of the several States, or by Conventions in three fourths thereof, as the one or the other Mode of Ratification may be proposed by the Congress; Provided that no Amendment which may be made prior to the Year One thousand eight hundred and eight shall in any Manner affect the first and fourth Clauses in the Ninth Section of the First Article; and that no State, without its Consent, shall be deprived of its equal Suffrage in the Senate.

Amendments may be proposed in either of two ways: a two-thirds vote of each chamber (Congress) or at the request of two-thirds of the states. Ratification of amendments may be carried out in two ways: by the legislatures of three-fourths of the states or by the voters in three-fourths of the states. No state may be denied equal representation in the Senate.

---

11. Repealed by the Thirteenth Amendment.

Article VI. (National Supremacy)

Clause 1: Existing Obligations. All Debts contracted and Engagements entered into, before the Adoption of this Constitution shall be as valid against the United States under this Constitution, as under the Confederation.

During the Revolutionary War and the years of the Confederation, Congress borrowed large sums. This clause pledged that the new federal government would assume those financial obligations.

Clause 2: Supreme Law of the Land. This Constitution, and the Laws of the United States which shall be made in Pursuance thereof; and all Treaties made, or which shall be made, under the Authority of the United States, shall be the supreme Law of the Land; and the Judges in every State shall be bound thereby, any Thing in the Constitution or Laws of any State to the Contrary notwithstanding.

This is typically called the supremacy clause; it declares that federal law takes precedence over all forms of state law. No government at the local or state level may make or enforce any law that conflicts with any provision of the Constitution, acts of Congress, treaties, or other rules and regulations issued by the president and his or her subordinates in the executive branch of the federal government.

Clause 3: Oath of Office. The Senators and Representatives before mentioned, and the Members of the several State Legislatures, and all executive and judicial Officers, both of the United States and of the several States, shall be bound by Oath or Affirmation, to support this Constitution; but no religious Test shall ever be required as a Qualification to any Office or public Trust under the United States.

Every federal and state official must take an oath of office promising to support the U.S. Constitution. Religion may not be used as a qualification to serve in any federal office.

Article VII. (Ratification)

The Ratification of the Conventions of nine States shall be sufficient for the Establishment of this Constitution between the States so ratifying the Same.

Nine states were required to ratify the Constitution. Delaware was the first and New Hampshire the ninth.

Done in Convention by the Unanimous Consent of the States present the Seventeenth Day of September in the Year of our Lord one thousand seven hundred and Eighty seven and of the Independence of the United States of America the Twelfth. In witness whereof we have hereunto subscribed our Names,

Attest William Jackson Secretary

DELAWARE
Geo. Read
Gunning Bedford jun
John Dickinson
Richard Bassett
Jaco. Broom

MARYLAND
James McHenry
Dan of St. Thos. Jenifer
Danl. Carroll

VIRGINIA
John Blair
James Madison Jr.

NORTH CAROLINA
Wm. Blount
Richd. Dobbs Spaight
Hu. Williamson

SOUTH CAROLINA
J. Rutledge
Charles Cotesworth Pinckney
Charles Pinckney
Pierce Butler

GEORGIA
William Few
Abr. Baldwin

Go. WASHINGTON
Presid't. and deputy from Virginia

NEW HAMPSHIRE
John Langdon
Nicholas Gilman

MASSACHUSETTS
Nathaniel Gorham
Rufus King

CONNECTICUT
Wm. Saml. Johnson
Roger Sherman

NEW YORK
Alexander Hamilton

NEW JERSEY
Wh. Livingston
David Brearley
Wm. Paterson
Jona. Dayton

PENNSYLVANIA
B. Franklin
Thomas Mifflin
Robt. Morris
Geo. Clymer
Thos. FitzSimons
Jared Ingersoll
James Wilson
Gouv. Morris

Articles in addition to, and amendment of, the Constitution of the United States of America, proposed by Congress and ratified by the Legislatures of the several states, pursuant to the Fifth Article of the original Constitution.

Amendments to the Constitution of the United States

(The Bill of Rights)[12]

Amendment I.
(Religion, Speech, Assembly, and Petition)

Congress shall make no law respecting an establishment of religion, or prohibiting the free exercise thereof; or abridging the freedom of speech, or of the press; or the right of the people peaceably to assemble, and to petition the Government for a redress of grievances.

Congress may not create an official church or enact laws limiting the freedom of religion, speech, the press, assembly, and petition. These guarantees, like the others in the Bill of Rights

(the first ten amendments), are not absolute—each may be exercised only with regard to the rights of other persons.

Amendment II.
(Militia and the Right to Bear Arms)

A well regulated Militia, being necessary to the security of a free State, the right of the people to keep and bear Arms, shall not be infringed.

To protect itself, each state has the right to maintain a volunteer armed force. States and the federal government regulate the possession and use of firearms by individuals.

Amendment III.
(The Quartering of Soldiers)

No Soldier shall, in time of peace be quartered in any house, without the consent of the Owner, nor in time of war, but in a manner to be prescribed by law.

Before the Revolutionary War, it had been common British practice to quarter soldiers in colonists' homes. Military troops do not have the power to take over private houses during peacetime.

Amendment IV.
(Searches and Seizures)

The right of the people to be secure in their persons, houses, papers, and effects, against unreasonable searches and seizures, shall not be violated, and no Warrants shall issue, but upon probable cause, supported by Oath or affirmation, and particularly

---

12. On September 25, 1789, Congress transmitted to the state legislatures twelve proposed amendments, two of which, having to do with congressional representation and congressional pay, were not adopted. The remaining ten amendments became the Bill of Rights. In 1992, the amendment concerning congressional pay was adopted as the Twenty-seventh Amendment.

describing the place to be searched, and the persons or things to be seized.

Here the word warrant means "justification" and refers to a document issued by a magistrate or judge indicating the name, address, and possible offense committed. Anyone asking for the warrant, such as a police officer, must be able to convince the magistrate or judge that an offense probably has been committed.

Amendment V.
(Grand Juries, Self-Incrimination, Double Jeopardy, Due Process, and Eminent Domain)

No person shall be held to answer for a capital, or otherwise infamous crime, unless on a presentment or indictment of a Grand Jury, except in cases arising in the land or naval forces, or in the Militia, when in actual service in time of War or public danger; nor shall any person be subject for the same offence to be twice put in jeopardy of life or limb; nor shall be compelled in any criminal case to be a witness against himself, nor be deprived of life, liberty, or property, without due process of law; nor shall private property be taken for public use, without just compensation.

There are two types of juries. A grand jury considers physical evidence and the testimony of witnesses and decides whether there is sufficient reason to bring a case to trial. A petit jury hears the case at trial and decides it. "For the same offence to be twice put in jeopardy of life or limb" means to be tried twice for the same crime. A person may not be tried for the same crime twice or forced to give evidence against herself or himself. No person's right to life, liberty, or property may be taken away except by lawful means, called the due process of law. Private property taken for use in public purposes must be paid for by the government.

Amendment VI.
(Criminal Court Procedures)

In all criminal prosecutions, the accused shall enjoy the right to a speedy and public trial, by an impartial jury of the State and district wherein the crime shall have been committed, which district shall have been previously ascertained by law, and to be informed of the nature and cause of the accusation; to be confronted with the witnesses against him; to have compulsory process for obtaining witnesses in his favor, and to have the Assistance of Counsel for his defence.

Any person accused of a crime has the right to a fair and public trial by a jury in the state in which the crime took place. The charges against that person must be indicated. Any accused person has the right to a lawyer to defend him or her and to question those who testify against him or her, as well as the right to call people to speak in his or her favor at trial.

Amendment VII.
(Trial by Jury in Civil Cases)

In Suits at common law, where the value in controversy shall exceed twenty dollars, the right of trial by jury shall be preserved, and no fact tried by jury, shall be otherwise re-examined in any Court of the United States, than according to the rules of the common law.

A jury trial may be requested by either party in a dispute in any case involving more than $20. If both parties agree to a trial by a judge without a jury, the right to a jury trial may be put aside.

Amendment VIII.
(Bail, Cruel and Unusual Punishment)

Excessive bail shall not be required, nor excessive fines imposed, nor cruel and unusual punishments inflicted.

Bail is that amount of money that a person accused of a crime may be required to deposit with the court as a guarantee that she or he will appear in court when requested. The amount of bail required or the fine imposed as punishment for a crime must be reasonable compared with the seriousness of the crime involved. Any punishment judged to be too harsh or too severe for a crime shall be prohibited.

Amendment IX.
(The Rights Retained by the People)

The enumeration in the Constitution, of certain rights, shall not be construed to deny or disparage others retained by the people.

Many civil rights that are not explicitly enumerated in the Constitution are still held by the people.

Amendment X.
(Reserved Powers of the States)

The powers not delegated to the United States by the Constitution, nor prohibited by it to the States, are reserved to the States respectively, or to the people.

Those powers not delegated by the Constitution to the federal government or expressly denied to the states belong to the states and to the people. This amendment in essence allows the states to pass laws under their "police powers."

Amendment XI.
(Ratified on February 7, 1795—
Suits against States)

The Judicial power of the United States shall not be construed to extend to any suit in law or equity, commenced or prosecuted against one of the United States by Citizens of another State, or by Citizens or Subjects of any Foreign State.

This amendment has been interpreted to mean that a state cannot be sued in federal court by one of its own citizens, by a citizen of another state, or by a foreign country.

Amendment XII.
(Ratified on June 15, 1804—
Election of the President)

The Electors shall meet in their respective states, and vote by ballot for President and Vice-President, one of whom, at least, shall not be an inhabitant of the same State with themselves; they shall name in their ballots the person voted for as President, and in distinct ballots the person voted for as Vice-President, and they shall make distinct lists of all persons voted for as President, and of all persons voted for as Vice-President, and of the number of votes for each, which lists they shall sign and certify, and transmit sealed to the seat of the government of the United States, directed to the President of the Senate;—The President of the Senate shall, in the presence of the Senate and House of Representatives, open all the certificates and the votes shall then be counted;—The person having the greatest number of votes for President, shall be the President, if such number be a majority of the whole number of Electors appointed; and if no person have such majority, then from the persons having the highest numbers not exceeding three on the list of those voted for as President, the House of Representatives shall choose immediately, by ballot, the President. But in choosing the President, the votes shall be taken by States, the representation from each State having one vote; a quorum for this purpose shall consist of a member or members from two-thirds of the States, and a majority of all States shall be necessary to a choice. [And if the House of Representatives shall not choose a President whenever the right of choice shall devolve upon them, before the fourth day of March next following, then the Vice-President shall act as President, as in the case of the death or other constitutional disability of the President.][13]—The person having the

greatest number of votes as Vice-President, shall be the Vice-President, if such number be a majority of the whole number of Electors appointed, and if no person have a majority, then from the two highest numbers on the list, the Senate shall choose the Vice-President; a quorum for the purpose shall consist of two-thirds of the whole number of Senators, and a majority of the whole number shall be necessary to a choice. But no person constitutionally ineligible to the office of President shall be eligible to that of Vice-President of the United States.

The original procedure set out for the election of president and vice president in Article II, Section 1, resulted in a tie in 1800 between Thomas Jefferson and Aaron Burr. It was not until the next year that the House of Representatives chose Jefferson to be president. This amendment changed the procedure by providing for separate ballots for president and vice president.

Amendment XIII.
(Ratified on December 6, 1865—
Prohibition of Slavery)

Section 1.
Neither slavery nor involuntary servitude, except as a punishment for crime whereof the party shall have been duly convicted, shall exist within the United States, or any place subject to their jurisdiction.

Some slaves had been freed during the Civil War. This amendment freed the others and abolished slavery.

Section 2.
Congress shall have power to enforce this article by appropriate legislation.

Amendment XIV.
(Ratified on July 9, 1868—
Citizenship, Due Process, and
Equal Protection of the Laws)

Section 1.
All persons born or naturalized in the United States, and subject to the jurisdiction thereof, are citizens of the United States and of the State wherein they reside. No State shall make or enforce any law which shall abridge the privileges or immunities of citizens of the United States; nor shall any State deprive any person of life, liberty, or property, without due process of law; nor deny to any person within its jurisdiction the equal protection of the laws.

---

13. Changed by the Twentieth Amendment.

Under this provision, states cannot make or enforce laws that take away rights given to all citizens by the federal government. States cannot act unfairly or arbitrarily toward, or discriminate against, any person.

Section 2.

Representatives shall be apportioned among the several States according to their respective numbers, counting the whole number of persons in each State, excluding Indians not taxed. But when the right to vote at any election for the choice of electors for President and Vice President of the United States, Representatives in Congress, the Executive and Judicial officers of a State, or the members of the Legislature thereof, is denied to any of the male inhabitants of such State, being [twenty-one][14] years of age, and citizens of the United States, or in any way abridged, except for participation in rebellion, or other crime, the basis of representation therein shall be reduced in the proportion which the number of such male citizens shall bear to the whole number of male citizens twenty-one years of age in such State.

Section 3.

No person shall be a Senator or Representative in Congress, or elector of President and Vice President, or hold any office, civil or military, under the United States, or under any State, who having previously taken an oath, as a member of Congress, or as an officer of the United States, or as a member of any State legislature, or as an executive or judicial officer of any State, to support the Constitution of the United States, shall have engaged in insurrection or rebellion against the same, or given aid or comfort to the enemies thereof. But Congress may by a vote of two-thirds of each House, remove such disability.

This provision forbade former state or federal government officials who had acted in support of the Confederacy during the Civil War to hold office again. It limited the president's power to pardon those persons. Congress removed this "disability" in 1898.

Section 4.

The validity of the public debt of the United States, authorized by law, including debts incurred for payment of pensions and bounties for services in suppressing insurrection or rebellion, shall not be questioned. But neither the United States nor any State shall assume or pay any debt or obligation incurred in aid of insurrection or rebellion against the United States,

14. Changed by the Twenty-sixth Amendment.

or any claim for the loss or emancipation of any slave, but all such debts, obligations and claims shall be held illegal and void.

Section 5.

The Congress shall have power to enforce, by appropriate legislation, the provisions of this article.

Amendment XV.
(Ratified on February 3, 1870— The Right to Vote)

Section 1.

The right of citizens of the United States to vote shall not be denied or abridged by the United States or by any State on account of race, color, or previous condition of servitude.

No citizen can be refused the right to vote simply because of race or color or because that person was once a slave.

Section 2.

The Congress shall have power to enforce this article by appropriate legislation.

Amendment XVI.
(Ratified on February 3, 1913— Income Taxes)

The Congress shall have power to lay and collect taxes on incomes, from whatever source derived, without apportionment among the several States, and without regard to any census or enumeration.

This amendment allows Congress to tax income without sharing the revenue so obtained with the states according to their population.

Amendment XVII.
(Ratified on April 8, 1913— The Popular Election of Senators)

Section 1.

The Senate of the United States shall be composed of two Senators from each State, elected by the people thereof, for six years; and each Senator shall have one vote. The electors in each State shall have the qualifications requisite for electors of the most numerous branch of the State legislatures.

Section 2.

When vacancies happen in the representation of any State in the Senate, the executive authority of such State shall issue writs of election to fill such vacancies: Provided, That the legislature of any State may empower the executive thereof to make temporary appointments until the people fill the vacancies by election as the legislature may direct.

Section 3.

This amendment shall not be so construed as to affect the election or term of any Senator chosen before it becomes valid as part of the Constitution.

This amendment modified portions of Article I, Section 3, that related to election of senators. Senators are now elected by the voters in each state directly. When a vacancy occurs, either the state may fill the vacancy by a special election, or the governor of the state involved may appoint someone to fill the seat until the next election.

Amendment XVIII.
(Ratified on January 16, 1919— Prohibition)

Section 1.

After one year from the ratification of this article the manufacture, sale, or transportation of intoxicating liquors within, the importation thereof into, or the exportation thereof from the United States and all territory subject to the jurisdiction thereof for beverage purposes is hereby prohibited.

Section 2.

The Congress and the several States shall have concurrent power to enforce this article by appropriate legislation.

Section 3.

This article shall be inoperative unless it shall have been ratified as an amendment to the Constitution by the legislatures of the several States, as provided in the Constitution, within seven years from the date of the submission hereof to the States by the Congress.[15]

This amendment made it illegal to manufacture, sell, and transport alcoholic beverages in the United States.

Amendment XIX.
(Ratified on August 18, 1920— Women's Right to Vote)

Section 1.

The right of citizens of the United States to vote shall not be denied or abridged by the United States or by any State on account of sex.

Section 2.

Congress shall have power to enforce this article by appropriate legislation.

---

15. The Eighteenth Amendment was repealed by the Twenty-first Amendment.

Women were given the right to vote by this amendment, and Congress was given the power to enforce this right.

Amendment XX.
(Ratified on January 23, 1933— The Lame Duck Amendment)

Section 1.

The terms of the President and Vice President shall end at noon on the 20th day of January, and the terms of Senators and Representatives at noon on the 3d day of January, of the years in which such terms would have ended if this article had not been ratified; and the terms of their successors shall then begin.

This amendment modified Article I, Section 4, Clause 2, and other provisions relating to the president in the Twelfth Amendment. The taking of the oath of office was moved from March 4 to January 20.

Section 2.

The Congress shall assemble at least once in every year, and such meeting shall begin at noon on the 3d day of January, unless they shall by law appoint a different day.

Congress changed the beginning of its term to January 3. The reason the Twentieth Amendment is called the Lame Duck Amendment is because it shortens the time between when a member of Congress is defeated for reelection and when he or she leaves office.

Section 3.

If, at the time fixed for the beginning of the term of the President, the President elect shall have died, the Vice President elect shall become President. If a President shall not have been chosen before the time fixed for the beginning of his term, or if the President elect shall have failed to qualify, then the Vice President elect shall act as President until a President shall have qualified; and the Congress may by law provide for the case wherein neither a President elect nor a Vice President elect shall have qualified, declaring who shall then act as President, or the manner in which one who is to act shall be selected, and such person shall act accordingly until a President or Vice President shall have qualified.

This part of the amendment deals with problem areas left ambiguous by Article II and the Twelfth Amendment. If the president dies before January 20 or fails to qualify for office, the presidency is to be filled as described in this section.

Section 4.

The Congress may by law provide for the case of the death of any of the persons from whom the House of Representatives may choose a President whenever the rights of choice shall have devolved upon them, and for the case of the death of any of the persons from whom the Senate may choose a Vice President whenever the right of choice shall have devolved upon them.

Congress has never created legislation pursuant to this section.

Section 5.

Sections 1 and 2 shall take effect on the 15th day of October following the ratification of this article.

Section 6.

This article shall be inoperative unless it shall have been ratified as an amendment to the Constitution by the legislatures of three-fourths of the several States within seven years from the date of its submission.

Amendment XXI.
(Ratified on December 5, 1933—
The Repeal of Prohibition)

Section 1.

The eighteenth article of amendment to the Constitution of the United States is hereby repealed.

Section 2.

The transportation or importation into any State, Territory, or possession of the United States for delivery or use therein of intoxicating liquors, in violation of the laws thereof, is hereby prohibited.

Section 3.

This article shall be inoperative unless it shall have been ratified as an amendment to the Constitution by conventions in the several States, as provided in the Constitution, within seven years from the date of the submission hereof to the States by the Congress.

The amendment repealed the Eighteenth Amendment but did not make alcoholic beverages legal everywhere. Rather, they remained illegal in any state that so designated them. Many such "dry" states existed for a number of years after 1933. Today, there are still "dry" counties within the United States, in which the sale of alcoholic beverages is illegal.

Amendment XXII.
(Ratified on February 27, 1951—
Limitation of Presidential Terms)

Section 1.

No person shall be elected to the office of the President more than twice, and no person who has held the office of President, or acted as President, for more than two years of a term to which some other person was elected President shall be elected to the office of President more than once. But this Article shall not apply to any person holding the office of President when this Article was proposed by the Congress, and shall not prevent any person who may be holding the office of President, or acting as President, during the term within which this Article becomes operative from holding the office of President or acting as President during the remainder of such term.

Section 2.

This article shall be inoperative unless it shall have been ratified as an amendment to the Constitution by the legislatures of three-fourths of the several States within seven years from the date of its submission to the States by the Congress.

No president may serve more than two elected terms. If, however, a president has succeeded to the office after the half-way point of a term in which another president was originally elected, then that president may serve for more than eight years, but not to exceed ten years.

Amendment XXIII.
(Ratified on March 29, 1961—
Presidential Electors for
the District of Columbia)

Section 1.

The District constituting the seat of Government of the United States shall appoint in such manner as the Congress may direct:

A number of electors of President and Vice President equal to the whole number of Senators and Representatives in Congress to which the District would be entitled if it were a State, but in no event more than the least populous State; they shall be in addition to those appointed by the States, but they shall be considered, for the purposes of the election of President and Vice President, to be electors appointed by a State; and they shall meet in the District and perform such duties as provided by the twelfth article of amendment.

Section 2.

The Congress shall have power to enforce this article by appropriate legislation.

Citizens living in the District of Columbia have the right to vote in elections for president and vice president. The District of Columbia has three presidential electors, whereas before this amendment it had none.

Amendment XXIV.
(Ratified on January 23, 1964—
The Anti–Poll Tax Amendment)

Section 1.

The right of citizens of the United States to vote in any primary or other election for President or Vice President, for electors for President or Vice President, or for Senator or Representative in Congress, shall not be denied or abridged by the United States, or any State by reason of failure to pay any poll tax or other tax.

Section 2.

The Congress shall have power to enforce this article by appropriate legislation.

No government shall require a person to pay a poll tax to vote in any federal election.

Amendment XXV.
(Ratified on February 10, 1967—
Presidential Disability and
Vice Presidential Vacancies)

Section 1.

In case of the removal of the President from office or of his death or resignation, the Vice President shall become President.

Whenever a president dies or resigns from office, the vice president becomes president.

Section 2.

Whenever there is a vacancy in the office of the Vice President, the President shall nominate a Vice President who shall take office upon confirmation by a majority vote of both Houses of Congress.

Whenever the office of the vice presidency becomes vacant, the president may appoint someone to fill this office, provided Congress consents.

Section 3.

Whenever the President transmits to the President pro tempore of the Senate and the Speaker of the House of Representatives his written declaration that he is unable to discharge the powers and duties of his office, and until he transmits to them a written declaration to the contrary, such powers and duties shall be discharged by the Vice President as Acting President.

Whenever the president believes she or he is unable to carry out the duties of the office, she or he shall so indicate to

Congress in writing. The vice president then acts as president until the president declares that she or he is again able to carry out the duties of the office.

Section 4.

Whenever the Vice President and a majority of either the principal officers of the executive departments or of such other body as Congress may by law provide, transmit to the President pro tempore of the Senate and the Speaker of the House of Representatives their written declaration that the President is unable to discharge the powers and duties of his office, the Vice President shall immediately assume the powers and duties of the office as Acting President.

Thereafter, when the President transmits to the President pro tempore of the Senate and the Speaker of the House of Representatives his written declaration that no inability exists, he shall resume the powers and duties of his office unless the Vice President and a majority of either the principal officers of the executive department or of such other body as Congress may by law provide, transmit within four days to the President pro tempore of the Senate and the Speaker of the House of Representatives their written declaration that the President is unable to discharge the powers and duties of his office. Thereupon Congress shall decide the issue, assembling within forty-eight hours for that purpose if not in session. If the Congress, within twenty-one days after receipt of the latter written declaration, or, if Congress is not in session, within twenty-one days after Congress is required to assemble, determines by two-thirds vote of both Houses that the President is unable to discharge the powers and duties of his office, the Vice President shall continue to discharge the same as Acting President; otherwise, the President shall resume the powers and duties of his office.

Whenever the vice president and a majority of the members of the cabinet believe that the president cannot carry out her or his duties, they shall so indicate in writing to Congress. The vice president shall then act as president. When the president believes that she or he is able to carry out her or his duties again, she or he shall so indicate to the Congress. However, if the vice president and a majority of the cabinet do not agree, Congress must decide by a two-thirds vote within three weeks who shall act as president.

Amendment XXVI.
(Ratified on July 1, 1971—
Voting Rights for Eighteen-Year-Olds)

Section 1.

The right of citizens of the United States, who are eighteen years of age or older, to vote shall not be denied or abridged by the United States or by any State on account of age.

No one eighteen years of age or older can be denied the right to vote in federal or state elections by virtue of age.

Section 2.

The Congress shall have power to enforce this article by appropriate legislation.

Amendment XXVII.
(Ratified on May 7, 1992—
Congressional Pay)

No law, varying the compensation for the services of the Senators and Representatives, shall take effect, until an election of representatives shall have intervened.

This amendment allows the voters to have some control over increases in salaries for congressional members. Originally submitted to the states for ratification in 1789, it was not ratified until 203 years later, in 1992.

Appendix C

Federalist Papers No. 10 and No. 51

In 1787, after the newly drafted U.S. Constitution was submitted to the thirteen states for ratification, a major political debate ensued between the Federalists (who favored ratification) and the Anti-Federalists (who opposed ratification). Anti-Federalists in New York were particularly critical of the Constitution, and in response to their objections, Federalists Alexander Hamilton, James Madison, and John Jay wrote a series of eighty-five essays in defense of the Constitution. The essays were published in New York newspapers and reprinted in other newspapers throughout the country.

For students of American government, the essays, collectively known as the Federalist Papers, *are particularly important because they provide a glimpse of the founders' political philosophy and intentions in designing the Constitution—and, consequently, in shaping the American philosophy of government.*

We have included in this appendix two of these essays: Federalist Papers *No. 10 and No. 51. Each essay has been annotated by the authors to indicate its importance in American political thought and to clarify the meaning of particular passages.*

Federalist Paper No. 10

Federalist Paper No. 10, penned by James Madison, has often been singled out as a key document in American political thought. In this essay, Madison attacks the Anti-Federalists' fear that a republican form of government will inevitably give rise to "factions"—small political parties or groups united by a common interest—that will control the government. Factions will be harmful to the country because they will implement policies beneficial to their own interests but adverse to other people's rights and to the public good. In this essay, Madison attempts to lay to rest this fear by explaining how, in a large republic such as the United States, there will be so many different factions, held together by regional or local interests, that no single one of them will dominate national politics.

Madison opens his essay with a paragraph discussing how important it is to devise a plan of government that can control the "instability, injustice, and confusion" brought about by factions.

Among the numerous advantages promised by a well-constructed Union, none deserves to be more accurately developed than its tendency to break and control the violence of faction. The friend of popular governments never finds himself so much alarmed for their character and fate as when he contemplates their propensity to this dangerous vice. He will not fail,

therefore, to set a due value on any plan which, without violating the principles to which he is attached, provides a proper cure for it. The instability, injustice, and confusion introduced into the public councils have, in truth, been the mortal diseases under which popular governments have everywhere perished, as they continue to be the favorite and fruitful topics from which the adversaries to liberty derive their most specious declamations. The valuable improvements made by the American constitutions on the popular models, both ancient and modern, cannot certainly be too much admired; but it would be an unwarrantable partiality to contend that they have as effectually obviated the danger on this side, as was wished and expected. Complaints are everywhere heard from our most considerate and virtuous citizens, equally the friends of public and private faith and of public and personal liberty, that our governments are too unstable, that the public good is disregarded in the conflicts of rival parties, and that measures are too often decided, not according to the rules of justice and the rights of the minor party, but by the superior force of an interested and overbearing majority. However anxiously we may wish that these complaints had no foundation, the evidence of known facts will not permit us to deny that they are in some degree true. It will be found, indeed, on a candid review of our situation, that some of the distresses under which we labor have been erroneously charged on the operation of our governments; but it will be found, at the same time, that other causes will not alone account for many of our heaviest misfortunes; and, particularly, for that prevailing and increasing distrust of public engagements and alarm for private rights which are echoed from one end of the continent to the other. These must be chiefly, if not wholly, effects of the unsteadiness and injustice with which a factious spirit has tainted our public administration.

Madison now defines what he means by the term faction.

By a faction I understand a number of citizens, whether amounting to a majority or minority of the

367

whole, who are united and actuated by some common impulse of passion, or of interest, adverse to the rights of other citizens, or the permanent and aggregate interests of the community.

Madison next contends that there are two methods by which the "mischiefs of faction" can be cured: by removing the causes of faction or by controlling their effects. In the following paragraphs, Madison explains how liberty itself nourishes factions. Therefore, to abolish factions would involve abolishing liberty—a cure "worse than the disease."

There are two methods of curing the mischiefs of faction: the one, by removing its causes; the other, by controlling its effects.

There are again two methods of removing the causes of faction: the one, by destroying the liberty which is essential to its existence; the other, by giving to every citizen the same opinions, the same passions, and the same interests.

It could never be more truly said than of the first remedy that it was worse than the disease. Liberty is to faction what air is to fire, an aliment without which it instantly expires. But it could not be a less folly to abolish liberty, which is essential to political life, because it nourishes faction than it would be to wish the annihilation of air, which is essential to animal life, because it imparts to fire its destructive agency.

The second expedient is as impracticable as the first would be unwise. As long as the reason of man continues fallible, and he is at liberty to exercise it, different opinions will be formed. As long as the connection subsists between his reason and his self-love, his opinions and his passions will have a reciprocal influence on each other; and the former will be objects to which the latter will attach themselves. The diversity in the faculties of men, from which the rights of property originate, is not less an insuperable obstacle to a uniformity of interests. The protection of these faculties is the first object of government. From the protection of different and unequal faculties of acquiring property, the possession of different degrees and kinds of property immediately results; and from the influence of these on the sentiments and views of the respective proprietors ensues a division of the society into different interests and parties.

The latent causes of faction are thus sown in the nature of man; and we see them everywhere brought into different degrees of activity, according to the different circumstances of civil society. A zeal for different opinions concerning religion, concerning government, and many other points, as well of speculation as of practice; an attachment to different leaders ambitiously contending for pre-eminence and power; or to persons of other descriptions whose fortunes have been interesting to the human passions, have, in turn, divided mankind into parties, inflamed them with mutual animosity, and rendered them much more disposed to vex and oppress each other than to co-operate for their common good. So strong is this propensity of mankind to fall into mutual animosities that where no substantial occasion presents itself the most frivolous and fanciful distinctions have been sufficient to kindle their unfriendly passions and excite their most violent conflicts. But the most common and durable source of factions has been the various and unequal distribution of property. Those who hold and those who are without property have ever formed distinct interests in society. Those who are creditors, and those who are debtors, fall under a like discrimination. A landed interest, a manufacturing interest, a mercantile interest, a moneyed interest, with many lesser interests, grow up of necessity in civilized nations, and divide them into different classes, actuated by different sentiments and views. The regulation of these various and interfering interests forms the principal task of modern legislation and involves the spirit of party and faction in the necessary and ordinary operations of government.

No man is allowed to be a judge in his own cause, because his interest would certainly bias his judgment, and, not improbably, corrupt his integrity. With equal, nay with greater reason, a body of men are unfit to be both judges and parties at the same time; yet what are many of the most important acts of legislation but so many judicial determinations, not indeed concerning the rights of single persons, but concerning the rights of large bodies of citizens? And what are the different classes of legislators but advocates and parties to the causes which they determine? Is a law proposed concerning private debts? It is a question to which the creditors are parties on one side and the debtors on the other. Justice ought to hold the balance between them. Yet the parties are, and must be, themselves the judges; and the most numerous party, or in other words, the most powerful faction must be expected to prevail. Shall domestic manufacturers be encouraged, and in what degree, by restrictions on foreign manufacturers? [These] are questions which would be differently decided by the landed and the manufacturing classes, and probably by neither with a sole regard to justice and the public good. The apportionment of taxes on the various descriptions of property is an act which seems to require the most exact impartiality; yet there is, perhaps, no legislative act in which greater opportunity and temptation are given to a predominant party to trample on the rules of justice. Every shilling with which they overburden the inferior number is a shilling saved to their own pockets.

It is in vain to say that enlightened statesmen will be able to adjust these clashing interests and render them all subservient to the public good. Enlightened statesmen will not always be at the helm. Nor, in many cases, can such an adjustment be made at all without taking into view indirect and remote considerations, which will rarely prevail over the immediate interest which one party may find in disregarding the rights of another or the good of the whole.

The inference to which we are brought is that the causes of faction cannot be removed and that relief is only to be sought in the means of controlling its *effects.*

Having concluded that "the causes of faction cannot be removed," Madison now looks in some detail at the other method by which factions can be cured—by controlling their effects. This is the heart of his essay. He begins by positing a significant question: How can you have self-government without risking the possibility that a ruling faction, particularly a majority faction, might tyrannize over the rights of others?

If a faction consists of less than a majority, relief is supplied by the republican principle, which enables the majority to defeat its sinister views by regular vote. It may clog the administration, it may convulse the society; but it will be unable to execute and mask its violence under the forms of the Constitution. When a majority is included in a faction, the form of popular government, on the other hand, enables it to sacrifice to its ruling passion or interest both the public good and the rights of other citizens. To secure the public good and private rights against the danger of such a faction, and at the same time to preserve the spirit and the form of popular government, is then the great object to which our inquiries are directed. Let me add that it is the great desideratum by which alone this form of government can be rescued from the opprobrium under which it has so long labored and be recommended to the esteem and adoption of mankind.

Madison now sets forth the idea that one way to control the effects of factions is to ensure that the majority is rendered

incapable of acting in concert in order to "carry into effect schemes of oppression." He goes on to state that in a democracy, in which all citizens participate personally in government decision making, there is no way to prevent the majority from communicating with one another and, as a result, acting in concert.

By what means is this object attainable? Evidently by one of two only. Either the existence of the same passion or interest in a majority at the same time must be prevented, or the majority, having such coexistent passion or interest, must be rendered, by their number and local situation, unable to concert and carry into effect schemes of oppression. If the impulse and the opportunity be suffered to coincide, we well know that neither moral nor religious motives can be relied on as an adequate control. They are not found to be such on the injustice and violence of individuals, and lose their efficacy in proportion to the number combined together, that is, in proportion as their efficacy becomes needful.

From this view of the subject it may be concluded that a pure democracy, by which I mean a society consisting of a small number of citizens, who assemble and administer the government in person, can admit of no cure for the mischiefs of faction. A common passion or interest will, in almost every case, be felt by a majority of the whole; a communication and concert results from the form of government itself; and there is nothing to check the inducements to sacrifice the weaker party or an obnoxious individual. Hence it is that such democracies have ever been spectacles of turbulence and contention; have ever been found incompatible with personal security or the rights of property; and have in general been as short in their lives as they have been violent in their deaths. Theoretic politicians, who have patronized this species of government, have erroneously supposed that by reducing mankind to a perfect equality in their political rights, they would at the same time be perfectly equalized and assimilated in their possessions, their opinions, and their passions.

Madison now moves on to discuss the benefits of a republic with respect to controlling the effects of factions. He begins by defining a republic and then pointing out the "two great points of difference" between a republic and a democracy: a republic is governed by a small body of elected representatives, not by the people directly; and a republic can extend over a much larger territory and embrace more citizens than a democracy can.

A republic, by which I mean a government in which the scheme of representation takes place, opens a different prospect and promises the cure for which we are seeking. Let us examine the points in which it varies from pure democracy, and we shall comprehend both the nature of the cure and the efficacy which it must derive from the Union.

The two great points of difference between a democracy and a republic are: first, the delegation of the government, in the latter, to a small number of citizens elected by the rest; secondly, the greater number of citizens and greater sphere of country over which the latter may be extended.

In the following four paragraphs, Madison explains how in a republic, particularly a large republic, the delegation of authority to elected representatives will increase the likelihood that those who govern will be "fit" for their positions and that a proper balance will be achieved between local (factional) interests and national interests. Note how he stresses that the new federal Constitution, by dividing powers between state governments and the national government, provides a "happy combination in this respect."

The effect of the first difference is, on the one hand, to refine and enlarge the public views by passing them through the medium of a chosen body of citizens, whose wisdom may best discern the true interest of their country and whose patriotism and love of justice will be least likely to sacrifice it to temporary or partial considerations. Under such a regulation it may well happen that the public voice, pronounced by the representatives of the people, will be more consonant to the public good than if pronounced by the people themselves, convened for the purpose. On the other hand, the effect may be inverted. Men of factious tempers, of local prejudices, or of sinister designs, may, by intrigue, by corruption, or by other means, first obtain the suffrages, and then betray the interests of the people. The question resulting is, whether small or extensive republics are most favorable to the election of proper guardians of the public weal; and it is clearly decided in favor of the latter by two obvious considerations.

In the first place it is to be remarked that however small the republic may be the representatives must be raised to a certain number in order to guard against the cabals of a few; and that however large it may be they must be limited to a certain number in order to guard against the confusion of a multitude. Hence, the number of representatives in the two cases not being in proportion to that of the constituents, and being proportionally greatest in the small republic, it follows that if the proportion of fit characters be not less in the large than in the small republic, the former will present a greater option, and consequently a greater probability of a fit choice.

In the next place, as each representative will be chosen by a greater number of citizens in the large than in the small republic, it will be more difficult for unworthy candidates to practice with success the vicious arts by which elections are too often carried; and the suffrages of the people being more free, will be more likely to center on men who possess the most attractive merit and the most diffusive and established characters.

It must be confessed that in this, as in most other cases, there is a mean, on both sides of which inconveniencies will be found to lie. By enlarging too much the number of electors, you render the representative too little acquainted with all their local circumstances and lesser interests; as by reducing it too much, you render him unduly attached to these, and too little fit to comprehend and pursue great and national objects. The federal Constitution forms a happy combination in this respect; the great and aggregate interests being referred to the national, the local and particular to the State legislatures.

Madison now looks more closely at the other difference between a republic and a democracy—namely, that a republic can encompass a larger territory and more citizens than a democracy can. In the remaining paragraphs of his essay, Madison concludes that in a large republic, it will be difficult for factions to act in concert. Although a factious group— religious, political, economic, or otherwise—may control a local or regional government, it will have little chance of gathering a national following. This is because in a large republic, there will be numerous factions whose work will offset the work of any one particular faction ("sect"). As Madison phrases it, these numerous factions will "secure the national councils against any danger from that source."

The other point of difference is the greater number of citizens and extent of territory which may be brought within the compass of republican than of democratic government; and it is this circumstance principally which renders factious combinations less to be dreaded in the former than in the latter. The smaller the society, the fewer probably will be the distinct parties and interests composing it; the fewer the distinct parties and interests, the more frequently will a majority be found of the same party; and the smaller the number of individuals composing a majority, and the smaller the compass within which they are placed, the more easily will they concert and execute their plans of oppression. Extend the sphere and you take in a greater variety of parties and interests; you make it less probable that a majority of the whole will have a common motive to invade the rights of other citizens; or if such a common motive exists, it will be more difficult for all who feel it to discover their own strength and to act in unison with each other. Besides other impediments, it may be remarked that, where there is a consciousness of unjust or dishonorable purposes, communication is always checked by distrust in proportion to the number whose concurrence is necessary.

Hence, it clearly appears that the same advantage which a republic has over a democracy in controlling the effects of faction is enjoyed by a large over a small republic—is enjoyed by the Union over the States composing it. Does this advantage consist in the substitution of representatives whose enlightened views and virtuous sentiments render them superior to local prejudices and to schemes of injustice? It will not be denied that the representation of the Union will be most likely to possess these requisite endowments. Does it consist in the greater security afforded by a greater variety of parties, against the event of any one party being able to outnumber and oppress the rest? In an equal degree does the increased variety of parties comprised within the Union increase this security. Does it, in fine, consist in the greater obstacles opposed to the concert and accomplishment of the secret wishes of an unjust and interested majority? Here again the extent of the Union gives it the most palpable advantage.

The influence of factious leaders may kindle a flame within their particular States but will be unable to spread a general conflagration through the other States. A religious sect may degenerate into a political faction in a part of the Confederacy; but the variety of sects dispersed over the entire face of it must secure the national councils against any danger from that source. A rage for paper money, for an abolition of debts, for an equal division of property, or for any other improper or wicked project, will be less apt to pervade the whole body of the Union than a particular member of it, in the same proportion as such a malady is more likely to taint a particular county or district than an entire State.

In the extent and proper structure of the Union, therefore, we behold a republican remedy for the diseases most incident to republican government. And according to the degree of pleasure and pride we feel in being republicans ought to be our zeal in cherishing the spirit and supporting the character of federalists.

Publius
(James Madison)

Federalist Paper No. 51

Federalist Paper No. 51, also authored by James Madison, is another classic in American political theory. Although the Federalists wanted a strong national government, they had not abandoned the traditional American view, particularly notable during the revolutionary era, that those holding powerful government positions could not be trusted to put national interests and the common good above their own personal interests. In this essay, Madison explains why the separation of the national government's powers into three branches—executive, legislative, and judicial—and a federal structure of government offer the best protection against tyranny.

To what expedient, then, shall we finally resort, for maintaining in practice the necessary partition of power among the several departments as laid down in the Constitution? The only answer that can be given is that as all these exterior provisions are found to be inadequate the defect must be supplied, by so contriving the interior structure of the government as that its several constituent parts may, by their mutual relations, be the means of keeping each other in their proper places. Without presuming to undertake a full development of this important idea I will hazard a few general observations which may perhaps place it in a clearer light, and enable us to form a more correct judgment of the principles and structure of the government planned by the convention.

In the next two paragraphs, Madison stresses that for the powers of the different branches (departments) of government to be truly separated, the personnel in one branch should not be dependent on another branch for their appointment or for the "emoluments" (compensation) attached to their offices.

In order to lay a due foundation for that separate and distinct exercise of the different powers of government, which to a certain extent is admitted on all hands to be essential to the preservation of liberty, it is evident that each department should have a will of its own; and consequently should be so constituted that the members of each should have as little agency as possible in the appointment of the members of the others. Were this principle rigorously adhered to, it would require that all the appointments for the supreme executive, legislative, and judiciary magistracies should be drawn from the same fountain of authority, the people, through channels having no communication whatever with one another. Perhaps such a plan of constructing the several departments would be less difficult in practice than it may in contemplation appear. Some difficulties, however, and some additional expense would attend the execution of it. Some deviations, therefore, from the principle must be admitted. In the constitution of the judiciary department in particular, it might be inexpedient to insist rigorously on the principle: first, because peculiar qualifications being essential in the members, the primary consideration ought to be to select that mode of choice which best secures these qualifications; second, because the permanent tenure by which the appointments are held in that department must soon destroy all sense of dependence on the authority conferring them.

It is equally evident that the members of each department should be as little dependent as possible on those of the others for the emoluments annexed to their offices. Were the executive magistrate, or the judges, not independent of the legislature in this particular, their independence in every other would be merely nominal.

In the following passages, which are among the most widely quoted of Madison's writings, he explains how the separation of the powers of government into three branches helps to counter the effects of personal ambition on government. The separation of powers allows personal motives to be linked to the constitutional rights of a branch of government. In effect, competing personal interests in each branch will help to keep the powers of the three government branches separate and, in so doing, will help to guard the public interest.

But the great security against a gradual concentration of the several powers in the same department consists in giving to those who administer each department the necessary constitutional means and personal motives to resist encroachments of the others. The provision for defense must in this, as in all other cases, be made commensurate to the danger of attack. Ambition must be made to counteract ambition. The interest of the man must be connected with the constitutional rights of the place. It may be a reflection on human nature that such devices should

be necessary to control the abuses of government. But what is government itself but the greatest of all reflections on human nature? If men were angels, no government would be necessary. If angels were to govern men, neither external nor internal controls on government would be necessary. In framing a government which is to be administered by men over men, the great difficulty lies in this: you must first enable the government to control the governed; and in the next place oblige it to control itself. A dependence on the people is, no doubt, the primary control on the government; but experience has taught mankind the necessity of auxiliary precautions.

This policy of supplying, by opposite and rival interests, the defect of better motives, might be traced through the whole system of human affairs, private as well as public. We see it particularly displayed in all the subordinate distributions of power, where the constant aim is to divide and arrange the several offices in such a manner as that each may be a check on the other—that the private interest of every individual may be a sentinel over the public rights. These inventions of prudence cannot be less requisite in the distribution of the supreme powers of the State.

Madison now addresses the issue of equality among the branches of government. The legislature will necessarily predominate, but if the executive is given an "absolute negative" (absolute veto power) over legislative actions, this also could lead to an abuse of power. Madison concludes that the division of the legislature into two "branches" (parts, or chambers) will act as a check on the legislature's powers.

But it is not possible to give to each department an equal power of self-defense. In republican government, the legislative authority necessarily predominates. The remedy for this inconveniency is to divide the legislature into different branches; and to render them, by different modes of election and different principles of action, as little connected with each other as the nature of their common functions and their common dependence on the society will admit. It may even be necessary to guard against dangerous encroachments by still further precautions. As the weight of the legislative authority requires that it should be thus divided, the weakness of the executive may require, on the other hand, that it should be fortified. An absolute negative on the legislature appears, at first view, to be the natural defense with which the executive magistrate should be armed. But perhaps it would be neither altogether safe nor alone sufficient.

On ordinary occasions it might not be exerted with the requisite firmness, and on extraordinary occasions it might be perfidiously abused. May not this defect of an absolute negative be supplied by some qualified connection between this weaker department and the weaker branch of the stronger department, by which the latter may be led to support the constitutional rights of the former, without being too much detached from the rights of its own department?

If the principles on which these observations are founded be just, as I persuade myself they are, and they be applied as a criterion to the several State constitutions, and to the federal Constitution, it will be found that if the latter does not perfectly correspond with them, the former are infinitely less able to bear such a test.

In the remainder of the essay, Madison discusses how a federal system of government, in which powers are divided between the states and the national government, offers "double security" against tyranny.

There are, moreover, two considerations particularly applicable to the federal system of America, which place that system in a very interesting point of view.

First. In a single republic, all the power surrendered by the people is submitted to the administration of a single government; and the usurpations are guarded against by a division of the government into distinct and separate departments. In the compound republic of America, the power surrendered by the people is first divided between two distinct governments, and then the portion allotted to each subdivided among distinct and separate departments. Hence a double security arises to the rights of the people. The different governments will control each other, at the same time that each will be controlled by itself.

Second. It is of great importance in a republic not only to guard the society against the oppression of its rulers, but to guard one part of the society against the injustice of the other part. Different interests necessarily exist in different classes of citizens. If a majority be united by a common interest, the rights of the minority will be insecure. There are but two methods of providing against this evil: the one by creating a will in the community independent of the majority—that is, of the society itself; the other, by comprehending in the society so many separate descriptions of citizens as will render an unjust combination of a majority

of the whole very improbable, if not impracticable. The first method prevails in all governments possessing an hereditary or self-appointed authority. This, at best, is but a precarious security; because a power independent of the society may as well espouse the unjust views of the major as the rightful interests of the minor party, and may possibly be turned against both parties. The second method will be exemplified in the federal republic of the United States. Whilst all authority in it will be derived from and dependent on the society, the society itself will be broken into so many parts, interests and classes of citizens, that the rights of individuals, or of the minority, will be in little danger from interested combinations of the majority. In a free government the security for civil rights must be the same as that for religious rights. It consists in the one case in the multiplicity of interests, and in the other in the multiplicity of sects. The degree of security in both cases will depend on the number of interests and sects; and this may be presumed to depend on the extent of country and number of people comprehended under the same government. This view of the subject must particularly recommend a proper federal system to all the sincere and considerate friends of republican government, since it shows that in exact proportion as the territory of the Union may be formed into more circumscribed Confederacies, or States, oppressive combinations of a majority will be facilitated; the best security, under the republican forms, for the rights of every class of citizen, will be diminished; and consequently the stability and independence of some member of the government, the only other security, must be proportionally increased. Justice is the end of government. It is the end of civil society. It ever has been and ever will be pursued until it be obtained, or until liberty be lost in the pursuit. In a society under the forms of which the stronger faction can readily unite and oppress the weaker, anarchy may as truly be said to reign as in a state of nature, where the weaker individual is not secured against the violence of the stronger; and as, in the latter state, even the stronger individuals are prompted, by the uncertainty of their condition, to submit to a government which may protect the weak as well as themselves; so, in the former state, will the more powerful factions or parties be gradually induced, by a like motive, to wish for a government which will protect all parties, the weaker as well as the more powerful. It can be little doubted that if the State of Rhode Island was separated from the Confederacy and left to itself, the insecurity of rights under the popular form of government within such narrow limits would be displayed by such reiterated oppressions of factious majorities that some power altogether independent of the people would soon be called for by the voice of the very factions whose misrule had proved the necessity of it. In the extended republic of the United States, and among the great variety of interests, parties, and sects which it embraces, a coalition of a majority of the whole society could seldom take place on any other principles than those of justice and the general good; whilst there being thus less danger to a minor from the will of a major party, there must be less pretext, also, to provide for the security of the former, by introducing into the government a will not dependent on the latter, or, in other words, a will independent of the society itself. It is no less certain than it is important, notwithstanding the contrary opinions which have been entertained, that the larger the society, provided it lie within a practicable sphere, the more duly capable it will be of self-government. And happily for the republican cause, the practicable sphere may be carried to a very great extent by a judicious modification and mixture of the *federal principle*.

Publius
(James Madison)

Government Spending and Revenue Charts

Do you find some of these percentages surprising? If so, which ones?

Federal Government Spending

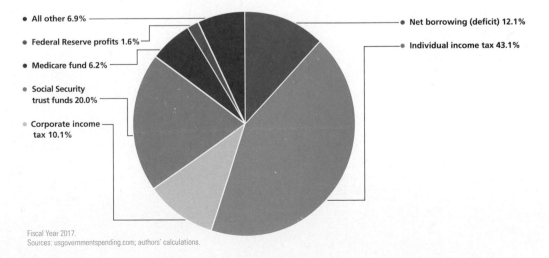

- Everything else 13.2%
- Interest on debt 7.3%
- Veterans' benefits 4.4%
- Military defense 14.9%
- Miscellaneous low-income support 6.7%
- SNAP and nutrition 2.6%

- Social Security 23.6%
- Medicare 14.6%
- Medicaid and CHIP 12.7%

Federal Government Revenues

- All other 6.9%
- Federal Reserve profits 1.6%
- Medicare fund 6.2%
- Social Security trust funds 20.0%
- Corporate income tax 10.1%

- Net borrowing (deficit) 12.1%
- Individual income tax 43.1%

Fiscal Year 2017.
Sources: usgovernmentspending.com; authors' calculations.

Glossary

A

Actual Malice Either knowledge of a defamatory statement's falsity or a reckless disregard for the truth.

Advice and Consent Terms in the Constitution describing the U.S. Senate's power to review and approve treaties and presidential appointments.

Affirm To declare that a court ruling is valid and must stand.

Affirmative Action A policy in educational admissions or job hiring that gives special attention or compensatory treatment to traditionally disadvantaged groups in an effort to overcome present effects of past discrimination.

Affordable Care Act (ACA) A law passed in 2010 that seeks, among other things, to provide health-care insurance to all American citizens. The act has been nicknamed "Obamacare."

Agency Capture The act by which an industry being regulated by a government agency gains direct or indirect control over agency personnel and decision makers.

Agenda Setting Determining which public-policy questions will be debated or considered.

***Amicus Curiae* Brief** A written legal argument filed by a third party, or *amicus curiae* (Latin for "friend of the court"), who is not directly involved in the litigation but who has an interest in the outcome of the case.

Anti-Federalist An individual who opposed the ratification of the new Constitution in 1787. The Anti-Federalists were opposed to a strong central government.

Appellate Court A court having jurisdiction to review cases and issues that were originally tried in lower courts.

Appointment Power The president's authority to fill a government office or position.

Appropriation The passage, by Congress, of a spending bill specifying the amount of authorized funds that actually will be allocated for an agency's use.

Arraignment The first act in a criminal proceeding, in which the defendant is brought before a court to hear the charges against him or her and enter a plea of guilty or not guilty.

Australian Ballot A secret ballot prepared, distributed, and tabulated by government officials at public expense. Since 1888, all states have used the Australian ballot rather than an open, public ballot.

Authoritarianism A type of regime in which only the government itself is fully controlled by the ruler. Social and economic institutions exist that are not under the government's control.

Authority The right and power of a government or other entity to enforce its decisions and compel obedience.

Authorization A formal declaration by a legislative committee that a certain amount of funding may be available to an agency. Some authorizations terminate in a year. Others are renewable automatically without further congressional action.

B

Bias An inclination or a preference that interferes with impartial judgment.

Bicameral Legislature A legislature made up of two parts, called chambers. The U.S. Congress, composed of the House of Representatives and the Senate, is a bicameral legislature.

Bicameralism The division of a legislature into two separate assemblies.

Bill of Attainder A law that inflicts punishment without a trial.

Bill of Rights The first ten amendments to the U.S. Constitution.

Block Grant A federal grant that provides funds to a state or local government for a general functional area, such as criminal justice or mental-health programs.

Blog A regular updating of one's ideas on a specific website. The word comes from Web log.

Budget Deficit Government expenditures that exceed receipts.

Bureaucracy A large organization that is structured hierarchically to carry out specific functions.

C

Cabinet An advisory group selected by the president to aid in making decisions. The cabinet includes the heads of fifteen executive departments and others named by the president.

Cabinet Department One of the fifteen major departments of the executive branch.

Capitalism An economic system characterized by the private ownership of wealth-creating assets, free markets, and freedom of contract.

Case Law Judicial interpretations of common law principles and doctrines, as well as interpretations of constitutional law, statutory law, and administrative law.

Casework Personal work for constituents by members of Congress.

Categorical Grant A federal grant to a state or local government for a specific program or project.

Caucus System A meeting of party members to select candidates and propose policies.

Checks and Balances A major principle of the American system of government whereby each branch of the government can check the actions of the others.

Chief Diplomat The role of the president in recognizing foreign governments, making treaties, and effecting executive agreements.

Chief Executive The role of the president as head of the executive branch of the government.

Chief Legislator The role of the president in influencing the making of laws.

Chief of Staff The person who is named to direct the White House Office and advise the president.

Civil Disobedience A nonviolent, public refusal to obey allegedly unjust laws.

Civil Liberties Those personal freedoms, including freedom of religion and of speech, that are protected for all individuals in a society.

Civil Rights Generally, all rights rooted in the Fourteenth Amendment's guarantee of equal protection under the law.

Civil Service A collective term for employees of the government. Generally, *civil service* is understood to apply to all those who gain government employment through a merit system.

Civil Service Commission The initial central personnel agency of the national government, created in 1883.

Class-Action Suit A lawsuit filed by an individual seeking damages for "all persons similarly situated."

Closed Primary A type of primary in which the voter is limited to choosing candidates of the party of which he or she is a member.

Cold War The ideological, political, and economic confrontation between the United States and the Soviet Union following World War II.

Commander in Chief The role of the president as supreme commander of the military forces of the United States and of the state National Guard units when they are called into federal service.

Commerce Clause The section of the Constitution in which Congress is given the power to regulate trade among the states and with foreign countries.

Commercial speech Advertising statements, which increasingly have been given First Amendment protection.

Common Law The body of law developed from judicial decisions in English and U.S. courts, not attributable to a legislature.

Concentrated Benefits and Dispersed Costs The theory that a minority benefiting from a government program will make a stronger effort to keep it than the majority will ever make to abolish it.

Concurrent Powers Powers held jointly by the national and state governments.

Concurring Opinion A separate opinion prepared by a judge who supports the decision of the majority of the court but for different reasons.

Confederal System A system consisting of a league of independent states, in which the central government created by the league has only limited powers over the states.

Confederation A political system in which states or regional governments retain ultimate authority except for those powers they expressly delegate to a central government.

Conference Committee A special joint committee appointed to reconcile differences when bills pass the two chambers of Congress in different forms.

Consensus General agreement among the citizenry on an issue.

Conservatism A set of beliefs that includes advocacy of a limited role for the national government in helping individuals, support for traditional values and lifestyles, and a cautious response to change.

Conservative Movement An American movement launched in the 1950s that provides a comprehensive ideological framework for conservative politics.

Constituent One of the persons represented by a legislator or other elected or appointed official.

Constitutional Power A power vested in the president by Article II of the Constitution.

Containment A U.S. diplomatic policy adopted by the Truman administration to contain Communist power within its existing boundaries.

Continuing Resolution A temporary funding law that Congress passes when an appropriations bill has not been passed by the beginning of the new fiscal year on October 1.

Cooperative Federalism A model of federalism in which the states and the national government cooperate in solving problems.

Cracking In gerrymandering, splitting the opposing party's voters into many different districts.

Credentials Committee A committee used by political parties at their national conventions to determine which delegates may participate.

D

De Facto **Segregation** Racial segregation that occurs because of patterns of racial residence and similar social conditions.

De Jure **Segregation** Racial segregation that occurs because of laws or administrative decisions by public agencies.

Defamation of Character Wrongfully hurting a person's good reputation.

Defense Policy A subset of national security policy concerning the U.S. armed forces.

Democracy A system of government in which political authority is vested in the people.

Democratic Party One of the two major American political parties evolving out of the Republican Party of Thomas Jefferson. It was formed in 1828.

Democratic Republic A republic in which representatives elected by the people make and enforce laws and policies.

Détente A French word meaning a relaxation of tensions. The term characterized U.S.-Soviet relations as they developed under President Richard Nixon and Secretary of State Henry Kissinger.

Devolution The transfer of powers from a national or central government to a state or local government.

Diplomacy The process by which states carry on political relations with each other. Also, the process of settling conflicts among nations by peaceful means.

Diplomatic Recognition The formal acknowledgment of a foreign government as legitimate.

Direct Democracy A system of government in which political decisions are made by the people directly, rather than by their elected representatives.

Direct Primary A primary election in which voters decide party nominations by voting directly for candidates.

Direct Technique An interest group technique that uses direct interaction with government officials to further the group's goals.

Discharge Petition A procedure by which a bill in the House of Representatives may be forced (discharged) out of a committee that has refused to report it for consideration by the House.

Dissenting Opinion A separate opinion in which a judge dissents from (disagrees with) the conclusion reached by the majority of the court and expounds his or her own views about the case.

Diversity of Citizenship The condition that exists when the parties to a lawsuit are from different states or when the suit involves a U.S. citizen and a government or citizen of a foreign country. Diversity of citizenship can provide a basis for federal jurisdiction.

Divided Government A situation in which one major political party controls the presidency and the other controls one or more chambers of Congress, or in which one party controls a state governorship and the other controls the state legislature.

Divided Opinion Public opinion that is polarized between two different positions.

Domestic Policy All government laws, planning, and actions that concern internal issues of national importance, such as health care, the environment, and the economy.

Dual Federalism A model of federalism that looks on national and state governments as co-equal sovereign powers. Neither the state government nor the national government should interfere in the other's sphere.

E

Earmarks Special provisions in legislation to sct aside funds for projects that have not passed an impartial evaluation by agencies of the executive branch. Also known as *pork*.

Economic Aid Assistance to other nations in the form of grants, loans, or credits to buy the assisting nation's products.

Elastic Clause, or Necessary and Proper Clause The clause in Article I, Section 8, that grants Congress the power to do whatever is necessary to execute its specifically delegated powers.

Elector A member of the electoral college, which selects the president and vice president. Each state's electors are chosen in each presidential election year according to state laws.

Electoral College A group of persons, called electors, that officially elects the president and the vice president of the United States. The electors are selected by each state and the District of Columbia.

Elite Theory The argument that society is ruled by a small number of people who exercise power to further their self-interest.

Emergency Power An inherent power exercised by the president during a period of national crisis.

Enabling Legislation A statute enacted by Congress that authorizes the creation of an administrative agency and specifies the name, purpose, composition, functions, and powers of the agency being created.

Entitlement Program A government program that entitles a defined class of people to obtain benefits. Entitlements operate under open-ended budget authorizations that do not limit how much can be spent.

Enumerated Powers Powers specifically granted to the national government by the Constitution. The first seventeen clauses of Article I, Section 8, specify most of the enumerated, or expressed, powers of the national government.

Equality As a political value, the idea that all people are of equal worth.

Establishment Clause The part of the First Amendment prohibiting the establishment of a church officially supported by the national government.

Ex Post Facto Law A law that inflicts punishment for an act that was not illegal at the time it was committed.

Exclusionary Rule A judicial policy prohibiting the admission at trial of illegally seized evidence.

Executive Agreement An international agreement made by the president, without senatorial ratification, with the head of a foreign state.

Executive Budget The budget prepared and submitted by the president to Congress.

Executive Office of the President (EOP) An organization established by President Franklin Roosevelt to assist the president in carrying out major duties.

Executive Order A rule or regulation issued by the president that has the effect of law.

Executive Privilege The right of executive officials to withhold information from, or to refuse to appear before, a legislative committee or a court.

Expressed Power A power of the president that is expressly written into the Constitution or into statutory law.

F

Fall Review The annual process in which the OMB, after receiving formal federal agency requests for funding for the next fiscal year, reviews the requests, makes changes, and submits its recommendations to the president.

Federal Election Commission (FEC) The federal regulatory agency with the task of enforcing federal campaign laws. As a practical matter, the FEC's role is largely limited to collecting data on campaign contributions.

Federal Mandate A requirement in federal legislation that forces states and municipalities to comply with certain rules.

Federal Open Market Committee The most important body within the Federal Reserve System. The Federal Open Market Committee decides how monetary policy should be carried out.

Federal Question A question that has to do with the U.S. Constitution, acts of Congress, or treaties. A federal question provides a basis for federal jurisdiction.

Federal Register A daily publication of the U.S. government that prints executive orders, rules, and regulations.

Federal Reserve System (the Fed) The system created by Congress in 1913 to serve as the nation's central banking organization.

Federalist An individual who was in favor of the adoption of the U.S. Constitution and the creation of a federal union with a strong central government.

Feminism The movement that supports political, economic, and social equality for women.

Filibuster The use of the Senate's tradition of unlimited debate as a delaying tactic to block bills or nominations.

First Budget Resolution A resolution passed by Congress in May that sets overall revenue goals and spending targets for the following fiscal year.

Fiscal Having to do with government revenues and expenditures.

Fiscal Federalism A process by which funds raised through taxation or borrowing by one level of government (usually the national government) are spent by another level (typically, state or local governments).

Fiscal Policy The federal government's use of taxation and spending policies to affect overall business activity.

Fiscal Year (FY) A twelve-month period that is used for bookkeeping or accounting purposes. Usually, the fiscal year does not coincide with the calendar year. For example, the federal government's fiscal year runs from October 1 through September 30.

Focus Group A small group of individuals who are led in discussion by a professional consultant to gather opinions on, and responses to, candidates and issues.

Foreign Policy A nation's external goals and the techniques and strategies used to achieve them.

Fracking Also called hydraulic fracturing, the injection of a high-pressure solution of water, sand, and chemicals into hydrocarbon-bearing rocks, releasing oil or natural gas.

Framing In a media report, the technique of embedding an issue in particular examples or story lines to alter public perceptions of the issue.

Free Exercise Clause The provision of the First Amendment guaranteeing the free exercise of religion.

Free-Rider Problem The difficulty that interest groups face in recruiting members when the benefits they achieve can be gained without joining the group.

Front-Loading The practice of moving presidential primary elections to the early part of the campaign to maximize the impact of these primaries on the nomination.

Front-Runner The presidential candidate who appears to be ahead at a given time in the primary season.

G

Gender Discrimination Any practice, policy, or procedure that denies equality of treatment to an individual or to a group because of gender.

Gender Gap The difference between the percentage of women who vote for a particular candidate and the percentage of men who vote for the candidate.

General Election An election, normally held on the first Tuesday in November, that determines who will fill various elected positions.

General Jurisdiction A court's authority to hear cases that is not significantly restricted. A court of general jurisdiction normally can hear a broad range of cases.

Generational Effect A long-lasting effect of the events of a particular time on the political opinions of those who came of political age at that time.

Gerrymandering The drawing of legislative district boundary lines for the purpose of obtaining partisan advantage.

A district is said to be gerrymandered when its shape is altered substantially to determine which party will win it.

GOP A nickname for the Republican Party, which stands for "grand old party."

Government The preeminent institution within a society. Government has the ultimate authority to decide how conflicts will be resolved and how benefits and privileges will be allocated.

Government Corporation An agency of government that administers a quasi-business enterprise. These corporations are used when government activities are primarily commercial.

Government in the Sunshine Act A law that requires all committee-directed federal agencies to conduct their business regularly in public sessions.

Grandfather Clause A device used by southern states to disenfranchise African Americans. It restricted voting to those whose ancestors had voted before 1867.

Great Compromise The compromise between the New Jersey and Virginia plans that created one chamber of the Congress based on population and one chamber representing each state equally; also called the Connecticut Compromise.

Gross Domestic Product (GDP) The dollar value of all final goods and services produced in a one-year period.

H

Hatch Act An act passed in 1939 that restricted the political activities of government employees. It also prohibited a political group from spending more than $3 million in any campaign and limited individual contributions to a campaign committee to $5,000.

Head of State The role of the president as ceremonial head of the government.

Hispanic Someone who can claim a heritage from a Spanish-speaking country. Hispanics may be of any race.

House Effect In public opinion polling, an effect in which one polling organization's results consistently differ from those reported by other poll takers.

I

Imminent Lawless Action Test The current standard established by the Supreme Court for evaluating the legality of advocacy speech. Such speech can be forbidden only when it is "directed to inciting . . . imminent lawless actions."

Impeachment An action by the House of Representatives to accuse the president, vice president, or other civil officers of the United States of committing "Treason, Bribery, or other high Crimes and Misdemeanors."

Incorporation Theory The view that the protections of the Bill of Rights apply to state governments through the Fourteenth Amendment's due process clause.

Independent A voter or candidate who does not identify with a political party.

Independent Executive Agency A federal agency that is not part of a cabinet department but reports directly to the president.

Independent Expenditures Unregulated political expenditures by PACs, organizations, and individuals that are not coordinated with candidate campaigns or political parties.

Independent Regulatory Agency An agency outside the major executive departments charged with making and implementing rules and regulations within a specific area.

Indirect Primary A primary election in which voters choose convention delegates, and the delegates determine the party's candidate in the general election.

Indirect Technique An interest group technique that uses third parties to influence government officials.

Inflation A sustained rise in the general price level of goods and services.

Inherent Power A power of the president derived from the statements in the Constitution that "the executive Power shall be vested in a President" and that the president should "take Care that the Laws be faithfully executed."

Initiative A procedure by which voters can petition to vote on a law or a constitutional amendment.

Institution An ongoing organization that performs certain functions for society.

Instructed Delegate A legislator who is an agent of the voters who elected him or her and who votes according to the views of constituents, regardless of personal beliefs.

Intelligence Community The government agencies that gather information about the capabilities and intentions of foreign governments or that engage in covert actions.

Interest Group An organized group of individuals sharing common objectives who actively attempt to influence policymakers.

Intermediate, or Exacting, Scrutiny A judicial standard used to determine whether a law or government action unconstitutionally discriminates against women.

Internet Service Provider (ISP) A corporation or service that sells access to the Internet.

Interstate Compact An agreement between two or more states.

Invisible Primary The preprimary campaign to win supporters among elected officials, fund-raisers, interest groups, and opinion leaders.

Iron Triangle A three-way alliance among legislators in Congress, bureaucrats, and interest groups to make or preserve policies that benefit their respective interests.

Isolationist Foreign Policy A policy of abstaining from an active role in international affairs or alliances, which characterized U.S. foreign policy toward Europe during most of the 1800s.

Issue Advocacy Advertising Advertising paid for by interest groups that support or oppose a candidate's position on an issue without mentioning the candidate, voting, or elections.

Issue Network A group of individuals or organizations— which may consist of legislators and legislative staff members, interest group leaders, bureaucrats, scholars and other experts, and media representatives—that supports a particular policy position on a given issue.

J

Joint Committee A legislative committee composed of members from both chambers of Congress.

Judicial Activism A doctrine holding that the federal judiciary should take an active role by using its powers to check the activities of governmental bodies when those bodies exceed their authority.

Judicial Implementation The way in which court decisions are translated into action.

Judicial Restraint A doctrine holding that courts should defer to the decisions made by the elected representatives of the people in the legislative and executive branches when possible.

Judicial Review The power of the Supreme Court or any court to examine and possibly declare unconstitutional federal or state laws and other acts of government.

Jurisdiction The authority of a court to decide certain cases. Not all courts have the authority to decide all cases. Where a case arises and what its subject matter is are two jurisdictional issues.

Justiciable Controversy A controversy that is real and substantial, as opposed to hypothetical or academic.

K

Keynesian Economics A school of economic thought that favors active federal government policymaking to stabilize economy-wide fluctuations, including the use of discretionary fiscal policy.

Kitchen Cabinet The informal advisers to the president.

L

Labor Movement The economic and political expression of working-class interests.

Latino An alternative to the term *Hispanic* that is preferred by many.

Lawmaking The process of establishing the legal rules that govern society.

Legislature A governmental body primarily responsible for the making of laws.

Legitimacy Popular acceptance of the right and power of a government or other entity to exercise authority.

Libel A written defamation of a person's character or reputation. The defamatory statement must be observed by a third party.

Liberalism A set of beliefs that includes advocacy of positive government action to improve the welfare of individuals, support for civil rights, and tolerance for political and social change.

Libertarianism A political ideology based on skepticism or opposition toward most government activities.

Liberty The greatest freedom of the individual that is consistent with the freedom of other individuals in the society.

Limited Government A government with powers that are limited either through a written document or through widely shared beliefs.

Limited Jurisdiction A court's authority to hear cases that is restricted to certain types of claims, such as tax claims or bankruptcy petitions.

Line Organization In the federal government, an administrative unit that is directly accountable to the president.

Literacy Test A test administered as a precondition for voting, often used to prevent African Americans from exercising their right to vote.

Litigate To engage in a legal proceeding or seek relief in a court of law. To carry on a lawsuit.

Lobbyist An organization or individual who attempts to influence the passage, defeat, or content of legislation and the government's administrative decisions.

Loophole A legal method by which individuals and businesses are allowed to reduce the tax liabilities they owe to the government.

M

Madisonian Model A structure of government proposed by James Madison, in which the powers of the government are separated into three branches: executive, legislative, and judicial.

Majoritarianism A political theory holding that in a democracy, the government ought to do what the majority of the people want.

Majority Leader of the House A leader elected by the majority party in the House to assist the Speaker and foster party cohesion.

Majority Opinion A court opinion reflecting the views of the majority of the judges.

Majority Rule A basic principle of democracy asserting that the greatest number of citizens in any political unit should select officials and determine policies.

Media The channels of mass communication.

Medicaid A joint state-federal program that provides medical care to the poor (including indigent elderly persons in nursing homes). The program is funded out of general government revenues.

Medicare A federal health-insurance program that covers U.S. residents over the age of sixty-five. The costs are met in part, by a tax on wages and salaries.

Merit System The selection, retention, and promotion of government employees on the basis of competitive examinations.

Midterm Elections National elections in which candidates for president are not on the ballot. In midterm elections, voters choose all members of the U.S. House of Representatives and one-third of the members of the U.S. Senate.

Minority Leader of the House The party leader elected by members of the minority party in the House.

Monetary Policy The use of changes in the amount of money in circulation to alter credit markets, employment, and the rate of inflation.

Monroe Doctrine A policy statement made by President James Monroe in 1823. The United States would not accept any new European intervention in the Western Hemisphere. In return, the United States would not meddle in European affairs.

Moral Idealism A philosophy that views nations as normally willing to cooperate and to agree on moral standards for conduct.

N

National Committee A standing committee of a national political party established to direct and coordinate party activities between national party conventions.

National Convention The meeting held every four years by each major party to select presidential and vice-presidential candidates, write a platform, choose a national committee, and conduct party business.

National Security Council (NSC) An agency in the Executive Office of the President that advises the president on national security.

National Security Policy Foreign and domestic policy designed to protect the nation's independence and political integrity. Policy that is concerned with the safety and defense of the nation.

Natural Rights Rights held to be inherent in natural law, not dependent on governments. John Locke stated that natural law, being superior to human law, specifies certain rights of "life, liberty, and property."

Net Neutrality The principle that an ISP should treat all traffic equally.

Normal Trade Relations (NTR) Status A status granted through an international treaty by which each member nation must treat other members as well as it treats the country that receives its most favorable treatment. This status was formerly known as *most-favored-nation status.*

O

Office of Management and Budget (OMB) A division of the Executive Office of the President. The OMB assists the president in preparing the annual budget, clearing and coordinating departmental agency budgets, and supervising the administration of the federal budget.

Ombudsperson A person who hears and investigates complaints by private individuals against public officials or agencies (from the Swedish word *ombudsman*, meaning "representative").

Open Primary A primary in which any voter can vote in either party primary (but must vote for candidates of only one party).

Opinion A statement by a judge or a court of the decision reached in a case. An opinion sets forth the applicable law and details the reasoning on which the ruling was based.

Opinion Leader One who is able to influence the opinions of others because of position, expertise, or personality.

Opinion Poll A method of systematically questioning a small, selected sample of respondents who are deemed representative of the total population.

Oral Arguments The arguments presented in person by attorneys to an appellate court.

Order A state of peace and security. Maintaining order by protecting members of society from violence and criminal activity is the oldest purpose of government.

Oversight The process by which Congress follows up on laws it has enacted to ensure that they are being enforced and administered in the way Congress intended.

P

Packing In gerrymandering, packing as many voters as possible of the opposing party into a single district.

Pardon A release from the punishment for, or legal consequences of, a crime. A pardon can be granted by the president before or after a conviction.

Party Identification Linking oneself to a particular political party.

Party Organization The formal structure and leadership of a political party, including election committees; local, state, and national executives; and paid professional staff.

Party Platform A document drawn up at each national convention, outlining the policies, positions, and principles of the party.

Patronage The practice of rewarding faithful party workers and followers with government employment and contracts.

Peer Group A group consisting of members who share common social characteristics. Such groups play an important part in the socialization process, helping to shape attitudes and beliefs.

Pendleton Act (Civil Service Reform Act) An act that established the principle of federal government employment based on merit and created the Civil Service Commission to administer the personnel service.

Pluralism A theory that views politics as a conflict among interest groups. Political decision making is characterized by bargaining and compromise.

Plurality A number of votes cast for a candidate that is greater than the number of votes for any other candidate but not necessarily a majority.

Plurality Opinion An opinion by a minority of the Court that decides a case because it is supported by one or more concurring opinions.

Pocket Veto A special veto exercised by the chief executive after a legislative body has adjourned. Bills not signed by the chief executive die after a specified period of time.

Police Power The authority to legislate for the protection of the health, morals, safety, and welfare of the people. In the United States, most police power is reserved to the states.

Policy Demanders Individuals or interest group members who participate in political parties with the intent to see that certain policies are adopted or specific groups favored.

Political Action Committee (PAC) A committee set up by and representing a corporation, labor union, or interest group. PACs raise campaign donations.

Political Consultant A paid professional hired to devise a campaign strategy and manage a campaign.

Political Culture The patterned set of ideas, values, and ways of thinking about government and politics that characterizes a people.

Political Ideology A comprehensive set of beliefs about the nature of politics and the role of government.

Political Party A group of political activists who organize to win elections, operate the government, and determine public policy.

Political Question An issue that a court believes should be decided by the executive or legislative branch, or both.

Political Realism A philosophy that views each nation as acting principally in its own interest.

Political Socialization The process by which people acquire political beliefs and values.

Political Trust The degree to which individuals express trust in the government and political institutions, usually measured through a specific series of survey questions.

Politics The struggle over power or influence within organizations or informal groups that can grant or withhold benefits or privileges.

Poll Tax A special tax that had to be paid as a qualification for voting. The Twenty-fourth Amendment to the Constitution outlawed the poll tax in national elections, and in 1966, the Supreme Court declared it unconstitutional in state elections as well.

Popular Sovereignty The concept that ultimate political authority is based on the will of the people.

Precedent A court ruling bearing on subsequent legal decisions in similar cases. Judges rely on precedents in deciding cases.

President pro tempore The senator who presides over the Senate in the absence of the vice president.

Presidential Primary A statewide primary election of delegates to a political party's national convention, held to determine a party's presidential nominee

Primary Election An election in which political parties choose their candidates for the general election.

Priming In a media report, using only certain facts to shape the public's response to an issue.

Prior Restraint Restraining an activity before it has actually occurred. When expression is involved, this means censorship.

Privatization The replacement of government services with services provided by private firms.

Progressive A popular alternative to the term *liberal*.

Progressive Tax A tax that rises in percentage terms as incomes rise.

Property Anything that is or may be subject to ownership.

Public Agenda Issues that are perceived by the political community as meriting public attention and governmental action.

Public Figure A public official, movie star, or other person known to the public because of his or her positions or activities.

Public Interest The best interests of the overall community. Also, the national good, rather than the narrow interests of a particular group.

Public Opinion The aggregate of individual attitudes or beliefs shared by some portion of the population.

Public, or National, Debt The total amount of debt carried by the federal government.

R

Ratification Formal approval.

Rational Basis Review A judicial standard for assessing a law or government action that is employed when neither strict nor intermediate scrutiny apply.

Realignment A large-scale, lasting change in the types of voters who support each of the major political parties.

Reapportionment The allocation of seats in the House of Representatives to each state after a census.

Recall A procedure allowing the people to vote to dismiss an elected official from office before his or her term has expired.

Recession An economic downturn, usually characterized by a fall in the GDP and rising unemployment.

Reconciliation A special rule that can be applied to budget bills sent from the House of Representatives to the Senate. Reconciliation measures cannot be filibustered.

Redistricting The redrawing of the boundaries of the congressional districts within each state.

Referendum An electoral device whereby legislative or constitutional measures are referred by the legislature to the voters for approval or disapproval.

Registration The entry of a person's name onto the list of registered voters for elections. To register, a person must meet certain legal requirements of age, citizenship, and residency.

Regressive Tax A tax that falls in percentage terms as incomes rise.

Remand To send a case back to the court that originally heard it.

Representation The function of members of Congress as elected officials representing the views of their constituents as well as larger national interests.

Representative Assembly A legislature composed of individuals who represent the population.

Representative Democracy A form of government in which representatives elected by the people make and enforce laws and policies, but in which the monarchy may be retained in a ceremonial role.

Reprieve A formal postponement of the execution of a sentence imposed by a court of law.

Republic A form of government in which sovereign power rests with the people, rather than with a king or a monarch.

Republican Party One of the two major American political parties. It emerged in the 1850s as an antislavery party and consisted of former northern Whigs and antislavery Democrats.

Reverse To annul or make void a court ruling on account of some error or irregularity.

Reverse Discrimination Discrimination against individuals who are not members of a minority group.

Rule of Four A United States Supreme Court procedure by which four justices must vote to grant a petition for review if a case is to come before the full court.

Rules Committee A standing committee of the House of Representatives that provides special rules under which specific bills can be debated, amended, and considered by the House.

S

Sampling Error The difference between a sample result and the true result if the entire population had been interviewed.

Second Budget Resolution A resolution passed by Congress in September that sets binding limits on taxes and spending for the following fiscal year.

Select Committee A temporary legislative committee established for a limited time period and for a special purpose.

Senate Majority Leader The chief spokesperson of the majority party in the Senate, who directs the legislative program and party strategy.

Senate Minority Leader The party officer in the Senate who commands the minority party's opposition to the policies of the majority party and directs the legislative program and strategy of his or her party.

Senatorial Courtesy In federal district court judgeship nominations, a tradition allowing a senator to veto a judicial appointment in her or his state.

Seniority System A custom followed in both chambers of Congress specifying that the member of the majority party with the longest term of continuous service will be given preference when a committee chairperson (or a holder of some other significant post) is selected.

Separate-but-Equal Doctrine The doctrine holding that separate-but-equal facilities do not violate the equal protection clause of the Fourteenth Amendment to the U.S. Constitution.

Separation of Powers The principle of dividing governmental powers among different branches of government.

Service Sector The sector of the economy that provides services— such as health care, banking, and education— in contrast to the sector that produces goods.

Sexual Harassment Unwanted physical or verbal conduct or abuse of a sexual nature that interferes with a recipient's job performance, creates a hostile work environment, or carries with it an implicit or explicit threat of adverse employment consequences.

Signing Statement A written declaration that the president may make when signing a bill into law. It may contain instructions to the bureaucracy on how to administer the law or point to sections of the law that the president considers unconstitutional or contrary to national security interests.

Slander The public uttering of a false statement that harms the good reputation of another. The statement must be made to, or within the hearing of, someone other than the defamed party.

Social Contract A voluntary agreement among individuals to secure their rights and welfare by creating a government and abiding by its rules.

Social Movement A movement that represents the demands of a large segment of the public for political, economic, or social change.

Socialism A political ideology based on strong support for economic and social equality. Socialists traditionally envisioned a society in which major businesses were taken over by the government or by employee cooperatives.

Socioeconomic Status The value assigned to a person due to occupation or income. A professional person with a substantial income, for example, has high socioeconomic status.

Soft Money Campaign contributions unregulated by federal or state law, usually given to parties and party committees to help fund general party activities.

Sound Bite A brief, memorable comment that can easily be fit into news broadcasts.

Soviet Bloc The Soviet Union and the Eastern European countries that installed Communist regimes after World War II and that were dominated by the Soviet Union.

Speaker of the House The presiding officer in the House of Representatives. The Speaker is chosen by the majority party and is the most powerful and influential member of the House.

Spin An interpretation of political events that is favorable to a candidate or officeholder

Spin Doctor A political adviser who tries to convince journalists of the truth of a particular interpretation of events.

Splinter Party A new party formed by a dissident faction within a major political party. Often, splinter parties have emerged when a particular personality was at odds with the major party.

Spoils System The awarding of government jobs to political supporters and friends.

Spring Review The annual process in which the Office of Management and Budget (OMB) requires federal agencies to review their programs, activities, and goals, and submit their requests for funding for the next fiscal year.

Standing Committee A permanent committee in the House or Senate that considers bills within a certain subject area.

Stare Decisis To stand on decided cases—the judicial policy of following precedents established by past decisions.

State A group of people occupying a specific area and organized under one government. It may be either a nation or a subunit of a nation.

State Central Committee The principal organized structure of each political party within each state. This committee is responsible for carrying out policy decisions of the party's state convention.

State of the Union Message An annual message to Congress in which the president proposes a legislative program. The message is addressed not only to Congress but also to the American people and to the world.

Statutory Power A power created for the president through laws enacted by Congress.

Straight-Ticket Voting Voting exclusively for the candidates of one party.

Strict Scrutiny A judicial standard for assessing the constitutionality of a law or government action when the law or action threatens to interfere with a fundamental right or potentially discriminates against members of a suspect classification.

Suffrage The right to vote.

Super PAC A political organization that aggregates unlimited contributions by individuals and organizations to be spent independently of candidate committees.

Superdelegate A party leader or elected official who is given the right to vote at the party's national convention. Superdelegates are not elected at the state level.

Supremacy Clause The constitutional provision that makes the Constitution and federal laws superior to all conflicting state and local laws.

Supremacy Doctrine A doctrine that asserts the priority of national law over state laws. This principle is stated in Article VI of the Constitution.

Suspect Classification A classification, such as race, religion, or national origin, that triggers strict scrutiny by the courts when a law or government action potentially discriminates against members of the class.

Symbolic Speech Expression made through articles of clothing, gestures, and other forms of nonverbal conduct.

T

Terrorism A systematic attempt to inspire fear to gain political ends, typically involving the indiscriminate use of violence against noncombatants.

Third Party A political party other than the two major political parties (Republican and Democratic).

Totalitarian Regime A form of government that controls all aspects of the political, social, and economic life of a nation.

Tracking Poll A poll that is taken continuously—sometimes every day—to determine how support for an issue or candidate changes over time.

Transgender Persons Persons who experience a mismatch between their gender identity and the gender assigned to them at birth.

Treasuries U.S. Treasury securities—bills, notes, and bonds. Debt issued by the federal government.

Trial Court The court in which most cases begin.

Truman Doctrine The policy adopted by President Harry Truman in 1947 to halt Communist expansion.

Trustee A legislator who acts according to her or his conscience and the broad interests of the entire society.

Twelfth Amendment An amendment to the Constitution, adopted in 1804, that specifies the separate election of the president and the vice president by the electoral college.

Twenty-fifth Amendment A 1967 amendment to the Constitution that establishes procedures for filling presidential and vice-presidential vacancies and makes provisions for presidential incapacity.

Two-Party System A political system in which only two parties have a reasonable chance of winning.

U

Unanimous Opinion A court opinion or determination on which all judges agree.

Unemployment The inability of those who are in the labor force to find a job.

Unicameral Legislature A legislature with only one legislative chamber, as opposed to a bicameral (two-chamber) legislature, such as the U.S. Congress.

Unit Rule A rule by which all of a state's electoral votes are cast for the presidential candidate who receives a plurality of the votes in that state.

Unitary System A centralized governmental system in which ultimate governmental authority rests in the hands of the national, or central, government.

Universal Suffrage The right of all adults to vote for their representatives.

V

Veto Message The president's formal explanation of a veto, which accompanies the vetoed legislation when it is returned to Congress.

Vote-Eligible Population The number of people who, at a given time, enjoy the right to vote in national elections.

Voter Turnout The percentage of citizens taking part in the election process. Also, the number of eligible voters who actually "turn out" to cast their ballots.

Voting-Age Population The number of people of voting age living in the country at a given time, regardless of whether they have the right to vote.

W

War Powers Resolution A law passed in 1973 spelling out the conditions under which the president can commit troops without congressional approval.

Wave Election An election in which voters display dissatisfaction with one of the major parties through a "wave" of support for the other. In contrast to a realigning election, the results of a wave election are not permanent.

Whig Party A major party in the United States during the first half of the nineteenth century, formally established in 1836. The Whig Party was anti-Jackson and advocated spending on infrastructure.

Whip A member of Congress who aids the majority or minority leader of the House or the Senate.

Whistleblower In the context of government, someone who brings gross governmental inefficiency or an illegal action to the public's attention.

White House Office The personal office of the president, which tends to presidential political needs and manages the media.

White Primary A state primary election that restricted voting to whites only. Outlawed by the Supreme Court in 1944.

Working Class Currently, those with no college education. Traditionally, individuals or families in which the head of household was employed in manual or unskilled labor.

Writ of *Certiorari* An order issued by a higher court to a lower court to send up the record of a case for review.

Writ of *Habeas Corpus* *Habeas corpus* means, literally, "you have the body." A writ of *habeas corpus* is an order that requires jailers to bring a prisoner before a court or judge and explain why the person is being held.

Index

F

Facebook, 135, 136, 137
  impact on public opinion, 122
Factions, among delegates to Constitutional Convention, 31
Fairness and Accuracy in Reporting, 143
Fairness Doctrine, 121
Faithless electors, 188
Fall review, 220
False Claims Act, 263
Family, political socialization and, 120
Fannie Mae, 259
Farm Bureau, 149
Faubus, Orval, 96, 290
Fed. *See* Federal Reserve System (Fed)
Federal budget, 218–222
  budget deficit and Keynes, 310
  budget resolutions and crisis, 221–222
  categories of spending, 252–253
  Congress and, 221
  continuing resolution, 221
  debt ceiling and, 222
  defense spending, 253
  deficit (*See* Budget deficit)
  election-year budgets, 221
  executive budget, 218, 220
  preparing budget, 220–221
  size of, 252–253
  social spending of, 252–253
Federal Circuit, 276
Federal Communications Commission (FCC), 257
  Fairness Doctrine, 121
  net neutrality and, 137
Federal court system, 273–279
  alien "removal" courts, 278
  basic judicial requirements for cases, 274
  constitutional authority for, 274
  executive checks, 289–290
  FISA court, 277–278
  impact of lower courts on, 291
  judicial activism, 287
  judicial appointment, 282–286
  judicial restraint, 287
  judicial traditions and doctrine, 291
  jurisdiction, 274
  legislative checks, 290
  parties to lawsuits, 274
  policymaking function of, 286–291
  procedural rules, 274–275
  Supreme Court (*See* Supreme Court of United States)
  suspected terrorist detainees, 278–279
  types of courts
    administrative law tribunals, 276
    courts of appeals, 276
    district courts, 275–276
    Supreme Court, 276
    as three-tiered system, 275–276
  war on terrorism and, 277–279
Federal Deposit Insurance Corporation (FDIC), 258, 259
Federal Election Campaign Act (FECA), 178–179
Federal Election Commission (FEC), 168
  creation of, 179
  501(c)4 organizations, 181–182
Federal Employees Political Activities Act, 262

Federal government. *See* National government
Federal grants
  block, 59
  categorical, 58–59
  conditions attached to, 59–60
Federal Home Loan Mortgage Corporation, 259
Federalism, 44–63
  arguments against, 48–49
  arguments for, 46–47
  benefit of, for United States, 47
  characteristics of, 46
  constitutional basis for, 49–53
  cooperative, 57–58
  devolution, 58
  dispute over division of power, 53–60
  dual, 56–57
  fiscal federalism, 59
  politics of, 58
  Supreme Court and
    early years, 53–56
    today, 61–62
Federalist Papers, 34, 36, 37, 48, 147, 206
Federalists, 161
  ratification of Constitution, 36–37
Federal mandates, 60
Federal National Mortgage Association, 259
Federal Open Market Committee, 313
Federal question, 274, 276
Federal Register, 238, 265, 266
Federal Regulation of Lobbying Act, 155
Federal Reserve System (Fed)
  Board of Governors of, 313
  defined, 313
  functions of, 313
  organization of, 313
Federal system, 46. *See also* Federalism
Federal Trade Commission (FTC), 265
Federal Trade Commission Act, 265
Feminine Mystique, The (Friedan), 109
Feminism, 109
Fertility rate, 105
Fifteenth Amendment, 56, 93, 95, 193
Fifth Amendment, 69, 79, 83
Filibuster, 205, 206
  advantages and disadvantages of, 207
  constitutionality of, 206
  increased use of, 205
  nuclear option, 206
  reconciliation, 205
Films. *See* Movies
First Amendment
  clear and present danger, 74
  commercial speech, 74
  cross burning, 74
  establishment clause, 69–70
  federal employees and, 261
  flag burning, 73
  freedom of press (*See* Press, freedom of)
  freedom of religion (*See* Religion, freedom of)
  freedom of speech (*See* Speech, freedom of)
  free exercise clause, 72–73
  hate speech, 67
  imminent lawless action test, 75
  incorporation theory, 68–69
  interest groups and, 147
  privacy rights and, 79

  symbolic speech, 73
First Bank of the United States, 53
First budget resolution, 221
First Continental Congress, 25
First Gulf War, 324
FISA court, 277–278
Fiscal federalism, 59
Fiscal policy, 310–313
  criticism of Keynes, 310–311
  defined, 59, 310
  discretionary fiscal policy, 310
  government spending and borrowing, 310
  timing problem of, 310
Fiscal year cycle, 220
Fisher v. University of Texas, 103
501(c)4 organizations, 181–182
527 organizations, 181
Flag Protection Act, 73–74
Flynn, Michael, 264, 334
Focus group, 178
Food stamps, 253
Ford, Gerald, armed forces ordered by into combat without congressional approval, 335
Foreign Affairs, 337
Foreign governments, lobbying by, 152–153
Foreign Intelligence Surveillance Act (FISA), 277
Foreign Intelligence Surveillance Act (FISA) court
  after September 11, 277–278
  establishment of, 277
  National Security Agency and, 278
Foreign policy, 320–341
  Afghanistan and, 325
  Arab Spring, 322–323
  China and, 330–331
  civil war in Syria and rise of ISIS, 326–327
  Congressional powers and, 335–336
  containment policy, 337
  defense policy, 321
  defined, 321
  diplomacy, 321
  economic troubles in Europe, 331–333
  human rights and, 341
  intelligence community and, 335
  Iraq, wars in, 324–325
  isolationist, 336
  Israel and Palestinians, 329–330
  moral idealism and, 322
  National Security Council and, 334
  national security policy and, 321
  nuclear weapons, 327–329
  political realism and, 322
  presidential powers and, 333
  process of, 321
  September 11, 2001 and changed view of, 320–321
  State Department and, 334
  techniques and strategies of, 321
  terrorism and, 323–324
  themes in, 336–341
    formative years, 336–337
    internationalism, 337–338
    superpower relations, 338–341
    Truman Doctrine, 337–338
Forward guidance, 315
Four-cornered ideological grid, 16–17